AMERICAN CHILDHOOD

AMERICAN CHILDHOOD

A Research Guide
and
Historical Handbook

Edited by
JOSEPH M. HAWES
and
N. RAY HINER

Greenwood Press
Westport, Connecticut • London, England

Library of Congress Cataloging in Publication Data

Main entry under title:

American childhood.

  Bibliography: p.
  Includes index.
  1. Children—United States—History—Addresses, essays,
lectures. I. Hawes, Joseph M. II. Hiner, N. Ray.
HQ792.U5A525 1985   305.2'3'0973   84-15708
ISBN 0-313-23337-3 (lib. bdg.)

Library of Congress Catalog Card Number: 84-15708
ISBN: 0-313-23337-3

First published in 1985

Greenwood Press
A division of Congressional Information Service, Inc.
88 Post Road West
Westport, Connecticut 06881

Printed in the United States of America

10 9 8 7 6 5 4 3 2 1

Dedicated to the memory of
Peter Romanofsky

Contents

Preface

Historical studies have undergone a profound change in the last two decades. Where politics and a concern for political events once dominated the study of the past, historians now are attempting to learn about all aspects of the past—its social, economic, intellectual, scientific, cultural, public, private, and gender-related activities in addition to a host of interconnections among these categories. As a result, the study of history is richer, more varied, and much more complex than it used to be. The last and smallest (in physical size) of the groups to interest historians are children. As historians seek to gain knowledge in these new areas, they have had to develop new methods and to rely on the methods and insights of many other disciplines. Each new approach to the past and each effort to understand the diverse groups of the human family have brought with them new justifications for the study of the past and new ways to look at human development over time. Ethnic history, women's history, and "history from the bottom up"—the history of inarticulate masses—have all appeared recently, and all have added to the fund of historical knowledge.

We are beginning to understand why knowledge of past politics is not enough, why economic changes have a widespread influence on social and cultural developments, why private lives can diverge sharply from public expectations, and much more. In short, we have gained a greater understanding of a larger part of the past by using new approaches and by focusing on excluded groups. Still, the picture is far from complete. We can add enormously to our understanding of the past—of the history of the family—of the economic roles and functions of the members of the family—of how past societies regarded the future and so on—by looking at the history of childhood. Simply put, much more of the past becomes understandable when we focus on children. As a result of that focus, we can discover the many different social and personal meanings of children, and we can see how these meanings changed over time. In addition, we can discern the main patterns in adult thinking about children—what adults thought should be done to and with children. As we do this, we are forced to admit that children were not simply the passive recipients of adult actions and thought. They, too, were historical actors who had their own subjective experience and who influenced adults as well.

During the last ten years a substantial, but widely scattered, literature about the history of American children has appeared. A few monographs are available, but the bulk of the information is to be found in articles appearing in scholarly journals. A central purpose of this collection is to provide a guide to that literature. At the same time the authors of the separate essays have sought to define and explain the major developments within their areas and during the time periods listed. We are pleased to make this information available in this form because we believe that this present work will make the information accessible to the largest group of scholars and students in the most efficient manner. Our purpose in undertaking this work is to promote the study of children in the American past. To that end we hope that this volume assists those engaged in that pursuit and stimulates others to begin it.

American Childhood is organized primarily in a chronological fashion, from the seventeenth century to the present. Each of the chapters has been written by a recognized authority in the history of childhood or related fields. Some of the chapters depart from the focus on chronological periods to treat specialized topics—ethnicity, gender, and children's literature—in greater depth. The authors have provided a comprehensive review of the available literature, assessed the relative merits of the literature they discuss, and described the most important developments involving children during each period. In addition to the chapter bibliographies we have included a comprehensive bibliography that lists the published works cited by the various contributors. We have also included a chronology of the important dates in the history of American childhood and a list of child-helping agencies around the country. As editors, we believe that the diversity of the following material is an accurate reflection of a complex new field, and we are also impressed with the range and quality of scholarship in this new field. We hope that others agree.

Joseph M. Hawes and N. Ray Hiner

Acknowledgments

This work is primarily that of the contributors whose chapters follow. Our job has been one of assembling and compiling and working with the scholars whose qualifications made them the logical choices for the various chapters. The project originated with a letter from Marilyn Brownstein of Greenwood Press. We found that working together seemed a natural way to proceed from this beginning. We also acknowledge the assistance we have received from the Bureau of General Research at Kansas State University, the History Department at the University of Kansas, the History Department at Kansas State University, and the School of Education of the University of Kansas.

Joseph M. Hawes and N. Ray Hiner

AMERICAN CHILDHOOD

Introduction

Joseph M. Hawes
N. Ray Hiner

THE HISTORIOGRAPHY OF AMERICAN CHILDHOOD

One of the most influential early works in the history of childhood is
Philippe Aries's *Centuries of Childhood: A Social History of Family Life*.[1]
Concerned with the origins of the modern family, Aries succinctly expressed what many Americans had come to understand, that "our experience of the modern demographic revolution has revealed to us the
importance of the child's role in this silent history." Furthermore, Aries
challenged traditional assumptions about the changelessness of childhood and argued instead that the idea of childhood had not even existed
before the fifteenth or sixteenth centuries. Before this period, during
the Medieval Era, Aries says "children were mixed with adults as soon
as they were considered capable of doing without their nannies," and
were in some respects better off than children in later periods when,
under the influence of the modern idea of childhood, adults began to
deprive children of their freedom, confine them to prison-like schools,
and subject them to the severe discipline of schoolmasters.

Although not everyone shared Aries's nostalgia for the Medieval period, his basic thesis that childhood was in part a social category and
therefore subject to the historical process proved to be an immensely
popular idea among American social historians and helped to justify
research into its historical development. *Centuries of Childhood* has recently
been labeled "a superb piece of rhetoric," and Aries has been justly
criticized for his selective and sometimes uncritical use of evidence, but
no one has successfully challenged his essential point that childhood is
not an immutable stage of life, free from the influence of historical
change.

Another European scholar who had considerable influence on the

development of the history of childhood during the 1960s and 1970s is
Erik Erikson, the well-known child analyst and psychohistorian who emigrated to the United States in the 1930s. His first book, *Childhood and
Society*,[2] written in the 1940s and published in the 1950s, was not widely
discussed by American historians until the 1960s when his interdisciplinary approach, which integrated psychological, social, and cultural perspectives, took on a special relevance for many Americans who were
puzzling over the many complex issues raised by the post-World War II
generation. Scholars were now more willing to consider the implications
of Erikson's critical observation in *Childhood and Society* that "one may
scan work after work on history, society, and morality and find little
reference to the fact that all people start as children and that all peoples
begin in their nurseries."

Erikson's developmental or epigenetic model of psychosocial stages
which he described in *Childhood and Society* attracted a favorable response
from several historians, including John Demos, who used it to assess the
experience of children in his important and well-received study of seventeenth-century Plymouth published in 1970.[3] Demos argued that, unlike the approach followed by scholars such as Aries, "who study the
child as a kind of mirror which focuses and reflects back cultural themes
of central importance," Erikson's model encouraged historians to treat
the child as "not just a mirror, not only the creature, but also the creator
of culture, and in this sense, a dynamic force in his own right."

Whereas Erikson and Demos sought to establish the historical importance of children and childhood, Lloyd deMause went even further and
asserted that children and parent-child relations constitute "the central
force for change in history," independent to some extent from social
and technological trends.[4] According to deMause, a scholar with training
in pyschoanalysis, political science, and history, the primary source of
this change lies in "the ability of successive generations of parents to
regress to the psychic age of their children and work through the anxieties of that age in a better manner the second time they encounter
them than they did during their own childhood." DeMause therefore
concluded that each generation of parents grew in their capacity to love
and care for children, became better parents than those of previous
generations, and thereby provided an essential foundation for general
social progress. For deMause, then, "the history of childhood is a nightmare from which we have only recently begun to awaken. The further
back in history one goes, the lower the level of child care, and the more
likely children are to be killed, abandoned, beaten, terrorized, and sexually abused." Thus, deMause completely reversed the portrayal of childhood provided by Aries. DeMause and Aries agree on one point, however,
that childhood as an experience and a social category is part of the
historical process and subject to change over time.

In 1966, Robert H. Bremner, a respected social historian at Ohio State

University, began a major research project initiated by the American
Public Health Association, funded by the U.S. Children's Bureau and
designed to update Grace Abbott's classic, *The Child and the State*, published in 1938. The result of this research project was the publication
of *Children and Youth in America*, a massive three-volume documentary
history of public policy toward children and youth which appeared between 1970 and 1974.[5] Even though Bremner says that it does not comprise a history of childhood in America, and, although the collection is
by definition heavily institutional in focus, a cursory glance at its contents
reveals that it offers great insight into the historical experience of children in America. *Children and Youth in America* also demonstrates the
relevance a knowledge of the history of childhood has for the discussion
and formulation of public policy affecting children.

Another significant area for the history of children is in the field of
the history of education. Long dominated by a focus confined almost
totally to institutions, historians of education until the 1960s concentrated on schools, their organization, administration, and curriculum
and gave little attention to children as children. However, a more comprehensive view of education as a psychological, social, and cultural
process has emerged, and historians of education are now more inclined
to include the perspective of the child as "learner" in their research.
Two important works that reflect this new awareness of children are Sol
Cohen's comprehensive, five-volume *Education in the United States: A Documentary History*[6] and Barbara Finkelstein's anthology, *Regulated Children/
Liberated Children: Education in Psychohistorical Perspective*.[7] As more historians of education have come to share Cohen's and Finkelstein's sensitivity to the historical importance of children, the history of education
has become an increasingly valuable source of insight for the historian
of childhood.

Also important for the history of childhood is the rapidly expanding
history of the family, which, since the early 1970s has produced an
enormous volume of studies either directly or indirectly concerned with
children. As family historians extended the scope of their inquiry beyond
an emphasis on household structure and began to investigate the nature
of emotional relationships within the family, they produced a substantial
body of knowledge vital to an understanding of the daily lives of children.
Several important collections of articles and documents in this field are
now available. Among the most valuable are Michael Gordon's *The American Family in Social-Historical Perspective* (1978);[8] *Loving, Parenting and
Dying: The Family Cycle in England and America, Past and Present* (1980)
edited by Vivian C. Fox and Martin H. Quitt;[9] Mel Albin's and Dominick
Cavallo's *Family Life in America, 1620–2000* (1981);[10] and *America's Families: A Documentary History* (1982) edited by Donald M. Scott and Bernard
Wishy.[11]

As noted above, the richness and complexity of this new field can be found in the article literature scattered throughout professional journals. Our primary purpose in this collection is to provide a guide to that literature. Before we move to the detailed discussion of it, we believe it is appropriate to indicate how we view the history of American childhood. Necessarily, that history must be seen as falling within the context of American social history, and it is against the broad canvas of that emerging field that we have developed a brief history of American childhood.

AN OVERVIEW OF THE HISTORY OF AMERICAN CHILDHOOD

In the early seventeenth century when English settlement began in North America, the most common form of social organization was a tightly knit pre-industrial farming village. These villages predominated in New England, while in the Chesapeake region settlement was dispersed. In both areas, however, the family was the basic social unit and was expected to carry out a series of social functions. Among the functions of the family in the seventeenth century were economic production, education, religious emphasis, social welfare, and social control.

In this world children had a critical economic function; they were a vital part of the labor force and assisted the family as it sought economic self-sufficiency. Of course, children were important for other reasons as well. Colonial parents were deeply concerned for their children's physical and spiritual welfare and, like modern parents, felt threatened when their children did not embrace prevailing religious and moral values. Parents and other adults sought to mold colonial children to values and norms of their community. How the community accomplished this task of socialization and enculturation varied greatly according to the religious beliefs, economic status, ethnic identity, and geographical location of the child's family of origin.[12]

We may never know with full confidence how seventeenth-century parents felt about their children. We do know that pre-industrial families were larger than the urban middle-class families which became the dominant family type in the late nineteenth century, and we also know that children began to work and contribute to the economic fortunes of their families at an early age. Most children learned their adult roles as apprentices—in their own homes. Boys worked beside their fathers in the fields, girls beside their mothers inside the house and nearby. The world in which these children lived was structured so that everyone had a place in a social hierarchy. This hierarchy reflected an awareness of mutual dependence and found expression in the relationships between parents and children. Children worked not only to earn their own keep but also to help the family survive. In return for this labor parents were obliged to give their children a start in life. Ideally, for sons this meant that the father had to provide them with land and a home so that the sons could have families of their own. Daughters received the necessary items to set up housekeeping in their new home.

In the eighteenth century this essentially agrarian world began to change. Increased trade, immigration, and a rapid natural increase in population (due in large part to a decline in the death rate) combined with the influence of the Enlightenment and the Great Awakening to make life in the thirteen British colonies more heterogeneous, complex, and cosmopolitan. As the economy of eighteenth-century North America quickened its pace, cities grew and some sons sought their fortunes there rather than on farm land. The small number of families who lived in these cities saw their internal relationships begin to change as husbands now left home for work and wives found their productive roles narrowed as they became managers rather than producers. Thus, as the eighteenth century neared its end, a new pattern of family life was emerging—the urban middle-class family. In this family the economic meaning of children had begun to change. In middle-class families children's economic role was oriented to consumption rather than production. These new middle-class urban families had fewer children in part because they saw the future in a different light, in part because they no longer needed the labor of their children, and in part because women's roles had changed.[13]

Social assumptions about children's inner natures also changed. John Locke's famous view of children as being blank slates (which could be interpreted to mean that they were morally neutral) gained wide acceptance during the eighteenth century as an alternative to the grim view that infants were innately depraved held by orthodox Calvinists.[14] At the same time women began to assume greater responsibility for the moral education of their children. In the pre-industrial world fathers had had this responsibility, but their absence from the home combined with a new sense of women as being morally superior to men led to this shift.[15] Economic and social patterns had changed so much that children could no longer be prepared to enter the world in the same way their mothers and fathers had. Not all young men would be farmers, and young women would have greater responsibilities for the moral education of children when they became wives and mothers. Consequently, formal schooling assumed a new social significance, and from this point on there was no question that coeducation would be the norm.

Life was different for the poorer families who lived in cities. Their families were still large, and their children began to work at an early age. As soon as they were able, boys sought paid employment, while girls remained at home to help with domestic tasks. Sometimes younger children who could not work outside the home provided child care so that older children and the parents could seek work. This urban family pattern—which in some ways resembles the pre-industrial family—was especially characteristic of immigrant families. Sometimes these working-class families did not survive the rigors of nineteenth-century urban life, and homeless children, living by their wits on city streets, became a disturbing reality.

Nineteenth-century reformers, concerned about both the homeless children on their city streets and what they took to be a rising crime rate, began to build a series of institutions designed to meet the problem of these neglected and potentially criminal children. The most notable of these institutions were the urban public schools.[16] In addition, the reformers created a series of juvenile institutions designed to deal with those young people who were already destitute or criminal (to most nineteenth-century reformers the distinction was not important). The first of these was the New York House of Refuge, founded in 1825. It combined the functions of a school, a welfare institution, and a jail for children in much the same way that workhouses had done for all members of the "dangerous classes." As the cities grew, the number of children who appeared to need reforming outstripped the capacities of these juvenile prisons, and new approaches had to be found. Typical of the new approaches was the Children's Aid Society founded in New York in 1853 by Charles Loring Brace, a New England minister who prided himself on sweeping children off the city streets into waiting Western families. He argued that his procedure was in accordance with the laws of supply and demand.[17]

Brace's approach met with wide public acclaim—in part because it was consistent with the changing meaning of children in different parts of American society. Middle-class urban dwellers did not regard their own children as valued members of a struggling economic enterprise; instead, they saw their children as (among other things, of course) objects whose dress and behavior (and whose smaller numbers compared to working-class families) testified to their father's middle-class status and affluence. But these same middle-class families recognized that children meant something different to farm families where labor was still very much in short supply. Thus, as American society became more complicated, differing views of the economic meaning of children coexisted.

Late in the nineteenth century, middle-class city dwellers began to look upon their way of life with increasing anxiety. It seemed to them that society was out of control and therefore in need of serious reform. They were concerned about rising industrialism and a political system that seemed more given to corruption than to effective government. Public-spirited reformers moved to restrict immigration, install sanitary sewers, clean up city hall, improve the efficiency of social welfare, and control the future. In these tasks they were aided by the appearance of "professional" disciplines and callings such as economics, sociology, psychology, and medicine. The culmination of all this effort has been commonly labeled the Progressive Movement. Much of this effort to reshape American society focused on children. Reformers tried to eliminate juvenile prostitution and the exploitation of children by professional beggars. In founding the Society for the Prevention of Cruelty to Children, they demonstrated a concern about child abuse and child abandonment. They built more juvenile prisons and tried to apply the principles of juvenile prisons to older young people. They tinkered with the internal workings of these juvenile prisons and called them reform schools; they tried new systems of dealing with juvenile offenders, developing the system of probation. Others crusaded against child labor, trying at first to reduce it at the work site and finally gaining some success by passing compulsory school attendance laws. Still others founded the juvenile court and completed the process of separating youthful offenders from adult criminals in the criminal justice system. In addition, more earnest middle-class reformers sought to tame the evils of massive urban growth and the influx of immigrants by creating playgrounds and supervising children's activities on them.[18]

Reformers focused much of their attention on children because they represented the future. This sense of the public meaning of children had always been a part of American culture, but it had never had so great an impact on public policy before the Progressive Era. Significantly, in this period reformers and civic leaders sought to influence the behavior of children directly as individuals rather than as members of families—a practice that had begun with the creation of public schools but one that intensified in the late nineteenth century. So important were the children for the future that a new discipline, child psychology, appeared. The leading figure in this new area was G. Stanley Hall, the president of Clark University and the author of *Adolescence*, a two-volume compendium of material on what was claimed to be a new phase in human development and human history.[19] Child psychology provided one of the building blocks of the new expertise on the family that characterized the twentieth century.

One of the themes of the Progressive Era was the rise of governmental regulation of all sorts of social activity: child labor laws, pure food and drug laws, laws regulating business and economic activity, laws designed to eliminate corruption and prostitution. Many of these new laws were federal and marked the beginning of the entrance of the Federal Government into the arena of business and social regulation for the public good. One consequence of this new climate was the creation of two new governmental bureaus—one for children and one for women. The Children's Bureau was largely the creation of the reformers who had campaigned against child labor. With no very clear mission, the Children's

Bureau tried to do everything: reduce child labor, increase child health, promote justice for juvenile offenders, and advise mothers about the latest scientific information on how to care for their children.[20] The Federal Women's Bureau in the Department of Labor concerned itself with the conditions of work for women and paid little attention to children until the 1960s.

Since the founding of the Children's Bureau early in the twentieth century, the most potent force in public policy affecting children has been the Federal Government. During the 1920s the government, under the auspices of the Sheppard-Towner Act, sought to improve child health directly by granting money to community groups that would stress such measures as improved prenatal care. They also tried to protect children's health by giving welfare aid to mothers. By the 1970s, the descendant of that approach, Aid to Families with Dependent Children, was the largest single category of welfare in the country.[21]

As the government expanded its services for children, two other social developments also occurred. The first was the rise of a new type of expert and the second, flowing from the first, was a new ideal defining the private meaning of children within families. The new experts on children could be found in the disciplines of sociology and psychology (and related fields such as home economics and education), and, as they studied children and the contexts in which these young people lived, worked, and played, the experts began to prescribe techniques for teaching them, supervising their play, and nurturing them generally. As those experts looked at the twentieth-century family, they concluded that it was totally different from its predecessors. For them, the essential meaning of the family was now emotional and psychological rather than economic. Affection was the chief characteristic of the family, and parents could concentrate on loving their offspring since there were now fewer children in the typical middle-class family.[22]

While the Federal Government and the experts were expanding services for children and attempting to explain their meaning and their behavior, young people moved to define part of their own lives by means of the peer group. Beginning in the early twentieth century, young people developed a code of behavior for themselves and thereby gained a measure of control over their own lives independent from adult authority. Of course, peer groups were not new for American youth in the twentieth century, but earlier peer groups lacked the ability to control youthful behavior as effectively as the twentieth-century groups did. Youthful peer groups first demonstrated their importance among college students in the 1920s. As the century progressed, youthful peer groups became more important—until in the 1960s youth constituted a "counterculture."[23]

In looking at the history of American children in broad outline form, it is easy to overlook some of the important exceptions to this pattern. Young women, for example, have a different history in our culture than do young men. The children of native Americans have a history almost totally different from that of the dominant European culture. Among other things they were the first children to come under the influence of the Federal Government. It is possible, in fact, to draw parallels between the Federal Government's treatment of Indian children and its increasing activity on behalf of children in the twentieth century.[24]

Understanding black children requires a thorough knowledge of black history and culture. In particular, it requires an awareness that black culture—specifically Afro-American culture—existed under slavery. Of course, the process of growing up for black children was in many ways similar to that for other children, but it was sufficiently different as to require special attention from historians. Black children had to face the realities of slavery and the continuing racism of American society after the Civil War.[25]

Other patterns, equally important for a discussion of the social meaning of children and for an understanding of the history of American childhood, also appeared. After World War II more people chose to remain single or live together without marrying. Most people saw the problem as one of trying to maintain separate but equal values in a very difficult world. There were obvious signs of family decline: divorces, childless marriages, greater numbers of people remaining single longer and, those who married but chose to remain childless. Experts who see these trends as a rejection of children and the family ignore the reasons for these developments. The people who decided to choose an alternative to the typical nineteenth-century middle-class family did not necessarily reject the family—or children; they were simply trying to live up to the expectations articulated by the experts in the earlier part of the twentieth century. They sought both personal happiness and individual autonomy, and they wanted the same things for their partners and their children.[26]

NOTES

1. Philippe Aries, *Centuries of Childhood: A Social History of Family Life*, Robert Baldick, trans. (New York: Random House, 1962).

2. Erik H. Erikson, *Childhood and Society* (2d ed., New York: W. W. Norton, 1963).

3. John Demos, *A Little Commonwealth: Family Life in Plymouth Colony* (New York: Oxford University Press, 1970).

4. Lloyd deMause, ed., *The History of Childhood* (New York: Psychohistory Press, 1974).

5. Robert H. Bremner, et al., *Children and Youth in America: A Documentary History*, 3 vols. (Cambridge, Mass.: Harvard University Press, 1970–1974).

6. Sol Cohen, ed., *Education in the United States: A Documentary History*, 5 vols. (New York: Random House, 1974).

7. Barbara Finkelstein, ed., *Regulated Children/Liberated Children: Education in Psychohistorical Perspective* (New York: Psychohistory Press, 1979).

8. Michael Gordon, ed., *The American Family in Social-Historical Perspective* (2d ed., New York: St. Martin's Press, 1978).

9. Vivian C. Fox and Martin H. Quitt, eds., *Loving, Parenting and Dying: The Family Cycle in England and America, Past and Present* (New York: Psychohistory Press, 1980).

10. Mel Albin and Dominick Cavallo, eds., *Family Life in America, 1620–2000* (St. James, N.Y.: Revisionary Press, 1981).

11. Donald M. Scott and Bernard Wishy, eds., *America's Families: A Documentary History* (New York: Harper & Row, 1982).

12. For a discussion of this area, see Philip Greven, *The Protestant Temperament: Patterns of Child-Rearing, Religious Experience, and the Self in Early America* (New York: Alfred A. Knopf, 1977).

13. See Demos, *Little Commonwealth*.

14. For a discussion of this process, see Peter G. Slater, *Children in the New England Mind in Death and Life: From the Puritans to Bushnell* (Hamden, Conn.: Archon Books, 1977).

15. See Nancy Cott, *The Bonds of Womanhood: Woman's Sphere in New England, 1780–1835* (New Haven: Yale University Press, 1977).

16. See, for example, Michael Katz, *The Irony of Early School Reform* (Cambridge, Mass.: Harvard University Press, 1968).

17. Joseph M. Hawes, *Children in Urban Society: Juvenile Delinquency in the Nineteenth Century* (New York: Oxford University Press, 1971).

18. See, for example, Steven Schlossman, *Love and the American Delinquent: The Theory and Practice of "Progressive" Juvenile Justice, 1825–1920* (Chicago: University of Chicago Press, 1977); Anthony Platt, *The Child Savers: The Invention of Delinquency* (Chicago: University of Chicago Press, 1969); Hawes, *Children in Urban Society*; and Dominick Cavallo, *Muscles and Morals: Organized Playgrounds and Urban Reform, 1880–1920* (Philadelphia: University of Pennsylvania Press, 1981).

19. Joseph Kett, *Rites of Passage: Adolescence in America: 1790 to the Present* (New York: Basic Books, 1977).

20. See Bremner, et al., *Children and Youth in America*.

21. Ibid.

22. Christopher Lasch, *Haven in a Heartless World: The Family Besieged* (New York: Basic Books, 1977).

23. Paula Fass, *The Damned and the Beautiful: American Youth in the 1920s* (New York: Oxford University Press, 1977).

24. Barbara Finkelstein, "Uncle Sam and the Children: History of Government Involvement in Childrearing," *Review Journal of Philosophy and Social Science* (India) 3 (1978): 139–153.

25. David Wiggins, "The Play of Slave Children," *Journal of Sport History* (Summer 1980): 21–39.

26. See, for example, Glen H. Elder, *Children of the Great Depression* (Chicago: University of Chicago Press, 1976); Kenneth Keniston, *All our Children: The*

American Family Under Pressure (New York: Harcourt Brace, 1977); Christopher Lasch, *The Culture of Narcissism: American Life in an Age of Diminishing Expectations* (New York: W. W. Norton, 1979); Carl Degler, *At Odds: Women and the Family in America from the Revolution to the Present* (New York: Oxford University Press, 1980); and Daniel Yankelovich, *New Rules: Searching for Self Fulfillment in a World Turned Upside Down* (New York: Random House, 1981).

1

The Child in Seventeenth-Century America

Ross W. Beales, Jr.

The last two decades have witnessed a revolution in the study of colonial America, especially in the area of family history, with scholars providing significant insights into that most basic of all human institutions. The history of childhood has become a challenging area of investigation as historians have utilized the methodologies of demography, anthropology, sociology, and psychology to interpret sometimes frustratingly elusive and ambiguous data.[1] With the publication of a revised edition of Edmund S. Morgan's classic *The Puritan Family* (1966) and other significant studies of family and community life by John Demos, Philip J. Greven, Jr., and Kenneth A. Lockridge, the early American family has become an important field of research.[2]

This chapter is divided into two parts: a summary of the demographic characteristics of family life; and an examination of the stages of growth experienced by seventeenth-century children, including infancy, childhood, and adolescence. Throughout, it is important to emphasize that there has been considerable debate over the nature and consequences of childhood experiences. Furthermore, recent work on the Chesapeake portrays conditions of family life far different from those in New England.

The demographic history of seventeenth-century American family life must include a consideration of immigration patterns, ages at marriage (especially for women), life expectancies (for both parents and children), and family size and household composition, since all these circumstances affected the lives of children.[3]

Research for much of this chapter was made possible by a National Endowment for the Humanities Fellowship at the American Antiquarian Society. Portions were delivered at the Duquesne University History Forum, October 21, 1982.

The differences in immigration patterns to New England and the Chesapeake are important in terms of numbers, duration, composition, and status. Immigration to New England began with the settlement of Plymouth Colony in 1620 and was especially concentrated in the 1630s after the founding of Massachusetts Bay. These immigrants, numbering about 20,000, formed the essential reproductive core for a population increase to nearly 100,000 by 1700. This growth reflected an extremely favorable demographic environment when compared to England and especially to the Chesapeake and Caribbean: a balanced sex ratio among immigrants; large numbers of persons who paid their own passage and were thus not prevented from marrying by virtue of indentured servitude; a generally healthful climate, which reduced seasoning morbidity and mortality; abundant land, good diet, and ample fuel supplies; relatively low rates of maternal mortality; and generally long life expectancies, especially for those who survived childhood.[4] These conditions resulted in low death rates; early marriages for women; few spinsters or bachelors; relatively low rates of infant and childhood mortality; large families, few of which were broken in their early years by parental death; parents' provision for their children through gifts or inheritances of land; and large numbers of older people.

In an important early essay on immigration to America, Herbert Moller concluded that men outnumbered women by about three to two among immigrants to New England. This would support the assumption that most women would marry, and at early ages, because of the larger male population. Recent studies find that seventeenth-century New England women typically first married in their late teens or early twenties. These findings, especially when compared with markedly higher ages at marriage for women in England, are certainly compatible with an uneven sex ratio among immigrants, which would have given women a wider choice of husbands and encouraged them to marry at earlier ages. However, in a reexamination of the immigrant lists, T. H. Breen and Stephen Foster find a more even sex ratio. How, then, might one explain the low ages at marriage among first-generation women? One possibility is as much ideological as social: the desire to establish a flourishing Puritan community. In discussing the "astoundingly high" birth rate in Dedham, 1636–1645, Lockridge speculates that "the challenge of founding a town in the wilderness brought a demographic response. Voluntarily or involuntarily the first townspeople seem to have produced children as if their success depended on it."[5]

Early marriages among immigrant women provided one condition for rapid population growth by increasing a woman's childbearing years. A typical couple conceived a child within a year of marriage (the rate of premarital conceptions in seventeenth-century New England was relatively low), and the average woman bore children at roughly two-year intervals until her late thirties or early forties, with the interval between the second-to-last and last child greater as she approached menopause.[6]

While risks of illness and death resulting from childbirth were considerably higher than today, mortality among New England women during the childbearing years may have been much lower than previously assumed. Death rates for women of childbearing age in Andover and Ipswich were comparable to those for men of the same age, although in Plymouth the risk of death for women during their childbearing years was significantly higher than the risk of death for men of the same age.[7]

Rates of remarriage provide another clue concerning risks of death during women's childbearing years. In Andover, "marriages broken by premature deaths clearly were the exceptions, not the general rule, since both men and women lived much longer than many of us have realized." In the case of Plymouth Colony, "the old stereotype of the doughty settler going through a long series of spouses one after the other needs to be quietly set aside."[8]

The consequences of this marital stability for family life in general, and for children in particular, are important for understanding childhood and for underscoring the dramatic contrasts in family life between New England and the Chesapeake. Early marriages for women, combined with relatively low rates of bereavement during the childbearing years, resulted in large New England families and few stepchildren. The size of completed families—those in which the wife survived to age forty-five—provides striking evidence of a major source of population growth in New England. In Andover and Plymouth Colony the average completed family had between seven and nine children. In Ipswich, the mean number of children in completed families was smaller, but women who married between ages fifteen and nineteen had an average of more than seven children.[9]

Historians generally agree that the importance of these large families lies not so much in the number of children born (although a woman's survival and continued childbearing were important), but in relatively low mortality rates for both children and adults. Although deaths were significantly underregistered, rates of infant mortality were not as high as previously assumed and certainly compare favorably with rates in pre-industrial England. In Plymouth Colony and Andover, rates of infant and childhood mortality were no more than 25 percent. Greven concludes that "even with allowances made for gaps in the records and under-recording of deaths, the fact remains that in Andover during the 1650's and 1660's there was an unusually high proportion of survivors among the infants and children born in the wilderness community." One important result was a long life expectancy for individuals who attained adult years. In Plymouth Colony, for example, men had a life expectancy of almost seventy years, while women could expect to live to their early sixties. Conditions were even more favorable in Andover, where the average first-generation men and women lived until their early seventies.[10]

Large families and favorable life expectancies did not necessarily result in large or complex household structures. Families were nuclear in structure (that is, consisting of parents and their children), and households, on the average, were small. Extended families (three generations in the same household) were relatively uncommon. Elderly parents might live with an adult child and grandchildren—for example, with a son to whom the parental homestead might be deeded in exchange for lifetime care. Such arrangements, however, affected only *one* child, for, as John J. Waters urges, "the question to ask is not how many households had grandparents, but rather how many grandparents shared households with a son or daughter and their children." Among those who wrote wills in seventeenth-century Barnstable, at least one-third and possibly one-half lived with their children.[11]

The 1689 census for Bristol, Rhode Island, reveals that, although households ranged in size from one to fifteen persons, those containing four, five, or six persons were most common. Household size depended on two principal variables: the parents' ages and the number of servants. Young couples would not have many children, while elderly couples would have few children still living at home. Thus, a couple in their early forties, with the wife perhaps still bearing children, would have a large household.[12]

While household structure was usually simple and household size varied with the parents' ages, more complex family relationships formed outside the home. Most families were nuclear for most of their existence, but adult longevity and the great numbers of surviving children inevitably resulted in extended kinship ties. Although Demos believes that such ties had relatively little strength or meaning in Plymouth Colony, other historians have demonstrated their importance in settlement patterns and in the services that distant relatives could provide. Thus, in Andover, where almost 80 percent of second-generation sons remained, an elaborate network of persons related by blood and marriage emerged in the seventeenth century and became increasingly complex in the eighteenth. More subtly, naming patterns recognized and strengthened kin connections. Even when geographically separated, families relied on distant relatives for apprenticeships and other forms of education for their children. Thus, the seventeenth-century New England population experienced unprecedented, rapid demographic growth and stability: families persisted in terms of both geographical location over extended periods and the survival of large numbers of parents and children.[13]

In contrast to early New England, the demographic history of the Chesapeake colonies was bleak. Because of extraordinarily high death rates among all ages, both sexes, and all classes, the population of Virginia and Maryland could not sustain itself by natural increase and grew only through migration from Europe and Africa. Families experienced chronic and pervasive instability at all levels of society. Life expectancy was low; completed families were unusual; parents rarely lived to see their grandchildren; children frequently lost one parent; and orphans were common. As a result, families and households were frequently altered in size and composition by death and remarriage. "Judged in terms of natural increase," concludes Russell R. Menard, "the Puritan settlements were a demographic success, Virginia and Maryland failures."[14]

Under the Virginia Company, the colony was a "death trap" for immigrants, but even after the Company's dissolution, Virginia remained an early graveyard for most immigrants. In the years 1635–1699, more than 80,000 people arrived in Virginia, yet the population was only about 60,000 in 1700. Immigrants to Maryland fared no better: although between 23,500 and 38,000 Europeans arrived in the years 1634–1681, by the latter date whites numbered only about 19,000. The contrast between the Chesapeake and New England is sobering: although the regions had roughly equal populations at the end of the seventeenth century, the Chesapeake had received perhaps seven or eight times the number of European immigrants. Not until late in the century did changing conditions in the Chesapeake allow the growth of population through natural increase. As John Oldmixon observed, "Twas a long time before Virginia saw a Race of English on the Spot."[15]

Menard and other Chesapeake scholars identify three circumstances that restricted the white population's natural increase: a shortage of women, high rates of disease and death, and late marriages. The shortage of women reflected the character of European immigration to the Chesapeake. In Virginia's early development, when the Company hoped to exploit native labor and find quick riches, there was little reason to send women to the colony. Even after development of tobacco as a cash crop, Virginia resembled, in Edmund S. Morgan's appropriate phrase, a "boom town," pervaded by an "atmosphere of transience," where "women were scarcer than corn or liquor . . . and fetched a higher price." Unlike immigration to New England, which was characterized by family groups and an age distribution resembling a settled population, immigration to the Chesapeake consisted largely of young, single males, many arriving as indentured servants to satisfy the tobacco economy's "voracious" demands for labor.[16]

The preponderance of males placed a premium on women, and most female immigrants were of marriageable age. In other circumstances, most women would have married early, but their servant status delayed marriage, and many died as servants (perhaps 40 percent in mid-seventeenth-century Maryland, for example). Female indentured servants who survived seasoning and servitude quickly found husbands, but most marriages were short-lived, with few children born and fewer surviving to maturity. Since immigrant women typically married in their mid-twenties, they had already lost up to ten years of their reproductive lives and the possibility of bearing four or five additional children.[17]

Life expectancies were sharply reduced in the Chesapeake's exceptionally hostile disease environment, where immigrants encountered dysentery, typhoid, influenza epidemics, and "a malarial fever which apparently approached pandemic proportions." Men in their early twenties were likely to live for only an additional twenty to twenty-five years, and death rates among infants and children were even more devastating. In Maryland, for example, as many as one-fourth to one-third of all male children died before their first birthdays, and 45 to 55 percent died before age twenty.[18]

High death rates among all age groups, combined with relatively late marriages for immigrant women, resulted in small families that were frequently broken by parental death. Thus, in 1625, more than 60 percent of the couples in Virginia had no surviving children, and couples who did usually had no more than one or two. Not only was family size reduced by infant and childhood mortality, but also the number that might have been conceived by a couple was limited by the relatively high ages at marriage for immigrant women and by the death of either husband or wife. As Lorena S. Walsh notes, "the life cycle of growing up, marrying, procreating, and dying was compressed within a short span of years." Thus, in one Maryland county in the second half of the century, half of the marriages lasted less than seven years. Parents had no realistic expectation of a long marriage or many children, much less of seeing their grandchildren. As John M. Murrin observes, grandparents may have been a uniquely New England "invention."[19]

Under such conditions, many children were orphaned. In Middlesex County, Virginia, "parental death was a part of the fabric of life," for nearly 25 percent of children lost one or both parents before age five, 50 percent by age thirteen, and nearly 75 percent by age twenty-one or marriage, whichever came first. Because of the probability that a surviving parent would remarry, children were likely to spend part of their lives with one or more stepparents. The structure of Chesapeake households tended to be both complex and impermanent. A household was likely to contain, in the Rutmans' words, a mixture of "orphans, half-brothers, stepbrothers and stepsisters, and wards running a gamut of ages. The father figure in the house might well be an uncle or a brother, the mother figure an aunt, elder sister, or simply the father's 'now-wife'—to use the wording frequently found in conveyances and wills."[20]

Family life in the seventeenth-century Chesapeake was thus characterized by a profound instability deriving from the age and sex characteristics of the population, relatively late ages at marriage among immigrant women, and exceptionally high rates of morbidity and mortality. The resulting small families were frequently broken by parental death and just as often re-formed by the remarriage of surviving parents and the merging of sometimes quite disparate households.

Conditions began to change toward the end of the century, primarily because of earlier and hence more prolific marriages among native-born white women: while immigrant women married in their mid-twenties, most of their daughters married well before age twenty-one. In Somerset County, Maryland, some girls married as early as twelve, and among those born before 1670 the mean age of marriage was sixteen and one-half years.[21]

Early marriages among native-born white women, longer life expectancies, and a balanced sex ratio in the native-born population resulted in significant natural population growth toward the end of the century. Early eighteenth-century census figures for Maryland suggest the importance and magnitude of this natural increase. Between 1704 and 1710, years of low immigration, the white population grew by more than 2.5 percent a year, from 30,164 to 35,794.[22]

The growing native-born population was crucial not merely in terms of numbers but also for social stability. The increasingly balanced ratio of men to women, which stemmed from declining immigration in the late seventeenth century and the growth of the native-born population, resulted in a smaller proportion of young, unmarried, and often landless males who had little stake in society and whose tenuous status had exacerbated the turmoils of Bacon's Rebellion.[23]

The growth of the native-born population contributed to the emergence of elaborate and important networks of kin. Since most immigrants arrived as single individuals, it is not surprising that, at death, those who had married left few relatives other than a spouse and children. The native-born population was more fortunate and, in times of crisis, especially when children were orphaned, could seek assistance from an expanding range of kin and quasi-kin. As the Rutmans note with respect to orphans, "what we might take for the disruption of childhood involved, conversely, a system for rooting the parentless child within the society" through the reciprocal bonds of kinship and quasi-kinship. In other words, the importance of extended kin was enhanced in a society that frequently confronted crises of parental death and orphanhood. If the "startling contrast" in mortality figures between New England and the Chesapeake is substantiated by additional research in New England, the Rutmans conclude "that we are dealing with two entirely different types of childhood along the seventeenth-century Anglo-American coast— in New England one lived more in a parental situation; in the Chesapeake area one lived more in a kinship situation."[24]

The contrasts in the population histories of the two regions are significant in virtually every respect: the characteristics of the settlers, health conditions, mortality among all ages and groups, age at marriage, family size, household structure, duration of marriages and rates of remarriage, life expectancies, and age structure. Immigration to New England, which was mostly concentrated into little more than a decade, was a movement of families, including a fairly even sex ratio, an age distribution that was typical of a settled population, and relatively few servants whose status delayed marriage. By comparison, immigration to the Chesapeake occurred throughout the century (although not at a uniform rate),[25] with the proportion of white and black immigrants shifting significantly in the later decades. The movement of Europeans to the Chesapeake was dominated by young, single males, and both men and women usually spent several years under indenture contracts.

Ages at first marriage reflected the differences in the immigration patterns to New England and to the Chesapeake. In New England first-generation women tended to marry young, while their husbands' ages at marriage approximated the higher European patterns. Age at marriage rose for women in subsequent generations, but their ages at marriage remained well below those of European women.

Upon arrival in the colonies, newcomers encountered very different conditions. In New England, the brief but devastating starving time suffered by the Pilgrims, which has been enshrined in the national mythology, was succeeded by generally healthful conditions in which epidemic diseases such as smallpox occurred only in port towns like Boston. Not until the eighteenth century did New Englanders face major changes in their disease environment when an increasingly densely settled landscape created conditions where epidemics such as the "throat distemper" (diphtheria) spread far and wide. By contrast, Virginia's starving time and the subsequent decades of disease and death in the Chesapeake have never been a subject of reverence. Indeed, only recently have historians understood the health problems that debilitated and decimated the European population. The effects of these two sharply contrasting environments on family life and population growth are dramatic. In New England, life expectancy was high; rates of maternal, infant, and childhood mortality were low; families were nuclear, large, and infrequently broken by the death of one partner in their early years; the structure of households was simple; and the number of elderly people was large. In the Chesapeake, these conditions were reversed: life expectancy was low; pregnant women were exposed to a variety of life-threatening conditions; risks of death at childbirth, or from causes related to parturition, were high, as was infant and childhood mortality; families were small, but households were complex; widows and widowers abounded, and while widows quickly remarried, significant numbers of men never mar-

ried despite what Carr and Walsh have termed "a pattern of serial pol-
yandry, which enabled more men to marry and to father families than
the sex ratios otherwise would have permitted"; there were few elderly
persons; and traditional classifications such as "nuclear" or "extended"
inadequately describe marriages and families that were frequently visited
by death and often re-formed by the surviving members of broken
families.[26]

In comparing the Chesapeake and New England to England and continental Europe, historians have noted that demographic conditions were
more favorable in New England than in the pre-industrial England which
Peter Laslett has described in *The World We Have Lost*. By contrast, conditions in the Chesapeake, which made life so precarious and families
so unstable, might not have seemed unusual to Europeans who had
experienced wars, famines, epidemic diseases, and considerable geographic movement of individuals, families, and groups. Nonetheless,
some characteristics of the Chesapeake were exceptional, even by European standards: the extreme imbalance in the sex ratio; a new disease
environment; delayed marriages among immigrant women, unusually
early marriages among native-born white women, and no marriages for
many men; especially high rates of premarital sexual activity; and extraordinarily complex and unstable family and household structures.[27]

In comparing recent work on the Chesapeake with New England, John
M. Murrin warns that the Puritans should not provide the norms by
which to measure others' deficiencies, for they were "just about the
oddest group ever to brave the Atlantic crossing, at least until the Quaker
migration of the 1680s." Murrin has in mind much more than the demographic characteristics of the migration to New England and the
conditions that resulted in remarkable population growth: "The ... people who settled New England in family groups and invested its stingy
soil with millennial expectations that could never be met were truly
unusual, weird even by seventeenth-century standards." Other scholars
make essentially the same point, although perhaps not so forcefully. In
addition, some urge a reexamination of seventeenth-century New England to determine, with greater precision, whether the studies published
in the 1960s and early 1970s should be revised. It would also be worthwhile to accumulate data on New York under both Dutch and English
rule and on the initial decades of settlement in Pennsylvania,[28] so that
the demographic characteristics of all the colonies might be compared.

For better or worse, however "weird" or "odd" the Puritans and their
descendants might have been, they assiduously recorded information
about their culture, gave advice and admonitions to all who would listen
(as well as to those who would not), and reflected and anguished, both
publicly and privately, about the nature and results of their special en-

terprise. Much of this literature reveals a pervasive concern for their children individually and, in characteristic language, for the "rising generation."

In examining New Englanders' ideas about and their treatment of children, historians have disagreed about the nature and duration of childhood, the quality of childhood experiences, and the influence of parental attitudes and practices on children. One of the most interesting debates focuses on the duration of childhood, Puritans' perceptions of their children, and the existence of adolescence in anything but a physiological sense.

In this respect, the New England Puritans have fascinated—and sometimes repelled—several generations of historians. While scholars have disagreed on many aspects of Puritan religious, political, economic, and social life, with respect to childrearing there is substantial agreement on one point. Almost without exception, from Alice Morse Earle in the 1890s to John Demos and Philip Greven in the 1970s, historians have concluded that Puritan childrearing ideas and practices had devastating effects on the development of healthy personalities.[29]

In part, this assessment is based on the assumption that modern styles of childrearing are appropriate for other cultures and eras and that, lacking the insights of modern psychology, Puritans could not possibly have nurtured healthy children. Some accounts of childhood in early America manifest a smug superiority, a gush of sentimentality, or even blank incomprehension. In response to Cotton Mather's account that he told his daughter he would die shortly and she must always remember her own sinful nature, Earle could "hardly understand" why Mather, "who was really very gentle to his children, should have taken upon himself to trouble this tender little blossom with dread of his death." Earle was less charitable toward Nathaniel Mather's expression of guilt for whittling on the Sabbath: "It is satisfactory to add that this young prig of a Mather died when nineteen years of age."[30]

Also contributing to the conclusion that Puritans badly handled their responsibilities as parents is the widely held belief that they—and others as well—had no concept of childhood and treated children as miniature adults. Recent examinations of New England laws, the role of children in the churches, children's literature, ideas about the ages of man and childrearing, and portraiture demonstrate that Puritans, while certainly different from us in many respects, considered childhood as a distinct phase of life.[31]

For those who believe that Puritans regarded children as miniature adults, it follows that Puritans did not recognize adolescence. "All the evidence we have," writes Demos, "suggests that adolescence as we know it—a turbulent period of inner stress—barely existed before the twentieth century. Here, it seems, is a developmental crisis largely created, or at least sharply intensified, by the progress of modern history." Recent scholarship, however, challenges this view. Indeed, the discovery of childhood and adolescence in colonial America is part of a larger reassessment of childhood and youth in Europe and a growing critical awareness of the deficiencies of Philippe Aries's *Centuries of Childhood* which suggested that Europeans did not recognize childhood as a stage of life before the seventeenth century.[32]

The Puritans' relationship with and responsibility and love for their children began well before birth, for Puritanism not only strongly sanctioned marriage for the purpose of procreation, but also posited, in John Cotton's words, that children were "capable of the habits and gifts of grace from their first Conception." According to English Puritan Isaac Ambrose, infancy began in the womb, and parents were obliged to pray for an unborn child because it was conceived in sin. A mother also had to take special care to ensure safe delivery. Citing Judges 13:7, Ambrose asked, "Why was the Charge of *abstaining from Wine, strong Drink, and unclean Things*, given to *Manoah's Wife*, but because *of the Child which she had conceived?*" Thus, prenatal care was both spiritual and physiological. Noting that an unborn child had an immortal soul, Joseph Belcher asked, "is not this enough to make a Fathers Prayers and Cryes for his Child *Anticipate* his kisses and embraces of it?"[33]

Childbirth took place in the home, with a midwife directing the delivery and assisted by neighborhood women. Childbirth was part of a network of female friendships and mutual assistance, and, while husbands were frequently nearby, there is no evidence that they witnessed or assisted at the birth.[34]

The bonds between a mother and her newborn would develop in the hours, days, and weeks following birth. Puritans were amazed by the very rapid recovery of Indian women after delivery, for their own experience—indeed, that of the English more generally—differed significantly. Following childbirth, an English mother was likely to be confined for a period of weeks, first to her bed, then to her room, and finally to her home. She might be helped by her family, servants, neighbors, or persons who were specifically brought into the home to care for the infant. However, unless she had difficulty in nursing or had the means and desire to hire a wet-nurse, mother and infant were in each other's presence much of the time.[35]

The importance of the bonding of mother and nursing child was readily acknowledged by Puritans. As John Robinson pointed out, "Children, in their first days, have the greater benefit of good mothers, not only because they suck their milk, but in a sort, their manners also, by being continually with them, and receiving their first impressions from them." Ambrose noted the mother's special responsibility for a nursing child, as it was her duty "to take all the pains she possibly may, for the

Education of her Child; and especially to give her Child suck, if she be able thereto." Not only was this nature's way, but it was also sanctioned by Scripture, and Ambrose cited nine biblical passages in favor of breast-feeding one's own child. John Cotton believed that "love makes a Nurse very painfull about her childe, you shall not have so much service from any servant you keep as that service a Nurse performs; she doth it freely and readily, love will make us serviceable without measure."[36]

While recognizing the special bonds between infant and mother or nurse, Puritan fathers may not have always been entirely sympathetic to a mother's grief upon a child's death. Thus, following the death of her child, the younger John Cotton's wife was "most desolate and pensive, and did yesternight fall afresh to mourning, as if she had nothing else to doe." Cotton asked Increase Mather to send some "lines...for her direction and comfort, and for mine also."[37]

Child-naming also reveals how parents invested part of themselves in their children. Parents customarily named children after themselves, with the mother's name given to a daughter as often as the father's was given to a son. Naming children after the parents was one way to draw children into a familial network of kin, some of whom were immediate and living, others more distant or deceased.[38]

While the choice of a name might strengthen familial ties and create reciprocal obligations between the person so honored and the namesake, devout New Englanders often chose biblical names. The editors of the Geneva Bible (1560) had lamented that

the wickednes of time, and the blindnes of the former age hathe bene suche that all things altogether have bene abused and corrupted, so that the very right names of diverse of the holie men named in the Scriptures have bene forgotten, and now seme strange unto us, and the names of infants that shulde ever have some godlie advertisements in them, and shulde be memorials and markes of the children of God received into his housholde, hathe bene hereby also changed and made the signes and badges of idolatrie and heathenish impietie.

They therefore appended a table of Old Testament names and their meanings

partly to call backe the godlie from that abuse, when they shal know the true names of the godlie fathers, and what they signifie, that their children now named after them may have testimonies by their very names, that they are within that faithful familie that in all their doings had ever God before their eyes, and that they are bounde by these their names to serve God from their infancie and have occasion to praise him for his workes wroght in them and their fathers: but chiefly to restore the names to their integritie, whereby many places of the Scriptures and secret mysteries of the holie Gost shal better be understand [sic].[39]

Puritans also looked to providential events in selecting names. Thus, John Cotton baptized his first child "Seaborn" to commemorate his birth during the voyage to New England. When a child died, parents commonly gave its name to the next-born, same-sex sibling. While the reasons for this practice are not entirely clear, scattered records are suggestive. When Thomas Shepard's first son and namesake died, he named his second son Thomas, "which name I gave him because we thought the Lord gave me the first son I lost on sea in this again, and hence gave him his brother's name." Similarly, following the death of his son Benjamin, John Paine named his next-born son "in remembrance of my dear Son Benjamin who latly departed this life."[40] Such cases suggest that reusing a name was a remembrance of the deceased, a way to express yet limit the grief resulting from the loss of a child.

The death of children was often a grim reality for New England parents. While infant and childhood mortality rates were lower in New England than in other parts of the world, death was an ever-present but unpredictable possibility. Life was fragile, the child like "a bubble, or the brittle glass," in Anne Bradstreet's apt metaphor.[41]

While the reuse of dead children's names might have permitted parents to handle feelings of grief, some historians suggest that death posed far deeper problems for Puritan parents. The fear of infant damnation, Peter G. Slater suggests, "cast its shadow over Puritan households in mourning for deceased babies." John Philip Hall asserts that "a child who lived only one hour could hardly be brought into salvation by faith, and New England Calvinism did not even have a Limbo for those who died so young." In Michael Wigglesworth's *Day of Doom* (1662), God consigned infants who died without baptism to "the easiest room in Hell."[42]

This view is partly a misunderstanding on the part of Puritanism, for the Westminster Confession of Faith (1647) provided that "elect infants, dying in infancy, are regenerated and saved by Christ through the Spirit, who worketh when, and where, and how he pleaseth."[43] And, as noted above, John Cotton had argued that children were "capable of the habits and gifts of grace from their first Conception." Did parents have grounds for hope that dead children might be saved, enjoying the delights of heaven rather than suffering the torments of hell? Certainly, parents' pain at a child's death was intense; it would have been excruciating if they thought that their child's soul was consigned to eternal suffering.

Cotton Mather, himself frequently bereaved, articulated his own faith following the death of one of his children. Acknowledging "*the multitude of my Thoughts within me,*" he asked his congregation to follow the counsel which he gave himself. By his covenant with Abraham, God promised to be a God to both Abraham and his seed; this covenant had passed to the Gentiles through Christ, and therefore Mather rejoiced:

But if the Great God, will be a God unto my *Children*, Triumph, O my *Faith*, in a joyful Assurance That He will *Raise them from the Dead*, and that *He has prepared for them a Room in his Heavenly City*. My *Dead Children* are to *Live again*; They are only *Entered into their Chambers*, and *Shut up*, and *Hidden*, and for a *Little moment*, until the *Indignation of God against a wicked world be over past*. A *Dew* from God, the Regenerating and Enlivening *Spirit* of God falling like a *Dew* upon them (which in their *Baptism* has been *Sealed* unto them) shall fetch them out like *Herbs*, at the *Spring of the Resurrection*.[44]

Mather conceded the difficulty of explaining how "the *Souls* of any *Infants* are Sanctified," but he was unwilling to sorrow for his children, "as the Pagans do, who have *no Hope* for theirs." Rather, he would forfeit all earthly treasure before doubting that his children had an eternal inheritance in heaven. "I do *Hope* (and God forbid that I should easily *Cast away the Confidence*!) That when my *Children* are *Gone*, they are not *Lost*; but carried unto the *Heavenly Feast* with *Abraham*, whose *Blessing* is come upon them through Jesus Christ."[45]

This reasoning, which was not unique to Mather, helps us to understand parental reflections and expressions upon the death of children. In consoling a member of the Winthrop family, Samuel Sewall noted, " 'Tis the Happiness of Christian Parents, more especially respecting their Infant-Children, that they sorrow not as those without Hope"; as "a most sweet and rich Cordial," he cited appropriate passages from Isaiah and Corinthians. John Paine turned to verse when his second Benjamin died:

> I hope in heaven my precious Babe is blest
> and that with Jesus he is now at rest
> The lord gives and the lord takes away
> Blessed be the name of the lord
> our Earthly Comforts are but mercys lent us
> and of Such blessings Soon may death prevent us.

Such consolatory reflections, offered by friends and relatives or expressed by parents, were pervasive in the colonial period. Although parents grieved at a child's death, Puritanism provided strong hope, if not absolute confidence, that a dead child would be saved. If parents suspected that children went even to Wigglesworth's "easiest room in Hell,"[46] such fears are hidden by this rhetoric.

Puritanism admonished believers to love God more than His creatures and to look toward the eternal delights of heaven rather than the transitory pleasures of earth. Within these limitations, Puritan parents loved their children. In a world where early death was far more frequent than today, Puritanism provided a check on one's loving emotions and, equally important, sustained hope and provided consolation upon the death of loved ones.[47]

Barring illness or accident, the first year or two of an infant's life may have been "a relatively comfortable and tranquil time." At the center of attention, it was comfortably dressed, often warmed by a fire, and allowed ready access to its mother's breast. This image of early life is plausible, but, as David J. Rothman suggests, one might draw an opposite conclusion: "Since the household was small and the mother burdened with many duties, the infant always seemed underfoot; breast feeding was rushed and impersonal, at the mother's convenience. The noise level in the house was high (with people working, eating, playing, and visiting), so that the baby slept fitfully and was frequently startled; when he added his own cries to the din, he was perfunctorily moved or attended to." Bradstreet, whose "Childhood" recalls "Infancy" in "Of the Four Ages of Man," lends some support to the image of a loving, but also harried, mother:

> My mother still did waste as I did thrive,
> Who yet with love and all alacrity,
> Spending, was willing to be spent for me.
> With wayward cries I did disturb her rest,
> Who sought still to appease me with the breast:
> With weary arms she danced and "By By" sung,
> When wretched I, ingrate, had done the wrong.

Historians will never know with certainty what actually transpired, for details of nursing, dress, toilet-training, and other aspects of daily care were so unremarkable, so mundane in their regularity, that they were seldom mentioned, much less systematically recorded. Church records mark the early baptism of many children (commonly within two weeks of birth), and diaries occasionally note the weaning of a child (typically twelve to eighteen months after birth). But it would be difficult to generalize from Bradstreet's observation that "some children are hardly weaned; although the teat be rubbed with wormwood or mustard they will either wipe it off, or else suck down sweet and bitter together."[48]

Further compounding the difficulty of generalization is sibling rank, for the experiences of a first-born child and of the last-born some twenty years later might have differed radically. The accumulation of direct childrearing experience, the effects of children on their parents, and elder siblings' care for a newborn may have differentiated, perhaps significantly, and affected successive children within a family.[49] In the absence of direct evidence, however, this remains at best conjecture.

Demos urges historians to identify patterns of language and adult behavior which might suggest hypotheses about treatment of children.

In Plymouth Colony, he argues, the ideas of separatist minister John Robinson were especially important. Robinson believed that all children possessed, in varying degrees, "a stubbornness, and stoutness of mind arising from natural pride," which parents were obligated to break and beat down. The result would be "humility and tractableness," upon which parents might build other virtues. Parents were to restrain and repress children's wills at an early age, "lest sooner than they imagine, the tender sprigs grow to that stiffness, that they will rather break than bow." Ideally, "children should not know, if it could be kept from them, that they have a will in their own, but in their parents' keeping."[50]

Although Robinson nowhere stated the ages at which children would be subject to his advice, Demos speculates that such discipline might have been imposed upon a one- to two-year-old, thus coinciding with weaning, the birth of a rival sibling, and a child's increasing physical mobility, dexterity, and expressions of will. Drawing on an Eriksonian model of personality development, he hypothesizes that the crushing of a child's efforts to achieve autonomy left it with a lasting sense of shame and doubt that would later be manifested in extremely litigious behavior over issues of trespass and slander as well as in the public humiliations that were characteristic Puritan punishments.

Despite Demos's ingenuity in developing an arresting hypothesis about early childhood discipline and its effects on a child's personality, one cannot, as Demos acknowledges, go beyond hypothesis. In part, Robinson's advice exemplifies the interpretive difficulties that Jay Mechling delineates in his "Advice to Historians on Advice to Mothers." Since twentieth-century mothers frequently subscribe to one childrearing model and yet act differently, one cannot assume that mothers in past times were more consistent. Thus, advice on childrearing is not descriptive of actual practice and, in fact, is evidence only about the advice-giver's state of mind.[51]

Robinson presents special problems of interpretation, for not only was he a member of that highly educated—and therefore exceptional—profession that provides most extant childrearing advice for the colonial period, but as a separatist he was exceptional even among Puritans. Furthermore, he died in the Netherlands. It is especially difficult to link the written advice of a dead minister with the childrearing practices of people who were geographically far removed and among whom literacy may not have been widespread. In addition, however abstractly compelling Robinson's advice might have been, his childrearing observations and experiences as a male were probably quite different from the actual experiences of the women who were responsible for day-to-day care of infants and small children.

Finally, at least some of Robinson's contemporaries had substantially different perceptions of children. John Cotton, for example, urged his congregation to be as little children if they were to be children of God (Matthew 18:3, "Except ye be converted, and become as little children, ye shall not enter into the kingdom of heaven"). Those who wanted their sins forgiven were "to be of Child-like dispositions, free from ambition, and malice, and revenge, to frame themselves to humility, and innocency, and meeknesse, and simplicity, and contentment, and resting on promise and hopes."[52]

Puritans recognized a child's limited abilities. Cotton noted that, although children might "spend much time in pastime and play," this was not idleness, "for their bodies are too weak to labour, and their minds to study are too shallow." When children arrived at "riper years," they should be employed, but the first seven years were "spent in pastime, and God looks not much at it." While Samuel Sewall might condemn mischievous behavior on April Fool's Day ("anniversary days for sinfull vanities, are Damnable"), casual references to children at play suggest that the Puritans sanctioned children's play if it did not lead to mischief or disrupt the sabbath.[53]

While parents might not be unduly concerned about play among very young children, by age seven a child would have begun several significant transitions that were manifested by changes in clothing and embodied in the child's introduction to the doctrines and rituals of religious life, the world of print, and the responsibilities of work. In addition, some children would be placed into an apprenticeship or put out into other homes.

While few examples of seventeenth-century children's clothing survive, there is no evidence that infants were swaddled, and there is some agreement that boys and girls were probably dressed similarly "in a kind of long robe which opened down the front." This garment, while similar to a woman's dress, was set off by a pair of ribbons which hung from the shoulders—perhaps relics of leading strings. How long children wore this robe is unclear, although Bradstreet's advice suggests that it may have been somewhat modified as soon as a child could walk and run: "A prudent mother will not cloth her little child with a long and cumbersome garment; she easily forsees what events it is like to produce, at the best, but falls and bruises or perhaps somewhat worse."[54]

By about age five or six, boys' and girls' clothing became distinct. While it might appear that children were now dressed as miniature adults and were symbolically entering the world of adulthood, changes in clothing can also be interpreted simply as gender differentiation. Karin Calvert's recent study of colonial portraiture suggests something more subtle. While a boy of six or seven gave up petticoats and now wore breeches,

the junior status of boys in their mid-teens or younger can be read in portraiture, for artists commonly depicted breeched youths in conventional feminine poses, surrounded by a flutter of drapery (a device used for women's portraits), or holding a feminine prop. Boys of this age were never depicted with such standard male props as an account ledger, military baton, or Bible, that indicated occupation or achievement, though they did carry artifacts that symbolized masculinity and social status, such as gloves, walking stick, or sword. A third of the boys between the ages of seven and fourteen posed with a feminine prop such as fruit, flowers, or pets—a last tie to the subordinate class from which they were emerging.[55]

Costume thus signalled the beginning of a transition into the adult world rather than an abrupt and complete entry.

A child's initiation into the symbolic and ritual dimensions of religious life began at an early age. Born into a pious family, it would have been surrounded with religious ceremony and expressions of piety from the moment of birth, including all aspects of daily family devotion, such as prayer, psalm-singing, and Bible readings, as well as the special character of sabbath observances. As early as 1648, heads of families were required by law "once a week (at the least) [to] catechize their children and servants in the grounds and principles of Religion," and when ministers assumed the burden of catechizing groups of children, these classes included children of seven or eight years and older. Just how soon children were introduced to the public aspects of religious ceremony is not clear. Joseph Belcher's advice indicates a willingness to exclude infants and perhaps small children from church services: parents were admonished to bring children to church as soon as they were old enough "to be benefited themselves and the Congregation not disturbed by 'em." John Cotton recognized the limited capacity of small children to absorb complex doctrine: "bring them to Church, and help them to remember something, and tell them the meaning of it, and take a little in good part, and encourage them, and that will make them delight in it."[56]

A child's introduction to print and literacy was connected to the family's and community's religious life, for a limited number of texts—the Bible, a catechism, a primer—provided entry into a world of "intensive" readers and "steady sellers." As David D. Hall observes, seventeenth-century readers treasured certain texts—the Bible and books of devotion—which "gained in meaning as time went by." This was not a modern world in which readers sought new or novel ideas but rather a conservative world in which "certain formulas had enduring significance."[57]

Historians have yet to determine the extent and quality of literacy among colonial Americans. Even for New England the answer is ambiguous. At the heart of the problem is the fact that reading and writing were separate skills, learned at different ages and under different circumstances. As Increase Mather recalled, "I learned to read of my mother. I learned to write of Father, who also instructed me in grammar learning,

both in the Latin and the greeke Tongues."[58] Not only does this suggest
the separate and sequential steps in the acquisition of the skills of literacy,
but it also underscores the mother's subordinate role in a world in which
her ability to read, but not necessarily to write, provided reinforcement
for cultural norms.

According to Kenneth A. Lockridge, in 1660 only 60 percent of New
England men who left wills could write their names; the other 40 percent
signed with a mark. The male signature-literacy rate rose to 70 percent
by 1710 and to nearly 90 percent by 1790. Among the few women who
left wills, only one-third who died before 1670 signed their names; this
figure rose to nearly 45 percent for the rest of the colonial period.
Lockridge concludes that the incidence of signatures on wills is a reliable
indicator of literacy rates in the entire population, as biases in the sample
(for example, age, wealth, occupational status, feebleness, forgetfulness,
and educational opportunity) tend to cancel each other. As Harvey J.
Graff points out, however, such biases in the data may not offset each
other.[59]

This emphasis on signature rates obscures an even more important
issue: the quality of a population's literacy. Those who have studied
literacy point out that signing one's name was an intermediate step between reading and writing. That is, a person who signed his or her name
could almost certainly read but could not necessarily write anything more
than a signature. What qualitative judgments can be made about the
reading literacy of a person who could only sign his or her name? David
Hall provides the most persuasive insight into the culture of literacy.
His emphasis on the "intensive" quality of reading and the rote manner
in which reading skills were acquired suggests that the literacy of much
of the seventeenth-century New England population was profoundly
conservative, reinforcing the culture's values rather than providing access to new ideas or information.

Just as a child acquired reading skills through rote and repetition, so,
too, initiation into the world of work involved imitation and observation.
As a child grew in strength and dexterity, and with practice, he or she
would move from simple to more complex tasks, each perhaps more
demanding but also comprehensible and accessible because few callings
were primarily intellectual in nature. In both the male and the female
worlds of work, many tasks quickly became matters of routine, to be
carried out as regularly, and perhaps as monotonously, as the rising and
setting of the sun and the passing of the seasons.

The age at which children began to assume work responsibilities marked
another transition for those who became apprentices or who were placed
in other households for a period of service. In Plymouth Colony, Demos
finds that six to eight years was apparently "the most common age for
such arrangements." Morgan, on the other hand, places the timing of

a boy's choice of a calling at age ten to fourteen. In a largely agricultural economy, apprenticeships presumably affected a relatively small proportion of children—those, for example, who entered trades closely allied with agriculture, or children from more urban backgrounds, or those whose parents could afford the expenses that might have been part of a contract or understanding with a master or another family.[60]

Those children who were put out into other households present an intriguing interpretive challenge. In some cases, the reasons were clear: the child might obtain valuable training either for a calling or in literacy. Morgan notes, however, that "Puritan children were frequently brought up in other families than their own even when there was no apparent educational advantage involved." Because New Englanders did not record their motives, Morgan speculates that the practice reflected an older English custom which the Puritans continued because they "did not trust themselves with their own children" and feared that too much affection would spoil them. The removal of a child from its parents may have had a sound psychological basis:

The child left home just at the time when parental discipline causes increasing friction, just at the time when a child begins to assert his independence. By allowing a strange master to take over the disciplinary function, the parent could meet the child upon a plane of affection and friendliness. At the same time the child would be taught good behavior by someone who would not forgive him any mischief out of affection for his person.[61]

Morgan's hypothesis has been generally accepted, although without supporting evidence. Charles G. Steffen has shown that the Sewall family placed their children into a web of extended kin, and therefore "relatives remained figures of authority for the youths."[62] The Sewalls' status— and that of many others who left records of placing their children into other households—reminds us of the highly selective and fragmentary evidence on which discussions of putting out have relied. The practice may have been largely that of the upper social strata—perhaps consciously emulating English practice and thereby indicating membership in a wider Anglo-American colonial class system. Historians have not determined whether their less advantaged neighbors or co-religionists had inclination or opportunity to place their children into other homes primarily for psychological reasons.

The case of the Sewall children suggests another hypothesis: namely, that a family's structure and life cycle may have influenced the decision to place children outside the home. For example, the number and sex composition of a family's children may have encouraged parents to place some of them into other households, thereby alleviating crowdedness and disposing of surplus labor. Similarly, families at different stages of

the life cycle may have needed additional labor either to care for very
small children or to replace grown children who had left the household.
Finally, the fact that Samuel and Hannah Sewall placed their infants in
the household of Samuel's parents may have been an acknowledgment
of grandfather Henry Sewall's continuing exercise of authority in familial
affairs.[63] It may also have reflected mutual needs: the grandparents'
need for children as objects of affection and the parents' need for more
freedom.

By the age of five or six, then, children's roles in the culture were
significantly expanded: dressed so as to be distinguished by gender,
learning to read and perhaps to write, acquiring the rudiments of religious doctrine, and developing initial skills as workers, they were becoming contributing members of their families and, in some cases, of
other households. They were not expected, however, to perform tasks
more suitable for older persons. As Bradstreet admonished, "A wise
father will not lay a burden on a child of seven years old which he knows
is enough for one of twice his strength."[64] New Englanders thus recognized childhood as a distinct phase of development, although their
society was hardly as age-graded as ours; furthermore, transitions from
one stage of life to another were much less abrupt.

Puritans also recognized important changes in the early teens, and in
their vocabulary the word "youth" had connotations similar to "adolescence" in our own culture. As catechumens, older boys were separated
from younger ones at age twelve or thirteen. In Massachusetts, fourteen
was the legal age of discretion for slander, while in Plymouth Colony,
sixteen was the age of discretion in cases of slander and lying. Orphans
were permitted to choose their own guardians at fourteen, and a sod-
omist under fourteen was severely punished rather than executed. The
increasing maturity of teenagers—sexual, moral, and intellectual—implicit in these legal provisions was acknowledged by Thomas Shepard
when he admonished his fourteen-year-old son, who was entering Harvard in 1672, to "Remember ... that tho' you have spent your time in
the vanity of Childhood; sports and mirth, little minding better things,
yet that now, when come to this ripeness of Admission to the College,
that now God and man expects you should putt away Childish things:
now is the time come, wherein you are to be serious, and to learn sobriety,
and wisdom in all your ways which concern God and man." In the early
eighteenth century, the Reverend Benjamin Colman of Boston articulated the seriousness of purpose toward life which youth were expected
to adopt. Now was their *"chusing time"* and often their *"fixing time,"* he
declared.

Now you commonly chuse your *Trade*; betake your selves to your business for
life, show what you incline to, and how you intend to be imploy'd all your days.

Now you chuse your *Master* and your Education or Occupation. And now you dispose of your self in *Marriage* ordinarily, place your *Affections*, give away your hearts, look out for some *Companion* of life, whose to be as long as you live.[65]

The tasks of youth were thus similar to those of twentieth-century adolescents: to determine what they wished to become and to obtain appropriate education or training so that they could be economically self-sufficient.

In preparing to assume adult roles and responsibilities, in answering basic questions about identities separate from parents, and in developing the independence and autonomy of adults, Puritan youth inevitably worried and sometimes exasperated their parents and other figures of authority. Intergenerational conflict, however, was hardly as widespread or intense as in later periods; indeed, there is little evidence of such discord until the 1660s and 1670s, when second-generation Puritan ministers developed their characteristic sermon, the jeremiad. Changes in Puritan society—the death of the founding generation, a loss of zeal, growing prosperity—may well have provided conditions under which elements of a youth culture and adolescent behavior could emerge sufficiently to evoke widespread comment and response.[66]

Not surprisingly, comment and response came from the ministry and the churches alike. Both, however, had difficulty in accommodating the needs of the young, for neither Puritan theology nor experience provided much evidence that teenagers were likely subjects of conversion and church membership. While God would not discriminate on the basis of age, it was usually between ages twenty and forty, in Thomas Hooker's words, that "a man is able to conceive and partake of the things of grace." The ages at which men and women became communicants substantiated what ministers preached. Except during religious revivals (for example, Solomon Stoddard's five "harvests" at Northampton and the Great Awakening of the 1740s), few persons became church members before age twenty.[67]

Admission to communicant membership symbolized, for many individuals, achievement of full adult status within the community. The ages at which New Englanders commonly became communicants thus placed youth in an anomalous situation: past the age of discretion and urged to be concerned for their souls' sake, they were warned that conversion was neither easy nor universal, and that their religious experiences would be closely scrutinized when they sought membership. Furthermore, it was not unusual for individuals to marry and have children before becoming communicants, a situation that compounded their difficulty: only communicants in the early New England churches could have their children baptized. The Synod of 1662 provided a partial solution: when grown, baptized children of communicants came "*personally under the*

Watch, Discipline and Government" of their parents' church, but they were not admitted to communion without suitable religious experience. The Synod's fifth proposition set forth what became known as the halfway covenant: children of baptized noncommunicants could be baptized if their parents understood and publicly accepted "*the Doctrine of Faith*," led upright lives, and "owned" the church's covenant, giving themselves and their children to the Lord and subjecting themselves to the church's discipline. Some churches, such as Dorchester, not only adopted the halfway covenant but also developed a ceremony in which all "children of the church"—that is, children of communicants—over sixteen years, whether married or not, publicly submitted to the church's government. Furthermore, in some cases, the halfway covenant became a means by which pious but unconverted individuals, who were single and therefore had no children to baptize, could publicly declare their commitment to God. For still others, owning the covenant preceded baptism.[68]

The adoption and expansion of the halfway covenant and the mass covenant-owning ceremonies which were developed after 1662 were thus means by which New Englanders sought to influence the "rising generation." At Northampton, Solomon Stoddard discovered an alternative: in 1690, he introduced an open communion, which any person over age fourteen and "Civilized and Cathechised," could receive. In Stoddard's view, communion was a converting ordinance rather than a privilege of the converted. It appears, however, that few young people availed themselves of the open communion, for the five revivals during Stoddard's ministry particularly affected young persons. Revivals, rather than open communion, thus became the means by which the young could be brought into the church.[69]

In Boston, Cotton Mather developed a different approach to youth by encouraging the formation of young men's societies that met regularly to pray, sing psalms, hear or repeat sermons, and discuss religious subjects. These groups, which first emerged in the 1690s, became an important feature and focal point of youthful religious activities in the eighteenth century.[70]

The emergence of adolescence in the seventeenth century—or at least society's perception that youth required exhortation, remediation, and closer supervision by parents, magistrates, and ministers—may have been related to a weakening of parental control over their children's lives. In explaining the problem of youth, preachers of the jeremiads pointed to a waning of both piety and parental authority as well as to the inherent characteristics of youth as a stage of life. Although the loss of piety can be measured in declining church membership, the weakening of parental authority is more difficult to pinpoint. Greven's study of the first four generations in Andover demonstrates significant changes in the relationships between fathers and sons. Andover's long-lived settlers typically exercised control over their sons well beyond their relatively late marriages. Fathers settled sons on family lands but withheld title. Thus, many second-generation sons did not attain full economic independence until late in their fathers' lives or at their fathers' deaths. This pattern of late marriages and prolonged economic dependence, "above all, was of the utmost importance in creating, and in maintaining, the extended patriarchal families characteristic of the first and second generations in Andover. In this seventeenth-century American community, at least, patriarchalism was a reality, based firmly upon the possession and control of the land."[71]

The transition from one generation to another and the erosion of authority cannot be measured precisely, but the Andover tax list for 1685 is one indicator of the shift: among 120 taxpayers, only 15 were first-generation settlers. The relationship between second-generation fathers and their sons differed from the relationship between the first two generations. With less abundant resources, the second generation had to adopt more flexible strategies to provide for their sons, some of whom married as early as the 1680s and 39 percent of whom moved away from Andover. Patriarchal authority remained a strong force in Andover, but, as Philip Greven observes,

in contrast to the earlier period, some third-generation sons managed to gain their autonomy relatively early, often with the encouragement and the assistance of their fathers, who either settled them in trades for their livelihoods, gave them deeds for their land, or helped them to emigrate to other places, often at considerable distances from Andover, to live and raise their families.[72]

The strength of fathers' authority is evident in the fact that sons of men who died early married earlier than sons of men who survived to old age, although this pattern weakened in the eighteenth century. An erosion of authority is also implicit in rising rates of premarital pregnancy late in the century. For whatever reasons—weakening supervision by parents and communities or a failure to instill sufficient self-restraint in their offspring—through their premarital sexual activities, children may have been forcing their parents' hands. Thus, recognition of youth as a distinct—and difficult—stage of life may have reflected shifting levels of religiosity, prosperity, and patriarchalism in New England families and communities.[73]

The strength of patriarchalism in New England family life offers an appropriate starting point for comparing childrearing attitudes and practices in New England with those in the Chesapeake. New England patriarchalism was based on religion, strong cultural sanctions supporting the family as the basic social unit, and exceptionally long life expectancies. Conditions in the Chesapeake were dramatically different, for religion was less important, many men never married, life expectancies were short, and marriages were typically brief. Early deaths and broken families prevented fathers from exercising effective, long-term control over their children.

The emotional relationships between children and parents must have been conditioned and perhaps made more distant by the expectation of early bereavement and by the frequent necessity of adding new and perhaps unrelated members to the household unit. In New England, Bradstreet might anticipate death at childbirth and ask her husband to guard her children "from step-dame's injury," but the chances that her children would be orphaned were far fewer than the children of Chesapeake families, most of whom would in fact spend part of their minority with a stepparent. And, as Lorena Walsh points out,

the potential for conflict was great in situations where children of more than one marriage lived together in a family. Each parent naturally tended to favor his own children and to discriminate against those from a partner's previous marriage. Parental favoritism only heightened conflicts between stepchildren already competing for their parents' attention and affection.[74]

The Rutmans suspect that children matured early under the conditions of life and death in the Chesapeake: "there seems little enough of that emotional content of family life which gives meaning to childhood as we know it—little time for it given the fact of many children and the shortness of life itself." Furthermore, Hecht suggests that childhood may have been "more a social status than a biological stage of development" for the poor and the orphaned who had to assume significant responsibilities at early ages.[75]

The effects of parental death, whether actual or anticipated, can be seen in several aspects of childhood. In the area of education, Chesapeake parents wanted their children "brought up in Civility good litterature and the feare of God," but, as Walsh points out, this goal was frequently not realized because of parental death and the lower priority that guardians, stepparents, or masters placed on educating a child. Given small families, the labor-intensive nature of tobacco cultivation, and the absence of a significant nonagricultural sector of the economy, parents had no rationale for arranging apprenticeships for their children. When a family was broken by the father's early death, the widow might bind out her sons to learn how to make a living and her daughters to learn housekeeping.[76]

The large numbers of orphans (defined in the Chesapeake as children who had lost their fathers) and the prospect of early death prompted several responses. Acknowledging the odds against a long life and recognizing that stepfathers and guardians might not adequately care for a fatherless child or his estate, fathers attempted to ensure their children's well-being. They frequently deeded cattle to their sons at birth and appointed trustees to see that the children received the cattle's female increase at marriage or majority; as a result, orphans were among the principal owners of cattle in Virginia. Likewise, fathers often provided in their wills for sons to assume early responsibility over their inheritances. The Chesapeake colonies developed and elaborated legal mechanisms to guard both orphans and their property. In finding guardians for their children, fathers looked to kin whenever possible or, in the case of Maryland Catholics and some Protestants as well, chose godparents who would take special interest in a child's well-being. Given the number of children whose estates were vulnerable to unscrupulous guardians or stepparents, the Rutmans find relatively few assaults upon orphans' property. Perhaps a golden rule of necessity encouraged men to be honest in administering orphans' estates because they hoped that other men would do the same for their children.[77]

The actual or prospective status of heir or heiress helped to mature children, for fathers tried to advance their sons' legal maturity, and teenage heirs frequently assumed an active role in preserving their inheritances. Even when sons reached majority, fathers often granted them independence as quickly as possible: with early parental death and youthful inheritances the norm, long-lived fathers may have felt compelled to help their sons keep up with their peer group.[78]

The early maturation of children in the Chesapeake may not have been universally smooth. On the one hand, the Rutmans argue that the potential for conflict between the generations hardly existed in Middlesex County, Virginia, where half the sons were orphaned before marriage or legal majority. For those families in which parents lived to see their children grown, fathers tended to grant independence to sons in their early twenties. On the other hand, Walsh discerns elements of an adolescent crisis among boys. "Especially in families where the father had died, teenaged sons argued with their parents, sought to escape from work and from the authority of others, spent their inheritances imprudently, and got into scrapes with the law."[79]

Parental death also affected the conditions under which Chesapeake children married. Daughters of immigrant women married much earlier than their mothers; as a result, they were less often pregnant at marriage. Moreover, parental supervision seems to have affected rates of bridal pregnancy: girls whose fathers were dead were much more likely to become pregnant before marriage than girls whose fathers were still living. For many young men and women in Maryland, parental wishes or supervision had little effect on the timing of marriage or the choice of a spouse, since parents frequently died before their children married, and stepparents or guardians could control their charges only until majority.[80]

Thus, from birth to marriage, the experiences of childhood and of childrearing in the seventeenth-century Chesapeake were markedly different from those in New England. Chesapeake children were frequently orphaned; received poorer educations; might experience the tensions of living in ever-changing households containing an extraordinary range of relatives and strangers; were given earlier responsibilities in managing property; and had little parental guidance in choosing a spouse and in the timing of marriage. By contrast, New England children grew up in stable households under strict discipline; received better educations (at least in terms of literacy training); assumed responsibilities more gradually; and were sometimes denied full economic and psychological independence until relatively late in life.

While differences abound, there were also similarities. If anticipation of early death prompted Chesapeake fathers to provide for their sons, and if death curtailed their direct influence over their children's lives in such matters as marriage, patriarchal authority in New England was also eroding at the end of the century. While the nuclear family was unstable in the Chesapeake, the networks of extended kin that emerged toward the end of the century resembled networks that had formed quite early in New England. Furthermore, while the kin networks in the Chesapeake were more complex and their individual members assumed heavier burdens than those of New Englanders, networks in both regions functioned similarly. Finally, if the deaths of parents, guardians, siblings, and other relatives taught Chesapeake children that life was transitory,[81] New England Puritans would have understood and applauded this lesson.

This is not to say that conditions or values in the two societies were converging or that their similarities were more important than their differences, but rather to emphasize the difficulty of making generalizations about the "colonial family" without reference to variables of place, time, class, and family structure. Certainly the history of childhood in New England can no longer serve as a proxy for the colonial experience. It remains to be seen, however, whether patterns of family life and childhood in the Chesapeake will replace New England as the paradigm in understanding colonial family life.

NOTES

The following abbreviations are used in the notes:

AQ   *American Quarterly*
CMHS   *Collections of the Massachusetts Historical Society*
EIHC   *Essex Institute Historical Collections*

tr42   Ross W. Beales, Jr.

y

HCQ   *History of Childhood Quarterly*
JIH   *Journal of Interdisciplinary History*
JSH   *Journal of Social History*
NEHGR   *New England Historical and Genealogical Register*
PAAS   *Proceedings of the American Antiquarian Society*
WMQ   *William and Mary Quarterly, 3d ser.*

1. Historiographical articles include N. Ray Hiner, "The Child in American Historiography: Accomplishments and Prospect," *Psychohistory Review* 7 (1978): 13–23; idem, "Wars and Rumors of Wars: The Historiography of Colonial Education as a Case Study in Academic Imperialism," *Societas* 8 (1978): 89–114; and Daniel Blake Smith, "The Study of the Family in Early America: Trends, Problems, and Prospects," *WMQ* 39 (1982): 3–28.

2. Edmund S. Morgan, *The Puritan Family: Religion and Domestic Relations in Seventeenth-Century New England* (Rev. ed., New York: Harper & Row, Harper Torchbooks, 1966); John Demos, "Notes on Life in Plymouth Colony," *WMQ* 22 (1965): 264–286; idem, "Families in Colonial Bristol, Rhode Island: An Exercise in Historical Demography," *WMQ* 25 (1968): 40–57; Philip J. Greven, Jr., "Family Structure in Seventeenth-Century Andover, Massachusetts," *WMQ* 23 (1966): 234–256; idem, "Historical Demography and Colonial America: A Review Article," *WMQ* 24 (1967): 438–454; Kenneth A. Lockridge, "The Population of Dedham, Massachusetts, 1636–1736," *Economic History Review*, 2d ser., 19 (1966): 318–344; John Demos, *A Little Commonwealth: Family Life in Plymouth Colony* (New York: Oxford University Press, 1970); Philip J. Greven, Jr., *Four Generations: Population, Land, and Family in Colonial Andover, Massachusetts* (Ithaca, N.Y.: Cornell University Press, 1970); Kenneth A. Lockridge, *A New England Town, The First Hundred Years: Dedham, Massachusetts, 1636–1736* (New York: W. W. Norton, 1970).

Review essays include James A. Henretta, "The Morphology of New England Society in the Colonial Period," *JIH* 2 (1971): 379–398; Rhys Isaac, "Order and Growth, Authority and Meaning in Colonial New England," *American Historical Review* 76 (1971): 728–737; John M. Murrin, "Review Essay," *History and Theory* 11 (1972): 226–275; Richard S. Dunn, "The Social History of Early New England," *AQ* 24 (1972): 661–679; Jack P. Greene, "Autonomy and Stability: New England and the British Colonial Experience in Early Modern America," *JSH* 7 (1974): 171–194.

Important recent studies of family life and childrearing include Joseph E. Illick, "Child-Rearing in Seventeenth-Century England and America," in Lloyd deMause, ed., *The History of Childhood* (New York: Psychohistory Press, 1974), 303–350; James Axtell, *The School upon a Hill: Education and Society in Colonial New England* (New Haven: Yale University Press, 1974); Philip Greven, *The Protestant Temperament: Patterns of Child-Rearing, Religious Experience, and the Self in Early America* (New York: Alfred A. Knopf, 1977). See also Vivian C. Fox and Martin H. Quitt, "Uniformities and Variations in the English and American Family Cycle: Then and Now," in Fox and Quitt, eds., *Loving, Parenting and*

Dying: The Family Cycle in England and America, Past and Present (New York: Psychohistory Press, 1980), 3–90, and Peter Wagner, "A Note on Puritans and Children in Early Colonial New England," *Amerikastudien* 25 (1980): 47–62.

3. Because of the paucity of data, this essay does not consider the experience of black parents and children. On the black family, see Allan Kulikoff, "The Beginnings of the Afro-American Family in Maryland," in Aubrey C. Land, Lois Green Carr, and Edward C. Papenfuse, eds., *Law, Society, and Politics in Early Maryland: Proceedings of the First Conference on Maryland History, June 14–15, 1974* (Baltimore: Johns Hopkins University Press, 1977), 171–196 (hereafter cited as *Law, Society, and Politics*).

4. For discussions of these circumstances, see Lockridge, "Population of Dedham"; Susan L. Norton, "Population Growth in Colonial America: A Study of Ipswich, Massachusetts," *Population Studies* 25 (1971): 433–452.

5. Herbert Moller, "Sex Composition and Correlated Culture Patterns of Colonial America," *WMQ* 2 (1945): 118; Greven, *Four Generations*, 33; Demos, *Little Commonwealth*, 193; Lockridge, "Population of Dedham," 326–327, 330; Norton, "Population Growth," 445; T. H. Breen and Stephen Foster, "Moving to the New World: The Character of Early Massachusetts Immigration," *WMQ* 30 (1973): 189–222.

6. Daniel Scott Smith and Michael S. Hindus, "Premarital Pregnancy in America, 1640–1971: An Overview and Interpretation," *JIH* 5 (1975): 537–570. On patterns of conception, see Demos, *Little Commonwealth*, 68, 133; Greven, *Four Generations*, 30, 112; Lockridge, "Population of Dedham," 332.

7. Greven, *Four Generations*, 27–28 (a better measure of the risk of death during the childbearing years would include ages forty to forty-five); Demos, *Little Commonwealth*, 193; Norton, "Population Growth," 441–442.

8. Greven, *Four Generations*, 27–29; Demos, *Little Commonwealth*, 67, 194.

9. Greven, *Four Generations*, 31, 111; Demos, *Little Commonwealth*, 192; Norton, "Population Growth," 444.

10. Demos, "Notes on Life in Plymouth," 270–271; Greven, *Four Generations*, 25–26, 30; Demos, *Little Commonwealth*, 66, 192; Maris A. Vinovskis, "Angels' Heads and Weeping Willows: Death in Early America," *PAAS* 86 (1976): 282. On underregistration, see Norton, "Population Growth," 439; Lockridge, "Population of Dedham," 319; and David E. Stannard, "Death and the Puritan Child," *AQ* 26 (1974): 464–465.

11. John Demos, "Demography and Psychology in the Historical Study of Family-Life: A Personal Report," in Peter Laslett and Richard Wall, eds., *Household and Family in Past Time* ... (Cambridge: At the University Press, 1972), 562; John J. Waters, "The Traditional World of the New England Peasants: A View from Seventeenth-Century Barnstable," *NEHGR* 130 (1976): 8.

12. Demos, "Families in Colonial Bristol," 44, 46.

13. Demos, *Little Commonwealth*, 124; Greven, *Four Generations*, 39; idem, "Family Structure in Seventeenth-Century Andover," 244–256; Ralph J. Crandall, "Family Types, Social Structure, and Mobility in Early America: Charlestown, Massachusetts, a Case Study," in Virginia Tufte and Barbara Myerhoff, eds., *Changing Images of the Family* (New Haven: Yale University Press, 1979), 67–69; Daniel Scott Smith, "Child-Naming Patterns and Family Structure Change: Hingham, Massachusetts, 1640–1880," Newberry Papers in Family and Community His-

tory, Paper 76–5 (Chicago: Newberry Library, 1977); Charles G. Steffen, "The Sewall Children in Colonial New England," *NEHGR* 131 (1977): 163–172; Thomas R. Cole, "Family, Settlement, and Migration in Southeastern Massachusetts, 1650–1805: The Case For Regional Analysis," *NEHGR* 132 (1978): 175–178.

14. See particularly Darrett B. Rutman and Anita H. Rutman, "Of Agues and Fevers: Malaria in the Early Chesapeake," *WMQ* 33 (1976): 31–60; Russell R. Menard, "Immigrants and Their Increase: The Process of Population Growth in Early Colonial Maryland," in Land, et al., eds., *Law, Society, and Politics*, 88–110; Carville V. Earle, "Environment, Disease, and Mortality in Early Virginia," in Thad W. Tate and David L. Ammerman, eds., *The Chesapeake in the Seventeenth Century: Essays on Anglo-American Society* (Chapel Hill: University of North Carolina Press, 1979), 96–125 (hereafter cited as *Chesapeake in Seventeenth Century*); Lorena S. Walsh, " 'Till Death Us Do Part': Marriage and Family in Seventeenth-Century Maryland," in Tate and Ammerman, eds., *Chesapeake in Seventeenth Century*, 126–152; and Darrett B. and Anita H. Rutman, " 'Now-Wives and Sons-in-Law': Parental Death in a Seventeenth-Century Virginia County," in Tate and Ammerman, eds., *Chesapeake in Seventeenth Century*, 153–182.

15. Menard, "Immigrants and Their Increase," 102; Edmund S. Morgan, *American Slavery, American Freedom: The Ordeal of Colonial Virginia* (New York: W. W. Norton, 1975), 158–159; Robert V. Wells, *Revolutions in Americans' Lives: A Demographic Perspective on the History of Americans, Their Families, and Their Society* (Westport, Conn.: Greenwood Press, 1982), 29; Menard, "Immigrants and Their Increase," 90–91, 102. The Oldmixon quotation is in Russell R. Menard, "The Tobacco Industry in the Chesapeake Colonies, 1617–1730: An Interpretation," *Research in Economic History* 5 (1980): 119.

16. Menard, "Immigrants and Their Increase," 97, 102–103; Edmund S. Morgan, "The First American Boom: Virginia, 1618 to 1630," *WMQ* 28 (1971): 178–179; James Horn, "Servant Emigration to the Chesapeake in the Seventeenth Century," in Tate and Ammerman, eds., *Chesapeake in Seventeenth Century*, 61–62; Morgan, *American Slavery*, 163; Russell R. Menard, "From Servant to Freeholder: Status Mobility and Property Accumulation in Seventeenth-Century Maryland," *WMQ* 30 (1973): 47; Irene W. D. Hecht, "The Virginia Muster of 1624/5 As a Source for Demographic History," *WMQ* 30 (1973): 71.

17. Horn, "Servant Emigration," 65; Walsh, " 'Till Death,' " 132; Menard, "Immigrants and Their Increase," 93; Lois Green Carr and Russell R. Menard, "Immigration and Opportunity: The Freedman in Early Colonial Maryland," in *Chesapeake in Seventeenth Century*, 208–209; Lois Green Carr and Lorena S. Walsh, "The Planter's Wife: The Experience of White Women in Seventeenth-Century Maryland," *WMQ* 34 (1977): 552. On the incidence of bastardy and premarital conceptions, see Carr and Walsh, "Planter's Wife," 547–549.

18. Lorena S. Walsh and Russell R. Menard, "Death in the Chesapeake: Two Life Tables for Men in Early Colonial Maryland," *Maryland Historical Magazine* 69 (1974): 215, 222, 225–226; Rutman and Rutman, "Of Agues," 50, 52; Menard, "Immigrants and Their Increase," 93; Daniel Blake Smith, "Mortality and Family in the Colonial Chesapeake," *JIH* 8 (1978): 413–414, 416.

19. Hecht, "Virginia Muster," 84; Smith, "Mortality and Family," 418–419; Walsh, " 'Till Death,' " 128; Murrin, "Review Essay," 238.

20. Hecht, "Virginia Muster," 84; Rutman and Rutman, " 'Now-Wives,' " 153, 158, 167; Smith, "Mortality and Family," 422; Walsh, " 'Till Death,' " 128, 143.

21. Carr and Walsh, "Planter's Wife," 564.

22. Menard, "Immigrants and Their Increase," 97, 102.

23. Morgan, *American Slavery*, 238–240; Carr and Menard, "Immigration and Opportunity," 209.

24. Carr and Walsh, "Planter's Wife," 565–566; Lois Green Carr, "The Development of the Maryland Orphans' Court, 1654–1715," in Land, et al., eds., *Law, Society, and Politics*, 41–42; Walsh, " 'Till Death,' " 131; Rutman and Rutman, " 'Now-Wives,' " 168, 173; idem, "Of Agues," 57–58.

25. On the ebb and flow of immigration, see Wesley Frank Craven, *White, Red, and Black: The Seventeenth-Century Virginian* (Charlottesville: University Press of Virginia, 1971), and Edmund S. Morgan, "Headrights and Head Counts: A Review Article," *Virginia Magazine of History and Biography* 80 (1972): 361–371.

26. Carr and Walsh, "Planter's Wife," 560; on the complexity of families and household structure, see Rutman and Rutman, "Of Agues," 57–59, and John M. Murrin, review of *Chesapeake in Seventeenth Century* in *WMQ* 38 (1981): 118.

27. Peter Laslett, *The World We Have Lost* (New York: Charles Scribner's Sons, 1965); idem and John Harrison, "Clayworth and Cogenhoe," in H. E. Bell and H. L. Ollard, eds., *Historical Essays, 1600–1750, Presented to David Ogg* (New York: Barnes & Noble, 1963), 157–184; Hecht, "Virginia Muster," 91.

28. Murrin, review of *Chesapeake in Seventeenth Century*, 120; Greene, "Autonomy and Stability," 173; Rutman and Rutman, " 'Now-Wives,' " 171–173 and n. 39. See also Richard S. Dunn, "The Barbados Census of 1680: Profile of the Richest Colony in English America," *WMQ* 26 (1969): 3–30; Robert V. Wells, "Quaker Marriage Patterns in a Colonial Perspective," *WMQ* 29 (1972): 415–442; Barry Levy, " 'Tender Plants:' Quaker Farmers and Children in the Delaware Valley, 1681–1735," *Journal of Family History* 3 (1978): 125–126. Maris A. Vinovskis summarizes "Recent Trends in American Historical Demography: Some Methodological and Conceptual Considerations," *Annual Review of Sociology* 4 (1978): 603–627.

29. Alice Morse Earle, *Child Life in Colonial Days* (New York: Macmillan Co., 1899); Arthur W. Calhoun, *A Social History of the American Family from Colonial Times to the Present* (Cleveland: Bobbs-Merrill, 1917); Sandford D. Fleming, *Children & Puritanism: The Place of Children in the Life and Thought of the New England Churches, 1620–1847* (New Haven: Yale University Press, 1933); Demos, *Little Commonwealth*; Greven, *Protestant Temperament*. The major exception is Morgan, *Puritan Family*.

30. Fleming, *Children & Puritanism*, 60; Alice Morse Earle, *Customs and Fashions in Old New England* (New York: Charles Scribner's Sons, 1896), 13, 15. See Elizabeth Bancroft Schlesinger, "Cotton Mather and His Children," *WMQ* 10 (1953): 181–189, and especially N. Ray Hiner, "Cotton Mather and His Children: The Evolution of a Parent Educator, 1686–1728," in Barbara Finkelstein, ed., *Regulated Children/Liberated Children: Education in Psychohistorical Perspective* (New York: Psychohistory Press, 1979), 24–43.

31. Demos, *Little Commonwealth*, 57–58, 139–140; idem, "The American Family in Past Time," *American Scholar* 43 (1974): 422–446; Ross W. Beales, Jr., "In Search of the Historical Child: Miniature Adulthood and Youth in Colonial New

England," *AQ* 27 (1975): 379–398; Hiner, "Child in American Historiography," 16–17; Stannard, "Death and Puritan Child," 457–459; Crandall, "Family Types," 62; C. John Sommerville, "English Puritans and Children: A Social-Cultural Explanation," *Journal of Psychohistory* 6 (1978): 113–137.

32. Demos, "Demography and Psychology," 564–565; idem, *Little Commonwealth*, 145–150; idem and Virginia Demos, "Adolescence in Historical Perspective," *Journal of Marriage and the Family* 31 (1969): 632–638; Joseph F. Kett, "Adolescence and Youth in Nineteenth-Century America," *JIH* 2 (1971): 283–298; idem, *Rites of Passage: Adolescence in America, 1790 to the Present* (New York: Basic Books, 1977), 11–14. Axtell, *School upon a Hill*, 201–202 (suggesting that only the colonial colleges provided conditions in which adolescence could be manifested); N. Ray Hiner, "Adolescence in Eighteenth-Century America," *HCQ* 3 (1975): 253–280; Beales, "Historical Child"; Vivian C. Fox, "Is Adolescence a Phenomenon of Modern Times?" *Journal of Psychohistory* 5 (1977): 271–290; Karin Calvert, "Children in American Family Portraiture, 1670 to 1810," *WMQ* 39 (1982): 87–113. On Aries's *Centuries of Childhood: A Social History of Family Life*, Robert Baldick, trans. (New York: Vintage Books, 1962), see Richard T. Vann, "The Youth of *Centuries of Childhood*," *History and Theory* 21 (1982): 279–297. Important revisions of Aries are Natalie Zemon Davis, "The Reasons of Misrule: Youth Groups and Charivaris in Sixteenth-Century France," *Past and Present*, No. 50 (1971): 41–75; Steven R. Smith, "The London Apprentices as Seventeenth-Century Adolescents," *Past and Present*, No. 61 (1973): 149–161; idem, "Religion and the Conception of Youth in Seventeenth-Century England," *HCQ* 2 (1975): 493–516; idem, "Almost Revolutionaries: The London Apprentices During the Civil War," *Huntington Library Quarterly* 42 (1979): 313–328. See also Susan Brigden, "Youth and the English Reformation," *Past and Present*, No. 95 (1982): 37–67; Anne Yarbrough, "Apprentices as Adolescents in Sixteenth Century Bristol," *JSH* 13 (1979): 67–81.

33. Morgan, *Puritan Family*, ch. 2; John Cotton, *A Practical Commentary . . . upon the First Epistle Generall of John* (London, 1656), 100. See also Joseph Belcher, *Two Sermons Preached in Dedham* (Boston, 1710), 8–10; Isaac Ambrose (1604–1664), *The Well-Ordered Family . . .* (Boston, 1762), 10–11; Belcher, *Two Sermons*, 10. See also R. V. Schnucker, "The English Puritans and Pregnancy, Delivery and Breast Feeding," *HCQ* 1 (1974): 637–658.

34. Laurel Thatcher Ulrich, *Good Wives: Image and Reality in the Lives of Women in Northern New England, 1650–1750* (New York: Alfred A. Knopf, 1982), 126–135.

35. On maternal-infant bonding, see Selma Fraiberg, *Every Child's Birthright: In Defense of Mothering* (New York: Basic Books, 1977), chs. 1–2.

36. *The Works of John Robinson, Pastor of the Pilgrim Fathers, with a Memoir and Annotations*, ed. Robert Ashton (London: John Snow, 1851), 1:244; Ambrose, *Well-Ordered Family*, 10; Cotton, *Practical Commentary*, 274.

37. John Cotton to Increase Mather, Plimouth, 19 January 1677, in *CMHS*, 4th ser., 8 (1868): 231.

38. Smith, "Child-Naming Patterns."

39. *The Geneva Bible: A Facsimile of the 1560 Edition* (Madison: University of Wisconsin Press, 1969); Sommerville, "English Puritans and Children," 115.

40. Axtell, *School upon a Hill*, 8–10; Illick, "Child-Rearing," 324–325; Smith,

"Child-Naming Patterns," 6; *God's Plot: The Paradoxes of Puritan Piety, Being the Autobiography and Journal of Thomas Shepard*, ed. Michael McGiffert (Amherst: University of Massachusetts Press, 1972), 34; "Deacon John Paine's Journal," *Mayflower Descendant* 9 (1907): 137.

41. *The Works of Anne Bradstreet*, ed. Jeannine Hensley (Cambridge, Mass.: Harvard University Press, 1967), 236. See Ross W. Beales, Jr., "Anne Bradstreet and Her Children," in Finkelstein, *Regulated Children/Liberated Children*, 10–23.

42. Peter G. Slater, " 'From the *Cradle* to the *Coffin*': Parental Bereavement and the Shadow of Infant Damnation in Puritan Society," *Psychohistory Review* 6 (1977–1978): 5; John Philip Hall, "The Journal of James Weston, Cordwainer, of Reading, Massachusetts, 1788–1793," *EIHC* 92 (1956): 201; Michael Wigglesworth, *The Day of Doom* (1662), stanza 181, in Harrison T. Meserole, ed., *Seventeenth-Century American Poetry* (New York: New York University Press, 1968), 102. See Marion L. Starkey, "The Easiest Room in Hell," *EIHC* 92 (1956): 33–42.

43. Philip Schaff, ed., *Bibliotheca Symbolica Ecclesiae Universalis: The Creeds of Christendom, with a History and Critical Notes* (4th ed., New York: Harper & Brothers, 1919), 3:625.

44. Cotton Mather, *Meat Out of the Eater* (Boston, 1703), 27–28, 96–98.

45. Ibid., 98–100; Mather, *Nepenthes Evangelicum* (Boston, 1713), 25–26; Benjamin Colman, *A Devout Contemplation on the Meaning of Divine Providence* (Boston, 1714), 19.

46. Samuel Sewall to John Winthrop, 8 April 1717, in *CMHS*, 6th ser., 2 (1888): 69; "Paine's Journal," 139; Gerhard T. Alexis, "Wigglesworth's 'Easiest Room,' " *New England Quarterly* 42 (1969): 573–583.

47. For another perspective on Puritans and death, see David E. Stannard, *The Puritan Way of Death: A Study in Religion, Culture, and Social Change* (New York: Oxford University Press, 1977), ch. 3.

48. Demos, *Little Commonwealth*, 134; David J. Rothman, "Documents in Search of a Historian: Toward a History of Childhood and Youth in America," *JIH* 2 (1971): 369; Bradstreet, *Works*, 53, 279; Ulrich, *Good Wives*, 138–144.

49. For children's effects on parents, see Hiner, "Cotton Mather and His Children"; on sibling rank, see Wells, *Revolutions*, 55.

50. Demos, *Little Commonwealth*, 134–139; idem, "Developmental Perspectives on the History of Childhood," *JIH* 2 (1971): 319; Robinson, *Works* 1:246–247.

51. Jay Mechling, "Advice to Historians on Advice to Mothers," *JSH* 9 (1975): 44–63. On Demos, see Dunn, "Social History of Early New England," 672; Rothman, "Documents," 369, 374; Greene, "Autonomy and Stability," 186.

52. Cotton, *Practical Commentary*, 87.

53. Ibid., 124–125, citing Zechariah 8:5; Samuel Sewall to Ezekiel Cheever and Nathaniel Williams, 1 April 1708, in *CMHS*, 6th ser., 1 (1866): 365; *The Diary of Edward Taylor*, ed. Francis Murphy (Springfield, Mass.: Connecticut Valley Historical Museum, 1964), 17–18 (12 January 1672); *Winthrop's Journal "History of New England," 1630–1649*, ed. James Kendall Hosmer (New York: Charles Scribner's Sons, 1908), 1:207 (December 10, 1636), 2:209–210 (17 September 1644); "Rev. Samuel Danforth's Records of the First Church in Roxbury, Mass.," *NEHGR* 34 (1880): 362 (14 May 1673); *The Diary of Samuel Sewall, 1674–*

1729, ed. M. Halsey Thomas (New York: Farrar, Straus & Giroux, 1973) 1:142 (6 June 1687).

54. Demos, *Little Commonwealth*, 132–133, 140; Bradstreet, *Works*, 279.

55. Demos, *Little Commonwealth*, 57–58; Calvert, "Family Portraiture," 97 (she relies principally on eighteenth-century portraits).

56. *The Laws and Liberties of Massachusetts: Reprinted from the Copy of the 1648 Edition in the Henry E. Huntington Library*, ed. Max Farrand (Cambridge, Mass., 1929), 11; Belcher, *Two Sermons*, 12; Cotton, *Practical Commentary*, 102. On religious observances, see Winton U. Solberg, *Redeem the Time: The Puritan Sabbath in Early America* (Cambridge, Mass.: Harvard University Press, 1977); Charles E. Hambrick-Stowe, *The Practice of Piety: Puritan Devotional Disciplines in Seventeenth-Century New England* (Chapel Hill: University of North Carolina Press, 1982); Beales, "Historical Child," 385.

57. David D. Hall, "The World of Print and Collective Mentality in Seventeenth-Century New England," in John Higham and Paul K. Conkin, eds., *New Directions in American Intellectual History* (Baltimore: Johns Hopkins University Press, 1979), 166–180; idem, "The Uses of Literacy in New England, 1600–1850," in William L. Joyce et al., eds., *Printing and Society in Early America* (Worcester, Mass.: American Antiquarian Society, 1983), 20-26.

58. "The Autobiography of Increase Mather," ed. M. G. Hall, *PAAS* 71 (1961): 278.

59. Kenneth A. Lockridge, *Literacy in Colonial New England: An Enquiry into the Social Context of Literacy in the Early Modern West* (New York: W. W. Norton, 1974), 7–13, 38; Harvey J. Graff, "Literacy in History," *History of Education Quarterly* 15 (1975): 472. Linda Auwers examines signatures and marks on deeds, "Reading the Marks of the Past: Exploring Female Literacy in Colonial Windsor, Connecticut," *Historical Methods* 13 (1980): 204–214.

60. Demos, *Little Commonwealth*, 140; Morgan, *Puritan Family*, 68.

61. Morgan, *Puritan Family*, 76–78.

62. Demos, *Little Commonwealth*, 73–74; Stannard, "Death and the Puritan Child," 466; Wells, *Revolutions*, 58; Fox and Quitt, "Uniformities and Variations," 40; Steffen, "Sewall Children," 167. See also Alan Macfarlane, *The Family Life of Ralph Josselin, a Seventeenth-Century Clergyman: An Essay in Historical Anthropology* (Cambridge: At the University Press, 1970), 205–210.

63. Steffen, "Sewall Children," 165.

64. Bradstreet, *Works*, 280.

65. Beales, "Historical Child," 384, 394.

66. Perry Miller, "Declension in a Bible Commonwealth," *PAAS* 51 (1941): 37–94.

67. *Thomas Shepard's Confessions*, eds. George Selement and Bruce C. Woolley, Publications of the Colonial Society of Massachusetts, Collections 58 (Boston: The Society, 1981), 4; Beales, "Historical Child," 387.

68. Williston Walker, ed., *The Creeds and Platforms of Congregationalism* (1893; Boston: Pilgrim Press, Pilgrim Paperbound, 1960), 326, 328; Ross W. Beales, Jr., "The Half-Way Covenant and Religious Scrupulosity: The First Church of Dorchester, Massachusetts, as a Test Case," *WMQ* 31 (1974): 465–480; Robert G. Pope, *The Half-Way Covenant: Church Membership in Puritan New England* (Princeton: Princeton University Press, 1969).

69. Patricia J. Tracy, *Jonathan Edwards, Pastor: Religion and Society in Eighteenth-Century Northampton* (New York: Hill & Wang, 1980), 23.

70. N. Ray Hiner, "The Cry of Sodom Enquired into: Educational Analysis in Seventeenth-Century New England," *History of Education Quarterly* 13 (1973): 15–16; idem, "Adolescence in Eighteenth-Century America," 265.

71. Kenneth A. Lockridge, "The History of a Puritan Church, 1637–1736," *New England Quarterly* 40 (1967): 399–424; Greven, *Four Generations*, 39, 98–99. For a different interpretation of the level of church membership, see Robert G. Pope, "New England Versus the New England Mind: The Myth of Declension," *JSH* 3 (1969–70): 95–108.

72. Greven, *Four Generations*, 38, 126. From a more impressionistic reading of Plymouth Colony records, Demos, *Little Commonwealth*, 169–170, finds "*little warrant . . . for any general assumption that parents deployed their ownership of property so as to maintain effective control over their grown children.*"

73. Morgan, *Puritan Family*, chs. 2–3; Smith and Hindus, "Premarital Pregnancy," 553–554; Daniel Scott Smith, "Parental Power and Marriage Patterns: An Analysis of Historical Trends in Hingham, Massachusetts," *Journal of Marriage and the Family* 35 (1973): 419–428. On the long-term erosion of patriarchal authority, see Greven, *Four Generations*, 279–282; Edwin G. Burrows and Michael Wallace, "The American Revolution: The Ideology and Psychology of National Liberation," *Perspectives in American History* 6 (1972): 165–306; Greven, *Protestant Temperament*, 339–341.

74. Bradstreet, *Works*, 224; Walsh, " 'Till Death,' " 144.

75. Rutman and Rutman, " 'Now-Wives,' " 169; Hecht, "Virginia Muster," 84.

76. Walsh, " 'Till Death,' " 148–150.

77. Morgan, *American Slavery*, 168–169; Walsh, " 'Till Death,' " 135, 143, 147; Carr and Walsh, "Planter's Wife," 558–560; Carr, "Maryland Orphans' Court," 41–62; Rutman and Rutman, " 'Now-Wives,' " 166–167.

78. Rutman and Rutman, " 'Now-Wives,' " 170.

79. Ibid., 173; Walsh, " 'Till Death,' " 147.

80. Carr and Walsh, "Planter's Wife," 564–565; Walsh, " 'Till Death,' " 131.

81. Rutman and Rutman, " 'Now-Wives,' " 168.

BIBLIOGRAPHY

Anderson, Terry L., and Thomas, Robert Paul. "The Growth of Population and Labor Force in the 17th-Century Chesapeake." *Explorations in Economic History* 15 (1978):290–312.

Aries, Philippe. *Centuries of Childhood: A Social History of Family Life.* Translated by Robert Baldick. New York: Vintage Books, 1962.

Auwers, Linda. "Reading the Marks of the Past: Exploring Female Literacy in Colonial Windsor, Connecticut." *Historical Methods* 13 (1980):204–214.

Axtell, James. *The School upon a Hill: Education and Society in Colonial New England.* New Haven: Yale University Press, 1974.

Bailyn, Bernard. *Education in the Forming of American Society: Needs and Opportunities for Study.* Chapel Hill: University of North Carolina Press, 1960.

Beales, Ross W., Jr. "Anne Bradstreet and Her Children." In *Regulated Children/*

Liberated Children: Education in Psychohistorical Perspective, edited by Barbara Finkelstein, pp. 10–23. New York: Psychohistory Press, 1979.

———. "The Half-Way Covenant and Religious Scrupulosity: The First Church of Dorchester, Massachusetts, as a Test Case." *William and Mary Quarterly* 31 (1974):465–480.

———. "In Search of the Historical Child: Miniature Adulthood and Youth in Colonial New England." *American Quarterly* 27 (1975):379–398.

Breen, T. H., and Foster, Stephen. "Moving to the New World: The Character of Early Massachusetts Immigration." *William and Mary Quarterly*, 3d ser., 30 (1973):189–222.

Brigden, Susan. "Youth and the English Reformation." *Past and Present*, No. 95 (1982):37–67.

Brown, Richard D. "Modernization and the Modern Personality in Early America, 1600–1865: A Sketch of a Synthesis." *Journal of Interdisciplinary History* 2 (1972):201–228.

Byman, Seymour. "Child Raising and Melancholia in Tudor England," *Journal of Psychohistory* 6 (1978):67–92.

Cable, Mary. *The Little Darlings: A History of Child Rearing in America.* New York: Charles Scribner's Sons, 1975.

Calvert, Karin. "Children in American Family Portraiture, 1670 to 1810." *William and Mary Quarterly*, 3d ser., 39 (1982):87–113.

Carr, Lois Green. "The Development of the Maryland Orphans' Court, 1654–1715." In *Law, Society, and Politics in Early Maryland: Proceedings of the First Conference on Maryland History, June 14–15, 1974*, edited by Aubrey C. Land, Lois Green Carr, and Edward C. Papenfuse, pp. 41–62. Baltimore: Johns Hopkins University Press, 1977.

———, and Menard, Russell R. "Immigration and Opportunity: The Freedman in Early Colonial Maryland." In *The Chesapeake in the Seventeenth Century: Essays on Anglo-American Society*, edited by Thad W. Tate and David L. Ammerman, pp. 206–242. Chapel Hill: University of North Carolina Press, 1979.

———, and Walsh, Lorena S. "The Planter's Wife: The Experience of White Women in Seventeenth-Century Maryland." *William and Mary Quarterly*, 3d ser., 34 (1977):542–571.

Cole, Thomas R. "Family, Settlement, and Migration in Southeastern Massachusetts, 1650–1805: The Case for Regional Analysis." *New England Historical and Genealogical Register* 132 (1978):171–185.

Crandall, Ralph J. "Family Types, Social Structure, and Mobility in Early America: Charlestown, Massachusetts, A Case Study." In *Changing Images of the Family*, edited by Virginia Tufte and Barbara Myerhoff, pp. 61–81. New Haven: Yale University Press, 1979.

Cremin, Lawrence A. *American Education: The Colonial Experience, 1607–1783.* New York: Harper & Row, 1970.

Davis, Natalie Zemon. "The Reasons of Misrule: Youth Groups and Charivaris in Sixteenth-Century France." *Past and Present*, No. 50 (1971):41–75.

Demos, John. "The American Family in Past Time." *American Scholar* 43 (1974):422–446.

———. "Demography and Psychology in the Historical Study of Family-Life: A

Personal Report." In *Household and Family in Past Time: Comparative Studies in the Size and Structure of the Domestic Group over the Last Three Centuries in England, France, Serbia, Japan and Colonial North America, with Further Materials from Western Europe*, edited by Peter Laslett and Richard Wall, pp. 561–569. Cambridge: At the University Press, 1972.

———. "Developmental Perspectives on the History of Childhood." *Journal of Interdisciplinary History* 2 (1971):315–327.

———. "Families in Colonial Bristol, Rhode Island: An Exercise in Historical Demography." *William and Mary Quarterly*, 3d ser., 25 (1968):40–57.

———. *A Little Commonwealth: Family Life in Plymouth Colony*. New York: Oxford University Press, 1970.

———. "Notes on Life in Plymouth Colony." *William and Mary Quarterly*, 3d ser., 22 (1965):264–286.

———. "Underlying Themes in the Witchcraft of Seventeenth-Century New England." In *Colonial America: Essays in Politics and Social Development*, edited by Stanley N. Katz, pp. 114–133. Boston: Little, Brown & Co., 1971.

———, and Demos, Virginia. "Adolescence in Historical Perspective." *Journal of Marriage and the Family* 31 (1969):632–638.

Demos, John Putnam. *Entertaining Satan: Witchcraft and the Culture of Early New England*. New York: Oxford University Press, 1982.

Dunn, Richard S. "The Barbados Census of 1680: Profile of the Richest Colony in English America." *William and Mary Quarterly*, 3d ser., 26 (1969):3–30.

———. "The Social History of Early New England." *American Quarterly* 24 (1972):661–679.

Earle, Alice Morse. *Child Life in Colonial Days*. New York: Macmillan Co., 1899.

Earle, Carville V. "Environment, Disease, and Mortality in Early Virginia." In *The Chesapeake in the Seventeenth Century: Essays on Anglo-American Society*, edited by Thad W. Tate and David L. Ammerman, pp. 96–125. Chapel Hill: University of North Carolina Press, 1979.

Finkelstein, Barbara, ed. *Regulated Children/Liberated Children: Education in Psychohistorical Perspective*. New York: Psychohistory Press, 1979.

Fleming, Sandford. *Children & Puritanism: The Place of Children in the Life and Thought of the New England Churches, 1620–1847*. New Haven: Yale University Press, 1933.

Fox, Vivian C. "Is Adolescence a Phenomenon of Modern Times?" *Journal of Psychohistory* 5 (1977):271–290.

———, and Quitt, Martin H., eds. *Loving, Parenting and Dying: The Family Cycle in England and America, Past and Present*. New York: Psychohistory Press, 1980.

Frost, J. William. *The Quaker Family in Colonial America: A Portrait of the Society of Friends*. New York: St. Martin's Press, 1973.

Frost, Jerry W. "As the Twig Is Bent: Quaker Ideas of Childhood." *Quaker History* 60 (1971):67–87.

Gemery, Henry A. "Emigration from the British Isles to the New World, 1630–1700: Inferences from Colonial Populations." In *Research in Economic History: A Research Annual*, edited by Paul Uselding, Vol. 5, pp. 179–231. Greenwich, Conn.: JAI Press, 1980.

Graff, Harvey J. "Literacy in History." *History of Education Quarterly* 15 (1975):467–474.

Greene, Jack P. "Autonomy and Stability: New England and the British Colonial Experience in Early Modern America." *Journal of Social History* 7 (1974):171–194.

Greven, Philip J., Jr. "Family Structure in Seventeenth-Century Andover, Massachusetts." *William and Mary Quarterly*, 3d ser., 23 (1966):234–256.

———. *Four Generations: Population, Land, and Family in Colonial Andover, Massachusetts.* Ithaca, N.Y.: Cornell University Press, 1970.

———. "Historical Demography and Colonial America: A Review Article." *William and Mary Quarterly*, 3d ser., 24 (1967): 438–454.

———. *The Protestant Temperament: Patterns of Child-Rearing, Religious Experience, and the Self in Early America.* New York: Alfred A. Knopf, 1977.

Hall, David D. "The Uses of Literacy in New England, 1600–1850." In *Printing and Society in Early America*, edited by William L. Joyce et al., pp. 1–47. Worcester, Mass.: American Antiquarian Society, 1983.

———. "The World of Print and Collective Mentality in Seventeenth-Century New England." In *New Directions in American Intellectual History*, edited by John Higham and Paul K. Conkin, pp. 166–180. Baltimore: Johns Hopkins University Press, 1979.

Hambrick-Stowe, Charles E. *The Practice of Piety: Puritan Devotional Disciplines in Seventeenth-Century New England.* Chapel Hill: University of North Carolina Press, 1982.

Hecht, Irene W.D. "The Virginia Muster of 1624/5 As a Source for Demographic History." *William and Mary Quarterly*, 3d ser., 30 (1973):65–92.

Henretta, James A. "The Morphology of New England Society in the Colonial Period." *Journal of Interdisciplinary History* 2 (1971):379–398.

Hiner, N. Ray. "Adolescence in Eighteenth-Century America." *History of Childhood Quarterly* 3 (1975):253–280.

———. "The Child in American Historiography: Accomplishments and Prospect." *Psychohistory Review* 7 (1978):13–23.

———. "Cotton Mather and His Children: The Evolution of a Parent Educator, 1686–1728." In *Regulated Children/Liberated Children: Education in Psychohistorical Perspective*, edited by Barbara Finkelstein, pp. 24–43. New York: Psychohistory Press, 1979.

———. "The Cry of Sodom Enquired into: Educational Analysis in Seventeenth-Century New England." *History of Education Quarterly* 13 (1973):3–22.

———. "Wars and Rumors of Wars: The Historiography of Colonial Education as a Case Study in Academic Imperialism." *Societas* 8 (1978):89–114.

Homan, Walter Joseph. *Children & Quakerism: A Study of the Place of Children in the Theory and Practice of the Society of Friends, Commonly Called Quakers.* New York: Arno Press, 1972 (Berkeley: Gillick Press, 1939).

Horn, James. "Servant Emigration to the Chesapeake in the Seventeenth Century." In *The Chesapeake in the Seventeenth Century: Essays on Anglo-American Society*, edited by Thad W. Tate and David L. Ammerman, pp. 51–95. Chapel Hill: University of North Carolina Press, 1979.

Illick, Joseph E. "Child-Rearing in Seventeenth-Century England and America."

In *The History of Childhood*, edited by Lloyd deMause, pp. 303–350. New York: Psychohistory Press, 1974.

Isaac, Rhys. "Order and Growth, Authority and Meaning in Colonial New England." *American Historical Review* 76 (1971):728–737.

Kett, Joseph F. "Adolescence and Youth in Nineteenth-Century America." *Journal of Interdisciplinary History* 2 (1971):283–298.

———. *Rites of Passage: Adolescence in America, 1790 to the Present*. New York: Basic Books, 1977.

Kulikoff, Allan. "The Beginnings of the Afro-American Family in Maryland." In *Law, Society, and Politics in Early Maryland: Proceedings of the First Conference on Maryland History, June 14–15, 1974*, edited by Aubrey C. Land, Lois Green Carr, and Edward C. Papenfuse, pp. 171–196. Baltimore: Johns Hopkins University Press, 1977.

Land, Aubrey C.; Carr, Lois Green; and Papenfuse, Edward C., eds. *Law, Society, and Politics in Early Maryland: Proceedings of the First Conference on Maryland History, June 14–15, 1974*. Baltimore: Johns Hopkins University Press, 1977.

Laslett, Peter. *The World We Have Lost*. New York: Charles Scribner's Sons, 1965.

Levy, Barry. " 'Tender Plants:' Quaker Farmers and Children in the Delaware Valley, 1681–1735." *Journal of Family History* 3 (1978):116–135.

Lockridge, Kenneth A. *Literacy in Colonial New England: An Enquiry into the Social Context of Literacy in the Early Modern West*. New York: W. W. Norton, 1974.

———. *A New England Town, the First Hundred Years: Dedham, Massachusetts, 1636–1736*. New York: W. W. Norton, 1970.

———. "The Population of Dedham, Massachusetts, 1636–1736." *Economic History Review*, 2d ser., 19 (1966):318–344.

McCracken, Grant. "The Exchange of Children in Tudor England: An Anthropological Phenomenon in Historical Context." *Journal of Family History* 8 (1983):303–313.

Macfarlane, Alan. *The Family Life of Ralph Josselin, a Seventeenth-Century Clergyman: An Essay in Historical Anthropology*. Cambridge: At the University Press, 1970.

Mechling, Jay. "Advice to Historians on Advice to Mothers." *Journal of Social History* 9 (1975):44–63.

Menard, Russell R. "From Servant to Freeholder: Status Mobility and Property Accumulation in Seventeenth-Century Maryland." *William and Mary Quarterly*, 3d ser., 30 (1973):37–64.

———. "The Growth of Population in the Chesapeake Colonies: A Comment." *Explorations in Economic History* 18 (1981):399–410. Reply by Terry L. Anderson, "From the Parts to the Whole: Modeling Chesapeake Population," ibid., pp. 411–414.

———. "Immigrants and Their Increase: The Process of Population Growth in Early Colonial Maryland." In *Law, Society, and Politics in Early Maryland: Proceedings of the First Conference on Maryland History, June 14–15, 1974*, edited by Aubrey C. Land, Lois Green Carr, and Edward C. Papenfuse, pp. 88–110. Baltimore: Johns Hopkins University Press, 1977.

———. "The Tobacco Industry in the Chesapeake Colonies, 1617–1730: An

Interpretation." In *Research in Economic History*, edited by Paul Uselding, Vol. 5, pp. 109–177. Greenwich, Conn.: JAI Press, 1980.

Middlekauff, Robert. "Piety and Intellect in Puritanism." *William and Mary Quarterly*, 3d ser., 22 (1965):457–470.

Molen, Patricia A. "Population and Social Patterns in Barbados in the Early Eighteenth Century." *William and Mary Quarterly*, 3d ser., 28 (1971):287–300.

Morgan, Edmund S. *American Slavery, American Freedom: The Ordeal of Colonial Virginia*. New York: W. W. Norton, 1975.

———. "The First American Boom: Virginia, 1618 to 1630." *William and Mary Quarterly*, 3d ser., 28 (1971):169–198.

———. "Headrights and Head Counts: A Review Article." *Virginia Magazine of History and Biography* 80 (1972):361–371.

———. *The Puritan Family: Religion and Domestic Relations in Seventeenth-Century New England*. Rev. ed., New York: Harper & Row, Harper Torchbooks, 1966.

———. Review of *The Chesapeake in the Seventeenth Century: Essays on Anglo-American Society*, edited by Thad W. Tate and David L. Ammerman (Chapel Hill: University of North Carolina Press, 1979). *William and Mary Quarterly*, 3d ser., 38 (1981):115–121.

———. *Visible Saints: The History of a Puritan Idea*. 1963. Ithaca, N.Y.: Cornell University Press, Cornell Paperbacks, 1965.

Murrin, John M. "Review Essay." *History and Theory* 11 (1972):226–275.

Norton, Susan L. "Population Growth in Colonial America: A Study of Ipswich, Massachusetts." *Population Studies* 25 (1971):433–452.

Pollock, Linda A. *Forgotten Children: Parent-Child Relations from 1500 to 1900*. Cambridge: Cambridge University Press, 1983.

Pope, Robert G. *The Half-Way Covenant: Church Membership in Puritan New England*. Princeton: Princeton University Press, 1969.

Rothman, David J. "Documents in Search of a Historian: Toward a History of Childhood and Youth in America." *Journal of Interdisciplinary History* 2 (1971):367–377.

Rutman, Darrett B., and Rutman, Anita H. " 'Now-Wives and Sons-in-Law': Parental Death in a Seventeenth-Century Virginia County." In *The Chesapeake in the Seventeenth Century: Essays on Anglo-American Society*, edited by Thad W. Tate and David L. Ammerman, pp.153–182. Chapel Hill: University of North Carolina Press, 1979.

———. "Of Agues and Fevers: Malaria in the Early Chesapeake." *William and Mary Quarterly*, 3d ser., 33 (1976):31–60.

Schlesinger, Elizabeth Bancroft. "Cotton Mather and His Children." *William and Mary Quarterly*, 3d ser., 10 (1953):181–189.

Schnucker, R. V. "The English Puritans and Pregnancy, Delivery and Breast Feeding." *History of Childhood Quarterly* 1 (1974):637–658.

Shepard, Thomas. *God's Plot: The Paradoxes of Puritan Piety, Being the Autobiography and Journal of Thomas Shepard*. Edited by Michael McGiffert. Amherst: University of Massachusetts Press, 1972.

Slater, Peter Gregg. *Children in the New England Mind: In Death and in Life*. Hamden, Conn.: Archon Books, 1977.

————. " 'From the *Cradle* to the *Coffin*': Parental Bereavement and the Shadow of Infant Damnation in Puritan Society." *Psychohistory Review* 6 (1977–1978):4–24.

Smith, Daniel Blake. "Mortality and Family in the Colonial Chesapeake." *Journal of Interdisciplinary History* 8 (1978):403–427.

————. "The Study of the Family in Early America: Trends, Problems, and Prospects." *William and Mary Quarterly*, 3d ser., 39 (1982):3–28.

Smith, Daniel Scott. "Child-Naming Patterns and Family Structure Change: Hingham, Massachusetts, 1640–1880." Newberry Papers in Family and Community History, Paper 76–5. Chicago: Newberry Library, 1977.

————. "The Demographic History of Colonial New England." *Journal of Economic History* 32 (1972):165–183.

————. "Old Age and the 'Great Transformation': A New England Case Study." In *Aging and the Elderly: Humanistic Perspectives in Gerontology*, edited by Stuart F. Spicker, Kathleen M. Woodward, and David D. Van Tassel, pp. 285–302. Atlantic Highlands, N.J.: Humanities Press, 1978.

————. "Parental Power and Marriage Patterns: An Analysis of Historical Trends in Hingham, Massachusetts." *Journal of Marriage and the Family* 35 (1973):419–428.

————. "A Perspective on Demographic Methods and Effects in Social History." *William and Mary Quarterly*, 3d ser., 39 (1982):442–468.

————, and Hindus, Michael S. "Premarital Pregnancy in America, 1640–1971: An Overview and Interpretation." *Journal of Interdisciplinary History* 5 (1975):537–570.

Smith, Steven R. "Almost Revolutionaries: The London Apprentices During the Civil Wars." *Huntington Library Quarterly* 42 (1979):313–328.

————. "The London Apprentices as Seventeenth-Century Adolescents." *Past and Present*, No. 61 (1973):149–161.

————. "Religion and the Conception of Youth in Seventeenth-Century England." *History of Childhood Quarterly* 2 (1975):493–516.

Solberg, Winton U. *Redeem the Time: The Puritan Sabbath in Early America*. Cambridge, Mass.: Harvard University Press, 1977.

Sommerville, C. John. "English Puritans and Children: A Social-Cultural Explanation." *Journal of Psychohistory* 6 (1978):113–137.

Stannard, David E. "Death and the Puritan Child." *American Quarterly* 26 (1974):456–476.

Starkey, Marion L. *The Devil in Massachusetts: A Modern Enquiry into the Salem Witch Trials*. New York: Alfred A. Knopf, 1949.

————. "The Easiest Room in Hell." *Essex Institute Historical Collections* 92 (1956):33–42.

Steffen, Charles G. "The Sewall Children in Colonial New England." *New England Historical and Genealogical Register* 131 (1977):163–172.

Tate, Thad W., and Ammerman, David L., eds. *The Chesapeake in the Seventeenth Century: Essays on Anglo-American Society*. Chapel Hill: University of North Carolina Press, 1979.

Vann, Richard T. "The Youth of *Centuries of Childhood*." *History and Theory* 21 (1982):279–297.

Vinovskis, Maris A. "Angels' Heads and Weeping Willows: Death in Early America." *Proceedings of the American Antiquarian Society* 86 (1976):273–302.

———. "Mortality Rates and Trends in Massachusetts Before 1860." *Journal of Economic History* 32 (1972):184–213.

———. "Recent Trends in American Historical Demography: Some Methodological and Conceptual Considerations." *Annual Review of Sociology* 4 (1978):603–627.

Wagner, Peter. "A Note on Puritans and Children in Early Colonial New England." *Amerikastudien* 25 (1980):47–62.

Walsh, Lorena S. " 'Till Death Us Do Part': Marriage and Family in Seventeenth-Century Maryland." In *The Chesapeake in the Seventeenth Century: Essays on Anglo-American Society*, edited by Thad W. Tate and David L. Ammerman, pp. 126–152. Chapel Hill: University of North Carolina Press, 1979.

———, and Menard, Russell R. "Death in the Chesapeake: Two Life Tables for Men in Early Colonial Maryland." *Maryland Historical Magazine* 69 (1974):211–227.

Waters, John J. "The Traditional World of the New England Peasants: A View from Seventeenth-Century Barnstable." *New England Historical and Genealogical Register* 130 (1976):3–21.

Weissbach, Lee Shai. "The Townes of Massachusetts: A Pilot Study in Genealogy and Family History." *Essex Institute Historical Collections* 118 (1982):200–220.

Wells, Robert V. "Quaker Marriage Patterns in a Colonial Perspective." *William and Mary Quarterly*, 3d ser., 29 (1972):415–442.

———. *Revolutions in Americans' Lives: A Demographic Perspective on the History of Americans, Their Families, and Their Society*. Contributions in Family Studies, No. 6. Westport, Conn.: Greenwood Press, 1982.

Wilson, Adrian. "The Infancy of the History of Childhood: An Appraisal of Philippe Aries." *History and Theory* 19 (1980):132–153.

Yarbrough, Anne. "Apprentices as Adolescents in Sixteenth Century Bristol." *Journal of Social History* 13 (1979):67–81.

Ziff, Larzer. *The Career of John Cotton: Puritanism and the American Experience*. Princeton: Princeton University Press, 1962.

Zuckerman, Michael. "William Byrd's Family." *Perspectives in American History* 12 (1979):255–311.

2

Children and Childhood in the Eighteenth Century

Constance B. Schulz

Historians who have written or spoken during the past two decades about children in the eighteenth century provide a resounding echo to the conclusions arrived at by Glenn H. Elder, Jr., in his perceptive essay reviewing the present state of theoretical and practical approaches to the history of the family: the study of the history of childhood, like that of the history of the family from which it springs, is increasingly a "Discovery of Complexity."[1] Until very recently, the historical understanding of childhood in the colonial period was bracketed by scholarly exigeses on the text of the New England Primer's admonition "In Adam's Fall We Sinned all" and Alice Morse Earle's lively descriptions of children's cradles and clothing. New England children typified all children; the seventeenth and eighteenth centuries were no more separated in the historical imagination than Georgia and Boston where child life was concerned. An early pioneer, Edmund Sears Morgan, dared to suggest that *The Puritan Family* and *Virginians at Home* represented two quite different times, places, and milieus within which colonial children were born, nurtured, educated, and ushered into adulthood, but for the most part the understanding of children and their past looked no further.[2]

The study of American children in the eighteenth century has changed dramatically since the publication of Philippe Aries's groundbreaking study, *Centuries of Childhood: A Social History of Family Life*, in 1962. Whether or not one agrees with Aries that childhood itself was not discovered until the relatively recent seventeenth century, most historians did not discover childhood until the mid-twentieth century. The emergence of new techniques, new approaches, new questions, and new concerns has led historians into a creative burst of activity demonstrating both directly and indirectly the inadequacy of earlier generalizations about colonial children. To write of "children in the eighteenth century" one must first ask, "Which children?": children of New England, or of the Chesapeake, or perhaps of Pennsylvania or the Carolinas? Farming youngsters of Dedham, Massachusetts, in 1700 or sons and daughters of Boston merchants in 1799? Irish apprentices in Philadelphia or German schoolchildren in Frederick, Maryland? Slave infants on a South Carolina plantation or youthful female converts at a Connecticut revival? Historians have studied all of these and more, and from their recent contributions have emerged fascinating contradictions, as well as an overwhelming quantity of detail that seems to defy easy comparison, let alone lend itself to the building of useful generalizations.[3]

A practical way to get around this dilemma is to approach the history of childhood in the eighteenth century not by asking *what* historians now think they know about those children, but *how* we know about them. What sources have historians tapped in their curiosity about this important corner of the past, and how have they used those sources to explain children and the adults who have dealt with them? Historians have turned to three sorts of evidence to reconstruct the varied and elusive lives of children: literary evidence, most of it necessarily reflecting the views of adults who observed, worried about, regulated, or instructed the child; quantitative evidence painstakingly pieced together from comprehensive family or community reconstitution studies that delineate the child within the larger context of intricately interwoven adult economic and social patterns; and the mute testimony of material culture, evidence that hauntingly places the child in a spatial dimension in its own world but requires careful translation and explication in order to speak to ours. These three forms of source material have been used, sometimes in creative combination, and with varying degrees of success, in answering the four questions N. Ray Hiner has proposed as the basic inquiries that any investigation into the history of childhood must address:

1. What have been the attitudes of adults toward children and childhood? . . . 2. What are the conditions which helped to shape the development of children? . . . 3. What has been the subjective experience of childhood in the past? . . . 4. How have children and childhood influenced adults?[4]

Some, like John Demos in his study of seventeenth-century Plymouth and Robert Gross in his description of Concord, Massachusetts, on the eve of the American Revolution, have imaginatively combined all three methodologies to recreate worlds of which children formed an important element. In these and similar studies, however, children and their concerns are seldom the central focus of attention.[5] Moreover, in spite of the renewed interest in childhood, and the expanding quantity of information about children of the past, much of the basic research remains to be done before interpretive essays can be written. This chapter will explore the realms of eighteenth-century childhood that historians have begun to map and describe, as a step toward seeing where the gaps remain, where the terrain is still largely unknown, and where the questions have not yet been asked.

THE HISTORIAN AND LITERARY EVIDENCE ABOUT CHILDREN

Literary evidence, in the broadest sense of that term, is the raw material with which the majority of historians trained before 1960 were most familiar. Alice Morse Earle, whether describing *Child Life in Colonial Days* (New York, 1899) or home life or colonial costume,[6] utilized photographs and illustrations of artifacts in her descriptive catalogues of the behavior and appearance of past youngsters, but much of her re-creation of the lives of children relied heavily on the diaries and letters of parents, childrearing literature, and children's schoolbooks. With the exception of the occasional letters and diaries of children, literary evidence is almost exclusively a record of the concerns, observations, and theories of adults about the children they knew, or of their writings for those children. Although some insight into the subjective experience of children can be extracted from it, it lends itself more directly to the study of adult attitudes toward children and the institutions of childhood.

The earliest studies of eighteenth-century childhood focused on the mutually dependent educational and religious training of children. Sanford Fleming, in *Children and Puritanism: The Place of Children in the Life and Thought of the New England Churches, 1620–1847*, relied heavily on the literature of catechism and conversion to paint a static picture of rigid Calvinist orthodoxy that doomed children to harsh discipline of both their bodies and their minds, stimulated children terrified for their souls to a religious precocity that seemed pitiful to its twentieth-century chroniclers, and left no room for adults who enforced it to appreciate the natural joyfulness or spontaneity of children. Fleming acknowledged that there was within New England a liberal group that was "much more sympathetic to the real religious needs of children" but found in the eighteenth century no change from the predominant Calvinist values. A child-oriented concept of Christian education did not develop until Horace Bushnell preached a doctrine of "Christian Nurture" in the 1840s.[7]

Fleming and others used literary sources to describe the secular and religious content of early education for children. Monica Kiefer used the same sources to rediscover the children themselves in her 1948 study,

American Children Through Their Books, 1700–1835.[8] Agreeing that there was a "sovereignty of religion in every phase of child life," in which children "had no special religious status, but shared that of their elders," Kiefer's study of a wide range of children's literature nevertheless revealed a change in the status of the child and of adult views of the education suitable for children. Around the time of the American Revolution, the child gradually emerged "from a submerged position in an adult world" into "a position of honor as a cherished social entity."[9] Despite the permeation of children's literature with moral instruction and religious content, Kiefer discovered there a constant adult concern for the behavior and health of the children under their care, a diversity of educational subject matter, and evidence that children during the eighteenth century, at least those of the middle classes in the middle and northern colonies, routinely amused themselves with games and toys.

It was Bernard Bailyn who transformed the study by historians of education, both its impact on children and its meaning for adults, by calling in 1960 for a new use of literary and other sources to investigate education "not only as a formal pedagogy but as the entire process by which a culture transmits itself across the generations." In the seventeenth century, education as cultural transmission was a process in which the family had a predominant role, shared with the community and the church. By the beginning of the nineteenth century, it had been "transformed in the jarring multiplicity, the raw economy, and the barren environment of America" into a "controversial, conscious, constructed" effort, focusing on formal education. Education and its instrument, the school, became "an agency of rapid social change, a powerful internal accelerator" that "distinctively shaped the American personality."[10]

Although Bailyn's conclusions about the changing impact of formal education on society at large as well as on the child directly have been both expanded on and criticized,[11] his invitation to regard education as a much larger process, and his observation that the history of the family and its crucial historical role in education "has been almost entirely neglected by American historians," helped to inspire a new approach to the child in which literary materials lent themselves to two quite different explorations of the world of childhood.[12] One group of historians has extended the study of education forward into adulthood, filling out Bailyn's perception that education is nothing less than the process of creating the intelligence and culture of a people. The history of education in their hands has been transformed from study of the creation of institutions to far more wide-ranging questions of intellectual, cultural, and religious history in which the child and its formal and informal training became the fertile ground for transforming republican ideology into republican economic, social, and political institutions. Yet Bernard Wishy, *The Child and the Republic, The Dawn of Modern American Child Nurture*, and Daniel Calhoun, *The Intelligence of a People*, have been less interested in histories of the children themselves than in what their education symbolizes about a changing society and the culture it transmits.[13]

Drawing insight from the theoretical writings of psychology and anthropology and assuming that education begins at birth, another group of historians has described and analyzed patterns of childrearing, and their impact on the early psychological development of the child. From this focus on the family as the primary force forming the child's personality, and perhaps thereby affecting the whole character of the society, emerged developmental questions about swaddling, breast-feeding, weaning, toilet-training, physical discipline in breaking the child's will, parental affection, male-female role models and sex specific clothing, and adolescent behavior. Contributions to understanding of childhood through understanding of family dynamics have come both from content analysis of literary sources, and from interpretive use of the results of the burgeoning number of quantitative studies of the family.

The application of psychological theories to the changes in childhood in the eighteenth century has ranged from the "psychogenic theory of history" postulated by Lloyd deMause and his followers to the matter-of-fact acceptance of concepts of "self-identity" and "emotional security" by Daniel Blake Smith. Psychogenic theory operates on "the radical premise that the evolution of childhood within the family is the root *cause* of the evolution of society," and constructs an "evolutionary, psychoanalytical theory of human history."[14] In applying psychoanalytical behavioral theory to the evolution of parent-child relations in the eighteenth century, John F. Walzer characterized parents as holding and acting on diametrically opposed attitudes toward their children. The ambivalent parental desires to simultaneously reject and cling to their children were clearly a positive step forward from the earlier and more barbarous practices of outright rejection and infanticide. Nevertheless, while fostering feelings of affection in and for their children, these not-yet-modern parents continued to expose them unthinkingly to the hazards of weather, open fires, and disease, sent them away to wet-nurses and to schools at very early ages, and attempted to install in them obedience, manners, and religion through harsh physical punishment and shame. The parents' ambivalence was reflected in an equal ambivalence among the children, who wished to be independent and yet remain dependent. Walzer argues that this "causally reciprocal" shift in attitudes marked the beginning of a psychological evolution in the eighteenth century toward individualism.[15]

The problem with such generalizations, useful as they are in raising questions about the psychological content of parent-child relationships, is that they suggest that all eighteenth-century parents nurtured their children alike. The ways in which parents gave guidance to their children varied substantially, however. The ways in which parents gave guidance to their children varied substantially, however. Recent historians, recognizing this diversity, have differentiated between systems of parental childrearing behavior, demonstrating that the answers to Hiner's first question, "What have been the attitudes of adults toward children and childhood?" are complex. Philip Greven divided childrearing patterns on the basis of the temperament of the adults, perceiving temperament to be shaped by the demands of the religious ideology embraced by the community of which the parents were a part. Others have sought out the nurturing methodologies of particular groups of parents whose childrearing patterns reflected ethnic, or geographic, or denominational values and circumstances.

Greven used many of the same literary sources that earlier students of education and the family had explored, and assumed with them the central importance of religious experience for children as for adults. Shifting from the institutional and formal educational focus of earlier histories, he analyzed instead the impact of differing theologies on family emotional structures as they affected children from infancy through adolescence. He categorized adult behavior into authoritarian families practicing evangelical modes of childrearing, authoritative families practicing moderate modes of childrearing, and affectionate families practicing genteel modes of childrearing. Greven argues that these patterns persisted over time and were transferred from one generation to the next.

Evangelical parents isolated themselves and their offspring in tightly regulated nuclear families to have better control over their children, insulating them both from the temptations of the less pious members of the larger community and from the indulgences of grandparents. Their theological dependence on a God of judgment led them to "break the wills" of children through rigorous physical, verbal, and emotional punishment, and encouraged self-suppression, guilt, and shame in adolescents. Evangelical patterns of childrearing were strongest in the seventeenth century. Increasingly throughout the eighteenth century, such evangelical families were in a minority and were more likely to be representative of newer, rural, or frontier communities, than of older and wealthier centers of population.[16]

Moderates became increasingly the majority model for childrearing practices throughout all the colonies in the eighteenth century. Focusing on "love and duty" rather than on "love and fear" as the principal familial obligations, these parents strove to bend rather than break the wills of their children, to control rather than destroy the child's conception of self, to bind the child through the obligations of connection to an organic and complex world rather than to isolate him or her from temptation and sin. This child- and world-view differed from evangelical Calvinism in placing more stress on reason, moderation, and the liberty of the human will. Discipline appropriate to the child's age and stage of development was derived from a view of the infant as innocent though corruptible, rather than inherently sinful. Internalization of a sense of duty and obligation permitted adolescents to take their eventual places as sober, virtuous, and pious citizens in an orderly if complex society governed by rules of law and nature.[17]

Attachment to moderate childrearing practices crossed economic, ethnic, and geographic barriers. John and Abigail Adams and their friends Mercy and James Warren stressed to their children and to each other the merits of moderation, virtue, duty, and obedience. Quaker assumptions that children were born innocent and righteous, and remained so until they reached an age sufficient to reason or experience the inner light, steered parental discipline and childrearing practices toward moderate rather than toward evangelical patterns. The second and third generations of the Shippen family of Pennsylvania, and the family of Eliza Lucas Pinckney in South Carolina, were reared to adulthood by parents who were confident that moderate and loving methods would instill in children piety, virtue, and a sense of duty to family and community. Colonel Landon Carter, a wealthy Virginia planter, and Benjamin Franklin, a middle-class Philadelphia printer, stressed alike the usefulness of reason for controlling the passions, and the necessity of instilling self-control and moderation in the consciences of children.[18]

Where evangelicals and moderates stressed control of children, whether imposed by external discipline or internalized self-control, genteel parents preferred indulgence over discipline in rearing children. Freed by servants from the day-to-day responsibility for molding willful children into acceptable human beings—the servants fed, disciplined, and nursed their offspring—wealthy parents as portrayed by Greven seemed impervious to inner threats and anxieties and displayed a remarkable self-assurance in their childrearing habits. For parents and children alike, activity and purpose were shaped, not by piety, but by pleasure. Dances, games, races, assemblies, dinners, fashion, gossip, and sociability formed the daily lives of adults, and children were socialized into that existence by an education that stressed the polite and mannerly skills of young gentlemen and the feminine arts of docility and domesticity, rather than mastery of scripture and theology. Easily accepting their own importance, secure in knowledge of their right to affection and power, and trained from infancy in the genteel habits of command and authority, such children readily took their positions of political and social leadership when they reached adulthood.[19]

Greven recognized that wealth and class were determining factors in the emergence of the genteel temperament. Daniel Blake Smith and Jan Lewis suggest through their studies of Maryland and Virginia that these childrearing patterns were also a geographic and temporal phenomenon, located primarily in the southern and middle colonies, and emerging largely after the 1750s. Smith argues that Chesapeake parents did discipline their children, although they did so by adopting a Lockean style that emphasized affection and the development of autonomy rather than submission to parental authority and breaking or bending the child's will. Their economic circumstances in an uncrowded plantation environment "allowed planters to raise their children under more optimistic and permissive assumptions about childhood and parental conduct."[20] Yet the prolonged dependence that Charles Carroll of Annapolis enforced on his son Charles Carroll of Carrollton and the severe developmental regimen revealed in the correspondence between "Papa" and "Charlie" contradicts Smith's portrayal.[21] Moreover, for young women, the genteel childrearing patterns of the Chesapeake stressed softness and compliance, and emphasized natural beauty and feminine charms rather than independence. In a study of Virginia gentry, Jan Lewis suggests that parental attachment to their offspring lacked emotional intensity; Virginia ladies and gentlemen managed personal relationships behind a screen of manners, geniality, and self-assurance that allowed them to maintain domestic tranquility, and judged failure by the absence of that tranquility occasioned by the behavior of their offspring.[22]

The variety of adult attitudes toward childhood apparent in divergent childrearing practices is not reflected in the place of children in the legal system. Law is fundamentally much more conservative than the society for which it serves as an organizing force; as the official statement of culture, it is often the last to conform to change. American family law in the eighteenth century was still firmly bound to its English origins, rooted in English common law, in regulation of marriage by the established church, and in colonial and parliamentary statute law. During the eighteenth century, both local court customs and informal mechanisms developed outside of the legal system in conformity with community folkways and institutions began to respond to the changing perceptions of childhood that were emerging in community practice, but family law itself did not change substantially. The "unity of husband and wife" that was marriage conveyed to the husband absolute ownership of his wife's personal property, any income she might earn, and lifetime control of her lands, and denied to her custody of her children in the rare case of divorce. Fathers had absolute authority over the person and property of their children. The child was, in a manner of speaking, a servant to whose services the father had an absolute right. "The law, to be sure, recognized certain primary duties, such as protection, support, and education, that every parent owed to his children, but these it held to be exclusively moral obligations." The exception to this general paternal authority arose under poor laws, which Maxwell Bloomfield has described as the "reverse image of the common law doctrines governing persons of property." Children could be separated from their parents and forced to work for others, or grandparents could be compelled to support them if their parents were incapable of doing so.[23]

Apart from the special position of the poor, children in colonial society became a concern of the law when they misbehaved or threatened order in the community, when they were orphaned and provision had to be made for care of their persons or their property, or when they were involved in legal contracts, most frequently indentures of apprenticeship. In Puritan New England, biblical sanctions were added to common law practices to provide for the death penalty for a "stubborn or rebellious son ... which will not obey the voice of his Father, or the voice of his Mother." These "stubborn child" laws, first enacted in Massachusetts in 1646 and repeated in other colonies, were never enforced, for in practice difficult children were bound away from their parents as apprentices; parents having problems controlling a willful son over sixteen could turn to the courts to compel obedience.[24]

In common and statute law, there was no provision for assigning parents to the orphaned child. Yet in colonial Chesapeake, "family disruption resulting from frightfully high mortality" and the absence of immediate family frequently left children orphaned without proper custodial arrangements made for their persons or property. Using Charles County, Maryland, as a case study, Lorena Walsh demonstrated that by the early eighteenth century, "a reasonably effective mechanism" had developed from Orphans Court practices. Designed originally to protect property, over time they came to protect the rights of the children. In many cases, custody and power over the estate given to mothers enlarged in practice a legal ability that women did not yet have under strict adherence to common law.[25] In Massachusetts, a number of mechanisms arose that in effect created a practice of adoption even though no laws permitted it: the apprenticeship system of indentured servitude was sometimes used to create a legal bond where an affectionate one already existed. Wills could transfer inheritance to a child thus "created" through indenture, and parents seeking to safeguard the interests of such an "adoptee" could petition the General Court for permission to change the child's name.[26]

The literary evidence of statute and case law, combined with analysis of childrearing patterns, informs us about a wide variety of adult attitudes toward children and childhood, but does not necessarily tell us about the daily experiences of children. Just as strict laws did not always reflect actual practice, nurturant patterns that adults advocated, and perhaps followed, did not always result in obvious differences in their childrens' lives. "It is easy to imagine . . . two different childrearing value orientations resulting in the same overt childrearing behavior," notes Jay Mechling in profferring "Advice to Historians on Advice to Mothers." Nevertheless, by combining information about the children themselves found in studies of adult childrearing practices with that found in histories of education and religion, and insight from the history of medicine, it is possible to compile an overview of the lives of eighteenth-century children.[27]

Childbearing itself reminded evangelical parents of the short and unpredictable course of life and the awfulness of divine judgment. In Puritan New England, death in childbirth was not as common as has sometimes been thought, although advice literature such as Cotton Mather's *Elizabeth in Her Holy Retirement, An Essay to Prepare a Pious Woman for Her Lying-in* (Boston, 1710) warned pregnant women: "Your death has entered into you, you may have conceived that which determines but about Nine Months more at the most for you to live in the World."[28] In using pregnancy to enforce piety, this literature may have put a special emotional burden on evangelical women as they prepared for parenthood; yet other parents also feared the dangers of childbed. Children were born in their own homes, although some women chose to return to their parents' homes for delivery rather than risk the ministrations of unfamiliar neighbors or less solicitous in-laws. Until late in the eighteenth century, mothers were assisted in delivery by a midwife and her female assistants. Female control of the birth process was first seriously challenged in 1763 in Philadelphia when William Shippen established a practice of male-midwifery, initially to ease difficult births by utilizing forceps, but eventually building a large clientele for normal births as well.[29]

The majority of American mothers nursed their infants, although a few of the wealthy put their children to a hired wet-nurse, or a slave. For those who could not nurse their children themselves, or afford the services of a wet-nurse, the only alternative was "hand feeding." Cow's milk, skimmed of its cream and boiled, perhaps diluted somewhat, could be given even newborn infants through a device known as a "bubby-pot," a small vessel, usually pewter, with a spout ending in a bulbous knob with a small hole that enabled the baby to suck for his nourishment.[30] Some evangelicals made of weaning an early test of parental control over the infant. Yet available evidence suggests that most colonial mothers, evangelical, moderate, or genteel, weaned children sometime between the first and second birthdays, usually when the baby began to acquire enough teeth to make nursing uncomfortable.

Breast-feeding their infants had the additional merit for mothers that it delayed conception and helped space children two years or more apart. This had an important consequence for the children, for it determined both their relationships to siblings and the length of time in which an infant had the more concentrated attention of both its parents before a new baby diverted and divided that concern. The findings of Darrett and Anita Rutman have suggested that nursing had an even more important consequence for Chesapeake infants: in a society constantly weakened by endemic malaria, infants fed at the breast of an immune mother ingested a temporary immunity themselves. With weaning, that immunity ended, and children two to four years of age suffered a proportionally higher rate of mortality compared to newborn infants than in other regions.[31]

Infant mortality from disease during the eighteenth century insured that, despite an average birth-spacing of between two and three years, even children born into large families did not necessarily live in households with great numbers of other children. N. Ray Hiner has demonstrated this phenomenon in an illuminating chart illustrating at a glance the life course of Cotton Mather's family. Although his wives bore him sixteen children in twenty-six years, in only two of those years were more than two children under the age of five present in the household.[32] The death rates for children under the age of five were high, particularly in the coastal regions of the South. Daniel Blake Smith estimates that in the first third of the eighteenth century the mortality rate for children under four reached 180 per 1,000 in Charles Parish, Virginia. Even in colonial New England where the isolation of villages from each other prevented some of the worst ravages of spreading epidemics, John Demos has estimated that in Plymouth in the seventeenth century, 25 percent of all children born died during the first decade of life. Mortality rates were highest for the very youngest: in colonial Andover and Salem between 10 and 30 percent of children born did not survive until their first birthday. A young couple beginning a family could confidently expect that at least two or three of their children would die in early childhood.[33]

These frightening statistics are in part attributable to the periodic epidemics that swept the North American continent throughout the colonial period; epidemics in 1702, 1721, 1730, and 1752 doubled and tripled the normal average of approximately 30 deaths per 1,000 in Boston in those years. Small children were particularly susceptible to the ravages of smallpox, yellow fever, adult respiratory diseases, agues and fevers, intestinal diseases, and influenza. Smallpox was especially terrifying during most of the seventeenth and eighteenth centuries. The practice of inoculation—deliberately inducing the disease by implanting pus from a victim under the skin of a healthy person—was at least in part introduced in Boston in 1721 by Cotton Mather and Zabdial Boylston to protect young Samuel Mather from contracting the dread disease "in the natural way." This "variolation" provoked considerable opposition from both the clergy and physicians in the early eighteenth century, but its significant reduction of deaths led eventually to its more widespread adoption by late in the century. Progressive parents like the Mathers, the Adamses, and Benjamin Franklin willingly inoculated their children. During the height of epidemics in Philadelphia in 1730 and 1750, in Charleston, South Carolina, in 1738 and 1760, and in Boston in 1764 and 1776, large numbers of residents of those cities, including children of all classes, submitted to variolation. In Boston in 1730, the fatality rate from the disease among the 400 inoculated was 3 percent compared to 12.5 percent of the 4,000 who caught the disease naturally. By 1792, when over 9,000 Bostonians were inoculated, the death rate from variolation was only 1 in 55.[34]

Some epidemics found their victims almost exclusively among young children in the eighteenth century. Diptheria, or "throat distemper," and scarlet fever (which were sometimes difficult for colonial parents and physicians to distinguish) were often fatal for children under fifteen. Almost unknown in the seventeenth century, diptheria first reached epidemic proportions only after 1730. John Duffy reports that in the New England diptheria epidemic of 1736–1737, twenty families in one town buried all of their children, another community lost more than half of all its children under fifteen years of age, and New Hampshire children under ten accounted for 802 of 948 deaths from the disease in a fourteen-month period. Noah Webster, in *A Brief History of Epidemic and Pestilential Diseases* (Hartford, Conn., 1799), wrote that "It was literally the *plague among children*. Many families lost three or four children—many lost all."[35] The disease spread to other regions only slowly; Philadelphia had its first serious outbreak in 1746, New York in the period between 1750 and 1755, and South Carolina in the winter of 1750–1751. These epidemic disease tolls must be added to a background incidence of mortality from endemic children's diseases—measles, whooping cough, and mumps, which themselves occasionally reached epidemic proportions—and help explain the almost pathological fears and forebodings for the children of parents like Cotton Mather.[36]

Slave children were exposed to additional life-threatening factors. Kenneth and Virginia Kipple argue that malnutrition, particularly shortages of trace elements such as calcium, iron, and magnesium in the diet, and a vitamin D deficiency, was responsible for a mortality rate for black children under four that was double that of whites. This occurred, not because of deliberate starvation by owners who had much to lose from the deaths of slave infants, but because of the inability of children whose bodily mechanisms were designed for survival in West Africa to absorb nutritional elements from their marginal diet. Indeed, planters misunderstood the distended bellies that are evidence of protein-calorie malnutrition for evidence that children in the "quarters" were thriving. They blamed infant deaths on "teething," "rickets," "worms," and "dirt-eating."[37]

Surprisingly little study has been conducted on the effect of this tragic element of eighteenth-century childhood on the children themselves. Eighteenth-century children were intimately acquainted with death, not of the elderly, but of children like themselves. For New England children, evangelical children, and Quaker children, this encounter with death was heightened by theological tenets that demanded that a child repent of his or her sins before life ended. Children were offered not comfort, but a terrifying picture of the fate of the unregenerate. "Puritan diaries and sermons were filled with references to . . . childhood responses to the terrors of separation, mortality, and damnation," but the interpretive energy of most recent historians has been directed more fully at the fears and mourning of their parents than at a comprehensive analysis of the way the children themselves perceived death and accepted the suffering of disease.[38]

Disease was not the only physical threat to children's lives and health. The frequent references to childish accidents in parental diaries suggests that in busy eighteenth-century households, toddlers and young children were not always closely watched. Perhaps suspecting that a distraught mother feared for her absent husband's anger as well as her burned son's injuries, Dr. John Warren wrote to reassure the child's father that she

had at the moment of the accident's taking place just stepped out of the chamber door to speak to a servant, and before she could turn herself the child was in a blaze. This instance is a proof how ineffectual are the utmost care, vigilance and attention for preventing misfortunes of this kind; and we infrequently have occasion to wonder at the escape of children that seem to have no care taken of them at all.[39]

Cotton Mather recorded his children falling into the fire or catching their clothes afire with a candle on several occasions. Other youngsters, not entirely unlike their counterparts in the twentieth century, fell into rivers, stuffed nutshells up their noses, swallowed pins (in the days before the invention of the safety pin), and ate poisonous berries, nuts, seeds, and plants.[40]

During the eighteenth century, the dividing line between "infancy" and "childhood" was still blurred, and the terms were often used interchangeably. As in the seventeenth century, somewhere between a child's fifth and seventh birthdays the universal dress-like frock of infancy was replaced by sex-differentiated apparel. Some historians argue that the gowns were intended by the parents who put them on male and female children alike as clothing appropriate to females and as a reinforcement of powerlessness; "Clothing symbolized the feminization of children." Such clothing also allowed parents to pass clothing from one child to another regardless of gender; gowns were both less likely to be outgrown by young boys than breeches, and easier for immature hands to cope with removing when natural bodily functions required. The age of five or six when most small boys were "breeched," often in a ceremonial occasion, marks the stage in their development of manual dexterity when they become able to manage buttons.[41]

The children who survived infancy entered a world where the way in which they spent their days was in part determined by their geographic location, gender, and economic status. Very young children could assist in household chores, and girls were taught early to spin, weave, make, and mend clothing. Urban families that could afford them kept domestic animals, and in the predominantly rural settings in which most children grew to adulthood, the need for constant daily labor in a wide variety of chores meant that young boys and girls were rarely idle.[42] In cities, children of the working poor were bound out as apprentices at an early age or were given tasks such as collecting kindling wood, herding livestock, or delivering dairy products from the nearby countryside to supplement family income. Poor children not apprenticed by their parents might be bound to a master through public intervention. Under Boston's Act of 1735, half of 1,100 children of the poor bound out between 1734 and 1805 were between the ages of five and nine. The boys were apprenticed to tradesmen and to husbandry; the girls were sent out chiefly to serve as housemaids.[43]

Indentures were not confined to the very poor but continued to be a method of training children for future adult employment in skilled crafts or trades. Recent scholarship on parental control of adolescents in New England has disputed the argument of Edmund Sears Morgan in *The Puritan Family* that children of relatively well-to-do parents were also apprenticed as domestic labor, or sent to relatives to live, in order to relieve the tensions created by adolescent challenges to parental authority. James Axtell notes that widespread use of locally apprenticed youngsters as household servants did spill over into the eighteenth century, even as apprenticeship changed drastically and increasingly involved Irish or other immigrants rather than native-born children of the "middling sort."[44]

Children in the eighteenth century played as well as worked, and even among groups like the Quakers, toys and games for children were given adult approval. "Girls had swings, drew on slates, cut out paper dolls with scissors, recited poetry, and played with doll houses and cradles. Boys flew kites, sailed boats, constructed wigwams and played at being Indians, rode hobby horses and later real ponies, collected rocks and bird eggs, attempted scientific experiments, gardened, and made pets of squirrels, guinea hens, dogs and cats." Such playfulness continued into early adolescence for at least a few; ingenious pranks came to be expected as a part of collegiate life, although tutors could hardly have approved of those who "put cows in the college pulpit, burned the fellows' privy, or cut the rope of the college bell." At mid-century such pranks at Harvard nearly degenerated into riots and led to heavy fines, degradation, and expulsion.[45]

For a few very small children gathered into "Dames schools," and for many children over seven, formal schooling was also a part of daily routine. Lawrence Cremin has suggested that education took place in three distinctive types of institutions: the "English," or common school, the Latin School, distinguished primarily by the presence of instruction in the classical languages, and the academy, which combined the common school practical subjects with the grammar school classical subjects and even some collegiate ones. Moreover, a number of children were also educated by private tutors like Philip Fithian at Nomini Hall, or by pastors of sectarian churches whose duties included education as well as preaching, or with a wide variety of entrepreneurial teachers who advertised particular skills such as needlework, cyphering, and dancing.[46]

New England from its inception required some sort of public education for all of its children, although Kenneth Lockridge has pointed out that Puritan school laws were initially ineffective because populations were not dense enough to support them, and that these schools systematically offered less instruction to female children, creating a higher rate of illiteracy among women. In rural New England in the early eighteenth century, the rising concentration of population meant an increased likelihood that young boys, and to a lesser extent, young girls, would attend school at least part of the year. By 1720, Boston had five public or "free schools" and a wide range of private schools and academies, though a small payment of "entrance and fire money" for the free schools probably kept the poorest from attending. The law authorizing the Boston Overseers of the Poor to apprentice indigent children required the new masters to provide for their education, although this was not always carefully enforced. Boys were to be taught reading and writing, and girls reading only.[47] The availability of education also expanded outside of New England during the eighteenth century. In a study of the growth of public and private schooling in Philadelphia and New York, Lawrence Cremin calculated that the ratio of school-aged children to instructors, after rising dramatically between 1689 and 1735, dropped significantly by the end of the century, making the availability of education markedly more available at the end of the century than it had been in the beginning.[48]

The likelihood that the majority of children would have an opportunity to attend school was much smaller in the southern colonies, but even there, many children between the ages of five and sixteen spent some portion of their time in school. In Elizabeth City County, Virginia, the Syms free school and the Eaton charity school provided free education during much of the eighteenth century, and other counties also provided some institutions for education of poor children.[49] For dissenters throughout the South, as for the South Carolina frontier parishes of the Anglican Church, preachers also served as teachers. Among the gentry, a tutor might be hired for sons, or boys were sent off to board with a clergyman who, for a fee, took in scholars to be taught Greek and Latin. Thomas Jefferson first learned to love classical languages and to distrust the established clergy while a student boarding at the Reverend James Maury's home. In Maryland, it was fashionable for wealthy Catholic families to send young boys to France for a proper education, while the first families of Virginia sent many of their youths to England.[50]

The schools of sectarian and ethnic communities also served to socialize those children into the specialized values and cultures of their parents. Germans in Frederick, Maryland, in the 1740s provided religious and secular instruction in the German language as a consciously adopted "means of passing their cultural heritage on to their children." In contrast, by the late eighteenth century the Germans in Germantown, Pennsylvania, settled nearly half a century earlier than the western Maryland communities, supported the building of a Union school (rather than a number of competing parochial schools) where the German language was only one of several offered in the secular course of instruction. In that community a child's attendance at a particular school, parochial, Union, or public, seems to have been based on neighborhood residence rather than denomination or language.[51]

Quaker schools were only available where there was a density of Quaker population sufficient to support them, primarily in Pennsylvania and New Jersey. Philadelphia had nine schools supervised by the Friends in 1779. Colony-wide, the Pennsylvania Quakers supported forty schools for children ranging in age from three to fourteen. Some of the Quaker community schools were coeducational—although boys and girls were not allowed to talk to each other unless they were brother and sister— but towns that could do so provided separate schools for girls, who were taught to sew and knit, and were required to complete intricate samplers. Quakers had quite a different language problem than that confronting German schools; plain Friends were hostile to classical education, while its proponents argued that Greek and Latin, as languages of learned men, were essential to a good education. As some Pennsylvania Quakers moved increasingly from "Meeting House to Counting House," one method of distinguishing themselves as merchants from the mechanics and the ruder sorts of people was to educate their sons in a classical grammar school education.[52]

Matriculation at college was the pinnacle of education, and for the small minority of young men who participated in it, the means of so- cialization into the leadership roles they would take in a hierarchical society. That was an opportunity that had expanded significantly during the eighteenth century from the "single collegiate institution available in 1689" to the thirteen colleges empowered by charter to grant degrees by 1789. It was an opportunity from which female adolescents were systematically excluded. Lawrence Cremin has compiled an extensive bibliography describing the institutions, the curriculum, the faculty, the ideological ferment, and the political importance of particular institu- tions, an extended review of which is beyond the scope of this chapter. Two studies are of particular note for their attempt to describe the behavior and experiences of young American students within a context of changing dynamics in American higher education at the end of the century. Phyllis Vine's perceptive analysis of the role of "shame" points to the importance for young men of public participation in a specialized culture where conformity to community values became a rite of passage, ensured by public acquisition of "honor." The other study by Stephen J. Novak of *The Rights of Youth: American Colleges and Student Revolt, 1798– 1815,* though mainly an adult view of student unrest, details student rebellion against this system of conformity and the students' ultimately futile effort to create a cause in which to demonstrate their own identity and manhood.[53]

These studies are particularly remarkable because most of the exten- sive literature on eighteenth-century education focuses on institutions, and adult perceptions of those institutions, without considering the role of the children themselves in the learning process. Visualizing learners as "essentially passive," these studies of education have, in the words of Barbara Finkelstein, proceeded "as though children were cavernous holes into which are poured status, skills, books, curricula, and out of which emerge formed human beings."[54] Only rarely do studies of education attempt to portray the child's physical, subjective experience within the classroom. Both J. William Frost's chapter on "Quaker School Life" and James Axtell's chapter on "Whipt Eminence" manage to convey in some detail the routine events and the character of the eighteenth-century schoolrooms. Axtell concludes that in those schoolrooms, significant changes had occurred during the course of a century, including a diminution of the heavy-handed physical punishment that had characterized rote instruction. Moreover, although their acceptance was not universal, girls had begun to be admitted into the grammar schools.[55]

Whether young people attended grammar schools or colleges, remained as laborers in their families, or were indentured or apprenticed to learn a trade, there is increasing evidence during the course of the eighteenth century that the transition from childhood to adulthood did not take place as smoothly as adults would have liked. Even after historians made a discovery of childhood, the belief persisted that adolescence remained a more modern invention. "The concept of adolescence, as generally understood and applied," John and Virginia Demos stated in 1969, "did not exist before the last two decades of the nineteenth century," while Joseph F. Kett in a 1971 article on "Adolescence and Youth in Nineteenth Century America," affirmed that verbal distinctions between childhood and youth were rare and exceptional in the eighteenth century. The Demoses admit that the emergence of an adult recognition of the concept in the early twentieth century is a response to an observable fact—"the fact of a youth culture, of many young people seemingly in distress (or at least behaving in ways that distressed their elders)." Kett later developed an explanation for the uncertain movement of early nineteenth-century male youths through a prolonged period of semidependence.[56]

N. Ray Hiner has argued persuasively that the restlessness among their youth that concerned eighteenth-century parents bears a clear resemblance to what twentieth-century parents recognize as adolescence. Although Hiner is concerned primarily with New England youth, his reasoning needs to be applied to the literary evidence available for young people in other settings, for some of the tensions facing Puritans confounded Quaker and other parents as well.[57] Ambivalence over the expanding range of vocational and other choices, challenges to traditional forms of adult authority, growing awareness of and experience with their own sexual development, all were heightened in young people by the simultaneous expansion of adult awareness of their children, and expectations that youth could be molded to redeem the future. A "choosing time" of prolonged dependency as the eighteenth century waned coincided with a weakening of traditional controls over young men and women that sometimes led them to seek outlets for their ambivalence.

For some, the result was a change in sexual behavior; yet the upsurge in premarital pregnancy in eighteenth-century Massachusetts has been interpreted, not as a youthful challenge to mores, but as a means of forcing parents to relinquish control and sanction marriage.[58] For others, spurred on by the optimistic hopes of their parents that the new piety would lead to a return to traditional values, religious conversion offered a chance both to identify with other young people and to find meaning for their own lives.[59]

There were marked differences in experiences of adolescence among young men and young women. For well-bred girls, the imperative of young womanhood was still "How to get and keep your man," and the advice literature directed to the adolescent female reinforced the lessons of docility and domesticity which many of them had already learned in school and at home. Modesty was still the key to finding a husband and keeping him pleased. "Encourage not a train of admirers, lest their envy and jealousy of each other cast an odium on thy conduct." The advice coincided with a popular cultural emphasis on romantic love that reinforced young women's ideas of marriage as an ideal.[60] Yet for New England women, that advice became increasingly more difficult to implement at the close of the eighteenth century, as the ratio of women to men increased. The choices made by young women were more narrowly circumscribed than those Kett has described for young men, and the disruption of the daughter's place in the colonial household by industrial manufacture of clothing made those choices even fewer. It was no coincidence that the emotional release of the Second Great Awakening found large numbers of unmarried young women between twelve and twenty-five among its converts.[61]

QUANTITATIVE METHODOLOGY, THE HISTORIAN, AND THE HISTORY OF CHILDHOOD IN THE EIGHTEENTH CENTURY

Literary evidence has enabled scholars to describe with some complexity the attitudes of adults toward children and childhood, and the stages of passage from infancy through childhood to adolescence. Historians have examined what children did, how they were treated, and what adults thought about their activities and their attitudes, although with a number of gaps and with disproportionate attention to some children at the expense of others. New England and Quaker children have received the most attention. In the middle colonies, work has begun, although even there far more is known about Pennsylvania children than about those in New York.[62] Childrearing patterns among the Chesapeake elite have received attention, both in a general analysis and in the biographical monographs on its leading citizens. Almost nothing has appeared on family structures and the emotional roles of children in Georgia and the Carolinas, although evidence about wealthier Charleston families does appear in Philip Greven's defense of temperament as an organizing theme for understanding childhood and in Lawrence Cremin's comprehensive analysis of American education.

More disquieting than the geographic imbalance however, has been the bias of literary sources toward economically more affluent and stable families, and the experience of children in them. Literary sources necessarily reflect literacy, and during the eighteenth century literacy continued to reflect wealth and power, although it did make some inroads into the lower classes. To correct this imbalance, during the past two decades historians have turned to the methodologies of sociologists, historical demographers, and anthropologists, combined with the technological tools of the computer age, in an attempt to rediscover the inarticulate, to rethink history "from the bottom up."[63] The resulting explosion of work committed to discovery of the past through quantification and social history, particularly historical demography, has virtually revolutionized the understanding of American colonial history. Where earlier studies had focused on legal, political, and economic institutions, the new social history concentrates on the interwoven developments of the family and the community. Daniel Blake Smith has recently summarized and organized this research into "two thematic and methodological waves" in an important review essay, "The Study of the Family in Early America: Trends, Problems, and Prospects."[64] During the 1970s, important work by John Demos, Philip Greven, Kenneth Lockridge, Bernard Farber, and Michael Zuckerman utilized computer-assisted analysis, and the new techniques of family and community reconstitution pioneered by English historical demographers under Edward A. Wrigley and the Cambridge group, to reconstruct interactions within and among families in New England towns.[65]

Inspired by these studies, other historians began to adapt them to communities in the middle states. Jessica Kross argues that in important family as well as political and economic developments, New Town, New York experienced many of the same processes and stages of growth and change that have been described for New England. Stephanie Grauman Wolf used community reconstitution techniques to investigate Germantown, Pennsylvania, a community where pragmatic Germans committed to advancing their own prosperity molded private and public institutions to fit a heterogeneous, highly mobile population. Elizabeth Kessel concerned herself with a group of Germans quite different from their Germantown counterparts. Recent arrivals, with no nearby Philadelphia influence to challenge their attempts to preserve their culture, Germans in Frederick County, Maryland, developed mechanisms for interacting smoothly with the dominant English system and struck a subtle balance between cultural persistence and accommodation to the majority culture. Billie G. Smith has applied the techniques for investigating a geographically defined community to examine the conditions of an economically defined community: the laboring poor of Philadelphia in the last half of the eighteenth century. While reconstructing slave families from plantation records does not involve precisely the same techniques as that followed in reconstructing New England families from town records, the pioneering work by Allan Kulikoff on Maryland slave families and by Herbert Gutman on South Carolina slave plantations is within the same tradition.[66] Community study monographs using demographic techniques coincided with an expansion of other work more strictly devoted to historical demography. Much of it has been highly detailed and devoted to fairly narrow geographic regions, most notably New England and the Chesapeake, but Robert Wells has contributed two book-length studies that bring together population information for all of British North America in the eighteenth century.[67]

The combination of family and demographic analyses has highlighted some highly suggestive shifts that had a profound long-term impact on children in America. During the eighteenth century, immigration shifted from English to non-English in character, until by 1775, almost half of the population had non-English origins. Of these, blacks formed the largest number, nearly 20 percent of the total population. Children in the eighteenth century were thus more likely to be, or to have some contact with, non-English "outsiders" than seventeenth-century children. Family life stabilized in the areas in the South and the Chesapeake where high male-female ratios during the first half of the colonial period had produced a gender imbalance and discouraged family formation. In the early part of the eighteenth century, the combination of relatively early marriage (compared to Europe) and a slight improvement in life expectancy produced an increase in fertility. This was reversed at the end of the century when fertility began to decline in some parts of the population, a trend that gathered momentum and accelerated through the nineteenth and twentieth centuries.[68]

Although there were regional variations and differences between the beginning and end of the century, the average family size of free persons varied between five and seven persons, and a married couple could expect to have between six and eight children. Although relatively few families bore twelve or more children, and 10 percent of all couples had three children or less, large families were the norm for more children than for parents: the 35.9 percent of families that bore nine or more children contained in them 50.7 percent of all children in the eighteenth century. Throughout the century, the proportion of children in the total population rose gradually; in the British colonies on the eve of the Revolution, children under sixteen comprised between 45 and 50 percent of the population.

The rise in fertility and the large-scale immigration of the eighteenth century combined to make the total population grow rapidly, doubling every quarter-century. Yet, although the total economy grew, only in the middle colonies did growth of trade with England exceed the population growth. During the eighteenth century, the poorest segment of the population controlled a shrinking share of its resources: in 1748, the poorest 30 percent of taxpayers in Chester County, Pennsylvania, had 13 percent of its resources, but in 1802 their share was only 4 percent. Throughout the century, larger proportions of the population owned no property at all. Although this society could not yet be called child-oriented, children formed a near majority in it almost everywhere. For increasing proportions of those children, their family's share of total wealth was diminishing, and their access to the diet, housing, clothing, education, and toys associated with that wealth diminished.[69]

Some children had no access to such privileges. Slave children born of African or African-descended parents did not form a significant group in the seventeenth century, but any discussion of eighteenth-century children must include them as an important subgroup of American childhood. Few direct studies have been made of eighteenth-century slave family patterns; the following description is based on the important work of Allan Kulikoff for Prince Georges County, Maryland. Because large-scale importation of slaves did not begin until the end of the seventeenth century, at the beginning of the eighteenth century the early imbalance between men and women meant that African men had difficulty finding wives. When they did marry, the limited evidence for this early period suggests that their wives and children often lived on other plantations and belonged to other masters. Thus, black children in Maryland at the beginning of the century were more likely to live with their mothers, who "taught them the broad values they brought from Africa and related the family's history in Africa and the Chesapeake. When the children began working in the fields, they learned from their mothers how to survive a day's work and how to get along with master and overseer." As the century progressed, however, demographic changes substantially altered this picture: black population density grew, the improved sex ratio among adults made family formation easier, and the increase in the number of large plantations made it possible for families to remain together.[70]

In Maryland by the 1750s, the number of slaves who lived on plantations with more than twenty others increased significantly, and the proportion of blacks in the total population reached half or more by the end of the century. The result was the rise of a complex kin network, not patterned directly after specific African tribal kinship systems, but informed by a shared African belief in "kinship as the principal way of ordering relationships between individuals." The result for African-American children was that over half under the age of ten on large plantations lived with both of their parents, and even after the age of ten when they were more likely to live away from one or both parents, they continued to be part of kinship networks that could embrace several plantations, or an entire county.[71]

"For the first few months of life, a newborn infant...received his identity...from his mother," who took him to the field with her, frequently nursing him. Young children "were left, during a great proportion of the day, on the ground at the doors of their own huts, to their own struggles and efforts," although slightly older children might take some responsibility for younger siblings.[72] Slave children lived in communities with others their own age as well as in nuclear family units that often contained both parents. Although a few privileged boys might learn a skilled craft, either from whites or their skilled kinfolk, most children, male and female, began fieldwork between the ages of seven and ten, and that work coincided with their departure from home as they were sold away or sent to work the fields of other plantations owned by their masters. Slave men typically did not marry until their mid- or late twenties, but girls married in their late teens. The work by Herbert Gutman demonstrating the slaves' creation of their own distinctive cultural and family patterns, though primarily focused on South Carolina plantations in the nineteenth century, suggests that patterns similar to those found by Kulikoff in Maryland earlier developed throughout the plantation South during the eighteenth century.[73]

Just as demographic methodology has helped some scholars to re-create slave family patterns and revise earlier conclusions about the nature of slave family existence, it can also reveal the experience of poor white families for whom there is little or no written record. In an attempt to answer the question whether the "lower sort" in Philadelphia had a relatively high standard of living and an optimistic outlook for the future for themselves and their children, Billie Smith has analyzed the material wealth and household budgets of the laboring poor—cordwainers, tailors, laborers, and mariners—in a way that throws considerable light on the lives of their children. "People who lived just below the poverty line and generally did not receive public assistance," these groups formed more than half of the bottom third of taxable residents and approximately half of the free male workers of Philadelphia in the last half of the eighteenth century. Most families of the laboring poor were young and small: households averaged 4.5 persons each, and three-quarters of these households included young children. Older children were apprenticed out during hard times when the family income fell and parents could not afford their keep. Such families lived on a diet heavy on grain, with small quantities of cheap meat. Their housing, usually rented and often shared with boarders, consisted of small, narrow wooden buildings. A twelve by eighteen foot tenement, perhaps with two stories, might contain two families in a few crowded rooms with no separate kitchen. Many of the wealthier citizens of Philadelphia owned brick kitchen outbuildings that were more commodious than the homes of the men who delivered their firewood. In such crowded homes, there was little furniture and few utensils or other amenities; children shared a bed with each other, or with their parents, and drank soups or stews from communal "pitchers."[74]

Even the costs of this minimal standard of living were often beyond the wages of the laborers, "who encountered very serious difficulties in meeting their families' basic needs." Despite low wages and few opportunities, therefore, the wages of women and very young children were essential to the survival of these families. Although some wills indicate that poor parents wanted education for their children, for most that was a luxury denied by the need for the pittance earned by a child's labor. Smith suggests that the result was a material vulnerability, but also an attitude of affection and concern bred from a rough equality among the members of laboring families: husband and children alike respected the mother as an essential wage-earner; fathers had little or no economic leverage over their children; isolated from kin or friendship networks, these families had no one to turn to but each other.[75]

The evidence painstakingly gathered through family and community reconstitution, or demographic analysis of whole populations or particular and specialized groups, is important in beginning to frame answers to Hiner's second question, "What are the conditions which helped to shape the development of children." But they cannot re-create the physical world in which children actually lived with the vividness that the artifacts surviving from the eighteenth century do. For that we must turn our attention to the third category of source material from which historians have drawn insight into the lives of children: material culture.

MATERIAL CULTURE AND EIGHTEENTH-CENTURY CHILDHOOD

Precisely because of an interest in people whose lives left little written record, historians wishing to understand the past have turned increasingly to the use of evidence that can help reconstruct the lives of ordinary people. Everyone who lives in a society uses objects and depends for existence on material things. Material culture therefore offers an opportunity to re-create the total spectrum of human experience. It reflects changes over time in the lives of rich and poor alike and serves to "illustrate current solutions to everyday problems . . . and to document the technology of the time." The styles embodied in material things "help to define both the taste of an age and its characteristic form preference." Variations in this style can throw light on regional and national differences, and on the influence of various groups who contributed to the American culture. Artifacts can also have an economic bias, of course: many of the materials preserved over long periods of time have survived because they are beautiful, or were valuable at the time of their creation, and thus expensive to those who bought or commissioned or created them. Just as historians using literary materials have turned to the work of psychology and literary analysis for assistance, and the historians working with quantification techniques have adopted the tools and theories of economists, demographers, sociologists, and anthropologists, so too have historians wanting to learn from artifacts turned to the work of historical archaeologists, folklorists, anthropologists, museum curators, and art historians.[76]

Material culture can serve a twofold purpose for the historian interested in children in the eighteenth century. The artifacts, the objects themselves, help to give a visual, spatial, tactile dimension to the world children inhabited two centuries ago: real children played with this silver rattle, sat in that Windsor chair, stitched this now-faded sampler, sucked nourishment through the unyielding metallic knob of this "bubby pot," and perhaps were enchanted with artists' re-creation of their faces in unique portraits. Although we cannot really know the answer to Hiner's third question, "What has been the subjective experience of childhood in the past?" through such objects, we can (very carefully, sometimes, under the watchful eye of the curators under whose control and protection such artifacts are now placed) hold in our hands a tiny bit of a child's objective experience. The second purpose material culture serves is to give another dimension to the answers we have begun to formulate about the child's subjective experience, and to the conditions that helped to shape the development of children, by giving us another way of examining the culture in which those children functioned, affecting the adults who were socializing them to that culture just as the children themselves were becoming acculturated within it. The objects that adults allowed children to use, or created for them, tell us as surely as do childrearing manuals and school textbooks what those adults thought was the proper place of those children in that culture.

Of the historical literature surveyed in this chapter, material culture studies are least apt to focus directly on children as suitable subjects of study. This brief essay on material culture and children is therefore highly interpretive and is meant to suggest areas where study needs to be done as much as it reports on what we actually now know about children from such sources. Three areas of study seem potentially most fruitful: the depiction of children in the art of the eighteenth century (the visual dimension); the archaeological and preservationist recovery of the houses in which children lived, played, and worked (the spatial dimension); and the description of the objects that children made, played with, or used in their daily tasks (the tactile dimension).

The most fully developed study of children in material culture is in the realm of portraiture. Because of the large expense of having a portrait painted, the children portrayed are the children of the wealthy. In early child portraiture, the paintings themselves are often as much a catalogue of the wealth of the parents, in their ostentatious display of laces, rich fabrics, ornate jewelry, and props, as a record of the appearance of children. By the late eighteenth century, the more readily available talents of itinerant "limners" and primitive local artists meant that members of the middle class could also afford likenesses of their children.[77] The growth of interest in childhood as an historic subject has provided the inspiration for exhibits specifically devoted to children in regional museums, where insights drawn from paintings as well as from scholarly studies of the status of the child have provided a setting and a context for other material objects included in the display. Although children were not the principal focus, the recent exhibit (October 28, 1982–January 2, 1983) illustrating the wide-ranging contributions of Charles Willson Peale at the National Portrait Gallery demonstrated both his devotion to his own children and his unique painterly appreciation for the special relationship between children and adults, as well as the impact of his children upon him. Peale saw family harmony as a metaphor for public harmony, and he painted most of the few known eighteenth-century multigenerational portraits of children, parents, and grandparents working and relaxing together.[78]

Recently, three important studies have applied computer-assisted quantitative methods to the portraits of hundreds of individual children to draw general conclusions about the changing adult perception of childhood as conveyed through adult-commissioned paintings.[79] Charles Cohen focused his analysis of 82 portraits of children and 181 portraits of adults on the relative frequency of full-length and partial poses within each group, although he also considered the content of images. Without proposing an explanation for the artistic decision, he argues that artists clearly recognized childhood as a distinctively different subject, whose treatment in portraits required the convention of full-length depiction.

In contrast, their elders were far less frequently portrayed with lower limbs. He also found in the portraits he studied a recognition of adolescence as a stage of life separate both from adults and from the world of childhood. Although he recognizes a qualitative difference between children and adolescents, mostly in portrayal of a dreamy detachment in adolescents, Cohen also believes that beginning around the time of the Revolution, adolescents were more likely to appear in three-quarter-length portraits than the full portaits of children or the half-length portraits of adults.[80]

Stephen Brobeck worked with a sample of 152 family group portraits and 99 individual child portraits to study the relationship between children and adults depicted by artists for the enjoyment and satisfaction of their families. At first, families pictured rarely included both parents. Before the mid-eighteenth century, groups most commonly portrayed stiffly posed children, or a mother and her offspring. Even when fathers become a part of the family group later, Brobeck notes that parents rarely touch or look at each other, while siblings are quite likely to be portrayed in physical contact, increasingly so in the early nineteenth century. Toys and playthings appear more frequently as props in canvases painted after the Revolution, and so, too, does a less restrained appearance among children, who abandon stiff poses for a more natural playfulness. He recognizes that each of these phenomena is more likely to be representative of changing artistic convention than of changed child behavior, but he argues that this reflects changes in adult attitudes toward childhood and the cultural standards for what behavior is appropriate, tolerated, or appreciated in children.[81]

The most complex analysis of children pictured by eighteenth-century artists is that of Karin Calvert. She, too, argues, however, that a distinctive change occurred in portraiture between 1750 and 1770. Through content analysis of clothing, hairstyle, props, and the formality or informality of poses, Calvert traces an important shift in painting conventions that reflects a corresponding change in cultural evaluation of childhood and adolescence. Late seventeenth-century portraits contained highly stylized depictions of two distinct groups: dominant men and breeched boys, and subordinate females and young children in petticoats. By the early nineteenth century, this polarization had been replaced by a more complex family system in which six groups received distinctive "vocabularies" of pictorial representation, allowing distinctions to emerge between dependent males in three stages of development distinguished by clothing, and for the first time permitting an intermediate stage of adolescence between adulthood and womanhood depicted through costume and hairstyle for young women (the sixth stage was infancy). This complexity also broke "the link between femininity and childishness," and coincided with a "new freedom accorded children and a new fondness for, or at least acceptance of, childish behavior" in portraiture. Indeed, by the end of the eighteenth century, instead of children being dressed as copies of adults, the new styles reflected in the portraiture showed adults adopting the fashions of childhood. Men assumed the long trousers previously worn as an intermediate stage of male costume by their immature sons, and women borrowed the white empire dress from the muslin frocks their adolescent daughters had been wearing for thirty years. Finally, Calvert argues, the very proliferation of complete families in portraiture illustrates "a new interest in the nuclear family as a unit" and the importance of the "inner life" rather than the material possessions of that family unit.[82]

Child portraiture, although it conveys a visual sense of the appearance of real children from the past, nevertheless sees those children through the lens of adult preconceptions of what children ought to look like. Placing children within the spatial dimension of the buildings that were their homes moves completely away from focus on the child, however. Long the province of the aesthetic analysis of art and architectural historians, studies of buildings as evidence of the values of the culture they serve have recently drawn the interest of a wider range of scholarship. In contrast to the study of painting, this scholarship has virtually ignored the question of whether children and their needs were a consideration in expressing those values. Although Gwendolyn Wright combined social, cultural, and architectural history in *Building the Dream* and argued that domestic architecture is "a way of encouraging certain kinds of family and social life," that "domestic environments can reinforce certain character traits, promote family stability, and assure a good society," she virtually ignores the changing role of children in her analysis of cultural values in the domestic built environment.[83] Nevertheless, her focus on ordinary housing, built in great numbers, often without the assistance of professional architects, is part of the growing respectability of vernacular architecture among architectural historians interested in the colonial and early national period. Sparked by James Deetz's creative description of the relationship of New England housing to both its English origins and its Puritan purposes, recent studies have attempted to see how, when, and why that domestic architecture changed its character. The most fascinating attempt at explanation has been the structuralist study by the folklorist Henry Glassie, based on intensive fieldwork observations of a limited geographic area of Virginia. Although critics have questioned some of his assumptions about static persistence of populations over long periods of time, other analyses of vernacular domestic architecture agree with Glassie's painstakingly demonstrated conclusion that between 1750 and 1800 a profound change occured in folk archi-

tecture. The "hall and parlor" form of construction in which homes
focused most domestic activities in a central room, or hall, where cooking,
spinning, eating, playing, mending, and socializing all competed with
one another for space, gradually gave way to a new tripartite, more
symmetrical form of structure where each activity had its own space.
Privacy in the older, unsymmetrical form was reserved for the highly
formal "parlor" where ceremonial activities took place, and where parents might have their sleeping quarters; in smaller buildings, persons
seeking privacy there had to pass through the public hall and all the
people in it. Small loft-like upper rooms were used as storage space for
the family "lumber" (that catch-all colonial phrase for the odds and ends
of domestic paraphernalia) and for children and servants to sleep. In
the newer architectural style, more privatized rooms were separated
from each other by a central hallway, and individual rooms had specified
purposes, separating activities that had previously shared space and creating opportunity for segregating children's activities from those of
adults.[84]

Dorothy Smith has argued in "Household Space and Family Organization" that spatial usage lets us know about the inner life of a family.
Using the differentiation devised by Erving Goffman and others of "front"
and "back" regions of home or property as the proper spaces, respectively, for carrying on public or ceremonial and private behavior, she
observes in twentieth-century households that while the "front" regions
have a certain shared accessibility, most dwellings feature an orientation
that puts children's activities in "back" regions, while adult activities are
concentrated in "front" regions. Did such distinctions, which have been
observed by anthropologists in modern primitive societies, have meaning
in eighteenth-century America? What does it mean for children in those
families to have had "public" and "private" spaces change so dramatically? Did children's activities become less public and, therefore, less
subject to rigorous control and discipline as they no longer were visible
for public judgment and approbation?[85]

David Flaherty, in commenting on early home spaces and privacy,
argued that, while children and parents were forced into daily contact
with each other by lack of privacy, rather than choosing such contact,
children nevertheless "interfered minimally in the private lives of their
parents" because of their unlimited access to an unstructured outdoor
world. As housing became more congested in urban centers, did children's impact on their parents become more oppressive and inspire an
unarticulated architectural response both to parental desire for privacy
and to changing perceptions of childhood? The connection is important
from the point of view of Hiner's fourth question, "How have children
and childhood influenced adults?" We simply do not know the answers

to these and other important questions related to the link between child-hood and the architecture that framed children's spatial perceptions.[86]

It is in the "Small Things Forgotten" of childish "lumber" that his-torians with imagination are most likely to feel the presence of actual children. Here the studies often concern themselves directly with chil-dren's things, but the framework is most often that of the antiquarian, the collector, or the museum curator. Museum exhibits designed to por-tray the lives of women and of children bring some of these objects together in an interpretive way,[87] but more often the historian of child-hood must bring his or her own insight to highly descriptive catalogues of objects. A child's silver whistle and bell made in Philadelphia around 1750, a child's initialed silver porringer given by Josiah Quincy to his granddaughter in 1763, a child's or a doll's carefully carved high post bed from 1800, indicate clearly that families of wealth purchased spe-cially made small items for children's use in living and playing.[88] Sur-viving material objects made for or used by poorer children, because they were made of cruder and less durable materials, are far rarer. Here again, the desire to utilize material culture to regain the lives of the "lower sort" has led instead to studies that enrich our perceptions of the better off, but leave us wondering still about the ordinary lives of a large number of eighteenth-century children.

One of the few categories of small things that has stimulated some analysis by collectors is the sampler. This activity was worked by countless small girls at home or at school as a demonstration of their skills at the stitchery tasks essential to their future role in providing, marking, and mending family linens and clothing. A middle-class activity, samplers were divided into two types: plain sewing, whose alphabets and numbers would identify the contents of linen chests; and more complicated display pieces that contained pictorial elements and were made under careful instruction to be framed and kept as a momento of a young lady's school-ing or accomplishments. From mid-century, samplers produced in America began to take on a less formal, disciplined, or symmetrical appearance rather than the English style on which they had previously been modeled. Many of the late eighteenth-century examples show a high degree of individuality. Where earlier samplers had been devoted to pious verses and stylized decorations, later ones featured patriotic themes or included small figures of parents and likenesses of a girl's home. Children as young as seven produced quite intricate designs in tiny stitches, signing their handiwork with their names, ages, and the date. Samplers reveal both the shift from religious preoccupation to more secular concerns in the schools for middle-class young women. They also testify to the discipline required of very young children throughout the eighteenth century, and they make historians, convinced that childhood had at last been recognized as a specialized part of life, pause briefly at the still-marked contrasts between expectations of children then and now. Few twentieth-century children of any age could be compelled to complete work of the sort undertaken by very young eighteenth-century children as a matter of course.[89]

Needlework made for rather than by children also reveals something of the lives of those children and the affection and whimsy they sometimes inspired in their parents. Infants were kept in their mother's room at night, and in a cradle near the main fireplace during the day; eighteenth-century inventories routinely include cradles and the "ruggs" and sheets that kept small inhabitants snug and warm in poorly insulated houses. There are still in existence a few of the carefully stitched quilts that mothers or older sisters created late in the eighteenth century to fit small-sized beds. Their scale, as well as the motifs that decorate them, identify them clearly as objects made for children by people who saw childhood as a distinct and vulnerable stage of life with its own special needs.[90]

Nor were items for a child's comfort and convenience made only at home. For the children of the wealthy, by the late eighteenth century a wide range of specially sized furnishings demonstrated the finest cabinet-maker's art in a child's size. Child-sized furniture also had its still smaller counterpart in miniatures made for the dolls and dollhouses of genteel children. The wealthy did not have a monopoly on child-sized items. The case of chairs is perhaps an example. Throughout the seventeenth century, chairs were relatively rare in households: most homes contained but one, whose use by the father signified his importance and authority. By the mid-eighteenth century, even in the homes of the middling sort, chairs began to appear in larger numbers and in diverse varieties. The emergence of local manufacturers of seating equipment created a distinctly American style of sturdy but relatively cheaply constructed furniture, and Windsor chairs were made in matched sets like their more expensive Queen Anne and Chippendale counterparts. The proliferation of chairs for adults is matched by the manufacture of a number of different kinds of Windsor chairs for children as well: small armchairs and rockers, child-sized settees, highchairs for an infant to sit at the table with adults (even one example of a double-seated highchair for twins or children close in age), and small side chairs fitted with a chamber pot. Although we cannot see the way in which such furniture was used, its existence suggests that children for whom such items were purchased had acquired an increased importance in their own households and that adults saw children as having special physical needs that adult items could not satisfy.[91]

Quilts and chairs have a utilitarian function for children, but parents in the eighteenth century were willing to buy items for their children's amusement as well. Wealthy parents indulged little girls with miniature versions of the matched imported pottery and porcelain sets that graced adult tables. George Washington's stepchildren submitted a Christmas list that included "A Tunbridge Tea Sett" and "A Prussian Dragoon," in 1759. A Tory shopkeeper in New York in 1777 advertised "Christmas Presents for the Young FOLKS who have an affection for the Art Military Consisting of Horse, Foot and Dragoons Cast in metal, in beautiful uniform, 18 S a dozen." Nor were all toys imported from Europe and expensive: local craftsmen from New Hampshire to Georgia could carve a "Ball and cup" or a "bullroarer," hoops and kites, or a crude pair of wooden skates for winter play. That there was enough demand for such items from fond parents to make it profitable for shopkeepers to advertise them is an indication that children and their desires had become an important consideration for significant numbers of adults.[92]

Although children and childhood were not inventions of the eighteenth century, the extensive changes in the lives of ordinary people in the last half of the eighteenth century, which have been labeled part of "modernization" and attributed to the process of industrialization, made children into an increasingly differentiated and important part of their society. As in all changes, this one did not affect all children at once; it did not reach some children until well into the nineteenth century. All children who lived as children during some part of the eighteenth century felt its effects; those whose childhoods began with the century were the adults who in their old age were baffled by the new importance of the young; those who were children at mid-century knew a world of schools and clothing and material possessions and other opportunities *as children* that their parents had never known. Those who were themselves children after the Revolution imbibed a new and freer spirit of childhood. Its evidence is in houses that gave children more (and more private) space, in schools that began educating them for a more worldly and independent life, in clothing that distinguished them by increasingly complex age groupings, in books and toys that catered to their desires, in more openly affectionate parental behavior and less demanding physical discipline. Not all children knew yet what it was like to be children: the Irish indentured servants of Boston and Philadelphia, the hardworking offspring of laborers and mariners in Philadelphia, the slave children of Maryland and South Carolina were caught in conditions where children might be loved by both parents who could not afford the luxury of relieving them of adult tasks and responsibilities. Yet the institutions were already beginning to develop that would enforce a different childhood on even these children: a culture beginning to sentimentalize childhood as a "place apart" began to look at those children as children rather than as poor or slave peoples, and to demand that their very childhood entitled them to something better. The roots of the nineteenth-century reform movements that would insist on a social policy for children that would set them apart from other humans had their spring growth in the eighteenth century.

NOTES

1. Glenn H. Elder, Jr., "History and the Family: The Discovery of Complexity," *Journal of Marriage and the Family* 43 (1981): 489–519.

2. Alice Morse Earle, *Child Life in Colonial Days* (New York: Macmillan Co., 1899); Edmund Sears Morgan, *The Puritan Family: Essays on Religion and Domestic Relations in Seventeenth Century New England* (Boston: Little, Brown & Co., 1944); *Virginians at Home: Family Life in the Eighteenth Century* (Charlottesville: Colonial Williamsburg, 1952).

3. Studies that encompass some of these possibilities include Philip J. Greven, Jr., *The Protestant Temperament* (New York: Alfred A. Knopf, 1977); Daniel Blake Smith, *Inside the Great House: Planter Family Life in Eighteenth Century Chesapeake Society* (Ithaca, N.Y.: Cornell University Press, 1980); Kenneth A. Lockridge, *A New England Town: The First Hundred Years* (New York: W. W. Norton, 1970); Peter Dobkin Hall, "Marital Selection and Business in Massachusetts Merchant Families, 1700–1900," reprinted in Michael Gordon, ed., *The American Family in Social-Historical Perspective* (2d ed., New York: St. Martin's Press, 1978), 101–114; Dennis Clark, "Babes in Bondage: Indentured Irish Children in Philadelphia in the Nineteenth Century," *Pennsylvania Magazine of History and Biography* 101 (1977): 475–486; Elizabeth A. Kessel, " 'A Mighty Fortress Is Our God'; German Religious and Educational Organizations on the Maryland Frontier 1734–1800," *Maryland Historical Magazine* 77 (1982): 370–387; Kenneth F. Kiple and Virginia H. Kiple, "Slave Child Mortality: Some Nutritional Answers to a Perennial Puzzle," *Journal of Social History* 10 (1977): 284–309, reprinted as chapter 7, "The Children," in Kenneth F. Kiple and Virginia Himmelsteib King, *Another Dimension in the Black Diaspora: Diet, Disease, and Racism* (Cambridge: Cambridge University Press, 1981), 91–116; Nancy F. Cott, "Young Women in the Second Great Awakening in New England," *Feminist Studies* 3 (1975): 15–29.

4. N. Ray Hiner, "The Child in American Historiography: Accomplishments and Prospects," *Psychohistory Review* 7 (1978–1979): 13–23.

5. John Demos, *A Little Commonwealth: Family Life in Plymouth Colony* (New York: Oxford University Press, 1970); Robert Gross, *The Minute Men and Their World* (New York: Hill & Wang, 1976).

6. Alice Morse Earle, *Home Life in Colonial Days* (New York: Macmillan Co., 1898) and *Two Centuries of Costume in America* (New York: Macmillan Co., 1903).

7. Sanford Fleming, *Children and Puritanism: The Place of Children in the Life and Thought of the New England Churches, 1620–1847* (New York: Arno Press, 1969), p. 3. This is a reprint of the original 1933 Yale University Press edition, part of a series on "American Education, Its Men, Ideas, and Institutions," which

also includes: George Stewart, Jr., *A History of Religious Education in Connecticut to the Middle of the Nineteenth Century* (New York: Arno Press, 1969), originally published by Yale University Press in 1924; Clifton Hartwell Brewer, *The History of Religious Education in the Episcopal Church to 1835* (New York: Arno Press, 1969); and Thomas Woody, *Quaker Education in the Colony and State of New Jersey, A Source Book* (New York: Arno Press, 1969), originally published by the University of Pennsylvania in 1923. Woody in particular was a prolific writer on the subject of colonial education. The reprints in this series form only a small part of what Bernard Bailyn has described as an "astonishingly large" corpus of early studies on colonial education; see his "Bibliographical Essay," and the selected "List of References" in *Education in the Forming of American Society* (Chapel Hill: University of North Carolina Press, 1960).

8. Monica Kiefer, *American Children Through Their Books, 1788–1835* (Philadelphia: University of Pennsylvania Press, 1948).

9. Ibid., 225.

10. Bailyn, *Education*, 15, 49.

11. See especially Lawrence A. Cremin, *American Education: The Colonial Experience, 1607–1783* (New York: Harper & Row, 1970) and Kenneth A. Lockridge, *Literacy in Colonial New England: An Enquiry into the Social Context of Literacy in the Early Modern West* (New York: W. W. Norton, 1974).

12. Bailyn, *Education*, 76.

13. Bernard Wishy, *The Child and the Republic, The Dawn of Modern American Child Nurture* (Philadelphia: University of Pennsylvania Press, 1968), and Daniel Calhoun, *The Intelligence of a People* (Princeton: Princeton University Press, 1973).

14. Glenn Davis, *Childhood and History in America* (New York: Psychohistory Press, 1976), 13–14.

15. John F. Walzer, "A Period of Ambivalence: Eighteenth-Century American Childhood," in Lloyd deMause, ed., *The History of Childhood* (New York: Psychohistory Press, 1974), 351–382.

16. Greven, *Protestant Temperament*, "Part Two: The Evangelicals: The Self Suppressed," 21–61, spells out in detail the practices and successes of evangelical parents in achieving these goals. Rhys Isaac, *The Transformation of Virginia, 1740–1790* (Chapel Hill: University of North Carolina Press, 1982) suggests the importance of class and geographical location in the creation of a battleground between rival cultural systems. The patterns Isaac ascribes to the evangelicals as a political, social, and economic group correspond closely to the distinctions assigned to them by Greven as a temperamental and psychological community. Greven's argument for the persistence of evangelical childrearing patterns over time and between generations is supported by the comparison of three generations of prominent evangelical fathers and sons in William G. McLoughlin, "Evangelical Child-Rearing in the Age of Jackson: Francis Wayland's View on When and How to Subdue the Willfulness of Children," *Journal of Social History* 9 (1975): 21–43.

17. Greven, *Protestant Temperament*, "Part Three, The Moderates: The Self Controlled," 151–191.

18. The concerns of the Adamses for the proper rearing of their children

dominate the first two volumes of Lyman H. Butterfield, et al., eds., *Adams Family Correspondence* (Cambridge, Mass.: Harvard University Press, 1963–); on Abigail's particular influence on John Quincy Adams, see Joseph E. Illick, "John Quincy Adams: The Maternal Influence," *Journal of Psychohistory* 4 (1976): 185–195. Concerns about their children are present in the correspondence between Mercy Otis Warren and Abigail Adams, some of it reprinted in *Warren-Adams Letters: Being Chiefly a Correspondence Among John Adams, Samuel Adams, and James Warren*, Massachusetts Historical Society, *Collections* 72–73 (Boston, 1917–1925). On Quakers as moderates, see J. William Frost, *The Quaker Family in Colonial America: A Portrait of the Society of Friends* (New York: St. Martin's Press, 1973), esp. ch. 4, "Childhood: As the Twig is Bent," 73–79. The Shippen and Pinckney families are discussed in Raldolph Shipley Klein, *Portrait of an Early American Family: The Shippens of Pennsylvania Across Five Generations* (Philadelphia: University of Pennsylvania Press, 1975); Elise Pinckney and Marvin R. Zahniser, eds., *The Letterbook of Eliza Lucas Pinckney 1739–1762* (Chapel Hill: University of North Carolina Press, 1972); and Harriott Horry Ravenel, *Eliza Pinckney* (New York: Charles Scribner's Sons, 1896). On Carter and Franklin, see Jack P. Greene, ed., *The Diary of Colonel Landon Carter of Sabine Hall, 1752–1778*, 2 vols. (Charlottesville: University of Virginia Press, 1965); Henry Steele Commager, ed., *The Autobiography of Benjamin Franklin and Selections from His Other Writings* (New York, 1950); Claude-Anne Lopez and Eugenia W. Herbert, *The Private Franklin: The Man and His Family* (New York, 1975).

19. Greven, *Protestant Temperament*, "Part Four, The Genteel: The Self Asserted," esp. 265–295.

20. Smith, *Inside the Great House*, 49.

21. Ronald Hoffman, "Forging a Worthy Heir: The Testing of Charles Carroll of Carrollton," unpublished paper delivered in December 1982 at the University of Maryland seminar in Early American History and Culture. This paper will be published in revised form as part of the introduction to the edition of the Charles Carroll of Carrollton papers to be published by the Institute of Early American History and Culture, Williamsburg, Virginia.

22. Smith, *Inside the Great House*, 61–68; Jan Lewis, "Domestic Tranquility and the Management of Emotion Among the Gentry of Pre-Revolutionary Virginia," *William and Mary Quarterly*, 3d ser., 39 (1982): 135–149, reprinted in Jan Lewis, *The Pursuit of Happiness: Family and Values in Jefferson's Virginia* (Cambridge: Cambridge University Press, 1983).

23. Maxwell Bloomfield, *American Lawyers in a Changing Society, 1776–1876* (Cambridge, Mass.: Harvard University Press, 1976), ch. 4, "The Family in Antebellum Law," 94–100; see also Jamil S. Zainaldin, *Law in Antebellum Society: Legal Change and Economic Expansion* (New York: Random House, 1983). I am indebted in this summary of the relationship between legal and social change to the guidance of Dr. Zainaldin.

24. John R. Sutton, "Stubborn Children: Law and the Socialization of Deviance in the Puritan Colonies," *Family Law Quarterly* 15 (1981): 31–64, argues that these laws were radically modern, rather than mere enforcement of common law parental authority: they worked toward "socialization of law and family,"

coopting the family to further the values of the community, and they developed a formal means of surveillance of behavior that was judged deviant, providing a process for "normalization and universalization of deviance."

25. Lorena Walsh, "Child Custody in the Early Chesapeake: A Case Study," unpublished paper delivered at the Berkshire Conference of Women Historians, Vassar College, June 1981.

26. Joseph Ben-Or, "The Law of Adoption in the United States: Its Massachusetts Origins and the Statute of 1851," *New England Historical and Genealogical Register* 130 (1976): 259–272. See also Stephen B. Presser, "The Historical Background of the American Law of Adoption," *Journal of Family Law* 11 (1971): 443–516; and Jamil S. Zainaldin, "The Emergence of a Modern Family Law: Child Custody, Adoption, and the Courts, 1796–1851," *Northwestern University Law Review* 73 (1979): 1038–1089. Zainaldin's work is based in part on the author's 1976 University of Chicago Ph.D. dissertation, "The Origins of Modern Legal Adoption: Child Exchange in Boston, 1851–1893."

27. Jay Mechling, "Advice to Historians on Advice to Mothers," *Journal of Social History* 9 (1975): 53. The following summary of children's experiences in the eighteenth century should be read cautiously; even when the daily events of children's lives seem to have been quite similar, the particular circumstances of individual children and groups of children profoundly affected the ways in which those children perceived or reacted to events that are described here as essentially universal.

28. Catherine M. Scholten, "On the Importance of the Obstetrick Art: Changing Customs of Childbirth in America, 1760–1825," *William and Mary Quarterly*, 3d ser., 34 (1977): 428. See also James Axtell, *The School upon a Hill, Education and Society in Colonial New England* (New Haven: Yale University Press, 1974), 61–69.

29. Scholten, "Changing Customs of Childbirth," 434–435; by 1820, the process of birth had virtually been taken over in Philadelphia by male practitioners. For a review essay of recent studies of childbirth customs in America, see Nancy Schrom Dye, "History of Childbirth in America," *Signs* 6 (1980): 97–108. At the same time, the romanticization of motherhood, the emergence of companionate marriages, and the rise of a more child-centered culture led to the post-1820 phenomenon described by Jill Suitor of "Husbands' Participation in Childbirth: A Nineteenth Century Phenomenon," *Journal of Family History* 6 (1981): 278–293. On Shippen's medical career, see also Klein, *Portrait of an Early American Family*.

30. Walzer, "Period of Ambivalence," 354; Axtell, *School upon a Hill*, 75–79; Frost, *Quaker Family*, 71–73; Julia Cherry Spruill, *Women's Life and Work in the Southern Colonies* (New York: Russell & Russell, 1969, reissue of 1938 University of North Carolina Press Edition), 55–58. On hand feeding, see Thomas E. Cone, *Two Hundred Years of Feeding Infants in America* (Columbus, Ohio: Ross Laboratories, 1976), 8–9, 14–15.

31. For a detailed analysis of nursing and its impact on birth-spacing, see Paula A. Treckel, "Breastfeeding as a Method of Birth Control in Colonial America," paper delivered at the Duquesne History Forum, Fall 1982. Daniel

Blake Smith, "Mortality and the Family in the Colonial Chesapeake," *Journal of Interdisciplinary History* 8 (1978): 412, draws conclusions about mother-dependent immunity based on the work of the Rutmans reported in "Of Agues and Fevers: Malaria in the Early Chesapeake," *William and Mary Quarterly*, 3d ser., 33 (1976): 31–60.

32. N. Ray Hiner, "Cotton Mather and His Children: The Evolution of a Parent Education," in Barbara Finkelstein, ed., *Regulated Children/Liberated Children: Education in Psychohistorical Perspective* (New York: Psychohistory Press, 1979), 30.

33. Smith, "Mortality and Family," 412–413. Demos, *Little Commonwealth*, 66; Maris A. Vinovskis, "Mortality Rates and Trends in Massachusetts Before 1860," *Journal of Economic History* 32 (1972): 184–213, and "Angel's Heads and Weeping Willows: Death in Early America," *Proceedings of the American Antiquarian Society* 86, Part 2 (1977): 273–302, reprinted in Gordon, *American Family*, 2d ed., 552. See also David E. Stannard, *The Puritan Way of Death: A Study in Religion, Culture, and Social Change* (New York: Oxford University Press, 1977), esp. ch. 3, "Death and Childhood," which originally appeared under the title "Death and the Puritan Child," in *American Quarterly* 26 (1974): 456–476; Peter Gregg Slater, *Children in the New England Mind in Death and in Life: From the Puritans to Bushnell* (Hamden, Conn.: Archon Books, 1977), a revision of the author's 1970 University of California at Berkeley Ph.D. thesis, "Views of Children and Child Rearing During the Early National Period: A Study in the New England Intellect."

34. John Duffy, *Epidemics in Colonial America* (Baton Rouge: Louisiana State University Press, 1953), 33–37; see also Thomas E. Cone, *History of American Pediatrics* (Boston: Little, Brown & Co., 1979), 32–36.

35. Webster is quoted in Duffy, *Epidemics*, 118–119; see also 123–125.

36. Duffy, *Epidemics*, ch. 5, "Measles, Whooping Cough, and Mumps," 164–183. Cone, *History of Pediatrics*, reprints on page 33 (Cotton Mather's anguish over his 1721 decision to inoculate Sammy, then aged fifteen, against smallpox; see also 36–47.

37. Kiple and Kiple, "Slave Child Mortality," 284–309.

38. Stannard, *Puritan Way of Death*, 68–69, quotes the concern of Samuel Sewall's seven-year-old daughter Elizabeth for her soul, but the bulk of his own concern is for New England adults, particularly in the chapters "Death and Childhood" and "Death and Dying." Slater, too, in *Children in the New England Mind*, Part One, "The Dead Child," is preoccupied with the impact of infant deaths on parents rather than on the children themselves. Frost, *Quaker Family*, 69–71, suggests the same phenomenon among Quakers. Yet even this is more illuminating than materials on death for the Chesapeake, where almost all of the present historical literature is more concerned with the quantitative and demographic aspects of the death of children than with the emotional and psychological. Peter Uhlenberg, "Death and the Family," *Journal of Family History* 5 (1980): 313–320, reprinted in Michael Gordon, *The American Family in Social-Historical Perspective* (3d ed., New York: St. Martin's Press, 1983), 169–177, has written a perceptive essay on the impact of declining death rates on families in the twentieth century, suggesting that areas in which we might expect to find an impact on children would be in parent-child and in sibling relationships.

39. Manfred Waserman, "Relieving Parental Anxiety: John Warren's 1792 Letter to the Father of a Burned Child," *New England Journal of Medicine* 299 (1978): 135–136.

40. Hiner, "Cotton Mather and His Children," 32; Cone, *History of Pediatrics*, 47–48.

41. Smith, *Inside the Great House*, 56; Greven, *Protestant Temperament*, 46. For descriptions of children's clothing, see Earle, *Child Life*, ch. 2. This is not to suggest that toilet-training was an overwhelming concern of eighteenth-century parents. Arlene W. Scadron, "The Formative Years: Childhood and Child-Rearing in Eighteenth Century Anglo-American Culture" (Ph.D. dissertation, University of California at Berkeley, 1979), ch. 2, has found almost no evidence that this was an issue in any of the childrearing literature prior to 1800. She concludes that there was "little interest in controlling the child's sphincter, . . . a great deal of concern about controlling his will or in training him to control it himself," 314.

42. Frost, *Quaker Family*, 83; Earle, *Home Life*, "Girl's Occupations."

43. On occupations of children, see Billie G. Smith, "The Material Lives of Laboring Philadelphians, 1750–1800," *William and Mary Quarterly*, 3d ser., 38 (1981): 188. On indentures, see Lawrence W. Turner, "The Indentures of Boston's Poor Apprentices, 1734–1805," *Publications of the Colonial Society of Massachusetts* 43 (1962): 417–434; the indentures of 1,100 named young apprentices are appended to Turner's article. See also Clark, "Babes in Bondage," 475–486, which argues that young Irishmen formed the majority of indentured labor in Philadelphia in the eighteenth century.

44. In addition to Morgan, see also Axtell, *School upon a Hill*, 134. Bailyn, *American Education*, 31–34, theorizes briefly about the changing educational role of apprenticeships during the colonial period, and he provides a bibliographical essay on relevant literature. The classic study of apprenticeship is still worth consulting: Marcus Wilson Jernegan, *Laboring and Dependent Classes in Colonial America, 1607–1783; Studies of the Economic, Educational, and Social Significance of Slaves, Servants, Apprentices, and Poor Folk* (Chicago: University of Chicago Press, 1931). Another aspect of the use of indentured labor resulted from the familial nature of the living arrangements; David H. Flaherty, *Privacy in Colonial New England* (Charlottesville: University Press of Virginia, 1967), 60, notes that in the one-third of New England homes that housed servants during the century before the Revolution, apprentices reduced still further the already limited privacy available.

45. Frost, *Quaker Family*, 82–83; Axtell, *School upon a Hill*, 236–237. See also Earle, *Child Life*; Kiefer, *American Children*, 191–221.

46. The "Dames schools," like modern nursery schools, seem in some cases to have functioned as much as relief for parents from constant watchfulness as for real instruction. Peter Kalm reported, in amusement, of schools for three-year-olds that "They probably realized that such little children would not be able to read much, but they would be rid of them at home and thought it would protect them from any misbehavior. Also they would acquire a liking for being with other children." Cremin, *American Education*, 500, 544.

47. Lockridge, *Literacy in Colonial New England*, 50–51; Towner, "Boston's Apprentices," 424–425; Stanley K. Schultz, *The Culture Factory, Boston Public Schools, 1789–1860* (New York: Oxford University Press, 1973), 5–7.

48. Cremin, *American Education*, 538–540.

49. Ibid., 531–534.

50. Ibid., 450–451; Hunter Dickinson Farish, ed., *Journal and Letters of Philip Vickers Fithian, 1773–1774: A Plantation Tutor of the Old Dominion* (Williamsburg, Va.: Colonial Williamsburg, 1943); Ronald Hoffman, "Forging a Worthy Heir;" Lucille Griffin, ed., "English Education for Virginia Youths: Some Eighteenth Century Ambler Family Letters," *Virginia Magazine of History and Biography* 69 (1961): 14–16. On Jefferson, see Dumas Malone, *Jefferson the Virginian* (Boston: Little, Brown & Co., 1948), 40–46, and Constance B. Schulz, "The Radical Religious Ideas of Thomas Jefferson and John Adams, A Comparison," Ph.D. dissertation, University of Cincinnati, 1973.

51. Kessel, "Mighty Fortress"; Stephanie Grauman Wolf, *Urban Village, Population, Community and Family Structure in Germantown, Pennsylvania, 1683–1800* (Princeton: Princeton University Press, 1977), 238–242.

52. Frost, *Quaker Family*, 96–105, 120–121; Frederick B. Tolles, *Meeting House and Counting House: The Quaker Merchants of Colonial Philadelphia, 1682–1763* (New York, 1948).

53. Cremin, *American Education*, p. 509; see esp. 661–662 of Cremin's bibliographical essay. Phyllis Vine, "Preparation for Republicanism: Honor and Shame in the Eighteenth-Century College," Chapter 3 in Finkelstein, *Regulated Children/Liberated Children*, 44–62; see also her study of "The Social Function of Eighteenth-Century Higher Education," *History of Education Quarterly* 16 (1976): 409–424. Stephen J. Novak, *The Rights of Youth: American Colleges and Student Revolt, 1798–1815* (Cambridge, Mass.: Harvard University Press, 1977).

54. Finkelstein, *Regulated Children/Liberated Children*, introduction, 1.

55. Frost, *Quaker Family*, 121–127; Axtell, *School upon a Hill*, 166–200.

56. John Demos and Virginia Demos, "Adolescence in Historical Perspective," *Journal of Marriage and the Family* 31 (1969): 632–638; Joseph F. Kett, "Adolescence and Youth in Nineteenth Century America," *Journal of Interdisciplinary History* 2 (1971): 283–298; Joseph F. Kett, *Rites of Passage: Adolescence in America 1790 to the Present* (New York: Basic Books, 1977).

57. N. Ray Hiner, "Adolescence in Eighteenth Century America," *History of Childhood Quarterly* 3 (1975): 253–280; Frost, *Quaker Family*, 134–136.

58. Daniel Scott Smith and Michael S. Hindus, "Premarital Pregnancy in America, 1640–1971," *Journal of Interdisciplinary History* 5 (1975): 537–570; Maris A. Vinovskis, "An 'Epidemic' of Adolescent Pregnancy? Some Historical Considerations," *Journal of Family History* 6 (1981): 226–228.

59. Philip J. Greven, Jr., "Youth, Maturity, and Religious Conversion: A Note on the Ages of Converts in Andover, Massachusetts, 1711–1749," *Essex Institute Historical Collections* 108 (1972): 119–134; Cushing Strout, "Fathers and Sons: Notes on 'New Light' and 'New Left' Young People as a Historical Comparison," *Psychohistory Review* 6 (1977): 25–31.

60. Susan R. Falb, "How to Get and Keep Your Man: Advice to American

Women, 1600–1982," unpublished lecture, College of Wooster, April 1983; Herman R. Lantz, "Pre-Industrial Patterns in the Colonial Family in America: A Content Analysis of Colonial Magazines," *American Sociological Review* 33 (1968): 413–426.

61. Nancy F. Cott, *The Bonds of Womanhood, "Woman's Sphere" in New England, 1780–1835* (New Haven: Yale University Press, 1977); Cott, "Young Women in the Second Great Awakening in New England," 15–29.

62. Mary P. Ryan, *Cradle of the Middle Class, The Family in Oneida County, New York, 1790–1865* (New York: Cambridge University Press, 1981) describes the domestic arrangements of frontier New Yorkers at the end of the eighteenth century; Thomas J. Archdeacon, *New York City, 1664–1770: Conquest and Change* (Ithaca, N.Y.: Cornell University Press, 1976); and Jessica Kross, *The Evolution of an American Town: Newtown, New York 1642–1775* (Philadelphia: Temple University Press, 1983). Both include children at least peripherally in their analysis of town social developments.

63. Kenneth A. Lockridge, "Historical Demography," in Charles F. Delzell, ed., *The Future of History* (Nashville: Vanderbilt University Press, 1977), 53–64, writes an infectiously enthusiastic endorsement of the ability of these tools, the materials they provide, and the analyses they support, to "gain the best and most accurate sense of what it meant to be a man, or a woman." Jesse Lemisch and John K. Alexander, "The White Oaks, Jack Tar, and the Concept of the 'Inarticulate,' " *William and Mary Quarterly*, 3d ser., 29 (1972), 134n., have been less certain that demography can recover subjective lives as well as objective profiles of the people we have lost.

64. Daniel Blake Smith, "The Study of the Family in Early America: Trends, Problems, and Prospects," *William and Mary Quarterly*, 3d ser., 39 (1982): 3–28.

65. Demos, *Little Commonwealth*, Philip J. Greven, Jr., *Four Generations: Population, Land and Family in Colonial Andover, Massachusetts* (Ithaca, N.Y.: Cornell University Press, 1970); Bernard Farber, *Guardians of Virtue: Salem Families in 1800* (New York: Basic Books, 1972); Lockridge, *A New England Town*; Michael Zuckerman, *Peaceable Kingdoms, New England Towns in the Eighteenth Century* (New York: Alfred A. Knopf, 1970); E. A. Wrigley, ed., *An Introduction to English Historical Demography* (New York: Basic Books, 1966) and *Population and History* (New York: McGraw-Hill, 1969).

66. Kross, *American Town*, see esp. introduction, xii–xiii and xvi–xvii; Wolf, *Urban Village*; Elizabeth Kessel, "Germans on the Maryland Frontier: A Social History of Frederick County, Maryland, 1730–1800" (Ph.D. dissertation, Rice University, 1981); Billie G. Smith, "Struggles of the 'Lower Sort': The Lives of Philadelphia's Laboring People, 1750–1800" (Ph.D. dissertation, University of California, Los Angeles, 1981); Herbert G. Gutman, *The Black Family in Slavery and Freedom, 1750–1925* (New York: Pantheon Books, 1976).

67. On the Chesapeake, see Allan Kulikoff, "Tobacco and Slaves: Population, Economy and Society in Eighteenth Century Prince George's County Maryland" (Ph.D. Dissertation, Brandeis University, 1975); Daniel Blake Smith, "Mortality and Family in the Colonial Chesapeake," 403–427. On New England, see Nancy Osterud and John Fulton, "Family Limitation and Age at Marriage: Fertility

Decline in Sturbridge, Massachusetts, 1730–1850," *Population Studies* 30 (1973): 481–494; Daniel Scott Smith, "The Demographic History of Colonial New England," *Journal of Economic History* 32 (1972): 165–183; Maris A. Vinovskis, *Fertility in Massachusetts from the Revolution to the Civil War* (New York: Academic Press, 1981) and "Mortality Rates and Trends in Massachusetts Before 1860," 184–213; Lynne E. Withey, "Household Structure in Urban and Rural Areas: The Case of Rhode Island, 1774–1800," *Journal of Family History* 3 (1978): 37–50. Robert Wells began his demographic work in studies of Pennsylvania Quakers; see "Family Size and Fertility Control in Eighteenth Century America: A Study of Quaker Families," *Population Studies* 25 (1971): 73–82. Beginning with his article "Family History and Demographic Transition," *Journal of Social History* 9 (1975): 1–19, Wells began to develop a theory of a major demographic shift toward smaller family size in the late eighteenth century. That idea is more fully articulated in *The Population of the British Colonies in America Before 1776: A Survey of Census Data* (Princeton: Princeton University Press, 1975) and *Revolutions in Americans' Lives: A Demographic Perspective on the History of Americans, Their Families and Their Society* (Westport, Conn.: Greenwood Press, 1982).

68. Wells, *Revolutions in Americans' Lives*. Marriage patterns shifted for reasons varying from the approaching parity of gender in the Chesapeake to the weakening of parental power over children in Massachusetts with opposite results in trends of age at marriage. See Lois Green Carr and Lorena S. Walsh, "The Planter's Wife: The Experience of White Women in Seventeenth-Century Maryland," *William and Mary Quarterly*, 3d ser., 34 (1977), reprinted in Gordon, *American Family*, 3d ed., 336–337; and Daniel Scott Smith, "Parental Power and Marriage Patterns: An Analysis of Historical Trends in Hingham, Massachusetts," *Journal of Marriage and the Family* 35 (1973): 419–428, also reprinted in Gordon, *American Family*, 3d ed., 255–268.

69. Philip J. Greven, "The Average Size of Families and Households in the Province of Massachusetts in 1764 and in the United States in 1790: An Overview," in Peter Laslett and Richard Wall, eds., *Household and Family in Past Time* (Cambridge: Cambridge University Press, 1972), 552; Wells, *Demographic Revolution*, 43–44, 50, 79–81; Wells, *Population of the British Colonies*, 268; James A. Henretta, *The Evolution of American Society, 1700–1815: An Interdisciplinary Analysis* (New York: D. C. Heath & Co., 1973), 103.

70. Allan Kulikoff, "The Beginnings of the Afro-American Family in Maryland," in A. C. Land, Lois Green Carr, and Edward C. Papenfuse, eds., *Law, Society, and Politics in Early Maryland* (Baltimore: Johns Hopkins University Press, 1977), reprinted in Gordon, ed., *American Family*, 2d ed., 447–448.

71. Ibid., 446.

72. Samuel Stanhope Smith, *An Essay on the Causes of the Variety of Complexion and Figure in the Human Species* (Philadelphia, 1787), quoted in Gordon, ed., *American Family*, 457.

73. Gutman, *Black Family*.

74. Billie Smith, "Philadelphia's Laboring Poor," 276, 301.

75. Smith, "Material Lives," 201; "Philadelphia's Laboring Poor," 313.

76. One of the earliest voices calling on historians to interpret American

culture through its surviving artifacts was that of E. McClung Fleming, in "Early American Decorative Arts as Social Documents," *Mississippi Valley Historical Review* 45 (1958): 278, 282. Decorative arts attracted Fleming's attention because their antique value has led to their collection and preservation and, therefore, has made them widely available for study. In 1972 Harold Skramstad observed that Fleming's invitation has been "primarily pursued by art historians, whose first interest is artistic and esthetic, only secondarily viewing the object as an indicator of a 'fundamental attitude toward the world' "; see "American Things: A Neglected Material Culture," *American Studies* 10 (1972): 13. While cultural and social historians have recently responded to that invitation too, the field is still so new that its followers are attempting to define "material culture." James Deetz has proposed a fairly simple definition that upon examination proves to be almost too inclusive: "Consider material culture as that segment of man's physical environment which is purposely shaped by him according to culturally dictated plans," in "Material Culture and Archaeology—What's the Difference," in Leland G. Ferguson, ed., *Historical Archeology and the Importance of Material Things*, Special Publications Series No. 2 (Society for Historical Archeology, 1977), 10. For other definitions of "material culture," see James Deetz, *In Small Things Forgotten: The Archaeology of Early North American Life* (New York: Doubleday, 1977), 24–25; and Thomas J. Schlereth, *Material Culture Studies in America* (Nashville: American Association for State and Local History, 1982), 3 and 356–357. Schlereth's volume brings together in one place a number of important interpretive essays on the theory, methodology, and practice of material culture studies, introduced by his comprehensive review of the history of those studies in America. The *Winterthur Portfolio*, a lavishly illustrated journal published three times a year by the Winterthur Museum, is the most important outlet for scholarly contributions in this multidisciplinary field. Cary Carson has cautioned the non-historians this encompasses that for historians using artifacts, their "subject is the history of people, not things, and [the] object is to explain the changing patterns of behavior," not the artistic or intrinsic character of the material studied. In choosing which objects to study and how to use them, even the new historians will work with artifacts as sources of ideas." Cary Carson, "Doing History with Material Culture," in Ian M. Quimby, ed., *Material Culture and the Study of American Life* (New York: W. W. Norton, 1978), 43–45.

77. Folk and primitive portraiture has received increasing recognition from collectors and critics, and historians interested in studying it can find it in well-produced catalogues. See, for instance, the numerous striking full-color illustrations of children in Richard B. Woodward, *American Folk Painting: Selections from the Collection of Mr. and Mrs. William E. Wiltshire III* (Richmond: Virginia Museum, 1977), a catalogue of an exhibit at the museum, November 29, 1977–January 8, 1978; and Beatrix T. Rumford, gen. ed., Abby Aldrich Rockefeller Folk Art Series, *American Folk Portraits: Paintings and Drawings from the Abby Aldrich Rockefeller Folk Art Center* (Boston: New York Graphic Society, 1981).

78. Catalogues for two such exhibits devoted entirely to children include both objects and paintings: Sandra Brant and Elissa Cullman, *Small Folk, A Celebration of Childhood in America* (New York: E. P. Dutton and the Museum of American

Folk Ark, 1980); and Rosamond Olmsted Humm, *Children in America: A Study of Images and Attitudes* (Atlanta: High Museum of Art, 1978), a catalogue of an exhibit, September 30, 1978–May 27, 1979. On Peale, see Edgar P. Richardson, Brooke Hindle, and Lillian B. Miller, *Charles Willson Peale and His World* (New York: Harry N. Abrams, 1982).

79. Charles Cohen, "Palatable Children: White American Attitudes Toward Children in Paintings, 1670–1860," unpublished seminar paper, University of California at Berkeley, 1975, loaned to me through the courtesy of Joseph Illick; Stephen Brobeck, "Images of the Family: Portrait Paintings as Indices of American Family Culture, Structure, and Behavior, 1730–1860," *Journal of Psychohistory* 5 (1977): 81–106; and Karin Lee Calvert, "Children in American Family Portraiture, 1670–1810," *William and Mary Quarterly*, 3d ser., 39 (1982): 87–113, a revision of the author's more extensive but unpublished University of Delaware 1980 M.A. thesis, "The Perception of Childhood in America: 1670–1870."

80. Cohen, "Palatable Children."

81. Brobeck, "Images of the Family."

82. Calvert, "Children in Portraiture," 112–113.

83. Gwendolyn Wright, *Building the Dream: A Social History of Housing in America* (New York: Pantheon Books, 1981), xv–xvii.

84. Modern interest among historians in vernacular or folk architecture was to some degree prefigured by the monumental work of Thomas Jefferson Wertenbaker, *The Founding of American Civilization: The Middle Colonies*, in which he examined the domestic architecture of each immigrant group as a means of tracing its contributions to the common culture. Deetz, *In Small Things Forgotten*; Henry Glassie, *Folk Housing in Middle Virginia: A Structural Analysis of Historic Artifacts* (Knoxville: University of Tennessee Press, 1975). For a review of both of these studies, see Harvey Green, "Exploring Material Culture," *American Quarterly* 32 (1980): 222–228. The most comprehensive analysis of the older "hall and parlor" style of building, which persisted well into the eighteenth century, is Abbott Lowell Cummings, *The Framed Houses of Massachusetts Bay, 1625–1725* (Cambridge: Harvard University Press, 1979). Relatively few examples of "hall and parlor" architecture survive in the South, and the reasons for their impermanence as well as their cultural links with England are traced in Cary Carson, Norman F. Barka, William L. Kelso, Garry Wheeler Stone, and Dell Upton in "Impermanent Architecture in the Southern Colonies," *Winterthur Portfolio* 16 (1981): 135–196. Other descriptions of vernacular architecture and its cultural meaning include Dell Upton, "Toward a Performance Theory of Vernacular Architecture: Tidewater Virginia as a Case Study," *Folklore Forum* 12 (1979): 173–196; Carl Lounsbury, "The Development of Domestic Architecture in the Albemarle Region," *North Carolina Historical Review* 54 (1977): 17–48; James A. Crutchfield, "Pioneer Architecture in Tennessee," *Tennessee Historical Quarterly* 35 (1976): 162–174; Edward A. Chappell, "Acculturation in the Shenandoah Valley: Rhenish Houses of the Massanutten Settlement," *Proceedings of the American Philosophical Society* 124 (1980): 55–89; Robert L. Alexander, "Baltimore Row Houses of the Early Nineteenth Century," *American Studies* 16 (1975): 65–76.

85. Dorothy Smith, "Household Space and Family Organization," *Pacific Sociological Review* 14 (1971): 53–58; the "Goffman Model" is described in Erving Goffman, *The Presentation of Self in Everyday Life* (New York: Doubleday, 1959), and the relationship between "front" and "back" spaces and children is discussed further in Alice W. Portnoy, "A Microarchaeological View of Human Settlement Space and Function," in Richard A. Gould and Michael B. Schiffer, eds., *Modern Material Culture: The Archeology of Us* (New York: Academic Press, 1981), 213–224.

86. Flaherty, *Privacy in Colonial New England*, 56–57, and much of ch. 1, "The Home," and ch. 2, "The Family." For a discussion of the dwellings of elites as they relate to changes in style, form, and function, the best overview is Alan Gowans, *Images of American Living: Four Centuries of Architecture and Furniture as Cultural Expression* (Philadelphia: V. P. Lippincott, 1964).

87. See, for instance, Linda Grant DePauw and Conover Hunt, *Remember the Ladies: Women in America, 1750–1815* (New York: Viking Press, 1976), and the catalogues by Brant, *Small Folk* and Humm, *Children in America*.

88. DePauw, *Remember the Ladies*, 30–33; Herbert F. Schiffer and Peter B. Schiffer, *Miniature Antique Furniture* (Wynnewood, Penn.: Livingston Publishing Co., 1972), 33–34.

89. Anne Sebba, *Samplers, Five Centuries of a Gentle Craft* (New York: Thames & Hudson, 1979), esp. the chapter on "America's Blossoming Tradition," 81–112. Sebba includes in her illustrations a sampler worked in Hebrew by a young eighteenth-century Jewish girl. The section on "Samplers" in Margaret B. Schiffer, *Historical Needlework of Pennsylvania* (New York: Charles Scribner's Sons, 1968), 17–89, also includes a good discussion of the education of young girls as it related to the creation of samplers.

90. Bruce Johnson, *A Child's Comfort: Baby and Doll Quilts in American Folk Art* (New York: Harcourt Brace Jovanovich, 1977), although it deals primarily with nineteenth-century quilts, illustrates earlier quilt patterns. Thomas K. Woodward and Blanche Greenstein, *Crib Quilts and Other Small Wonders* (New York: E. P. Dutton, 1981) begins a volume otherwise devoted to nineteenth-century quilts with an excellent introductory discussion of bedding and sleeping arrangements that includes descriptions of eighteenth-century materials.

91. On the change in usage of chairs, see Deetz, *In Small Things Forgotten*, 120–122. Some fine examples of a wide variety of children's furnishings are found in Charles Santore, *The Windsor Style in America: A Pictorial Study of the History and Regional Characteristics of the Most Popular Furniture Form of Eighteenth Century America, 1739–1830* (Philadelphia: Running Press, 1981), esp. 160–176; in Jane Toller, *Antique Miniature Furniture in Great Britain and America* (London: G. Bell & Sons, 1966), esp. 77–107; and in Schiffer and Schiffer, *Miniature Antique Furniture*, esp. 23–29.

92. Brant and Cullman, *Small Folk*, esp. Part 4, "A Child's Delight." On miniature porcelain, see Katherine Morrison McClinton, *Antiques in Miniature* (New York: Charles Scribner's Sons, 1970), 127–142. On toys, see Dan Foley, *Toys Throughout the Ages* (New York: Chilton Books, 1969), 95; Inez McClintock and Marshall McClintock, *Toys in America* (Washington, D.C.: Public Affairs Press,

1961), 27; and Bernard Barenholtz, *American Antique Toys: 1830–1900* (New York: Harry N. Abrams, 1980), 24–28.

BIBLIOGRAPHY

Alexander, Robert L. "Baltimore Row Houses of the Early Nineteenth Century." *American Studies* 16 (1975): 65–76.

American Folk Portraits: Paintings and Drawings from the Abby Aldrich Rockefeller Folk Art Center. Boston: New York Graphic Society, 1981. Abby Aldrich Rockefeller Folk Art Series, Beatrix T. Rumford, gen. ed.

Archdeacon, Thomas J. *New York City, 1664–1770: Conquest and Change.* Ithaca, N.Y.: Cornell University Press, 1976.

Axtell, James. *The School upon a Hill: Education and Society in Colonial New England.* New Haven: Yale University Press, 1974.

Bailyn, Bernard. *Education in the Forming of American Society.* Chapel Hill: University of North Carolina Press, 1960.

Barenholtz, Bernard. *American Antique Toys: 1830–1900.* New York: Harry N. Abrams, 1980.

Ben-Or, Joseph. "The Law of Adoption in the United States: Its Massachusetts Origins and the Statute of 1851." *New England Historical and Genealogical Register* 130 (1976): 259–272.

Bloomfield, Maxwell. *American Lawyers in a Changing Society, 1776–1876.* Cambridge, Mass.: Harvard University Press, 1976.

Brant, Sandra, and Cullman, Elissa. *Small Folk, A Celebration of Childhood in America.* New York: E. P. Dutton and the Museum of American Folk Art, 1980.

Brewer, Clifton Hartwell. *The History of Religious Education in the Episcopal Church to 1835.* New York: Arno Press, 1969.

Brobeck, Stephen. "Images of the Family: Portrait Paintings as Indices of American Family Culture, Structure, and Behavior, 1730–1860." *Journal of Psychohistory* 5 (1977): 81–106.

Butterfield, Lyman H., et al., eds. *Adams Family Correspondence.* Cambridge, Mass.: Harvard University Press, 1963–   .

Calhoun, Daniel. *The Intelligence of a People.* Princeton: Princeton University Press, 1973.

Calvert, Karin Lee. "Children in American Family Portraiture, 1670–1810," *William and Mary Quarterly* 3d ser., 39 (1982): 87–113.

———. "The Perception of Childhood in America: 1670–1870." Unpublished M.A. thesis, University of Delaware, 1980.

Carr, Lois Green, and Walsh, Lorena. "The Planter's Wife: The Experience of White Women in Seventeenth Century Maryland." *William and Mary Quarterly*, 3d ser., 34 (1977): 542–571. Reprinted in *The American Family in Social-Historical Perspective*, 3d ed., edited by Michael Gordon, pp. 321–346. New York: St. Martin's Press, 1982.

Carson, Cary. "Doing History with Material Culture." In *Material Culture and the Study of American Life*, edited by Ian M. Quimby, pp. 41–64. New York: W. W. Norton, 1978.

Chappell, Edward A. "Acculturation in the Shenandoah Valley: Rhenish Houses of the Massanutten Settlement." *Proceedings of the American Philosophical Society* 124 (1980): 55–89.

Clark, Dennis. "Babes in Bondage: Indentured Irish Children in Philadelphia in the Nineteenth Century." *Pennsylvania Magazine of History and Biography* 101 (1977): 475–486.

Cohen, Charles. "Palatable Children: White American Attitudes Toward Children in Paintings, 1670–1860." Unpublished graduate seminar paper, University of California at Berkeley, 1975.

Commager, Henry Steele, ed. *The Autobiography of Benjamin Franklin and Selections from His Other Writings.* New York, 1950.

Cone, Thomas E. *History of American Pediatrics.* Boston: Little, Brown & Co., 1979.

———. *Two Hundred Years of Feeding Infants in America.* Columbus, Ohio: Ross Laboratories, 1976.

Cott, Nancy F. *The Bonds of Womanhood: "Woman's Sphere" in New England, 1780–1835.* New Haven: Yale University Press, 1977.

———. "Young Women in the Second Great Awakening in New England." *Feminist Studies* 3 (1975): 15–29.

Cremin, Lawrence A. *American Education: The Colonial Experience, 1607–1783.* New York: Harper & Row, 1970.

Crutchfield, James A. "Pioneer Architecture in Tennessee." *Tennessee Historical Quarterly* 35 (1976): 162–174.

Cummings, Abbott Lowell. *The Framed Houses of Massachusetts Bay, 1625–1725.* Cambridge, Mass.: Harvard University Press, 1979.

Davis, Glenn. *Childhood and History in America.* New York: Psychohistory Press, 1976.

Deetz, James. *In Small Things Forgotten: The Archaeology of Early North American Life.* New York: Doubleday, 1977.

———. "Material Culture and Archaeology—What's the Difference." In *Historical Archeology and the Importance of Material Things,* edited by Leland G. Ferguson. Society for Historical Archeology, Special Publications Series No. 2, 1977.

Delzell, Charles F. *The Future of History.* Nashville: Vanderbilt University Press, 1977.

deMause, Lloyd, ed. *The History of Childhood.* New York: Harper & Row, 1974.

Demos, John. *A Little Commonwealth: Family Life in Plymouth Colony.* New York: Oxford University Press, 1970.

———, and Demos, Virginia. "Adolescence in Historical Perspective." *Journal of Marriage and the Family* 31 (1969): 632–638.

DePauw, Linda Grant, and Hunt, Conover. *Remember the Ladies: Women in America, 1750–1815.* New York: Viking Press, 1976.

Duffy, John. *Epidemics in Colonial America.* Baton Rouge: Louisiana State University Press, 1953.

Dye, Nancy Schrom. "History of Childbirth in America." *Signs* 6 (1980): 97–108.

Earle, Alice Morse. *Child Life in Colonial Days.* New York: Macmillan Co., 1899.
———. *Home Life in Colonial Days.* New York: Macmillan Co., 1898.
———. *Two Centuries of Costume in America.* New York: Macmillan Co., 1903.
Elder, Glenn H., Jr. "History and the Family: The Discovery of Complexity." *Journal of Marriage and the Family* 43 (1981): 489–519.
Falb, Susan R. "How to Get and Keep Your Man: Advice to American Women, 1600–1982." Unpublished lecture, College of Wooster, April 1983.
Farber, Bernard. *Guardians of Virtue: Salem Families in 1800.* New York: Basic Books, 1972.
Farish, Hunter Dickinson, ed. *Journal and Letters of Philip Vickers Fithian, 1773–1774: A Plantation Tutor of the Old Dominion.* Williamsburg, Va.: Colonial Williamsburg, 1943.
Ferguson, Leland G., ed. *Historical Archeology and the Importance of Material Things.* Society for Historical Archeology, Special Publications Series No. 2, 1977.
Finkelstein, Barbara. *Regulated Children/Liberated Children: Education in Psychohistorical Perspective.* New York: Psychohistory Press, 1979.
Fischer, David Hackett. *Growing Old in America.* Expanded ed., New York: Oxford University Press, 1978.
Flaherty, David H. *Privacy in Colonial New England.* Charlottesville: University Press of Virginia, 1967.
Fleming, E. McClung. "Early American Decorative Arts as Social Documents." *Mississippi Valley Historical Review* 45 (1958): 276–284.
Fleming, Sanford. *Children and Puritanism: The Place of Children in the Life and Thought of the New England Churches, 1620–1847.* New Haven: Yale University Press, 1933. Reprint ed., New York: Arno Press, 1969.
Foley, Dan. *Toys Through the Ages.* New York: Chilton Books, 1969.
Frost, J. William. *The Quaker Family in Colonial America: A Portrait of the Society of Friends.* New York: St. Martin's Press, 1973.
Glassie, Henry. "Archeology and Folklore: Common Anxieties, Common Hopes." In *Historical Archeology and the Importance of Material Things*, edited by Leland G. Ferguson. Society for Historical Archeology, Special Publications Series No. 2, 1977.
———. *Folk Housing in Middle Virginia: A Structural Analysis of Historical Artifacts.* Knoxville: University of Tennessee Press, 1975.
Gordon, Michael, ed. *The American Family in Social-Historical Perspective.* 2d ed., New York: St. Martin's Press, 1978. 3d ed., New York: St. Martin's Press, 1982.
Gowans, Alan. *Images of American Living: Four Centuries of Architecture and Furniture as Cultural Expression.* Philadelphia: V. P. Lippincott, 1964.
Green, Harvey. "Exploring Material Culture." *American Quarterly* 32 (1980): 222–228.
Greene, Jack P., ed. *The Diary of Colonel Landon Carter of Sabine Hall, 1752–1778.* 2 vols., Charlottesville: University of Virginia Press, 1965.
Greven, Philip J., Jr. "The Average Size of Families and Households in the Province of Masssachusetts in 1764 and in the United States in 1790: An Overview." In *Household and Family in Past Time*, edited by Peter Laslett

and Richard Wall, pp. 545–560. Cambridge: Cambridge University Press, 1972.

———. *Four Generations: Population, Land and Family in Colonial Andover, Massachusetts*. Ithaca, N.Y.: Cornell University Press, 1970.

———. *The Protestant Temperament*. New York: Alfred A. Knopf, 1977.

———. "Youth, Maturity, and Religious Conversion: A Note on the Ages of Converts in Andover, Massachusetts, 1711–1749." *Essex Institute Historical Collections* 108 (1972): 119–134.

Griffin, Lucille, ed. "English Education for Virginia Youths: Some Eighteenth Century Ambler Family Letters." *Virginia Magazine of History and Biography* 69 (1961): 14–16.

Gross, Robert. *The Minute Men and Their World*. New York: Hill & Wang, 1976.

Gutman, Herbert G. *The Black Family in Slavery and Freedom, 1750–1925*. New York: Pantheon Books, 1976.

Hall, Peter Dobkin. "Marital Selection and Business in Massachusetts Merchant Families, 1700–1900." In *The American Family in Social-Historical Perspective*, edited by Michael Gordon, pp. 101–114. 2d ed., New York: St. Martin's Press, 1978.

Henretta, James A. *The Evolution of American Society, 1700–1815: An Interdisciplinary Analysis*. New York: D. C. Heath & Co., 1973.

Hiner, N. Ray. "Adolescence in Eighteenth Century America." *History of Childhood Quarterly* 3 (1975): 253–280.

———. "The Child in American Historiography: Accomplishments and Prospect." *Psychohistory Review* 7 (1978–1979): 13–23.

———. "Cotton Mather and His Children: The Evolution of a Parent Education." In *Regulated Children/Liberated Children: Education in Psychohistorical Perspective*, edited by Barbara Finkelstein, pp. 24–43. New York: Psychohistory Press, 1979.

Hoffman, Ronald. "Forging a Worthy Heir: The Testing of Charles Carroll of Carrollton." Unpublished paper delivered in December 1982 at the University of Maryland seminar in Early American History and Culture.

Humm, Rosamond Olmsted. *Children in America: A Study of Images and Attitudes*. Atlanta: High Museum of Art, 1978.

Illick, Joseph E. "John Quincy Adams: The Maternal Influence." *Journal of Psychohistory* 4 (1976): 185–195.

Isaac, Rhys. *The Transformation of Virginia, 1740–1790*. Chapel Hill: University of North Carolina Press, 1982.

Jernegan, Marcus Wilson. *Laboring and Dependent Classes in Colonial America, 1607–1783; Studies of the Economic, Educational, and Social Significance of Slaves, Servants, Apprentices, and Poor Folk*. Chicago: University of Chicago Press, 1931.

Johnson, Bruce. *A Child's Comfort: Baby and Doll Quilts in American Folk Art*. New York: Harcourt Brace Jovanovich, 1977.

Kessel, Elizabeth A. " 'A Mighty Fortress Is Our God'; German Religious and Educational Organizations on the Maryland Frontier 1734–1800." *Maryland Historical Magazine* 77 (1982): 370–387.

———. "Germans on the Maryland Frontier: A Social History of Frederick County, Maryland, 1730–1800." Ph.D. dissertation, Rice University, 1981.

Kett, Joseph. "Adolescence and Youth in Nineteenth Century America." *Journal of Interdisciplinary History* 2 (1971): 283–298.

———. *Rites of Passage: Adolescence in America 1790 to the Present.* New York: Basic Books, 1977.

Kiefer, Monica. *American Children Through Their Books, 1788–1835.* Philadelphia: University of Pennsylvania Press, 1948.

Kiple, Kenneth F., and Kiple, Virginia H. "Slave Child Mortality: Some Nutritional Answers to a Perennial Puzzle." *Journal of Social History* 10 (1977): 284–309.

Klein, Randolph Shipley. *Portait of an Early American Family: The Shippens of Pennsylvania Across Five Generations.* Philadelphia: University of Pennsylvania Press, 1975.

Kross, Jessica. *The Evolution of an American Town: Newtown, New York, 1642–1775.* Philadelphia: Temple University Press, 1983.

Kulikoff, Allan. "The Beginnings of the Afro-American Family in Maryland." In *Law, Society, and Politics in Early Maryland,* edited by A. C. Land, Lois Green Carr, and Edward C. Papenfuse. Baltimore: Johns Hopkins University Press, 1977. Reprinted in *American Family in Social-Historical Perspective,* edited by Michael Gordon, pp. 444–466. 2d ed., New York: St. Martin's Press, 1978.

———. "Tobacco and Slaves: Population, Economy and Society in Eighteenth Century Prince George's County Maryland." Ph.D. Dissertation, Brandeis University, 1975.

Lantz, Herman R. "Pre-Industrial Patterns in the Colonial Family in America: A Content Analysis of Colonial Magazines." *American Sociological Review* 33 (1968): 413–426.

Laslett, Peter, and Wall, Richard, eds. *Household and Family in Past Time.* Cambridge: Cambridge University Press, 1972.

Lewis, Jan. "Domestic Tranquility and the Management of Emotion Among the Gentry of Pre-Revolutionary Virginia." *William and Mary Quarterly,* 3d ser., 39 (1982): 135–149.

Lockridge, Kenneth A. "Historical Demography." In *The Future of History,* edited by Charles F. Delzell, pp. 53–64. Nashville: Vanderbilt University Press, 1977.

———. *Literacy in Colonial New England: An Enquiry into the Social Context of Literacy in the Early Modern West.* New York: W. W. Norton, 1974.

———. *A New England Town: The First Hundred Years.* New York: W. W. Norton, 1970.

Lopez, Claude-Anne, and Herbert, Eugenia W. *The Private Franklin: The Man and His Family.* New York, 1975.

Lounsbury, Carl. "The Development of Domestic Architecture in the Albemarle Region." *North Carolina Historical Review* 54 (1977): 17–48.

McClintock, Inez, and McClintock, Marshall. *Toys in America.* Washington, D.C.: Public Affairs Press, 1961.

McClinton, Katherine Morrison. *Antiques in Miniature*. New York: Charles Scribner's Sons, 1970.

McLoughlin, William G. "Evangelical Child-Rearing in the Age of Jackson: Francis Wayland's View on When and How to Subdue the Willfulness of Children." *Journal of Social History* 9 (1975): 21–43.

Malone, Dumas. *Jefferson the Virginian*. Boston: Little, Brown & Co., 1948.

Mechling, Jay. "Advice to Historians on Advice to Mothers." *Journal of Social History* 9 (1975): 44–63.

Morgan, Edmund Sears. *The Puritan Family: Essays on Religion and Domestic Relations in Seventeenth Century New England*. Boston: Little, Brown & Co., 1944.

———. *Virginians at Home: Family Life in the Eighteenth Century*. Charlottesville: Colonial Williamsburg, 1952.

Novak, Stephen J. *The Rights of Youth: American Colleges and Student Revolt, 1798–1815*. Cambridge, Mass.: Harvard University Press, 1977.

Osterud, Nancy, and Fulton, John. "Family Limitation and Age at Marriage: Fertility Decline in Sturbridge, Massachusetts, 1730–1850." *Population Studies* 30 (1973): 481–494.

Pinckney, Elise, and Zahniser, Marvin R., eds. *The Letterbook of Eliza Lucas Pinckney 1739–1762*. Chapel Hill: University of North Carolina Press, 1972.

Portnoy, Alice W. "A Microarchaeological View of Human Settlement Space and Function." In *Modern Material Culture: The Archeology of Us*, edited by Richard A. Gould and Michael B. Schiffer, pp. 213–224. New York: Academic Press, 1981.

Presser, Stephen B. "The Historical Background of the American Law of Adoption." *Journal of Family Law* 11 (1971): 443–516.

Rabb, Theodore K., and Rotberg, Robert I., eds. *The Family in History: Interdisciplinary Essays*. New York: Harper & Row, 1973.

Ravenel, Harriott Horry. *Eliza Pinckney*. New York: Charles Scribner's Sons, 1896.

Richardson, Edgar P.; Hindle, Brooke; and Miller, Lillian B. *Charles Willson Peale and His World*. New York: Harry N. Abrams, 1982.

Rutman, Darrett, and Rutman, Anita. "Of Agues and Fevers: Malaria in the Early Chesapeake." *William and Mary Quarterly*, 3d ser., 33 (1976): 31–60.

Ryan, Mary P. *Cradle of the Middle Class, The Family in Oneida County, New York, 1790–1865*. New York: Cambridge University Press, 1981.

Santore, Charles. *The Windsor Style in America: A Pictorial Study of the History and Regional Characteristics of the Most Popular Furniture Form of Eighteenth Century America, 1739–1830*. Philadelphia: Running Press, 1981.

Scadron, Arlene W. "The Formative Years: Childhood and Child-Rearing in Eighteenth Century Anglo-American Culture." Ph.D. dissertation, University of California at Berkeley, 1979.

Schiffer, Herbert F., and Schiffer, Peter B. *Miniature Antique Furniture*. Wynnewood, Penn.: Livingston Publishing Co., 1972.

Schiffer, Margaret B. *Historical Needlework of Pennsylvania*. New York: Charles Scribner's Sons, 1968.

Schlereth, Thomas J. *Material Culture Studies in America*. Nashville: American Association for State and Local History, 1982.

Scholten, Catherine M. "On the Importance of the Obstetrick Art: Changing Customs of Childbirth in America, 1760–1825." *William and Mary Quarterly*, 3d ser., 34 (1977): 426–445.

Schultz, Stanley K. *The Culture Factory, Boston Public Schools, 1789–1860*. New York: Oxford University Press, 1973.

Sebba, Anne. *Samplers, Five Centuries of a Gentle Craft*. New York: Thames & Hudson, 1979.

Skramstad, Harold. "American Things: A Neglected Material Culture." *American Studies* 10 (1972): 11–22.

Slater, Peter Gregg. *Children in the New England Mind in Death and in Life: From the Puritans to Bushnell*. Hamden, Conn.: Archon Books, 1977.

Smith, Billie G. "The Material Lives of Laboring Philadelphians, 1750–1800." *William and Mary Quarterly*, 3d ser., 38 (1981): 163–202.

———. "Struggles of the 'Lower Sort': The Lives of Philadelphia's Laboring People, 1750–1800." Ph.D. dissertation, University of California, Los Angeles, 1981.

Smith, Daniel Blake. "Autonomy and Affection: Parents and Children in Eighteenth Century Chesapeake Families." *Psychohistory Review* 6 (1977): 32–51.

———. *Inside the Great House: Planter Family Life in Eighteenth Century Chesapeake Society*. Ithaca, N.Y.: Cornell University Press, 1980.

———. "Mortality and the Family in the Colonial Chesapeake." *Journal of Interdisciplinary History* 8 (1978): 403–427.

———. "The Study of the Family in Early America: Trends, Problems, and Prospects." *William and Mary Quarterly*, 3d ser., 39 (1982): 3–28.

Smith, Daniel Scott. "The Demographic History of Colonial New England." *Journal of Economic History* 32 (1972): 165–183.

———. "Parental Control and Marriage Patterns: An Analysis of Historical Trends in Hingham, Massachusetts." *Journal of Marriage and the Family* 35 (1973): 419–428.

——— and Hindus, Michael S. "Premarital Pregnancy in America, 1640–1971." *Journal of Interdisciplinary History* 5 (1975): 537–570.

Smith, Dorothy. "Household Space and Family Organization." *Pacific Sociological Review* 14 (1971): 53–78.

Spruill, Julia Cherry. *Women's Life and Work in the Southern Colonies*. Chapel Hill: University of North Carolina Press, 1938. Reissued New York: Russell & Russell, 1969.

Stannard, David E. *The Puritan Way of Death: A Study in Religion, Culture, and Social Change*. New York: Oxford University Press, 1977.

Stewart, George, Jr. *A History of Religious Education in Connecticut to the Middle of the Nineteenth Century*. New Haven: Yale University Press, 1924. Reprinted New York: Arno Press, 1969.

Strout, Cushing. "Fathers and Sons: Notes on 'New Light' and 'New Left' Young People as a Historical Comparison." *Psychohistory Review* 6 (1977): 25–31.

Suitor, Jill. "Husbands' Participation in Childbirth: A Nineteenth Century Phenomenon." *Journal of Family History* 6 (1981): 278–293.

Sutton, John R. "Stubborn Children: Law and the Socialization of Deviance in
the Puritan Colonies." *Family Law Quarterly* 15 (1981): 31–64.

Toller, Jane. *Antique Miniature Furniture in Great Britain and America.* London: G.
Bell & Sons, 1966.

Tolles, Frederick B. *Meeting House and Counting House: The Quaker Merchants of
Colonial Philadelphia, 1682–1763.* New York, 1948.

Treckel, Paula A. "Breastfeeding as a Method of Birth Control in Colonial
America." Unpublished paper delivered at the Duquesne History Forum,
Fall 1982.

Turner, Lawrence W. "The Indentures of Boston's Poor Apprentices, 1734–
1805." *Publications of the Colonial Society of Massachusetts* 43 (1962): 417–
434.

Uhlenberg, Peter. "Death and the Family." *Journal of Family History* 5 (1980):
313–320. Reprinted in *The American Family in Social-Historical Perspective*,
edited by Michael Gordon, pp. 169-177.3d ed., New York: St. Martin's
Press, 1983.

Upton, Dell. "Toward a Performance Theory of Vernacular Architecture: Tidewater Virginia as a Case Study." *Folklore Forum* 12 (1979): 173–196.

Vine, Phyllis. "Preparation for Republicanism: Honor and Shame in the Eigh-
eenth-Century College." In *Regulated Children/Liberated Children: Education
in Psychohistorical Perspective*, edited by Barbara Finkelstein, pp. 44–62.
New York: Psychohistory Press, 1979.

———. "The Social Function of Eighteenth-Century Higher Education." *History
of Education Quarterly* 16 (1976): 409–424.

Vinovskis, Maris A. "An 'Epidemic' of Adolescent Pregnancy? Some Historical
Considerations." *Journal of Family History* 6 (1981): 205–230.

———. "Angel's Heads and Weeping Willows: Death in Early America." *Pro-
ceedings of the American Antiquarian Society* 86, Part 2 (1977): 273–302.
Reprinted in *The American Family in Social-Historical Perspective*, edited by
Michael Gordon, pp. 546–563. 2d ed., New York: St. Martin's Press, 1978.

———. *Fertility in Massachusetts from the Revolution to the Civil War.* New York:
Academic Press, 1981.

———. "Mortality Rates and Trends in Massachusetts Before 1860." *Journal of
Economic History* 32 (1972): 184–213.

Walsh, Lorena. "Child Custody in the Early Chesapeake: A Case Study." Unpublished paper delivered at the Berkshire Conference on the History of
Women, Vassar College, June 1981.

Walzer, John F. "A Period of Ambivalence: Eighteenth-Century American Childhood." In *The History of Childhood*, edited by Lloyd deMause, pp. 351–382.
New York: Psychohistory Press, 1974.

Waserman, Manfred. "Relieving Parental Anxiety: John Warren's 1792 Letter
to the Father of a Burned Child." *New England Journal of Medicine* 299
(1978): 135–136.

Wells, Robert V. "Family History and Demographic Transition." *Journal of Social
History* 9 (1975): 1–19.

———. "Family Size and Fertility Control in Eighteenth Century America: A Study of Quaker Families." *Population Studies* 25 (1971): 73–82.

———. *The Population of the British Colonies in America Before 1776: A Survey of Census Data.* Princeton: Princeton University Press, 1975.

———. "Quaker Marriage Patterns in Colonial Perspective." *William and Mary Quarterly.* 3d ser., 29 (1972): 415–442.

———. *Revolutions in Americans' Lives: A Demographic Perspective on the History of Americans, Their Families and Their Society.* Westport, Conn.: Greenwood Press, 1982.

Wishy, Bernard. *The Child and the Republic: The Dawn of Modern American Child Nurture.* Philadelphia: University of Pennsylvania Press, 1968.

Withey, Lynne E. "Household Structure in Urban and Rural Areas: The Case of Rhode Island, 1774–1800." *Journal of Family History* 3 (1978): 37–50.

Wolf, Stephanie Grauman. *Urban Village, Population, Community and Family Structure in Germantown, Pennsylvania, 1683–1800.* Princeton: Princeton University Press, 1977.

Woodward, Richard B. *American Folk Painting: Selections from the Collection of Mr. and Mrs. William E. Wiltshire III.* Richmond: Virginia Museum, 1977.

Woodward, Thomas K., and Greenstein, Blanche. *Crib Quilts and Other Small Wonders.* New York: E. P. Dutton, 1981.

Woody, Thomas. *Quaker Education in the Colony and State of New Jersey, A Source Book.* Philadelphia: University of Pennsylvania Press, 1923. Reprinted New York: Arno Press, 1969.

Wright, Gwendolyn. *Building the Dream: A Social History of Housing in America.* New York: Pantheon Books, 1981.

Wrigley, E. A., ed. *An Introduction to English Historical Demography.* New York: Basic Books, 1966.

———. *Population and History.* New York: McGraw-Hill, 1969.

Zainaldin, Jamil S. "The Emergence of a Modern Family Law: Child Custody, Adoption, and the Courts, 1796–1851." *Northwestern University Law Review* 73 (1979): 1038–1089.

———. *Law in Antebellum Society: Legal Change and Economic Expansion.* New York: Random House, 1983.

Zuckerman, Michael. *Peaceable Kingdoms, New England Towns in the Eighteenth Century.* New York: Alfred A. Knopf, 1970.

3

Casting Networks of Good Influence: The Reconstruction of Childhood in the United States, 1790–1870

Barbara Finkelstein

This chapter describes and explains the shape children's experiences began to take in the period from 1790 to 1870. It is based on the assumption that the contours of childhood can best be understood by paying close attention to the networks of association, the structures of authority, and the character of activities that connect children to social worlds outside their particular subjectivities. Although the uses to which young people put their experiences are also of fundamental importance, this chapter focuses on transformations in the kinds of experiences constructed for children in the first two-thirds of the nineteenth century.

Nineteenth-century Americans did not discover childhood vulnerability. Nor did they invent the notion that children required protection and supervision. What they originated was a disposition to define, build, and organize learning communities for the young—specialized educational settings in which their moral and cognitive capacities would be especially attended. Indeed, the eighty years from 1790 to 1870 were momentous ones for children and youth in the United States.

It was during two generations, from 1790 to 1835 and from 1835 to 1870, that Americans constructed a dazzling array of educational settings, "tutelary complexes" specifically to serve the young. From 1800 to 1835, they built Sunday schools for infants in factories, monitorial schools for children in densely populated settlements, refuges and orphanages for abandoned children. From 1840 to 1860, they expanded

This chapter evolved out of work originating in the spring of 1977 in preparation for the Charles Riley Armington Seminar, held annually at Case Western Reserve University. I am indebted to Bertram Wyatt-Brown and Barry Levy who gave me the opportunity to participate in the seminar and to Michael Grossberg who criticized the paper so thoroughly and so well at that time.

their institution-building efforts, constructing public schools, parochial schools, boarding schools, and reform schools and reconstructing environments housing the deviant, delinquent, neglected, and abandoned. It was during these eighty years that the acquisition of literacy, that is, of formal learning, was extended to the masses, becoming an important developmental task for almost all children between the ages of six and twelve. During the middle decades of the century, reformers also attempted to influence the character of domestic nurture and to transform the family into a tutorial environment, as well as a unit of reproduction and a source of social order. They also attempted to substitute public for private authorities and to place certain classes of children under the control of teachers rather than employers. In short, concern for the young and very young increasingly found expression in the creation of educational blueprints and in the construction of educational settings that irreversibly transformed the meaning of childhood and childrearing.

As they explain the emergence of specialized institutions for the young and very young, historians have adopted a variety of descriptive and explanatory modes, which, in one way or another, typically neglect to recover the whole of the context of children's lives. The nature and character of associations into which children entered as they grew up have been virtually unexplored, as have the processes through which their consciousness might have been informed, their affiliative loyalties organized, and their behavior influenced. In other words, historians have typically paid more attention to structures of authority than to their persuasive capacity and possibility. As a consequence, they have ignored the psychological and social meanings of transformations in childhood experience, and have neglected to explore the processes that influenced the manners, morals, mentalities, dispositions, and sentiments of the rising generation.

Some historians such as Steven L. Schlossman, Michael B. Katz, and Elizabeth Badinter, have represented the institutional innovations of the ante-bellum period as nothing more or less than strategies to create, train, and prepare a docile labor force for a newly emerging industrial order. For these historians, the emergence of schools, reformatories, orphanages, and houses of refuge constituted a response to industrialization, urbanization, and demographic shifts occurring in early nineteenth-century cities.[1] Implicitly defining children's institutions as nothing more or less than structures of domination and control, they root the emergence of specialized institutions in the bedrock of economic structure, viewing ideas and institutions as weapons used by elites in an unending struggle for power. Historians of this school describe the emergence of tutorial complexes as driven by rational calculations of consciously recognized personal advantage. Some, like Jacques Donzelot and Christopher Lasch, regard nurture writers and other educational

reformers as class representatives, middle-class manipulators constructing social spaces or complexes through which they could transform and
thereby control the socialization of working- or laboring class children.[2]
Others define the array of educational institutions as attempts to undermine the capacity of laboring families to control the terms by which
their children entered the labor force.[3] No subtleties here. Defining
institutionalization narrowly, strictly as a strategy of domination, they
have obscured the existence of motives other than greed and ambition
as galvanizing mechanisms in the transformation of children's lives.

Other historians—Joseph M. Hawes studying juvenile justice, Charles
Strickland exploring early childhood education, John Duffy examining
children's health, and Bertram Wyatt-Brown examining child abuse—
have explained the emergence of institutional complexes for children
and youth as a product of humanitarian concern and benevolent sentiment. Defining the emergence of children's institutions as a step forward in the realization of more humane institutions, they define public
schools as structures of opportunity, rather than of regulation, and describe hospitals, asylums, refuges, and orphanages as creative, scientifically more advanced institutional innovations.[4] Rooting their analyses
in the rhetoric of social reform, the intentions of social planners, and
the blueprints of institution-building, they have been more sensitive to
the character of moral and social concern than they have been to the
economic realities and political complexities out of which institutional
innovations evolved. For these historians, the stated intentions of reformers were compelling as explanations of change. As David J. Rothman has put it, "the movement to incarcerate the orphan, the abandoned
child, the youngster living in dire poverty, the juvenile vagrant and the
delinquent promised enormous benefits with small risks."[5]

Similarly, certain historians of education—R. Freeman Butts and
Lawrence A. Cremin among them—have emphasized the promises rather
than the realities, the benefits rather than the costs of educational expansion. Focusing on the enabling character of literacy and on the benefits of tutorial environments for the prospects of individual mobility,
these historians have been virtually insensitive to processes of education
and exercises of authority as they proceeded in small circles of association
within family, church, and neighborhood. They have ignored tensions
between planners and recipients of social services—simply disregarding
transformations within families and churches. These historians also
underestimated the capacity of public authority to satisfy diverse interests
and needs.[6]

Providing creative variations on the humanitarian theme are certain
historians of childhood like Lloyd deMause, who define institutional
transformations as a reflection of new and more enlightened dispositions
toward the young. For this group of historians, the construction of tu-

torial complexes for children represented the triumph and expression of a particular mode of childrearing, experienced in childhood by reformers who took charge of defining nineteenth-century social structures.[7] More concerned with children's institutions as they reflected transformations in the capacity of human beings to love and nurture than they are in the capacity of educational structures to influence and inform thought and action, these historians tend to obscure the force of external circumstance on the evolution of children's social consciousness, sentiments, actions, and choices.

decline family church auth.

There are still other historians who, adopting the perspectives of sociological functionalism, define the emergence of children's institutions as reflections of a decline in family and church authority.[8] No longer able to preside effectively over their children, adult authorities, that is, parents and ministers, turned to schools and other social institutions to govern their young. Unable typically to provide all their children with land, property, or even vocational preparation, they vested schools with social missions that they could no longer perform. Defining schools, asylums, refuges, and orphanages as specialized institutions, with specialized functions, historians of this school—Michael Igniateff, Carl Kaestle and Maris Vinovskis, Bernard Bailyn—see the emergence of tutorial environments in the decline of other authoritative structures. Inherently descriptive rather than analytic, the sociological approach to educational expansion obscures human agency and social options, ignoring the importance of relationships between structure and consciousness, structure and process.[9]

Still other historians like Michel Foucault combine the sociological interest in institutional socialization with a belief in the compelling power of words and ideas. Describing the emergence of tutorial environments in the nineteenth century as an elaboration of enlightenment commitments to reason and rational planning in human affairs, reformers, as historians tell the tale, tried to bring "madness under the unbending control of reason,"[10] and to bring children under the command of rules and regulations in environments that would organize and discipline their unseemly and unpredictable impulses and dispositions.[11] These historians recognize the emergence of schools, refuges, asylums, and reformatories as an attack on informal customary modes of authority in family and church in favor of an authority of rules, clocks, fines, and increasing supervision in schools. For these historians, the orgy of institution-building characterizing the first seventy years of the nineteenth century represented nothing more or less than an attempt of reformers to place children in settings that would effectively bind their impulses and imaginations, substitute the rule of reason for the rule of passion, and bring emotion under the control of reason.

Finally, there are historians—David Rothman, Carroll Smith-Rosenberg, Nancy Cott—who harbor a more complex and historically more complete view of the expansion of institution-building in the nineteenth century, although they have not focused their expositions on children's institutions.[12] They recognize the force of economic circumstance in human affairs, without assuming that they are beyond the reach of human agency. They proceed on the assumption that psychological factors are compelling ones without simultaneously denying the importance of political, economic, and other stratificatory realities on the consciousness of human beings. They know that the power of words and ideas is fundamental, but recognize that they derive meaning and significance from the social contents within which human beings function and define the world. Finally, they recognize the existence of complexity and ambiguity in human motivation, feeling no discomfort with the notion that reformers might simultaneously harbor benevolent sentiments and imperial dispositions and might act out of motives that are political, economic, and sentimental, all at the same time.

While none of the more sophisticated historical treatments has as yet attended specifically to the character and evolution of childhood and childrearing, there are nonetheless several useful principles that we can apply as we seek to make sense out of the nature of social transformations between 1790 and 1870. Whether they have explored institutions, as David Rothman and Barbara Brenzel have done,[13] or whether they focus on the character of human experiences as Nancy Cott and Caroll Smith-Rosenberg have done, they have used organizing concepts that implicitly connect social structure and individual consciousness, stratificatory realities and affiliative loyalties, material and psychological factors.[14] Complex thinkers, they define the evolution of new ideas and social institutions as the products of human agency and of human fears. They pay very close attention to relationships between social structure and human consciousness, seeking explicitly to recover the whole of a social context, eschewing reductive explanations of social change, treating institutions as economic, political, social, and cultural entities simultaneously, defining human motivations as psychological, moral, intellectual, and sentimental as well as political, economic, and cunning.

What follows is an attempt to explain the evolution of childhood and childrearing in the period between 1790 and 1870, seeking insofar as possible to avoid determinisms and to recover the social and psychological contexts from which reform evolved. It is assumed that the contours of childhood can be best comprehended if we pay close attention to transformations in the networks of association, the structures of authority, and the character of the activities that informed the consciousness, compelled the behavior, and otherwise shaped the consciousness of children throughout the nineteenth century.

Early nineteenth-century English-speaking Americans inherited "tem-

116   Barbara Finkelstein

plates," or blueprints of childrearing processes that evolved in the seventeenth and eighteenth centuries when the search for community
cohesion and identity was regnant, the fear of the polluting power of
alien communities ever present.[15] Reflected in a psychologically and socially segmented society, a mosaic of educational structures separated
children into communities of ethnic, religious, and racial similarity.[16]
Formal education might have proceeded within families, churches, or
within schools, if it occurred at all. When it occurred in schools, they
were homogeneously arranged. There were schools for rich and for
poor, for blacks and for whites, for boys and for girls, for Catholics and
for Protestant groups—for Quakers, Lutherans, Anglicans, Congrega-
tionalists, and so on. Whether they lived in the country or the city, in
the South or the North, East, or West, children grew up in small circles
of association immersed in clusters of likemindedness, shielded from
strangers by walls of social, political, and intellectual protection.[17] And
they participated fully in the life of the community, attending church
services, working the farms, tending households along with their parents,
and acquiring the rudiments of literacy in between all of this other
activity.

Immersed in the traditional language, culture, myths, mores, and manners of their parents, children received the whole of their education in
the presence of parent-approved mentors, within households, churches,
and communities, in the fields, on the streets, or in the workplace. For
children in the early nineteenth century, public and private space was
typically indistinguishable, the relationship among their mentors was
reinforcing, their universe of shared symbols in harmony.[18]

If an environment purged of alien influence inspired the construction
of communities of likemindedness among settlers, their modes of social
control were unequal to, if not subversive of, orderliness and obedience
in the younger generation. By the early decades of the nineteenth century, apprenticeship arrangements had lost their compelling power; young
people headed for cities in search of work and for new lands in search
of opportunity.[19] Girls as well as boys deserted farm communities, seeking to earn a living and at the same time to reconstruct communities
within new factory towns and frontier settlements.[20] Fear of community
disintegration and of social pollution was, it is likely, reinforced by the
arrival in the 1830s and 1840s of large numbers of Irish Catholic and
German-speaking immigrants into the city and country. An increasingly
visible class of cultural strangers and destitute and dirty children appeared. Marginal as their fear of social disorder may have been in the
awareness of early nineteenth-century social leaders, they reacted as they
had learned to react from their progenitors: as vigilant and intrusive
stewards of the young.

TWO GENERATIONS OF REFORMERS: TINKERERS AND TRANSFORMERS

Like their forbears, the new social leaders were aware of childhood vulnerabilities and believed that children required protection and supervision. But unlike previous generations of English-speaking Americans, they attempted to remove children from workplace and tavern, from centers of urban and rural sociability, commerce, and adult intimacies. Indeed, they engaged in systematic attempts to purify the environments of the young, to withdraw them from debasing community temptations, and to immerse them in networks of good influence.[21]

This is the hidden logic to be found in the evolution of childhood environments from 1790 to 1870. It is the psycho-socio-logic of multiple attempts to structure and organize a coherent reality for the young in a world of expanding possibility and diverse world-views. It reflected a growing consciousness of children as learners, vulnerable to the force of circumstance and subject to multiple influences. It involved systematic attempts to fix their identities, their affiliative loyalties during times in their development when, reformers thought, they were psychologically most vulnerable to the force of circumstance and the binding power of love and/or habit. It represented an attempt to control the experiences and, after 1830, to narrow the range of association for the young, creating tutorial environments with exemplary adults who would engage in attempts to predefine the terms by which the younger generation entered the world outside of their immediate families. It constituted an elaborate, if only implicitly understood, strategy to steward, shepherd, control, and otherwise organize the character of social change, the processes that historians like to call modernization. The instruments of reform were political and educational. The object was moral regulation, character development, and ultimately control over the consciousness of the rising generation.

The process of narrowing the range of association for the young was not uniform. Nor did it happen to all children at the same time. In fact, it appears to have proceeded in two waves: the first, occurring roughly between 1800 and 1835; the second between 1835 and continuing until very recently. Beginning early in the century, a first wave of reformers concentrated their efforts on providing children with the rudiments of literacy, creating schools in the multiplicity of work, church, and community settings in which children spent their time. For a relatively small group of children from laboring and poor classes who, for one reason or another were orphaned, impoverished, ill, neglected, or delinquent, reformers constructed refuges or asylums. Satisfied in this early period to make opportunities for schooling and worship available, they did not

seek to substitute school for work or to transform the character of relationships between parents and children. This sort of work became the
burden and the joy of a second generation of reformers.

TINKERERS: THE REFORMERS AND THEIR REFORMS:
1790–1835

For the first half of the nineteenth century, coalitions of moral reformers, including physicians, education reformers, and middle-class
and high-born women, began consciously to conceptualize children as
learners in need of carefully structured tutorial environments in which
their physical, intellectual, imaginative, and moral capacities would be
especially attended and nurtured. They began to define, organize, and
then to build organized learning communities for the young—projecting
special guardians, prescribing particular practices, and otherwise defining what children should know, do, and feel.

Among the first objects of protective concern were children of the
poor and laboring classes who, for one or another reason were orphaned,
impoverished, ill, neglected, or declared criminal. Seeking to withdraw
these young people from association with adult criminals in institutions
that co-mingled young and old, murderers and thieves, self-styled humanitarian reformers like John Griscom, Thomas Eddy, and Isabella
Graham in New York, Benjamin Rush and the Sisters of Charity in
Philadelphia, and Samuel Gallaudet in Boston constructed specialized
institutions: houses of refuge specifically for children.[22] Further to disentangle juvenile criminals from those who were merely unfortunate,
reformers in cities as diverse as New York, Baltimore, Boston, and Philadelphia constructed houses of reformation to incarcerate juvenile criminals.[23] Throughout the length and breadth of the then United States,
orphan asylums emerged to house and superintend children without
families. In Charleston (1792), child reformers removed all dependent
children to a public orphanage.[24] A City Council Rule for the Government of the Almshouse in New York City (1800) required the construction of a children's section with presiding nurses, educational facilities,
and a schoolmaster.[25] Asylums for female orphans emerged in Boston,
Philadelphia, New York, Baltimore, Savannah, and Washington, D.C.,
that is, wherever Female Benevolent Associations did their work.

The disposition to withdraw dependent children from association with
adults and juvenile offenders and to separate girls and boys represented
an attempt to immerse them in carefully structured tutorial environments in which their physical, intellectual, imaginative, and moral capacities would be especially attended and nurtured. The tutorial
environment of the early nineteenth-century reform imagination was
one that resembled the ideal domestic environment as it was defined by

the generality of Protestant settlers in the seventeenth and eighteenth centuries.[26] For these reformers, as it had been for divines like Cotton Mather, prayers, books, and sermons constituted the ideal focus of adult-child relationships. Through a process of vigilant tutorship, children would learn to govern their passions, not primarily by being whipped or otherwise beaten into submission, but by attending to the task of formal learning—memorizing and reciting passages from the Bible, learning to read and write, that is, deriving from books and especially worthy adults a vocabulary through which to organize and understand reality. Finding approval in formal intellectual expression, young people would somehow use their minds to direct their emotions, or so the reformers seemed to believe.

Their belief in the capacity of intellectual exercise to overwhelm emotional excesses and to deflect corruption is reflected in the disposition of reformers to describe the array of institutions housing dependent and delinquent children as educational. Indeed, they referred to asylums as schools, inmates as scholars, guards as teachers, and incarceration as a pedagogical necessity rather than a punishment.[27] It is reflected as well in the aims of incarceration as they were defined by reformers.

The children shall be educated, fed and clothed at the expense of the Society, and at the Asylum. They must have religious instruction, moral example, and habits of industry inculcated on their minds. As soon as the age and acquirements of the Children ... shall render them capable of earning their living, they must be bound out to some reputable persons or families.[28]

The commitment to the suppression of emotion through the cultivation of intellect is symbolized by the pride with which humanitarian reformers celebrated their successes with residents of one of the female refuges in New York City in 1825: "3,052 female students had memorized 25,030 catechism answers, 144,685 answers to McDowell's questions, 189,191 scripture verses, and 26,500 hymn verses."[29] In a memorial to the legislature of New York requesting a charter for the creation of a first house of refuge in New York City, the directors of the New York Society for the Reformation of Juvenile Delinquents asserted the then widespread conviction that specialized tutorial environments would salvage the young from certain corruption and dissolution.

.... in an asylum, in which boys under a certain age, who become subject to the notice of our Police, either as vagrants, or houseless, or charged with petty crimes, may be received, be judiciously classed according to their degrees of depravity or innocence, put to work at such employments as will tend to encourage industry and ingenuity, taught reading, writing, and arithmetic, and most carefully instructed in the nature of their moral and religious obligations, while at the same time, they are subjected to a course of treatment, that will afford a prompt and energetic corrective of their vicious propensities.... Such an institution would in time exhibit scarcely any other than the character of a decent school and manufactury.[30]

The work of child-saving was not confined to the construction of asylums, specialized networks of association for homeless or delinquent young people. Constructing Sunday schools, infant schools, monitorial schools as well as asylums and refuges, a remarkable array of male and female moral reformers hoped to stem, if not to divert, a tide of moral contagion which they believed had spilled over onto the city streets. Benjamin Rush reflected what appears to have been a fundamental fear of social pollution:

The children of poor people form a great proportion of all communities. Their ignorance and vices when neglected are not confined to themselves; they associate and contaminate the children of persons in the higher ranks of society.... They have a complexion to the morals and manners of the people ... where the common people are ignorant and vicious ... a republican nation, can never be long free and happy.[31]

Proceeding on the assumption that the ability to read and write would have a disinfecting effect on the children of the laboring classes, early nineteenth-century educational reformers constructed schools in multiple settings. They built infant schools in factories, monitorial schools in cities and on army posts, and arranged low-cost schooling in the countryside.

Captivated by a view that literacy and restraint proceeded simultaneously, and that children, if they learned to read and write, would in the process learn to be good, Lancaster found a way to provide schooling at small cost where a single master could provide schooling for as many as 1,000 students simultaneously. Joseph Lancaster, an English Quaker and school reformer, provided a model for countless teachers in the early years of the nineteenth century. In his manuals, Lancaster left no minute of the day unexplained, left no student unattended. The plans were symbolized by his declaration, "A place for everything and everything in its place."[32] Lancaster arranged the instructional system so that students would at all times be responsible to designated authorities. There were monitors to take attendance, monitors to keep order, monitors for recess, and monitors in charge of monitors. The beauty of the system, remarked an English traveler, is that "nothing is trusted to the boy himself; he does not only repeat the lesson before a superior, but he learns it before a superior ... under the eye and command of a master."[33]

Not only did the monitorial system provide for a hierarchy of offices to which every student was bound by threat of physical or mental punishment, but the Lancasterian masters enforced rules and regulations that proscribed every conceivable physical movement of the students as well. In effect, teachers forced students to suspend their impulses; to derive their standards of conduct from the will of the monitors and master. The elaborate and carefully enforced rituals were designed to substitute the mechanical and systematic for the spontaneous and unpredictable. Not only did students have to hang up their coats on signal, but they also had to perform intellectual tasks in proper physical form.

While reading, as the eye rises to the top of the right hand page, the right hand is brought to the position, with the forefinger under the leaf, the hand is slid down to the lower corner, and retained there during the reading of the page. ... This also is the position in which the book is to be held when about to be closed; in doing which the left hand, being carried up to the side, supports the book firmly and unmoved, while the right hand turns the part it supports over the left thumb.... The thumb will then be drawn out between the leaves and placed on the cover; when the right hand will fall by the side.[34]

A student who attended a monitorial school in New York City recalled that every boy had to have "his left hand enclosed in his right...in a sort of self-handcuffed state, and woe be to him who is not paying attention when the order is given.... 'Hadn't hands behind' was a significant offense in this school."[35]

Whether they were sponsored by public or quasi-public school societies; whether they were conducted in churches, factories, building basements, or especially built school houses; whether they housed boys or girls, three years old as they might have been in infant schools or sixteen or eighteen as they commonly were in factories, children learned to read and write in an atmosphere of relentless regulation. It was an atmosphere designed to stamp out differences among individual students, to secure a rigid conformity to rules and regulations as dictated by teachers, to substitute the rule of law for the rule of personal persuasion, to disconnect children from networks of personal communication and engage them, instead, in a highly controlled world of books and print.[36] For these children, learning to read and write constituted a process that detached the written word from the public world of face-to-face communication. As they entered school, they entered an isolating world in which teachers used the printed word to effect a psychological transformation in their students. The schoolroom was a place in which learning to be a student meant learning to withdraw from informal sociability and to present a prescribed self—to develop, in short, a public or social personality.[37]

Infant schools, flourishing for a half-century from around 1790 to about 1838, served the children of working-class parents in factories.[38] Enjoying a vogue with certain groups of factory owners and humanitarian reformers who feared the dissolution of morality and manners among the children of their employees, infant schools provided children with periodic daily infusions of instruction in the three R's. The enthusiasm with which teachers entered into the task of imparting the rudiments of literacy to young children is reflected in the critical disposition of certain members of the Boston Infant School Society in 1833: "the schools are made into mere pieces of machinery for developing the intellect"[39] Engaged in the mass production of literacy, infant school advocates instituted the monitorial or lancasterian system, impressing visitors by presenting children who had become "prodigies in mere intellect," doing "those infantile feats which would have done more honor to learned brutes than to beings endowed with wisdom."[40]

Seeking to immerse children in networks of association that would assure their moral and intellectual nurture, reformers also constructed Sunday schools to serve children whom they believed to be deprived of decent influences.[41] Typically part of the missionary efforts of various religious denominations, Sunday schools, like infant and free schools, were designed to supplement, if not to displace, parents as moral and cognitive nurturers. The hopes of Sunday school reformers were reflected in the rhetoric of Samuel Slater, a preeminent factory owner and moral reformer of the early nineteenth century:

The introduction of manufacturing was . . . a harbinger of moral and intellectual improvement, to the . . . numerous operatives from remote and secluded parts of the country. . . . Hundreds of families . . . originally from places where the general poverty had precluded schools and public ownership, brought up illiterate and without religious instruction, and disorderly and vicious in consequence of their lack of regular employment, have been transplanted to these new creations of skill and enterprise; and by the ameliorating effects of study, industry, and instruction, have been reclaimed, civilised, Christianised.[42]

As they secured support for, planned, organized, and constructed refuges to house abandoned children, and schools for others to attend, reformers—the city's elites—chose schooling, in one form or another, to uplift, correct, and direct some of the children of laboring classes. Like the legions of Protestant settlers who preceded them, early nineteenth-century reformers defined systematic intellectual training as indispensable instruments of moral and social order.

They did not seek to substitute school for work, or to transform the character of relationships between parents and children. Nor did they seek to impose institutional constraints and regulations on children by detaching them systematically and legally from their families. The efforts of early nineteenth-century reformers to enclose children in circles of protection led them to build asylums and schools, but not to reconstruct the nature of childrearing and the meaning of childhood. This sort of work became the burden of reformers and the characteristic of reform efforts after 1830.

TRANSFORMERS: CONSTRUCTING TWO CIRCLES OF PROTECTION, HOME AND SCHOOL, 1835–1870

Attempts to purify the environments of the young, and to limit and/ or reorganize their networks of association, were made manifest in a stunning effusion of new reform sentiment, strategies, and structural rearrangements of childhood experience in the period between 1830 and 1870. An almost obsessive attention to sources of moral corruption appears to have inspired a preoccupation with the means of moral education in the years from 1830 to 1870. The commitment to purity involved the projection of women as proper guardians of moral sensibility in the young, and of families as moral refuges from the corrupting influences of strangers and workplaces. It united a coalition of physicians, ministers, and middle-class women.[43] It involved the discovery of child abuse and neglect, and of corrupt families bereft of pedagogical fathers and nurturing mothers. It involved a reconstruction of refuges and asylums to reflect domestic rather than military models of discipline.[44] The construction of reform schools and industrial schools and the identification of foster families were similarly the work of purity coalitions. It was central to the mentalities of school reformers, who, as they constructed common schools and kindergartens in the nineteenth century, defined schools as they had once defined families—as cognitive and psychological bridges between the increasingly differentiated world of family and workplace, men and women, children and adults. It was through transformed networks of influence and authority that children would build their moral armentaria.

During these thirty-five years, reformers constructed blueprints, or, as Clifford Geertz likes to call them, "templates of experience"[45] for the young, and proceeded to advocate, and finally to build a dazzling array of tutorial environments. So powerful was the force of their commitment to social purification that reformers constructed blueprints requiring the construction of more schools, more laws to effect the substitution of public for private authority over the disposition of activities for certain classes of children, and to effect a substitution of the authority of teachers for that of employers. They projected teachers as specialized nurturers, acting in place of parents in the important work of cultivating the intellect. They defined schools as transitional institutions, crucibles in which to place children and from which they would emerge freed from narrowmindedness and privatism while simultaneously armed with the cognitive wherewithal, that is, internal moral gyroscopes with which to thread their way through turbulent and unpredictable social seas, to resist temptation, as well as to work in a rapidly changing labor market.[46]

It is possible to explore the precise dimension of transformations in childrearing sentiments and social practices by exploring the ways in which stages of childhood came to be understood and then socially organized. Perhaps reflecting their discomfort with unchecked and uncontrolled environments, reformers seemed to proceed on the assumption that children required circles of protection that would shield them from adverse influence.

Very young children, those at birth to about the age of five or six, required an environment purged of worldly character. Projecting an isolated domestic sphere as a fit environment for infants, reformers sought to withdraw them from association with almost any adult besides their mothers. Older children, those from about the ages of five or six to fourteen or fifteen, required formal education. For these young people, reformers projected schools as ideal environments, seeking to withdraw children from the workplace, the streets, the fields, and from informal sociability with unspecified adults and peers. Between 1835 and 1870, reformers engaged in a formidable array of activities designed to reorganize the structures of persuasion into which children would enter, to narrow their range of association, and to control the character of their associates.

CONSTRUCTING INFANCY: REFUGES FOR THE YOUNG, 1835–1870

Between 1835 and 1870, there was a veritable outpouring of opposition to premature mental, emotional, and social exertion in a literature of domestic advice, in the reports of educational administrators, progressive pedagogs, and in the pages of professional education journals.[47] Defining education as a two-way interaction between children and adults, reformers, educationists, physicians, and moralists of one sort or another began to distinguish a period of infancy from one of childhood. In their infancy—from birth to the ages of five or six years old—children, they argued, were essentially under the control of animal impulses. Active beings, all of them, very young children required guidance, not repression, activity rather than confinement, sensitive tutoring from a totally available, benevolent mentor.[48]

Vulnerable in the extreme to corruption and overexcitement, they required protection—a purging of their environment of vulgar and debasing influences. Protection had a number of meanings. For some reformers it meant protection from premature association with people outside the immediate domestic circle of mothers and fathers.[49] Charles

Strickland explained the purification process as it was understood by Bronson Alcott:

Required, he [Alcott] thought, was a secluded setting for ideal child-rearing: one which would screen out such harmful influences as relatives, who might be inclined to rely more on tradition and custom than on the latest child-rearing wisdom. Bad influences would include also neighbors, who in their ignorance would invade the household, bringing along noxious diseases and subjecting the babies to fondling, jostling, tossing, bounding, rocking—all disturbing the infants. Still another threat... was posed by servants, especially Irish girls, who, with their boisterous ways and vulgar speech, might contaminate both the morals and the speech of the youngsters.... Vulgar books and vulgar behavior of neighboring children, especially working-class children, posed a threat to the antiseptic atmosphere which the parents labored to create.[50]

Not the least of moral dangers confronting children was intimate contact with wet-nurses—strangers from whom children might draw bad habits. In an attempt to dissuade mothers from hiring nurses for their infants, reformers implicitly gave educational dimension to the mothers' role in infant life. "With the mother's milk, the young child drinketh education," stated one of them.[51] Defining the ideal household as a place apart, "a utopian retreat from the city," a "haven," an antidote from "fever nests and centers of ignorance and crime,"[52] reformers also articulated a norm of maternal perfection, what Jane Mulligan has called the Maternal Redeemer complex. Mothers, by virtue of their inherent gentleness and moral superiority, were the proper agents of moral education. The work of moral nurture required the social isolation of mother and child and an intensification in their relationships. Not only was the ideal household understood to protect children from the contagion of unhealthy social influences and of corrupt values, but it also placed mothers in a position of strategic importance for the developing sensibility of the child. She became responsible for control over the entire environment in which the young child would grow and develop.[53]

Afraid of sexual and social precocity, reformers were equally fearful of premature mental exertion. Apparently proceeding as though they believed that children were corrupted by ambitious parents, reformers directed a veritable avalanche of advice to parents, encouraging them to attend to moral and psychological, rather than intellectual, nurture.[54]

One important ingredient in the prescriptive diet being fed to parents was an injunction against intellectual forcefeeding. Emphasizing the gradual and constant unfolding of the mental powers, reformers as diverse as Bronson Alcott, George Combe, Thomas Gallaudet, Jacob Abbot, and Lydia Childs, all called for a new form of moral culture for the young child, emphasizing the need for some physical and emotional space. Moral reformers of the 1830s, 1840s, and 1850s rejected traditional evangelical notions—that children should be engaged as early as possible in the tasks of formal education—learning to read, write, and recite. As part of an emerging commitment to domesticity, reformers reconceptualized the ideal parent-child relationship as organized not around the tasks of formal instruction, but around the requirements of a growing child.[55] "In attempting to call forth and cultivate the intellectual faculties of children before they are six or seven years old ... lasting injury has been done both to body and mind," asserted Amariah Brigham, a popular physician.[56] "Early mental excitement will only serve to bring beautiful, but premature flowers which are destined to wither away." "Don't teach infants their letters ... lest they develop a fatal langor resulting from premature mental exertion," intoned William Woodbridge.[57]

Rejecting a rigidly tutorial environment for young children, reformers substituted a view of parents as moral and psychological midwives, gently molding the growth of children. Mothers ought to drench their children in sensuous experience, surrounding them in a world of natural and attractive objects. Orson Fowler advised mothers to "replace school lessons and sedentary task lessons with nature walks," where the first reasoning power is cultivated.[58] Wrote a woman named Robinson in a prize-winning essay, "during the period of infancy, children should experience books as a form of amusement, at the domestic hearth."[59] "Allow children a quiet pursuit of their observations," advised Jacob Abbot, author of the Rollo books and innumerable childrearing manuals.[60] Lydia Childs offered this advice in the Mothers' Book: "First stimulate bodily senses, by presenting attractive objects to the child ... things of bright and beautiful colors ... and sounds pleasant and soft to the ear."[61] The newly idealized family involved mothers in close observation of children, instructive conversation, and organization of children's play.

An environment purged of worldly character, the domestic sphere of the reformer's imagination, placed a shield of morality around the young child, disentangling her or him from the corrupting influence of the streets, the workplace, and even the schools. Not trusting the willingness of mothers to assume the considerable burdens of moral nurture, reformers also sought to bar young children from attendance at school.

Their commitment to environmental purification inspired political as well as rhetorical activity. In a creative study of Massachusetts education, Carl F. Kaestle and Maris A. Vinovskis have identified the existence of educational spokespersons and medical authorities who "waged a slow but successful battle with parents" to keep their young children at home.[62] Defining intellectual precocity as a disease and schools as bastions of bad influence for young children, reformers wrote school attendance regulations excluding children under the age of six from attending public schools. While there was no agreement about an appropriate age for schoolgoing, reformers were nonetheless united in a commitment to constructing personal, domesticated enclosures for children under the ages of six or seven, agreed on the devastating effects of premature association with teachers, students, and systematic intellectual drill. "Those who proscribe precocity equated it with premature sophistication, premature independence, and intellectual over-exertion."[63] "The legitimate purpose of [infant] schools," reported the Boston Infant School Society in 1838, "was not for making prodigies in mere intellect, but as an aid for a time, for parental care."[64] "Many parents who have both the leisure and ability to instruct their children themselves and at home, through idleness or fondness for company send mere infants from parental influence, and from home, and thrust them into a public school.... In most there is danger of improper associations." Or, so argued Reverend Daniel Smith of New York in 1838.[65] In a discussion of the need to nurture moral sensibilities in the young child, Bronson Alcott described the ideal mentor: "He is to inform the understanding by chastening the appetites, allaying the passions, softening the affections . . . giving pliancy and force to the will.... Much systematic instruction is repulsive to the habits and feelings of infancy."[66] Horace Mann apparently agreed. Children, he argued in 1842, "should be prepared to acquire knowledge as they needed it and not to be loaded like beasts of burden"[67]; "what was called the love of knowledge," he wrote in another place, "was necessarily crammed into a love of books."[68] Even school committees began to reflect a belief in the dangers of premature schooling. The school committee of Weymouth, Massachusetts, put its objective in this way:

Children under four years of age, should not be sent to school.... If such children (sixty six of whom have been in our schools the last year) are required to attend school that their minds may be tasked with the discipline of study, it should be understood that this is generally injurious to the child's mental and physical frame.[69]

So successful were the reformers that not a single school statute regulating school attendance included children under the ages of six or seven as fit objects for compulsory instruction at public expense.

Directed primarily at middle-class and high-born women, the campaign to transform and re-create the substance of nurture within the household was hortatory and didactic, rather than systematic or coercive. Seeking to protect the young child from an array of perceived dangers, reformers imagined a wall of psychological protection that would simultaneously withdraw young children from too-early public association with strangers and dangers, while providing them with suitable guardians for their moral well-being. Indeed, one of the more interesting tutorial environments emerging in the 1860s and 1870s was the kindergarten. The Children's Gardens were understood to be extensions of domestic nurture, helping to produce morally autonomous human beings—self-governed, self-motivated, self-disciplined, self-controlled. Viewing themselves as pedagogical midwives, rather than drillmasters, engaging each child as a separate moral entity, and preferring object lessons to drill, kindergartners institutionalized a new kind of tutorial environment. Neither wholly domestic nor fully public, the Kindergarten was a specialized educational institution, drawing children into a protected, quasi-public environment that was moral and personal rather than cognitive and impersonal in its deliberate emphases.[70]

The assumption that public schools, public streets, and public associations were inappropriate social spaces for very young children informed the substance of advice to parents, inspired the conception of the kindergarten, and shaped the character of some political activity. With the exception of the campaign to push young children out of schools, domestic reformers did not seek to compel parents through the use of institutional constraints and simulations. Nor did they seek government intervention. Instead, they relied on the power of persuasion, seeking a transformation of the family from within it.[71] They convinced parents, and most especially mothers, to seize on medical and ministerial exhortations and "to use them to free children from the allegedly stifling grip of domestic servants and social promiscuities, construing around the child an educative model ... what Jacques Donzelot calls a process of 'protected liberation'."[72]

CONSTRUCTING INFANCY FOR LABORING AND DEPENDENT CLASSES

The construction of infancy proceeded on a different channel for the children of the urban lower classes, and most especially for the children of immigrant families. Less confident, or, as it may have happened, less able to engage the attention or sympathies of these families, reformers supplemented prescription and exhortation with institutional constraints and stimulations. Aimed at making the moral nurture of children the center of family life as they had tried to do with middling and highborn parents, they also constructed the legal means by which to remove children from households where families were failing in the task of moral instruction, and placed children in asylums, refuges, and the like. The purposes of the Children's Aid Society, and the rhetoric of its founder, Charles Loring Brace, were suffused with intense moral concern and belief in the power of moral education, the sentiments echoed by all manner of nineteenth-century child-savers:[73]

We have attempted to reach but one portion [of the poor in cities]—the children, believing that effort for them is the most hopeful and practical and that, through them, the parents can best be effected. Our objects have been the improvement and elevation of the vagrant and poor children of the street, boys and girls; and of those engaged in the petty outdoor trades; and those who beg or pilfer, or pick the streets for a living, and those who are driven by homelessness and poverty to the prison, and who are confined there for petty crimes.... the feeling with those engaged in this enterprise, is that childhood is never to be despaired of; that the habits and passions of the street boy or girl, can never be beyond the reach of kindly or religious influences, and that their faults are to be mildly judged, in memory of the pressing temptations and the hard circumstances which have surrounded them.[74]

Reformers did not attempt to mute the force of circumstances only by constructing schools for the mass of urban poor families to use on a voluntary basis. After 1835, they also engaged local and state governments in the work of moral reform by seeking to bring children under the control of public authorities. What this meant in the mid-nineteenth century was a transfer of authority over children from fathers to governments, from private families to public agencies when parents appeared incapable of or unwilling to govern their children and provide them with networks of good influence. Denying a writ of habeus corpus to the father of Mary Ann Crouse who had petitioned the managers of the House of Refuge in Philadelphia to return custody of his daughter, the Pennsylvania court defined moral education to be a public as well as a private concern:

The object of the charity is reformation, by training its inmates to industry; by imbuing their minds with principles of morality and religion; by furnishing them with means to earn a living; and above all, by separating them from the corrupting influence of improper associates. To this end, may not the natural parents, when unequal to the task of education, or unworthy of it, be superseded by the parents patria, or common guardian of the community? It is to be remembered that the public has a paramount interest in the virtue and knowledge of its members and that, of strict right, the business of education belongs to it. That parents are ordinarily entrusted with it, is because it can seldom be put in better hands; but where they are incompetent or corrupt, what is there to prevent the public from withdrawing their faculties, held, as they obviously are, at its sufferance? The right of parental control is a natural, but not an inalienable one.[75]

The court gave effective voice to those who had identified infancy as a stage in the life cycle when children were entitled to publicly sanctioned and supported networks of good influence. Its educative meaning was well understood by legions of Catholic ministers. Recognizing that moral nurture was no longer assumed to be the province of families or of churches, Levi Silliman Ives, minister and philanthropist, objected:

Steps are taken...to place a bar between these children and their parents...
they [the children] are undergoing a secret process by which it is hoped, that
every trace of their early faith and filial attachment will be rooted out; and
finally, that their transportation to that indefinite region, "the far west," with
changed names and low parentage, will effectually destroy every association
which might revive in their hearts a love for the religion of which they had been
robbed—the religion of their parents.[76]

Referring to the practice of fostering or binding out children to rural
Protestant families, what the Children's Aid Society called a policy of
emigration, Ives recognized that moral concern for the young had become a strategy of cultural domination as well as an attempt to minister
to the "captives of urban wretchedness." The product not only of status
anxieties, but also economic necessities, totalitarian aims, and even expert
advice, new structures of persuasion and nurture emerged out of a fear
of worldliness and a recognition of new social, moral, and individual
liberties and dangers.

What is intriguing about the social and psychological structures that
were created for the moral nurture of young children in the nineteenth
century was that they only rarely required "bully club coercion."[77] While
in certain cases legal authority for the custody of the very young was,
in fact, transferred from the family to the state, in general families were
persuaded rather than coerced. The product of a fascinating alliance
among physicians, women, middle-class Protestant, Jewish, even some
Catholic families, ministers of multiple denominations, and a small cadre
of organized working-class groups, the transformation of authority and
processes of nurture did not centralize and regulate childrearing processes for the very young. In fact, nineteenth-century domestic reformers
decentralized moral nurture, investing mothers with greater power over
the nurture of their children than had their seventeenth- and eighteenth-
century forbears.[78] Bequeathing social arrangements and mythic structures that tied the fate of women and young children inexorably together, reformers attempted to withdraw children from community
centers into households, from public to private spheres, from the authority of fathers to that of mothers.

Attempts to immerse young children in personal and intense associations with women of exemplary character within a family or kindergarten constituted but one form of a multifaceted attempt to narrow the
range of association for the young—the better to provide them with
sensitive moral guardians.

CONSTRUCTING CHILDHOOD: THE FATE OF
CHILDREN SIX TO FOURTEEN

For older children, those roughly between the ages of six and fourteen
years, reformers turned to schools, rather than families and churches,

as environments that offered the most promising networks of good influence for the rising generation. Following the paths of political reform that had characterized the work of child-savers in the cities, a coalition of ministers, physicians, women, humanitarians, and workingmen engaged in a series of slowly evolving, but ultimately successful, attempts to disengage children from workplaces, and from small circles of values, beliefs, and associations in family and church.[79] For the architects of public education, schools appeared to be the best institutions in which to provide highly controlled networks of association that were smaller, more protected, and more controllable than the marketplace, the street, or field, but larger than the immediate circles of parents, ministers, and playmates. Horace Mann gave voice to these sentiments: "At school... every child succeeds to so much more in the property of the community as is necessary for his education... not in the form of gold and silver, but in the form of knowledge and training of good habits."[80]

The moral possibilities of schooling did not elude countless other public school advocates. William A. Mowry, a professional teacher in rural schools for over half a century, suggested that country schools and teachers performed a unique socializing function. The farm, he explained, "furnished the members of only one family as companions." But the district school, to a large extent, remedied this defect and gave the very best social stimulus to children:

Here the boys receive their first lessons in true democracy. All children of the neighborhood meet on a common level. To all are accorded the same rights, to all are assigned the same tasks, in all the same powers are developed, and all are subject to the same discipline. Each boy measures himself with his peers.[81]

"A school..." recalled a Southern gentleman who had attended old field schools in the South in the 1840s and 1850s, "is a world within itself. In it the inhabitants learn to give and take as they must do in the larger world after school days are over."[82] And a New England master who had taught in the 1820s, 1830s, and 1840s remembered years later that he "had charge of forty children... from every kind of family, representing every phase of human nature. The bright and the stupid, the roguish and the ugly, the restless and the turbulent were all huddled in together, a little world in embryo...."[83] "[Q]uite apart from any special subject matter," remarked Henry Johnson, "we received our most amazing practice in fundamental social virtues."[84]

However inadvertently, public school advocates had become aware of the uses of literacy in the service of organizing civic consciousness and of defining a civil as well as a religious core of symbolism for students to internalize. Their concern with morality took the form of a commitment to civic education in public schools.

Common school reformers knew that the processes of learning to read and write could induce young people to loosen bonds of affiliation as well as to reinforce them. The acquisition of literacy, after all, involves people in what Walter J. Ong has called "a silent world of books and print."[85] Projected into a world of orderly structure and sequence, of fixed and contained culture, students experienced a different sort of learning reality from that which is defined in personal face-to-face communities,[86] almost forcing an evaluation of their experience.

Aiming to undermine the authority of churchmen and the binding power of religious commitments, public school advocates were attentive to the fund of allusion, fable, and sentiment that could be made available in schools. A veritable avalanche of new textbooks and reading materials for children of school age evolved in the nineteenth century. The heroes and heroines of the texts were national figures, patriots who were moral because they were honest, diligent, and enterprising. They were public servants rather than ministers, political stewards rather than religious authorities, politicians rather than churchmen.[87]

Some of the new heroines and heroes were boys and girls, living virtuous lives in public. "In hundreds of thin and predictable narratives," writes Anne S. MacCleod, "the example of the good child was opposed to the example for the wayward, and the advantage of goodness over evil demonstrated. Bad children came to grief swiftly and surely; good children found rewards of happiness, approval, and . . . worldly success." Obedient, self-disciplined, self-governed, and self-controlled, the idealized child of the writer's imagination was obedient to authority and engaged in the world of commerce and trade.[88] There is no small irony in the fact that the child of their fictional imaginations was a public child, engaged in the world, but the schoolchild was a child withdrawn.

Seeking to provide children with an alternative symbolic universe and a succession of worldly little role models, common school advocates also sought to inform the consciousness of the young by providing exemplary teachers. As concerned with the moral dispositions as with the intellectual attainments of students and teachers alike, they projected women as the proper guardians of classrooms—the creators of self-governed, self-controlled, self-disciplined, and virtuous republicans—who could embody in their behavior and disposition a fusion of public and private good. Unlike men, for whom teaching was but a temporary way station to the world, women would provide stability, giving "the scholars the advantage of having the same instructress throughout the year."[89] Possessing a "native tact" in the management of young minds, women were infinitely preferable as stewards of school-age children. "They would conduce to the improvement of manners and morals in the schools, since females attached more importance to these than men." Women also possessed a peculiar power of awakening sympathies in children and inspiring them with a desire to learn.[90] In other words, women were ideally suited to act as molders of moral sensibilities and architects of restraint.

The deliberate construction of virtuous citizens required a new code of discipline as well as a new core of symbolism and new forms of authority in the classroom. Through the agency of schools, reformers also hoped to create public personalities deliberately. A distaste for corporal punishment permeates the literature of school reform.[91] Arguing that corporal punishment hardened and debased rather than softened and elevated, a bevy of reformers counseled restraint—and for social as well as humanitarian and religious ends. Advocating the use of moral persuasion rather than physical coercion, they implicitly redefined the role of the teacher—from intellectual steward and moral guide, to social guardian and organizer of conscience. Concern with the moral effects of corporal punishment inspired Lyman Cobb to identify moral concern as a political necessity as well as an aid to salvation: "[the student] must be convinced that it is not only his duty and his interest to be good; that he will be more respected, more happy . . . when he leaves school. . . . He [should be] influenced and controlled by reason."[92] What moral persuasion might have meant in practice is reflected in this song of praise to a Boston teacher who had the following reaction to a boy who had shouted, "by Moses, ain't it cold," as he entered a Boston classroom:

. . . she sketched, in language suited for childish comprehension, the early history of the exposure of the "pretty infant" in a "little rush cradle" on the shore of the Nile . . . how the good God had called him to set free so many slaves; what a humility and reverence he always showed . . . how many trials he went through . . . how, at last, after all his labors, he was not allowed to enjoy the beautiful prospect along the Jordan. . . . Don't you think Moses deserves more respect and honor than Oscar showed to his name when he used it in the form of swearing, yesterday?[93]

After she had finished the lecture, she sent the students home in order to think about the processes through which they had gone to expunge improper words from their vocabularies. A less gentle, though nonetheless real, appeal to conscience is described by a student whose teacher announced publicly that she was not a fit person to be in school with such a good name. A New York City teacher explained to a visitor that they maintained order by appealing to the "self-respect of the girls themselves, and the older show an example to the younger."[94] Aimed at exposing unacceptable behavior to public observation, the appeal to shame implicitly gave moral awareness a public dimension.

The templates of experience created by public school ideologies constituted a radical re-imagination of the structures of persuasion that would inform the consciousness of children between the ages of six and fourteen. The structures would weave around children a network of female rather than male associations. They would provide them with an altered cloth of allusion, fable, and sentiment that would re-present, ideal-lize, and civil-ize the world outside their small networks of association in family and church. The new structures of persuasion would, if prop-erly constructed, provide a window on the world, revealing its contours and possibilities, rather than the whole of its realities and degradations—a disinfected if not entirely purified educative environment.[95] By 1870, it involved all children, rich and poor, black and white; it was defined as a universal necessity.

The blueprints called for the construction of schools and for the sub-stitution of the authority of teachers for that of employers. They proj-ected teachers as specialized nurturers—a supplement and a substitute for parents. Transitional institutions—the public schools of the reform imagination—were new and specialized transitions to the world, a kind of crucible in which to place children together and through which they would emerge, freed from narrow clusters of likemindedness and pri-vatism. And they would be armed—with the moral and cognitive where-withal to resist temptation, impulse, and aggression as well as to work in a rapidly changing labor market. Through extended schooling, they would acquire an internalized moral gyroscope to guide them through dangerous social seas.

To these ends, reformers rewrote textbooks, constructed teacher train-ing institutions, and initiated licensing procedures. They wrote, and they politicked in behalf of laws requiring school attendance and limiting child labor. The dazzling multiplicity of their efforts constituted a fun-damental modification of, if not an all-out attack on, informal and tra-ditional modes of personal and patriarchal authority in favor of the authority of rules—the invariable characteristic of modern institutional life.[96]

CONCLUSION

Paradoxically, mid-nineteenth-century reformers had actually imag-ined the conditions of political freedom and liberation to require a web of restraints. It was a web to be weaved first by mothers in the home and then by teachers in schools.

Recognizing the inadequacy of traditional modes of authority, nine-teenth-century reformers turned to women and to families to organize learning and establish identity initially for most, if not all, infants. They turned to schools and teachers to undo the effects—to qualify and rein-form the fund of allusion, fable, and sentiment, that is, the consciousness that children had acquired at home. Defining the family as the source of community stability or disintegration, they defined the schools as instruments of detribalization.[97] Taken together, these two educative agencies would engage young people in processes that would link them to the community and individualize them simultaneously, leading them out from under the influence of their own baser instincts as well as society's debasing ones, and thereby prepare them to reform the larger society into which they entered, or so the reformers hoped.

By the end of the nineteenth century, more and more children between the ages of six and fourteen were spending more and more time in school. Younger children were spending less and less.[98] No matter how inchoate or marginal to their awareness, educators had built the social structures and psychological meaning of infancy and childhood that would be scientifically described and politically advanced in the latter part of the nineteenth and early decades of the twentieth centuries by physicians, health professionals, scientists, and organized educators.

NOTES

1. For examples of excellent histories that demonstrate this approach, see Steven L. Schlossman, *Love and the American Delinquent: The Theory and Practice of Progressive Juvenile Justice, 1825–1920* (Chicago: University of Chicago Press, 1977); Raymond A. Mohl, *Poverty in New York, 1783–1825* (New York: Oxford University Press, 1971); Michael B. Katz, *The Irony of Early School Reform: Educational Innovation in Mid-Nineteenth Century Massachusetts* (Cambridge, Mass.: Harvard University Press, 1968); Elizabeth Badinter, *L'Amour en Plus: Histoire de l'Amour Maternel, 17éme-20éme Siècles* (Paris: Flamarrion, 1980); Joseph F. Kett, *Rites of Passage: Adolescence in America, 1790 to the Present* (New York: Basic Books, 1977).

2. This approach is especially exemplified in Schlossman's monograph where attempts to disentangle children from the streets or factories and to place them instead in school settings lead him to assert that the intention was to uplift and establish surveillance over the lower orders of society, assuming that this was somehow a principal sentiment driving reform. See Schlossman, *Love and the American Delinquent*, 20.

3. The shortcoming of this approach and interpretive scheme can be seen with particular clarity in David Nasaw, *Schooled to Order: A Social History of Public Schooling in the United States* (New York: Oxford University Press, 1980). For a systematic criticism, see Barbara Finkelstein, "Educational History in the Pursuit of Justice," *Reviews in American History* 8, No. 1 (March 1980): 122–128.

4. For examples of excellent histories using this approach, see Joseph M. Hawes, *Children in Urban Society: Juvenile Delinquency in Nineteenth Century America* (New York: Oxford University Press, 1971); John Duffy, "School Buildings and the Health of American School Children in the Nineteenth-Century," in Charles E. Rosenberg, ed., *Healing and History* (New York: Basic Books, 1979); Charles E. Strickland, "Paths Not Taken: Seminal Models of Early Childhood Education in Jacksonian America," in Bernard Spodek, ed., *Handbook of Research on Early Childhood Education* (New York: Free Press, 1982), ch. 14; Robert H. Bremner,

et al., *Children and Youth in America: A Documentary History* (Cambridge, Mass.: Harvard University Press, 1979), Vol. 1, 1600–1865; Bertram Wyatt-Brown, "Child Abuse, Public Policy, and Child-rearing in America: An Historical Approach," Working Paper No. 2 (College Park, Md.: University of Maryland, Center for the Study of Education Policy and Human Values, 1981).

5. David J. Rothman, *The Discovery of the Asylum: Social Order and Disorder in the New Republic* (Boston: Little, Brown & Co., 1971), ch. 9.

6.. For examples, see R. Freeman Butts, *Public Education in the United States: From Revolution to Reform* (New York: Holt, Rinehart & Winston, 1978); Lawrence A. Cremin, *American Education: The Colonial Experience, 1607–1782* (New York: Harper & Row, 1970); *American Education: The National Experience, 1783–1876* (New York: Harper & Row, 1980).

7. For particularly graphic examples, see "The Evolution of Childhood," in Lloyd deMause, ed., *The History of Childhood* (New York: Psychohistory Press, 1974). DeMause's scheme places nineteenth-century institutionalization in the context of newly emerging childrearing modes that enabled certain classes of reformers to perceive that children needed protection and nurture, restraint rather than punishment. He calls this newly emerging mode the socialization mode, suggesting that it represented a progressive step forward in the evolution of parent-child relationships. Its social products were schools and school teachers, and an emphasis on moral rather than physical modes of persuasion.

8. For example, see Carl F. Kaestle and Maris A. Vinovskis, "From Apron Strings to ABCs: Parents, Children and Schooling in Nineteenth-Century Massachusetts," in John Demos and Sarane Spence Boocock, eds., *Turning Points: Historical and Sociological Essays on the Family* (Chicago: University of Chicago Press, 1978), S39–S81; Bernard Bailyn, *Education in the Forming of American Society: A Reinterpretation* (Chapel Hill: University of North Carolina Press, 1960); Lawrence Stone, *The Family, Sex, and Marriage in England, 1500–1800* (New York: Harper & Row, 1977).

9. See also Carl F. Kaestle, "Social Change, Discipline and the Common School in Early Nineteenth-Century America," *Journal of Interdisciplinary History* 10, no. 1 (Summer 1978): 1–17.

10. For examples, see Michael Ignatieff, "Prison and Factory Discipline: The Origins of an Idea," unpublished manuscript delivered at the annual meeting of the American Historical Association, Washington, D.C., 1976. The corpus of work done by Michel Foucault on prisons, sexuality, madness, work, and punishment all reflect the wedding of intellectual history and sociological functionalism. I am indebted to David Rothman's useful summary of approaches to the study of asylums for this observation. See Rothman, *Discovery of the Asylum*, xvi.

11. Barbara Finkelstein, "Pedagogy as Intrusion: Teaching Values in Popular Primary Schools in Nineteenth-Century America, 1820–1880," in Donald R. Warren, ed., *History, Education and Public Policy: Recovering the American Educational Past* (Berkeley, Calif.: McCutchan Co., 1978); "The Moral Dimensions of Pedagogy: Teaching Values in Popular Primary Schools in the Nineteenth-Century," *American Studies* 2 (Fall 1974): 79–91; "In Fear of Childhood: Relationships Between Parents and Teachers in Nineteenth-Century America," *History of Childhood Quarterly* 3, no. 3 (Winter 1976): 321–337.

12. For particularly brilliant examples, see Rothman, *Discovery of the Asylum*;

Carroll Smith-Rosenberg, "Sex as Symbol of Victorian Purity: An Ethnohistorical Analysis of Jacksonian America," in Demos and Boocock, eds., *Turning Points,* §212–248; Nancy F. Cott, *The Bonds of Womanhood: "Woman's Sphere" in New England, 1780–1835* (New Haven and London: Yale University Press, 1977); Barbara Laslett, "The Family as a Public and Private Institution: An Historical Perspective," in Arlene Skolnick and Jerome Skolnick, eds., *Intimacy, Family, and Society* (Boston: Little, Brown & Co., 1974), 94–114.

   13. Barbara M. Brenzel, "Domestication as Reform: A Study of the Socialization of Wayward Girls, 1856–1905," *Harvard Educational Review* 50, no. 2 (May 1980): 196–213; Rothman, *Discovery of the Asylum,* 197.

   14. Cott, *Bonds of Womanhood;* Smith-Rosenberg, "Sex as Symbol of Victorian Purity." See also Barbara Finkelstein, "Reading, Writing and the Acquisition of Identity in the United States: 1790–1860," in Barbara Finkelstein, ed., *Regulated Children/Liberated Children: Education in Psychohistorical Perspective* (New York: Psychohistory Press, 1979), ch. 5.

   15. My approach to the historical materials has been importantly molded by the work of several historians, sociologists, and anthropologists beyond the ones already cited. See Clifford Geertz, *The Interpretation of Cultures* (New York: Basic Books, 1973); Richard Sennett, *The Uses of Disorder: Personal Identity and City Life* (New York: Alfred A. Knopf, 1970); Philippe Aries, *Centuries of Childhood: A Social History of Family Life,* Robert Baldick, trans. (New York: Alfred A. Knopf, 1962); Jacques Donzelot, *The Policing of Families* (New York: Pantheon Books, 1st English ed., 1979); Thomas Bender, *Community and Social Change in America* (New Brunswick, N.J.: Rutgers University Press, 1978).

   16. For colonial educational arrangements and transformations, see Cremin, *American Education;* Robert Wiebe, *The Segmented Society* (New York: Oxford University Press, 1975), preface. See also the summaries of Bender, *Community and Social Change;* Barbara Finkelstein, "Exploring Community in Urban Educational History," in Diane Ravitch and Ronald R. Goodenow, eds., *The Community Study of Urban Educational History* (New York: Holmes & Meier, 1983), forthcoming.

   17. For an elaboration, see Finkelstein, ed., *Regulated Children/Liberated Children,* Introduction; Bender, *Community and Social Change,* 19–50; Wiebe, *Segmented Society,* passim.

   18. See Finkelstein, "Reading, Writing and the Acquisition of Identity in the United States"; Barbara Welter, *Dimity Convictions: The American Woman in the Nineteenth Century* (Athens, Ohio: Ohio University Press, 1976). For a few examples of ethnic subgroups, see Anthony F.C. Wallace, *The Death and Rebirth of the Seneca* (New York: Alfred A. Knopf, 1970).

   19. Excellent treatments of transformations in social and economic structure and consciousness can be found in Cott, *Bonds of Womanhood.* New community histories are a rich source of data on evolving colonial communities. See Richard Bushman on Connecticut towns; Kenneth Lockridge on Dedham; Philip Greven on Andover; John Demos on Plymouth Colony. See also Michael Zuckerman, *Peaceable Kingdoms* (New York: Alfred A. Knopf, 1970). For studies of poverty and its treatment, see Bernard J. Klebaner, "Poverty and Its Relief in American Thought, 1815–1916," *Social Service Review* 38 (1964): 382–399; Stephan Thernstrom and Richard Sennett, eds., *Nineteenth-Century Cities* (New Haven: Yale University Press, 1969). See also Bailyn, *Education in the Forming of American*

Society. Splendid bibliographies can be found in Cremin, *American Education: The Colonial Experience,* and *American Education: The National Experience.*

20. Studies of families in newly evolving factory towns and young men in cities reflect the reality of mobility and choice for young Protestants moving to new economic opportunities. For an exploration of the meaning of mobility for the evolution of children's institutions, see Robert Mennell, *Thorns and Thistles* (Hanover, N.H.: University Press of New England, 1973); Joseph M. Hawes, *Children in Urban Society: Juvenile Delinquency in Nineteenth-Century America* (New York: Oxford University Press, 1971). The nature of social transformations and responses is also explored in Mohl, *Poverty in New York*; Carroll Rosenberg, *Religion and the Rise of the American City* (Ithaca, N.Y.: Cornell University Press, 1971); Carl F. Kaestle, *The Evolution of an Urban School System* (Cambridge, Mass.: Harvard University Press, 1973).

21. Aries, deMause, Stone, and Donzelot have all placed this kind of concern in the mid-sixteenth century, though they describe it as crude and formative at this time. It is expressed in laws barring infanticide, in the construction of schools where age-grading emerged, in the evolution of convents acting as educational institutions, and so on.

For explorations of colonial childrearing attitudes and practices, see John Demos, *A Little Commonwealth: Family Life in Plymouth Colony* (New York: Oxford University Press, 1970); Philip Greven, *The Protestant Temperament: Patterns of Child-Rearing, Religious Experience, and the Self in Early America* (New York: Alfred A. Knopf, 1977); Edmund S. Morgan, *The Puritan Family: Essays on Religion and Domestic Relations in Seventeenth-Century New England* (Revised ed., New York: Harper & Row, 1964); N. Ray Hiner, "The Child in American Historiography," *Psychohistory Review* 11, no. 1 (Summer 1978): 13–23.

The theme of purification is, of course, not original. My views are derivative of those of Richard Sennett who has discussed its expression in suburban flights and other excluding behaviors in *The Uses of Disorder: Personal Identity and City Life*; see also Smith-Rosenberg, "Sex as Symbol of Victorian Purity."

There are innumerable diaries and autobiographies documenting the existence and character of tutorial parenthood. See Finkelstein, "Introduction," and "Reading, Writing and the Acquisition of Identity," in Finkelstein, ed., *Regulated Children/Liberated Children*, 137–138; and Greven, *Protestant Temperament*.

22. For summaries and analyses of the emergence of asylums and other child-saving activities, see Schlossman, *Love and the American Delinquent*; Bremner, et al., eds., *Children and Youth in America*, Vol. 1; Sol Cohen, *Education in the United States: A Documentary History* (New York: Random House, 1974), Vol. 2; Rothman, *Discovery of the Asylum*; Mohl, *Poverty in New York*, 576–599.

23. The widespread disposition of charitable societies to create asylums for children led Bremner and his associates to speak of a refuge movement, and Rothman to characterize it as a fundamental social response to the possibilities of disorder. See ch. 9; in Bremner, see *Children and Youth in America*, 1: 674–695.

24. 275–276.

25. Ibid., pp. 276–277. For summaries, rather than a complex analysis of the work of female voluntary networks, see Barbara J. Berg, "The City as School: Female Voluntary Societies: 1800–1860," in Diane Ravitch and Ronald R. Good-

enow, eds., *Educating an Urban People* (New York: Teachers College Press, 1980).
See also Barbara Finkelstein, "Education and the Cult of Domesticity," unpublished paper presented at Berkshire Conference of Women Historians, Bryn Mawr College, 1976.

26. This sentiment is so universally expressed that it is difficult even to begin to cite works; they would run literally into hundreds of items. The explication of this theme has been brilliantly presented in relation to political theory by Albert O. Hirschman, *The Passions and the Interests: Political Arguments for Capitalism Before Its Triumph* (Englewood Cliffs, N.J.: Prentice-Hall, 1977).
For an elaboration of traditional views of parents and children, see N. Ray Hiner, "Cotton Mather and His Children," in Finkelstein, ed., *Regulated Children/Liberated Children*, ch. 2, 24–44; and Ross W. Beales, "Anne Bradstreet and Her Children," in Finkelstein, ed., *Regulated Children/Liberated Children*, ch. 1, 10–24.
Philip Greven's *Protestant Temperament* contains the most detailed analyses of this mentality in the chapters exploring the meaning of evangelical childrearing. For Quaker attitudes, see Barry Levy, "Tender Plants: Quaker Farmers and Children in the Delaware Valley, 1681–1735," *Journal of Family History* 3 (June 1978): 116–133; and Greven, "Moderate" Child-rearing, in *Protestant Temperament*.

27. I am indebted for this insight to Steven L. Schlossman who articulated it in *Love and the American Delinquent*, p. 22.

28. "Constitution of the Washington, D.C. Female Orphan Society, from the Ladies' Minutes, 1815–1851," Washington City Orphan Asylum, Hillcrest Childrens' Center Papers: Library of Congress Manuscript Collections, Box 1 of 21.

29. Children's Aid Society, *First Annual Report*, passim.

30. New York Society for the Reformation of Juvenile Delinquents, "Memorial to the Legislature of New York . . . on the Subject of Creating a House of Refuge," 22.

31. Benjamin Rush, "Letter to the Citizens of Philadelphia and of the District of Southward and the Northern Liberties," in the *Independent Gazateer*, 27 March 1787, in Lyman H. Butterfield, ed., *Letters of Benjamin Rush* (Princeton: Princeton University Press, 1951), Vol. 1, 413–431.

32. Joseph Lancaster, *The British System of Education: Being a Complete Epitome of the Improvements and Inventions Practised by Joseph Lancaster: To Which Is Added a Report of the Trustees of the Lancaster School at Georgetown, Columbia* (Washington, D.C.: Joseph Milligan, 1812); Joseph Lancaster, *The Lancasterian System of Education with Improvements by Its Founder* (Baltimore: Published for the author, 1821), 4. The sources for this discussion of Lancasterian schools portray schools in Eastern cities—New York, Philadelphia, Washington, Baltimore, Pittsburgh. But there is guidance to suggest that monitorial schools in cities further west resembled those of the Eastern metropolises. Civic leaders from places such as Cincinnati and Lexington dispatched men to study schools in Baltimore, Philadelphia, New York, and Boston. Richard C. Wade, *The Urban Frontier: The Rise of Western Cities, 1790–1830* (Cambridge, Mass.: Harvard University Press, 1959), 105–125. Articles appear frequently in the *American Annals of Education and Instruction* and describe the progress made by Western cities in establishing monitorial schools.
Allusions to Lancasterian schools can also be found in other periodicals. See, for example, *American Journal of Education 1826–1830; Western Academician and Journal of Education and Science.*

The Joseph Lancaster Papers located in the American Antiquarian Society in Worcester, Massachusetts, also contain references to Lancasterian schools in many cities and military posts.

Manuals, prepared by Masters of Lancasterian schools in particular locations, also indicate their omnipresence. See, for example, William Dale, *A Manual of the Albany Lancasterian School* (Albany: n.p., 1820).

Some monographs also describe the development of Lancasterian schools. See Ronald Rayman, "Joseph Lancaster Monitorial System of Instruction and American Education, 1815–38," *History of Education Quarterly* 21, no. 4 (Winter 1981): 395–411; Charles Calvert Ellis, *Lancasterian Schools in Philadelphia* (Philadelphia: n.p., 1907); John Franklin Reigart, *The Lancasterian System of Instruction in the Schools of New York City* (New York: Teachers College Press, 1916). Several other historians allude to the presence of Lancasterian schools in particular states. See, for example, Moses Edward Ligon, *A History of Public Education in Kentucky* (Lexington: University of Kentucky Press, 1942), 33; Charles Lee Coon, *North Carolina Schools and Academies: 1790–1840: A Documentary History* (Raleigh: Edwards & Broughton Printing Co., 1915), 722–745; William Arthur Maddox, *The Free School Idea in Virginia before the Civil War* (New York: Teachers College Press, 1915).

33. Quoted in Paul Monroe, *The Founding of the American Public School System: A History of Education in the United States* (New York: Macmillan Co., 1940), 369.

34. Almost all authors describe this kind of physical uniformity. For example, see "My School-Boy Days in New York City Forty Years Ago," *New York Teacher and American Educational Monthly* 6 (March 1869), passim; Edward Strutt Abdy, *Journal of a Residence and Tour in the United States and North America* (London: John Murray, 1834), 152–153; Anne Royall, *Sketches of History, Life, Manners in the United States* (New Haven: Printed for the Author, 1826), 256; William Bentley Fowle, "Boston Monitorial Schools," *American Journal of Education* 1, no. 1 (January 1826): 39–40; John Griscom, *Memoir* (New York: Robert Carter & Brothers, 1859), 209; Thomas Hamilton, *Men and Manners in America* (2d American ed., Philadelphia: Carey, Lea, & Blanchard, 1833), 52–57; Basil Hall, *Travels in North America in the Years 1827 and 1828* (London: Simpkin & Marshall, 1829), 24–30; Carl David Arfwedson, *The United States and Canada in 1832, 1833, and 1834* (London: R. Bentley, 1834), 240.

35. "My School-Boy Days in New York City Forty Years Ago," 95.

36. Walter J. Ong, *Interfaces of the Word* (Ithaca, N. Y.: Cornell University Press, 1977); Marshall McLuhan, *The Gutenberg Galaxy: The Making of Typographic Man* (Toronto: University of Toronto Press, 1962); Ong, *The Presence of the Word* (New Haven: Yale University Press, 1967); Ong, *Knowledge and the Future of Man* (Ithaca, N.Y.: Cornell University Press, 1968); Ong, *Rhetoric, Romance, and Technology* (Ithaca, N.Y.: Cornell University Press, 1973).

37. For an elaboration of the process of learning to read and write among children of laboring and dependent classes, see Barbara Finkelstein, "Reading, Writing, and the Acquisition of Identity," in Finkelstein, ed., *Regulated Children/ Liberated Children*, 119–124; "Pedagogy as Intrusion," in Warren, ed., *History, Education and Public Policy.*

38. For an analysis of the Infant School Movement, see Dean May and Maris A. Vinovskis, "A Ray of Millenial Light: Early Education and Social Reform in

the Infant School Movement in Massachusetts, 1826–1840," in Tamara Hareven, ed., *Family and Kin in Urban Communities* (New York: Basic Books, n.d.), 62–100.

39. "Report of the Boston Infant School Society," *American Annals of Education* (1830), 3: 296–298.

40. Horace Mann, *Life and Work*, (1846), 4: 130.

41. Explorations of the Sunday school can be found in Kaestle, *Origins of an Urban School System* and Cremin, *American Education*.

The work of the various Sunday school teachers can be examined through study of the missionary efforts of various religious societies as well as in the pages of professional education journals, such as the *American Annals of Education, Transactions of the Western Literary Institute, College of Professional Teachers*, and the *Common School Journal*, and in the records of various philanthropic societies.

42. Quoted in Cohen, *Education in the United States*, 2: 976.

43. The following historians explore the withdrawal of children from the community into specialized settings: Aries, *Centuries of Childhood*; deMause, ed., *History of Childhood*, introductory essay entitled "The Evolution of Childhood"; Edward Shorter, *The Making of the Modern Family* (New York: Basic Books, 1975); Stone, *Family, Sex and Marriage in England*; Donzelot, *Policing of Families*. See also Badinter, *L'Amour en Plus*; Arthur Hippler, "Cultural Evolution: Some Hypotheses Concerning the Cognitive and Affective Interpenetration During Latency," *Journal of Psychohistory*, 4 (Spring 1978): 419–439; Jules Henry, *Culture Against Man* (New York: Vintage Books, 1963).

44. The most useful from my own point of view have been Donzelot, *Policing of Families*; Christopher Lasch, *Haven in a Heartless World: The Family Besieged* (New York: Basic Books, 1979); Kett, *Rites of Passage*; Dominick Cavallo, "The Politics of Latency: Kindergarten Pedagogy, 1860–1930," in Finkelstein, ed., *Regulated Children/Liberated Children* 8, 158–184. See also my introduction.

There is a rich and varied literature describing an array of political alliances, and there are deep differences among historians of education about the nature of political support. For an exploration of controversy among historians, see any of the works of Michael B. Katz, or, for alternative definitions, those of R. Freeman Butts, and Diane Ravitch. The most recent work has been done by Paul Peterson of the University of Chicago and David Angus of Michigan describing the enormous difficulties of defining the bases of political support for public school effort.

45. I am greatly in debt to the brilliant essay by Clifford Geertz, "Ideology as a Cultural System," in *Interpretation of Cultures*, exploring ideology as templates or blueprints of experience rather than deliberate instruments of mystification. We should note that this has not been an invariable pattern. In Amish communities and Mormon communities, Chasidic communities as well as certain black communities, children remain in public, and lead public lives in school and community. See also John H. Marx, "The Ideological Construction of Post-Modern Identity Models in contemporary Movements," in Roland Robertson and Burkart Holzner, *Identity and Authority: Explorations in the Theory of Society* (New York: Alfred A. Knopf, 1979), ch. 5, 145–190.

46. With this interpretation I am insisting that transformations of social structure should not be defined as exclusively labor-market sensitive. Ethnicity, age, gender, beliefs, values, and feelings have emerged as equally useful and as

comprehensive. This is not to say that those who have identified institutionalization as a product of economic realities rather than consciousness have not contributed to our understanding of both. See, for example, the variety of work by Michael B. Katz of the University of Pennsylvania and Marvin Lazerson of the University of British Columbia. For an excellent explanation of intellectual origins, see Michael Ignatieff, "Prison and Factory Discipline, 1770–1800"; see also the work by Carl Kaestle, University of Wisconsin, who is now emphasizing the strategic importance of ethnicity, and by David Angus who is emphasizing age. For other explanations, see Rothman, *Discovery of the Asylum*; Michel Foucault, *Power/Knowledge: Selected Interviews and Other Writings, 1972–77* (New York: Basic Books, 1980), passim.

47. The sentiment is so universal among middle-class reformers as to be universally expressed in nurture manuals, the minutes of school administrators, medical texts, and popular magazines. See "On Physical Education," *Parents' Magazine* 2 (June 1842): 217. See also Thomas Gallaudet, *Child's Books on the Soul* (Hartford, Conn.: Cooke, 1831), Part I. The work of Jacob Abbott has been beautifully explicated in Gregory Nenstiel, "Jacob Abbott: The Evolution of a Nineteenth-Century Educator," (Ph.D. dissertation, University of Maryland, College Park, 1979); Lydia M. Child, *The Mother's Book* (2d ed., Boston: Carter, Hendee & Babcook, 1831); Heman Humphrey, *Domestic Education* (Amherst: J. S. & C. Adams, 1844), 11–12; George Combe, *Lectures on Popular Education* (Boston: Marsh, Capon, & Lyon, 1834).

48. An excellent chapter exploring advice to parents is contained in Anne L. Kuhn, *The Mother's Role in Childhood Education: New England Concepts, 1830–1860* (New Haven: Yale University Press, 1947), ch. 5. See also Kaestle and Vinovskis, "From Apron Strings to ABCs," in Demos and Boocock, eds., *Turning Points*, S39–81. For the medical literature, see Joseph Kett, "Curing the Disease of Precocity," in Demos and Boocock, eds., *Turning Points*, 183–212; Amos Bronson Alcott, *Observations on the Principles and Methods of Infant Instruction* (Boston: Carter & Hendee, 1830), 4–13; "On Physical Education," 217. See also Gallaudet, *Child's Books on the Soul*, Part I; Nenstiel, "Jacob Abbott"; Child, *Mother's Book*; Humphrey, *Domestic Education*, 11–12; Combe, *Lectures on Popular Education*.

49. For an elaboration of their fears and childrearing practices, see Finkelstein, "Reading, Writing, and the Acquisition of Identity," in Finkelstein, ed., *Regulated Children/Liberated Children*, ch. 6, 124–127.

50. Charles Strickland, "Families, Children and Women: The Revolt Against the Victorian Model," unpublished paper, 1979, 14.

51. For an exploration of the family as a retreat from the world, see the following secondary sources: Kuhn, *Mother's Role in Childhood Education*; Bernard Wishy, *The Child and the Republic: The Dawn of Modern American Child Nurture* (Philadelphia: University of Philadelphia Press, 1968); Kirk Jeffrey, "The Family as Utopian Retreat from the City: The Nineteenth-Century Contribution," *Soundings* 55 (1972): 21–41; Walter Houghton, *The Victorian Frame of Mind, 1830–1870* (New Haven: Yale University Press, 1957). Among reformers, one can pick almost at random from the voluminous literature of domestic advice published in the middle decades of the nineteenth century, whether it is in the popular womens' magazines—*Ladies Godeys Book, Mothers Magazine, Parents Magazine*—or

in the literature of advice written by William Andrus Alcott, Jacob Abbot, Lydia Signourey, Horace Bushnell, or a host of others.

52. See Kirk Jeffrey, "The Family as Utopian Retreat."

53. Jane Silverman Mulligan, "The Madonna and Child in American Culture," (Ph.D. dissertation, University of California at Los Angeles, 1975), 38–43, and *passim*. See also Michelle Rosoldo and Louis Lamphere, *Women, Culture and Society* (Stanford, Calif.: Stanford University Press, 1974), 26. Excellent elaborations can also be found in Ann Douglas, *The Feminization of American Culture* (New York: Avon Books, 1977), esp. ch. 3; Nancy F. Cott, *The Bonds of Womanhood: "Woman's Sphere" in New England, 1780–1835* (New Haven: Yale University Press, 1977); Kathryn Kish Sklar, *Catherine Beecher: A Study in American Domesticity* (New Haven: Yale University Press, 1973).

54. See note 47.

55. For an elaboration of the content of these newly emerging sentiments, see Sterling Fishman, "The Double Vision of Education: The Romantic and the Grotesque"; Judith Plotz, "The Perpetual Messiah: Romanticism, Childhood, and the Paradoxes of Human Development," in Finkelstein, ed., *Regulated Children Liberated Children*, chs. 4 and 5. See also deMause. "The Evolution of Childhood."

56. Amariah Brigham, *Remarks on the Influence of Mental Cultivation and Mental Excitement on Health* (2d ed. Boston, 1833), 55.

57. William Woodbridge, "The Duties of Women," in the *Young Woman's Gift* (Boston, 1851).

58. Orson Fowler, *Loc. cit.*

59. Quoted in Kuhn, *Mother's Role*, 108.

60. Quoted in Nenstiel, "Jacob Albott" passim.

61. Child, "Mother's Book, 3."

62. Kaestle and Vinovskis, "From Apron Strings to ABCs" in Demos and Boocock, eds., *Turning Points*, S39–S81.

63. Kett, 'Curing the Disease of Precocity," in Demos and Boocock, eds., *Turning Points*, S187.

64. "Report of the Boston Infant School Society," 296–98.

65. Reverend Daniel Smith, *The Parent's Friend: or, Letters on the Government and Education of Children and Youth* (New York: T. Mason & G. Lane, 1838), 41.

66. Amos Bronson Alcott, *Observations on the Principles and Methods of Infant Instruction*; as quoted in Cohen, *Education in the United States*, 2: 207. See also Orson Fowler, quoted in Kuhn, *Mother's Role*, 116; William Crandall, *Three Hours School a Day: A Talk with Parents* (Albany: C. Van Thuisen, 1854), 28; Humphrey, *Domestic Education*.

67. Mary Peabody Mann, ed., *Life and Work of Horace Mann*, Fourth Annual Report for 1846.

68. Ibid.

69. Quoted in Kaestle and Vinovskis in Demos and Boocock, eds., *Turning Points*, 40.

70. For excellent discussions of the Kindergarten, see Marvin Lazerson, "Urban Reform and the Schools: Kindergartens in Massachusetts, 1870–1915" in Michael B. Katz, ed., *Education in American History* (New York: Harper & Row, 1973), 224–228; Evelyn Weber, *The Kindergarten: Its Encounter with Educational*

Thought in America (New York: Teachers College Press, 1969); Dale Ross, *The Kindergarten Crusade* (Athens: Ohio University Press, 1976). The most insightful analysis of the meaning of moral nurture in the Kindergarten can be found in Cavallo, "The Politics of Latency" in Finkelstein, ed., *Regulated Children/Liberated Children*, ch. 8.

71. For a sophisticated and original elaboration of the variety and complexity of family policy, see Donzelot, *Policing of Families*, xxi.

72. Ibid., xxi, and passim. Although the American and French experiences are dissimilar, as are the mechanisms of social control that have developed in the two countries, his argument is nonetheless broadly applicable, a description of two kinds of efforts to transform families in similar educative directions.

73. Children's Aid Society, *Second Annual Report* (February 1855), 4; see also Josiah Quincy, "Report of the Committee on the Subject of Pauperism and a House of Industry in the Town of Boston," (Boston, 1821), 8–10; *Niles Weekly Register*, 15 December, as quoted in Bremner, et al., *Children and Youth in America*, 753; "Boys as Leaders of the Mob in N.Y.," *Harpers Weekly* (26 July, 1863) 466, in Bremner, et al., *Children and Youth in America*, 757; Rebecca Gratz, *Report from the Female Association for the Relief of Women and Children in Reduced Circumstances*. See also reports from the Philadelphia Orphan Society, the Hebrew Sunday School Society, and the Jewish Foster Home, in Bremner, et al., *Children and Youth in America*, 1: 1661. Catholic philanthropic societies also flourished.

74. Charles Loring Brace, *The Crusade for Children: A Review of Child Life in New York During 75 Years, 1853–1928* (New York: Children's Aid Society, 1928), 10. See also Children's Aid Society, *Second Annual Report* (February 1855), 4.

75. *Ex parte Crouse*, 4 Wharton, Penn. 9 (1838). Cited in Bremner, et al., *Children and Youth*, Vol. 1, 691–692.

76. Levi Silliman Ives, "The Protection of Destitute Catholic Children," New York Catholic Protectory, *First Annual Report* (New York, 1863), quoted in Bremner, et al., *Children and Youth*, 1: 747.

77. The lovely phrase is Bertram Wyatt-Brown's. See "The Mission and the Masses: The Moral Imperatives of the City Bourgeoisie," *Reviews in American History* (1979): 527–534.

78. To my knowledge, there is only one history that explicitly recognizes this transfer of authority: see Cott, *Bonds of Womanhood*.

79. There is a rich and varied literature describing an array of political alliances, and there are deep differences among historians of education about the nature of political support. For an exploration of controversy among historians, see any of the works of Michael B. Katz, or, for alternative definitions, those of R. Freeman Butts and Diane Ravitch. The most recent work has been done by Paul Peterson of the University of Chicago and David Angus of Michigan describing the enormous difficulties of defining the bases of political support for public school effort.

80. Mann, *Life and Work* (1846), 4: 130.

81. William Augustus Mowry, *Recollections of a New England Educator* (New York: Silver-Burdett & Co., 1908), 15. See also Isaac Hall Freeman, *School from Three to Eighty: Pictures of American Life, 1825–1925* (Pittsfield, Mass.: n.p., 1927), 89; *John Dean Caton Family Papers*, Manuscript Division, Library of Congress;

William Andrus Allcott, *Confessions of a School Master* (Andover, Mass., 1889), passim.

82. John George Clinkscales, *On the Old Plantation: Reminiscences of His Childhood* (Spartanburg, S.C.: Band & White, 1916), 89. For particularly graphic descriptions, see the following: for New England: "Common Schools of Connecticut," *American Annals of Education and Instruction* 2 (15 April 1839): 249; for the West: Seymour D. Carpenter, *Genealogical Notes of the Carpenter Family Including the Autobiography and Personal Reminiscences of Dr. Seymour D. Carpenter* (Springfield, Ill.: Illinois State Journal Co., 1907), 77; William Dean Howells, *A Boy's Town* (New York: Harper & Brothers, 1904), 35; James Langdon Hill, *My First Years as a Boy* (Andover, Mass.: Andover Press, 1878), 99–100; for the Middle states: William Summers, "Early Public Schools in Norristown," Historical Society of Montgomery County, Pennsylvania *Proceedings* 6 (1929): 351; and for the South: John Lewis Herring, *Saturday Night Sketches; Stories of Old Wiregrass Georgia* (Boston: Gorham Press, 1918); George Clark Rankin, *The Story of My Life, or More Than a Half-Century As I Lived It* (Nashville: Smith & Lamar, 1912).

83. Hiram Orcutt, *Reminiscences of School Life* (Cambridge: Cambridge University Press, 1898), 50; Mrs. Francis Edward Clark, *The Little Girl That Once Was I* (Boston: International Society of Christian Endeavor, 1936), 48.

84. Henry Johnson, *The Other Side of Main Street: A History Teacher from Sauk Centre* (New York: Columbia University Press, 1935), 34; James P. Logan, "An Old-time Pedagogue: Memories of a Country District School in Civil War Days," *Proceedings of the New Jersey Historical Society* 55, no. 4 (October 1937): 265.

85. Ong, *Interfaces of the Word*, passim.

86. McLuhan, *Gutenberg Galaxy;* Ong, *Presence of the Word; Knowledge and the Future of Man*; and *Rhetoric, Romance, and Technology*.

87. There are several good studies of the social, political, economic, racial, moral, and cultural ideas contained in American textbooks. Ruth Miller Elson, *Guardians of Tradition: American Schoolbooks of the Nineteenth Century* (Lincoln: University of Nebraska Press, 1964); John A. Nietz, *Our Textbooks* (Pittsburgh: University of Pittsburgh Press, 1961); Richard Mosier, *Making the American Mind* (New York: Kings Crown Press, 1947); Charles H. Carpenter, *History of American Schoolbooks* (Philadelphia: University of Pennsylvania Press, 1963).

88. Anne S. MacCleod, "American Childhood in the Early 19th Century: Myths and Realities," an unpublished manuscript.

89. George B. Emerson and Alonzo Potter, *The School and the Schoolmaster* (Boston: W. B. Fowle, N. Capen, 1845). These sentiments were shared widely: Horace Mann advocated feminization of the teaching force, in the Second, Fourth, and Sixth Annual Reports. See also Catherine Beecher, *Suggestions on Improvements in Education* (Boston, 1929); *Essay on the Education of Female Teachers* (New York, 1835); and Jacob Abbott, *Gentle Measures in the Management of the Young* (New York: Harper, 1847).

90. See the following excellent interpretive histories exploring feminization and domesticity in the nineteenth century: Deborah Fitts, "Una and the Lion: The Feminization of District School-Teaching and Its Effects on the Roles of Students and Teachers in Nineteenth-Century Massachusetts," in Finkelstein, ed., *Regulated Children/Liberated Children*, ch. 7, 140–158; Sklar, *Catharine Beecher*; Wishy, *Child and the Republic*; Kuhn, *Mother's Role in Childhood Education*; Fink-

elstein, "The Nineteenth-Century School: An Institution of Domesticity," an unpublished paper. See also Strickland, "Paths Not Taken," in Spodek, ed., *Handbook of Research on Early Childhood Education*.

91. For example, see Donald R. Raichle, "The Abolition of Corporal Punishment in New Jersey Schools," *History of Childhood Quarterly* (Summer 1974): 53–77; Horace Mann, *Annual Reports*, Henry Barnard, Catharine Beecher, Lydia Childs, and many more.

92. Lyman Cobb, *The Evil of Corporal Punishment as a Means of Moral Discipline in Families and Schools* (New York: Mark A. Levinan & Co., 1847), 1115–B; see also Abbott, *Gentle Measures in the Management of the Young*.

93. "A Mother's Visit to a Primary School," *Massachusetts Teacher* 22 (April, 1869): 159–160; Thomas Garth, ed., *Old School Days: Being Reminiscences of a Passing Generation* (Ann Arbor: Edwards Brothers, n.d.), 40; Frederick William Ballinger, *Recollections of an Old Fashioned New Englander* (New York: Round Table Press, 1941), 15.

94. David Macrae, *The Americans at Home: Pen-and-Ink Sketches of American Men, Manners, and Institutions* (Popular ed. rev., Glasgow: John S. Marr & Sons, 1875), 473.

95. See Note 45 above.

96. See Note 46 above.

97. This is, of course, the basis for most twentieth-century social scientific definitions of the role of the schools as instrumental and of families as affective. Oversimplified to be sure, the categories are now undergoing modification. See, for example, Lasch, *Haven in a Heartless World*; and Bender, *Community and Social Change*, passim.

98. For examples of studies that contain good descriptions and analyses of school demographics, see Kaestle and Vinovskis, "From Apron Strings to ABCs"; Ronald Cohen, "Schooling and Age-Grading in American Society since 1800: The Fragmenting of Experience," unpublished paper; and Kett, *Rites of Passage*, ch. 1.

BIBLIOGRAPHY

Abbott, Jacob. *Gentle Measures in the Management of the Young*. New York, 1847.

Alcott, Amos Bronson. *Observations on the Principles and Methods of Infant Instruction*. Boston, 1830.

Allcott, William Andrus. *Confessions of a School Master*. Andover, Mass., 1889.

Aries, Philippe. *Centuries of Childhood: A Social History of Family Life*. Translated by Robert Baldick. New York, 1962.

Bailyn, Bernard. *Education in the Forming of American Society*. Chapel Hill, 1960.

Ballinger, Frederick William. *Recollections of an Old Fashioned New Englander*. New York, 1941.

Beales, Ross W., Jr. "Anne Bradstreet and Her Children." In *Regulated Children/ Liberated Children: Education in Psychohistorical Perspective*, edited by Barbara Finkelstein. New York, 1979.

Beecher, Catherine. *Suggestions on Improvements in Education*. Boston, 1929.

Bender, Thomas. *Community and Social Change in America*. New Brunswick, N.J., 1978.

Berg, Barbara J. "The City as School: Female Voluntary Societies: 1800–1860." In *Educating an Urban People*, edited by Diane Ravitch and Ronald R. Goodenow. New York, 1980, 10–23.

Brace, Charles Loring. *The Crusade for Children: A Review of Child Life in New York During 75 Years, 1853–1928*. New York, 1928.

Brenzel, Barbara. "Domestication as Reform: A Study of the Socialization of Wayward Girls, 1856–1905." *Harvard Education Review* 50, no. 2 (May 1980): 196–213.

Brigham, Amariah. *Remarks on the Influence of Mental Cultivation and Mental Excitement on Health*. Boston, 1833.

Butts, R. Freeman. *Public Education in the United States: From Revolution to Reform*. New York, 1978.

Child, Lydia Maria. *The Mother's Book*. Boston, 1831.

Clark, Francis Edward. *The Little Girl That Once Was I*. Boston, 1936.

Clinkscales, John George. *On the Old Plantation: Reminiscences of His Childhood*. Spartanburg, S.C., 1916.

Cobb, Lyman. *The Evil of Corporal Punishment as a Means of Moral Discipline in Families and Schools*. New York, 1847.

Combe, George. *Lectures on Popular Education*. Boston, 1834.

"Common Schools of Connecticut." *American Annals of Education and Instruction* 2 (15 April 1839): 249.

Cott, Nancy F. *The Bonds of Womanhood: "Woman's Sphere" in New England, 1785–1835*. New Haven, 1977.

Crandall, William. *Three Hours School a Day: A Talk with Parents*. Albany, 1854.

Cremin, Lawrence A. *American Education: The Colonial Experience, 1607–1782*. New York, 1970.

———. *American Education: The National Experience, 1783–1876*. New York, 1980.

Dale, William. *A Manual of the Albany Lancasterian School*. Albany, 1820.

deMause, Lloyd, ed. *The History of Childhood*. New York, 1974.

Demos, John. *A Little Commonwealth: Family Life in Plymouth Colony*. New York, 1970.

———, and Boocock, Sarane, eds. *Turning Points: Historical and Sociological Essays on the Family*. Chicago, 1978.

Donzelot, Jacques. *The Policing of Families*. New York, 1979.

Douglas, Ann. *The Feminization of American Culture*. New York, 1977.

Duffy, John. "School Buildings and the Health of American School Children in the Nineteenth Century." In *Healing and History*, edited by Charles E. Rosenberg. New York, 1979.

Ellis, Charles Calvert. *Lancasterian Schools in Philadelphia*. Philadelphia, 1907.

Elson, Ruth Miller. *Guardians of Tradition: American Schoolbooks of the Nineteenth Century*. Lincoln, 1964.

Emerson, George B., and Potter, Alonzo. *The School and the Schoolmaster*. Boston, 1845.

Finkelstein, Barbara. "Education and the Cult of Domesticity." Unpublished paper given at the Berkshire Conference on Women's History, 1976.

———. "Educational History in the Pursuit of Justice." *Reviews in American History* (March 1980): 122–128.

———. "Exploring Community in Urban Educational History." In *The Community*

Study of Urban Educational History, edited by Diane Ravitch and Ronald R. Goodenow. New York, 1984.

———. "In Fear of Childhood: Relationships Between Parents and Teachers in Nineteenth-Century America." *History of Childhood Quarterly* 3, no. 3 (Winter 1976): 321–337.

———. "The Moral Dimensions of Pedagogy: Teaching Values in Popular Primary Schools in the Nineteenth Century." *American Studies* 2 (Fall 1974): 79–91.

———. "Pedagogy as Intrusion: Teaching Values in Popular Primary Schools in Nineteenth-Century America, 1820–1880." In *History, Education and Public Policy: Recovering the American Educational Past*, edited by Donald R. Warren. Berkeley, Calif., 1978.

———. "Reading, Writing and the Acquisition of Identity in the United States: 1790–1860." In *Regulated Children/Liberated Children: Education in Psychohistorical Perspective*, edited by Barbara Finkelstein. New York, 1979.

Fishman, Sterling. "The Double Vision of Education: The Romantic and the Grotesque." In *Regulated Children/Liberated Children: Education in Psychohistorical Perspective*, edited by Barbara Finkelstein. New York, 1979.

Fitts, Deborah. "Una and the Lion: The Feminization of District School Teaching and Its Effects on the Roles of Students and Teachers in Nineteenth-Century Massachusetts." In *Regulated Children/Liberated Children: Education in Psychohistorical Perspective*, edited by Barbara Finkelstein. New York, 1979.

Fowle, William Bentley. "Boston Monitorial Schools." *American Journal of Education* 1, no. 1 (January 1826): 39–40.

Freeman, Isaac Hall. *School from Three to Eighty: Pictures of an American Life, 1825–1925*. Pittsfield, Mass., 1927.

Gallaudet, Thomas. *Child's Books on the Soul*. Hartford, Conn., 1831.

Garth, Thomas, ed. *Old School Days: Being Reminiscences of a Passing Generation*. Ann Arbor, n.d.

Geertz, Clifford. *The Interpretation of Cultures*. New York, 1973.

Greven, Philip. *The Protestant Temperament: Patterns of Child-Rearing, Religious Experience, and the Self in Early America*. New York, 1977.

Griscom, John. *Memoir*. New York, 1859.

Hall, Basil. *Travels in North America in the Years 1827 and 1828*. London, 1829.

Hamilton, Thomas. *Men and Manners in America*. Philadelphia, 1833.

Hawes, Joseph M. *Children in Urban Society: Juvenile Delinquency in Nineteenth-Century America*. New York, 1971.

Henry, Jules. *Culture Against Man*. New York, 1963.

Herring, John Lewis. *Saturday Night Sketches: Stories of Old Wiregrass Georgia*. Boston, 1918.

Hill, James Langdon. *My First Years as a Boy*. Andover, Mass., 1878.

Hiner, N. Ray. "The Child in American Historiography." *Psychohistory Review* 11, no. 1 (Summer 1978): 13–23.

———. "Cotton Mather and His Children." In *Regulated Children/Liberated Children: Education in Psychohistorical Perspective*, edited by Barbara Finkelstein. New York, 1979.

Hippler, Arthur. "Cultural Evolution: Some Hypotheses Concerning the Cognitive and Affective Interpenetration During Latency." *Journal of Psychohistory* 4 (Spring 1978): 419–439.

Hirschman, Albert O. *The Passions and the Interests: Political Arguments for Capitalism Before Its Triumph.* Englewood Cliffs, N.J., 1977.

Howells, William Dean. *A Boy's Town.* New York, 1904.

Humphrey, Heman. *Domestic Education.* Amherst, Mass., 1844.

Ignatieff, Michael. "Prison and Factory Discipline: The Origins of an Idea." Unpublished paper presented at the annual meeting of the American Historical Association, 1976.

Jeffrey, Kirk. "The Family as Utopian Retreat from the City: The Nineteenth-Century Contribution." *Soundings* 55 (1972): 21–41.

Johnson, Henry. *The Other Side of Main Street: A History Teacher from Sauk Centre.* New York, 1935.

Kaestle, Carl F. *The Evolution of an Urban School System.* Cambridge, Mass., 1973.

———. "Social Change, Discipline and the Common School in Early Nineteenth-Century America." *Journal of Interdisciplinary History* (Summer 1978): 1–17.

———, and Vinovskis, Maris A. "From Apron Strings to ABCs: Parents, Children and Schooling in Nineteenth-Century Massachusetts." In *Turning Points: Historical and Sociological Essays on the Family*, edited by John Demos and Sarane Boocock. Chicago, 1978.

Katz, Michael. *The Irony of Early School Reform: Educational Innovation in Mid-Nineteenth Century Massachusetts.* Cambridge, Mass., 1968.

———, ed. *Education in American History.* New York, 1973.

Kett, Joseph F. "Curing the Disease of Precocity." In *Turning Points: Historical and Sociological Essays on the Family*, edited by John Demos and Sarane Boocock. Chicago, 1978.

———. *Rites of Passage: Adolescence in America, 1790 to the Present.* New York, 1977.

Klebaner, Bernard J. "Poverty and Its Relief in American Thought, 1815–1916." *Social Service Review* 38 (1964): 382–399.

Kuhn, Anne L. *The Mother's Role in Childhood Education: New England Concepts, 1830–1860.* New Haven, 1947.

Lancaster, Joseph. *The British System of Education: Being a Complete Epitome of the Improvements and Inventions Practised by Joseph Lancaster: To Which Is Added a Report of the Trustees of the Lancaster School at Georgetown, Columbia.* Washington, D.C., 1812.

———. *The Lancasterian System of Education with Improvements by Its Founder.* Baltimore, 1821.

Lasch, Christopher. *Haven in a Heartless World: The Family Besieged.* New York, 1979.

Laslett, Barbara. "The Family as a Public and Private Institution; An Historical Perspective." In *Intimacy, Family, and Society*, edited by Arlene Skolnick and Jerome Skolnick. Boston, 1974.

Lazerson, Marvin. "Urban Reform and the Schools: Kindergartens in Massachusetts, 1870–1915." In *Education in American History*, edited by Michael Katz. New York, 1973.

Levy, Barry. "Tender Plants: Quaker Farmers and Children in the Delaware Valley, 1681–1735." *Journal of Family History* 3 (June 1978): 116–133.

Ligon, Moses Edward. *A History of Public Education in Kentucky.* Lexington, Ky., 1942.

Logan, James P. "An Old Time Pedagogue: Memories of a Country District School in Civil War Days." *Proceedings of the New Jersey Historical Society* 55, no. 4 (October 1937): 265.

McLuhan, Marshall. *The Gutenberg Galaxy: The Making of Typographic Man.* Toronto, 1962.

Macrae, David. *The Americans at Home: Pen-and-Ink Sketches of American Men, Manners, and Institutions.* Glasgow, 1875.

Maddox, William Arthur. *The Free School Idea in Virginia Before the Civil War.* New York, 1915.

May, Dean, and Vinovskis, Maris. "A Ray of Millenial Light: Early Education and Social Reform in the Infant School Movement in Massachusetts, 1826–1840." In *Family and Kin in Urban Communities*, edited by Tamara Hareven. New York, n.d.

Mennel, Robert. *Thorns and Thistles.* Hanover, N.H., 1973.

Mohl, Raymond. *Poverty in New York, 1783–1825.* New York, 1971.

Monroe, Paul. *The Founding of the American Public School System: A History of Education in the United States.* New York, 1940.

Morgan, Edmund S. *The Puritan Family: Essays on Religion and Domestic Relations in Seventeenth-Century New England.* New York, 1964.

Mosier, Richard. *Making the American Mind.* New York, 1947.

Mowry, William Augustus. *Recollections of a New England Educator.* New York, 1908.

Mulligan, Jane Silverman. "The Madonna and Child in American Culture." Ph.D. dissertation, University of California at Los Angeles, 1975.

Nasaw, David. *Schooled to Order: A Social History of Public Schooling in the United States.* New York, 1980.

Nenstiel, Gregory. "Jacob Abbott: The Evolution of a Nineteenth-Century Educator." Ph.D. dissertation, University of Maryland, 1979.

Nietz, John A. *Our Textbooks.* Pittsburgh, 1961.

Ong, Walter J. *Interfaces of the Word.* Ithaca, N.Y., 1977.

———. *Knowledge and the Future of Man.* Ithaca, N.Y., 1968.

———. *The Presence of the Word.* New Haven, 1967.

———. *Rhetoric, Romance, and Technology.* Ithaca, N.Y., 1973.

"On Physical Education." *Parents' Magazine* 2 (June 1842): 217.

Orcutt, Hiram. *Reminiscences of School Life.* Cambridge, Mass., 1898.

Plotz, Judith. "The Perpetual Messiah: Romanticism, Childhood, and the Paradoxes of Human Development." In *Regulated Children/Liberated Children: Education in Psychohistorical Perspective*, edited by Barbara Finkelstein. New York, 1979.

Raichle, Donald R. "The Abolition of Corporal Punishment in New Jersey Schools." *History of Childhood Quarterly* (Summer 1974): 53–77.

Rankin, George Clark. *The Story of My Life, or More than A Half-Century As I Lived It.* Nashville, 1912.

Ravitch, Diane, and Goodenow, Ronald R. *The Community Study of Urban Educational History.* New York, 1983.

———. *Educating an Urban People.* New York, 1980.

Rayman, Ronald. "Joseph Lancaster's Monitorial System of Instruction and American Education, 1815–38." *History of Education Quarterly* 21, no. 4 (Winter 1981): 395–411.

Reigart, John Franklin. *The Lancasterian System of Instruction in the Schools of New York City.* New York, 1916.

"Report of the Boston Infant School Society," *American Annals of Education* 3 (1830): 296–298.

Robertson, Roland, and Holzner, Burkart. *Identity and Authority: Explorations in the Theory of Society.* New York, 1979.

Rosenberg, Carroll. *Religion and the Rise of the American City.* Ithaca, N.Y., 1971.

Rosenberg, Charles E., ed. *Healing and History.* New York, 1979.

Rosoldo, Michelle, and Lamphere, Louis. *Women, Culture and Society.* Stanford, Calif., 1974.

Ross, Dale. *The Kindergarten Crusade.* Athens, Ohio, 1976.

Rothman, David J. *The Discovery of the Asylum: Social Order and Disorder in the New Republic.* Boston, 1971.

Royall, Anne. *Sketches of History, Life, Manners in the United States.* New Haven, 1826.

Schlossman, Steven L. *Love and the American Delinquent: The Theory and Practice of Progressive Juvenile Justice, 1825–1920.* Chicago, 1977.

Sennett, Richard. *The Uses of Disorder: Personal Identity and City Life.* New York, 1970.

Sklar, Kathryn Kish. *Catherine Beecher: A Study in American Domesticity.* New Haven, 1973.

Smith, Daniel (Reverend). *The Parent's Friend; or, Letters on the Government and Education of Children and Youth.* New York, 1838.

Smith-Rosenberg, Carroll. "Sex as Symbol of Victorian Purity: An Ethnohistorical Analysis of Jacksonian America." In *Turning Points: Historical and Sociological Essays on the Family,* edited by John Demos and Sarane Boocock. Chicago, 1978.

Spodek, Bernard, ed. *Handbook of Research on Early Childhood Education.* New York, 1982.

Stone, Lawrence. *The Family, Sex and Marriage in England, 1500–1800.* New York, 1977.

Strickland, Charles E. "Paths Not Taken: Seminal Models of Early Childhood Education in Jacksonian America." In *Handbook of Research on Early Childhood Education,* edited by Bernard Spodek. New York, 1982.

Summers, William. "Early Public Schools in Norristown." Historical Society of Montgomery County. Pennsylvania *Proceedings* 6 (1929): 351.

Thernstrom, Stephan, and Sennett, Richard, eds. *Nineteenth-Century Cities.* New Haven, 1969.

Wade, Richard C. *The Urban Frontier: The Rise of Western Cities, 1790–1830.* Cambridge, Mass., 1959.

Wallace, Anthony F.C. *Death and Rebirth of the Seneca.* New York, 1970.

Weber, Evelyn. *The Kindergarten: Its Encounter with Educational Thought in America.* New York, 1969.

Wiebe, Robert. *The Segmented Society.* New York, 1975.

Wishy, Bernard. *The Child and the Republic: The Dawn of Modern American Child Nurture.* Philadelphia, 1968.

Woodbridge, William. *The Young Woman's Gift.* Boston, 1851.

Wyatt-Brown, Bertram. "Child Abuse, Public Policy, and Child-Rearing in America, An Historical Approach." Working paper no. 2. Center for the Study of Educational Policy and Human Values, University of Maryland, 1981.

———. "The Mission and the Masses: The Moral Imperatives of the City Bourgeoisie." *Reviews in American History* (1979): 527–534.

Zuckerman, Michael. *Peaceable Kingdoms.* New York, 1970.

4

Growing Up Female in Young America, 1800–1860

Anne M. Boylan

"It is surely not accidental," writes Carl Degler in his history of women and the family in America, "that the century of the child is also the century of the Cult of True Womanhood."[1] The nineteenth century was indeed both. In countless advice books, magazines, and learned tomes, Americans delineated both new views of children and childhood and new prescriptions for female behavior. And often, as Degler notes, the two intertwined. Just as prescriptive literature portrayed women as more sensitive, caring, and emotional than men, so too it depicted children as experiencing the world primarily through their "affections," not their conscious minds. Women and children were bound together both by a common popular imagery and by nineteenth-century sex-role definitions that gave women almost exclusive control over child care and nurture.

In both its guises—as "the century of the child" and as "the century of the Cult of True Womanhood"—the nineteenth century has generated a good deal of historical literature. Little has been done, however, on the history of female children. The historian looking for accounts of what it was like to grow up female must examine the literature of both the history of childhood and the history of women. Even at that, one often catches only a glimpse of female childhood because in neither field have historians done much to focus on the distinctively female aspects of growing up or the distinctly child-oriented aspects of the female experience. In this chapter, both of these issues are examined. In doing so, the hope is to elucidate how changing attitudes toward childhood and adolescence affected girls, how the experience of growing up female in the early nineteenth century changed, and how nineteenth-century ideals of womanhood influenced and were transmitted to girls.

PRESCRIPTIVE IDEALS

Views of childhood changed dramatically in the early nineteenth century. At least on the level of prescription, nineteenth-century adults expressed very different perceptions of childhood from those of earlier times. To begin with, adults now viewed childhood as important both in itself and as preparation for one's future life. A missionary traveling in the South in 1831 was quite appalled to discover parents who viewed childhood as "the period for unrestrained indulgence and gaiety—a season which should be left run to waste."[2] His horror at this perspective reflected his acceptance of the notion, common among those who advised parents on childrearing, that an individual's childhood could set the course for his or her future life. To let it "run to waste" was to destroy an entire life. Likewise, as nineteenth-century biographers and auto-biographers devoted increasing amounts of space to their subjects' childhoods, they expressed the belief that the roots of future actions were to be found in childhood experience. Parson Weems's invention of the story of the cherry tree had its counterpart in hundreds of other books that traced their subjects' adult greatness back to childhood roots.

With its importance newly recognized, childhood became a period much more subject to scrutiny than ever before, and from this scrutiny emerged a new child psychology stressing the centrality of the "affections" in the child's personality. According to this view, which was widely held by the 1820s, children were primarily sentient creatures who experienced the world through their feelings (their "hearts"), unlike adults who operated through reason. (This new psychology owed much to the Scottish Common Sense philosophers who argued that different mental "faculties" developed at different rates.) "Youth is the season of susceptibility," wrote one amateur psychologist in 1825, "the heart is tender; the affections are lively and glowing. The wax is warmed and softened by the heat of youthful feeling, and awaits the impressions which we are desirous of fixing upon it." The very images this author employed— plasticity, softness, malleability—recurred frequently in writings on childhood and underlined the adult view that children were peculiarly susceptible to adult manipulation. "Adults are fixed, and with difficulty wrought on," noted the managers of an institution for children in 1819; "children are pliable."[3]

While this view of children's natures was widespread by the early nineteenth century, it was susceptible to different interpretations, as Peter Slater has shown. Thus, transcendentalists like Bronson Alcott and reformers like Lydia Maria Child subscribed to an essentially romantic view of children. In language worthy of Wordsworth's "Intimations of Immortality," Child stated flatly that children "come to us from heaven, with their little souls full of innocence and peace." At the opposite end of the ideological spectrum lay the Calvinist theorists of childhood who wrestled long and hard to square the doctrine of original sin with belief in children's malleability. Between the romantic and Calvinist extremes lay the Lockean and Arminian views of people like John Abbott. To them the child was John Locke's immortal *tabula rasa*, a blank slate upon which experience and environment would draw the lines of character.[4]

This belief in the plasticity of children's natures led to a new stress on the importance of the environment in childrearing. Advice-givers argued that children received "impressions" from their environments that were all-important in shaping their personalities. Strong impressions (whether pleasant or unpleasant) left their mark on children much more than did rational arguments or appeals to abstract reasoning. Thus, it was important that from an early age children received the correct kinds of impressions. Example, not precept, made the requisite impression on children, who were likely to be shaped more by what their care-givers did than what they said. "Children will quickly detect any inconsistency that may exist between our instructions and our examples," noted one publication for teachers, reflecting the contemporary stress on correct example, as well as the notion that children had peculiarly keen insights into others' motives.[5]

Given the importance of the impressions children received from their environments, most childrearing theorists agreed that parents and not servants should take primary responsibility for children's upbringing. More to the point, mothers seemed best cut out, not only by opportunity but also by temperament, to rear children. Whereas earlier childrearing books had often been aimed at the father or had depicted him as the ultimate disciplinarian and final authority in families, the new works that poured from the popular presses after 1820 portrayed the mother as having primary responsibility for children's socialization. Fathers had a place, to be sure, especially in training sons as they got older, but it was a distinctly secondary place. Whether this "unequivocal affirmation of the mother's predominance" reflected a "real increase in mothers' presence and authority and a decline in fathers' presence and authority," is, as Nancy Cott has noted, highly questionable. Mothers had always had primary responsibility for the care of young children. Rather, the new stress on mothers' role in childrearing reflected both adults' new evaluation of childhood's importance and women's new concentration on their childrearing tasks, a concentration made possible by changes in women's own household roles.[6]

New ideas about childhood, then, went hand-in-hand with new prescriptions for female behavior. More to the point, they were a direct result of new female role-prescriptions. Between 1780 and 1830, before the proliferation of new concepts of childhood, Americans fundamentally redefined womanhood. The "cult of domesticity" that emerged in those years focused particularly on women's mothering capabilities, re-evaluating women's role in society in terms of their functions as child-rearers. As a result, women gained new status in society as wives and mothers and were able to ascribe new importance to both childhood and childrearing.

One of the first historians to delineate nineteenth-century cultural ideals of womanhood was Barbara Welter, who, in a now classic article entitled "The Cult of True Womanhood," outlined the prescriptive ideals with which young women were presented in the antebellum years. Four norms—piety, purity, submissiveness, and domesticity—constituted the sum total of acceptable behavior for girls, according to Welter. More important, she argued that these norms were created for women by "the nineteenth-century American man," who, feeling guilty about neglecting "the religious values of his forebears," "salved his conscience" by turning woman into "a hostage . . . to all of the values which he held so dear and treated so lightly." In similar vein, Gerda Lerner argued that the Cult of True Womanhood led to a sharp differentiation between the lives of middle-class and lower-class women, and a deterioration in women's economic and political status. Picking up on a theme popular among historians of women since the 1930s, Lerner suggested that women had enjoyed higher status and more opportunities for individual choice in the colonial era than they did in the nineteenth century.[7]

In the past fifteen years, other historians have challenged these arguments from several perspectives. Some, like Ronald Hogeland, have shown that there was a variety of role-prescriptions available to nineteenth-century women, not the one "Cult of True Womanhood" Welter posited. Others have attacked the notion of a colonial "golden age" for women, pointing to the universally inferior status of women in the colonies and the low cultural estimation of women's activities. More importantly, many historians have begun to look for the roots of nineteenth-century role-prescriptions in Revolutionary-era experiences and to point to the very real benefits women derived from the nineteenth century's high evaluation of their mothering functions. In addition, historians like Kathryn Kish Sklar have shown that it was women, not men, who were instrumental in redefining their own cultural roles.[8]

Although these subjects remain controversial, many historians now agree that the redefinition of womanhood was essentially complete by 1830 and that it had its origins, first, in the Revolutionary experiences of American women and, second, in the economic and social transformation of American society in the years that followed. Two recent books, Mary Beth Norton's *Liberty's Daughters* and Linda K. Kerber's *Women of the Republic*, have shown how the Revolution transformed both women's self-concept and their cultural image by giving patriotic value to their traditional tasks (weaving homespun, for example), "politicizing" the household economy through women's participation in boycotts, and requiring them to carry on male tasks during wartime. These experiences helped make women bolder about demanding their rights in a republican society (as seen, for example, in increases in woman-initiated divorce petitions) and anxious to formulate a new conception of their place in such a society. That formulation, which Kerber has dubbed "the Republican Mother," enabled women to see a connection between their biological destiny and their social role by suggesting that women could influence the destiny of the nation through correct childrearing. After the Revolution, as American society underwent a "wide and deep-ranging transformation," the separation of home and work and the decline in domestic production because of the rise of factories led women to focus more of their energies on child care. As they did, they sought, through reformers like Catharine Beecher, to elevate motherhood to a cultural virtue and to carve out a separate (but equal) sphere for themselves in American life.[9]

In this context, the new nineteenth-century interest in childhood becomes explicable. As motherhood gained in status, so did childhood. As mothers translated their knowledge of children into common wisdom through domestic advice books, so did they begin to redefine children's natures. Thus, as Mary Ryan has argued, it may have been women's assumption of responsibility for their children's religious training and their formation of maternal associations that led to major shifts in such theological axioms as infant depravity. The picture of the malleable child, subject to molding by proper nurture, emerged as women concentrated their lives on childrearing.[10]

In addition, this picture linked women to children in ways that suggested that, both within and without the family, female nurture was best. Insofar as their "affections" ruled their personalities and their "hearts" to precedence over their heads, women could reach and teach children on their own level in a way that men could not. Thus, arguments for using exclusively female teachers in schools explicitly connected women's and children's natures, assuming that they were natural allies because they had so much in common. Catharine Beecher, for example, argued that since "the mind is to be guided chiefly by means of the affections . . . is not *woman* best fitted to accomplish these important objects?" Others, especially other female educators, stressed similar themes. When Mary Lyon begged money for her new female seminary in 1836, she stated flatly that training "a multitude of benevolent, self-denying female teachers" was one of the "means essential to the safety of the nation."[11] Through such arguments, reformers like Beecher and Lyon asserted not only women's control over family child care but also their right to run schools, Sunday schools, and other institutions for children, institutions that could become powerful agencies for the transmission of feminine ideals to future generations.

GIRLHOOD

To turn from examining new ideas about children and women to examining mothers' behavior or girls' actual experiences is to enter uncharted territory, for if historians have delineated these new ideas in detail, they have found it a good deal more difficult to determine how these ideas affected women and girls. Thus Carl Degler, in his history of women and the family, devotes much of a chapter on childrearing techniques to fathers' methods, not mothers', and to mother-son interactions, not mother-daughter. Even Charles Strickland's lengthy and fascinating analysis of Bronson Alcott's childrearing methods actually reveals rather little about his daughters' upbringing or childhoods, partly because Alcott's observational diaries record primarily his abstract musings on childhood, partly because he relegated much of the girls' day-to-day care to their mother, who did not always implement her husband's theories. With the exception of biographical and autobiographical works, there are available few detailed analyses of how women reared their daughters or how daughters experienced their childhoods.[12]

Further complicating the problem is the fact that most available evidence comes from the white middle and upper classes. Not only were they the ones most likely to read childrearing advice literature, they were also most likely to have the leisure and opportunity to record their practices. We have little information, for example, on how slave mothers reared their daughters. If twentieth-century practices obtained in the nineteenth, then we can assume that lower-class families were less influenced by new childrearing theories than their middle-class counterparts. At the same time, girls of all social backgrounds could not escape the effects of new developments—such as the emergence of institutions like schools—that affected the treatment of nineteenth-century children. Finally, it is well to keep in mind, as Ray Hiner reminds us, that in the past, as in the present, parental treatment of children varied considerably from family to family. Even in our own day, when societal concern and care for children's welfare are unquestionable, some parents neglect children while others nurture them, and some abuse them while others love them. If today "the capacity to love children is not distributed evenly among the population," we would do well to avoid the mistake of assuming that nineteenth-century parents were different.[13]

If we do not really know whether parents translated new ideas into actual practice in rearing their children, if we do not know how these ideas affected the experience of growing up, we do know some things about nineteenth-century childhood that enable us to raise questions about the shape of nineteenth-century girlhood. We know, for example, that the nineteenth century saw the emergence of greater parental interest in children. Parents began to celebrate children's birthdays, purchase books and toys for them, assign them individual names (rather than giving the name of a dead sibling to the next child of the same sex), and encourage them to use affectionate titles such as Mama and Papa. In addition, the urban middle classes began consciously to restrict the number of children they bore, in order to give a larger share of family resources—both monetary and psychological—to each child. In Utica, New York, for example, the average size of native-born families declined from 5.8 children in the 1810s to 3.6 in the 1830s. Even in rural Sturbridge, Massachusetts, the average number of children born to couples married in the 1820s and 1830s was 5.3, as compared to 6.02 for couples married during the preceding two decades.

Perhaps most importantly, we know that in the early nineteenth century, children were increasingly relegated to the care of women. In the home, where women's traditional responsibility as childrearers was intensified by the attenuation of domestic production, and in the schools and Sunday schools, where women teachers gradually came to outnumber men, children moved in a largely female world. The implications of this last change for children's actual experience of childhood deserve further exploration, especially as this change affected each sex differently. Did boys, as Nancy Cott has suggested, discover an increased conflict between the values taught them by their mothers and teachers, and those exemplified by their fathers—between the values of home and those of the marketplace? Did girls, on the other hand, experience a socialization characterized by "comparative seamlessness" in that they were brought up, unlike their brothers, "to be comfortable in an all-female world?" How did the shift to female teachers affect girls? Deborah Fitts has argued that it was problematic for boys, especially those in adolescence, leading them to abandon school at earlier ages. Historians of women, on the other hand, have pointed to the benefits girls derived from contact with female teachers—the possibility of close friendships, the availability of role models, and the improvement of job opportunities, to name a few. Still other historians have wondered whether these benefits were offset by the limitations imposed by the "cult of domesticity." Did the emergence of new ideas about women's place introduce fundamental discontinuities between girlhood in the colonial period and in the nineteenth century, and make more difficult the nineteenth-century girls's transition to adulthood? Or did nineteenth-century girls perceive domesticity as elevating women's status and look forward to marriage and motherhood because these functions were more positively evaluated by their culture?[14]

To examine these issues from the standpoint of girls growing up in the nineteenth century is to ask how the experience of female childhood changed and whether the changes brought with them improvements in girls' lives. Having done that, one needs to investigate the experience of female adolescence and the transition to womanhood, in order to determine how teenage girls perceived and experienced the maturation process.

By a variety of objective measures, nineteenth-century girlhood seems to have represented a real improvement over girlhood in the colonies. Certainly, in terms of the physical care they received, many nineteenth-century girls were the beneficiaries of the new "scientific" ideas of the century, which encouraged parents to believe that they could influence their children's health. Thus, many middle-class mothers sought to provide proper care for their daughters by breast-feeding them, on demand, for eight to twelve months, dressing them in loose, light clothing, permitting them to crawl as soon as they were able, and encouraging them to stand and walk early. Not only were such practices in keeping with contemporary parenting literature, they also probably helped reduce the incidence of infant diarrhea and thus of infant death. Outside the middle class, some girls may have encountered a lower level of physical care, especially if their families lived in crowded lower-class sections of cities, where epidemics of cholera or yellow fever were commonplace. Still, many cities undertook public health measures that improved the lives of their citizens, particularly in providing clean water supplies by the 1830s. Even among slave families, there is good evidence of generally better treatment for all slaves by the early nineteenth century, an improvement that would have benefited slave children as well as adults.[15]

From another objective standpoint—access to schooling—most nineteenth-century girls were better off than their colonial counterparts. The proliferation of schools—both private and public—brought vastly increased educational opportunities that bore fruit in rising female literacy rates. By 1850, except in the South, the "literacy gap" between white men and women had closed, and the United States could claim one of the highest female literacy rates in the world. To be sure, the arguments for female education were almost as grudging in the 1830s as they had been when they originated in the 1780s, stressing as they did the need to educate girls so that they could better fulfill their future roles as wives and mothers. Linda Kerber has traced the emergence of female seminaries in the post-Revolutionary years to the belief that women carried out their duty to society as the wives and mothers of its male citizens. Only by being educated in useful subjects and trained to be independent could women truly act the part of the "Republican Mother." Although the terms changed somewhat, with "democracy" coming to replace republicanism as a justification for female education, most of the arguments for educating girls remained utilitarian and family-oriented. Likewise, the opportunities for girls' education in the early nineteenth century were often catch-as-catch-can, with common schooling available only in brief summer sessions or at ephemeral female academies. And girls had to struggle against a common contempt for female intelligence which viewed intellectual women as "unsexed." Still, by the 1850s, most Northern states had created free public school systems that were equally available to girls and boys, and at least in Massachusetts, the proportion of girls attending school between the ages of five and twelve exceeded that of boys.[16]

Despite these new opportunities, some have suggested that access to schooling and even attendance at school were not an unmixed blessing. Barbara Finkelstein has suggested, for example, that nineteenth-century parents sent children to school—often at age two or three—not so much for the children's benefit as to rid themselves of the burden of their care and supervision. Likewise, one might argue that attendance at school was ultimately frustrating for a girl because she became aware of the many limitations placed on her by a society that encouraged boys' aspirations to the fullest. Along these lines, Barbara Epstein has claimed that nineteenth-century girls were highly frustrated because of the contrast between the ideals of independence and liberty learned from books and the actuality that they had to confine their aspirations to marriage and motherhood.[17]

It is true, of course, that nineteenth-century parents often exhibited an unseemly eagerness to turn their children's care over to teachers. Lucy Larcom, who began to attend an informal neighborhood school when she was about two, recalled that it existed primarily because "the mothers of . . . large families had to resort to some means of keeping their little ones out of mischief, while they attended to their domestic duties." Indeed, educators, complaining that parents sent two- and three-year-olds to school to "get them out of the way," made successful efforts in the 1840s and 1850s to exclude children under four or five from schools. From the standpoint of children's experiences, however, parental motives may be irrelevant. Whether parents used schools for their own convenience and not their children's good, the children themselves were the beneficiaries of improved access to education. Furthermore, many adults were aware that children prized school attendance for the social opportunities it afforded them as well as for any learning they may have picked up.[18]

It seems equally unlikely that girls found their new opportunities for schooling ultimately frustrating. The effects of improved literacy on girls' lives can hardly be overstated. Not only did it open to them new avenues of intellectual stimulation, but it also made new aspirations possible for them. Through reading they could find female role models on whom to pattern their own dreams and lives, and evidence from autobiographies suggests that they did just that. At the same time, their new attainments made them more skilled than their illiterate or semiliterate colonial predecessors and hence gave them access to new occupations, however limited in scope. Ten-year-old Caroline Richards, for example, filled her diary in 1852 with accounts of the books she read or was given, including a volume of *Noble Deeds of American Women* presented by a teacher. She aspired to "write a book some day," reasoning that if "Miss Caroline Chesebro did ... I don't see why I can't." Her experience was repeated by millions of girls who read the women's history of their day in the spiritual memoirs and reminiscences that poured forth from the popular press. Although educators may have intended improved schooling only as a means of creating better mothers, they could not keep education from undermining those intentions by broadening girls' horizons and aspirations.[19]

Aside from schools, other institutions for children may have had a less salutary influence on girls' lives. On the one hand, the appearance of houses of refuge, orphanages and, later, industrial and reform schools signalled an adult willingness to treat girls differently from women if they ran afoul of the law, and to provide protection for orphaned or neglected girls. On the other hand, such institutions often permitted adults to remove from their families and institutionalize girls (though admittedly only a small percentage) who were merely troublesome or rebellious. Indeed, some families used institutions to rid themselves of problem daughters. The Lancaster Industrial School, founded by the state of Massachusetts in 1856, included among its inmates both girls who had committed crimes and those considered "likely to become criminals" either because they were "exposed to vice" or merely because they were truants. Thus, in the school's early years the major reasons for girls' commitment, in order of importance, were: "stubbornness and disobedience," larceny, and leading "an idle and vicious life." Unlike her colonial counterpart whose transgressions were handled within the community, the troublesome nineteenth-century girl might find herself removed from her family, forbidden to contact family members, placed in an institution, and eventually apprenticed as a servant to a new family in an unfamiliar locality. Passing through such institutions seems generally to have doomed girls to marginal lives with few opportunities for social or educational mobility.[20]

As the case of the Lancaster Industrial School suggests, the new nineteenth-century interest in children's psychological makeup and emotional needs could be a mixed blessing. From the child's standpoint, she was both beneficiary and victim of adults' newfound concern for her psychological health. Within the family as well, many nineteenth-century girls found themselves the object of greater parental attention, both because families were smaller and because early childhood training was now deemed essential to future development. Children were observed, studied, and even experimented on by mothers (and occasionally fathers) who kept observational journals, attended meetings of maternal associations, and generally sought to be consciously aware of the childrearing methods they practiced. If they followed the advice given in popular parenting literature, their methods probably included early religious training, intellectual stimulation without encouraging precocity, and psychological rather than physical methods of discipline. Their major goal, as most parents saw it, was to inculcate self-control in their children by developing healthy consciences in them. From the child's perspective, this parental attention had its drawbacks since it meant that her behavior was more carefully monitored, her transgressions more easily observed, and her activities more interfered with, but it also brought benefits in the form of greater intimacy and perhaps informality in relations with her mother and an increased sense of her own importance.[21]

Increased attention also brought with it the potential for battles of will with one's parents. Despite the gradual disappearance of Puritan-style admonitions for parents to break their children's wills, nineteenth-century parents continued to place great value on obedience in their children, and the historical record reveals many incidences of parent-child confrontations. The most famous case involved Francis Wayland's two-day battle with his fifteen-month-old son over the boy's refusal to obey Wayland's requests, but other nineteenth-century parents noted similar, if less dramatic, events. What is interesting about these squabbles is that most of the recorded ones involved boys, not girls. Perhaps parents were less likely to note confrontations with their daughters, but the lack of such incidents suggests that parents were more likely to provoke confrontations with boys by demanding obedient acquiescence to their wishes. Girls may have been more indulged or may have learned in other ways to be docile and obedient, perhaps through withdrawal of parental love. Bronson Alcott, for example, who went to extraordinary lengths to avoid spanking his daughters, may have been unusual in the nineteenth century, but his use of love-deprivation to enforce obedience was a commonly advocated tactic. If indeed parents did avoid direct confrontations with daughters, then girls may have found it more difficult than boys to separate themselves psychologically from their parents and thus reinforced their dependence and identification with them.[22]

Insofar as they received better physical care, had more attention paid to their emotional development, and experienced greater access to elementary schooling, nineteenth-century girls were better off than their colonial counterparts. Access to these improvements was not evenly spread throughout the population, however, and so some girls experienced a relative deterioration in their lives. To take an obvious example, the enactment of slave codes prohibiting slaves from learning to read and write meant that the slave girls' access to literacy declined in relation to that of white girls of their own era. Likewise, the South's failure to establish common schools widened the literacy gap between white girls in the North, some 55 to 75 percent of whom attended school by 1850, and their counterparts in the South, where only about a third of girls were similarly engaged. The spread of the market economy and the growth of commercial cities in the nineteenth century widened class differences, so that the opportunities available to middle- and upper-class urban girls were beyond the reach of their lower-class counterparts, many of whom were destined to spend their childhoods scavenging in city streets to earn money for their families, or being shunted about among various public institutions when their families could no longer care for them. Any assessment of nineteenth-century girlhood must take into account these variations in experience and opportunity.[23]

ADOLESCENCE

How nineteenth-century girls weathered their adolescence is a subject to which historians have devoted some attention. Whether the teen years brought with them the type of stress that is currently associated with adolescence is not entirely clear. Historians disagree on the extent to which nineteenth-century Americans recognized as a separate stage the period now termed adolescence. Furthermore, while there has been a good deal of recent research on the experiences of adolescent girls—particularly new opportunities in the areas of education, work, and friendship—historians do not agree on how young women perceived such opportunities. Did they, like Alexis de Tocqueville, contrast the freedom and opportunities of the teen years with the restrictions of marriage and motherhood and thus approach adulthood with trepidation? Or did they look forward to adulthood, anticipating new challenges and improved status?

Although the term "adolescence" was not widely used until the early twentieth century, a good deal of evidence points to early nineteenth-century Americans' awareness that emotional upheavals often accompanied the physical changes of puberty. Thus, there are many references in childrearing literature from the 1820s and 1830s to a "critical period" through which "youth" passed during the teen years. It was a critical period not only because the youth became exceedingly emotional and subject to the sway of his or her "passions," but also because the individual's entire future life might be determined by decisions made now. "During the eventful and critical period of youth (say from fourteen to eighteen or twenty)," wrote one observer in 1839, "the character usually becomes fixed for life, and for the most part for eternity."[24]

Much of this discussion centered, however, on boys, not girls. It was "large boys" who attracted the particular attention of commentators and around whom much of the anxiety about youth centered. "High-spirited, inclined to throw off restraints, often reckless, generally overestimating themselves, perfectly confident of their own wisdom, and somewhat ashamed to be numbered among children," these boys "who are just between the period of childhood and manhood," seemed to many observers troublesome and ripe for ruin. It was they who disrupted schools and "turned out" the schoolmaster, they who fell easy prey to the temptations of city life. Indeed, it seemed as though the opportunities and choices which nineteenth-century America offered boys—in jobs, locations, marriage partners—helped to make the mid-to-late teens especially volatile and dangerous.[25]

By contrast, female adolescence would seem to have been less anxiety-producing precisely because girls faced few major life-decisions and because training for womanhood began early. Joseph Kett, the leading historian of adolescence, has argued that nineteenth-century Americans saw female adolescence as less traumatic than male and has analyzed adolescent experience not in terms of age (because age distinctions were not finely drawn) but in terms of types of status. Thus, he suggests that different teenagers in the pre-1860 period passed through the stages of dependency, semidependency, and independence at varying ages, and that many of them achieved adult independence only after alternating between statuses for years. Applying his analysis to girls is problematic for two reasons: first, because there is evidence that some observers did see female adolescence as traumatic and second because his discussion of types of status is drawn exclusively from male sources. We need to examine, then, the available commentaries on female adolescence to learn how contemporaries saw teenage girls. In addition, we need to study the female experience to determine whether Kett's categories of status fit girls. If, for example, a girl went from living at home with her parents to living with a husband, did she ever achieve independence, or did she experience semidependence?[26]

When nineteenth-century commentators discussed female adolescence, they often used similar words and phrases to those used for males. According to Barbara Welter, nineteenth-century observers saw the teen years as ushering in a "brilliant and stormy crisis" during which a girl's "sensibilities were at their height." Likewise, Carroll Smith-Rosenberg has found evidence that nineteenth-century physicians saw the teen years as a " 'period of storm and stress' of 'brooding, depression and morbid introspection.' " Words like "crisis" and "critical period" cropped up frequently in reference to both male and female adolescence. There were significant differences, however, in how these words were applied to girls as opposed to boys. To begin with, many of the commentators on the female crisis were physicians who focused particularly on the experience of menarche as inaugurating the critical period. While they did see other manifestations of this trauma—such as rebelliousness, mother-daughter conflict, and moodiness—they generally traced these to physical causes. In discussing boys, as Carroll Smith-Rosenberg has noted, most writers associated the physical changes of puberty with growing power and vigor, whereas girls' puberty seemed to bring weakness and even monthly debility in the form of menstruation. Thus, while the social manifestations of the adolescent crisis were, in girls, tied directly to bodily changes, in boys they were seen as separate, less explicable, and consequently more dangerous. Adults, then, perceived both boys and girls as enduring a "critical period" but in different ways. Whereas this crisis manifested itself in boys through antisocial or destructive behavior, in girls it took the form of potentially weakening physical changes.[27]

By contrast to theoretical discussions of the adolescent crisis, girls' actual experiences of young womanhood, as we will see below, were often characterized by increased personal freedom and new vocational opportunities. To be sure, individuals' experiences varied according to their class and ethnic backgrounds, as well as their locations, but most were affected by the changing nineteenth-century economy which restructured girls' traditional work roles and by the redefinition of womanhood which occurred in the early nineteenth century. As a result of these economic and ideological changes, young women often found themselves offered new educational and vocational opportunities as well as greater freedom to form friendships and choose marriage partners. It seems puzzling, then, that adult observers should focus on the stressful aspects of adolescence when many girls themselves experienced it as a period of relative freedom. Perhaps the reported stress occurred because young women's relative freedom was constrained by the realization that it would soon have to be traded in for the narrow domestic sphere that the nineteenth century allotted adult women. Perhaps, as Alexis de Tocqueville argued, American girls were independent "mistresses of their own actions" who surrendered that independence "irrecoverably... in the bonds of matrimony." To analyze these issues further, we need to examine the work and educational experiences of teenage girls in the early nineteenth century, looking in particular at the effects these experiences had on young women.[28]

Within the family, the economic changes of the nineteenth century had their biggest impact on young women's traditional work roles. As Nancy Cott has shown, the work that adolescent girls in New England had traditionally done within the home—especially spinning—was transformed by the development of power-driven spinning and weaving devices at the turn of the century. As a result, many farm daughters began leaving their parents' households in the 1810s to take jobs at factories like Waltham and Lowell, earning wages for work they had traditionally done for their families. Other rural teenagers, who had served as "hired girls" (although their hire was not compensated in wages) at neighboring farms, followed suit. Still others found new opportunities in school teaching as local school districts became increasingly willing to hire women for regular positions during the school year. By the 1830s, thousands of farm girls, especially in the Northeast, were earning money as factory operatives, teachers, seamstresses, and the like.[29]

The question of how this transformation in their work affected women is one over which there has been considerable historical argument. Many historians, following the lead of Alexander Hamilton, have suggested that girls' factory labor was simply an extension of their family responsibilities, undertaken for family reasons. Writing in his 1791 "Report on Manufactures," Hamilton cited as one of the advantages of factories "the employment of persons who would otherwise be idle." In general, he suggested, "women and children are rendered more useful by manufacturing than they would otherwise be.... The husbandman [experiences] a new source of profit and support from the increased industry of his wife and daughters, stimulated by the demands of neighboring manufactories." Many of the factory girls themselves took a similar view, portraying their labor as dictated by family necessity. Thus, the stories and articles in the *Lowell Offering*, a factory operatives' magazine published from 1840 to 1845, invariably depicted the Lowell workers as self-sacrificing individuals whose work was paying off the family mortgage, putting a brother through school, or supporting a widowed mother. This picture has led many historians to argue that factory work did little to encourage girls' independence or to alter their self-perception. They left home briefly, stayed at Lowell for a few years under the watchful eyes of substitute mothers, fulfilled family responsibilities, and then returned home to take up family duties again through marriage and childbearing. To use Kett's categories, they remained semidependent even while working and living away from home. By the same logic, girls who worked as schoolteachers enjoyed a similar semidependent status. Although they left home and earned wages, the practice of "boarding around" among local families meant they were under adult care and scrutiny, and their wages may have gone to their families, not themselves.[30]

Thomas Dublin offers a contrasting view in his book *Women at Work* and in a recent collection of factory operatives' letters entitled *Farm to Factory*. Although agreeing that girls' work in very early textile manufacturing was family-based, Dublin argues that the development of the power loom and the establishment of a resident factory labor force by firms like the Boston Manufacturing Company offered single women between fifteen and thirty new opportunities for social and economic independence, opportunities to which they responded with alacrity. Through elaborate tracing of the operatives' backgrounds and an examination of their letters, Dublin establishes that most of them came from male-headed middle-income farm families, not the widow-headed destitute families depicted in the *Lowell Offering*. Rather than sending their daughters to work to help pay off the mortgage, Dublin argues, these families acquiesced in the girls' own desires for money-earning opportunities and may have been relieved because their departure lightened the burden of their financial support. There was often no conflict between families' needs and daughters' wishes. For their part, the girls often went to places like Lowell to fulfill some personal goal such as earning money for clothes, a dowry, or an education. In the process, "they experienced a new life and enjoyed the social and economic independence it provided." Even those who returned home to the farm could never be the same because they came back "with new clothes and with periodicals and more modern ideas picked up in the fluid urban setting." Only three in ten of those who married chose farmers for husbands (although two-thirds of their fathers were farmers); moreover, their ages at marriage were higher than average, and they bore fewer children than their contemporaries who stayed at home. Dublin suggests that the experience of mill work fundamentally changed the young women who underwent it and opened an unbridgeable chasm between them and the world of their childhoods.[31]

In contrast to Western Europe, where women's work in early industrialization was closely tied to family responsibilities, in the United States the development of textile factories seems to have given adolescents opportunities for greater individual freedom. One wonders if the same was the case with other occupations that opened up to young women in the early nineteenth century. Although teaching school was not, strictly speaking, a new occupation for women in the nineteenth century, the configurations of the job changed quite a bit. Whereas earlier women teachers were often widows supplementing their meager incomes by running casual "dame" schools, in the nineteenth century the expansion of schools and academies and the development of common schools opened up new, more regular teaching opportunities, especially for girls who had received some schooling themselves. Indeed, the popular female seminaries that developed in the 1820s seem to have met a growing demand for training girls to teach in these newly emerging common schools. As a result, thousands of young women between fifteen and thirty taught school for at least part of their young adult lives. So common was this phenomenon that two historians have concluded that in Massachusetts, fully 20 percent of women served as school teachers at some time in their lives.[32]

Although some evidence—particularly the practice of boarding teachers around in local families—suggests that girls who became teachers remained in a semidependent status even though no longer living at home, other evidence indicates that teaching and earning a living changed young women's lives fundamentally. Recent work by David F. Allmendinger and Anne Firor Scott has found that among women who attended the new female seminaries and then worked as teachers a high proportion never married. For example, Allmendinger found that 19 percent of girls who graduated from Mt. Holyoke Female Seminary between 1838 and 1850 and then taught remained single, as compared to 6 to 8 percent of American women as a whole. One could argue, of course, that these figures merely show that educated women teachers priced themselves out of the marriage market or were victims of the growing imbalance in the New England sex ratio caused by the westward migration of native-born men. It seems more likely, however, that their educations and teaching experiences gave them more freedom in the choice of a marriage partner and led them to contrast favorably the independence of the single life with the constraints placed on married women. In the 1830s, teacher Emily Chubbuck wondered in a letter to her brother about a suitor: "Shall I . . . tie myself to a person towards whom I feel perfect indifference for the sake of a home and protector?" Her negative answer was no doubt made possible by the fact that she was self-supporting.[33]

For other girls, however, the transformation of work in the early nineteenth century had different consequences. Particularly for lower-class whites, the disappearance of adolescents' traditional jobs often made their lives more insecure and marginal. Faye Dudden has documented the changing nature of household service in the nineteenth century and has noted the metamorphosis of the "hired girl" into the "domestic" by the latter half of the century. Whereas hired girls were usually neighbors who lived in rural households and shared the family's work, much as a teenage daughter would, domestics worked in city households for middle-class employers in a hierarchical relationship. The elimination of young women's traditional work from the family gradually ended the roles that hired girls played at the same time that increasing urban demand for servants brought more and more girls into the very different position of paid domestic. As a domestic, a girl was subject to constant supervision, long hours, and low wages, and enjoyed little free time. Small wonder, then, that few girls who could get other work would take such jobs, leaving them to a growing class of immigrants who had no other choice.[34]

Other lower-class girls pursued traditional female occupations such as sewing, but in the market economy of the early nineteenth century, these skills brought very small monetary rewards. More important, it cut girls loose from their families and condemned many of them to live very marginal existences in the growing commercial cities. The reports of benevolence societies in the 1820s and 1830s are filled with accounts of the extreme difficulty women encountered in finding regular, year-round, remunerative work when their skills involved only "coarse sewing." As a result, many lower-class girls drifted into occasional prostitution to support themselves. In a survey of 2,000 New York prostitutes taken in the 1850s, physician William Sanger found that some 300 had other means of support—usually domestic service or low-skilled female occupations. Evidence like this has led historian Christine Stansell to conclude that prostitution was an occasional occupation of perhaps thousands of urban girls, used to supplement the meager wages they received at other jobs.[35]

As the preceding discussion makes clear, for some young women improved job opportunities were tied up with increased access to education through female academies and seminaries. This connection was not, however, immediate or necessary. When women's academies first developed in the 1780s and 1790s, they had an important impact on their pupils' experiences and ideas, but they do not seem to have changed their future lives in any appreciable way. Most of their students were upper-class girls who went out from the academies to marry and preside over their own households. Still, attendance at schools like the Young Ladies' Academy of Philadelphia changed those who experienced it. They learned how to judge and be judged on merit alone—not wealth or family—and a few perceived the "contradictions between their education and their future." Most important, the very existence of academies gave succeeding generations of girls hope for their educations and models to emulate.[36]

The schools founded in the 1820s and 1830s (at least in the North) made the explicit connection between education and job training, and attempted to train girls for one specific career: teaching. Attended by somewhat older girls of much more modest means than those who had patronized earlier academies, schools like Emma Willard's Troy Female Seminary and Mary Lyon's Mt. Holyoke College offered a determinedly practical curriculum. Whether women or their families created the demand for such training is not clear. In his study of Mt. Holyoke students, David Allmendinger has argued that the demand for such schools was a product of demographic changes that forced girls and their families to plan their lives in new ways. As the age of marriage among native-born New England women rose in the early nineteenth century, he suggests, a new stage of the life cycle emerged—a stage between girlhood and womanhood—that was filled with school attendance and brief stints at teaching. As many Mt. Holyoke women came from families with disproportionately high numbers of daughters, families may have provided tuition money as a kind of dowry to older daughters, partly to bridge the widening gap between girlhood and marriage, partly to hedge against the possibility that marriage offers would not materialize. An alternative explanation is, of course, that women's school attendance itself helped cause the delay in marriage age and was a result of women's own attraction toward education and teaching. Just as farm girls going off to Lowell and other factory towns did so from a combination of circumstances—a desire to earn money, a family's willingness to part with a daughter whose labor was no longer essential, a quest for independence—so too girls may have been able to attend Troy or Mt. Holyoke both because they were attracted to its opportunities and because their families saw some advantage in it. After all, education could be a route to social mobility and, perhaps, an upwardly mobile marriage. In any case, there is enough evidence to indicate that once a girl got the ambition to attend a seminary, she bent all her efforts to fulfill that dream. Thus, Emily Chubbuck, who had begun working in a mill at age ten to help support her family, rejected her mother's suggestion that she become a milliner and set her sights on teaching. Once she had done so, she alternated her time between teaching a district school to earn money and attending an academy with her earnings. Eventually, she took a position at a female seminary which enabled her both to teach and to take training. Likewise, only one-third of Mt. Holyoke's early graduates completed the school course in the appointed three years. A full 41 percent completed the course in two years, undoubtedly to save money. Since these girls came from families of modest means and since the college required its students to do all its domestic work, it seems likely that many girls paid their own way through.[37]

SISTERHOOD

Whether they worked in mills or attended female seminaries, young women in the nineteenth century found their experience of adolescence transformed by the new opportunities they encountered. As many historians have pointed out, these opportunities made possible a qualitative difference in relationships among women. By collecting them in heavily female communities, the factories and seminaries created new peer groupings among women. The resulting sense of sisterhood has been widely discussed by historians, both for its impact on women's self-concept and for its implications for male-female relationships.

The classic statement of the role of sisterhood in nineteenth-century women's lives is Carroll Smith-Rosenberg's article, "The Female World of Love and Ritual." Through the study of a wide variety of upper-class and upper-middle-class women's letters and diaries, Smith-Rosenberg chronicled the prevalence of "intense, loving and openly avowed" friend-

ships between women which usually "began during the women's adolescence and, despite subsequent marriages and geographic separation,
continued throughout their lives." These friendships were made possible, she argued, by the "rigid gender-role differentiation" that characterized nineteenth-century society and segregated women into same-sex
institutions. In this context, "a specifically female world" developed that
was not only socially accepted and sanctioned but also provided women
with a series of female rituals around which they oriented their lives. By
contrast women's relations with men were often stiff and formal and
frequently "lacked the spontaneity and emotional intimacy that characterized bonds with other women."[38]

Other historians have described similar patterns among nineteenth-
century women and have elaborated on the cultural forms that permitted, indeed encouraged, the growth of close homosocial bonds. In her
book *The Bonds of Womanhood*, Nancy Cott has pointed to the close identification that nineteenth-century Americans made between women and
the emotions—the "heart"—an identification that drove them together
to find close personal intimacy. Cott has also shown how the growth of
women's schools reinforced this intimacy by bringing teenage girls together in peer groups and encouraging the notion that female friendships were purer than male-female ones. Likewise, religious beliefs that
stressed the importance of the "heart" in conversion experiences furthered the notion that women had more in common with each other
than they did with men. In fact, women's academies often became in-
cubators for very emotional mass conversions among pupils, conversions
that were "orchestrated" as Joan Jacobs Brumberg notes, by a combination of teacher pressure and peer persuasion. As a result, girls often
came to see each other as sisters in deeply spiritual and emotional ways,
tied together by almost sacred bonds of friendship and mutual religiosity.
By these means, succeeding generations of girls learned nineteenth-
century ideals of womanhood and were initiated into a woman-defined
culture.[39]

For historians of female adolescence, this recent emphasis on sisterhood raises several important questions. It indicates, for example, that
nineteenth-century girls had a difficult time making the transition to
womanhood and marriage because they could never duplicate with a
man, even a husband, the intimate friendship they enjoyed with women.
Nancy Cott, for example, suggests that the happiest adult women were
those who were able to combine marriage with sisterhood by bringing
a female relative to live with them after marriage. This emphasis on
sisterhood opens up the possibility that girls viewed heterosexual sex
with fear or disgust, contrasting the "pure" love of women for each other
with the "base" passion men felt for women. In an article attempting to
explain the emergence of Victorian ideas about women's "passionless-

ness," Cott has argued that women helped create these ideas in part because they gave them greater control over their husbands' sexual demands and in part because they replaced the traditional "sexual/carnal characterization of women with a spiritual/moral one, allowing women to develop their human faculties and their self-esteem."[40]

There is reason, however, to question some of these conclusions, as they refer both to married women and to teenage girls. Through examining letters and diaries, Carl Degler has persuasively shown that many nineteenth-century middle-class couples shared deep intimacy in marriage and that this intimacy sprang from the love and emotional dependence of the partners on one another. Degler has also pointed out that because of the wide range in styles of marriage, no one model fits all nineteenth-century couples—or even all middle-class white couples. While some may have had marriages based on formality and distance, others shared the kind of companionship often only associated with modern marriage. If this was the case, nineteenth-century girls were able to observe a wide variety of marital styles and to develop opinions about which style they found most attractive. In addition, one might argue that, even if most nineteenth-century girls found the marriages they observed unsatisfactory, their immediate response may not have been to envision similar results for their future unions, but to resolve to do things differently themselves. And such dreams were available. Just as modern teenagers learn about courtship behavior from movie screens and televison sets, nineteenth-century girls did so from novels and memoirs, often going so far as to replicate book-learned behavior in their own lives.[41]

Because of work like Smith-Rosenberg's and Cott's, we now recognize the strength and importance of sisterhood in the lives of nineteenth-century women. Yet there is reason to believe that historians have been too uncritical in their wholesale acceptance of the concept. Common sense should lead us to question Carroll Smith-Rosenberg's assertion that "an intimate mother-daughter relationship" based on "closeness and mutual emotional dependency" was the norm in the early nineteenth century and that "expressions of hostility . . . seem to have been uncommon indeed," especially when such conclusions are based on analyses of letters. Although letters are a highly useful source, the context in which they are written—separation, loneliness—makes them questionable sources for information on actual relationships. It is unlikely, of course, that daughters whose relationships with their mothers were very hostile would write warm, loving letters once separated from them, but the absence of epistolary expressions of mother-daughter hostility may reflect, not its absence in real life, but the unwillingness of women who had hostile relationships to correspond at all. Mother-daughter conflict may well have been less common or less intense in an era before the emergence of modern adolescence, but there is enough evidence from literature and autobiography to suggest that it was not wholly absent.[42]

While properly stressing the enormous importance of sisterhood to the women who experienced it, historians have also downplayed its limitations. Close female ties flourished at seminaries and places like Lowell when women shared common cultural, ethnic, and religious backgrounds. Sisterhood did not, however, enable women to transcend the racial, ethnic, class, religious, and cultural barriers that divided them in nineteenth-century America. Just as the Yankee Lowell workers were unable to develop friendships with the Irish girls who began entering the mills in the 1840s, girls attending Protestant seminaries would never have been able to forge sisterly ties with those in Catholic schools. Likewise, it is not necessary to suggest that sisterhood precluded close emotional ties with men. In a recent article on middle-class courtship, Ellen Rothman found that courting young men and women enjoyed "a degree of autonomy and privacy" that allowed them not only "to develop genuine closeness in their relationships" but also to express their affection for each other sexually. Thus, the same young women who experienced strong sisterly bonds with other women, in courtship engaged in open, playful, physical expressions of endearment. Furthermore, Rothman offered strong evidence that, contrary to the idea that girls internalized ideals of female passionlessness, young women frequently affirmed their "womanhood through sexuality," enjoying sexual activity (including coitus) while also advocating self-control for themselves and their young men. Restraint and self-control, not denial of sexual feelings, were what girls expected of themselves. Perhaps, as Rothman suggests, unmarried youths had greater freedom for cross-sex friendships and activities than they would have later as married people; her findings indicate that girls may indeed have experienced substantial discontinuity between their adolescent and their adult experiences and expectations of heterosexual sex. In light of Rothman's evidence, historians need to rethink the concept of sisterhood in order to understand how intense female friendships made room for close heterosexual ties.[43]

CONCLUSION

Despite the growth of historical interest in the two fields discussed here—history of childhood and history of women—there are major gaps in the historiography of growing up female in the nineteenth century. Both fields exhibit a plethora of studies of prescriptive ideas and a dearth of analyses of actual experience. We know a great deal, for example, about nineteenth-century Americans' theories about childhood and their prescriptions for the treatment of children. Likewise, we are inundated with discussions of prescriptive literature for women and girls and the female image in popular media. Harder to come by are studies of how parents actually treated their children, how socialization of girls in the family differed from that of boys, or how girls perceived and reacted to their upbringing. It is also interesting to note the lack of intersection between the interests of historians in the two fields. Historians of childhood have done relatively little to analyze the sex-specific aspects of nineteenth-century childhood, while historians of women have generally ignored the experience of girls, concentrating instead on studying adolescents and young women. Only in biographies—such as Jean Strouse's marvelous study of Alice James—does one get a clear-cut picture of how parents raised girls as opposed to boys and how a girl responded to her upbringing.[44]

Nor have historians in the two fields always agreed on the conclusions of their research. Whereas historians of childhood have tended to assume that the proliferation of new ideas and advice on children led to improvements in children's lives, historians of women have argued heatedly about whether women (and by extension girls) experienced a gain or loss in status as a result of the rise of the cult of domesticity. Much of the disparity in their conclusions stems from differences in focus and criteria. Depending on how one defines "status," for example, one can conclude that women gained or lost it in the nineteenth century. Clearly, women's political status as disfranchised citizens deteriorated as more white men were enfranchised after 1820; at the same time, however, their family status improved as wives' and mothers' activities received more cultural approbation. Many children, on the other hand, benefited from the improved attention to their health and welfare evident by the 1820s. How many benefited is not clear however. Nor is it clear whether girls participated equally with boys in improved treatment.

Both fields also continue to suffer from what Catherine Clinton has called "the New Englandization of women's history." That is to say, much of the available work on nineteenth-century female childhood and adolescence is based on studies of white, middle-class, New England sources. The pitfalls of basing generalizations on such narrowly focused information are obvious. By substantially ignoring the South, historians run the risk of assuming, erroneously, that similar patterns of childrearing and sex-role differentiation obtained in all sections of the country. In a recent analysis of Southern white families, Bertram Wyatt-Brown has argued that Southern childrearing differed substantially from Northern in the ante-bellum years. Whereas the "Northern mode" involved mother-run child care, in which the major goal was conscience building and the major technique withdrawal of affection, the "Southern [white] mode" was father-centered, oriented toward inculcation of family pride, and implemented through the use of honor and shame. The result, Wyatt-

Brown suggests, was an "attitude of bemused indulgence, pride in aggressiveness, and distracted child care" that contrasted sharply with Northern modes. In addition, he hints that the Southern white obsession with family pride and regional honor led parents to invest much more real and psychological capital in sons than in daughters, with the result that girls had few opportunities for the kind of independence Tocqueville observed in Northern young women. The fact that they generally married younger than Northern women reinforced their dependence. Other historians, notably Anne Firor Scott and Catherine Clinton, have delineated the differences between Southern and Northern ideals of womanhood;" yet we have few analyses of how Southern white girlhood and adolescence differed from Northern.[45]

The "New Englandization" of women's history has also meant a neglect of the experiences of black and rural girls. What little work we have on slave girlhood and adolescence suggests very different patterns of ideals and experience from the dominant white ones.[46] Likewise, Western and non-New England rural girls were obviously not affected by industrialization in the same way New England girls were until much later in the century. One wonders, then, whether older "colonial" patterns continued in rural America into the nineteenth century, or whether distinctive nineteenth-century styles of girlhood emerged among Western, rural folk.

The agenda for the future is a long one. Historians of female childhood will need to broaden the focus of their work to include regions other than New England and groups other than the white middle and upper classes. They will also need to shift their attention away from prescriptive literature toward material on adults' treatment of children. And they must generate much more detailed information—perhaps through intensive studies of autobiographies, diaries, memoirs, and biographies—on the actual experience of growing up. Finally, they will have to delineate both the patterns that were common to both sexes and those that were specifically male or female. When historians have completed these tasks, then we will be able to describe with some accuracy the varieties of growing up female in young America.

NOTES

1. Carl Degler, *At Odds: Women and the Family in America from the Revolution to the Present* (New York: Oxford University Press, 1980), 74.

2. Quoted in Ralph R. Smith, " 'In Every Destitute Place: The Missionary Program of the American Sunday School Union, 1817–1834" (Ph.D. dissertation, University of Southern California, 1973), 163.

3. Nancy F. Cott, "Notes Toward an Interpretation of Antebellum Child-rearing," *Psychohistory Review* 7 (1977–1978): 4–20; Anne M. Boylan, "Sunday

Schools and Changing Evangelical Views of Children in the 1820s," *Church History* 49 (1979): 325–328. The quotation is from W. F. Lloyd, *Teacher's Manual: or, Hints to a Teacher on Being Appointed to the Charge of a Sunday School Class* (Philadelphia: American Sunday School Union, 1825), 47–48.

4. Peter G. Slater, *Children in the New England Mind: In Death and in Life* (Hamden, Conn.: Archon Books, 1977), 128–158 (the quotation is from 151). See also Philip Greven, ed., *Child-Rearing Concepts, 1620–1861: Historical Sources* (Itasca, Ill.: F. E. Peacock, 1973), introduction; Anne L. Kuhn, *The Mother's Role in Childhood Education: New England Concepts* (New Haven: Yale University Press, 1947); Bernard Wishy, *The Child and the Republic: The Dawn of American Child Nurture* (Philadelphia: University of Pennsylvania Press, 1968), 11–23; William Bridges, "Family Patterns and Social Values in America, 1825–1875," *American Quarterly* 17 (1965): 3–11.

5. Joseph F. Kett, *Rites of Passage: Adolescence in America, 1790 to the Present* (New York: Basic Books, 1977), ch. 2; Cott, "Antebellum Childrearing," 9–10. The quotation is from *American Sunday School Magazine* 1 (November 1824): 135.

6. Cott, "Antebellum Childrearing," 8–9; Mary P. Ryan, *Cradle of the Middle Class: The Family in Oneida County, New York, 1790–1865* (New York: Cambridge University Press, 1981), 101–102; Kuhn, *Mother's Role in Childhood Education*, ch. 2; Wishy, *Child and the Republic*, 24–33.

7. Barbara Welter, "The Cult of True Womanhood, 1820–1860," *American Quarterly* 18 (1966): 151–174 (quotation, 151); Gerda Lerner, "The Lady and the Mill Girl; Changes in the Status of Women in the Age of Jackson," *Midcontinent American Studies Journal* 10 (1969): 5–15.

8. Ronald W. Hogeland, " 'The Female Appendage': Feminine Life-Styles in America, 1820–1860," *Civil War History* 17 (1971): 101–114; Mary Beth Norton, "The Myth of the Golden Age," in Carol Berkin and Mary Beth Norton, eds., *Women of America: A History* (Boston: Houghton Mifflin, 1979), 37–47; Anne M. Boylan, "Women's History: Some Axioms in Need of Revision," *Reviews in American History* 6 (1978): 340–347; Kathryn Kish Sklar, *Catharine Beecher: A Study in American Domesticity* (New Haven: Yale University Press, 1973).

9. Nancy F. Cott, *The Bonds of Womanhood: "Woman's Sphere" in New England, 1785–1835* (New Haven: Yale University Press, 1977); Mary Beth Norton, *Liberty's Daughters: The Revolutionary Experience of American Women, 1750–1800* (Boston: Little, Brown & Co., 1980), esp. Part II; Linda K. Kerber, *Women of the Republic: Intellect and Ideology in Revolutionary America* (Chapel Hill: University of North Carolina Press, 1980), chs. 2, 7, 9 (quotation, 41); Ruth H. Bloch, "American Feminine Ideals in Transition: The Rise of the Moral Mother, 1785–1815," *Feminist Studies* 4 (1978): 101–126; Sklar, *Catharine Beecher*, passim.

10. Ryan, *Cradle of the Middle Class*, ch. 2.

11. Sklar, *Catharine Beecher*, 113–115, 222–223 (quotation, 97); Sklar, "The Founding of Mount Holyoke College," in Berkin and Norton, eds., *Women of America*, 177–200 (quotation, 200). See also Keith Melder, *Beginnings of Sisterhood: The American Woman's Rights Movement, 1800–1850* (New York: Schocken Books, 1979), 23–27.

12. Degler, *At Odds*, 86–110; Charles Strickland, "A Transcendentalist Father: The Child-Rearing Practices of Bronson Alcott," *Perspectives in American History* 3 (1969): 5–73. See also Jay Mechling's timely piece on the dangers of using

prescriptive literature, "Advice to Historians on Advice to Mothers," *Journal of Social History* 9 (1975): 44–63.

13. N. Ray Hiner, "The Child in American Historiography: Accomplishments and Prospect," *Psychohistory Review* 7 (1978): 13–23 (quotation, 13).

14. Degler, *At Odds*, 71; Ryan, *Cradle of the Middle Class*, 155; Nancy Osterud and John Fulton, "Family Limitation and Age at Marriage: Fertility Decline in Sturbridge, Massachusetts, 1730–1850," *Population Studies* 30 (1976): 481–494; Cott, "Antebellum Childrearing," 16; Deborah Fitts, "Una and the Lion: The Feminization of District School Teaching and Its Effects on the Roles of Students and Teachers in Nineteenth-Century Massachusetts," in Barbara Finkelstein, ed., *Regulated Children/Liberated Children: Education in Psychohistorical Perspective* (New York: Psychohistory Press, 1979), 140–157.

15. Robert Sunley, "Early Nineteenth-Century American Literature on Child-Rearing," in Margaret Mead and Martha Wolfenstein, eds., *Childhood in Contemporary Cultures* (Chicago: University of Chicago Press, 1955), 150–168; Alice Judson Ryerson, "Medical Advice on Child Rearing, 1550–1900," *Harvard Educational Review* 31 (1961): 302–323; Willie Lee Rose, "The Domestication of Domestic Slavery" and "Childhood in Bondage," in *Slavery and Freedom* (New York: Oxford University Press, 1982), 18–36, 37–48. See also Cott, "Antebellum Childrearing," 7–8; Jacqueline Reinier, "Rearing the Republican Child: Attitudes and Practices in Post-Revolutionary Philadelphia," *William and Mary Quarterly* 39 (1982): 150–163; Wishy, *Child and the Republic*, 34–41.

16. Maris Vinovskis and Richard M. Bernard, "Beyond Catharine Beecher: Female Education in the Antebellum Period," *Signs* 3 (1978): 856–869, esp. Table 3; Kerber, *Women of the Republic*, 192–198, 203–214; Carl Kaestle and Maris A. Vinovskis, "From Apron Strings to ABCs: Parents, Children and Schooling in Nineteenth-Century Massachusetts," in John Demos and Sarane Spence Boocock, eds., *Turning Points: Historical and Sociological Essays on the Family* (Chicago: University of Chicago Press, 1978), 39–80.

17. Barbara Finkelstein, "In Fear of Childhood: Relationships Between Parents and Teachers in Popular Primary Schools in the Nineteenth Century," *History of Childhood Quarterly* 3 (1975–1976): 321–335; Barbara Leslie Epstein, *The Politics of Domesticity: Women, Evangelism and Temperance in Nineteenth-Century America* (Middletown, Conn.: Wesleyan University Press, 1981), 73–85.

18. Lucy Larcom, *A New England Girlhood* (1889; reprint edition New York: Corinth Books, 1961), 44; Kaestle and Vinovskis, "From Apron Strings to ABCs," 55–71 (quotation, 60). See also Joseph F. Kett, "Curing the Disease of Precocity," in Demos and Boocock, eds., *Turning Points*, 183–211.

19. Caroline Cowles Richards, *Village Life in America, 1852–1872* (New York: Henry Holt & Co., 1913), 2.

20. Robert Bremner, et al., eds., *Children and Youth in America: A Documentary History, Volume 1: 1600–1865* (Cambridge, Mass.: Harvard University Press, 1970), 686–704; Chaim Rosenberg and Herbert James Paine, "Female Juvenile Delinquency: A Nineteenth-Century Followup," *Crime and Delinquency* 19 (1973): 72–78; Carol Lasser, "A 'Pleasingly Oppressive' Burden: The Transformation of Domestic Service and Female Charity in Salem, 1800–1840," *Essex Institute Historical Collections* 116 (1980): 156–175.

21. Wishy, *Child and the Republic*, 42–49; Cott, "Antebellum Childrearing," 10–11.

22. Degler, *At Odds*, 87, 91–93; William G. McLoughlin, "Evangelical Child-Rearing in the Age of Jackson: Francis Wayland's Views on When and How to Subdue the Wilfulness of Children," *Journal of Social History* 9 (1975): 21–43; Strickland, "Transcendentalist Father," 44–70.

23. Vinovskis and Bernard, "Beyond Catharine Beecher," Table 3; Bremner, et al., ed., *Children and Youth in America*, 415–420. See also Mary Christine Stansell, "Women of the Laboring Poor in New York City, 1820–1860" (Ph.D. dissertation, Yale University, 1979), 29–31, and her "Women, Children and the Uses of the Street: Class and Gender Conflict in New York City, 1850–1860," *Feminist Studies* 8 (Summer 1982): 309–336.

24. Kett, *Rites of Passage*, ch. 1; John and Virginia Demos, "Adolescence in Historical Perspective," *Journal of Marriage and the Family* 31 (1969): 632–638; Anne M. Boylan, "The Role of Conversion in Nineteenth-Century Sunday Schools," *American Studies* 20 (1979): 35–48; the quotation is from F. A. Packard, *The Teacher Taught* (Philadelphia: American Sunday School Union, 1839), 87.

25. Asa Bullard, *Incidents in a Busy Life: An Autobiography* (Boston: Congregational Publishing Society, 1888), 193. See also Stephen J. Novak, *The Rights of Youth: American Colleges and Student Revolt, 1798–1815* (Cambridge, Mass.: Harvard University Press, 1977), 68–70.

26. Kett, *Rites of Passage*, ch. 1.

27. Barbara Welter, "Female Complaints: Medical Views of American Women (1790–1865)," *Dimity Convictions: The American Woman in the Nineteenth Century* (Athens: Ohio University Press, 1976), 61–62; Carroll Smith-Rosenberg, "Puberty to Menopause: The Cycle of Femininity in Nineteenth-century America," *Feminist Studies* (Winter-Spring 1973): 58–72 (quotation, 61); Welter, "Coming of Age in America: The American Girl in the Nineteenth Century," *Dimity Convictions*, 3–20.

28. Quoted in Nancy F. Cott, *Root of Bitterness: Documents in the Social History of American Women* (New York: E. P. Dutton & Co., 1972), 117–119. See also Nancy M. Theriot, "Mothers and Daughters in Nineteenth-Century America: Ideology, Experience, and Legacy" (M.A. thesis, University of New Mexico, 1979).

29. Cott, *Bonds of Womanhood*, ch. 1; Thomas Dublin, *Women at Work: The Transformation of Work and Community in Lowell, Massachusetts, 1826–1860* (New York: Columbia University Press, 1979), ch. 1.

30. Hamilton quoted in Bremner, et al., eds., *Children and Youth in America*, 172; Benita Eisler, ed., *The Lowell Offering: Writings of New England Mill Women (1840–1845)* (New York: Harper & Row, 1977).

31. Dublin, *Women at Work*, ch. 3; Thomas Dublin, ed., *Farm to Factory: Women's Letters, 1830–1860* (New York: Columbia University Press, 1981), introduction (quotation, 35–36).

32. Richard M. Bernard and Maris A. Vinovskis, "The Female School Teacher in Ante-Bellum Massachusetts," *Journal of Social History* 10 (1977): 332–345.

33. David F. Allmendinger, "Mount Holyoke Students Encounter the Need for Life-Planning, 1837–1850," *History of Education Quarterly* 19 (1979): 27–46; Anne Firor Scott, "The Ever Widening Circle: The Diffusion of Feminist Values

from the Troy Female Seminary, 1822–1872," *History of Education Quarterly* 19 (1979): 3–25; letter of Emily Chubbuck quoted in Joan Jacobs Brumberg, *Mission for Life: The Story of the Family of Adoniram Judson, the Dramatic Events of the First American Foreign Mission, and the Course of Evangelical Religion in the Nineteenth Century* (New York: Free Press, 1980), 122.

34. Faye Dudden, *Serving Women: Household Service in Nineteenth-Century America* (Middletown, Conn.: Wesleyan University Press, 1983), 1–71.

35. See William W. Sanger, *The History of Prostitution* (New York: Harper & Bros., 1858); *Report of the Committee of Advice on Behalf of the Society for Employing the Female Poor* (Boston, 1824), 1–7; Stansell, "Women of the Laboring Poor in New York City," 170–183. See also George Ellington, *The Women of New York; or, the Under-World of the Great City* (1869; reprint ed., New York: Arno Press, 1972), 497–505.

36. Ann D. Gordon, "The Young Ladies' Academy of Philadelphia," in Berkin and Norton, eds., *Women of America*, 69–91 (quotation, 82); Thomas Woody, *A History of Women's Education in the United States* (1929; reprint ed., New York: Octagon Books, 1966), Vol. 1.

37. Allmendinger, "Mount Holyoke Students," 37–40; Scott, "Ever Widening Circle," 3–10; Brumberg, *Mission for Life*, 119–122; Cott, *Bonds of Womanhood*, ch. 3.

38. Carroll Smith-Rosenberg, "The Female World of Love and Ritual: Relations Between Women in Nineteenth-Century America," *Signs* 1 (1975): 1–29; see also Melder, *Beginnings of Sisterhood*, ch. 3.

39. Cott, *Bonds of Womanhood*, ch. 5; Brumberg, *Mission for Life*, 30–36; Dublin, *Women at Work*, ch. 5.

40. Nancy F. Cott, "Passionlessness: An Interpretation of Victorian Sexual Ideology, 1790–1850," *Signs* 4 (1978): 219–236 (quotation, 233).

41. Degler, *At Odds*, 26–51.

42. Smith-Rosenberg, "Female World of Love and Ritual," 15.

43. Ellen Rothman, "Sex and Self-Control: Middle-Class Courtship in America, 1770–1870," *Journal of Social History* 15 (1982): 409–425.

44. Jean Strouse, *Alice James: A Biography* (Boston: Houghton Mifflin, 1980).

45. Catherine Clinton, *The Plantation Mistress: Woman's World in the Old South* (New York: Pantheon, 1982), preface; Anne Firor Scott, *The Southern Lady: From Pedestal to Politics, 1830–1930* (Chicago: University of Chicago Press, 1972); Bertram Wyatt-Brown, *Southern Honor: Ethics and Behavior in the Old South* (New York: Oxford University Press, 1982), 117–148, quotation, 143.

46. Herbert G. Gutman, *The Black Family in Slavery and Freedom, 1750–1925* (New York: Pantheon, 1976), esp. ch. 2.

BIBLIOGRAPHY

Allmendinger, David F. "Mount Holyoke Students Encounter the Need for Life-Planning, 1837–1850." *History of Education Quarterly* 19 (1979): 27–46.
American Sunday School Magazine 1 (November 1824): 135.
Bernard, Richard M., and Vinovskis, Maris A. "The Female School Teacher in Ante-Bellum Massachusetts." *Journal of Social History* 10 (1977): 332–345.

Bloch, Ruth H. "American Feminine Ideals in Transition: The Rise of the Moral Mother, 1785–1815." *Feminist Studies* 4 (1978): 101–126.

Boylan, Anne M. "The Role of Conversion in Nineteenth-Century Sunday Schools." *American Studies* 20 (1979): 35–48.

———. "Sunday Schools and Changing Evangelical Views of Children in the 1820s." *Church History* 49 (1979): 325–328.

———. "Women's History: Some Axioms in Need of Revision." *Reviews in American History* 6 (1978): 340–347.

Bremner, Robert, et al., eds. *Children and Youth in America: A Documentary History.* Volume 1: 1600–1865. Cambridge, Mass.: Harvard University Press, 1970.

Bridges, William. "Family Patterns and Social Values in America, 1825–1875." *American Quarterly* 17 (1965): 3–11.

Brumberg, Joan Jacobs. *Mission for Life: The Story of the Family of Adoniram Judson, the Dramatic Events of the First American Foreign Mission, and the Course of Evangelical Religion in the Nineteenth Century.* New York: Free Press, 1980.

Bullard, Asa. *Incidents in a Busy Life: An Autobiography.* Boston: Congregational Publishing Society, 1888.

Clinton, Catherine. *The Plantation Mistress: Woman's World in the Old South.* New York: Pantheon, 1982.

Cott, Nancy F. *The Bonds of Womanhood: "Woman's Sphere" in New England, 1785–1835.* New Haven: Yale University Press, 1977.

———. "Notes Toward an Interpretation of Antebellum Childrearing." *Psychohistory Review* 7 (1977–1978): 4–20.

———. "Passionlessness: An Interpretation of Victorian Sexual Ideology, 1790–1850." *Signs* 4 (1978): 219–236.

———. *Root of Bitterness: Documents in the Social History of American Women.* New York: E. P. Dutton & Co., 1972.

Degler, Carl. *At Odds: Women and the Family in America from the Revolution to the Present.* New York: Oxford University Press, 1980.

Demos, John, and Demos, Virginia. "Adolescence in Historical Perspective." *Journal of Marriage and the Family* 31 (1969): 632–638.

Dublin, Thomas, ed. *Farm to Factory: Women's Letters, 1830–1860.* New York: Columbia University Press, 1981.

———. *Women at Work: The Transformation of Work and Community in Lowell, Massachusetts, 1826–1860.* New York: Columbia University Press, 1979.

Dudden, Faye. *Serving Women: Household Service in Nineteenth Century America.* Middletown, Conn.: Wesleyan University Press, 1983.

Eisler, Benita, ed. *The Lowell Offering: Writings of New England Mill Women (1840–1845).* New York: Harper & Row, 1977.

Ellington, George. *The Women of New York: or, the Under-World of the Great City.* 1869; reprint ed., New York: Arno Press, 1972.

Epstein, Barbara Leslie. *The Politics of Domesticity: Women, Evangelism and Temperance in Nineteenth-Century America.* Middletown, Conn.: Wesleyan University Press, 1981.

Finkelstein, Barbara. "In Fear of Childhood: Relationships Between Parents and Teachers in Popular Primary Schools in the Nineteenth Century." *History of Childhood Quarterly* 3 (1975–1976): 321–335.

Fitts, Deborah. "Una and the Lion: The Feminization of District School Teaching and Its Effects on the Roles of Students and Teachers in Nineteenth-Century Massachusetts." In *Regulated Children/Liberated Children: Education in Psychohistorical Perspective*, edited by Barbara Finkelstein, pp. 140–157. New York: Psychohistory Press, 1979.

Gordon, Ann D. "The Young Ladies' Academy of Philadelphia." In *Women of America: A History*, edited by Carol Berkin and Mary Beth Norton. Boston: Houghton Mifflin, 1979.

Greven, Philip, ed. *Child-Rearing Concepts, 1620–1861: Historical Sources*. Itasca, Ill.: F. E. Peacock, 1973.

Gutman, Herbert G. *The Black Family in Slavery and Freedom, 1750–1925*. New York: Pantheon, 1976.

Hiner, N. Ray. "The Child in American Historiography: Accomplishments and Prospect." *Psychohistory Review* 7 (1978): 13–23.

Hogeland, Ronald W. " 'The Female Appendage': Feminine Life-Styles in America, 1820–1860." *Civil War History* 17 (1971): 101–114.

Kaestle, Carl, and Vinovskis, Maris A. "From Apron Strings to ABCs: Parents, Children and Schooling in Nineteenth-Century Massachusetts." In *Turning Points: Historical and Sociological Essays on the Family*, edited by John Demos and Sarane Spence Boocock. Chicago: University of Chicago Press, 1978: S39–80.

Kett, Joseph F. "Curing the Disease of Precocity." In *Demos, Turning Points: Historical and Sociological Essays on the Family*, edited by John Demos and Sarane Boocock: S183–211.

———. *Rites of Passage: Adolescence in America, 1790 to the Present*. New York: Basic Books, 1977.

Kerber, Linda K. *Women of the Republic: Intellect and Ideology in Revolutionary America*. Chapel Hill: University of North Carolina Press, 1980.

Kuhn, Anne L. *The Mother's Role in Childhood Education: New England Concepts*. New Haven: Yale University Press, 1947.

Larcom, Lucy. *A New England Girlhood*. 1889; reprint ed., New York: Corinth Books, 1961.

Lasser, Carol. "A 'Pleasingly Oppressive' Burden: The Transformation of Domestic Service and Female Charity in Salem, 1800–1840." *Essex Institute Historical Collections* 116 (1980): 156–175.

Lerner, Gerda. "The Lady and the Mill Girl: Changes in the Status of Women in the Age of Jackson." *Midcontinent American Studies Journal* 10 (1969): 5–15.

Lloyd, W. F. *Teacher's Manual: or, Hints to a Teacher on Being Appointed to the Charge of a Sunday School Class*. Philadelphia: American Sunday School Union, 1825.

McLoughlin, William G. "Evangelical Child-Rearing in the Age of Jackson: Francis Wayland's Views on When and How to Subdue the Wilfulness of Children." *Journal of Social History* 9 (1975): 21–43.

Mechling, Jay. "Advice to Historians on Advice to Mothers." *Journal of Social History* 9 (1975): 44–63.

Melder, Keith. *Beginnings of Sisterhood: The American Woman's Rights Movement, 1800–1850*. New York: Schocken Books, 1979.

Norton, Mary Beth. *Liberty's Daughters: The Revolutionary Experience of American Women, 1750–1800*. Boston: Little, Brown & Co., 1980.

———. "The Myth of the Golden Age." In *Women of America: A History*, edited by Carol Berkin and Mary Beth Norton. Boston: Houghton Mifflin, 1979: 37–47.

Novak, Stephen J. *The Rights of Youth: American Colleges and Student Revolt, 1798–1815*. Cambridge, Mass.: Harvard University Press, 1977.

Osterud, Nancy, and Fulton, John. "Family Limitation and Age at Marriage: Fertility Decline in Sturbridge, Massachusetts, 1730–1850." *Population Studies* 30 (1976): 481–494.

Packard, F. A. *The Teacher Taught*. Philadelphia: American Sunday School Union, 1839.

Reinier, Jacqueline. "Rearing the Republican Child: Attitudes and Practices in Post-Revolutionary Philadelphia." *William and Mary Quarterly* 39 (1982): 150–163.

Richards, Caroline Cowles. *Village Life in America, 1852–1872*. New York: Henry Holt & Co., 1913.

Rose, Willie Lee. "Childhood in Bondage." In *Slavery and Freedom*. New York: Oxford University Press, 1982: 37–48.

———. "The Domestication of Domestic Slavery." In *Slavery and Freedom*. New York: Oxford University Press, 1982: 18–36.

Rosenberg, Chaim, and Paine, Herbert James. "Female Juvenile Delinquency: A Nineteenth-Century Followup." *Crime and Delinquency* 19 (1973): 72–78.

Rothman, Ellen. "Sex and Self-Control: Middle-Class Courtship in America, 1770–1870," *Journal of Social History* 15 (1982): 409–425.

Ryan, Mary P. *Cradle of the Middle Class: The Family in Oneida County, New York, 1790–1865*. New York: Cambridge University Press, 1981.

Ryerson, Alice Judson. "Medical Advice on Child Rearing, 1550–1900." *Harvard Educational Review* 31 (1961): 302–323.

Sanger, William W. *The History of Prostitution*. New York: Harper & Bros., 1858.

Scott, Anne Firor. "The Ever Widening Circle: The Diffusion of Feminist Values from the Troy Female Seminary, 1822–1872." *History of Education Quarterly* 19 (1979): 3–25.

———. *The Southern Lady: From Pedestal to Politics*. Chicago: University of Chicago Press, 1972.

Sklar, Kathryn Kish. *Catharine Beecher: A Study in American Domesticity*. New Haven: Yale University Press, 1973.

———. "The Founding of Mount Holyoke College," In *Women of America: A History*, edited by Carol Berkin and Mary Beth Norton. Boston: Houghton Mifflin, 1979.

Slater, Peter G. *Children in the New England Mind: In Death and in Life*. Hamden, Conn.: Archon Books, 1977.

Smith, Ralph R. " 'In Every Destitute Place': The Missionary Program of the American Sunday School Union, 1817–1834." Ph.D. dissertation, University of Southern California, 1973.

Smith-Rosenberg, Carroll. "The Female World of Love and Ritual: Relations Between Women in Nineteenth-Century America." *Signs* 1 (1975): 1–29.

————. "Puberty to Menopause: The Cycle of Femininity in Nineteenth-Century America." *Feminist Studies* (Winter-Spring 1973): 58–72.

Stansell, Mary Christine. "Women of the Laboring Poor in New York City, 1820–1860." (Ph.D. dissertation, Yale University, 1979.

Strickland, Charles. "A Transcendentalist Father: The Child-Rearing Practices of Bronson Alcott." *Perspectives in American History* 3 (1969): 5–73.

Strouse, Jean. *Alice James: A Biography*. Boston: Houghton Mifflin, 1980.

Sunley, Robert. "Early Nineteenth-Century American Literature on Child-Rearing." In *Childhood in Contemporary Cultures*, edited by Margaret Mead and Martha Wolfenstein, pp. 150–168. Chicago: University of Chicago Press, 1955.

Theriot, Nancy M. "Mothers and Daughters in Nineteenth-Century America: Ideology, Experience, and Legacy." M.A. thesis, University of New Mexico, 1979.

Vinovskis, Maris A., and Bernard, Richard M. "Beyond Catharine Beecher: Female Education in the Antebellum Period." *Signs* 3 (1978): 856–869.

Welter, Barbara. "Coming of Age in America: The American Girl in the Nineteenth Century." In *Dimity Convictions: The American Woman in the Nineteenth Century*. Athens: Ohio University Press, 1976: 3-20.

————. "The Cult of True Womanhood, 1820–1860." *American Quarterly* 18 (1966): 151–174.

————. "Female Complaints: Medical Views of American Women (1790–1865)." In *Dimity Convictions: The American Woman in the Nineteenth Century*. Athens: Ohio University Press, 1976: 74.

Wishy, Bernard. *The Child and the Republic: The Dawn of American Child Nurture*. Philadelphia: University of Pennsylvania Press, 1968.

Woody, Thomas. *A History of Women's Education in the United States*. 1929; reprint ed., New York: Octagon Books, 1966.

Wyatt-Brown, Bertram. *Southern Honor: Ethics and Behavior in the Old South*. New York: Oxford University Press, 1982.

5

American Children's Literature, 1646–1880

Elizabeth A. Francis

In 1700 Cotton Mather published *A Token, for the Children of New-England*. Sequel and supplement to James Janeway's already celebrated *Token* (1671–1672),[1] Mather's Preface and tales define in brief the syntax, genres, and diction by which children of the late seventeenth and early eighteenth centuries understood the act of reading, and the aims and proprieties of formal writing. Mather's is a syntax of consequences where the reference of behavior is apocalypse: judgment is the guide of human action. The Preface begins with a negative conditional:

> If the Children of *New-England* should not with an *Early Piety*, set themselves to *Know* and *Serve* the Lord JESUS CHRIST, the *God of their Fathers*, they will be Condemned, not only by the *Examples* of *Pious Children* in other parts of the world, the Publish'd and Printed Acounts whereof have been brought over hither; but there have been *Exemplary Children* in the midst of *New-England* it self, that will Rise up again't them for their Condemnation.

The series of narratives amplifying the "if...then" constructions of the Preface are "true histories," not fiction, stories in outline (like the woodcuts of the day) which "represent" successful behavior. Particular children conform their lives to an ideal life, conform their language to a set of ideal inherited literary-religious texts, and thus become emblems with spiritual and social import. The children who live and die in Mather's tales become fit objects of meditation—patterns of spiritual self-discipline worth the attention of their peers. Mather composes for children from a strong sense of duty; his writing is hortatory, urgent, and formulaic.

Nathaniel Hawthorne, by contrast, composed *The Wonder Book for Girls and Boys* (1852)[2] in seven weeks during the summer of 1851 as a act of heady pleasure. Certain that his new work would be widely read and that his subject was fresh, he wrote with excitement and ease, retelling a set of Greek myths in a New England pastoral setting to children named by their association with flowers. If Mather drew on an English literary and homiletic tradition already transplanted to America by the time he wrote—a tradition defined by Janeway, Bunyan,[3] the emblem writers,[4] and Scripture—Hawthorne drew on and reclothed English pastoral and the classical heritage from which it derives according to American assumptions.[5] The key to Hawthorne's excitement in 1851 was freedom—freedom to compose older literary structures because he was certain the myths he retold were themselves enduring and constant in underlying shape, despite variations in surface expression. So with confidence he chose a "romantic" or "gothic" "tone" for his work, palliating the "cold touch of marble"[6] he associated with older tellings of the myths. Where Mather wrote from a profound and urgent sense of duty, Hawthorne wrote from and for pleasure. Where Mather faithfully reported the sources of his narrators, Hawthorne constructed a fictional narrator for his work who represents youth poised between "wonder" and adulthood. Hawthorne's children are receptive, amused, and carefree; intimately bound to a landscape they explore in its seasonal variety and in whose context they hear the tales.

The contrast between Hawthorne's and Mather's practice describes in extreme but real terms the history of American children's books from the early colonial period to the mid-nineteenth century. Their differences mark a radical shift in the intentions and subjects of children's books, the way the writer defines an audience for his work, the place of reading in intellectual and social experience, the character of the child as a moral, imaginative, and social being, the place of the child in an overriding concept of nature, and change in the uses of language itself. The contrasts are telling because comparisons between Hawthorne and Mather are legitimate. Both expected, and received, large audiences for their work. Both wrote in existing traditions which they approached critically and reinforced with care. Each made a view of nature fundamental to the structure of narrative he wrote. Each insisted that his writing depended on "intertextuality"—the interrelationships among literary texts. Both epitomized the syntax of their time; formed a close and as yet undescribed relationship among aim, audience, and style in their work; and embedded in their verbal structures important theoretical notions of the child as subject and object, presence and absence, a linguistic entity.

The movement from Mather to Hawthorne has been described largely in terms of a shift from Puritan theological strictures and codes, to quiet piety and "good" instruction in the Republican period, to celebration of fantasy and family in the years succeeding the publication of *Alice in Wonderland* (1864).[7] Critics and family historians alike have used juvenile literature to assess the changing status of the child in family and society, the role of the child in systems of ethics and work. Thus, in the most recent history of American juveniles (*From Dr. Mather to Dr. Seuss* [Boston, 1979]), Mary Lystad traces attitudes toward egalitarianism, self-expression, freedom of choice, and needs fulfillment over a 200-year period in an effort to understand American beliefs about the nature of children and proper methods of socialization. Influenced by studies of sex-role stereotyping in textbook illustrations,[8] Lystad undertakes "content analysis of a random sample of children's books in the Rare Books Division of the Library of Congress"[9] to produce statistical analysis and interpretation of fifty variables by period. Lystad adopts and quantifies a stance toward analysis already evident in the work of Monica Kiefer and Alice Morse Earle before her. Thus, Kiefer's intention is to "trace the changing status of the American child in the Colonial and early national periods as it is revealed in juvenile literature."[10] Juvenile literature serves as a valuable source of historical evidence; it "reveals" information about the status of the child. Certainly, Lystad's work on publishing history and socialization, Kiefer's detailed account of the content and focus of early American children's books, and Earle's inferences about the conditions of child life in early American upper-class families[11] provide important information for the family historian. But at least two criticisms of their methodology should be made. In his important review article, "The Study of the Family in Early America: Trends, Problems, and Prospects," Daniel Blake Smith compares the outcomes of demographic and psychosocial analysis with studies of private experience based on literary evidence:

...the insights gained from the exploration of the family's inner life come with numerous qualifications: literary evidence on early American families is very thinly and unevenly distributed across the centuries and geographic regions, and the available personal documents tell us very little about the poor, the ordinary, and the nonwhite. Students of *la vie intime*, dependent as they are on the writings of the articulate few, must therefore realistically confront—but need not be daunted by—the criticism that the history they recover is essentially elitist.[12]

Those who seek to recover psychosocial attitudes toward children and childrearing find different results depending on the kinds of source materials they use: "Prescriptive literature—sermons, tracts, advice books and the like—tends to present a disciplinary picture of child-rearing, while diaries and letters may convey a more affectionate, loving tone."[13] A further claim may be made. To say that children's books "reflect" prevailing cultural attitudes and expectations, to assume that books are indeed mirrors which retain and disclose the content of past experience, to focus on the translucency of the text rather than on the ways it calls attention to itself as an act of language, is to suppress what was most at stake in the shift from colonial to mid-nineteenth-century writing for children: change in the rhetorical, syntactic, and generic codes by which young readers learned to possess language itself.

The history of American children's books is in part a history of changing expectations about language. From early ABCs and didactic religious texts to instructional and fictional literature of the nineteenth century, American children's books focus on competence in language systems and insist that child readers evaluate, shape, and criticize speech. Studying the shift from formal sentence patterning overlaid by paradoxically sensual "figures" in early formal writing for children, to an easy handling of narrative at the end of the period under consideration, allows us to analyze patterns of cohesion and closure, sentence sequences characteristic of children's books from period to period, and thus contexts and codes of thought. The essay undertaken here does not ignore the shifting contents which Lystad, Kiefer, and Earle have discussed, but reads them in terms of the overriding issue of language and language formation. It asks what becomes of the voice of the child in books that posit the voice, how patterns of syntax and style shift from period to period, how the characteristic rhetorical patterns of children's books from dominant cultural groups compare with rhetoric in texts from the subcultures we can partially identify. Because much research remains to be done in the field, only partial answers to these questions can be given here, and even they are given with caution. Books "for children" were after all written by adults for adult purposes; we have little writing from children to confirm or criticize their effects. Even though we assume most children heard preaching in the earlier periods, we do not know in what proportion children were exposed to various kinds of texts. And we have little access to the strains of recitation, song, and story that underlay the texts of dominant groups in colonial America. Nevertheless some useful statements about change in language directed to children can be made if we examine in detail selected popular books. Let us now turn back to Cotton Mather and his contemporaries, recognizing that colonial literary culture was at once indigenous and borrowed, at once English and American.

On December 22–23, 1696, Samuel Sewall recorded his infant daughter's death:

This day I remove poor little Sarah into my Bed-chamber, where about Break of Day Dec. 23. she gives up the Ghost in Nurse Cowell's Arms. Born, Nov. 21, 1694. Neither I nor my wife were by: Nurse not expecting so sudden a change, and having promis'd to call us. I thought of Christ's Words, could you not watch with me one hour!... The Chapt. read in course on Dec. 23.m was Deut. 22, which made me sadly reflect that I had not been so thorowly tender of my daughter; nor so effectually carefull of her Defence and preservation as I should have been. The good Lord pity and pardon and help for the future as to those God has still left me.[14]

On the 25th he wrote:

Note. Twas wholly dry, and I went at noon to see in what order things were set; and there I was entertain'd with a view of, and converse with, the Coffins of my dear Father Hull, Mother Hull, Cousin Quinsey, and my Six Children: for the little posthumous was now took up and set in upon that that stands on John's: so are three, one upon another twice, on the bench at the end. My Mother ly's on a lower bench, at the end, with head to her Husband's head: and I order'd little Sarah to be set on her Grandmother's feet. 'Twas an awfull yet pleasing Treat; Having said, The Lord knows who shall be brought hither next, I came away.[15]

Written two days apart, the passages show us the codes by which a man and his culture marked death as a fact of childhood in the colonial period and closed the experience. The first acknowledges failures of attention and care. Likening himself to Saint Peter, Sewall uses Scripture to judge and correct his behavior. Biblical passages inform Sewall's writing, ready to the tongue and relevant to experience, human and divine speech alternating to diminish guilt and invite prayer. By contrast, the second passage celebrates a formal scene. Sewall arranges his dead children in relation to each other and their grandparents, forming a double emblem of family unity and insistent mortality. To form and contemplate the emblem is for Sewall "an awfull yet pleasing Treat." The words are highly significant. Good formal designs both teach and please, fulfilling the requirements of art Sidney and Spenser had described a century earlier.[16] Satisfied by his act and what it signifies, Sewall allows his grief to be resolved. Thus, he speaks the canonical sentence that ends the paragraph: "Having said, The Lord knows who shall be brought hither next, I came away."

Almost twenty years earlier Mrs. Rowlandson recorded the death of another "infant," a six-year-old daughter wounded in the raid on Lancaster:

I sat much alone with a poor wounded Child in my lap, which moaned night and day, having nothing to revive the body, or cheer the spirits of her, but in stead of that, sometimes one Indian would come and tell me one hour, that your Master will knock your Child in the head, and then a second, and then a third, your Master will quickly knock your child in the head.

This was the comfort I had from them, miserable comforters are ye all, as he said. Thus nine dayes I sat upon my knees, with my Babe in my lap, till my flesh was raw again; my Child being even ready to depart this sorrowfull world, they bade me carry it out to another Wigwam (I suppose because they would not be troubled with such spectacles) Wither I went with a very heavy heart, and down I sat with the picture of death in my lap. About two houres in the night, my sweet Babe like a Lambe departed this life, on Feb. 18, 1675.[17]

The "Babe" dies during the "third remove." During the eighth Mrs. Rowlandson meets her son Joseph, also a captive:

I asked him wither he would read; he told me, he earnestly desired it, I gave him my Bible, and he lighted upon that comfortable Scripture, Psal. 118. 17,18. I shall not dy but live, and declare the works of the Lord: the Lord hath chasteneth me sore, yet he hath not given me over to death. Look here, Mother (says he), did you read this? And here I may take occasion to mention one principall ground of my setting forth these Lines: even as the Psalmist sayes, To declare the Words of the Lord, and his wonderful Power in carrying us along, preserving us in the Wilderness, while under the Enemies hand, and returning us in safety again, And His goodness in bringing to my hand so many comfortable and suitable Scriptures in my distress.[18]

Although Mrs. Rowlandson cites Scripture sparingly, the words of the Psalms and of Job lace her writing at critical moments. Like Sewall, she derives comfort from the juxtaposition of her own words with Scripture and from the physical design or emblem of death she composes. Unable to bury her child, she still lies down all night with her dead babe, embracing the child she has held for days as a *pietà*. Two forms of articulation, "word" and "picture," enable these parents to interpret and alleviate their grief. Either they construct their syntax as an exchange between word and Word, making Scripture an intimate part of their personal language, or they compose physical designs with symbolic significance. The first act signifies human dependence on Scripture as an encompassing explanation of human experience; the second is a way of limiting fallible human emotion and speech.

The contrast between Joseph and the children at the center of Sewall's journal passage and Mrs. Rowlandson's narrative is striking. Like his mother and Sewall, Joseph is an accomplished reader of Scripture, making it a natural part of everyday speech (note the voice of "look here, Mother") and using it to interpret events. Instructed, he possesses the Word. By contrast, the Babe is inarticulate, vulnerable to sickness, pain, and death, capable only of a cry.

Spiritual Milk for Boston Babes, the first children's book written and published in America, forms a relation between the children Sewall and Rowlandson mourn and the child who can speak "comfortable Scripture." First published in America in 1684, *Spiritual Milk* is in fact a book of the 1640s, published in London in 1646 and written by John Cotton who emigrated from Lincolnshire to Boston in 1633.[19] This early American catechism, with the Assembly of Divines Catechism, fundamental to language acquisition in the seventeenth century, grounds the ultimate imperatives of the Ten Commandments in an exchange of voices, a dialogue initiated by the formal syntactic relationship of question and answer:

Q. What hath God done for you?

A. God hath made me (a) He keepeth me, and he can save me.

Q. Who is God?

A. God is a Spirit of (b) himself and for himself.

Q. How many Gods be there?

A. There is but one God in Three Persons (c) the Father, the Son, and the Holy Ghost.

Q. How did God make you?

A. In my first Parents (d) Holy and Righteous.

Q. Are you then born holy and righteous?

A. No, my first Father (e) sinned and I in him.

Q. Are you then born a sinner?

A. I was conceived in sin and born in iniquity.

Q. What is your birth sin?

A. Adam's sin imputed to me, (g) and a corrupt nature dwelling in me.

Q. What is your corrupt nature?

A. My corrupt nature is empty (h) of Grace, bent unto sin, and only unto sin.

Q. What is sin?

A. Sin is the Transgression of the Law.

Q. How many commandments of the Law be there?[20]

The voice of authority questions the child, and the voice of innocence replies. Cadence and rhythm contribute to the spoken quality of the writing and the ease with which the child reader becomes the new speaker of the text; many of the replies are in iambic pentameter or variations of it. Question and answer frame a logical and progressive exposition of fact, leading from a definition of the child's identity and situation, to the Ten Commandments' force as law, to a developed and closed argument stating the goals and consequences of human history. The opening exchange quoted above and the later applications of law to experience are psychologically and intellectually astute; the writer shows the child reader how to apply theory to example and how to think in relational ways. Thus, to honor father and mother means to honor "all our Superiours whether in Family, School, Church, and commonwealth." To steal means "to take away (d) another man's good without his leave; or to spend our own without benefit to ourselves or others." As a social document, *Spiritual Milk* teaches an exchange of dominance and obedience, authority and innocence, adult and child. As a religious document, it teaches the fundamental assertions of Puritan doctrine. As a linguistic and rhetorical document, it establishes the patterns and rules of formal exposition, and the relation between personal speech and abstract reasoning. As a psychological document, it co-opts and shapes the voice of the child, particularly its pronouns, positing a voice for the Babe's inarticulate cry. Both style and argument demand a committed and responsive reader, a reader humbled and then raised up by the "ministry of the Law," a reader who understands the act of reading as an argument that leads to a theory of closure, to the threshold of heaven or hell. The argument and formal design of the catechism assert a comparison between a finished, closed text and eternal consequences, and as such provides a model for ending other children's books. Children who memorize and recite this sequence of questions and answers commit themselves to its content by speaking its personal pronouns as their own. They learn a private liturgy that informs and conditions inner speech.

How then do we understand and account for the book's metaphoric title? When we look closely at the metaphor "spiritual milk," we find a concrete, tactile, and compelling complex of images. Recited and learned, *Spiritual Milk for Boston Babes* is, of course, the most basic of spiritual foods—liquid and easy to digest! More to the point, the metaphor acknowledges the nature and status of the child as a physical being in need of maternal sustenance, even as the book's argument teaches the reader to understand himself or herself as reasoner, subordinate, sinful Adam's heir. The metaphor "spiritual milk" (which labels the book "for children") briefly gives rein to imagination and physical experience despite the restricted patterns of thinking encouraged by the book as a whole. It suggests that metaphors are simultaneously abstract and concrete contexts for reasoning, and that important statements can be made by indirection.

The full significance of the gap between the title and conduct of *Spiritual Milk for Boston Babes* only becomes apparent when we look at the structure of another didactic text which is also among the earliest examples in the Rosenbach Collection of Early American Children's Books. Published in London in 1644 (Boston, 1682), *Rule of the New Creature* is a syllabus of didactic literary strategies and expectations that establishes a relation between figurative and reasoned language. To read the opening alone, as one suspects some cataloguers have done, is to find sentiments familiar enough: "Be sensible of thy Original Corruption daily, how it inclines thee to evil and indisposeth thee to good; groan under it, and bewail it as Paul did, Rom. 7.24. Also take special notice of your actual sins and daily infirmities in Thought, Word, and Deed."[21] The book begins with the fact of sin. To read further is to find it a rubric for overcoming the effects of corruption by encouraging the reader to act on his or her own spiritual behalf while acknowledging the sufficiency of Christ. Section I, taken as a whole, establishes a rhythm between two kinds of instructive language. Exert yourself against your sins at bedtime, the reader is told,

repenting and canvassing them

working your heart to grief for them

believing or casting yourself wholly on Christ's righteousness

cleaving to God's promise of pardon and peace

waiting till the Lord shall speak to you.[22]

Then the writer turns to reinforce and conclude what he has said:

Get your union with Christ, and interest Christ cleared and confirmed to you daily more and more, that you are a Branch in his Vine, a Member of his Body by daily renewal of faith...by examining your heart upon what ground you take Christ to be yours, by surveying and observing the manner you take Christ daily.[23]

The rhythm is clear enough. Metaphor crowns statement, image balances imperative. The metaphors are familiar and conventional, grounded in Scripture. But they are also concrete; they focus and settle the abstract processes enjoined in the earlier passage. At first, those metaphors are scriptural interpolations. But as the book continues, the alternation between imperatives cast in strict parallel structure and metaphor becomes more urgent, the figures themselves more concrete. The speaker recommends both an abstract and a tangible apprehension of sin, a sensuality of the spirit that reminds us of the first stage of the meditative poem as written by Robert Southwell and William Alabaster, Roman Catholic poets of the late sixteenth and early seventeenth centuries.[24] The writer expects the reader to be competent in shifting from reasoned to figurative language, and he begins to develop a series of metaphors with intrinsic emotional and imagistic associations. So in Section II he writes, "get your union with Christ" ... "by daily renewal of your Faith ...especially of the act of Faith, whereby the soul knits or ties itself unto Christ, casts or roules itself on Christ for Salvation." Shortly thereafter he writes:

1. Come to Christ empty of yourself
2. Lay hold on Christ alone with an empty hand of Faith
3. Find the Father drawing your heart after Christ so that the stream both of your judgment and affection run towards him.[25]

The contrast between emptiness and attraction describes an exchange between magnetic drawing power and the natural inclination of a stream. Divinity pulls and affection flows. Metaphors juxtaposed to reasoning enable faith to flow naturally toward its proper object; the metaphors of stream and attraction become metaphors for faith:

Labour to draw and derive from Christ (by the pulling attractive force of faith) ability sufficient for the day, acting faith daily in the promise of grace and strength...which are both security given you by God, that you shall receive grace, and conduit pipes or instruments of conveying the same (grace and strength) from Christ unto you.[26]

Developed and altered, these metaphors are the stylistic equivalent to the method of the book as a whole, which, though didactic in intent, persuades the reader to assent and is not entirely authoritarian. The writer acknowledges positive and almost pleasurable attitudes that are apparently absent from writing for children that concentrates on the description of judgment and hell. One of the earliest children's books published in New England and of undoubted popularity, *Rule of the New Creature*, suggests that at least in the earlier part of the seventeenth century it was possible to conceive of faith as a strongly compelling experience; of Christ offering delight, almost pleasure; and of the voice of the writer using the imperative not in the spirit of punishment but of spiritual encouragement.

The metaphoric power of Sections II and III is subtle preparation for increasingly concrete figures that continue to counterpoint the main text of *Rule*. Section IV establishes the quality of attention necessary to the daily activities of prayer, meditation, and reading. Section V describes "holy reasoning" itself. This section is especially important for the study of colonial children's literature because it predicts the habits of narration we have already begun to note in Mather's *Token*. Three kinds of "reasoning" are efficacious against temptation. One is reasoning from and to consequences, exemplified in a series of "if/then" sentences. A second is a study of precepts and examples that illustrate characteristic human traits or failings. We can fortify ourselves each morning against our "special lusts" "by pondering in your mind Precepts of God's book, against your sin, judgments threatened, or inflicted for it, on proud Herod, voluptuous Dives, churlish Nabal."[27] That is, this section permits stories as long as they illustrate biblical precept or contribute to spiritual self-discipline. Finally, we fortify ourselves "by applying promises of mortification close to your hearts as a plaster to the sore for subduing our iniquity" and "by drawing vertue from Christ's death into the soul."[28] Once again the writer uses metaphor to conclude and ground his point, adding it to the repertory of reasoning and implied moralized story by which the Christian prepares himself for struggle against the forces that condemn. What stands out in the last sentence quoted is "plaster to the sore"—an image of pain, disease, and inadequacy. In the meditative process defined for early seventeenth-century English Catholics by poets from Alabaster and Southwell to Donne, direct experience fully sensed is the prelude to understanding and then to colloquy with God. In the Puritan text before us, and indeed in the children's books we will soon describe, that process seems to work in reverse. As a didactic text goes on, the call to immediate experience increases, expressing itself in extremely concrete and sensory metaphors that provide a means and occasion for closing the literary work. So in the later sections of *Rule of the New Creature*, the writer tells the reader to "get and keep a savoury relish continually of your Christian privileges," a relish compounded of dignity, liberty, victory, safety, riches, joy, and pleasure. The rise in privilege from dignity to joy and pleasure accompanies a shift from explanatory imperative to ecstatic writing, indeed to the edge of spiritual apotheosis. The language of "joy and pleasure" yields to "peace inconceivable, . . . joy unspeakable." The passionate rise of Section VII ends in an extraordinary celebration of spiritual appetite in a passage that reminds us of Donne's funeral sermon:

Get your hearts affected with all these as being yours: chew and suck them by serious meditation, work and warm them on your hearts by close application, rubbing them into your affections; oppose these your spiritual privileges to all your temporal pleasures, setting the one against the other, as your heavenly friends to your earthly foes.[29]

At its most abstract, this style is most concrete. The intensity of the writing is undeniable at this, the "crisis" of the volume. The end of the book is slightly more ambivalent, playing between images of absence and presence, emptiness and attraction as the book correctly recommends that the Christian must imp himself on Christ and wean himself from the world:

Get your hearts weaned daily from the world, and from those creatures and comforts in it which are all dearest and sweetest unto you. as Wife, Children, Friends, goods, Liberty, House, Life. This Christ requires of those that follow him . . . this will prepare you either to suffer, or to die, either of which may put you upon it to lose all.
When we do come to be happy in heaven, we shall stand in no need of food,

rayment, physical marriage...we shall be like the Angels of God in heaven, we shall hunger no more, neither thirst any more. We shall live by the all sufficient spirit of God, which never needs refreshing; we shall be clothed with the long white robes of immortality.[30]

Rule of the New Creature, like Sewall's journal entry, ends with canonical words. Like *Spiritual Milk*, it remains ambivalent about the place and force of metaphor, but admits it to the didactic text. We note that the requirements of daily life and survival become the central metaphors of spiritual fitness—hunger, thirst, clothing, safety, absence of pain. We suck and chew on God's presence. At the same time the main text of the book is a sustained, indeed brilliant, exercise in parallel structure based on strong durative verbs cast in the imperative. As an intellectual process, the book values listing, parallel structure, processive argument, and apotheosis as closure. We end, as we do in *Spiritual Milk*, at the threshold of judgment. *Rule of the New Creature* is not a narrative work, but it provides for the possibility of narrative by including "example" as a legitimate means of holy reasoning. "Cruel Herod" and "voluptuous Dives" and "churlish Nabal" are cues to stories every competent reader knows. The stories the phrases denote are univalent; they value messages, not fiction for its own sake. Narrative, to the extent it exists at all in colonial published writing, is a subdivision of "holy reasoning," subordinate to aims other than its own. Indeed, ambivalence about the purpose and nature of narrative writing persisted in American children's books until the middle of the nineteenth century. Still the stories we infer from "proud" and "voluptuous" can be legitimately implied by the writer because they refer to the one story worth telling in colonial culture.

From the 1590s on, English poets and writers discussed the relative balance of pleasure and instruction in good writing, the necessity of both *dolce et utile*.[31] It seems clear that this concern persisted in partly conscious and altered forms among those who settled and wrote in America. We find traces of the balance in the syntax of religious and didactic writing, where the use of Scripture not only confirms the imperatives announced by the main text but also provides sweet relief from them and assurance of hope; and we find traces in the use of metaphors which, like scriptural citations, provide relief from the imperative and also make analogies between experience in the world and its eternal referent. The degree to which a profound sense of pleasure and joy could theoretically inform Puritan writing is explicit, and explained, in the opening section of *Pilgrim's Progress* (1678) which found its way to America in numerous editions from the date of its publication on.

Intending only to gratify himself, Bunyan "fell into an allegory."[32] He sets pen to paper with delight, not as a duty, though the work keeps him from sin, and when he has said "twenty" things, twenty more occur to him. In a passage reminiscent of Sidney and of the early important metaphors in *Rule of the New Creature*, Bunyan reports: "Still as I pull'd it came; and so I penn'd for length and breadth the bigness which you see."[33] Pulling is a wonderful metaphor for attraction, participation, and spontaneity in writing. The work comes as a small revelation, not as a conscious act of authority. The story that results from the inspiration described in the Apology is one of action, a step-by-step interpretation of the Christian life that keeps apocalypse in mind as its protagonist moves across a symbolic landscape. Bunyan justifies the use of metaphor on the ground that Scripture itself is metaphoric. In *Pilgrim's Progress* we find a controlled but real rhetoric of delight and a deliberate state- ment about God's pulling attractive power. Bunyan defends pleasure as a suitable means of instruction; after all, the fisherman has to "tickle" some fish. His acts as a writer are clear examples of the interpretations other readers of Scripture might perform: "My dark and cloudy words they do but hold/The truth, as cabinets enclose the gold." Bunyan "reads" by turning Scripture into allegory, into representative and exemplary history that stands behind writing for children from his own time to the work of Edith Nesbit, Charlotte Bronte, and Louisa May Alcott in the nineteenth century. Together with Milton in England (*Paradise Lost* [1667]) and Michael Wigglesworth in America (*The Day of Doom* [1662]), he demonstrates how a fully developed and psychologically complex nar- rative could result from holy aims. Bunyan, Milton, and Wigglesworth all confront the problem of matching authorial voice and epic ambition with Christian duty. Bunyan follows Christian's journey across a moral landscape from the City of Destruction to the river in the land of Beulah, converting the history of fall and judgment into an allegorical "life" comparable with the experience of his readers. Wigglesworth dares to imagine apocalypse, relishing the details of incipient pain but above all the differences between holy and false reasoning, the sophistry of the damned, discourse itself. If his verse is decidedly mediocre, his ambition was no less than that of the others. Milton takes us from God's first judgment against Satan to the threshold of history and the consequences of Adam's fall; inspired by Urania, that combination of revelation and classical muse, he justifies poetic ambition because it tells the one story worth telling.[34] *The Day of Doom, Pilgrim's Progress,* and *Paradise Lost* are ambitious narratives—detailed, psychologically interesting, conscious of the opportunities and dangers of language. Such narratives were con- scionable because they did not stand alone or apart from Scripture. All three imitate the original even as they are controlled by it.

Anxiety about admitting narrative to, or reconciling narrative impulses with, instruction was extremely strong in seventeenth-century Puritan writing for both adults and children, in England and America. This anxiety and the character of the large prose and verse narratives that arose from it resulted from the fact that there was only one true text and one story worth telling. Scripture, as we have begun to see, was at the heart of colonial life and colonial writing for children, an assumed part of speech itself. The Bible's power as a fund of story seems obvious enough. If the Christ child is seldom mentioned in Puritan writing as a model for children, Samuel, Timothy, Isaac, and Joseph are—examples of obedience and disobedience, but also examples of suffering, endurance, misapprehension, and success. The Bible does not flesh out the stories of children who are both victims and heroes; instead, it leaves their plots open, to be filled by reader and writer with details and interpretation. Their stories are small parts of the plot that includes all others, the plot outlined by the organization of Scripture. We may justly claim that this organization sets expectations for the conduct of other texts: the movement from creation to judgment, Genesis to Revelation, is in itself a concept of beginning, middle, and end, of inception and closure, which is authoritative, unambiguous, and final. Scripture thus influences other texts at the level of encompassing form, not just of quotable language and example. It predicts progression from sin to judgment, whether the new book is a version of apocalypse, a history of exemplary children, a catechism, or a primer. To understand Scripture as a narrative code is to see other works emulating its finality, its truthfulness, and its emphasis on Revelation. It is also to understand the Bible as an extremely eclectic document, unitary in aim but immensely diverse in structure. The Bible is a collection of books. Its eclecticism encourages other writers to practice the many small genres it includes: song, prophecy, sermon, parable, law, genealogy, and testimony, to name a few; and it permits discontinuity among the sections that compose a text as long as those sections contribute to a single end. The implications of the unified diversity of Scripture seem clear. Readers needed to do more than comprehend the language of the text. Competence meant the ability to apply, compare, and interpret. The reader of Scripture was to be engaged *with* the content of the text and *in* constant acts of comparison and contrast, cause and effect analysis, explanation, and application. We might claim that fully competent readers (and thus writers) possessed scriptural language as both a dialect of English and a set of rhetorical forms that governed formal speech. The more successful the new text, the more compelling its assimilation and reexpression of biblical language. Those who wrote for children at the turn of the eighteenth century had accepted Scripture as a standard to which all other ethical texts aspired and from which they declined. The texts and genres we associate with the literature of popular assent—primer, catechism, juvenile elegy, sermon—struggled with the perfect text as they celebrated and emulated its design.

The *Tokens* of Janeway and Mather drive a middle course between the spare eclecticism of the primer and the developed allegorical narrative. They are interesting and influential because they tell the stories of "real" children, not of Herod or Dives. In them the warmth and encouragement residually present in *Rule of the New Creature* and *Spiritual Milk* essentially disappear, yielding to a market in fear and a desire for exultation. Cotton Mather's children achieve freedom from pain and the possibility of salvation *if they can shape their language to the standard of the biblical text.*

"John Clap of Scituate," the first and most finished of Mather's tales, is an ideal example of the didactic narrative from the American Puritan standpoint.

Little more than Thirteen years old, was JOHN CLAP of *Scituate*, when he Dy'd; but it might very Truly be said of him, *That while he was yet Young, he began to seek after the God of his Father.* From his very Infancy he discovered a Singular Delight in the Holy Scripture, whereby he was made *Wise unto Salvation*; and he also made himself yet further Amiable, by his *Obedience* to his Parents, and his *Courtesy* to all his Neighbours. As he grew up he signalized his Concern for Eternity, not only by his diligent attendance upon both Publick and Private *Catechising*, but also by the like attendance on the *Ministry* of the Word, which he would Ponder and Apply, and Confer about, with much Discretion of Soul, and *Pray* for the Good effect thereof upon his own Soul.[35]

The words in emphatic position in these sentences are the watchwords of *Rule of the New Creature*, set in narrative form. "Wise unto Salvation" marks the outlines of a spiritual course; courtesy, obedience, catechizing, and praying establish a comparison between behavior in society and spiritual strength. Most important, this passage establishes a relation between knowledge of Scripture and the ability to speak in various forms. John delights in reading, catechizing (a pattern of speech), ministry of the Word, pondering, applying, and confering. The more one reads the passage, the more one is aware of its emphasis on language and language competence. This, in fact, is the theme of a tale ostensibly about the death of a pious child.

The early sections of the tale draw a parallel between John's careful attention to his father's "business" and spirituality, but as the tale goes on it gives over the theme of work and concentrates on an inverse relation between physical death and language competence. Even before his illness John excels in the many kinds of speech. He is constant in prayer, questioning, and exercises of devotion. His life forms itself as a relation between word and Word: "Yea, his Parents have affirmed, that for a Year or two before he Dy'd, They never heard an Unprofitable Word come out of his Mouth; but he would often bewayl the Idle, Tryfling, Vain Discourses of other People."[36] With fresh conviction of his "misery by reason of Sin both Original, & Actual," he "aggravates" his sinfulness with "Lamentations." Becoming ill, he follows "the Lord with Prayers, with Cries, with Tears." Then the Word has visible effect on his flesh:

It was also Observed and Admired, that when he was abroad at the Publick Worship, in the time of his Weakness, he would *stand* the whole time of the Long exercises, and be so affectionately attentive, that one might see every Sentence uttered in those Exercises, make some Impression upon him.[37]

John's body becomes an instrument of the Word. As the child approaches death, the instrumentality of the flesh and competence in holy speech become ever more pronounced.

God filled him with a marvellous Assurance of His Love, and so *Sealed* him with His own *Spirit*, that he Rejoyced *with Joy Unspeakable and full of Glory*. He would often be saying, *Whom have I in Heaven but thee? and there is none on Earth, that I desire beside thee*.... He would profess, that his Communion with the Lord Jesus Christ was *Inexpressible*; and the Spectaters judg'd his Consolations, to be as Great, as could be born, in a mortal Body. Being now asked, *Whether the Thoughts of Dying Troubled him not?* He replyed, *No, Death is no Terror to me*.[38]

The last paragraph is the most telling of all, for even in apparent silence there is speech, and it is urgent; through the child's shut teeth, those who lay their ears to his mouth hear him "continually expressing his comfort in God."

But just before his Death, his Teeth were opened; when he would often say, *Oh! how precious is the Blood of Christ, it is worth more than a Thousand Worlds!* and often pray, *Come, Lord Jesus, Come quickly!* and at Last, he gave himself to God, in those words, *Lord Jesus, receive my Spirit*. He desired his Mother to turn his *Face unto the Wall*; whereupon she said, *John, Dost thou now Remember Hezekiah's Turning his Face unto the Wall?* He said, *Yes, I do Remember it*: and as she Turned him in her Arms, he so quietly breathed his Soul into the Arms of his Blessed Saviour.[39]

The end of the tale reads as a consummation. The child who has been, like Christ, about "his father's business," commits himself to Christ in Christ's language, making his body and his speech the page of the text.

John can do everything—catechize, pray, confess, exhort, admonish, lament, ask, answer, complain, profess, justify, rejoice, say, cry, dispute, delight, express, quote, and tell. At the end of the story the narrator, who begins by "telling" us what John says, simply reports the child's words. What begins as an exemplum ends as verbal theater, forcing pity and terror on the reader. The adult at the conclusion of the tale is merely the elicitor of the child's speech. The child voice posited in the tale of John Clap is not only separate from adult voices, but also a purer and stronger example of them. John and his mother share texts and converse in their terms. "John Clap of Scituate" establishes a pattern for other juvenile elegies to follow. The rhetoric of the form emphasizes pathos and consummation; the plot of the genre concerns the inverse relationship between dying flesh and competence in speech. All books in the genre use the truthful testimony of observers to confirm what the plot says. Mather shows us that Puritan writers do not avoid pathos, since pathos is essential to persuasive force and to the formal close of the tale. In the early eighteenth century, the juvenile elegy flourished as it was to do for another hundred years. Both Benjamin Colman's *A Devout Contemplation on the Meaning of Divine Providence in the Early Death of Pious and lovely Children* (1714),[40] the story of Elizabeth Wainwright, and *A Legacy for Children, being Some of the Last Expressions and Dying Sayings of Hannah Hill, Junr.* (1717)[41] one from Boston and the other from Philadelphia, develop the emphasis on speech we have seen idealized in John Clap, allowing not only for the child's spiritual apotheosis and scriptural competence, but also for extended testimony of witnesses and the child's advice to others. We note that there seems to be little difference between the speeches of dying boys and girls, with the exception of Mather's adolescent Bethiah Longworth. A virgin fit for the bridegroom at an exceptionally early age, Bethiah wants to "sing" in Paradise. Mather thus lightly uses the language that was to describe women's poetry and to dominate women poets' conception of their art in the following two centuries.[42]

Early eighteenth-century children's books develop but do not essentially change the formal and syntactic patterns we have found in seventeenth-century writing for children. While European publishers began to print moralized fairy tales, nursery rhymes, and traditional short tales,[43] American writers and printers revised existing forms of instruction. We write the history of American children's books to at least 1760 in terms of the catechism, primer, textbook, juvenile elegy, advice book, sermon, and moralized "token" or example, genres that admitted narrative to their structures only for purposes of instruction.

Little needs to be said here about *The New England Primer*, since so much has already been written about it,[44] but three points should be made—two about the text and illustrations of the rhymed alphabet and one about the language of the Assembly of Divines Catechism. It is customary to trace the history of the *Primer* by marking the evangelization of the rhymed alphabet during the Great Revival.[45] And it is also customary to say that the only combination of rhyme and picture that remained unchanged throughout the history of the *Primer* was the first, "In Adam's fall/ We sinn'd all."[46] It may be claimed, first, that from the earliest version of the *Primer* "A" and "B" together, not "A" alone, provided a thesis statement for the act of learning, reducing biblical history to a minimum which was still complete. Second, the rhymed alphabet as a whole illustrates a symbiotic relationship between word and picture which recollects the attitudes of Sewall and Rowlandson and predicts the limits of children's book illustration until the nineteenth century. Like the noun-adjective combination in a phrase such as "proud Herod," the combination of picture and rhyme becomes an image that implies content. Used overtly as a mnemonic to teach the alphabet and doctrine, the collocation of rhyme and picture composes a formal emblem or sign of the type Francis Quarles printed.[47] It is particularly interesting to compare the rhymed alphabet with the first English translation of Perrault's fairy tales where the imaginative text of the tale is preceded by a woodcut that hypostasizes the story and is succeeded by a moral that states its social applications.[48] Third, the voice of the catechism usually printed at the end of the *Primer* differs fundamentally from the voice of *Spiritual Milk for Boston Babes*, which was occasionally printed with it. Where John Cotton uses "I" and "You" to elicit personal and emotional commitment for the child reciter, the Assembly of Divines Catechism[49] uses impersonal questions and answers dominated by the collective pronouns "we" and "us" to assert doctrine. Not only was the Westminster Catechism longer and more difficult to learn than *Spiritual Milk* (whose "breasts" Mather said should be drawn out on any occasion),[50] but it also enforced collective rather than personal assent to its content.

Textbooks, primers, catechisms, and advice books of the 1700–1760 period are eclectic documents that assert a comparison between religious and civil duty and a contrast between affection and discipline. Long before Lord Chesterfield mixed affection with advice in his letters to his son,[51] William Penn offered advice and counsel to his "dear Children" with respect to [their] Christian and Civil Capacity and Duty in the world."[52] We note the contrast between Penn's honest concern for the child and the sadistic solicitude of writers who took pleasure in describing the pains of hell. If it is true that a crescendo of interest in judgment accompanied a decline of colonial religious commitment in the first half of the eighteenth century,[53] then it is also true that change occurred within the language of that commitment. During the period, the advice book began to shift in aim from warnings about hell to warnings about social duty and social discomfiture, from methods of spiritual enlightenment to methods of patriotic and social success. By 1754, the *School of Good Manners* was published in America.[54] Other writers emphasized the importance of "useful" information. So George Fox's *Instructions for Right Spelling* (1st American ed. 1702, reprinted 1737 and 1769) is a compendium of "useful" knowledge, including the marks of the true Christian, the catechism, the names the children of God and the Devil are called by, proverbs, mathematical tables, the weights and measures in Scripture, and exercises in definition, childish sentence combining, and character description.[55] The last three point again to the interest in rhetoric we have seen in seventeenth-century writing as a whole, and the anxiety about narrative that persisted in eclectic "true" texts that emphasize accountability and consequences. We glimpse in the following passage the interest in fictional narrative that was to remain essentially suppressed in children's books until American publishers began to include titles such as *Robinson Crusoe,*[56] *Rasselas,*[57] *The Adventures of Urad,*[58] and *The Prodigal Daughter*[59] in their lists:

SARAH was a good Woman

JEZEBEL was a bad Woman, who killed the *Just,* and turned against the Lord's *Prophets,* with her attired *Head* and painted *Face,* peeping out the *Window.*[60]

In prefaces, in book conduct, and in printer's descriptions, we see an increasing concern for proper education and at least rudimentary recognition of the ability of the child to perceive, learn, and shape language differently at different ages. Even in *The Man of God Furnished* (1708)[61] Cotton Mather wrote a shortened version of *Spiritual Milk* so that children would learn it more easily. *Some Excellent Verses for the Education of Youth* (1708),[62] sections of which were much reprinted, distinguished between writing for older and younger children. We compare verses for youth with verses for infants:

> Young Isaacs who lift up their eyes
>   To meditate in Fields,
> Young Jacobs, who the blessing prize
>   This Age but seldom yields
> Few Samuels, leaving their playes
>   To Temple Work resign'd
> Few do as those in Youthful Dayes
>   Their great Creator mind.[63]

And,

> Though I am Young, a little one,
> If I can speak, and go alone,
> Then I must learn to know the Lord,
> And learn to read his holy Word,
> 'Tis time to seek to God and pray
> For what I want for every day:
> I have a precious Soul to save
> And I a mortal body have,
> Though I am Young, yet I may Die,
> And hasten to Eternity.
> There is a dreadful fiery Hell

> Where Wicked ones must always dwell
> There is a Heaven full of joy,
> Where Godly ones must always stay.[64]

The verse forms, syntax, and rhyme patterns differ markedly in these passages. We note not only the author's deliberate contrast between exemplary instruction and childish confession, but also the nursery rhyme quality of the verse attributed to the young child. The short quatrains that follow the last passage anticipate the popular use of hymns for children's instruction later in the eighteenth century.[65]

Finally, we find in eighteenth-century writing a slight shift or ambivalence in use of the word "child" associated by the end of the century with changed uses of "pious" and changed expectations about pleasure in writing. In his personal narrative, written after 1739, Jonathan Edwards distinguished between the pleasure he derived in boyhood from the performance of spiritual duties and the delight in divine things he experienced at his spiritual coming of age:

I was then very much affected for many months, and concerned about the things of religion, and my soul's salvation; and was abundant in duties. I used to pray five times a day in secret, and to spend much time in religious talk with other boys; and used to meet with them to pray together. I experienced I know not what kind of delight in religion. My mind was much engaged in it, and had much self-righteous pleasure; and it was my delight to abound in religious duties. . . .[66]

But I have often, since that first conviction, had quite another kind of sense of God's sovereignty than I had then. I have often since had not only a conviction, but a delightful conviction. The doctrine has very often appeared exceeding pleasant, bright, and sweet.[67]

Pleasure and delight flow from "ardor of soul," and from the "inward, sweet sense of Christ's redemption." As he walks in his father's pasture, Edwards perceives nature as a sign of God's majesty and grace, His "awful sweetness."[68] In an extended passage toward the end of the narrative in which he speaks of his love of the gospels (they have been "green pastures" for his soul, words that recall the moment of revelation in his father's fields where he stood as an instructed child), Edwards combines the notion of emptiness we saw in *Rule of the New Creature* with the text from Matthew which always potentially justified a contrast between the child and the "childlike" in Puritan writing:

I very often think with sweetness, and longings, and pantings of soul, of being a little child, taking hold of Christ, to be led by him through the wilderness of this world. That text, Math. xviii.3, has often been sweet to me, except ye be converted and become as little children, &. I love to think of coming to Christ, to receive salvation of him, poor in spirit, and quite empty of self, humbly exalting him alone; cut off entirely from my own root, in order to grow into, and out of Christ.[69]

The passage is remarkable because it associates the childlike with Christian emptiness and with nature. Jonathan Edwards elsewhere called children "vipers" in need of correction and wrote in *Images or Shadows of Divine Things* "That a Child needs correction, and the benefit of correcting Children, is a type of what is true with respect to God's children."[70] In a sense the latter statement suggests that, as in the metaphor, all those who accepted and lived the Puritan code were children in need of correction, and that there was little fundamental or doctrinal difference between the child and the adult. The first suggests, as has been assumed in all critical discussions about early American didactic and instructive literature for children, that children were imperfect creatures in need of correction, fear, and punishment. But Edwards's autobiographical writing offers another possibility, for it charts a movement from the child to the childlike. No one would claim that Jonathan Edwards contradicted or overturned prevailing notions of the child, but he did associate the childlike with spiritual enlightenment, natural splendor, and the words "delight" and "pleasure." The context and intensity of his writing—the obverse of the intensity we find in *Sinners in the Hand of an Angry God*—suggest that Edwards was as much a writer about the sublime as Joshua Reynolds or Joseph Turner and that he was in certain ways a pre-romantic. Emphatic as he was in his strictures, Edwards stated a biblically justified concept of the childlike as preliminary to union with Christ. His idea—the gospel's idea—was to be perfected in the secular language of Blake and Wordsworth, celebrated in the literature of "wonder" we associate with the nineteenth century.

In his classic study of English children's books,[71] F. J. Harvey Darton dates the history of children's literature proper to the founding of the Newbery Press in 1744. *A Little Pretty Pocketbook*, first of the Newbery Press books, was as eclectic as a Puritan text, but its intent was to give pleasure, and its contents represented the integration of a long-standing oral and chapbook tradition into a formal publishing market. Composed of disparate sections and small woodcuts, the *Pocketbook* drew on and combined material from romance, fable, and social instruction, titling descriptions of games with letters of the alphabet and offering missives from *Jack the Giant Killer*. Although its material was not combined in a coherent plot or organization, the book valued the elements that would eventually form the structure of the true children's novel.

The date of the founding of the Newbery Press was no accident: John Newbery, Oliver Goldsmith, Christopher Smart, and those who worked with them capitalized on elements of a literature already present and culturally viable, and on a market prepared by the running stationers throughout the first half of the eighteenth century. The stories of Bevis, Saint George, and Jack had been available as chapbooks during the seventeenth century, usually published in London but radiating out to other centers.[72] Chapbooks proliferated as printing costs fell. *The Arabian Nights*, the *Seven Champions of Christendom*, and Perrault's tales were widely known by mid-century, and shortly after their publication, Swift's *Gulliver's Travels* (1726) and Defoe's *Robinson Crusoe* (1719) were also appropriated by readers of all ages. Indeed, the history of children's literature parallels the early history of the novel and of popular journalism in the eighteenth century; all three forms were encouraged by a middle-class reading culture, and all three addressed the anxiety about free narrative evident in earlier literature. Defoe and Swift proposed a fiction of the distant and the upsidedown, a fiction of risk, possible because both writers were willing to "moralize" their texts. We see the enthusiasm to write narrative and the reluctance to let it speak for itself in the early English translations of Perrault; we see it also in *Robinson Crusoe* and *Moll Flanders* (1722), where fiction serves philosophical reflection in the one and justifies the description of secular—indeed sexual—conduct in the other. By mid-century Samuel Richardson's novel *Pamela* (1740) exhibited an extreme tension between "morality" and story; thus "moralized" fiction licenses voyeurism. The tension was theoretically, if not actually, resolved in Henry Fielding's *Tom Jones* (1749), where a theory of prose narrative as comic epic justified fiction written essentially for its own sake. The need to moralize died hard, in both England and America; as Puritan standards of writing relaxed after the Revolution, in part under the influence of the Newbery Press books, English children's publishing increasingly valued the moralism of Hannah More, Mrs. Trimmer, Mrs. Barbauld, and "Peter Parley."

The history of children's publishing in America from 1760 to 1830 is one of mixed aims and of the establishment of a mixed entrepreneurial market. From 1748 Benjamin Franklin and his partner David Hall published newer books alongside reissues of *Tokens* and primers. Isaiah Thomas founded his press at Worcester in 1779, pirating Newbery books, commissioning works on his own, and building a thriving business that maintained varied options in order to rival presses in New York, Philadelphia, and Boston. What strikes us in considering books preserved in the Rosenbach Collection, the Beinecke Library, and the American Antiquarian Society is the variety and number of books published by local houses at the turn of the nineteenth century, the slight but significant changes in language they exhibit, and the publishing formats that represent dominant themes and goals of the period. Phillip Freneau and Hugh Henry Brackenridge's poem "on the Rising Glory of America"

(1772)[73] anticipates the interest in American subjects evident in lists from the 1790s, when a *Life of Gen. Washington* (1794)[74] and several histories of America appeared. Books on American themes were informative as well as patriotic; long before Samuel Goodrich became Peter Parley, such expositions represented the combination of informative with didactic writing. In some instances patriotic literature was persuasive in tone, intending to create an American history and a set of national heroes with mythological force; John Davis's *Captain Smith and Princess Pocahontas, an Indian Tale* (1805)[75] does just that. In other texts the tone of the exposition was neutral. By the turn of the nineteenth century neutral expository writing contributed to books on natural as well as national history; "Charley Columbus' " *History of Beasts* (1794)[76] offers an example. In another book from 1794, however, translated from the Dutch, and in a small book published for the Bookbinder's Society in 1796, we find alternate attitudes toward nature which were to affect later writing. Johannes Martinet's *The Catechism of Nature*[77] justified study of natural history as a reverent act; *Rural Felicity*[78] valued pastoral life as an antidote to greed and associated it with happiness.

As informative and patriotic writing for children gained currency in America, so did a literature of the imagination. The Rosenbach Collection preserves *The Seven Voyages of Sinbad* (1794)[79] and *The Arabian Nights Entertainments* (1796)[80] after Galland. *The Arabian Nights* is a juxtaposition of tales with an account of Eastern manners and customs. As early as 1785 Thomas had published Stephanie Felicite de Genlis's *The Beauty and the Monster*[81] and *Hagar in the Desert*.[82] *Be Merry and Wise* followed in 1786,[83] together with *A Wonderful Discovery of a Hermit, Who lived upwards of two hundred years*.[84] We note that "Wonderful" in the last title is a descendant of "Notable Things" in Mather's Preface. By the turn of the nineteenth century, children's editions of *Robinson Crusoe, The Vicar of Wakefield*, and *Gulliver's Travels* had been published in America,[85] together with numerous chapbook versions of the "Babes in the Wood," "Jack the Giant Killer," "Dick Whittington," "Cock Robin," and "Tom Thumb." These titles formed a stable tradition of printed storytelling in America, while isolated titles offered newer subjects. Mrs. Pritchard's much reprinted *The Blind Child*[86] used a "true" story to distinguish between true and false sensibility as Jane Austen was soon to do. Samuel Spring's *Three Sermons to Little Children* described "the Nature and Beauty of the Dutiful Temper," adjusting moral definition to aesthetic language. *The Brother's Gift* (1795)[87] valued reformation, and *The Grateful Return* (1796) gratitude.

Nursery rhymes were also part of the newly published canon of imaginative literature based in oral traditions. *Mother Goose's Melody* appeared in a Thomas edition of 1794, reprinted from Newbery's volume of c. 1760; rhymes from the first part of *Mother Goose's Melody* appeared five years later as *Songs and Lullabies of the Good Old Nurses*.[88] Derived from

Perrault's "Contes de ma Mere l'Oye," both titles made folklore and
nursery rhymes the province of the fictional female storyteller; made
them, that is, separate by virtue of their narrators from the traditions
of writing for children dominant in the earlier period. We note that the
subtitle of *Mother Goose's Melody* framed and to some extent qualified the
imaginative text told by a female teller in ways comparable with the
woodcuts and morals printed adjacent to fairy tales. "Calculated to Amuse
Children. Embellished with Cuts; And illustrated with Notes and Maxims, Historical, Philosophical and Critical": rhymes could not yet stand
alone, though the desire to publish and read them was apparently very
strong. The writer was compelled to give a rational and critical context
to amusement (the *Arabian Nights* had also been qualified by an account
of manners). We find a similar strategy in the way another writer describes "trundling" and "kite-flying" in a book entitled *Children's
Amusements*:

TRUNDLING, or driving the hoop, is an innocent and healthful exercise; it is
diverting to see the agility and dexterity of the little lads as they pass along the
crowded streets of New-York, and of other cities, who, driving their hoops whilst
at full speed, generally avoid running against the many passengers that are
passing through the crowded streets.
  The ancient Greeks it is said, used this kind of diversion, and to please their
ears with a tinkling sound, had rings, or little plates of tin or brass fastened to
their hoops, to make a noise, as some of ours do here, for the same purpose.
This rational kind of play is best adapted to level grounds in the country, where
there are no foot passengers, or a few only to obstruct, or to be obstructed.

FLYING the kite, may properly be termed a rational and philosophical amusement, and is not only pleasing to the youth, but also to the reflecting mind, and
eye of age.[89]

"Rational" replaces "instruction" as a term of value in such writing.
  The Rosenbach Collection's holdings for 1805 aptly illustrate the variety and genres of short books for children available at the turn of the
nineteenth century, genres that remained separate rhetorical types for
the next thirty-five years. In addition to John Davis's *Captain Smith*, we
find Bunyan's *Grace Abounding to the Chief of Sinners*, Philip Doddridge's
The Principles of the Christian Religion, "Christopher Conundrum's" *A Pretty
Riddle Book*, a reprint of the *History of the Holy Jesus*, Maria Edgeworth's
Harry and Lucy, John Macgowan's *The Life of Joseph, the Son of Israel* (1805),
Priscilla Wakefield's *Domestic Recreation; or Dialogues illustrative of Natural
and Scientific Subjects*, and *Wisdom in Miniature: or the Young Gentleman and
Lady's Magazine*.
  But despite the diversity of texts available in short form during the

period, the dominant tone of many and the dominant form of publication for children remained the moralized tale. In its format, themes, and juxtapositions, we find both conservatism and change in the fundamental language of the children's book. What characterized the relationship between fictional and instructive writing at the turn of the nineteenth century? What was the fate of warning, punishment, pain, rules, Adam's fall, apocalypse, damnation, and catechizing? An 1824 version of Cock Robin's courtship and marriage, printed at Sidney's Press in New Haven,[90] sets the traditional poem against large, stylized woodcuts, making the first half of the little volume a version of the modern picture book. The rhyme speaks for itself. But the printer did not allow the rhyme to stand alone. He followed it with "The Last Dying Speech and Confession of Poor Puss," in which a cat tells a death bed tale of her own cruel nature and the cruelty of children. Juxtaposed to "Cock Robin" and having nothing to do with it, this death of an impious cat limits the imaginative text, and it is this tale we remember when we finish reading the book. The pendant text confesses that both men and beasts are cursed by their natures; pain, punishment, mutilation, and death result from following the dictates of nature and appetite. The final small rhyme in the book concerns a disobedient child who suffers scalding because she climbs on the back of a chair. We see quickly what has become of the pain and fear associated with expositions of sin in Puritan texts. The moralized tale at the turn of the nineteenth century is still a literature of consequences and of physical pain, but the consequences are earthly rather than eternal. Even informative accounts of children's amusements (a small genre of the children's book, 1800–1835) include warnings about bodily injury, whether from skating or shooting bows and arrows. And the darker fears evident in Puritan literature remain, couched in books of "juvenile trials" and in the last words of condemned criminal children. Juvenile trials describe the painful consequences of misbehavior;[91] *The Reprobate's Reward* (1798)[92] combines the circumstances of *The Beggar's Opera* with the old form of the confession of the dying child.

The moralized story intersected the imaginative text by juxtaposition, as we have seen in the case of Cock Robin. Moral and story also met in new small allegories. *The Two Lambs; an Allegorical History, by the Author of Margaret Whyte* (1828), published by Mahlon Day in New York,[93] at once emulates *Pilgrim's Progress* and *Rasselas*, and uses the language of Blake's *Songs of Innocence* and *Experience*. A good shepherd saves the lambs Inexperience and Peace, children of the ewe Innocence, from a ravening lion, and tends them in a valley among mountains. The twenty-two page allegory combines Christian pastoral with recent literary influences and Bunyan's language; the writer attempts a synthetic work. The persistence of *Pilgrim's Progress* and the synthetic impulse evident in the work of writers ambitious to write longer, sustained works for children account in some measure for the success of the children's novel after 1840.

Finally, we note a transformation of language evident everywhere in writing for children during 1800–1830, but especially clear in a pair of books reprinted by Arnold Arnold in *Pictures and Stories from Forgotten Children's Books*.[94] (John Ely had sounded the change earlier when he included descriptions of "good" and "bad" boys among extracts from recent writers in *The Child's Instructor* (1798).[95] Samuel Wood's *The Soliloquy of the Good Boy* (1822) and *The Soliloquy of the Good Girl* (1820) fully illustrate the linguistic descendants of "wicked" and "saved" in Puritan writing. In both books, a child speaks his or her social credo, and a culture's notion of the relationship between authority and submission, innocence and experience, imperative and confession. In his Preface to *The Good Boy's Soliloquy, Containing his Parents' instructions, relative to his disposition and manners*, the "Author" addresses the "Reader":

The favour which I solicit, is, that you will seriously practise the advice which I give you: doing all that I command, and avoiding all that I censure; as otherwise, instead of obtaining the character, to which I aspire, of a prudent and salutary monitor, I shall, on the contrary, be accused of putting a number of naughty things into your head, which it is most probable you never think of yourself.

As, I dare say, you are now impatient to proceed to the SOLILOQUY itself, I shall only detain you to observe, that you must consider it as spoken in your own person, and the name, at the conclusion, as representing your own name; and, consequently, that you may change Richard Roe, into John Doe, John O Nokes, Peter Stiles, or any other. If you can adapt the rhyme in the foregoing line to such change, so much the better; but if not, you will only experience a disappointment to which we rhymes are frequently subject.

Constituting himself an ethical speaker and condescending to the child, the author frankly *requests* that the reader do as he *commands*. He then writes the text as a soliloquy which the reader is to recite in his own voice, altering the last lines of the poem to rhyme with a given name. The strategy of the writer is the strategy of the catechist in *Spiritual Milk for Boston Babes*; the voice of the child takes for itself the strictures of authority:

> The things my parents bid me do,
> Let me attentively pursue;
> The things they bid me leave undone,
> Let me essay as much to shun;
> And that I may the better learn
> Their will at all times to discern,
> Let me their precepts now rehearse
> In memory-refreshing verse.

The child begins by reciting a version of the Ten Commandments (here understood as parents' instructions relative to disposition and manners), but the text goes on to value equally commandments, cleanliness, table manners, precautions against injury, nailbiting, tumbling, quarreling, and prohibitions against violence.

> I must, in short, from morn till night,
> Endeavour to do what is right;
> And as much, the whole day long,
> Endeavour to avoid what's wrong;
> And hence, I should the better grow,
> As long as I am RICHARD ROE.

Cause and effect, consequences, comparison and contrast (in paired rhymed lines), confession, warning, prohibition—are all here as the child-speaker internalizes the voice of authority as his own. But the opposition between damned and saved has softened. The oppositions this book and the literature that surrounds it attempt to understand are the recurrent pairs good/bad, idle/diligent, kind/unkind, happy/unhappy, vanity/modesty. The pains of hell have become the pains of social rejection and personal injury. *The Good Girl's Soliloquy* differs little from the *Good Boy's*, though it illustrates commonly held assumptions about male and female behavior:

> I must not slap, nor pinch, nor bite,
> Nor do a single thing in spite;
> Nor whistle, shout, or jump like boys,
> To vex the family with noise;
> I must not tell what's said or done
> In families, to any one—
> When I am eating bread or fruits,
> Or anything my palate suits,
> If I have more than I desire,
> I must not throw it in the fire—
> The morsel which I do not need,
> Might a young bird or chicken feed.
>
> I never must be vain in dress,
> Nor grudge what others may possess—

We find in verses such as these, in the frequent juxtaposition of moralized and purely imaginative texts, in the residual force of catechism and *Pilgrim's Progress*, a conservatism in form and language that allies nineteenth-century children's books with their Puritan forebears, but asserts the values of prudence, decorum, economy, and work.

If innovation in eighteenth-century publishing for children resulted from the pressure of popular oral literature against didactic forms, change in nineteenth-century writing derived from European literary and philosophical culture. The effects of Rousseau's *Emile* on theories of education and the nature of the child are well known. By 1794 William Blake, in *Songs of Innocence*, had replaced the traditional muses of poetry in the Western tradition with the child muse and had made the voice of the child a critique of repressive religious, political, economic, and social systems.[96] By 1800 Wordsworth declared the child father to the man, closer to revelation than the adult; the state of the child could be recovered only in appreciation and memory; Wordsworth valued the child who knew ecstatically, and nature, the child's teacher. At the same time folklore became a legitimate literary and philosophical interest. Walter Scott recorded Scottish ballads and stories at the end of the eighteenth century,[97] and by 1812–1816 the Grimms had collected and published the *Kinder und Hausmarchen*,[98] folktales recorded primarily from a female informant. The English translations of the Grimm's tales illustrated by George Cruikshank (1823),[99] and the translations of Hans Christian Andersen's tales by the Howitts in 1846,[100] counteracted the dominance of children's literature by Peter Parley and the English moralists, yielding John Ruskin's *King of the Golden River* by 1842, Charles Dickens's structural use of fairy tale in *Bleak House* by 1852–1853, and, in 1864, Charles Dodgson's *Alice in Wonderland*. We usually date the "flowering" of English children's books in the nineteenth century to the publication of *Alice*, assuming that the book had determining effects on both sides of the Atlantic. The history of American children's books in the nineteenth century is far more complex than the sea-change in English attitudes toward fairy tales during the 1846–1864 period could motivate. The force of Howard Pyle's *Men of Iron* and *The Wonder Clock*,[101] Alcott's *Little Women*, and the Horatio Alger stories derives in part from English influences, but also from the intersection of novel and fairy tale with the rhetoric of moral instruction and national pride, with themes of work, obedience, and family integrity, and above all with notions of pastoral and allegory which are both English and American.

In her recent book *The Lay of the Land*,[102] Annette Kolodny claims that American attitudes toward landscape and land use were colored from colonial times by a shifting interplay between the language of traditional pastoral poetry and language associating woman with the land. From colonial writings which viewed the American wilderness as a virgin paradise yielding fruits of itself without human labor, to later notions of the land as a virgin to be raped and left, American writers tied the enterprise of colonization to metaphors of planting, harvesting, and engendering. By the early nineteenth century, Washington Irving and James Fenimore Cooper had used the paired images of mother and whore to structure sections of their work, to assess stability in American social experience, and to describe the less stable life of the frontier. Kolodny's theory of an American pastoral, considered in relation to older notions of the "American Adam," accounts for important elements of Cooper's and Irving's practice. It cannot account for Hawthorne's children's books, where "wonder" results from the confrontation of American Puritan rhetoric and themes with nineteenth-century English revisions of the pastoral and a sudden understanding of "fairy." We note that *The Wonder Book for Girls and Boys* preceded the publication of *Alice in Wonderland* by thirteen years.

After the publication of *Preface to Lyrical Ballads*,[103] a subcurrent of literature in England valued the rural tale (Robert Bloomfield's *The Farmer's Boy* [1800] was reprinted in America as early as 1801).[104] Furthermore, the impulse that motivated Scott to record the superstitions of the highlands and the Grimms to record popular tales encouraged the publication of national myths and legends.[105] By 1830 the pull of small genres and national myths against the classical heritage and prevailing notions of the hero was strong. Young in the 1830s, Tennyson, for example, reconceived classical myths in *Ulysses* and *The Lotos-Eaters*, and then turned to compose nineteenth-century pastorals modeled both on Theocritus and on the new tradition of the rural tale. For educated readers of Tennyson, the "English Idyls" offer a delicated pleasure that comes in part from the writer's willingness to acknowledge contemporary culture, in part from his wish to reconcile modernity with his classical heritage.[106] When Hawthorne turned his hand to pastoral in *The Wonder Book for Girls and Boys*, he combined Tennyson's ambitions with problems in American writing he had already considered with profound tenseness, and with respect to extreme oppositions, in his short stories. We have already noted the fact that the narrator of Hawthorne's stories is adolescent, not adult, and that the children who hear the tales are named by their association with flowers. Hawthorne sets *The Wonder Book* in the Berkshires, using the intermittent occasions of storytelling to show us the seasons' effect on a landscape at once local and classically pastoral. Hawthorne offers the collection as a literary calendar, building into its fabric the theme of children's amusements we find in short books of the period 1800–1830. The setting of the book is an idealized New England landscape, and the tales themselves are cameos inside the double frame of the narration. We note that the innovative subject matter Hawthorne chooses—classical myth—is fully contained and controlled by the local rural frame. Hawthorne does what Tennyson does in his early poetry— he sets classical myth against contemporary subject matter and settings, making his tales delicate acts of revision. He differs from Tennyson by not writing directly about the heroic. Hawthorne did not explicitly set out to undo the effects of Peter Parley as "Summerly" did in England;

he shifts to a wider key, a wider literacy fundamental to the innovative literature that followed. The agent of change was not the fairy tale itself, but the image of a fairy glimpsed in the context of myth.

Hawthorne's myths offer curious transformations of now familiar themes. The story of Pandora, entitled "The Paradise of Children," is central to *The Wonder Book*. It recapitulates the themes discussed in this chapter. Epimetheus is a child without parents; Pandora is sent to comfort him:

It is thousands of years since Epimetheus and Pandora were alive; and the world, nowadays, is a very different sort of thing from what it was in their time. Then, everybody was a child. There needed no fathers and mothers to take care of the children; because there was no danger, nor trouble of any kind, and no clothes to be mended, and there was always plenty to eat and drink. Whenever a child wanted his dinner, he found it growing on a tree; and, if he looked at the tree in the morning, he could see the expanding blossom of that night's supper; or, at eventide, he saw the tender bud of tomorrow's breakfast. It was a very pleasant life indeed. No labor to be done, no tasks to be studied; nothing but sports and dances, and sweet voices of children talking, or carolling like birds, or gushing out in merry laughter, throughout the livelong day.[107]

This is the aboriginal paradise early colonists describe in certain accounts of America; and it is furthermore a world without authority. No need for parents when neither danger nor a need for rule exists. But it is also a world into which the myth of Eve's temptation and Adam's fall easily fits.

Pandora must know what is in Epimetheus's box and who sent it, though Epimetheus himself is content to remain in ignorance. Pandora tires of "merry times"; she has a taste for knowledge and thus for trouble. "I am so taken up with thinking about it all the time": "Most probably it contains pretty dresses for me to wear, or toys for you and me to play with, or something very nice for us both to eat."[108] And the box is beautiful, with faces and emblems carved on it that seem alive; the problem of the box is interesting in a world without toil.

After all, I am not quite sure that the box was not a blessing to her in its way. It supplied her with such a variety of ideas to think of, and to talk about, whenever she had anybody to listen! When she was in good humor, she could admire the bright polish of its sides, and the rich border of beautiful faces and foliage that ran all around it. Or, if she chanced to be ill tempered, she could give it a push, or kick it with her naughty little foot.[109]

Hawthorne writes a myth of dissatisfaction, obsession, and temptation, a critique of idleness and satiety, an account of vanity in the medium of the short tale. He affirms the outline of Eve's temptation and Adam's fall, rewriting the Genesis story in terms of a classical myth and reporting both from the context of an idealized American pastoral setting. We note that he emphasizes the boy's wish to obey authority, the boy's disappointment at the girl's obsessive desire for knowledge, the boy's need for companionship in a world without parents. And we note that Pandora's temptation is not only a version of Eve's, but also an attraction to a work of art, a curious and beautiful box holding voices, shadows, intellectually interesting possibilities. The box and its contents were brought to the cottage by Quicksilver, who laughed. The arrangement of the story confirms what we might have suspected from the publishing format of *Mother Goose's Melody* and the phrase "paradise of children." Curiosity, knowledge, disobedience, imagination, and nonsense are the province of undisciplined female desire. If "Historical, Philosophical, and Critical" maxims control and interpret the nursery rhymes, if Jezebel appears only momentarily with her painted face and attired head in a Puritan text, if the *Arabian Nights Entertainments* must be controlled by accurate accounts of manners and customs, then the story of Pandora needs to be controlled as well. Clearly Epimetheus has no power: dissatisfied with his companionless play, he finds storm clouds above his rural cottage; Troubles—Passions, Cares, Sorrows, Diseases, and Naughtiness—sting the children like bees and fly broadcast across the land. But Epimetheus finally helps Pandora raise the lid of the box a last time, releasing a tiny figure to counteract the effects of trouble. The children's act in releasing Hope expresses a sea-change in American children's literature itself. For Hope is a "fairy-like stranger" with rainbow wings, an antidote to human misery who anticipates the "aeranth" of George MacDonald[110] (as Hawthorne anticipates MacDonald's voice), and James Barrie's Tinker-Bell. Fairy legitimately enters an ethical literature in this passage, an ethical tale itself contained in the frame of an idealized English and American pastoral. The narrator's final lines connect the appearance of the fairy Hope with hope of eternal life:

No doubt—no doubt—the Troubles are still flying about the world, and have increased in multitudes rather than lessened, and are a very ugly set of imps, and carry most venomous stings in their tails. I have felt them already, and expect to feel them more, as I grow older. But then that lovely and lightsome little figure of Hope! What in the world could we do without her? Hope spiritualizes the earth; Hope makes it always new; and even in the earth's best and brightest aspect, Hope shows it to be only the shadow of an infinite bliss hereafter.[111]

Hawthorne thus connects the language of the fairy tale with the central plot and typical conclusion of Puritan writing. The fairy Hope is a guide to life—adult life as well as child life, a mechanism for expressing the fact and the consequences of disobedience. "The Paradise of Children" is a brilliant synthesis of English and American traditions, of myth, pastoral, moral tale, children's amusements, fairy story, and spiritual apotheosis. Hawthorne justifies imaginative literature as an agent of divine aims, as the advocate of moral virtue, not its adversary. He reconciles pleasure with instruction, not allowing them separate and equal places in a canon of children's books, but making them intrinsically related to one another. He understands pastoral at once as classical revision and rural tale, claiming the traditions of pastoral for a New England landscape. The fact that Hawthorne's writing came so easily, as Bunyan's had, testifies to the brilliance of Hawthorne's synthesis, the timeliness and completeness of his perception.

Only one more text need be considered. Alcott's *Little Women* recapitulates the history of American children's books in the ambitious form of the domestic novel. *Little Women* is a novel: it is also a pilgrim's progress, an advice book, a cautionary tale, a tentative excursion into fairy, an account of the goals and restrictions of women's lives, and an argument for marriage under changed social and educational conditions. Like Christina Rossetti in *Maude*,[112] Alcott studies the varieties of women's experience. Meg's life illustrates pure domesticity, the baseline of normality in the book. Amy chooses marriage when she has distinguished between "talent" and "genius," and when she has schooled herself to be a "gentle woman" matched with a gentle man. Both sisters reinterpret their mother's values, abandoning early ambitions for "mature" choices that disturb, and for many critics frustrate, the sense of high possibility open to American women in the early chapters of the book. Jo also marries, but her history of suppressed ambition, artistic error, and struggle, taken with Beth's slow dying, is in tension with the drive of the book toward novelistic form. Indeed, Jo's struggle represents and parallels Alcott's artistic process, for Alcott insists that the domestic novel is the proper outcome of earlier and less adequate genres of the children's book, many of which she includes and discards in her evolution of the novel's form, some of which she keeps as intrinsic to its structure. If we are to understand the significance of Alcott's formal choices and their relation to the history of the American children's book, we must observe the struggle among literary kinds Alcott deliberately creates, distinguishing between the intentions of Part I (1868) and Part II (1869).

Madelon Bedell has recently argued that Part I is a myth of female competence couched in the story of a matriarchy.[113] Marmee is indeed the controlling ethical and emotional force in Part I, valuing process, believing that play properly conducted is fundamental to "goodness." She has a theory of instruction which is also a theory of the text, and she centers her theory on a revised notion of Puritan literature and its relation to extended narratives. We have already seen that *Pilgrim's Progress* as a narrative interpretation of Scripture's central story remained current in American children's publishing through the eighteenth and nineteenth centuries. Alcott gives the symbiotic relationship between Bunyan's allegory and Scripture new force, allying it with Marmee's notion of play. On Christmas Day Marmee sets ethical tasks and offers instructive gifts to her daughters, shaping their lives for the coming year according to the scenario of *Pilgrim's Progress* and urging them to literalize the text in their daily lives and the architecture of the home. She gives them brightly covered copies of Scripture as "guidebooks" for the year's journey. Alcott's conscious use of bright colors pointedly argues for a connection between instruction and pleasure. Marmee uses Bunyan's plot to affirm her own, and Alcott's version, of the Carlylean doctrine of earnestness and to redefine the quest for the Celestial City:

"We are never too old for this my dear, because it is a play we are playing all the time in one way or another. Our burdens [of character, not sin] are here, our road is before us, and the longing for goodness and happiness is the guide that leads us through many troubles and mistakes to the peace which is the true Celestial City. Now, my little pilgrims, suppose you begin again, not in play, but in earnest, and see how far you can get before father comes home."[114]

Alcott excludes hell from the spiritual geography of the children's book but still centers ethical instruction and emotional growth on the quest for the Celestial City. In Part I, *Pilgrim's Progress* is a framework for literary inclusiveness and a corresponding social and ethical critique. Alcott, via Marmee, insists on a connection between the language of the imagination and moral/religious instruction. Chapters are exemplary tales within this overriding framework, illustrating the consequences of particular faults or sins: the cost of vanity in III, the foolishness of "complaint" in IV. Jo meets Apollyon and nearly allows Amy to drown; Beth falls ill because her sister is selfish. In Part I, consequences are potentially grave but averted, a series of social and physical "almosts" that increase in gravity as the sisters become increasingly able to "bear burdens." Alcott demonstrates her virtuosity by including recognizable elements from inherited genres for children in short passages—children's amusements, cautionary tales, good and bad boys' and girls' soliloquies—subordinating them all to the "progress" of the novel. Most important, within her organizing framework Alcott writes a sustained discourse about storytelling. In Chapter IV Alcott explicitly connects storytelling with ethical growth, and with the assumptions each character has about literary form. After a day of hard work, the sisters tell stories to reconcile themselves to frustration. When they have finished, Marmee tells two narratives, the second a transparent allegory integrating the girls' social confessions into an ethical tale. Like Alcott, Marmee forces her audience of young women to confront the relationship between play and high seriousness, fiction and sermon. The girls react as audiences in the text and according to conventions of the audience in traditional children's books:

> "Now, Marmee, that is very cunning of you to turn our own stories against us, and give us a sermon instead of a 'spin' ", cried Meg.

> "I like that kind of sermon; it is the sort father used to tell us," said Beth, thoughtfully, putting the needles straight on Jo's cushion.

> "I don't complain near as much as the others do, and I shall be more careful than ever now, for I've had warning from Susie's downfall," said Amy morally.

> "We needed that lesson, and we won't forget it. If we do, you just say to us as Old Chloe did in Uncle Tom, 'Tink ob yer marcies, chillen, tink ob yer marcies' ", added Jo, who could not for the life of her help getting a morsel of fun out of the little sermon, though she took it to heart as much as any of them.[115]

Alcott, then, writes a domestic novel by articulating a sustained critique of the adequacy of previous writing for children, and by limiting characters' reactions and understanding according to the language of texts they hear and recognize. Alcott thus opens the structure of the American children's book to include female domestic and emotional experience, but limits its implications by a sustained literary critique. Her book is at once traditionally American and new, sensitive to and inclusive of new populations and social issues, ready to account for the feminization of American culture in explicit terms.[116] But as the March sisters "play" themselves into moral adequacy, read and write themselves into appropriate work, they ultimately are controlled by the genres they come to affirm.

Little Women, Part I, subordinates inherited genres for children to the encompassing organization of *Pilgrim's Progress* and Scripture. This for Alcott was a just means of considering character on the verge between childhood and adolescence. Part II offers an altered rhetorical structure to account for the shift between adolescence and adulthood. Part II is not the story of a matriarchy, but of pairings. Even Marmee—preacher, teacher, and voice of authority in Part I—becomes one-half of a pair in Part II: wife to her preacher husband, "heart" in the partnership of "heart" and "mind." Like Tennyson in *The Princess*, Alcott argues for balanced marriages that permit childbearing and recognize male and female as "like in difference."[117] In order to assess marriage as the outcome of growth from childhood to adulthood, Alcott attaches each of the sisters' stories to a specific literary form: for Amy, literary romance; for Meg, domestic realism; for Jo, fairy tale. Beth retains her childhood association with *Pilgrim's Progress*. We need not follow the genres defined by Amy and Meg closely except to say that Amy's is a complex literary as well as emotional fate, determined as much by the conventions of English as American writing. Jo and Beth interest us most, for they exemplify the poles of female experience in the book and enable Alcott to revise assumptions and outcomes of inherited literary forms for children in terms of nineteenth-century literary expectations. Jo seeks her proper genre. Beth learns to die.

Never an integrated character from the author's standpoint until the end of the novel, Jo is troubled by questions of authority, authorship, and sexuality central to recent feminist criticism of nineteenth-century women's writing.[118] As a writer Jo tries a variety of genres in Part I, some for home and some for public audiences. She emerges from Part I confused about form and aim. The chapters entitled "Jo's Journal" and "A Friend" in Part II test Jo's literary capacities and serve as Alcott's polemic about appropriate writing for children. Alcott alternately uses her character as a valued surrogate in the text and as an object of criticism. In many respects, Jo's experience as a female writer becomes the stuff of a moral tale.

Jo arrives in New York having "tumbled," like Jack, "down the beanstalk" of authorship. Alcott refers to the familiar and often republished fairy tale in order to frame Jo's discovery that neither sensationalism (which sells) nor moralistic narrative modeled on Hannah More and Mrs. Trimmer (which doesn't sell) will do. Jo obediently learns what Alcott teaches: ends do not justify means; the writer has an ethical responsibility to the audience and honesty of the text. Then Jo tries a third form, juvenile literature:

Then she tried a child's story, which she could easily have disposed of if she had not been mercenary enough to demand filthy lucre for it. The only person who offered enough to make it worth her while to try juvenile literature, was a worthy gentleman who felt it his mission to convert all the world to his particular belief. But much as she liked to write for children, Jo could not consent to depict all her naughty boys as being eaten by bears, or tossed by mad bulls because they did not go to a particular Sabbath school, nor all the good infants who did go, of course, as rewarded by every kind of bliss, from gilded gingerbread to escorts of angels, when they departed this life, with psalms or sermons on their lisping tongues. So nothing came of these trials; and Jo corked up her inkstand, and said, in a fit of very wholesome humility,—

"I don't know anything; I'll wait till I do before I try again, and meantime, "sweep mud in the street," if I can't do better—that's honest, anyway." Which decision proved that her second tumble down the beanstalk had done her some good.[119]

When she corks up her inkstand, Jo has neither a rhetoric nor a voice. But Alcott frames her critique of the Sunday school tract nineteenth-

century version of the cautionary tale, with the promise of a new adequacy. All around Jo the signs of an appropriate language manifest
themselves if she will but "read" her experience correctly. Mr. Bhaer,
the German scholar who nurtures children, who reads Shakespeare,
Homer, Schiller, and Milton, who represents new immigrant energy in
American society, "schools" Jo in literary ethics and offers her an adequate genre fit for both life and art. Bhaer is the agent of Alcott's literary
polemic in the latter part of the novel, and the language Alcott uses to
describe the encounter between Bhaer and Jo expresses the literary hope
of the mid-nineteenth century—that fairy tale could indeed resolve plots
and give life form. Mr. Bhaer is an unlikely prince to Jo's Sleeping
Beauty, but "Sleeping Beauty" shapes the relationship even as it controls
plot in Tennyson's *The Princess*. Bhaer plays Bottom to Tina's Titania;
he affirms Marmee's notion of play when he teaches Jo German grammar
by obliging her to read the *märchen*, offering her "pills in jelly" more
effective as teaching tools than abstractions can be. It is important to see
that the fairy tales Bhaer places in Jo's hands are newly published works
by Andersen, coinages on the traditional tales Alcott has already acknowledged in the framing language of the chapter. Alcott criticizes
traditional expectations in writing as she proclaims the new validity of
the fairy tale, like Tennyson using fairy tale to argue for a qualified
earthly paradise at the end of the novel. Alcott, via Bhaer, offers a new
cultural language as well as an awakened sexuality to Jo; she confines
her character to a "female" role for the present but implies for her new
strength of authorship in the indefinite future. We may deeply regret
that Alcott diminishes Jo's intellectual aspirations and shifts to literary
polemic in the New York chapters, but we should see the power of her
critique: where Puritan writing for children moved from fall to apocalypse, fairy tale permits endings in the world. Ironically, it is fairy tale,
the form that liberated children's literature from the restrictions of didactic texts, that encouraged Alcott to limit female aspirations in the
mid-nineteenth-century domestic novel. The other was the residual power
of *Pilgrim's Progress*. We understand Alcott's anxious defense of a feminized American culture best if we see the ironic coincidence between
Alcott's literary and social choice, one she attaches to Beth at the crux
of the novel.

Beth is always "good," always childlike, a virgin who does not anticipate
marriage and childbearing. At the crisis of her first illness, she is a victim,
waxen, frail, and incoherent. Beth in Part II is a more complex character.
Alcott allows her to acknowledge failing health and its consequences, to
struggle against physical and existential fear. In "The Valley of the
Shadow," Alcott closely describes the stages of Beth's grief for herself;
Beth's wonted silence yields to authoritative speech, and Beth claims the
renunciation that love requires. The resurgence of *Pilgrim's Progress* as

a controlling rhetoric in this penultimate section of the novel, and Beth's force as a dying mentor, have special implications for Jo:

"You must take my place, Jo, and be everything to father and mother when I am gone. They will turn to you—don't fail them; and if it's hard to work alone, remember that I don't forget you, and that you'll be happier in doing that, than writing splendid books, or seeing all the world; for love is the only thing that we can carry with us when we go, and it makes the end so easy."[120]

Jo cedes her ambition "to a new and better one," accepting the discipline of her author and her sister. Then the language of literary suppression becomes the language of literary critique: Beth dies redefining one of the earliest genres of the American children's book.

So the spring days came and went, the sky grew clearer, the earth greener, the flowers were up fair and early, and the birds came back in time to say good-by to Beth, who, like a tired but trustful child, clung to the hands that had led her all her life, as father and mother guided her tenderly through the valley of the shadow, and gave her up to God.
Seldom, except in books, do the dying utter memorable words, see visions, or depart with beatified countenances; and those who have sped many parting souls know, that to most the end comes as naturally and simply as sleep. As Beth had hoped, the "tide went out easily": and in the dark hour before the dawn, on the bosom where she had drawn her first breath, she quietly drew her last, with no farewell but one loveing look and a little sigh.[121]

This is Alcott's new version of the "death of a pious child." Celebrating silence and peace, Alcott refuses apocalyptic endings. By implication Beth reaches the Celestial City, the first of her companions to cross the river; and she continues, a silent presence, conditioning family life.
Alcott resolves the novel in the chapter "Harvest Time," a canonical mid-nineteenth-century ending comparable with the conclusions of *Hard Times*, *Alice's Adventures in Wonderland*, *Goblin Market*, and *The Princess*. Jo the would-be author—like Alice the fantasist, Ida the seeker of female power, Sissie the child of the circus, Lizzie and Laura the tasters of forbidden fruit—is the bearer of children instead of works of the imagination. Like Alice, Sissie, Lizzie, and Laura, she becomes a teacher and storyteller for her own children, giving them limited access to her private imaginative life. This is where female power resides in a newly feminized American culture according to Alcott—in compromise, in the ability to form the imaginative and ethical lives of future generations, with spoken rather than written words. Alcott ends her novel with a sense of necessary limitation, limitation she accepts as just in a realist's world.
Little Women is a formal and intellectual watershed in the history of American writing for children. Immediately succeeding important work

by Dodgson, Dickens, and Hawthorne, immediately preceding novels of
heroic adventure by Pyle and Horatio Alger, *Little Women* epitomizes the
possibilities and restrictions inherent in the reconciliation of fairy, novel,
and didactic intent, the reconciliation of earthly and heavenly concerns.
Both the costs and the freedoms of Alcott's synthesis are great. The
domestic novel demands full exploration of family and women's lives;
fairy tale permits nearly explicit discussion of sexuality. But the newly
canonical forms and endings of fairy tale strictly define closure in the
domestic novel and thus limit the shape of the lives they describe. Alcott's
characters speak and think in generic terms, make choices according to
literary scenarios. Characters react according to the genres Alcott allows
them to know. And Alcott recommends their choices to the audiences
of her novel. Writing in the everyday speech rhythms of mid-nineteenth-
century life, using simple syntax to achieve extended narrative, Alcott
allows tradition and innovation in the language of the children's book
to become a determining force in nineteenth-century American culture.

NOTES

1. Cotton Mather, *A Token, for the Children of New-England. Or, Some Examples
of Children, In whom the Fear of God was Remarkably Budding, before they Dyed, in
Several Parts of New-England. Preserved and Published, for the Encouragement of Piety
in other Children.* (Boston: Printed by Timothy Green for Benjamin Eliot, 1700).
Supplement to James Janeway, *A Token for Children. Being an Exact Account of the
Conversion, Holy and Exemplary Lives and joyful Deaths of several young Children.*
(Boston, 1700). F.J. Harvey Darton, *Children's Books in England: Five Centuries of
Social Life* (2d ed., Cambridge: Cambridge University Press, 1958), 54–58, describes Janeway's text, its biographical origins and bibliographical history, and
its vogue in England, 1675–1720.
2. "Introductory Note," Nathaniel Hawthorne, *The Wonder Book for Girls
and Boys* (Boston and New York: Houghton Mifflin, 1900), xi. Hawthorne speaks
in the "Author's Preface," xiv, of "a task fit for hot weather, and one of the most
agreeable, of a literary kind, which he ever undertook...."; he concludes that
"he has generally suffered the theme to soar, whenever such was its tendency,
and when he himself was buoyant enough to follow without effort. Children
possess an unestimated sensibility to whatever is deep or high, in imagination
or feeling, so long as it is simple, likewise. It is only the artificial and the complex
that bewilder them."
3. The first American edition of *The Pilgrim's Progress from this World to that
which is to Come* was printed by Isaiah Thomas, at Worcester, 1790–1791, and
the second by J. M. M'Culloch at Philadelphia in 1793, but Bunyan was known
in America shortly after the initial publication of his works. *Grace Abounding to
the Chief of Sinners* was printed in the eighth edition (Boston: Printed by J. Allen
for Nicholas Boone) in 1717, and *Doctrine of the Law and Grace Unfolded . . .* in the
third edition (Boston: Printed by J. Draper for D. Henchman) in 1742.
4. Francis Quarles's *Emblemes* (London, 1635), asserts a correlation between

word and picture evident also in the patterned language of George Herbert's devotional poems "Easter Wings" and "The Altar" from *The Temple* (London, 1633). Quarles's *Emblemes* attaches a formal and decorative illustration as well as exposition in verse to selected biblical passages. In his address "To the Reader," Quarles writes: "An *Embleme* is but a silent Parable. Let not the tender Eye check, to see the allusion to our blessed Saviour figured in these Types. In holy Scripture, he is sometimes called a Sower; sometimes, a Fisher; sometimes a Physician: And why not presented so as well to the eye as to the ear? Before the knowledge of letters God was known by *Hieroglyphicks*; and, indeed, what are the Heavens, the Earth, nay every Crature, but *Hieroglyphicks* and *Emblemes* of His Glory?" *The Complete Works in Prose and Verse of Francis Quarles*, rep. Chertsey Worthies' Library, 3 vols. (New York, AMS Press, 1967), 3:45.

5. American pastoral ideas and the desire for a recovered Eden in the New World have been discussed at length by Frederick T. Carpenter, "The American Myth: Paradise (To Be) Regained," *Publications of the Modern Language Association* 74 (1959): 599–606; Alan Heimert, "Puritanism, The Wilderness and the Frontier," *New England Quarterly* 26 (1953): 361–381; Annette Kolodny, *The Lay of the Land* (Chapel Hill: University of North Carolina Press, 1975); R.W.B. Lewis, *The American Adam: Innocence, Tragedy and Tradition in the Nineteenth Century* (Chicago: University of Chicago Press, 1955); and A. W. Plumstead, "An Introductory Essay," *The Wall and the Garden: Selected Massachusetts Election Sermons 1670–1675* (Minneapolis: University of Minnesota Press, 1968).

6. Hawthorne, Letter to Fields, "Introductory Note," *The Wonder Book for Girls and Boys*, x–xi.

7. Mary Lystad, *From Dr. Mather to Dr. Seuss* (Boston: G. K. Hall & Co., 1980).

8. Cf. Lenore Weitzman, Deborah Effler, Elizabeth Hokada, and Catherine Ross, "Sex-Role Socialization in Picture Books for Preschool Children," *American Journal of Sociology* 77 (1972): 1125–1150.

9. Lystad, *From Dr. Mather to Dr. Seuss*, xii.

10. Monica Kiefer, *American Children Through Their Books* (Philadelphia: University of Pennsylvania Press, 1948), 1.

11. Alice Morse Earle, *Child Life in Colonial Days* (New York: Macmillan Co., 1904). Perhaps the most important section of Earle's study for the purposes of this chapter, in addition to the section on stories and picture books, is the concluding chapter entitled "Flower Lore of Children." Earle considers the language of traditional games, rhymes, and play.

12. Daniel Blake Smith, "The Study of the Family in Early America: Trends, Problems, and Prospects," *William and Mary Quarterly*, 3d ser., 39 (1983): 21–22.

13. Ibid., 13.

14. Samuel Sewall, "From the Diary," in Ray Harney Pearse, ed., *Colonial American Writing* (New York: Holt, Rinehart & Winston, 1950), 99.

15. Ibid., 100.

16. In "An Apology for Poetry," Sir Philip Sidney distinguishes poets from other artists by the relation between intent and subject. Poets "be they which most properly do imitate to teach and delight, and to imitate borrow nothing of what is, hath been, or shall be; but range, only reined with learned discretion,

into the divine consideration of what may be, and should be." Norton Anthology of English Literature, rev. ed., 2 vols. (New York: W. W. Norton, 1968), 1:480.

17. Mrs. Mary Rowlandson, "A Narrative of the Captivity and Restoration of Mrs. Mary Rowlandson" (Huntington Library MS.), in Richard Slotkin and James F. Folson, eds., *So Dreadful a Judgment: Puritan Responses to King Phillip's War, 1676–1677* (Middletown, Conn.: Wesleyan University Press, 1978), 328. Cf. Roy Harvey Pearce, "The Significances of the Captivity Narrative," *American Literature* 19 (1947): 1–20.

18. Ibid., 336.

19. *Spiritual Milk for Boston Babes. In either England; Drawn out of the breasts of both Testaments for their Souls nourishment. But may be of like use to any Children* (Boston, 1684). Described in A. S. W. Rosenbach, *Early American Children's Books* (New York: Kraus Reprint Corp., 1966; first printed Portland, Me., 1933), 3, Rosenbach No. 2. Rosenbach numbers refer henceforward to this volume and corresponding holdings in the Rare Book Department, Free Library, Philadelphia. Volumes cited from the Rosenbach Collection should be compared with comparable works cited in d'Alte A. Welch, *A Bibliography of American Children's Books Printed Prior to 1821* (Worcester, Mass.: American Antiquarian Society and Barre Publishers, 1972).

20. *Spiritual Milk*, 1.

21. *The Rule of the New-Creature. To be Practised every Day, in all the Particulars of it which are ten.* (Boston: Printed for Mary Avery, 1682), 3. Rosenbach No. 1.

22. Ibid., 1–2.

23. Ibid., 2.

24. Cf. Louis L. Martz, *The Poetry of Meditation; A study of English Religious Literature of the Seventeenth Century* (rev. ed., New Haven: Yale University Press, 1962). Louis L. Martz, ed., *The Meditative Poem: An Anthology of Seventeenth Century Verse* (New York: New York University Press, 1963).

25. *Rule of the New-Creature*, 5.

26. Ibid., 6, 7. See also p. 3: "You find the Father drawing your heart after Christ."

27. Ibid., 8.

28. Ibid.

29. Ibid., 11.

30. Ibid., 14.

31. An extreme example of parallel structure used to affirm a connection between reasoned human activity and religious inference is to be found in William Secker's *A Wedding Ring Fit for the Finger. Or, the Salve of Divinity on the Sore of Humanity . . . laid open in a Sermon at a Wedding in Edmonton. . . .* (Boston: Printed by T[imothy] G[reen] for N[icholas] Buttolph, 1705). Rosenbach No. 6.

32. John Bunyan, "The Author's Apology for his Book," *The Pilgrim's Progress from this World to that which is to Come*, ed. James Blanton Wharey; 2d ed., rev. by Roger Sharrock (Oxford: Clarendon Press, 1960), 1.

33. Ibid., 2.

34. For a description of Wigglesworth's poem, see Sandford Fleming, *Children and Puritanism* (New York: Arno Press and the New York Times, 1969), 82–85. *The Day of Doom* is particularly interesting as an early account of speech under controlled literary conditions: speakers confess and argue their cases,

demonstrating true and false reasoning. The tone of the poem contrasts sharply with that of an earlier work, Benjamin Keach's *War with the Devil, or, The Young Man's Conflict with the Powers of Darkness, in a Dialogue Discovering the Corruption and Vanity of Youth, the horrible Nature of Sin, and Deplorable Condition of Fallen Man....* (New York: William Bradford, 1707). Rosenbach No. 7.

35. Mather, *Token for the Children of New-England....*, 5.
36. Ibid., 6.
37. Ibid., 7–8.
38. Ibid., 9–10.
39. Ibid., 11.
40. Benjamin Colman, *A Devout Contemplation on the Meaning of Divine Providence, in the Early Death of Pious and lovely Children. Preached upon the Sudden and Lamented Death of Mrs. Elizabeth Wainwright Who departed this Life, April the 8th, 1714* (Boston: Printed by John Allen for Joanna Perry, 1714). Rosenbach No. 10.
41. *A Legacy for Children, being Some of the Last Expressions, and Dying Sayings of Hannah Hill, Junr. Of the City of Philadelphia, in the Province of Pennsilvania, in America, Aged Eleven Years and near Three Months* (3d ed., Philadelphia: Andrew Bradford, 1717). Rosenbach No. 13.
42. Christina Rossetti in "A Birthday" summarizes the association of women's lyric poetry and song when she writes "My heart is like a singing bird/ Whose nest is in a watered shoot,/ My heart is like an apple-tree/ Whose boughs are bent with thick-set fruit." Cf. Sandra Gilbert and Susan Gubar, *The Madwoman in the Attic* (New Haven and London: Yale University Press, 1980), 69, 539–563, and 586 for commentary on lyric poetry as a male tradition and the conventions of women writing lyric poetry through the nineteenth century.
43. Cf. Darton, *Children's Books in England*, 72–105.
44. Standard bibliography for the history and effects of *The New-England Primer* includes Wilberforce Eames, *Early New England Catechisms* (New York: Burt Franklin, 1898); Paul Leicester Ford, ed., *The New-England Primer: A History of Its Origin and Development* (New York: Teacher's College, Columbia University, 1962); Charles F. Heartman, *American Primers, Indian primers, Royal Primers, and thirty-seven other types of non-New-England primers issued prior to 1830; a Bibliographical Checklist embellished with twenty-six cuts, with an Introduction and Indexes* (Highland Park, N.J.: Printed for H. B. Weiss, 1935); Charles F. Heartman, *The New England Primer Issued Prior to 1830* (Privately printed, 1922); and George Emery Littlefield, *Early Schools and School-books of New England* (New York: Russell & Russell, 1965).
45. Cf. Ford, "Introduction," *New-England Primer*, 25–32.
46. Ibid., 26.
47. See note 4 above.
48. The first English edition of Charles Perrault's *Contes de ma Mere Loye* was printed in 1719. The Union List of Serials notes that an edition was printed in America as *Fairy Tales, or Histories of Past Times. With Morals* (Haverhill, Mass.: Peter Eden, 1794).
49. Ford, "Introduction," *New-England Primer*, 37–41.
50. The Assembly of Divines Catechism alternates between collective assent and third-person exposition of doctrine. We note the neutral and expository

tone of a passage such as the following: "Q. What are the Benefits which in this life do accompany or flow from Justification, Adoption & Sanctification? A. The Benefits which in this Life do accompany or flow from Justification, Adoption, or Sanctification, are assurance of God's love, peace of Conscience, Joy in the Holy Ghost, Increase of Grace and Perseverence therein to the end."

51. *Letters, written by the late Right Honourable Philip Dormer Stanhope, Earl of Chesterfield, to his son, Philip Stanhope esq., late envoy extraordinary at the court of Dresden. Together with other pieces on various subjects. Published by Mrs. Eugenia Stanhope, from the originals now in her possession* (London: J. Dodsley, 1774). The Rosenbach Collection includes an edition of the letters entitled *Principles of Politeness, and of Knowing the World* which is "Modernized and Digested under distinct Heads" (Norwich: John Trumbull, 1785). By 1828 an edition was published entitled *The American Chesterfield, or, Way to wealth, honour and distinction; being selections from the Letters of Lord Chesterfield to his son; and extracts from other eminent authors, on the subject of politeness: with alterations and additions, suited to the youth of the United States* (Philadelphia, J. Grigg).

52. William Penn, *Fruits of a Father's Love. Being the Advice of William Penn to His Children, Relating to Their Civil and Religious Conduct. . . .* (Printed London; Philadelphia, reprinted by Andrew Bradford, 1727), 7, 8. Rosenbach No. 21.

53. Kiefer, *American Children Through Their Books*, 29, writes: "The generation of 1700 showed signs of a weakening faith in the old religious codes based on hopes of heaven and fears of hell. Writers, in desperation, sought in the most terrifying manner to warn 'reprobates', however young, of the approaching 'Day of Doom' with its attendant terrors for the depraved and unrepentant sinner. The prevailing apathy against which the spiritually minded shattered their lances is reflected in the nervous apprehension and the vehement language of children's books and sermons."

54. Rosenbach No. 41 is a fifth edition published in New London by T. & J. Green, 1754.

55. *Instructions for Right-Spelling and Plain Directions for Reading and Writing True English. With several delightful things very Useful and Necessary, both for Young and Old, to Read and Learn* (Philadelphia: rep. by Reynier Jansen, 1702). Fox's version of "The Child's Lesson," 10, includes an interesting shift between the syntax of definition and belief: "Christ is the Truth, the Light, my Way, my Life, my Saviour, my hope of Glory, my Redeemer. . . . " Here definition becomes credo and assertion.

56. The earliest edition of *Robinson Crusoe* in the Rosenbach Collection is dated 1774 (Rosenbach No. 77). The collection includes fourteen editions, all prior to 1837.

57. Samuel Johnson, *The History of Rasselas, Prince of Abissinia. An Asiatic Tale*, 2 vols. in 1 (Philadelphia: Robert Bell, 1768). Rosenbach No. 60.

58. *The Adventures of Urad; or, the Fair Wanderer* (Boston: Mein & Fleeming, 1767). Rosenbach No. 58.

59. *The Prodigal Daughter; Or a strange and wonderful relation, shewing, how a Gentleman of a vast Estate in Bristol, had a proud and disobedient Daughter, who because her parents would not support her in all her extravagance, bargained with the Devil to poison them. How an Angel informed her parents of her design. How she lay in a trance four days; and when she was put in the grave, she came to life again, & &*, (Boston: I.

Thomas, [1771]). Rosenbach No. 70. Elizabeth Carroll Reilly, *A Dictionary of Colonial American Printers' Ornaments and Illustrations* (Worcester, Mass.: American Antiquarian Society, 1975), 331–337, prints several versions of five cuts from editions of *The Prodigal Daughter*, [1758?]–1772, which illustrate not only variations in the design of set images but also the movement of illustration toward storytelling. Images from *The Prodigal Daughter* should be compared with a similarly varied set of cuts from *The History of the Holy Jesus* which Reilly prints pp. 302–312. These cuts illustrate both anxiety about and movement toward illustrative storytelling in the context of biblical history for children.

60. Fox, *Instructions for Right Spelling*, 11.

61. Mather is concerned with *how* to catechize in this volume, the best methods of catechizing transplanted children (Boston, 1708).

62. [Richard Burton, i.e.; Nathaniel Crouch], *Some Excellent Verses for the Education of Youth, taken from Eccles. 12, 1. Remember thy Creator in the Dayes of thy Youth, &. To which are added Verses for Little Children* (Boston: Bartholomew Green, 1708).

63. Ibid., 5.

64. Ibid., 8.

65. The rhythmic, almost incantatory quality of the four stress lines quoted above gives place in the following passage to the cadences we associate with Isaac Watt's *Divine Songs for the Use of Children* (London, 1715):

And when my Days on Earth Shall end,
And I go hence and be no more,
Give me Eternity to spend,
My God to praise for evermore.

66. Pearce, ed., *Colonial American Writing*, 346.

67. Ibid., 348.

68. Ibid., 350.

69. Ibid., 357.

70. Ibid., 381, Section No. 129. For a complete modern edition of this text, see Jonathan Edwards, *Images or Shadows of Things Divine*, ed. Perry Miller (New Haven: Yale University Press, 1948).

71. Darton, *Children's Books in England*, 122–140, discusses the history of Newbery's career and press. Cf. also full discussion of Newbery texts and premises by Samuel E. Pickering, Jr., *John Locke and Children's Books in Eighteenth-Century England* (Knoxville: University of Tennessee Press, 1981), esp. 182–185 and 215–230.

72. Darton, *Children's Books in England*, 70–84. John Ashton, *Chap-Books of the Eighteenth Century* (New York: Benjamin Blom, 1966) reprints numerous chapbooks including "The History of Joseph and his Brethren," "Guy, Earl of Warwick," "The Pleasant and Delightful History of Jack and the Giants," "Tom Thumb," "The Life and Death of St. George," a brief version of Robinson Crusoe, "The World Turned Upside Down," "A True Tale of Robin Hood," and "God's Just Judgment on Blasphemer." The collection mixes narrative with warnings, wonders, judgments, and jests.

73. Philadelphia: Joseph Crukshank for R. Aitken, 1772.

74. *The Life of Gen. Washington, Commander in Chief of the American Army during the late War, and present President of the United States. Also, of the brave General Montgomery* (Philadelphia: Jones, Hoff & Derrick, 1794). Rosenbach No. 177. The pressure toward mythmaking in America during the early Republican period is well understood and need not be discussed here.

75. Philadelphia: Printed by Thomas L. Plowman for the Author, 1805. Rosenbach No. 302. The dedication to Edward Jenner is noteworthy, as is the book's interest in recovering myths of discovery and the first frontier. See also [W. D.] Cooper, *The History of North America. Containing, A Review of the Customs and Manners of the Original Inhabitants; the first Settlement of the British Colonies, their Rise and Progress, from the earliest Period to the Time of their becoming United, free, and independent States* (2d, American ed., Lansingsburgh: Silvester Tiffany for Thomas Spencer, 1795). Rosenbach No. 188.

76. *The Natural History of Beasts, Which are to be met with In the four Quarters of the Globe* (Worcester, Mass.: Isaiah Thomas, 1794).

77. Johannes Florentius Martinet, *The Catechism of Nature; for the use of Children*, John Hall, trans. (Philadelphia: Hoff & Derrick, 1794).

78. *Rural Felicity; or the History of Tommy and Sally* (New York: J. Oram for the Bookbinders Society, 1796). Collocating simple story with a rural theme, this book represents texts that anticipate the popularity of Robert Bloomfield's work in 1800; see note 104 below.

79. Philadelphia: H. & P. Rice, 1794. See Pickering, p. 61, for a discussion of Sinbad, and Darton, *Children's Books in England*, 71 and 90.

80. *Arabian Nights Entertainments; Being a collection of stories, told by the Sultaness of the Indies, To divert the Sultan from the Execution of a bloody Vow he had made to marry a Lady every Day, and have her head cut off next Morning, to avenge himself for the Disloyalty of the first Sultaness. Containing A better Account of the Customs, Manners, and Religion of the Eastern Nations, viz. Tartars, Persians, and Indians, than hitherto published* (Norwich: reprinted by Thomas Hubbard, 1796). Rosenbach No. 203. Interest in Eastern manners and customs remained high at the end of the eighteenth century, resulting in Daniel's prints in England, the juvenile poetry of Tennyson, and the "Hebrew Melodies" of Byron.

81. Stephanie-Felicite de Genlis, *The Beauty and the Monster, A Comedy* (Worcester, Mass.: Isaiah Thomas, 1785). Rosenbach No. 102. We note the use of "beauty" as a noun rather than a name in this early version, and the designation "comedy."

82. Stephanie-Felicite de Genlis, *Hagar in the Desert. Translated from the French, for the use of Children* (4th ed., Worcester, Mass.: Isaiah Thomas, 1785). Rosenbach No. 103. The woodcuts to the volume are particularly interesting, as is the force of the tale as both narrative and instruction.

83. *Be Merry and Wise; or, the Cream of the Jests, and the Marrow of Maxims, for the Conduct of Life. Published for the Use of all good Little Boys and Girls.* By Tommy Trapwit, Esq. (Worcester, Mass.: Isaiah Thomas, 1786). Rosenbach No. 106. Jests are tempered by maxims, humor by morals; this text illustrates the emergence of pleasure from instruction as a value in the children's text, and the genius of Isaiah Thomas in assessing the limitations and possibilities of his new market.

84. Worcester, Mass.: Isaiah Thomas, 1786. Rosenbach No. 107 notes that

this was a best-selling text of the year 1786. The tale itself includes actual discovery, abandonment, pathos, and romance.

85. *The Vicar of Wakefield*'s popularity is evident in both Rosenbach and Welch.

86. The Rosenbach Collection includes editions published in Boston, 1795, and Worcester, 1796. Published from a first London edition of 1791, *The Blind Child* anticipates Jane Austen's interest in sense and sensibility as it disciplines its audience's susceptibility to pathos.

87. *The Brother's Gift: or, The Naughty Girl Reformed* (3d ed., Worcester, Mass.: Isaiah Thomas, 1795), Rosenbach No. 187; and *The Grateful Return; An Entertaining Story, for Children* (Lansingsburgh: Luther Pratt & Co., 1796). Rosenbach No. 209.

88. *Mother Goose's Melody: or Sonnets for the Cradle, In Two Parts. Part I. Contains the most celebrated Songs and Lullabies of the good old Nurses, calculated to amuse Children and to excite them to sleep. Part II. Those of that sweet Songster and Nurse of Wit and Humour, Master William Shakespeare* (2d Wor. ed., Worcester, Mass.: Isaiah Thomas, 1794). Published from the text of John Newbery, *Mother Goose's Melody* illustrates the eclecticism of the text valued as didactic literature became entertaining. Both the reluctance to deny the usefulness of the text and the new focus of the children's book on the child are evident in the title of the text.

89. *Children's Amusements* (New York: Samuel Wood & Sons, 1822). Held by Beinecke Rare Book and Manuscript Library, Yale University.

90. *Cock Robin's Courtship and Marriage* (New Haven: Sidney's Press, 1824). Beinecke Rare Book and Manuscript Library, Yale University. See also *The Death of Cock Robin* (New Haven: Sidney's Press, 1826).

91. We find vestiges of such warnings and fear of bodily injury even in the plotting of *Little Women* where Alcott brings about meetings and turns in her plot, Part I, by a skating accident or the "boyish" adventures of Jo and Laurie.

92. *The Reprobate's Reward, or, a Looking-Glass for Disobedient Children, being a full and true Account of the barbarous and bloody Murder of one Elizabeth Wood, living in the city of Cork, by her own Son, as she was riding, upon the 28th day of July, to Kingsale market. How he cut her throat from ear to ear; as also how the murder was found out by her apparition or ghost; the manner of his being taken; his dying words at the place of execution....* (Philadelphia, 1798). The tone and focus of this dark piece contrast sharply with playful versions of children's errors, as in *Juvenile Trials for Robbing Orchards, telling Fibs, and other heinous Offences. By Master Tommy Littleton...with a Sequel by Dr. Aikin* (Boston: Printed for F. Nichols, 1797). Cf. Rosenbach No. 229 and 240.

93. Beinecke Rare Book and Manuscript Library, Yale University.

94. New York: Dover Publications, 1969. Arnold reprints brief sections from children's books in most popular genres c. 1800–1830.

95. Arnold, *Pictures and Stories*, 25.

96. Cf. *The Illuminated Blake*, ed. David V. Erdman (Garden City, Anchor Press/Doubleday, 1974), 41–69, for facsimile prints of *Songs of Innocence*.

97. Sir Walter Scott, *Minstrelsy of the Scottish Border* (Kelso: Printed by J. Ballantyne for T. Cadell, jun. and W. Davies, 1802).

98. Jakob Ludwig Karl Grimm, *Kinder und haus-marchen* (Berlin: Realschulbuchhand, 1812).

99. *German Popular Stories, trans. from the Kinder und hausmarchen, collected by M. M. Grimm, from oral tradition* (London: C. Baldwyn, 1823–1826).

100. *Wonderful Stories for Children, by Hans Christian Andersen, trans. from the Danish by Mary Howitt* (London: Chapman & Hall, 1846). Another English edition of the same year was *Danish fairy legends and tales* (London: W. Pickering, 1846). The first and second series of Mary Howitt's translations were also published in New York in 1846.

101. Cf. Darton, *Children's Books in England,* 224–258.

102. Cf. note 5 above.

103. Wordsworth's *Preface to Lyrical Ballads* claims the worth of rural speech for poetic composition, but does not directly argue for the composition of "rural tales." Wordsworth's practice in "Michael" and "Resolution and Independence," however, can be compared with the use of subject in true rural tales.

104. *The Farmer's Boy; A Rural Poem,* from 3d London ed. (Philadelphia: James Humphreys, 1801).

105. Cf., for example, T. C. Croker's *Fairy Legends,* 2 vols. (London, 1828); and Thomas Keightley, *The Fairy Mythology* (London: W. H. Ainsworth, 1828).

106. Cf. *The Poems of Tennyson,* ed. Christopher Ricks (London: Longman, 1969), 675–688, 700–714.

107. Hawthorne, *Wonder Book for Girls and Boys,* 88.

108. Ibid., 91.

109. Ibid., 95–96.

110. In *The Golden Key* (1867), George MacDonald writes a review of generic possibility even as he reconstructs the fairy tale as he received it from the Grimms, Andersen, and Dodgson. The aeranth is a bird/fish colored like the rainbow the children seek; it leads ultimately toward a spiritual apotheosis which we anticipate but do not see.

111. *Wonder Book for Girls and Boys,* 110–111.

112. For full discussion of Christina Rossetti's *Maude,* see Gilbert and Gubar, *Madwoman in the Attic,* 549–554.

113. Madelon Bedell, "Introduction," in Louisa M. Alcott, *Little Women* (New York: Modern Library, 1983).

114. Alcott, *Little Women,* 18.

115. Ibid., 59.

116. Ann Douglas, *The Feminization of American Culture* (New York: Avon Books, 1978), provides the intellectual context in which the discussion of a feminized American culture can take place.

117. Tennyson, *Princess,* VII, 262; Ricks, 838.

118. Cf. Gilbert and Gubar, *Madwoman in the Attic,* 3–104, for a theoretical discussion of these issues.

119. Alcott, *Little Women,* 439–440.

120. Ibid., 513.

121. Ibid., 513–514.

BIBLIOGRAPHY

Abbott, Jacob. *Gentle Measures for the Training of the Young.* New York: Harpers, 1872.

Alcott, Louisa May. *Louisa May Alcott: Her Life, Letters and Journals*. Edited by Ednah D. Cheney. Boston: Roberts, 1888.

Allen, Frederick. "Horatio Alger, Jr.," *Saturday Review of Literature* 18 (1938): 3–4, 16–17.

Arnold, Arnold. *Pictures and Stories from Forgotten Children's Books*. New York: Dover Publications, 1969.

Bedell, Madelon. *The Alcotts: Biography of a Family*. New York: Clarkson N. Potter, 1980.

———. "Introduction." Louisa May Alcott, *Little Women*. New York: Modern Library, 1983.

Blake, William. *The Illuminated Blake*. Edited by David V. Erdman. Garden City, N.Y.: Anchor Press/Doubleday, 1974.

Bunyan, John. *The Pilgrim's Progress from this World to that which is to Come*. Edited by James Blanton Wharey; 2d rev. ed. by Roger Sharrock. Oxford: Clarendon Press, 1960.

Carpenter, Charles. *History of American School Books*. Philadelphia: University of Pennsylvania Press, 1963.

Carpenter, Frederick T. "The American Myth: Paradise (To Be) Regained," *Publications of the Modern Language Association* 74 (1959): 599–606.

Children's Books in the Rare Book Division of the Library of Congress. Totowa, N.J.: Rowan & Littlefield, 1975.

Darton, F. J. Harvey. *Children's Books in England: Five Centuries of Social Life*. 2d ed. Cambridge: Cambridge University Press, 1958.

Douglas, Ann. *The Feminization of American Culture*. New York: Avon Books, 1978.

Eames Wilberforce. *Early New England Catechisms*. New York: Burt Franklin, 1898.

Earle, Alice Morse. *Child Life in Colonial Days*. New York: Macmillan Co., 1904.

"The Early History of Children's Books in New England." *New England Magazine* 26 (1899): 147–160.

Edwards, Johnathan. *Images or Shadows of Things Divine*. Edited by Perry Miller. New Haven: Yale University Press, 1948.

Elbert, Sarah. *So Sweet to Remember, Feminism and Fiction of Louisa May Alcott*. Philadelphia: Temple, 1983.

Ford, Paul Leicester. *The New-England Primer: A History of Its Origin and Development*. New York: Dodd, Mead, 1897; reprinted Teacher's College, Columbia University, 1962.

Freeman, Ruth S. *Yesterday's School Books*. Watkins Glen, N.Y.: Century House, 1960.

Gilbert, Sandra M., and Gubar, Susan. *The Madwoman in the Attic*. New Haven: Yale University Press, 1979.

Goodrich, Samuel. *Recollections of a Lifetime*. New York: Miller, Orton, 1857.

Halsey, Rosalie V. *Forgotten Books of the American Nursery*. Boston: Charles E. Goodspeed, 1911.

Hawthorne, Nathaniel. *The Wonder Book for Girls and Boys*. Boston and New York: Houghton Mifflin, 1900.

Heartman, Charles F. *American Primers, Indian Primers, Royal Primers, and Thirty-seven other types of non-New-England Primers issued prior to 1830; a Biblio-*

graphical *Checklist embellished with twenty-six cuts, with an Introduction and Indexes.* Highland Park, N.J.: Printed for H. B. Weiss, 1935.

———. *The New England Primer Issued Prior to 1830.* Privately Printed, 1922.

Heimert, Alan. "Puritanism, The Wilderness and the Frontier." *New England Quarterly* 26 (1953): 361–381.

Johnson, Clifton. *Old-Time Schools and School-Books.* New York and London: 1904; with a new introduction by Carl Withers, New York: Dover Publications, 1963.

Kiefer, Monica. *American Children Through Their Books.* Philadelphia: University of Pennsylvania Press, 1948.

Kolodny, Annette. *The Lay of the Land.* Chapel Hill: University of North Carolina Press, 1975.

Lewis, R.W.B. *The American Adam: Innocence, Tragedy and Tradition in the Nineteenth Century.* Chicago: University of Chicago Press, 1955.

Littlefield, Emery. *Early Schools and School-books of New England.* New York: Russell & Russell, 1965.

Livermore, George. *The Origin, History and Character of the New England Primer.* New York: C. F. Heartman, 1915.

Lystad, Mary. *From Dr. Mather to Dr. Seuss.* Boston: G. K. Hall & Co., 1980.

Martz, Louis L., ed. *The Meditative Poem: An Anthology of Seventeenth Century Verse.* New York: New York University Press, 1963.

———. *The Poetry of Meditation; A Study of English Religious Literature of the Seventeenth Century.* New Haven: Yale University Press, 1962.

Meigs, Cornelia L., ed. *A Critical History of Children's Literature.* New York: Macmillan Co., 1953.

———. *Invincible Louisa: The Story of the Author of Little Women.* Boston: Little, Brown & Co., 1933.

Nietz, John. *Old Textbooks.* Pittsburgh: University of Pittsburgh Press, 1961.

Payne, Alma. *Louisa May Alcott, A Reference Guide.* Boston: G. K. Hall & Co., 1980.

Pearce, Roy Harvey. "The Significances of the Captivity Narrative," *American Literature* 19 (1947): 1–20.

———, ed. *Colonial American Writing.* New York: Holt, Rinehart & Winston, 1950.

Pickering, Samuel E., Jr. *John Locke and Children's Books in Eighteenth-Century England.* Knoxville: University of Tennessee Press, 1981.

Plumstead, A. W. *The Wall and the Garden: Selected Massachusetts Election Sermons 1670–1675.* Minneapolis: University of Minnesota Press, 1968.

Reilly, Elizabeth Carroll. *A Dictionary of Colonial American Printers' Ornaments and Illustrations.* Worcester, Mass.: American Antiquarian Society, 1975.

Roselle, Daniel. *Samuel Griswold Goodrich, Creator of Peter Parley: A Study of His Life and Works.* Albany: State University of New York Press, 1968.

Rosenbach, A.S.W. *Early American Children's Books.* Portland, Me.: Southworth Press, 1933; reprinted New York: Kraus Reprint Corp., 1966.

Samuel Wood and Sons, *Early New York Publishers of Children's Books.* New York: New York Public Library, 1942.

Shipton, Clifford K. *Isaiah Thomas, Printer, Patriot and Philanthropist, 1749–1831.* Rochester, N.Y.: Printing House of Leo Hart, 1948.

Slotkin, Richard, and Olson, James F., eds. *So Dreadful a Judgment: Puritan Responses to King Phillip's War, 1676–1677.* Middletown, Conn.: Wesleyan University Press, 1978.

Smith, Daniel Blake. "The Study of the Family in Early America: Trends, Problems, and Prospects." *William and Mary Quarterly,* 3d ser. 39 (1982): 3–28.

Stern, Madeleine. *Louisa May Alcott.* Norman: University of Oklahoma, 1951; 1971.

Tebbel, John W. *From Rags to Riches: Horatio Alger, Jr., and the American Dream.* New York: Macmillan Co., 1963.

Tennyson, Alfred, Lord. *The Poems of Tennyson.* Edited by Christopher Ricks. London: Longman, 1969.

Thwaite, Mary F. *From Primer to Pleasure in Reading.* Boston: Horn Book, 1972.

Weitzman, Lenore; Effler, Deborah; Hokada, Elizabeth; and Ross, Catherine. "Sex-Role Socialization in Picture Books for Preschool Children," *American Journal of Sociology* 77 (1972): 1125–1150.

Welch, d'Alte A. *A Bibliography of American Children's Books Printed Prior to 1821.* Worcester, Mass.: American Antiquarian Society and Barre Publishers, 1972.

6

The City and the Child, 1860–1885

Priscilla Ferguson Clement

In 1872 Charles Loring Brace described a section of New York City as follows:

Every available inch of the ground [is] made use of for residences, so that each lot has that poisonous arrangement, a "double house," whereby the air is more effectually vitiated, and a greater number of human beings are crowded together. From this massing-together of families, and the drunken habits prevailing, it results very naturally that the children prefer outdoor life to their wretched tenements, and in the milder months, boys and girls live . . . on the docks and wood-piles, enjoying the sun and swimming, and picking up a livelihood by petty thieving and peddling.

Sometimes they all huddle together in some cellar, boys and girls, and there sleep. In winter they creep back to tenement-houses. . . . Ragged impudent, sharp, able "to paddle their canoe" through all the rapids of the great city—the most volatile and uncertain of children; today in school, to-morrow miles away.[1]

Youngsters with life-styles like those Brace described in New York could be found in other cities as well. Thousands of boys and girls adapted to the city environment as urbanization proceeded apace in America in the two decades after the Civil War. Spurred by technological change and a vast migration of men, women, and children from rural America and from Europe, cities grew in size and number. Between 1860 and 1890 the urban population of the United States more than tripled from 6,217,000 to 22,106,000 and the number of urban centers with 50,000 or more inhabitants rose from sixteen to fifty-eight.

The history of this urbanization process is ably detailed in several books of readings, including those edited by Alexander B. Callow, Jr., Charles N. Glaab, Raymond Mohl and James F. Richardson, and Bayrd Still. Some individual historians have also authored histories of the American

city in the late nineteenth century, perhaps the most clear and succinct
of which is that by Howard Chudacoff. He argues that the spread of
railroads (30,600 miles of track were laid by 1860), which largely linked
cities, stimulated urban growth, as did the use of steam engines fueled
by coal which freed factory owners from dependence on water power
and allowed them to locate their plants in cities. The older mercantile
centers of the Northeast and Mid-Atlantic regions grew most rapidly,
for commerce generated money for industrial development. "Commercial cities and the transportation revolution of the early nineteenth century bred the manufacturing cities and industrial revolution of the late
nineteenth century."[2]

Nonetheless, cities increased in number and size in the Midwest and
South as well. As Blake McKelvey has pointed out, many grew because
urban entrepreneurs developed manufacturing enterprises which exploited a nearby resource. Thus, Minneapolis capitalized on flour mill-
ing, Kansas City, on meatpacking, Milwaukee, on brewing, and Memphis,
on the production of cottonseed oil.[3]

Throughout the nation, urban growth was fueled by migration from
rural America and from abroad. While the number of farms in the nation
tripled from 1860 to 1900, so too did productivity vastly increase, driving
prices down and forcing farmers to work harder for less. Exhausted,
frustrated, and disillusioned, many white farm boys and girls moved to
Northeastern or Midwestern cities seeking easier work at higher pay.[4]
After the Civil War, blacks from the rural South also moved to nearby
cities to find jobs and a better education for their children. According
to Zane L. Miller (in Mohl and Richardson, *The Urban Experience, Themes
in American History*, 1973), by 1880 blacks constituted from 25 to 50
percent of the population of most Southern cities. They were, however,
segregated in small, scattered enclaves, subject to physical coercion by
whites, and relegated to the poorest paying jobs.[5] In contrast, according
to Bayrd Still, Northern cities in the later nineteenth century attracted
very few blacks; by 1860 they made up just 1 to 3 percent of the Northern
urban population. Treated as social inferiors, confined to segregated
schools and other institutions, forced to compete with immigrants for
the lowest paying jobs, and made the objects of physical abuse during
riots in Philadelphia and New York, blacks found it expedient to leave
Northern cities. More departed than entered urban areas above the
Mason-Dixon line in the latter half of the nineteenth century.[6]

Yet even as Northern cities lost some black residents, they gained
countless more people from abroad. The vast surge of immigration of
Irish Catholics, German Catholics and Protestants, English Protestants,
and Scandinavian Protestants, which began in the 1840s, peaked in the
1880s. Most entered through the Northeastern port cities, and many
settled there, though others moved a short distance onward to Paterson,

Newark, Providence, or Reading. By the 1850s, many of the Germans and Scandinavians followed the new transportation routes along rivers and railroads to cities in the Midwest and the Far West. Later, beginning in the 1890s, another distinctive group of immigrants, including Catholics from Eastern Europe, Italy, and Canada, as well as Jews from Russia and Eastern Europe, entered the United States in huge numbers. They too settled principally in cities. Because they were largely unskilled, non-Protestant, and often illiterate and unable to speak English, they were frequently made the objects of ridicule.[7] Such nativism was directed against immigrant children as well as their parents. Thus, even a sympathetic observer of the problems of children in cities, Jacob Riis, could say in 1892 in his book, *The Children of the Poor*:

Within a year there has been, through some caprice of immigration, a distinct descent in the quality of the children, viewed from even the standard of cleanliness that prevails at the Five Points [New York City slum]. Perhaps the exodus from Italy has worked farther south, where there seems to be an unusual supply of mud.[8]

The new immigrants generally settled in ghetto-like enclaves near the centers of cities. As Chudacoff explains, this residential pattern came about in part because of the way the transportation revolution of the later nineteenth century affected urban America. Until the 1850s, most cities in the United States were heterogeneous, with persons of all social, economic, and ethnic backgrounds living within walking distance of the downtown, where most jobs were to be found. From the eighteenth through the mid-nineteenth century, few people in Boston, New York, or Philadelphia lived farther than two miles from the center of their towns. Then in the 1830s, horsedrawn omnibuses moving along regular routes appeared in cities, followed in the 1860s by street railway cars pulled by horses on tracks laid in the city streets, and still later, by cable cars in San Francisco and Chicago, and finally by electric trolleys in most other cities. Upper- and middle-class urban dwellers took advantage of the new modes of transportation and moved out from crowded urban centers to less settled parts of cities or to the suburbs. Their former city residences were soon taken over by thousands of the new immigrants who could not afford to live beyond walking distance of their center city factory jobs. Neither could such migrants afford to pay much for rent, so many former single family dwellings were made over into multifamily structures to accommodate their new, less affluent residents. In the row houses of Philadelphia and Baltimore, there now lived four to six families in each home where there had been one before. In New England, where three-decker houses once contained one family per floor, there were soon two to three families living on each floor and others crowded into the lofts and cellars. In Detroit, Milwaukee, Omaha, and Seattle, the poor moved into old center city warehouses as well as into converted single family dwellings. In New York by the 1860s, such single family dwellings were torn down, and in their place, on each regulation 25 by 100 foot lot, there were erected four- to six-floor tenement buildings with tiny, windowless rooms, no kitchens, and no indoor plumbing. Often, as many as 150 people crowded into such dwellings.[9] These were the buildings from which Charles Loring Brace observed children fleeing in 1872. Later, Jacob Riis described the type of living quarters such youngsters left behind:

In one I visited very lately, the only bed was occupied by the entire family lying lengthwise and crosswise, literally in layers, three children at the feet, all except a boy of ten or twelve, for whom there was no room. He slept with his clothes on to keep warm, in a pile of rags just inside the door.[10]

Not surprisingly, with such poor housing conditions, city dwellers were prone to move frequently. Enormous geographical mobility was characteristic of the late nineteenth-century city. In Boston in just one decade, over one million people moved in and out of the city.[11]

In the crowded, constantly changing urban environment of the late nineteenth century, it would seem that family ties might have been hard to maintain. In actuality, such was not the case. Although extended families were rare and most urban families were nuclear, a significant minority took in lodgers, and frequently family members, sisters and brothers, parents and children, lived in the same neighborhoods.[12] Moreover, family insecurity could not have been too great, since most youngsters lived in two-parent households. Claudia Goldin's study of Philadelphia families through the 1880 census (in Theodore Hershberg, ed., *Philadelphia: Work, Space, Family, and Group Experience in the 19th Century*, 1981) indicates that 80 percent of native-born white families and 64 percent of all black families were headed by couples. Typically, white children also had mothers who remained at home as full-time caretakers. Black children were less likely to have nonworking mothers; more than one-fifth of all black married women in Philadelphia in 1880 were employed.[13]

By the late nineteenth century, almost all young urban dwellers, whatever their color, nationality, or sex, could take advantage of public schooling. Interestingly, however, a new study of Massachusetts in the nineteenth century by Carl F. Kaestle and Maris A. Vinovskis indicates that school attendance was consistently higher in rural areas than in cities. The authors theorize that because there were more jobs for teenagers in cities, more diversions other than schools, and more "alienation" from the educational system, urban children of all ages did not attend school in as large numbers as did their rural counterparts. Nonetheless, Kaestle and Vinovskis find that for those who did attend in cities, school sessions were longer than they were in the country, where only during the winter months, when their labor on farms was not required, did rural children spend time in classrooms. Yet, although among all city children from ages five to fifteen, urban school attendance figures were not as high as we might expect, a very large percentage of youngsters between eight and thirteen years of age enrolled in Massachusetts city schools.[14] Selwyn K. Troen in *The Public and the Schools* (1974) found the same high attendance pattern among youngsters between eight and eleven years in St. Louis.[15] Thus, for about three to six years of their lives, most youthful urban dwellers in late nineteenth-century America spent a good part of the year in public school classrooms.

The history of American urban public education has undergone considerable revision since the 1960s. Rejecting the older view that free public schools "were designed to promote true democracy, equality, or mobility," Michael Katz, in his study of Massachusetts schools in the last century, was the first to argue that America's elite responded to the disruption caused by large-scale immigration and the growth of manufacturing in cities by creating bureaucratic public school systems to control urban youth.[16] Later studies of New York City by Carl F. Kaestle and by Diane Ravitch, of Boston by Stanley K. Schultz, and of St. Louis by Selwyn K. Troen, confirmed that public school systems in these cities appeared in response to immigration and urban disorder and that they were characterized by "class bias, racism, and bureaucratic organization." Subsequently, educational historians William Bullough and David Tyack have each argued that as "all powerful professional and business elites" gained power and influence within cities in the late nineteenth century, they pressed for efficiency amid urban chaos. To achieve such efficiency, city school boards, "dominated by businessmen and other of the city's elites," delegated "more and more authority to professional superintendents, who built up their own bureaucracies."[17] More recently, historians of education, including collaborators Michael B. Katz, Michael J. Doucet, and Mark J. Stern, as well as Kaestle and Vinovskis, have turned from describing the original purposes of city schools and their bureaucratic structure to analyzing school attendance patterns and the effect of public education on various groups of children.

The discussion that follows draws on the work of all the above-named historians, as well as that of several Catholic historians, to tell the story of the evolution of America's city schools, public and parochial, in the late nineteenth century and their impact on urban youngsters.

Although Boston had a public school system by the late eighteenth century, in most other cities such systems did not develop until the nineteenth century. Then in Philadelphia, New York, and St. Louis, philanthropists established charity schools for the children of the poor. Eventually, these evolved into publicly funded schools, which nonetheless continued principally to enroll indigent youth. Middle- and upper-class parents educated their sons and daughters at home or sent them to private schools.[18] In the 1840s with the influx of large numbers of immigrant Irish Catholics into Eastern cities, urban reformers demanded that the children of the foreign-born be kept off the streets and Americanized in enlarged public schools. Such schools were presumably nondenominational, but within them lessons were punctuated by readings from the Protestant version of the Bible, the singing of Protestant hymns, and the reciting of Protestant prayers.[19]

Catholic leaders became alarmed at what appeared to be a public school plot to convert their children. Before the expansion of public education in the 1840s, Catholic children learned their lessons at home or not at all. However, as Glen Gabert, Jr., has pointed out (in *In Hoc Signo*, 1972), once urban public schooling became readily accessible, Catholic clerics feared that immigrant Catholic parents would be enticed into placing their children in public classrooms.[20] Consequently, New York's Bishop John Hughes, whose story is well told by Vincent P. Lannie, began a lengthy struggle with New York City to lessen the anti-Catholic bias of its public schools and later with New York state to obtain state monies for support of Catholic-run schools. Bishop Hughes lost on both fronts and subsequently determined that Catholics in New York should build their own school system. Leaders of the Church of Rome in other Eastern cities generally agreed with him, and by the late nineteenth century almost every diocese had its own parochial school system, though none was very large.[21] According to Marvin Lazerson (*The Origins of the Urban School*, 1971), the proportion of Boston children in Catholic schools rose from just 8 percent in 1888 to 15 percent in 1894.[22] Evidently, although Catholics built schools, they could not afford to construct enough for all Catholic youth, so that by 1890, James Hennesey reports (*American Catholics*, 1981), less than one-half of Catholic children in the United States were enrolled in parochial schools, most of them in the primary grades. There were very few Catholic secondary schools in America before 1900.[23]

Although many have admired Bishop Hughes and his supporters for their determination to protect Catholic youngsters from Protestant proselytizing in the public schools, others, including Diane Ravitch, have argued that his outspoken critique of public education stimulated nativism and made parochial schools a necessity if immigrant Catholic children were to be protected from the hostility of other Americans. Ravitch maintains that Hughes turned New York Catholics away from assimilation and stimulated a "ghetto mentality" among them.[24]

While Catholic schools developed in a climate of hostility in Eastern cities, quite the opposite was true in the Midwest. In St. Louis, Catholic schools were established long before public schools, and in Chicago and Milwaukee, as historian Timothy Walch has ably demonstrated (in "Catholic Social Institutions and Urban Development," 1978), civic leaders of the 1840s enthusiastically welcomed the establishment of Catholic schools and welfare asylums. Before mid-century, Chicago and Milwaukee were relatively new cities with large immigrant populations and few civic institutions. Government leaders and members of the press were delighted when Catholic dioceses in both cities quickly opened a number of schools that accepted Catholic and Protestant students alike. Even after public school systems in the two cities expanded later in the century, Catholic institutions continued to enjoy an enviable reputation in both.[25]

Whether in the Midwest or East, parochial schools were customarily administered by Church officials. In contrast, urban public school systems were at first directed by boards of unpaid laymen. However, as William Bullough explains in *Cities and Schools in the Gilded Age* (1974), by the Jacksonian era these board members found a constant round of school inspection and teacher training to be too time consuming, so they began to hire school superintendents to take over these and other chores.[26] Moreover, in this era, David Tyack reports (*The One Best System*, 1974), specialization of various city services such as firefighting, policing, and waste disposal became more common, and the employment of experienced educators was simply a part of this trend. Such educators soon determined that the ungraded school of the ante-bellum era was inefficient. Thus, by 1860 pupils in almost all city schools had been divided into various grades. Soon thereafter, the curriculum for each grade was standardized as well. Hence, the development of public school bureaucracies led to the creation of graded schools and the introduction of uniform study programs and examinations for each grade.[27]

Such changes were not always advantageous for children. According to Patricia Graham, "grade isolation emphasized the problems of those children who were not promoted and thus were forced to remain in the primary grades with children much smaller than they." She points out that a nonreading ten year old in a one-room school could at least be with his or her peers in the classroom and at recess, but in a large, graded public school he or she would constantly be with much younger children. Moreover, an immigrant child might move speedily through the curriculum in a one-room school, but would have to wait for official promotion before learning new material in a larger, graded school.[28]

Disregarding the special problems of both slow learners and extremely bright children, public school educators pressed on with graded schools and standardized curricula because both presumably promoted efficiency and order. In cities where houses, tenements, and streets were densely populated with an ethnically diverse population, children were certain to encounter petty crime, drunken brawls, and even prostitution. Educators believed that children living amid such tumult required some semblance of order in their lives if they were to grow up into responsible adults; the mission of the public schools was to supply such order. Accordingly, "punctuality," "regularity," "attention," and "silence" were expected of the urban public school student. Classrooms were scenes of military-like drill and were staffed by teachers who commonly attributed "intellectual failure" to "moral laxity."[29]

There were other unattractive features of urban public school classrooms in the late nineteenth century. As Bullough points out, they were grossly overcrowded, often with sixty students under the tutelage of one instructor. Moreover, in this era, thousands of children were actually denied access to public schools because there was no room for them. In 1881 New York City turned away over 9,000 children, and in 1882 Philadelphia turned away 60,000. A study conducted in 1882 revealed that there was not enough room in city schools for "55 percent of the nation's city children." Such limited facilities may also help to explain the relatively low urban school attendance figures of this era noted earlier in this chapter. Apparently, school construction programs simply could not keep pace with urban growth, especially during Depression years, as in the 1870s and 1890s, when citizens strongly objected to paying school taxes. Moreover, urban residential segregation caused by the transportation revolution increasingly divided the social classes; richer citizens did not understand the problems of the poor and protested against paying high school taxes to educate indigent children who, presumably, remained all too short a time in school largely because their parents preferred to withdraw the youngsters and put them to work.

Insufficient monies resulted not only in overcrowded schools, but also in inadequate facilities. Typically, classrooms were poorly ventilated, smelly, and dark.[30]

Moreover, through the doorways of such classrooms passed a constantly changing school population. Because of the high rate of urban mobility in the late nineteenth century, children did not remain in the same classrooms long. Lazerson notes that in Boston in 1882–1883, between 20 and 25 percent of children moved from one public school to another.[31]

The teachers that Boston children and others throughout the country encountered in the urban classroom were often themselves poorly trained. Frequently, both male and female teachers were appointed not because of their ability, but because of their political connections. As Bullough and Diane Ravitch point out, in the later nineteenth-century urban school boards became increasingly the province of local political machines. Gone were the school boards composed of educated laymen. In their place were boards of school directors made up wholly or in part of politicians. They used the schools for patronage purposes and appointed teachers who were politically acceptable, whether or not they were properly skilled.[32]

Sadly, even for the conscientious teacher, training was difficult to acquire. In the 1870s, some cities introduced teacher training institutes in August before classes began, but they were all too short in duration to be of much real use. Several city school boards after the Civil War also established normal schools designed to prepare teachers by providing them with the equivalent of the first two years of a high school education. However, normal schools admitted almost anyone, even those without a grammar school education, and less than one-quarter of their students actually completed the normal school program.[33]

Of course, teaching jobs were low-paying as well; an urban school teacher customarily earned about as much as would a male semiskilled artisan. Such wages discouraged able men from seeking employment as teachers, but not necessarily qualified women.[34] Since in this era teaching was one of the few respectable, professional-type jobs open to females, they eagerly sought it out, even though in cities like New York, according to Diane Ravitch, they were usually paid less than one-half of the already low wages paid male teachers.[35] David Tyack notes that in 1885 in ten cities, female teachers outnumbered male instructors by a ten to one margin. Tyack argues that school boards and school superintendents preferred to hire women because they were cheap and tractable. They obeyed orders, and they were willing to remain teachers while men took over school administrative posts.[36] As for women themselves, Sheila Rothman observes that they earned as much as teachers as they did as stenographers, the other seemingly "professional" job open to them at this time. In addition, teaching allowed women to use what was believed to be a skill unique to them: the ability to nurture children.[37]

Women not only filled most public school teaching slots, but they also staffed the majority of parochial schools. According to Catholic historian Glen Gabert, Jr., orders of nuns were in plentiful supply in America and quite willing to serve as teachers of Catholic youth. Fewer male than female religious orders established branches in the United States, and once here, male religious communities did not grow as fast as did convents. In addition, as with the public schools, female parochial school teachers were inexpensive to employ. "Brotherhoods cost about twice the amount that a comparable number of nuns would cost a parish."[38]

Whether parochial or public, the representative urban school of the late nineteenth century was a primary school, and, typically, it was sex-segregated. Coeducation was a rarity in both Catholic and public schools.

In 1870 according to Diane Ravitch, only five of New York City's ninety public grammar schools were open to both boys and girls, and by 1890 just 14 of 108 were coeducational.

Ravitch also discovered that in New York City black children were educated separately in segregated schools.[39] This same pattern held true in other cities North and South as well. In actuality, throughout the nation black children were customarily denied access to public education until after the Civil War, and even then they were assigned to special schools where facilities were usually poorer than in the classrooms whites attended. In St. Louis, "Negroes were educated in inadequate, inferior, and occasionally distant buildings, sometimes pursuing instruction at a different location each year."[40] Yet David Tyack maintains that segregated schools for blacks did have the advantage of providing black teachers with jobs and allowing black pupils to learn from some of the most well-educated members of their race. Unfortunately, when most Northern urban school systems abolished special schools for blacks at the end of the nineteenth century (the Massachusetts schools were the only ones desegregated before the Civil War), black teachers lost their jobs and black pupils came under the tutelage of white instructors exclusively.[41]

In the post-bellum era, not only were boys and girls, blacks and whites, assigned to separate grammar schools in cities, but also foreign-born children were sometimes segregated, although not always intentionally:

Actually, most schools, based as they were on residential patterns and before widespread school transportation was possible, served children in their immediate neighborhoods, and most neighborhoods were relatively homogeneous.... In New York City the schools were located in ethnic ghettos so that children of Little Italy attended school together while the school a few blocks south and east served the Jewish families in the Lower East Side.[42]

However, in schools that were more ethnically diverse, like many of those in Massachusetts, officials often found it more convenient to segregate children who were non-English speaking in their own special classrooms. Sometimes the teachers assigned to such classrooms or to schools in immigrant ghettos shared the same ethnic and linguistic background as their pupils, but just as often they did not.[43]

Of course, since many Eastern urban Catholic parishes were also ethnically homogeneous, clerics often invited a religious order from the country of origin of most students to staff the local parochial school.[44] For such youngsters, education was probably more easily acquired than it was for the non-English-speaking boys and girls in public primary schools who were assigned to teachers who were unfamiliar with any foreign language.

The situation was somewhat different in many Midwestern cities, at least for pupils of German origin. Tyack argues that because Midwestern Germans enjoyed a relatively high social status and exercised considerable political influence, they were able to secure bilingual education in public grammar schools in a number of cities including Cincinnati, Indianapolis, Louisville, St. Louis, and St. Paul. Moreover, as Gabert suggests, German Catholics in these and other Midwestern cities established German-speaking parochial schools in order to preserve both their language and their culture. By the 1880s, bilingualism in the public schools had some opponents who found it both costly and likely to retard the Americanization of pupils, but nonetheless, it lingered on through the rest of the century in several Midwestern cities.[45]

In these and other urban centers throughout the country in the last century, while the vast majority of pupils, whatever their sex, race, or ethnic background, attended primary schools, a few did enroll in public high schools. According to historian Edward A. Krug, most such public secondary schools were constructed in cities, and by the 1880s, they enrolled more students than did America's 1,600 private secondary academies. Nonetheless, in 1889–1890, less than 1 percent of the total population in the United States attended any secondary school.[46]

Most of the students who enrolled in public high schools were female. Boys generally left school earlier than girls in order to take jobs or to attend college. At this time, a secondary education was by no means a prerequisite for college entrance; universities did not require applicants to present a high school diploma, or even to demonstrate how many secondary school credits they had accumulated, but only to pass an entrance exam. As soon as they could pass, upper- and middle-class boys departed the primary and secondary schools they had attended, while their sisters often stayed on in the local urban high school, either because they had nothing else to do or because they expected a secondary education to prepare them for teaching.[47]

Even as public secondary education began to develop in cities in the late nineteenth century, so, too, did some pre-primary educational programs. After the Civil War, public kindergartens opened for the first time in Boston, Philadelphia, and St. Louis. These represented quite a significant educational innovation because, as Kaestle and Vinovskis argue, by the 1830s and 1840s in America, many educators registered strong objections to very young children attending school, and laws were passed to exclude from public education anyone below the age of six. Previously in the eighteenth and early nineteenth centuries, educators had believed children capable of learning to read at an early age. In the 1820s, the Infant School Movement spread from Europe to America, and boys and girls as young as eighteen months were admitted to such schools. By the Jacksonian era, educators had changed their minds and now frowned on such early exposure to schooling. Some stressed the sensitivity of the very young and emphasized the importance of the mother in educating the pliant toddler. Others argued, as did the popular Swiss educational reformer Johann Heinrich Pestalozzi, that very young boys and girls needed a balanced, gradual education rather than abrupt, early exposure to schools. Still others believed that early intellectual training might actually cause insanity. Although parents did not quickly accept these new theories, gradually they were forced by law to remove their very young sons and daughters from the public schools.[48]

Subsequently, as Margaret O'Brien Steinfels explains, the writings of the originator of the kindergarten in Germany, Friedrich Froebel, inspired Elizabeth Peabody (friend of Ralph Waldo Emerson and sister-in-law of educator Horace Mann) to establish a private kindergarten in Boston in 1860. Peabody's disciples eventually helped create the first public kindergarten in St. Louis in 1873.[49] This and public kindergartens in other cities, as both Troen and Rothman argue, were not designed to provide early intellectual training for the young, but rather to remove immigrant slum children from the city streets, where they were clearly learning wrong ideas and habits, and to Americanize them: "The kindergarten children in their daily games would march—and learn that their marching was part of an allegiance to country. They would set out to make a clock...and learn that the 'clock helps us to be good.' "[50] It was hoped that not only would the kindergarten "directly influence children, but through them it would also influence the immigrant family, perhaps even the entire foreign-born community."[51] Public educators approved the kindergarten because in it youngsters acquired "those virtues that formed such an important part of the district school curriculum—habits of regularity, punctuality, silence, obedience, and self-control."[52]

Eventually by the late 1870s, kindergartens came to be seen as a necessity for the rich as well as for the poor. Since wealthy parents might either neglect or overindulge their children, such youngsters required exposure to a kindergarten where they could develop "character" and creativity.[53] Yet despite its growing popularity in the late nineteenth century, the public kindergarten, like the public high school, served a small number of pupils. As late as 1920, less than 10 percent of American children received a kindergarten education.[54] Both public pre-primary and secondary education were late-nineteenth-century innovations in education that did not come fully into vogue until well into the twentieth century.

As for the children who enrolled in urban public kindergartens, grammar schools, and secondary schools in the nineteenth century, until recently historians have been able to describe them in only the most general terms. However, between 1975 and 1982 scholars made three separate comprehensive studies of large numbers of nineteenth-century schoolchildren: Selwyn K. Troen used the 1880 manuscript census of St. Louis to study students; Michael Katz, Michael Doucet, and Mark Stern relied on the manuscript censuses of 1851, 1861, and 1881 and some school attendance records to evaluate youth in Hamilton, Canada; and Carl F. Kaestle and Maris Vinovskis studied census and other related data on eight Massachusetts towns between 1860 and 1880 to describe urban schoolchildren in that state. Of course, these studies are confined to a few cities in selected years only. They are not exhaustive, but they do provide more information than we have had heretofore about youth in school from 1851 to 1881.[55]

The authors of all three studies discovered that nearly all children in the cities they studied, regardless of sex, social-class status, or ethnicity, attended school between ages eight and thirteen approximately. Those few children who were most likely to stay in school well into their teen years were the sons and daughters of the most affluent. Kaestle and Vinovskis found that among thirteen-to-nineteen-year-old youngsters living in cities, those most likely to be in school had fathers who were professionals or semiprofessionals, while those least likely to be in attendance were the offspring of skilled artisans or unskilled laborers. The authors theorize that perhaps long years of schooling were most useful to aspiring professionals, or possibly middle- and upper-class parents were trying to pass on social status to their children by educating them fully, or maybe richer parents simply could afford to keep their children in school longer.[56]

While the children of the most prosperous stayed in school the longest, sons of the well-to-do quit a little earlier than did their daughters. This pattern helps explain a phenomenon already noted: that more females than males attended urban high schools in the late nineteenth century. There was a wide range of job opportunities available to middle- and upper-class males and, as we have seen, many colleges were willing to accept them. Consequently, they departed grammar and secondary schools earlier than did their sisters who, until the end of the century, found few colleges willing to accept them, and, if they did not marry, had to choose between teaching and stenography, both of which customarily required some secondary school education.[57]

In contrast, urban working-class children rarely remained in school beyond grade six. To a certain extent, such youngsters were concentrated in the lower grades because of their erratic attendance patterns. In Hamilton, Canada, especially among lower-class boys and girls, attendance "peaked in the fall, fell away during the winter, increased in the spring to about its fall level, and finally, dropped off again during the summer." Moreover, in Hamilton, and no doubt in other cities, the enormous transiency among the working poor prevented their children from attending school on a regular basis.[58] Finally, it is probably true, as Joy

Parr has suggested in her study of child migrants from England to
Canada between 1869 and 1924, that urban-born children of the poor
between the ages of six and twelve customarily served as caretakers for
younger children and runners of errands for their parents. Often such
tasks prevented them from showing up in the classroom on a regular
basis.[59]

Other school enrollment patterns in late-nineteenth-century America
are worth noting. For example, evidence from the aforementioned studies of Massachusetts and Hamilton both indicate that sons and daughters
of widows were most likely to be withdrawn from school at an early age,
no doubt to work to help support their fatherless families. In addition,
these same studies reveal that: "the longer a child and his parents had
been in America, the greater the likelihood that the child would attend
school as a teenager."[60] Immigrant children generally quit school earlier
than did native-born youngsters, perhaps because of poverty or simply
because their lack of English-language skills kept them back in the lower
grades with younger children, a situation that they probably disliked and
that may have prompted them to leave school as soon as possible.[61]

Race also had some effect on school attendance. Urban black children
went to school in large numbers once public schooling was available to
them.[62] Interestingly, Claudia Goldin found that in Philadelphia in 1880
"black children remained in school more years than did the children of
immigrant families." She believes that this pattern developed because

black families were more willing to send both their married and widowed women
to work to enable their children to go to school.... Immigrants, in contrast,
appear to have foregone their children's education rather than send their married women to work in the labor market.

Goldin also suggests that black children stayed on longer in the classroom because, due to discrimination in employment practices, they were
unlikely to find work at an early age. "Textile mills and other industries
did not, in fact, hire black children, although they did employ a substantial percentage of the white children who worked for pay."[63]

Of course, eventually youngsters of all races and ethnic backgrounds
left school, and when they did, most by the age of twelve, they typically
went to work. According to the 1880 census, more than a million children
between the ages of ten and fifteen (one out of every six in that age
group) were employed. Walter I. Trattner, in his study of child labor in
the United States at the turn of the century, found that the few child
labor laws then on the books were generally not enforced. From the
beginnings of America, children had always worked, and most persons
believed they still should, if only to prevent delinquency.[64]

In the nineteenth century, however, those youngsters who went to work at an early age did so principally because they had to. Social-class status and the incidence of child labor were closely related. Goldin, in her study of Philadelphia families in 1880, found: "The higher the father's wage, the lower the probability of a child's participating in the labor force."[65] Michael R. Haines, in his survey of working-class families in Philadelphia in the same year, discovered that male family heads earned the most when they were in their thirties, but that their wages declined as they aged. Typically, as fathers grew older, they sent their eldest children out to work to make up for the shortfall in the family budget. White women rarely worked outside of the home; instead, their sons and daughters labored.[66] Moreover, as Joy Parr suggests, when youngsters between the ages of twelve and fourteen quit school and ceased serving as caretakers to younger brothers and sisters and instead became full-time workers who gave their earnings to their parents, the youngsters were "acknowledging the obligations they had accumulated as caretakers and dependents, making restitution to the family economy for the burden they had been in their earlier years."[67]

For these children, a variety of jobs were available in the late-nineteenth-century city. Many found employment in factories; others worked for their parents as apprentices; and still others plied various street trades as vendors of food, clothes, newspapers, or flowers. Boys were more likely to work than girls, probably because boys generally earned more than girls. In addition, there was a higher incidence of child labor among immigrants than among the native-born, presumably because of the greater degree of poverty among families of foreign birth. Interestingly, Goldin has found a slightly different pattern among blacks:

Even though black family incomes were lower than those of whites, black children up to the age of sixteen years...worked in the labor force to a lesser degree than did the children of immigrant families and about equal to those of native-born white parents.

The reasons for this anomaly have already been suggested. Apparently, black families kept their children out of the labor force and in school longer partly because black youngsters faced discrimination and could rarely find good-paying jobs, and partly because black women were more accustomed and more willing to labor outside of the home than were immigrant or native-born women.[68]

Since most children left urban public schools at such an early age to work, the little schooling they had by then acquired probably did not serve to prepare them in any significant way for the jobs they took. Nineteenth-century schools gave most children elementary training in language and mathematics and little else. They learned work skills on the job. In addition, Katz, Doucet, and Stern even argue that "school attendance itself . . . did virtually nothing to promote occupational mobility." Although they found that young men from working-class families in Hamilton generally obtained better manual type jobs than had their fathers:

education had not contributed to their occupational improvement. Its unimportance is reflected in the fact that working-class boys began to leave school earlier in order to work; employers clearly did not require prolonged schooling. Thus any improvement in the prospects of young men compared to those of their fathers should be credited to the expansion and industrialization of the economy rather than to the extension and modernization of schooling.[69]

In the post-bellum era, from the time most urban young people went to work in their early teens until they married in their twenties, they lived at home with their parents. Such a residence pattern does not seem unusual today, but, as Katz, Doucet, and Stern explain, it developed for the first time in nineteenth-century urban industrial centers. Previously, when young people went to work, often as apprentices, they left home to live in the families of their masters. However, even after apprenticeship declined in popularity, the practice of fostering out persisted. When boys and girls took their first jobs, they customarily went to board in other families, usually those of the more well-to-do: "It was a tradition that reflected an older social order in which the boundaries between family and community were indistinct and in which households, places of residence and work, were the basic units of organization."[70] Moreover, children also left home to live closer to their jobs. In early-nineteenth-century cities, where most shops and businesses employed only a few workers, there were few places where a child could find employment within walking distance of his or her family home. Thus, boys and girls moved out to live nearer to the jobs they took, but they did not live independently on their own in lodging houses or apartments. Because remaining within a family until marriage was still considered the only acceptable living arrangement for youths, in the pre-industrial city, most working-class youngsters boarded in families.

With industrialization came a change: after taking their first jobs, instead of moving out to live with other families, most young people remained in their own homes. By the late nineteenth century, this choice had become a viable alternative as large factories employing many persons (including children) were constructed within walking distance of most working-class homes. In addition, the specialization that accompanied industrial capitalism pulled family and community apart and diminished the sense of obligation to board working-class children previously felt by the wealthy. Still, working children could probably have moved out of their own family homes if they had so chosen; the wages they earned were adequate for self-support, and inexpensive lodging houses were readily available in most cities. Katz, Doucet, and Stern conclude:

Given these circumstances, the prolonged residence of young people in the homes of their parents reflects a conscious choice, not an adaptation to necessity. Young people apparently lived at home at least in part because they wanted to. Thus it is reasonable to suppose that during early industrialization ties between parents and their teenage children actually grew stronger.[71]

Of course, for some children in the late-nineteenth-century city, family ties were entirely dissolved. Parents died or deserted these youngsters or simply could not afford to support them. Such children created a very real and visible problem. They lived in the streets, slept out on park benches or in gutters, and committed petty thefts in order to survive. In 1872 Charles Loring Brace estimated their number in New York to be between 20,000 and 30,000.[72] Intervention by public and private helping agencies seemed a necessity. Consequently, to deal with the problems of poverty, dependency, and delinquency among urban youth in the late-nineteenth-century city, many social welfare agencies that had long been in existence stepped up their activities, and concerned philanthropists formed several new charities to provide assistance to needy youths.

The best general study of social welfare programs for dependent children is still that published in 1902 by social worker Homer Folks. In a straightforward fashion, he traces the development of public and private child welfare agencies throughout the country from the eighteenth through the nineteenth century. Also very useful is the multivolume series of documents on *Children and Youth in America* edited by Robert Bremner. Somewhat more specialized is a book by Andrew Billingsley and Jeanne M. Giovanonni on black children and social welfare, a small portion of which deals with the nineteenth century. As for Catholic agencies, the most accessible volume is a broad study by John O'Grady published in 1930, although Frances E. Lane's 1932 dissertation on immigrant Catholics in nineteenth-century New York and Massachusetts and the welfare programs on which the foreign-born and their children depended is still useful. In recent years, no histories devoted exclusively to impoverished, nondelinquent children in the nineteenth century have been published, although portions of books, like Robert Bremner's chronicle of the discovery of poverty between 1830 and 1925 and David Rothman's analysis of the growth of asylums, have dealt with children.[73]

By the time of the Civil War, the most common method of caring for homeless, needy, dependent, urban youth was to institutionalize them in public almshouses or in private orphanages. However, soon after mid-century, as Homer Folks explains, public objection to keeping children in almshouses intensified. Such asylums were places of incarceration for all sorts of poor; not only children, but also aged persons, prostitutes, vagrants, drunks, and insane persons were crowded into the foul-smelling, dark, and dirty wards of public poor houses. Commonly, adult paupers served as caretakers for child inmates. Reformers worried that such living arrangements perpetuated rather than alleviated poverty and subjected the most malleable and reformable of the poor, children, to the most terrible conditions. These concerns surfaced after the publication in 1856 of a state Senate Select Committee study of New York almshouses. As Folks explains, ten years later the first laws were passed ordering the removal of children from poor houses. In some states such as Ohio, Massachusetts, Michigan, Minnesota, Wisconsin, Rhode Island, and Connecticut, once children were withdrawn from almshouses they were placed in new public asylums constructed especially for them. In other states, such as Indiana and New Jersey, authorities established public agencies to place former youthful almshouse inmates in foster homes. In contrast, in New York, Pennsylvania, Maryland, and New Hampshire, once children were denied access to almshouses, public officials placed them in the care of private orphanages or foster care agencies.[74]

Yet despite all the public furor over children in almshouses, the process of removing them from such institutions was a gradual one. By the end of the century, as Folks discovered, only one-quarter of the states had passed laws ordering youngsters out of poor houses. Nonetheless, the number of boys and girls in public almshouses definitely diminished: in 1880 there were 7,770 youngsters between two and sixteen years of age in poor houses, and in 1890 there were 4,987, a drop of 36 percent. Thus, almshouses continued throughout the last century to accommodate indigent urban youth, albeit smaller numbers of them.[75]

In contrast, private orphanages for children grew rapidly: Homer Folks found that in 1851 there were 77 such institutions in the country, and by 1880 there were 613, housing 50,579 youngsters. Moreover, according to a 1910 U.S. government survey of benevolent institutions for children, another 474 orphanages were established between 1880 and 1899.[76] Such private child care institutions grew in number both in order to accommodate the large numbers of children who lost one or both parents as a consequence of the Civil War, disease, industrial accidents, or the grinding poverty of the new industrial cities, and in order to house youngsters excluded from almshouses.

In Eastern cities, Protestant men and women founded the first orphanages as early as the eighteenth century. Such asylums were financed by annual fees paid by members of the founding organizations, by donations from churches, and sometimes by large endowments contributed by wealthy philanthropists such as Stephen Girard of Philadelphia. Almost all the Protestant orphanages established through the Civil War era accommodated youngsters between the ages of two and twelve. In post-bellum years, Protestants experimented with industrial schools for teenagers which provided them with vocational skills, as well as with lodging houses for working youngsters and foundling hospitals for deserted infants.[77]

Eastern Catholics were slower than Protestants to enter the child welfare field. John O'Grady found just seventeen Roman Catholic orphanages in six cities by 1840. Of course, there were relatively few Catholics in the country at that time. All of these early Catholic orphanages were attached to parochial schools, where the fees contributed by pay pupils were used to help defray the cost of caring for orphans. Subsequently, the influx of Irish and German Catholics to Eastern cities in the 1840s occasioned the creation of many more orphanages, and by 1860 all Eastern dioceses maintained special institutions for needy Roman Catholic children under the age of twelve; older children were placed in public or Protestant asylums. After the Civil War Eastern Catholics became even more determined to care for all their needy young themselves. By then the Society of St. Vincent de Paul and other lay organizations created by Irish and German Catholics had grown in power and wealth and were anxious to save children both from indoctrination in Protestant orphanages and from the immorality of cities. Consequently, in urban Eastern parishes between 1860 and the end of the century, Catholics, like Protestants, founded many industrial schools and lodging houses for teenagers as well as some homes for infants and foundlings.[78]

To a certain extent, the development of orphanages in both the East and Midwest parallels the growth of public and parochial schools in these areas. Thus, in the older Eastern cities Protestants were the first to found not only grammar schools but also child care agencies, one function of both of which was to imbue children, Catholic and Protestant alike, with Protestant moral and religious doctrines. Not until the 1840s, with the immigration of thousands of Catholics, did the Catholic Church begin to establish numerous parochial schools and orphan asylums in the East to serve Catholic youth exclusively and thereby save them from the improper education they were likely to receive in the urban schools and orphanages controlled by Protestants. The reverse was true in several Midwestern cities. As Timothy Walch has explained, Chicago and Milwaukee were new urban centers in the 1830s and 1840s, and as such lacked both social welfare programs and public schools. When large numbers of foreign-born Catholics migrated to these cities in the 1840s, they founded the first orphan asylums and some of the earliest schools. Unlike Eastern cities, from the beginning these Midwestern Catholic institutions served both their own and Protestant youth. Because of lack of money, Protestants in Chicago and Milwaukee did not build social welfare institutions of their own, nor many public schools, until after 1850. From then on, in both cities, the relative importance of Catholic welfare agencies and parochial schools declined, but they continued to be much more widely accepted than their counterparts in Eastern cities.[79]

Also in common with parochial schools, and most especially with public schools, orphanages were designed to rescue needy youngsters from wicked urban haunts and to teach them to be obedient, neat, and quiet. Of course, since every orphanage was a live-in asylum, its training program was much more all-encompassing than that of any grammar school. Orphans generally wore uniforms, slept in large dormitories, all in identical beds, and spent what little time they had outside of the classroom doing household chores or performing military drills. Nonetheless, Protestant orphanages at least were not customarily permanent homes for children. Once a child was old enough to be of some use around a home or farm, Protestant institutions returned the youngster to relatives or placed him or her in a family home either in the city or in the surrounding countryside. Few asylums checked up on the boys and girls once released. It was assumed that after a child had been rescued from the city and properly trained in the orphanage, he or she was then prepared to return to regular family life. Catholic agencies placed children less frequently than did Protestant ones, presumably because there were fewer Catholic families willing and able to take in needy youngsters. Instead, Catholic orphans often advanced from asylum to asylum within the Church's system of charities until they were old enough to be released to find work on their own.[80]

Separation by sex and by race was also characteristic of most nineteenth-century urban orphanages, Catholic and Protestant alike. All of the earliest Catholic orphanages cared only for girls, apparently because they were viewed as more vulnerable than boys and in need of protection from the evils of cities.[81] As for black children, Billingsley and Giovanonni explain that members of the Society of Friends founded the first orphanages for nonwhites in the 1820s, although eventually members of other Protestant denominations as well as Catholics founded a few asylums for black youths. All such institutions were administered by whites, and none was integrated. Not until after the Civil War did blacks form some orphanages of their own in Southern cities. Unlike earlier child care asylums, they were not established by churches or groups of lay persons but by individuals. Such individuals had one prime concern: saving the lives of indigent and abandoned black children. They were much less interested than had been their white Protestant and Catholic predecessors in moral reform.[82]

Just as institution-building became the most popular method of dealing with orphans throughout the country in the nineteenth century, so too did it become the most accepted way of handling delinquents. The houses of refuge and reformatories founded before the Civil War were succeeded by reform schools and protectories in later years. These post-bellum institutions for youthful lawbreakers have proved much more interesting to historians than have orphanages, industrial schools, and foundling homes. Thus, there exists for late-nineteenth-century America, a larger body of literature on delinquency than on dependency. Recent histories of delinquency include Robert S. Pickett's largely descriptive account of the New York House of Refuge, as well as broader and more comprehensive studies of juvenile criminality by Joseph Hawes, Robert M. Mennel, and Steven L. Schlossman. In addition, David Rothman in his book on asylums, and Michael Katz in his study of Massachusetts public schools, both include interesting analyses of reform programs for delinquents.[83]

All of these historians agree that nineteenth-century Americans linked poverty, immigration, and urbanization with juvenile crime. The popular argument was that in cities the children of needy immigrants frequently fled their overcrowded homes and schools to drift in and about urban streets, saloons, pool halls, and gambling houses. Often youngsters were tempted to commit petty thefts to support their drinking or gambling habits.[84] Occasionally, youths even formed gangs and "prowled the streets after dark and sometimes fired pistols to frighten passers-by."[85] In New York such gangs were associated with saloon owners who relied on the youths to control voters in local elections, while in Philadelphia, according to Bruce Laurie, gangs were allied with local private fire companies. Since only the first fire company to arrive at the scene of a fire customarily received payment from grateful residents, gangs accompanied the fire companies to drive off rival firefighters.[86]

By the 1860s, some Americans blamed youthful criminality not only on the urban environment, but also on heredity. Presumably the children of lower-class, immigrant parents were the most prone to commit crime, and, consequently, the most likely to end up in juvenile reformatories.[87]

Between 1824, when the first house of refuge was founded in New York, and 1885, Americans established forty-five reform institutions for juveniles. Clearly, there were fewer asylums for delinquent than for dependent youth in nineteenth-century America. Moreover, nearly all of the juvenile reformatories were publicly supported, while most orphanages were maintained by private charitable groups.[88] Apparently in nineteenth-century cities, crime, whether committed by adults or juveniles, was a proper concern of public authorities, while poverty, especially among children, although not entirely outside of the public province, was usually more of a concern of private organizations.

Nonetheless, some religious controversy swirled about juvenile re-

formatories in the mid-nineteenth century, just as it did about orphanages and public schools. Even though most institutions for delinquents
were public asylums, they usually admitted only Protestant ministers to
preach to inmates on Sundays and thereby earned the enmity of Catholics, who in turn established a few reformatories of their own for in-
corrigible boys.[89] However, according to Aaron Abell, after 1870, when
public asylums for juveniles in New York, Philadelphia, Boston, Ohio,
and Massachusetts finally permitted Catholic inmates access to priests,
the Catholic Church largely abandoned construction of juvenile reformatories. Evidently, clerics preferred to utilize their limited funds to
maintain parochial schools and orphanages, which served a much larger
clientele than did reform schools for delinquents.[90]

For America's juvenile reformatories, the Civil War was a watershed.
As both Katz and Mennel demonstrate, the war led to a decrease in
crime among adult males and a corresponding increase among females
and juveniles. Men who became soldiers and were subjected to military
discipline proved less likely to commit crimes, but the wives and children
many of these soldiers left behind in cities often were unable to support
themselves and hence turned to thievery. Reformatories for children
were soon vastly overcrowded, and officials were forced to discharge
older delinquents to find employment, often in the military, in order to
make room for younger offenders.[91]

Moreover, high rates of admission combined with the inflation of the
war and postwar era put many reformatories in dire economic straits.
To supplement the inadequate sums of money they received from public
authorities, officials in most reformatories accepted payments from private contractors in return for the labor of youthful inmates. Such contractors set up shops within the reform schools where they supervised
youngsters as they labored at simple tasks such as the assembling of
umbrellas and brooms. Of course, contract labor in juvenile reformatories was not unknown in the ante-bellum era, but it became much more
common in such institutions during and after the Civil War. Eventually,
the opposition of organized labor to competition with unfree juvenile
laborers and the objection of reformers to youngsters working long
hours at tasks that did not prepare them in any meaningful way for life
outside of the asylum led to the abolition of contract labor in juvenile
reformatories in the 1880s and 1890s.

Of course, once contract labor was abolished, that did not mean that
all work programs in juvenile reformatories ended. Quite the contrary.
Instead of contractors supervising inmate laborers, asylum officials now
assumed this task.[92] Hard work remained as important a part of post-
bellum as it was of ante-bellum juvenile reform programs. Delinquents
had to learn discipline, obedience, and industry, and what better way to
teach them than through work?

Not only labor programs but also many other aspects of juvenile asylum regimens were the same in the late nineteenth century as they had been earlier. Delinquents were still expected to attend school within the institution for several hours each day, to exercise through military-like drill in large fenced playgrounds, and to behave as the authorities expected or face harsh punishments.

Moreover, in the late nineteenth century, nearly all juvenile reform asylums remained, as they had always been, segregated by sex and by race. Most reformatories continued to admit only white boys, but a few maintained separate quarters for some girls.[93] The first reform institution exclusively for female delinquents was the Massachusetts Industrial School for Girls, which opened in 1854. Its history is ably chronicled by Barbara Brenzel. In Massachusetts, as well as elsewhere in the country, girls were customarily incarcerated not because they had committed the petty larcenies that usually landed boys in asylums, but because of precocious sexual behavior, a "crime" with which boys were virtually never charged.[94] As for blacks, only a few institutions for juveniles admitted them at all, and those that did kept such youngsters rigidly segregated from whites. As a consequence, most black youths charged with crimes remained locked up in jails with adult criminals. Nineteenth-century reformers expressed much less interest in preventing exposure of black than they did white boys and girls to the contaminating influences of hardened criminals in public jails and prisons.[95]

Although many features of juvenile reform institutions remained unchanged throughout the last century, a few modifications were made in some asylums, most notably the abandonment of congregate or dormitory-like living arrangements and the introduction of cottage or family-style living. In several states and cities, officials became disillusioned by the failure of the early prison-like houses of refuge truly to reform youngsters. Prodded by the sharp criticism of institutionalization of boys and girls by Children's Aid Society founder Charles Loring Brace (see below), and inspired by the success of the family reform schools established by Johann Wichern in Germany and by Frederic DeMetz in France, reformers sought to redesign reformatories so as to isolate groups of twelve to thirty-six children in separate cottages under the supervision of mother and father-like figures. Each "family" would be composed of youngsters who were alike in sex, age, and perhaps in type of offense committed. Thus, the cottage-style plan would presumably allow for more specialized, as well as more humane and benevolent, treatment of delinquents. In 1854 the Massachusetts State Industrial School for Girls became the first cottage-style asylum, and the Ohio Reform School, opened in 1857, the second. Others were established in New Jersey and Indiana in the 1860s. In addition, some older juvenile reformatories, including the Massachusetts Reform School for Boys, the House of Refuge for

Western Pennsylvania, and the Philadelphia House of Refuge, converted
to cottage-style arrangements before the end of the century.[96] Nevertheless, older congregate-type institutions continued in existence and
were not without their own defenders. Steven L. Schlossman notes that
in 1857:

... the superintendent of the House of Refuge at Rochester, New York, decried
the excessive attention being paid [in cottage-style asylums] to the separation of
confirmed and relatively inexperienced lawbreakers. Careful classification of
inmates was unnecessary, he argued, because it was a positive good to have them
mix indiscriminately. "It seems to be one of the arrangements of Providence
that in society the virtuous and the vicious should in some respects be together.
... I do not think it wise to separate boys and girls from temptation. God has
not so ordered it."[97]

Another innovation in child welfare in the second half of the nineteenth century was the introduction of institutions intermediate between
orphanages and juvenile reformatories. Members of the Association for
Improving the Condition of the Poor helped create and secure state
funding for the first such institution, the New York Juvenile Asylum,
which opened in 1853. It admitted youngsters between the ages of seven
and fourteen who were a little too old to enter orphanages and a little
too young for juvenile reformatories. Some were brought by their parents; others (usually only young, first offenders) were committed by the
courts. The professed aim of the New York Juvenile Asylum was to
remove children from the contaminated urban environment, discipline
and educate them as their parents could or would not do for a period
of one to two years, and then return the youngsters to their own families
or indenture them out to farm families in the Midwest. It did not retain
children as long as did the typical orphanage, nor did it subject them to
as harsh discipline as did the typical asylum for delinquents. It did,
however, maintain the traditional Protestant orientation of most Eastern
urban child welfare agencies, as well as the conventional view that dependent and delinquent city children required a period of institutionalization if they were to be properly prepared to live useful lives.[98]

Because of its faith in institutionalization of the young, albeit for short
periods of time, the New York Juvenile Asylum came under attack by
proponents of foster care like Charles Loring Brace, who believed children were always better off in family homes. (See below for a fuller
discussion of Brace's views.) Other critics included Catholic clerics who,
while they accepted the necessity for institutionalization of poor and
delinquent youngsters, objected to the Protestant religious indoctrination which all youngsters, including Catholics, received in the Juvenile
Asylum. Eventually, members of the Catholic Church founded a com-

peting institution in 1863, the New York Catholic Protectory, which differed from its predecessor principally in religious orientation. Both the Protectory and the New York Juvenile Asylum aimed at saving the same types of youngsters, who were, in the words of Dr. Levi Silliman Ives, a founder of the Catholic Protectory: "defenseless young creatures ... wandering over the face of this great city, exposed to all the horrors of hopeless poverty, to the allurements of vice and crime in every disgusting and debasing form, bringing ruin on themselves and disgrace and obloquy." Evidently, both institutions met a real need, for they grew rapidly, the Catholic asylum more quickly than the Protestant, so that by 1875 the New York Catholic Protectory, with 2,000 inmates, was the largest child welfare asylum in the United States.[99]

In New York and other late-nineteenth-century cities, while younger delinquents might be sent to institutions like the Juvenile Asylum or the Catholic Protectory and older offenders to houses of refuge or reform schools, in Boston some youngsters convicted of crimes were not institutionalized at all but instead were placed on probation by the courts. John Augustus, a Boston shoemaker, is credited with originating the idea of probation. Informally, on his own, Augustus began to attend sessions of the Boston courts and in 1841 first provided bail for some adults. In 1846 he began his work with juveniles when he put up bail and agreed to supervise eleven boys convicted of larceny. Thenceforward, Augustus created for himself the role of juvenile probation officer.[100] While he was the first to occupy that role, Augustus was not the last. After his death Rufus R. Cook, chaplain of the Suffolk County Jail and later agent of the Boston Children's Aid Society, continued Augustus's work. In 1869 a state visiting agency was created in Massachusetts whose members served as probation officers and pressured the courts to place some convicted juveniles in their care. According to Homer Folks, from 1869 to 1885, thanks to the work of this agency, between 19 and 33 percent of youngsters brought before the courts annually were placed on probation. In addition, in 1878, local probation officers who represented the courts were appointed for the first time in Boston. However, this city was exceptional. Not until the turn of the century, with the creation of juvenile courts in many cities, did probation for juvenile offenders become a fairly widespread practice.[101]

The spread of probation in Massachusetts in the late nineteenth century was one small indication of a growing distrust of institutionalization of youngsters. However, the strongest attack on the incarceration of the young was launched elsewhere, in New York City, by a dynamic and seminal child welfare reformer named Charles Loring Brace.

Brace was born in 1826 in Connecticut, graduated from Yale, and later attended Yale Divinity School and the Union Theological Seminary. Though trained as a minister, he found the religion he learned in school "too technical and intellectualized" and instead preferred a more "practical piety" to help his fellow man.[102] After a trip to Europe in 1850–1851 where he studied various charities, Brace began his labors as a "practical" minister in New York City among adult prisoners and the slum poor. Soon he and others became convinced that the many homeless street children they encountered were in special need of Christian guidance. Therefore, Brace and other ministers organized "Boys Meetings" where they preached Christian principles to groups of youngsters who sometimes pelted them with stones, yelled derogatory comments, or conducted "a general scrimmage...over the benches."[103] Undeterred, Brace and other Protestant leaders tried a new tack: they founded the Children's Aid Society in 1853 to provide a more comprehensive rehabilitation program for New York's poor and delinquent youth.

Brace became the Society's first general secretary and a strong opponent of most other child-savers, who then relied so mightily on confinement of needy youngsters. Brace believed that asylums were overly costly and turned youngsters either into hypocrites, who behaved in a pious and moral fashion simply in order to avoid punishment, or into little automatons who were ill-prepared to live normal lives in society. He also objected to the method by which most institutions placed children upon release: through the signing of an indenture contract with the foster family. Brace felt such contracts were too restrictive: they did not allow easy removal of children from bad homes. He also felt they encouraged foster parents to treat youngsters placed with them as laborers rather than as full family members.

Under Brace's direction, the Children's Aid Society dealt with child vagrancy in a variety of ways, the most controversial of which was to remove slum children directly to farm homes in the Midwest. Here, the Society argued, in an intimate nuclear family setting, the youngster's character could best be reshaped. Agents of the Society canvassed New York slum neighborhoods and, when they found homeless or abused children, encouraged their parents or other relatives to release the youngsters to the Society, which then sent them in groups to various Midwestern communities. There, at citizens' meetings, residents observed the children and took home the most promising. No indentures were signed, and the child was free to leave his or her new home if he or she so chose. Most subsequent contact with the child was by letter, and the few Children's Aid Society agents stationed in the Midwest could not adequately supervise the over 60,000 youngsters the Society had placed by 1884.[104]

Brace's placing-out program had many critics. Roman Catholic officials complained that he sent Catholic youngsters to Protestant family homes. Asylum officials argued it was dangerous to send wild, rebellious children direct from city slums to country family homes without first teaching

them discipline and obedience in an institutional setting. And Midwesterners insisted that the Children's Aid Society was using their states as
dumping grounds for urban child vagrants and criminals. Brace responded vigorously to his critics but eventually turned his attention, even
before the 1890s, when several Midwestern states passed laws sharply
restricting the placement of children from out-of-state within their bor-
ders, to other parts of the Children's Aid Society program. He began to
emphasize several of the Society's projects which had long been in existence, including industrial schools, which trained urban youngsters for
useful jobs, and lodging houses for newsboys and working girls, which
provided inexpensive, comfortable housing for children engaged in street
trades.[105]

Brace's placing-out program did not die, but was taken up and modified by agencies in other cities, many of them modeled directly after
the New York Children's Aid Society. In Boston and in Philadelphia,
Children's Aid Societies began to investigate potential foster families and
to pay some of them to care for needy youths. These agencies also
checked up on youngsters carefully after placement.[106] Thus, Brace and
the Children's Aid Societies in New York and other cities must be given
credit for originating foster care, which, in the twentieth century, became
the preferred mode of caring for needy children.

Because of Charles Loring Brace's importance as a child welfare reformer, his work is discussed in almost every history that deals with
nineteenth-century reform. Until recently, most historians have maintained that Brace distrusted and disliked the city and its effect on young
people (he labeled urban youth "the dangerous classes"), and therefore
sought to remove children from urban areas and place them in more
healthful rural settings. However, a new view of Brace was introduced
by R. Richard Wohl in 1969 and Thomas Bender in 1975. Each argued
that Brace turned quite willingly from placing-out to industrial schooling
because he accepted the city and recognized that children had to be
helped to find their proper place within it. Bender also noted that Brace
was actually optimistic about urban environments, which he felt were
always in flux and thereby offered residents continual hope of advancement. Nonetheless, Bender also found that Brace was not an unqualified
defender of big city life; in fact, through his industrial schools, he tried
to bring many small town, middle-class values to urban children. Thus,
many of the staff members in these schools were middle-class volunteers
who were presumably "morally superior" to their students and whose
goal was to teach the urban poor to be like themselves: to work hard,
to be neat, clean, and moral.[107]

Brace's most recent interpreter, Paul Boyer, argues even more forcefully than Wohl and Bender that Brace was unique among nineteenth-
century reformers in that he accepted the city and admired the "tough

individualism and resourcefulness" of "slum urchins and street wan-
derers." Brace did worry about "their potential for destructive *collective*
action" but admired them as individuals. Boyer, in common with Bender,
also feels that Brace liked the city because he felt its openness let children
break away from their poor families and become better, hard-working
folk. However, Boyer goes a step further than preceding historians in
arguing that what Brace sought to do was not to place street youngsters
in family-type institutions or rebuild their families "but to complete the
break to freedom the child had already begun." To help youngsters
make this break and to encourage their independence, he created voluntary industrial schools and lodging houses to which children had to
pay fees to gain entrance. In contrast to Bender, Boyer believed the
schools were unconventional and discouraged "social and moral con-
formism." In addition, Boyer is the first to argue that Brace's placing-
out program was not an indication of his anti-urbanism. Rather, Boyer
feels Brace sought not to remove children from an evil city and place
them under the "control" of Western families, but rather to send them
to frontier areas where the youngsters' "freewheeling autonomy" would
have "a wider and more secure social arena in which to operate." Brace
did not tie children down with indentures because he wanted them to
be free and able to leave; he distrusted "all confining social institutions,
including the family."[108]

Just as Charles Loring Brace created in New York in the 1850s a child
welfare agency unlike any other before it and one that soon spawned
many imitators, so too did the members of the Society for the Prevention
of Cruelty to Animals (SPCA) create in the same city twenty years later
a unique child-helping program that became widely popular. Joseph
Hawes traces the origins of this new agency to the year 1874 when a
dying woman complained to a New York City missionary about a child
next door who was continually being beaten. Officials of the SPCA intervened and took the abused child's parents to court, and the agency
was subsequently granted custody of the child. This incident led to the
formation of the Society for the Prevention of Cruelty to Children (SPCC)
in 1875.[109] Its credo was well stated by one of its founders, the former
head of the SPCA, Henry Bergh: "The child is an animal.... If there is
no justice for it as a human being, it shall at least have the rights of the
stray cur in the street. It shall not be abused."[110] By 1880 similar agencies
had been established in ten other cities.

Like the New York Children's Aid Society, the Society for the Prevention of Cruelty to Children was interested in abused boys and girls,
but there the similarity ends. While the Children's Aid Society tried to
enroll such youngsters in industrial schools or, better yet, send them
west to new family homes, the SPCC worked through the court system
to prosecute their parents and gain custody of the youngsters. When

citizens complained, SPCC agents investigated charges of cruelty and neglect of children and, if necessary, took the offending adults before a magistrate. Soon New York court officials requested SPCC agents to investigate all cases of child neglect that came before the courts and to advise magistrates on what to do with youngsters removed from unsuitable family homes. As Homer Folks points out, SPCC agents were customarily given custody of such youngsters and in turn placed the boys and girls in institutions. Rarely did SPCC officials opt for foster care, perhaps because their work made them distrustful of families in general and maybe also because they felt that youngsters placed in asylums would be less accessible to the persons who had previously treated them cruelly.[111]

Because of its work in the courts and its sponsorship of legislation to prohibit children under fourteen from going to saloons, dance halls, and houses of prostitution or from just wandering about homeless, Hawes believes that the New York SPCC was a progenitor of the juvenile court.[112] The agency certainly had a great deal of power:

This society thus became, by 1890, the factor which actually controlled the reception, care, and disposition of destitute, neglected, and wayward children in New York City, thus practically controlling the lives of an average number of about fifteen thousand children, and an average annual expenditure for their support of more than one and one half million dollars.

Not surprisingly, poor persons became distrustful of an agency so powerful that it could dissolve family bonds, and thus they nicknamed it "The Cruelty."[113]

Nonetheless, the New York SPCC ended many practices harmful to children. It enforced a New York law that made child begging illegal and campaigned successfully to end the practice of young girls using flower selling as a cover for prostitution. In addition, the SPCC worked to eliminate the padrone system—a form of child slavery. A padrone would pay poor peasant families in Italy to turn over their children to him, and in turn he promised to take the youngsters to America for a few years, put them to work, and send their earnings back to their parents. Once in America, padrones physically forced their young charges to entertain in the streets and in bars, tasks for which neither the youngsters nor their parents were paid. After the SPCC cooperated with the Italian government in 1879 to apprehend the first child slaver in New York, the padrone system declined and eventually disappeared.[114]

To conclude, between the years 1860 and 1885, the effect of city living on children was varied. Urbanization introduced all young residents to a diversified and often exciting environment and provided almost all of them with the opportunity to acquire basic mathematical and language skills in public and parochial grammar schools. Between the ages of eight and thirteen, most city youngsters took advantage of free public education. They attended sexually and racially segregated, graded schools administered by a burgeoning, virtually all-male bureaucracy. They entered classrooms that were frequently overcrowded yet conducted in a strict, orderly fashion by female teachers, many of whom were inadequately trained for their jobs. And when the city child left school, he or she usually returned home to a two-parent household. Moreover, due to industrialization which accompanied urbanization, most city youngsters, whether they attended school or were employed, customarily lived with their families through their teen years until marriage.

Here the similarities in the life experiences of city-bred children end. Thereafter the effect of urban living on them varied, depending principally on their racial, ethnic, and socioeconomic backgrounds.

Black children living in cities attended school more years than did most whites, although the segregated schools in which blacks were enrolled were often physically inferior to comparable schools for white boys and girls. In addition, urban black children were more likely than white youngsters to have mothers who worked. Once black children left school, they faced considerable prejudice in the job market and usually had more difficulty finding work than did white youngsters. If they became homeless or delinquent, there were few orphanages or reformatories that would admit black children, so most languished in public almshouses or jails.

As for the children of the foreign-born, they too were often assigned to separate, special public schools. For the non-English-speaking immigrant child, language was a serious barrier unless the youngster happened to be either German and living in the Midwest, in which case he or she might attend a bilingual school, or Catholic and able to enroll in a parochial school, where the nuns were from the child's country of origin. Wherever they went to school, immigrant children were likely to quit the classroom earlier than the native-born in order to seek employment. In cities, jobs were plentiful and immigrant children usually had little trouble finding work.

The city-born child whose parents were well-to-do customarily lived some distance from the center of town because his or her parents could afford to take advantage of new modes of transportation like the trolley for commuting purposes. In addition, urban youngsters from affluent families, especially girls, usually attended school for many years, often from kindergarten through high school.

In contrast, working-class children usually lived in crowded housing within walking distance of the centers of cities where most employment opportunities were to be found. They attended school usually only through grade six, and then went to work. As for those among them who were extremely poor or who were orphaned or abused, there were many urban social agencies willing to help. By the late nineteenth century, few such needy youngsters ended up in public almshouses; many more were sent to Protestant or Catholic orphan asylums, often through the intervention of the Society for the Prevention of Cruelty to Children. Others attended industrial schools or were placed out of cities with farm families by agents of Children's Aid Societies. Those who were labeled delinquent, with the exception of the very few who were put on probation, generally ended up in large, congregate reformatories where they spent a couple of hours each day in the classroom, and many more laboring in the workrooms. However, some few delinquent boys and girls were more fortunate and entered the new cottage-style institutions, where living arrangements were more comfortable and punishments usually less harsh.

Generally speaking, in late-nineteenth-century America, the city affected all children in somewhat similar ways, but it also had a differential impact on its youngest residents, depending on whether they were black or white, foreign or native-born, affluent or poor.

NOTES

1. Charles Loring Brace, *The Dangerous Classes of New York and Twenty Years' Work Among Them* (New York: Wynkoop and Hallenbeck, 1872), pp. 330–331.

2. Alexander B. Callow, Jr., ed., *American Urban History, An Interpretive Reader with Commentaries*, 2d ed. (New York: Oxford University Press, 1973); Charles N. Glaab, ed., *The American City: A Documentary History* (Homewood, Ill.: Dorsey Press, 1963); Raymond Mohl and James F. Richardson, eds., *The Urban Experience, Themes in American History* (Belmont, Calif.: Wadsworth Publishing Co., 1973); Bayrd Still, *Urban America: A History with Documents* (Boston: Little Brown, 1974); Howard P. Chudacoff, *The Evolution of American Urban Society* (Englewood Cliffs, N.J.: Prentice Hall, 1975), pp. 28, 35–36, 87, quote 88.

3. Chapter by McKelvey in Callow, *American Urban History*, p. 162.

4. Chudacoff, *Evolution of American Urban Society*, p. 92.

5. Mohl and Richardson, *The Urban Experience*, pp. 47–48.

6. Still, *Urban America: A History with Documents*, pp. 127–128.

7. Chudacoff, *Evolution of American Urban Society*, pp. 93–94.

8. Jacob Riis, *The Children of the Poor* (New York: Charles Scribners Sons, 1892), p. 13.

9. Chudacoff, *Evolution of American Urban Society*, pp. 65, 68, 71–73, 79–80, 102–103.

10. Riis, *The Children of the Poor*, p. 39.

11. Chudacoff, *Evolution of American Urban Society*, p. 101.

12. Ibid., p. 111.

13. Claudia Goldin, "Family Strategies and the Family Economy in the Late Nineteenth Century: The Role of Secondary Workers," in Theodore Hershberg,

ed., *Philadelphia: Work, Space, Family and Group Experience in the 19th Century, Essays Toward an Interdisciplinary History of the City* (New York: Oxford University Press, 1981), pp. 297–298.

14. Carl F. Kaestle and Maris A. Vinovskis, *Education and Social Change in Nineteenth Century Massachusetts* (New York: Cambridge University Press, 1980), pp. 37, 75, 82–83.

15. Selwyn K. Troen, *The Public and the Schools: Shaping the St. Louis School System, 1838–1920* (Columbia, Mo.: University of Missouri Press, 1975), p. 121.

16. Ronald Cohen, "Schooling in Early Nineteenth-Century Boston and New York," *Journal of Urban History* 1 (November 1974): 119.

17. Ronald Cohen, "Urban Schooling in the Gilded Age and After," *Journal of Urban History* 2 (August 1976): 500.

18. Troen, *The Public and the Schools*, pp. 9–12.

19. Patricia Graham, *Community and Class in American Education, 1865–1918* (New York: John Wiley and Sons, 1974), pp. 5, 144; Vincent P. Lannie, *Public Money and Parochial Education, Bishop Hughes, Governor Seward, and the New York School Controversy* (Cleveland: Press of Case Western Reserve University, 1968), p. ix.

20. Glen Gabert, Jr., *In Hoc Signo? A Brief History of Catholic Parochial Education in America* (Port Washington, N.Y.: Kennikat Press, 1973), pp. 24–25.

21. Lannie, *Public Money and Parochial Education, passim.*

22. Marvin Lazerson, *The Origins of the Urban School: Public Education in Massachusetts, 1870–1915* (Cambridge, Mass.: Harvard University Press, 1971), p. 19.

23. James Hennesey, *American Catholics, A History of the Roman Catholic Community in the United States* (New York: Oxford University Press, 1981), pp. 186–187.

24. Diane Ravitch, *The Great School Wars, New York City, 1805–1973. A History of Public Schools as Battlefields of Social Change* (New York: Basic Books, 1974), pp. 80–81.

25. Timothy Walch, "Catholic Social Institutions and Urban Development: The View from 19th Century Chicago and Milwaukee," *Catholic Historical Review* 64 (1978): 16–27.

26. William Bullough, *Cities and Schools in the Gilded Age, The Evolution of an Urban Institution* (Port Washington, New York: Kennikat Press, 1974), pp. 44–46.

27. David Tyack, *The One Best System, A History of American Urban Education* (Cambridge, Mass.: Harvard University Press, 1974), pp. 30–32, 44–45.

28. Graham, *Community and Class in American Education, 1865–1918*, pp. 16–17.

29. Tyack, *The One Best System*, pp. 50, 55.

30. Bullough, *Cities and Schools in the Gilded Age*, quote p. 22; see also pp. 23, 26–27.

31. Lazerson, *The Origins of the Urban School*, pp. 15–16.

32. Bullough, *Cities and Schools in the Gilded Age*, pp. 62–71; Ravitch, *The Great School Wars*, pp. 88, 92–99.

33. Bullough, *Cities and Schools in the Gilded Age*, p. 34; Ravitch, *The Great School Wars*, p. 103.

34. Bullough, *Cities and Schools in the Gilded Age*, pp. 35, 39.

35. Ravitch, *The Great School Wars*, p. 103.

36. Tyack, *The One Best System*, pp. 60–61.

37. Sheila M. Rothman, *Woman's Proper Place: A History of Changing Ideals and Practices, 1870 to the Present* (New York: Basic Books, 1978), pp. 57–59.

38. Gabert, *In Hoc Signo? A Brief History of Catholic Parochial Education in America*, p. 31.

39. Ravitch, *The Great School Wars*, pp. 100–101.

40. Troen, *The Public and the Schools*, pp. 80–84, quote p. 85.

41. Tyack, *The One Best System*, pp. 109–125.

42. Graham, *Community and Class in American Education*, p. 9.

43. Lazerson, *The Origins of the Urban School*, pp. 15–16.

44. Troen, *The Public and the Schools*, pp. 37–39.

45. Tyack, *The One Best System*, pp. 106–109; Gabert, *In Hoc Signo? A Brief History of Catholic Parochial Education in America*, p. 59.

46. Edward A. Krug, *The Shaping of the American High School, 1880–1920* (Madison: University of Wisconsin Press, 1969), pp. 5, 11.

47. Ibid., pp. 6–7, 11–12; S. Rothman, *Woman's Proper Place*, p. 49.

48. Kaestle and Vinovskis, *Education and Social Change in Nineteenth Century Massachusetts*, pp. 46–63.

49. Margaret O'Brien Steinfels, *Who's Minding the Children? The History and Politics of Day Care in America* (New York: Simon and Schuster, 1973), p. 37.

50. S. Rothman, *Woman's Proper Place*, p. 100.

51. Ibid., p. 101.

52. Troen, *The Public and the Schools*, p. 104.

53. Ibid., p. 113.

54. S. Rothman, *Woman's Proper Place*, p. 99.

55. Troen, *The Public and the Schools*; Kaestle and Vinovskis, *Education and Social Change in Nineteenth Century Massachusetts*; Michael B. Katz, Michael J. Doucet, Mark J. Stern, *The Social Organization of Early Industrial Capitalism* (Cambridge, Mass.: Harvard University Press, 1982).

56. Kaestle and Vinovskis, *Education and Social Change in Nineteenth Century Massachusetts*, p. 90; Katz, et al., *The Social Organization of Early Industrial Capitalism*, pp. 270–272; Troen, *The Public and the Schools*, p. 126.

57. S. Rothman, *Woman's Proper Place*, p. 49.

58. Katz, et al., *The Social Organization of Early Industrial Capitalism*, p. 277.

59. Joy Parr, *Labouring Children: British Immigrant Apprentices to Canada, 1869 to 1924* (London: Croom Helm, 1980), pp. 17–20.

60. Kaestle and Vinovskis, *Education and Social Change in Nineteenth Century Massachusetts*, p. 91, quote p. 93; Katz, et al., *The Social Organization of Early Industrial Capitalism*, p. 273.

61. Katz, et al., *The Social Organization of Early Industrial Capitalism*, pp. 270, 277.

62. Tyack, *The One Best System*, pp. 109–125.

63. Goldin, "Family Strategies and the Family Economy," in Hershberg, *Work, Space, Family, and Group Experience in the 19th Century*, p. 298.

64. Walter I. Trattner, *Crusade for the Children: A History of the National Child Labor Committee and Child Labor Reform in America* (Chicago: Quadrangle Books, 1970), pp. 23–24, 30.

65. Goldin, "Family Strategies and the Family Economy," in Hershberg, *Work, Space, Family, and Group Experience in the 19th Century*, p. 290.

66. Michael R. Haines, "Poverty, Economic Stress, and the Family in a Late Nineteenth-Century City: Whites in Philadelphia, 1880," in Hershberg, *Work, Space, Family, and Group Experience in the 19th Century*, pp. 261–262.

67. Parr, *Labouring Children*, p. 21.

68. Goldin, "Family Strategies and the Family Economy," in Hershberg, *Philadelphia: Work, Space, Family, and Group Experience in the 19th Century*, pp. 284–285, 299, quote p. 298.

69. Katz, et al., *The Social Organization of Early Industrial Capitalism*, first quote p. 275, second quote p. 282.

70. Ibid., p. 240, quote pp. 249–250.

71. Ibid., pp. 245, 249–252, quote p. 283.

72. Brace, *The Dangerous Classes of New York*, p. 31.

73. Homer Folks, *The Care of Destitute, Neglected, and Delinquent Children* (New York: Johnson Reprint Co., 1970; reprint of 1901 ed.); Robert H. Bremner, ed., *Children and Youth in America, A Documentary History*, 3 vols. (Cambridge, Mass.: Harvard University Press, 1970–74); Andrew Billingsley and Jeanne M. Giovanonni, *Children of the Storm: Black Children and American Child Welfare* (New York: Harcourt Brace Jovanovich, 1972); John O'Grady, *Catholic Charities in the United States* (New York: Arno Press, 1971; reprint of 1930 ed.); Francis E. Lane, "American Charities and the Child of the Immigrant: A Study of Typical Child Caring Institutions in New York and Massachusetts Between the Years 1845 and 1880" (Ph.D. dissertation, Catholic University of America, 1932); Robert H. Bremner, *From the Depths: The Discovery of Poverty in the United States* (New York: New York University Press, 1956); David Rothman, *The Discovery of the Asylum: Social Order and Disorder in the New Republic* (Boston: Little Brown, 1971).

74. Folks, *The Care of Destitute, Neglected, and Delinquent Children*, pp. 4–7, 12, 37–39, 72–149.

75. Ibid., pp. 79–80.

76. Ibid., pp. 52–55; United States Bureau of the Census, *Benevolent Institutions, 1910* (Washington, D.C.: Government Printing Office, 1913), pp. 86–156.

77. Folks, *The Care of Destitute, Neglected, and Delinquent Children*, pp. 43–64.

78. O'Grady, *Catholic Charities in the United States*, pp. 71, 78–80, 33, 107, 111, 118, 122–124, 129, 132–135.

79. Walch, "Catholic Social Institutions and Urban Development," pp. 16–27.

80. D. Rothman, *The Discovery of the Asylum*, pp. 213–214, 228–229; Folks, *The Care of Destitute, Neglected, and Delinquent Children*, pp. 64–65; P. A. Baart, *Orphans and Orphan Asylums* (Buffalo: Catholic Publication Co., 1885), pp. 44–45.

81. O'Grady, *Catholic Charities in the United States*, pp. 7–8, 33.

82. Billingsley and Giovanonni, *Children of the Storm*, pp. 27, 30, 52–55.

83. Robert S. Pickett, *House of Refuge: Origins of Juvenile Reform in New York State, 1815–1857* (Syracuse: Syracuse University Press, 1969); Joseph M. Hawes, *Children in Urban Society: Juvenile Delinquency in Nineteenth-Century America* (New York: Oxford University Press, 1971); Robert M. Mennel, *Thorns and Thistles:*

Juvenile Delinquents in the United States, 1825–1940 (Hanover, N.H.: University Press of New England, 1973); Steven L. Schlossman, *Love and the American Delinquent. The Theory and Practice of "Progressive" Juvenile Justice, 1825–1920* (Chicago: University of Chicago Press, 1976); David Rothman, *The Discovery of the Asylum*; Michael B. Katz, *The Irony of Early School Reform* (Cambridge, Mass.: Harvard University Press, 1968).

84. Katz, *The Irony of Early School Reform*, pp. 172–173; Pickett, *House of Refuge*, pp. 105–106, 108–109.

85. Hawes, *Children in Urban Society*, p. 131.

86. Ibid. and Bruce Laurie, "Fire Companies and Gangs in Southwark: The 1840s," in Allen F. Davis and Mark Haller, *The Peoples of Philadelphia; A History of Ethnic Groups and Lower-Class Life, 1790–1940* (Philadelphia: Temple University Press, 1973), pp. 77–79.

87. Katz, *The Irony of Early School Reform*, pp. 180–181.

88. Folks, *The Care of Destitute, Neglected and Delinquent Children*, pp. 198–226.

89. Lane, "American Charities and the Child of the Immigrant," pp. 55–56, 121–124.

90. Aaron I. Abell, *American Catholicism and Social Action: A Search for Social Justice, 1865–1950* (Garden City, N.Y.: Doubleday, 1960), pp. 35–36.

91. Katz, *The Irony of Early School Reform*, p. 177; Mennel, *Thorns and Thistles*, pp. 57–58.

92. Mennel, *Thorns and Thistles*, p. 59; Katz, *The Irony of Early School Reform*, pp. 194–195; Folks, *The Care of Destitute, Neglected, and Delinquent Children*, pp. 227–228; Hawes, *Children in Urban Society*, pp. 134–136.

93. D. Rothman, *The Discovery of the Asylum*, pp. 257–264; Folks, *The Care of Destitute, Neglected, and Delinquent Children*, pp. 202, 207, 211, 214, 217, 219–220.

94. Barbara M. Brenzel, *Daughters of the State; A Social Portrait of the First Reform School for Girls in North America, 1856–1905* (Cambridge, Mass.: MIT Press, 1983), pp. 120, 122–123.

95. Cecilia Parris Remick, "The House of Refuge of Philadelphia" (Ed. D. dissertation, University of Pennsylvania, 1975), pp. 306–332. The Philadelphia House of Refuge was one of the few juvenile reform asylums to establish a segregated department for black boys and girls.

96. Folks, *The Care of Destitute, Neglected, and Delinquent Children*, pp. 210–221; Schlossman, *Love and the American Delinquent*, pp. 38–39.

97. Schlossman, *Love and the American Delinquent*, p. 37.

98. Hawes, *Children in Urban Society*, pp. 132–133.

99. O'Grady, *Catholic Charities in the United States*, quote p. 111. See also Folks, *The Care of Destitute, Neglected, and Delinquent Children*, pp. 61–64.

100. John Augustus, *John Augustus: First Probation Officer. John Augustus' Original Report of his Labors (1852)* (Montclair, N.J.: Patterson Smith, 1972), passim.

101. Mennel, *Thorns and Thistles*, p. 43; Folks, *The Care of Destitute, Neglected, and Delinquent Children*, pp. 229–236.

102. Thomas Bender, *Toward an Urban Vision: Ideas and Institutions in 19th Century America* (Lexington: University Press of Kentucky, 1975), pp. 136–139, quote p. 138.

103. Brace, *The Dangerous Classes of New York*, pp. 80–82, quote p. 80.

104. Ibid., pp. 84, 88, 76–77, 223–225, 227–268; Hawes, *Children in Urban Society*, p. 102.

105. Bender, *Toward an Urban Vision*, pp. 145–147; R. Richard Wohl, "The 'Country Boy' Myth and Its Place in American Urban Culture: The Nineteenth Century Contribution," *Perspectives in American History* 3 (1979): 118–119; Hawes, *Children in Urban Society*, pp. 103–107.

106. Folks, *The Care of Destitute, Neglected, and Delinquent Children*, pp. 68–71, 160–162, 182–185.

107. Wohl, "The 'Country Boy' Myth," pp. 77–156; Bender, *Toward an Urban Vision*, pp. 148–153.

108. All quotes from Paul Boyer, *Urban Masses and Moral Order in America, 1820–1920* (Cambridge, Mass.: Harvard University Press, 1978), pp. 96–101.

109. Hawes, *Children in Urban Society*, p. 138.

110. Riis, *Children of the Poor*, p. 143.

111. Folks, *The Care of Destitute, Neglected, and Delinquent Children*, pp. 172–177.

112. Hawes, *Children in Urban Society*, p. 139.

113. Folks, *The Care of Destitute, Neglected, and Delinquent Children*, quote p. 175. See also p. 177.

114. Hawes, *Children in Urban Society*, p. 138; Riis, *Children of the Poor*, pp. 148–149.

BIBLIOGRAPHY

Abell, Aaron I. *American Catholicism and Social Action: A Search for Social Justice, 1865–1950*. Garden City, N.Y.: Doubleday, 1960.

————. *The Urban Impact of American Protestantism, 1865–1900*. Cambridge, Mass.: Harvard University Press, 1943.

Augustus, John. *John Augustus: First Probation Officer. John Augustus' Original Report of his Labors (1852)*. Montclair, N.J.: Patterson Smith, 1972.

Baart, P. A. *Orphans and Orphan Asylums*. Buffalo: Catholic Publication Co., 1885.

Bender, Thomas. *Toward an Urban Vision: Ideas and Institutions in 19th Century America*. Lexington: University Press of Kentucky, 1975.

Billingsley, Andrew, and Giovanonni, Jeanne M. *Children of the Storm: Black Children and American Child Welfare*. New York: Harcourt Brace Jovanovich, 1972.

Boyer, Paul. *Urban Masses and Moral Order in America, 1820–1920*. Cambridge, Mass.: Harvard University Press, 1978.

Brace, Charles Loring. *The Dangerous Classes of New York and Twenty Years' Work Among Them*. New York: Wynkoop and Hallenbeck, 1872.

Bremner, Robert H., ed. *Children and Youth in America, A Documentary History*. 3 vols. Cambridge, Mass.: Harvard University Press, 1970–74.

Bremner, Robert H. *From the Depths, The Discovery of Poverty in the United States*. New York: New York University Press, 1956.

Brenzel, Barbara M. *Daughters of the State; A Social Portrait of the First Reform School for Girls in North America, 1856–1905*. Cambridge, Mass.: MIT Press, 1983.

Bullough, William. *Cities and Schools in the Gilded Age, The Evolution of an Urban Institution*. Port Washington, N.Y.: Kennikat Press, 1974.

Callow, Alexander B., Jr., ed. *American Urban History, An Interpretive Reader with Commentaries*. 2nd ed. New York: Oxford University Press, 1973.

Chudacoff, Howard P. *The Evolution of American Urban Society*. Englewood Cliffs, N.J.: Prentice Hall, 1975.

Cohen, Ronald. "Schooling in Early Nineteenth Century Boston and New York." *Journal of Urban History* 1 (November 1974): 116–23.

———. "Urban Schooling in the Gilded Age and After." *Journal of Urban History* 2 (August 1976): 499–506.

Cremin, Lawrence. *American Education, The National Experience, 1783–1876*. New York: Harper and Row, 1980.

———. *The Transformation of the School; Progressivism in American Education, 1876–1957*. New York: Knopf, 1961.

Davis, Allen F., and Haller, Mark. *The Peoples of Philadelphia; A History of Ethnic Groups and Lower-Class Life, 1790–1940*. Philadelphia: Temple University Press, 1973.

Folks, Homer. *The Care of Destitute, Neglected, and Delinquent Children*. New York: Johnson Reprint Co., 1970; reprint of 1901 edition.

Gabert, Glen, Jr. *In Hoc Signo? A Brief History of Catholic Parochial Education in America*. Port Washington, N.Y.: Kennikat Press, 1973.

Glaab, Charles N., ed. *The American City: A Documentary History*. Homewood, Ill.: Dorsey Press, 1963.

Graham, Patricia. *Community and Class in American Education, 1865–1918*. New York: John Wiley and Sons, 1974.

Hawes, Joseph M. *Children in Urban Society: Juvenile Delinquency in Nineteenth-Century America*. New York: Oxford University Press, 1971.

Hennesey, James. *American Catholics, A History of the Roman Catholic Community in the United States*. New York: Oxford University Press, 1981.

Hershberg, Theodore, ed. *Philadelphia: Work, Space, Family, and Group Experience in the 19th Century, Essays Toward an Interdisciplinary History of the City*. New York: Oxford University Press, 1981.

Jacoby, George. *Catholic Child Care in Nineteenth Century New York*. Washington, D.C.: Catholic University of America Press, 1941.

Kaestle, Carl F., and Vinovskis, Maris A. *Education and Social Change in Nineteenth Century Massachusetts*. New York: Cambridge University Press, 1980.

Katz, Michael B. *The Irony of Early School Reform*. Cambridge, Mass.: Harvard University Press, 1968.

Katz, Michael B.; Doucet, Michael J.; and Stern, Mark J. *The Social Organization of Early Industrial Capitalism*. Cambridge, Mass.: Harvard University Press, 1982.

Krug, Edward A. *The Shaping of the American High School, 1880–1920*. Madison: University of Wisconsin Press, 1969.

Lane, Francis E. "American Charities and the Child of the Immigrant: A Study of Typical Child Caring Institutions in New York and Massachusetts Between the Years 1845 and 1880." Ph.D. dissertation, Catholic University of America, 1932.

Lannie, Vincent P. *Public Money and Parochial Education, Bishop Hughes, Governor*

Seward, and the New York School Controversy. Cleveland: Press of Case Western Reserve University, 1968.

Lazerson, Marvin. *The Origins of the Urban School: Public Education in Massachusetts, 1870–1915.* Cambridge, Mass.: Harvard University Press, 1971.

McKelvey, Blake. *The Urbanization of America [1860–1915].* New Brunswick, N.J.: Rutgers University Press, 1963.

Mennel, Robert M. *Thorns and Thistles: Juvenile Delinquents in the United States, 1825–1940.* Hanover, New Hampshire: University Press of New England, 1973.

Mohl, Raymond, and Richardson, James F., eds. *The Urban Experience, Themes in American History.* Belmont, Calif.: Wadsworth Publishing Co., 1973.

O'Grady, John. *Catholic Charities in the United States.* New York: Arno Press, 1971; reprint of 1930 edition.

Parr, Joy. *Labouring Children: British Immigrant Apprentices to Canada, 1869 to 1924.* London: Croom Helm, 1980.

Pickett, Robert S. *House of Refuge: Origins of Juvenile Reform in New York State, 1815–1857.* Syracuse: Syracuse University Press, 1969.

Ravitch, Diane. *The Great School Wars, New York City, 1805–1973. A History of Public Schools as Battlefields of Social Change.* New York: Basic Books, 1974.

Remick, Cecilia Parris. "The House of Refuge of Philadelphia." Ed.D. dissertation, University of Pennsylvania, 1975.

Riis, Jacob. *The Children of the Poor.* New York: Charles Scribners' Sons, 1892.

Rothman, David J. *The Discovery of the Asylum: Social Order and Disorder in the New Republic.* Boston: Little Brown, 1971.

Rothman, Shelia M. *Woman's Proper Place: A History of Changing Ideals and Practices, 1870 to the Present.* New York: Basic Books, 1978.

Schlossman, Steven L. *Love and the American Delinquent. The Theory and Practice of "Progressive" Juvenile Justice, 1825–1920.* Chicago: University of Chicago Press, 1976.

Schultz, Stanley K. *The Culture Factory: Boston Public Schools, 1789 to 1860.* New York: Oxford University Press, 1973.

Steinfels, Margaret O'Brien. *Who's Minding the Children? The History and Politics of Day Care in America.* New York: Simon and Schuster, 1973.

Still, Bayrd. *Urban America: A History with Documents.* Boston: Little Brown, 1974.

Trattner, Walter I. *Crusade for the Children: A History of the National Child Labor Committee and Child Labor Reform in America.* Chicago: Quadrangle Books, 1970.

Troen, Selwyn K. *The Public and the Schools: Shaping the St. Louis School System, 1838–1920.* Columbia: University of Missouri Press, 1975.

Tyack, David. *The One Best System, A History of American Urban Education.* Cambridge, Mass.: Harvard University Press, 1974.

U.S. Bureau of the Census. *Benevolent Institutions, 1910.* Washington, D.C.: U.S. Government Printing Office, 1913.

Walch, Timothy. "Catholic Social Institutions and Urban Development: The View from 19th Century Chicago and Milwaukee." *Catholic Historical Review* 64 (1978): 16–32.

Wohl, R. Richard. "The 'Country Boy' Myth and Its Place in American Urban Culture: The Nineteenth Century Contribution." *Perspectives in American History* 3 (1979): 77–156.

7

Child-Saving and Progressivism, 1885–1915

Ronald D. Cohen

America was on the move as the nineteenth century waned. On every level activity was apparent. Population growth accelerated, the economy mushroomed, factories and cities appeared almost overnight, and immigrant cultures transformed the cultural landscape. Change was immense, generally welcomed, but had to be given some direction, some deliberate shape and substance. Every new benefit seemed to produce a new liability. Most important in the minds of thoughtful people, perhaps, were issues related to children. In Homestead, Pennsylvania, Margaret F. Byington discovered in 1909 the frightful results of uncontrolled change:

Summing up the results of indifference on one side and ignorance on the other, we find a high infant death-rate, a knowledge of evil among little children, intolerable sanitary conditions, a low standard of living, a failure of the community to assimilate this new race in its midst. As we waited in one of the little railroad stations in Homestead, a Slavak [*sic*] came in and sat down next to a woman and her two-year-old child. He began making shy advances to the baby, and coaxing her in a voice of heartbreaking loneliness. But she would not come to him, and finally the two left the room. As they went he turned to the rest of the company, and in a tone of sadness, taking us all into his confidence said simply, "Me wife, me babe [in] Hungar[y]." But were they here it would mean death for one baby in three, it would mean hard work in a dirty, unsanitary house for the wife, it would mean sickness and much evil. With them away, it means for him isolation and loneliness and the abnormal life of the crowded lodging-house.[1]

I am indebted to the astute criticism and comments of William J. Reese.

As a result of her investigation, Byington helped popularize some of the main themes of the child-saving movement at the turn of the century: broken and inadequate families, health, delinquency, morality, poverty, schooling, dependency and neglect, employment, discrimination, adolescence, recreation and play, and early child development. Adults worried about children—everyone's children, not just their own—for their own sake and also out of fear for the country's future. They also wanted to control them.

The scope of social change was vast indeed. Overall, the population increased from about 57 million in 1885 to over 100 million in 1915, almost a doubling in thirty years. Of the 76 million total population in 1900, perhaps 67 million were white. These were the years of the "new immigration," accounting for the rise from 334,000 entering the country in 1886, to 1,027,000 in 1905, with at least 750,000 for each year until 1914, when an additional 1,218,000 arrived; between 1900 and 1915 the total was almost 15 million. Primarily from Eastern and Southern Europe, Catholic, Orthodox, and Jewish in religion, mostly children and young adults, the new immigrants tended to settle in urban areas in the Northeast and North Central states. A parallel internal move, by both blacks and whites, from farm to city, added to the rapid shift from an agrarian to an urban society. In 1890 the rural population was almost twice as large as the urban: by 1910 they were approaching parity, with about 50 million in the countryside and 42 million in the cities. (Ten years later, there would be 3 million more in the cities.)

The economy galloped to keep up with the demographic changes. The gross national product more than doubled from 1890 to 1915, from about $27 billion to $62 billion (in 1929 prices). Heavy industry witnessed the largest increase in size with a jump in the industrial work force from approximately 2.7 million in 1880 to 8.4 million by 1920, with the majority working in factories with more than 500 employees. Bigness also meant managerial reorganization, the emergence of the modern corporation committed to long-range planning, cost cutting, and maximization of profits—in short, efficiency and rigidity. But the craving for organization and control stretched out from corporate capitalism, insinuating itself in many facets of life. The rise of professionalization was especially clear, marked by highly organized training programs, a growing reliance on expertise, bureaucratic structures, and an impersonal style of interaction. The machine became omnipresent. Moreover, as many became quite wealthy, or at least well off, countless others wallowed in poverty—the contrasts were becoming more apparent. Perhaps 40 percent of Americans were poor in 1900, according to James T. Patterson, because "the economy at that time was not abundant enough to prevent a uniquely high percentage of Americans of all ethnic backgrounds from falling into poverty."[2]

A wide range of concerned individuals tried to come to grips with this kaleidoscope of forces and pressures. They attempted to make sense out of the changes taking place by possibly channeling and controlling them, preserving some of the past while plunging into the future. The totality of this response is termed the Progressive Movement, a phrase as slippery and charged as an electric eel. Broadly encompassing the reforms and changes from the 1890s to roughly 1920, progressivism has been characterized as dominated by a humanitarian impulse, on the one hand, or the desire for efficiency and social control, on the other (although the two are not necessarily contradictory). It is the old story of the blind men and the elephant. Historians tended to emphasize the humanitarian thrust until the 1950s, when a quite different interpretation began to emerge. Dominated by the writings of Richard Hofstadter, Gabriel Kolko, Robert H. Wiebe, Samuel P. Hays, Melvin G. Holli, Otis L. Graham, and Christopher Lasch, this new approach, most simply (leaving aside major differences among them), has described progressivism as a conservative-oriented movement—one that sought to reassert the dominance of elites in society and politics, to restore the perceived freedom of the individual which was fast disappearing before the forces of immigration, industrialization, and urbanization. On the city level Progressives wanted to reorganize, restructure, and streamline government along efficient, businesslike lines; they were also suspicious of the federal and state governments. They were, generally, small town people who never felt comfortable in the modernized world of the twentieth century, yet could rely on the new business methods of order and bureaucracy to turn back the clock. Caught between past and future, these structural reformers relied on power and efficiency to secure an orderly society. The confusing nature of their response has recently been captured by T. J. Jackson Lears in *No Place of Grace* (1981).[3]

The humanitarian impulse has not been totally discarded, however. Many social reformers, often settlement workers and intellectuals, really believed in "the preventive possibilities of social action." Their basic concern was to improve—economically, socially, and culturally—the conditions of the poor in the cities. They may have often imposed their middle-class American values on these largely immigrant groups. Still, they also believed their first goal was to help others achieve a decent and more comfortable way of life. They have been aptly typed by Allen F. Davis in *Spearheads for Reform* (1967) as "a group of idealists who believed that they could solve some of the problems of the sprawling, crowded city by going to live in a working-class neighborhood." They were "optimists who were convinced that reform was not only necessary, but also possible, in an age when rapid industrialization and a deluge of immigrants exaggerated the social and economic differences in America and challenged the very tenets of democracy." Even thought they often shared with the structural reformers a suspicion of strong, centralized government, they accepted national legislation when it was in the interests of the poor, oppressed, or helpless. While highly critical of the by-products of urbanization, immigration, and industrialization—poverty, slums, social injustice, destruction of a homogeneous society, manipulation of women and children by factory owners, and the like—they still agreed with many of the structural reformers' beliefs and values.[4]

Historians of the child-saving movement of the Progressive period have mirrored the contradictory interpretations of the larger reform spirit. Early-twentieth-century chroniclers, such as Grace Abbott, Homer Folks, and William J. Schultz, had no doubts that the concern for the well-being of children stemmed from pure humanitarian motives. Children need help—food, clothing, shelter, schooling, a family environment, labor legislation and control over working conditions, delinquency prevention, supervised recreation, improved health—and people responded out of the goodness of their hearts. A somewhat modified version of this approach has most recently surfaced in Susan Tiffin's *In Whose Best Interest?* (1982), a sweeping review of most aspects of child welfare reform—childrearing practices, child labor regulation and compulsory education, child abuse, the mentally, physically, and morally handicapped, dependent and neglected children, public welfare, delinquents, the Children's Bureau, and the professionalization of child-saving. Tiffin notes that the movement was quite conservative. "The men and women who agitated for child welfare reform were mainly middle-class, native-born, urban-based professionals," she concludes. "The stable society they wished to ensure was one that was conducive to their own social and career aspiration. They did not wish a radical redistribution of wealth nor a basic restructuring of social relationships." Nonetheless, "at the same time they were also genuinely concerned about the plight of an unfortunate group of children." Indeed, this latter point becomes the book's major thrust. She echoes the dominant theme in Robert Bremner's *From the Depths* (1956) and in Walter Trattner's review of the history of social welfare, *From Poor Law to Welfare State* (1979), which traces "the evolving concept of man's responsibility to man and of the community's and the government's responsibility for the well-being of all citizens."[5]

A contrary note was sounded in the late 1960s by a group of revisionist historians, led by, among others, Christopher Lasch and Michael B. Katz. Using the term "the new radicalism," Lasch stressed the intellectual side of the reform spirit and its desire for social control. "Totalitarianism was hardly the goal toward which American Progressives were even unconsciously striving," he wrote. "But the manipulative note was rarely absent from their writings: the insistence that men could best be controlled and directed not by the old, crude method of force but by 'education' in its broadest sense." They were subtle but effective. Katz, contrarily, has taken a more structural approach, emphasizing the imperatives of the emerging capitalist system. His most recent study (with Michael Doucet and Mark Stern), *The Social Organization of Early Industrial Capitalism* (1982), while concerned with the mid-nineteenth century, has valuable insights for grasping the Progressive Era. For Katz, reforms have only served to adjust people to the built-in inequities of the system: "Despite occasional protest at moments when . . . new populations had to be incorporated into the industrial capitalist order, the most remarkable aspect of the history of inequality has been the degree to which it has been accepted or acquiesced in not only by its beneficiaries but by its casualties as well." A key institution has been public schooling, where children have learned "their first lesson in political economy: the unequal distribution of rewards mirrors the unequal distribution of ability. Those who achieve deserve their success; those who fail are, very simply, less worthy." Both the Lasch and Katz approaches have helped shape the revisionist perspective.[6]

The interpretive struggle between "liberals" and "revisionists" has concentrated on two areas, juvenile delinquency and public schooling, although other aspects of child-saving have been present on the battlefield. During the nineteenth century, reforms of various sorts had resulted in partially separating children and youth from adults while incarcerated. While the system was not perfect—indeed, extremely haphazard because of the bewildering variety of institutions and procedures established piecemeal over the years by local and state governments—some basic features were evident by 1890. Nearly every state outside the South had at least one reform school for boys, and perhaps a separate one for girls, normally controlled and supported by state and municipal governments—a movement distinct from the earlier private houses of refuge. Delinquents, those between roughly ten and sixteen who had committed a criminal act, could be sentenced to the reform schools by regular criminal courts, although others still wound up in the adult prisons. Laws and judicial practices were flexible. Neglected or deserted children, those accused of rebellion against their parents, and others of "decidedly mischievous propensities" were herded together with the rest. Supposedly places of "reformation, discipline and education," not punishment, they were grim indeed. Whether of the congregate or cottage type, discipline was harsh, control strict, and contact with the outside world limited. As a further refinement, starting in the 1870s some states opened reformatories for first-time male offenders ages sixteen to twenty-five.[7]

The treatment of delinquent, neglected, and dependent children was under serious review in the 1890s, leading to the establishment of the juvenile court system in Illinois in 1899. The first court quickly appeared in Chicago, within a decade ten states had followed suit, and by 1925 all but two states, Maine and Wyoming, had juvenile court laws. Informal, flexible, and paternalistic, the juvenile court depended heavily on treating separately each juvenile and his or her family; incarceration was rare, and most were put on probation, an indefinite status that kept them under the watchful eye of their parents (or guardians) as well as of the court.

Why were juvenile courts established, and what were their results? Perhaps the most positive treatment has been that of Joseph M. Hawes in *Children in Urban Society* (1971). Concerned with changing theories of juvenile delinquency, Hawes believes that "if the story has a theme, it is that of an increasing individualization of the treatment of juvenile delinquents, and a growing awareness on society's part that young offenders were individuals in need of help rather than members of a stereotyped group which merited society's condemnation." The juvenile court was designed to help, not hurt, the offender: "The judge in juvenile court was more concerned with what was best for the individual child before him than with whether or not that child had committed an offense. Here then was a new institution designed specifically for children." Hawes has taken the reformers at their word. The symbol of the humanitarian nature of the movement, Judge Ben Lindsey of the Denver court, has received laudatory treatment in Charles Larsen's *The Good Fight* (1972).[8]

Two years before Hawes's book appeared, Anthony Platt sounded a considerably more sour note. In *The Child Savers* (1969), the author, heavily influenced by the approach of Christopher Lasch, explored the central role played by middle-class women in the child-saving movement, culminating in the rise of the juvenile court. These women, concerned with protecting "parental authority, home education, domesticity, and rural values," as well as developing new careers in social work, were partially responsible for the repressive nature of the movement. Their conservative values meant that "the programs they enthusiastically supported diminished the civil liberties and privacy of youth. Adolescents were treated as though they were naturally dependent, requiring constant and pervasive supervision." Perhaps their motives were benign, but "their remedies seemed to aggravate the problem." Platt concentrated on the movement in Chicago and its leading child-savers, such as Louise de Koven Bowen and Jane Addams. In his broad-ranging study *Thorns and Thistles* (1973), perhaps the best overall treatment of the subject, Robert M. Mennel generally agrees with Platt. He notes the intrusive and arbitrary nature of the system, exemplified in the role played by the probation officers, a point overlooked by Platt: "Probation officers often exacerbated religious and ethnic tensions by assuming an authoritarian attitude toward probationers and their families, many of whom were both foreign-born and poor." And while probation was the norm, judges and probation officers could threaten, and resort to, incarceration if they so chose—"in short, juvenile courts, even those with a panoply of supporting staff and institutions, provided new bottles for old wine— ways of supervising delinquent children which, while not formally incarcerating them, provided penal sanctions for persistent wrongdoers." Mennel also notes that despite the general euphoria, from the beginning critics began to expose the system's faults.[9]

In the late 1970s criticism mounted. One approach, a detailed study of the Milwaukee Juvenile Court from 1901 to 1920, has been used by Steven L. Schlossman. Concerned more about the workings of the court than its intellectual roots, Schlossman takes a class view, believing "the juvenile court functioned as a public arena where the dependent status of children was verified and reinforced and where the incapacities of lower-class immigrant parents were, in a sense, certified. The juvenile court flunked parents just as the public school flunked children; in both instances, the lower-class immigrant was the principal victim." The court movement was marked by four innovations: the child's "condition" rather than specific acts was most important; separate detention facilities were provided; probation was stressed; and adults could be convicted for contributing to delinquency. Above all, the home was considered the center for treatment (not punishment). In theory, the court was to act out of love, not retribution, developing an emotional bond between the judges and probation officers and their clientele. In Milwaukee this did not usually occur. "By failing to approach the parents of children in court with kindness, compassion and sympathy," Schlossman concludes,

officers of the court undermined what made Progressive ideas unique in the first place, and left the promise of the juvenile court movement not only unrealized but untested. Ideally the court was a missionary agent for the educational and moral uplift of the poor. In practice it functioned more often than not as a source of arbitrary punitive authority, and an arena for the evocation of hostile emotions on all sides.

In a most provocative study, Schlossman cuts through the rhetoric to give a compelling portrayal of the actual workings of child-saving in the courts. Ellen Ryerson also emphasizes the importance of evaluating practice rather than theory. In her broad survey *The Best-Laid Plans*, she reviews the mediocre nature of early court personnel; few judges were of the caliber of Ben Lindsey, and the early volunteer probation officers were often failures. The procedures of the early courts were hardly scientific, and their success rates were quickly challenged. "The juvenile court movement had gained easy acceptance of its ideas but met disappointment and frustration in converting those ideas into reality," Ryerson sums up.[10]

Whether supportive or critical of the juvenile court movement, historians have generally stressed two points: that the courts were designed to bolster the family, and this was accomplished through extensive use of probation. Both premises have been challenged by David J. Rothman. In *The Discovery of the Asylum* (1971), Rothman launched a broad, learned attack on the rise of the institutional state in the mid-nineteenth century. In his followup *Conscience and Convenience* (1980), he limited his focus somewhat but still concentrated on the twentieth-century zeal to control and incarcerate the criminal, the delinquent, and the insane. In short, he believes that "progressive innovations may well have done less to upgrade dismal conditions than they did to create nightmares of their own." The juvenile court, for example, under the rubric of promoting the child's best interest, greatly extended the state's reach into the heart of the family, particularly among the lower classes and immigrants. The doctrine of *parens patriae*, the state as parent to the child, knew few bounds. For Rothman, the most chilling aspect of this situation, aside from the power and arrogance of judges and probation workers, was that "juvenile court reform did not significantly reduce rates of juvenile incarceration. It is unlikely that the number of commitments to training schools or reformatories diminished substantially as a result of the creation of the court." Moreover, the reformatories, despite Progressive rhetoric to the contrary, were essentially punitive. In a provocative chapter titled "When is a school not a school?" he examines the structure and routine of various reform schools, concluding that they "not only failed to do good, they frequently did harm." Rothman's sweeping attack, the most critical yet, presents a challenge to future historians who are reluctant to totally abandon the Progressives' hope for a humane, caring juvenile justice system.[11]

Recent studies of the juvenile court movement have contained an implicit bias—they have dealt almost exclusively with the treatment of males. The limitations of this unrealized emphasis have been demonstrated by Steven Schlossman and Stephanie Wallach, "The Crime of Precocious Sexuality" (1978). They make two basic points: females "were brought to court almost exclusively for alleged early sexual exploration," and because of this situation "were treated more punitively than males." For example, in Chicago more than half of the boys who appeared in court between 1899 and 1909 were put on probation, but for girls the figure was only 37 percent. And their reformatory sentences were frequently longer. Why? The reason, it appears, was a pervasive fear of female sexuality; by locking them away, they were forced to "save their sexual favors, moral reputations, and health until they were of marriageable age." Girls, in short, were more of a social threat than boys, particularly immigrant girls. Historians will hereafter have to be sensitive to gender (as well as racial and ethnic) differences when exploring the topic.[12]

While most studies of troubled and troublesome youth focus on the juvenile court, a few deal with other concerns in this direction. Most famous was the Junior Republic Movement founded by William R. George (1866–1936), better known as "Daddy" George. As depicted by Jack M. Holl, *Juvenile Reform in the Progressive Era* (1971), George was a typical middle-class reformer: a moderately wealthy, conservative Republican, believing in the new efficiency drive of the time. Working initially with gang members in New York City, he began a Fresh Air Camp in upstate New York in 1890, with the Junior Republic emerging in 1895. It was based on two principles: work and self-government. Soon the movement spread to other states, becoming attractive because "the Junior Republic was not a refuge from life, but rather brought the child face to face with the struggle for existence," combining aspects of a juvenile reformatory and a model vocational school. Moreover, the movement influenced various public school reforms, such as the introduction of student government. In 1913 George also proposed establishing Junior Municipalities in America's cities which would cooperate with the adult governments. The origin and checkered career of one such Boyville, in Gary, Indiana, founded by Willis Brown, has been explored by Steven Schlossman and Ronald Cohen. As for George and the Junior Republic, Holl concludes that for a brief time its influence was substantial, even if its legacy is questionable. It marked yet another attempt during the Progressive period both to idealize and to control adolescent boys in a "noninstitutional" institution.[13]

The Progressives' dependence on structural change in dealing with children and youth was most pronounced in their approach to schooling. What happened to public schooling, and why, has engendered controversy from then to now, and rightfully so, for this experience was becoming the central concern of children's lives. Modern scholarship starts with Lawrence A. Cremin's *The Transformation of the School* (1961). Still unsurpassed for its breadth and learning, Cremin's study was based on the belief that "progressive education began as part of a vast humanitarian effort to apply the promise of American life—the ideal of government by, of, and for the people—to the puzzling new urban-industrial civilization that came into being during the latter half of the nineteenth century." It was "a many-sided effort to use the schools to improve the lives of individuals." More recently, Cremin has broadened considerably his definition of education and dimmed somewhat his optimism—"the schools did extend opportunity to many whose familial education had been impoverished and constraining, and they extended even more opportunity to many whose familial education had been rich and liberating;

but such opportunity as they did extend was clearly inadequate for many individuals in both categories"—yet he refuses to be too critical.[14]

Many historians have parted company with Cremin and in the process have sharpened their interpretive skills. Some have adopted a more critical perspective, written from a multiplicity of ideological positions. Others adhere to a more positive approach. In a comparative study of four school systems—Johnson County, Indiana; Marquette County, Michigan; Butler County, Alabama; and New York City—Patricia A. Graham stresses geographical differences in school development, while underscoring their democratic rationale. Nonetheless, she does add that "crucial as the educational institutions were in the late nineteenth century, attendance at them did not guarantee full acceptance in the economic or social life of the nation," particularly for blacks.[15]

While there were significant local variations in the late nineteenth century, important changes were occurring nationally, particularly in cities, that would produce considerable uniformity among school systems (as well as among many other institutions). A foremost proponent of this approach is David B. Tyack. In *The One Best System* (1974), he traced the downfall of the community-controlled common school and its replacement after the turn of the century, when "an interlocking directorate of urban elites—largely business and professional men, university presidents and professors, and some 'progressive' superintendents—joined forces to centralize the control of schools." Professionals took over, the curriculum changed, and efficiency triumphed—almost. The urban elites were successful, but all did not necessarily profit, as they had assumed, for example, black and immigrant children. With Elisabeth Hansot, Tyack has extended his analysis of what he now calls the "Educational Trust" in *Managers of Virtue* (1982). They explore

the new leaders [who] thought they knew how to bring about a smoothly running, socially efficient, stable social order in which education was a major form of human engineering. Society would control its own evolution through schooling; professional management would replace politics; science would replace religion and custom as sources of authority; and experts would adapt education to the transformed conditions of modern corporate life.

In a finely tuned analysis, they expertly examine school "reform from the top down." While the male school managers held considerable power, their rule did not go unchallenged, for female teachers and administrators occasionally asserted their rights.[16]

As school leadership changed, reflecting new structures and values in American society, curricular and other innovations quickly appeared. Unfortunately, historians do not always distinguish between changes on the elementary and high school levels, often lumping programs together under the rubric of "Progressive education." Perhaps most innovations were in the upper grades, denoting the growing concern with the present and future conditions of teenagers. In an often neglected study, Edward Krug delineated *The Shaping of the American High School, 1880–1920* (1964). The public high school population exploded, from 203,000 in 1890 to 2.2 million in 1920, and the curriculum became more flexible and "practical." For Krug, the introduction of vocational and other programs marked the zeal for "education for social efficiency," a combination of a desire for social control and social service.[17]

In the 1970s, more specific studies appeared, broadening considerably our understanding of the origins and nature of educational change. In the *Origins of the Urban School* (1971), Marvin Lazerson noted that there were two distinct phases in the development of the new curriculum. Between 1870 and 1900, schooling was seen "as the basis of social amelioration," but after 1900, "the school's major function [became] the fitting of the individual into the economy. By the teaching of specific skills and behavior patterns, schools would produce better and more efficient workers and citizens, and they would do this through a process of selection and guidance." Lazerson focuses on the rise of the kindergarten, manual training, vocational education (particularly at the high school level), evening schools, and citizenship training. He connects the efficiency-oriented values of the school reformers and the development of specific programs. Joel Spring, in *Education and the Rise of the Corporate State* (1972), followed a similar line of argument with a more explicit connection between the business community and school reform. "Business supported many of the innovations in education because they promised a healthier and better trained worker," he argues. "Business also supported social activity programs in the school because they needed and wanted men who would cooperate with fellow workers. Organized industry wanted the organization man." Spring highlights the schools' socialization role by tracing the rise of vocational guidance, the junior high, and student government in high school—all designed to mold conformist citizens and workers.[18]

There are various ways of understanding the connection between the changing nature of schooling and the larger economic and social system then in the process of development. For Walter Feinberg, a philosopher, what was paramount was the reformers' acceptance of technology and its central role in modern society. "Technology, of course, meant more than the use of simple tools to create commodities and satisfy human wants," he explains.

It also indicated a high level of interdependence among various productive and social functions such that any given product was the result of many men interacting with each other and with the machine. Moreover such interaction had to be consciously planned and designed with the goals of production and efficiency in mind.

Thus, the demands of the machine, in a very broad sense, and particularly the need for "functional integration"—the whole is more important than the parts—dominated the thinking of Progressive educators. While Feinberg concentrates on technology as the lever of change, Samuel Bowles and Herbert Gintis in *Schooling in Capitalist America* put their emphasis on the omnipotence of corporate capitalism: "The legacy of the urban school reform movement... reflects both its strongly upper-class basis and its commitment to social control as the overriding objective of schooling.... The essence of Progressivism in education was the rationalization of the process of reproducing the social classes of modern industrial life." Most simply, schools could not, and did not, promote equality because the capitalist system demanded inequality.[19]

With broad strokes Feinberg, Bowles, and Gintis have sketched the motivating principles of educational change without differentiating between social and structural reformers. Moreover, they believe all children were affected by school policies, although minorities and the poor suffered inordinately. This has been the nature of the system. Others have directed their attention to the plight of working-class children, a particular target group of Progressive educators. In *The Training of the Urban Working Class*, Paul Violas studies seven prime innovations—compulsory school attendance, Americanization, the play movement, student extracurricular activities, vocational training, vocational guidance, and the emergence of the professional school administrator—familiar topics to recent historians. All were designed to control and influence working-class children, "to adjust those children to their inevitable industrial futures." Order and cooperation were paramount in the shop and office, so they became the prime educational goals. Paul Violas's structural approach leads him to conclude that since educators "felt it was in the student's best interests to share this industrial consciousness, the resultant programs emerged from an honest commitment." Honest, perhaps, but most unfortunate.[20]

If school innovations were primarily aimed at sorting and controlling the children of the working class, as Violas and others have argued, then it is most important to study the rise of vocational education. Crucial are the essays in *Work, Youth, and Schooling* (1982), edited by Harvey Kantor and David B. Tyack, which greatly extend our understanding of the interplay between economic and educational change. Large numbers of youth left work and went to school: "Between 1900 and 1920, the percentage of fourteen-to-eighteen-year-old males at work dropped from 43 to 23 percent, and females from 18 to 11 percent. At the same time, the high school enrollment of fourteen-to-seventeen-year-olds rose from approximately 8 percent in 1900 to over 44 percent in 1930." This, in turn, meant the restructuring of secondary education—the differentiated curriculum, vocational courses in the trades and business, guidance, and testing—and a reliance on "educational solutions to labor market problems." Why did these changes occur? W. Norton Grubb and Marvin Lazerson, in "Education and the Labor Market," offer some thoughtful suggestions concerning the link between extended schooling and jobs. The rise of large corporations produced the "fracturing of skill ladders, the development of internal labor markets, and the rationalization of hiring procedures," which "reinforced the economic values of staying in school." Simultaneously, rising age discrimination and the disappearance of some traditional youth jobs shrunk the labor market, while the expansion of managerial and office positions put a premium on learning new skills. Schools assumed a growing role in both "warehousing" youth, keeping them occupied during their idle years, and preparing them for future economic roles.[21]

The rapid spread and support of vocational education by World War I, capped by the passage of the Smith-Hughes Act in 1917 granting federal funds for vocational training, has been attributed to its central support by the business community. The programs were certainly marked by business-oriented values and behavior. Labor's role in this development has been more murky. The American Federation of Labor's early suspicion of vocational education was modified in 1910, and thereafter its support was lukewarm. The shift to guarded acceptance occurred for three possible reasons: the union believed high schools could be more interesting and attractive, business interests should not be allowed to monopolize the programs, and the vocational courses were necessary for skills training. Unions however, opposed separating vocational from academic and commercial programs, which would create an inferior track for working-class youth. The contest was heated in Illinois, as Julia Wrigley argues in *Class, Politics and Public Schools* (1982), where from 1913 to 1917 a battle raged in the state assembly between the Chicago Federation of Labor (and the Illinois State Federation of Labor) and the Commercial Club with its business allies over passage of the Cooley bill. The bill, which would establish separate vocational schools for working children over the age of fourteen, lost. This is only one example, among many, that Wrigley cites to demonstrate the power of organized labor in local and state politics. The violent conflict over introducing the Gary School Plan, with its marked vocational orientation, into the New York schools in 1917 was another example of labor's continuing suspicion of these schemes.[22]

The view that the transformation of public schooling must be seen as the work of business leaders and their allies has been modified in other ways. While the role of organized labor is scarcely known, partially reflecting the anemic state of the American Federation of Labor (AFL) at the time, historians have begun to focus on other grass-roots groups, such as Socialists, immigrants, and women. Non-elites had a hand both in shaping the form and content of schools, and in controlling their children's exposure to them. William J. Reese has taken the position that "a study of Milwaukee's socialist labor movement demonstrates how particular working people influenced school reform in a time of rapid social change, and it also demonstrates how they in turn were shaped by the reform groups that helped inaugurate many of the period's innovative education programs." Perhaps Milwaukee was too unique, with its Socialist mayor and radical labor movement, but Reese has extended his argument to understand educational change in Rochester, Toledo, and Kansas City as well. While this perspective might seem reminiscent of an earlier "democratic" interpretation, it is rather a forceful plea that the working class must be taken seriously in any understanding of public school affairs.[23]

More attention has been focused on the values and actions of various ethnic groups (who were heavily working class), who also had some volition. For David Hogan, at least in Chicago, "the working class made itself as much as it was made; the educational behavior was not the outcome of some vague process of modernization, or some form of ideological imposition, or some purely instrumental attitude to education, but primarily a response, mediated by cultural traditions, to the class structure of social relations of American society." In short, "all immigrant groups developed a positive, instrumental attitude toward education as a means of ensuring or enhancing the economic welfare of their children." The Americanization campaign of the early twentieth century, linked to the emerging heterogeneous nature of school programs and activities, was designed, it appears, to produce homogeneous children—good workers and good citizens. But the system was not omnipotent. The differential schooling of various immigrant groups occurred because the children and their parents made conscious decisions to control their lives. As Ronald Cohen and Raymond Mohl have stressed, in examining the interaction of immigrants and schooling in Gary, Indiana, "perhaps some ethnic groups sought to achieve mobility and economic success through education, while others sought the same goals through work." A common comparison has been made between Jewish and Southern Italian children, the Jewish having a greater interest in prolonged school attendance. While the common interpretation emphasizes a difference in traditional values, Miriam Cohen believes that the economic conditions of the groups must be considered. Southern Italian girls had to work to help support their families, while Jewish girls were somewhat freer to attend school because of slightly better financial circumstances. There was, indeed, great diversity in the attitudes and actions of ethnic groups in regard to public schooling, depending on a combination of values, economic circumstances, external influences, and generational differences. The growth of parochial schools partially resulted from this situation.[24]

The difficulty of generalizing about both the nature of educational change and the experiences of the children is highlighted by examining schooling for blacks. How were they affected by Progressive schooling? In the South galloping segregation doomed black children to a sorry plight. "The process of guaranteeing separate and unequal schooling in the South was completed in the 1890s," as Mary F. Berry and John Blassingame summarize the issue. "While blacks constituted 31.6 percent of the school-age population in the South in 1899, they received only 12.9 percent of public school funds." And conditions deteriorated: black teachers were paid less than whites, the school term was shorter, there were few high schools, and even the texts were different in some states. The title of J. Morgan Kousser's article captures the situation, "Progressivism—For Middle-Class Whites Only: North Carolina Education, 1880–1910."[25]

In the North, conditions were better but hardly adequate. While the inequalities were not as pronounced, segregation was the rule rather than the exception. New York State outlawed segregation in cities in 1900, thereby ending *de jure* black schools; *de facto* segregation continued, however. Similar conditions existed elsewhere. In Gary, Indiana, a separate black elementary school was established in 1908, two years after the city's founding, and by 1920 black children were either in segregated schools or denied equality in one large unit (K-12) school. The same situation prevailed in Indianapolis, according to Judy Jolley Mohraz:

Even a small percentage of Negroes in mixed schools produced distress among school officials. In 1909, 2,330 Negroes were enrolled in the school system. All but fifty of the children below the high school level attended one of the segregated schools, while about eighty Negroes attended each of the two high schools. The superintendent, G. N. Kendall, saw even this number of Negro students in classes with white pupils as objectionable.

Conditions were better in Chicago, where a modicum of integration existed, although there was constant friction as blacks resisted increased segregation. In Philadelphia, a majority of black children were in integrated schools; within ten years segregation had escalated, despite protests from the black community. They also objected to the introduction of manual training in more black than white elementary schools, a sign of the "industrialization" of their children's education. School officials, notes Vincent P. Franklin, argued "not only that it was educationally 'efficient' to keep blacks in separate schools, but also that they should have a special curriculum that would be better suited to their 'mental aptitudes' and future occupations"—common beliefs at the turn of the century.[26]

Historians are united in their critical analysis of growing school segregation, North and South, but are less certain of the meaning of other innovations. For example, what effect did the new school programs have on female students? The thrust of much recent research has been to connect skills and attitudes learned at school with job requirements, producing the trained, cooperative (male) worker. What were girls learning that would equip them for future roles as wives and mothers? Home economics courses proliferated, but we know little about them. Other vocational education courses have received somewhat more attention, however. Geraldine J. Clifford has attempted to account for the rise of vocational courses for girls:

the continued commitment to women's prime (that is, domestic) vocation; the desire to "do something" for the girls while the boys went off to their "real" vocational courses; the practical scheduling problems of balancing boys' offerings and girls' offerings so as to preserve the basic coeducational mix in the rest of the curriculum; the hope of prolonging school attendance by adding nonacademic subjects; and the goal of Americanizing the daughters of immigrants.

Specific job training, Clifford believes, was less important. And, depending on their ethnic background, girls often had a higher dropout rate than boys, for their place was assumed to be in the home once past fourteen. Those girls who continued on to high school preferred academic to commercial courses, however, some with the thought of going to college or into teaching.[27]

As children, and particularly youth, increased their school attendance (or stayed home, in the case of Italian girls, for example), child labor became less of a pressing issue. The connection between work and schooling is significant, but somewhat problematic is the cause and effect; did the enforcement of compulsory attendance laws and a revised curriculum precede or follow increased attendance? The regulation or elimination of child labor became an important element of Progressive childsaving, according to Walter Trattner in *Crusade for the Children*: (1970). The National Child Labor Committee was organized in 1904 to research and sponsor effective legislation, influence public opinion, and gather information. By 1912 there was some, but not widespread, regulation on the state level, leading the committee to begin support for federal legislation. The muckraking photo-journalism of Jacob Riis and Lewis Hine added to public concern and pressure. The Keating-Owen bill was passed in 1916, outlawing or limiting work in factories and mines for those under sixteen; it was declared unconstitutional two years later.

While success on the federal level was fleeting, gains were somewhat more visible in various states. In New York the Child Labor Committee, organized in 1902, helped pass a law controlling street trades, such as selling newspapers, and an improved factory bill. It had other victories over the years, but as Jeremy Felt concludes, "symbolic legislation made it possible for the public to believe that child labor was being checked and to ignore a considerable body of evidence demonstrating that the existing laws were badly enforced and that children were still working in tenements, in the streets, and on farms."[28]

Reformers attacked child labor without ever fully eliminating it. Miriam Cohen has even argued that "adequate enforcement of child labor and compulsory school laws would have had disastrous consequences for the schools. Even as large a public school system as New York was not adequate to accommodate all the children to the rapidly growing city." At the same time, however, certain jobs for young people were disappearing, as they were replaced by the cash register and the telephone, and employers began to prefer hiring older workers. One reason for the rise of the differentiated curriculum in high schools was to keep the newer, less academic students in school, but not bored. School populations grew rapidly, but attendance by some was sporadic, and others left after the age of fourteen (or sixteen). As of 1920, only 32 percent of youth ages fourteen to seventeen were enrolled in school, and only 17 percent had graduated from high school. Work remained the major pastime for teenagers, particularly for immigrants in the North and blacks in the South; economic necessity, mixed with parental values, still had the upper hand. Simultaneously, as Daniel T. Rodgers has shown, the cultural and intellectual meaning of work was undergoing a transformation—it was becoming less satisfactory.[29]

When they did go to school, many children were faced with hostile attitudes toward them. Teachers and school administrators, white and with Northern and Western European ancestry, had a natural inclination to look with disdain upon immigrant and black children whose physical and cultural differences were all too obvious. These prejudices became rationalized by "scientific" evidence of the children's innate inferiority. While the IQ test did not come into common use in public schools until the 1920s, its philosophical underpinnings reached back a few decades. Heredity was now seen as the key factor in molding intelligence and behavior. "While it would be inaccurate to say that most American experimentalists concluded as the result of the general acceptance of Mendelism by 1910 or so that heredity was all powerful and environment was of no consequence," writes Hamilton Cravens, "it was nevertheless true that heredity occupied a much more prominent place than environment in their writings." An extreme manifestation of this belief was the eugenics movement, the effort to improve the inborn characteristics of man by the study of human heredity and the application of those studies to human propagation. Eugenists grasped the important fact that a person's hereditary endowment is a major factor in his success and development, and they hoped to breed better people through encouraging propagation by those with desirable traits and through restricting propagation by those with undesirable traits.

The movement gathered momentum before World War I and gained success in the 1920s.[30]

If inherited characteristics were paramount, then it was necessary not only to control reproduction and immigration but also to measure and sort children in order to enhance their treatment. Testing and measurement (aptitude and skills as well as IQ) quickly became an accepted and efficient means of labeling and separating the young. That the movement had inherent racial and ethnic biases was perhaps only natural, given the homogeneous character of the scientists, schoolmen, and others who promoted it. Pioneered by Alfred Binet in France at the turn of the century, the concept of measuring intelligence migrated to the United States and soon appeared in the work of H. H. Goddard and Lewis Terman, the father of the Stanford-Binet test, which first appeared in 1916. According to Stephen Jay Gould,

American psychologists perverted Binet's intention and invented the hereditarian theory of IQ. They reified Binet's scores, and took them as measures of an entity called intelligence. They assumed that intelligence was largely inherited, and developed a series of specious arguments confusing cultural differences with innate properties. They believed that inherited IQ scores marked people and groups for an inevitable station in life. And they assumed that average differences between groups were largely the products of heredity, despite manifest and profound variation in quality of life.

The hereditarian theory of IQ fit perfectly, Gould notes, with American nativism, fear of radicalism, and "above all our persistent, indigenous racism." IQ testing did not become an educational tool until after World War I, but the belief in inherited characteristics highly influenced attitudes toward children during the previous two decades. For example, early "juvenile court workers and others concerned with crime and delinquency temporarily embraced mental testing as the key to their puzzle," Ellen Ryerson has written, which gave a pessimistic cast to their work.[31]

Child-savers were always searching for "the cause" of children's behavior. A "child study movement" emerged in the 1890s, led by G. Stanley Hall, president of Clark University and a leading psychologist. Hall's theory of recapitulation—that ontogeny (the development of the individual) mirrored phylogeny (the evolutionary development of mankind)—had little scientific foundation, but its popularity was widespread.

While the theory of recapitulation was quite mechanistic, Hall also emphasized other factors that were controllable, such as the importance of physical development and health. "The pervasive danger of disease and deviation which Hall and his colleagues pictured hanging over the younger generation had something to it of the old fear of sin," his biographer Dorothy Ross has written. "Although the studies of abnormalities in children were themselves meliorist in intent and enlightened in approach, some of the public apparently saw them in a traditional, pejorative light." There was much confusion as to what was preventable, and what was not.[32]

Running parallel with the belief in inherited or natural characteristics was a more pronounced argument that environmental circumstances were paramount. This conclusion was still disturbing to many, as T. J. Jackson Lears points out, because "if people were largely creatures of social circumstances or psychological drive, then personal moral responsibility was seriously eroded." Individual culpability was very popular in the nineteenth century, when character development was heavily stressed, but it began to lose importance by the turn of the century. As David Tyack and Michael Berkowitz argue in their study of the changing nature of the truant officer, "some social investigators were still censuring parents and children and waxing lyrical about the corrupting influence of poolrooms and dance halls. But the language of diagnosis was shifting from moral judgments about character to social scientific terminology, from 'vice' to 'maladjustment.' " The truant officer, similar to other social workers, was thereby transformed from an amateur to a scientifically trained professional. Indeed, the professional caseworker, emerging after the turn of the century as one example of the professionalization of society, was committed to efficient, scientific philanthropy through the individual approach. "Since each person was the sum of his individuality and social heritage, the guiding principle of casework was to treat unequal things unequally," writes Roy Lubove in *The Professional Altruist*. "Such 'differential social treatment' demanded 'special social skill,' whatever the institutional setting: school, workshop, hospital, court, or mental clinic." Professionals believed individual and social problems could be solved if enough evidence was gathered and scientific methods adhered to.[33]

The various strands that came together to form the Progressive child-saving movement can perhaps best be seen in the attitudes toward and treatment of adolescents or youth. The most comprehensive study is Joseph F. Kett's *Rites of Passage* (1977). Although limited to a discussion of the changing role of middle-class, white, male youth, Kett's analysis stresses the emergence of a separate stage of life termed "adolescence." Even before the word appeared, as the title of G. Stanley Hall's 1904 massive study, young people (that is, teenagers) were becoming a defined group: their organizations would be controlled by adults, they should be passive and not involved in adult activities. Youth was becoming more a stage of dependency, with the transition to adulthood—exit from school, entrance to the work force, departure from the family of origin, marriage, and establishment of a household—becoming regularized. After 1900 the concept took on shape and substance. "At the center of the change was the adolescent—vulnerable, awkward, incapacitated by the process of maturation, but simultaneously the object of almost rhapsodic praise, the very bud and promise of the race," Kett writes. "Adolescence, according to Hall, was a new birth, a wiping clean of the slate of childhood." Hall believed that adolescent males should be allowed to sow their wild oats, within reason, but others attempted to maintain firmer control.[34]

Various organizations and institutions emerged, including the junior high and high school, to supervise and control this burgeoning age group. The older means of social control—work, family, and community—were now considered inadequate. Kett mentions, for example, the Boy Scouts, established in the United States in 1912 and marked by "rigid organization, authoritarian control, and a disposition to view outdoor life as little more than a tool for toughening muscle fiber." For David I. McLeod, however, the Boy Scouts was, in fact, designed to "extend boyhood and distract boys from adolescence. . . . Boyish activism suffused Scouting." Because of its emphasis on woodcraft and badges, Scouting was most popular with boys twelve to fourteen, those just entering puberty. Macleod argues that older adolescents were more attracted to YMCA youth groups because of their team sports, leading him to conclude that youth "have subdivided each condition by age as well as gender and social class and have acted in terms of those finer gradations. To control them, adults have had to accede in part to their desires." Both the Boy Scouts and the YMCA aimed their message at urban middle-class boys, who were seen as being as vulnerable, but perhaps not as dangerous, as lower-class youth. Particularly problematic was the issue of masculinity. Increased sex education, on the one hand, and emphasis on virility, on the other, marked somewhat contrary tensions at the time.[35]

The playground movement emerged in the early twentieth century as yet one more manifestation of a desire to constructively channel the energies of children and youth. For Cary Goodman, in *Choosing Sides* (1979), the movement was a disaster:

Our grandparents lived and laughed and loved and grew to adulthood in the streets. The streets provided opportunities for community, kibitzing, and recreation. At the same time, the streets were centers of political action where soapboxers and strikes were a part of everyday life. In the streets, people struggled, loved, organized, and played, surrounded by familiar smells, sounds, people, and symbols. This book is about the streets and people of the Lower East Side of New York City during the years 1890–1914. It is about the destruction of immigrant, working-class street life accomplished through various means— not the least of which was the rise of organized play and the movement for social reform of which it was a major part.

Desiring to control the mobs of unruly children, whose unregulated play was considered unhealthy for them and a threat to society, reformers organized the Playground Association of America in 1906 and sprinkled the urban landscape with thousands of supervised public playgrounds. Its goals were "socialization for family life, for citizenship, and for production." In *Muscles and Morals* (1981), Dominick Cavallo takes a somewhat different view, although recognizing that "the playground was a vehicle of political socialization." Cavallo argues that carefully organized physical exercise "was an effective method of promoting stability in the child and reform in American society," particularly by promoting the team experience, which "was consciously designed by play organizers to generate an extreme form of peer dependence in adolescents." "Play organizers stressed social order over individual freedom, cooperation between groups instead of competition between individuals, and peer-approved goals rather than individual aspiration," he continues. "They did not, however, want to destroy the individual's freedom, his economic initiative, or his quest for advancement; they wanted to foster a new balance between these values and their counterparts, a balance that would harness individual drives to communal ends." Through bureaucratic administration, play organizers hoped to contribute significantly to society's present and future stability. While Cavallo does not romanticize street life, unlike Goodman, and draws on psychological models for his understanding of the reformers' objectives, he is nonetheless critical of their goals. They desired to prepare the (male) young for future roles in a corporate society.[36]

Contemporary observers of adolescence were split concerning its nature; some believed it was "a time for grappling with growth, development, and life purpose," while others "looked primarily to parents and society for solutions to" this "problematic time of life." It was a difference, perhaps, between those who stressed freedom and those who stressed control. A similar split developed among attitudes toward those just starting out in life. The kindergarten movement has been interpreted as a key element in understanding the developing status of little children in urban society. The kindergarten entered the country from Germany in the 1850s, based on Friedrich Froebel's theories of the importance of play in early childhood development. By the 1890s private charity kindergartens were visible in many cities, particularly in immigrant neighborhoods where they were located in settlement houses and churches, while others were in public schools. The early kindergartners stressed play and the child's autonomous development; the next generation was more concerned with social values. As Cavallo has written, "between 1890 and 1920, the years marking the struggle between orthodox and progressive kindergartners, progressives incessantly stressed the moral and intellectual inadequacies of the privatized model of family child-rearing." Similar to the motives of playground reformers, kindergartners distrusted the family, believing that public socialization of preschool children was necessary. This public experience was "designed to prepare youngsters for life in a technological, bureaucratic, interdependent, and democratic society, where untoward expressions of conflict and emotion retarded development of the capacity to calmly and objectively analyze complex social processes and problems." As Marvin Lazerson has demonstrated regarding kindergartens in Massachusetts, when they changed their methods in the twentieth century they ceased to be distinctive and became "simply an adjunct of the first grade." They also lost popularity. "As they became institutionalized in the urban public school," Lazerson continues, "kindergartens moved from the delicate balance they had earlier proposed between freedom and order, emancipation and discipline, to a clear and overriding commitment to control."[37]

Child-saving during the Progressive Era was not as altruistic as has been traditionally believed, according to many of the newer studies. The values of the reformers, who were predominantly middle-class WASPS (white—Anglo-Saxon—Protestant), combined with changing economic and social circumstances to influence them to stress "control" rather than "benevolence." In their own minds, perhaps, there was little difference. The one area where historians are the most charitable toward the reformers concerns the care of dependent, neglected, and destitute children, a much ignored area. In the broadest recent study, Susan Tiffin accepts partially the validity of the "social control" argument, yet clings to the view that "when considering the welfare reforms put forward during the Progressive era, it is clear that a genuine altruism was involved." One demonstration of this concern was the proliferation of charity organizations and their desire to improve home conditions, thereby helping the child and keeping the family together. At the same time they looked to the government, at all levels, for assistance and regulation.[38]

The fate of one group of dependent children, New York City's foundlings, has been analyzed by Peter Romanofsky. Two aspects of the treatment of orphans developed—public subsidies to private, largely sectarian charities; and the care of these children in homes and asylums. The Protestant charity societies attacked both practices, not wanting state money to go to Catholic institutions, as well as believing that adoption was preferable to institutionalization. They were successful, but only temporarily. In 1907 institutionalization returned, leading Romanofsky to conclude that "influenced by the Catholic charities position [New York City officials] helped to make the public care of dependent babies and foundlings, as it had been before, regressive." The division between those favoring family care over institutionalization was a long and bitter one, as was the struggle between Protestants and Catholics.[39]

Another division was between black and white. Standard histories of child-saving ignore provisions for black children. The gap has been partially filled by Andrew Billingsley and Jeanne Giovannoni, *Children of the Storm* (1972). As would be expected, services for black children were segregated, North and South. With little public support, private orphanages, day nurseries, kindergartens, and homes for working girls, under black control but often with white funding, emerged in the nineteenth century. Only two blacks participated in the first White House Conference on the Care of Dependent Children in 1909, one of whom was Booker T. Washington. As Billingsley and Giovanonni summarize the situation, "Up to the end of World War I, Black children were largely ignored by the established child welfare system, as they had been since the Civil War." Private efforts continued, however, as the black community struggled to save its own.[40]

At the heart of the reformers' concerns about children—black or white, Catholic or Protestant, rich or poor—lay their attitude toward the family, which was most ambiguous. On the one hand, they were strongly committed to saving and, if necessary, shoring up the family. As Tiffin has noted, social workers "shared the belief that family life was essential to the successful continuation of the capitalist economy and the existing sexual hierarchy and committed themselves to its preservation." Various methods were implemented to support the welfare of the home: keeping abused or neglected children with their natural parents as much as possible instead of transferring them to institutions or foster homes; establishing day nurseries for working mothers; promoting improved health care and housing; and providing private and public support for mothers' pensions, particularly aid to dependent children, with Illinois passing the first law in 1911. The juvenile courts' widespread use of probation also served this end. The development of the day nursery has been traced by Margaret O'Brien Steinfels, *Who's Minding the Children* (1973): "As the institutionalization of neglected and orphaned children came to be regarded then as abnormal, the ideal of philanthropic work became the preservation of the family, or the creation of family-like alternatives. The day nurseries fit perfectly into this view of things; the time was right for their large-scale development, which occurred between the 1870s and the First World War, not for the purpose of destroying the family but preserving it." Privately funded day nurseries not only took care of the children of working mothers, but they also often offered employment services and training programs for mothers interested in domestic employment. Supervision was lax before 1920, however, with little direct control being exerted by the National Federation of Day Nurseries, founded in 1898, or local federations. There is some question whether working mothers eagerly accepted day nurseries. "The clientele was generally made up of destitute and deserted wives who were unable to turn to friends or relatives for aid," Sheila M. Rothman argues. "Lacking all choice, they were forced to accept the charity of the middle class."[41]

In the early twentieth century, reformers focused increasing attention on the role of the mother in rearing children, for, as Carl N. Degler has written, "home and children were the world of most white women and an increasing number of black women as well"—only 5 percent of married white women worked outside the home. But mother and home were not enough. Public intervention was deemed essential. "While the Progressives were not the first to create special programs for children, no prior generation of reformers devoted as much attention or as much energy to their welfare," Sheila Rothman contends. "To an unprecedented degree, it became the charge of the mother and the state to pursue the best interests of the child." The *mother* and the *state*, both were required, and here was the dilemma. The more the state intervened, the less control the family possessed. W. Norton Grubb and Marvin Lazerson pose the problem:

But the irony is that even those practices designed to support home life, the "highest and finest product of civilization," had the contradictory result of expanding the state's role. The mothers' pensions, small as they were, still meant that the support of poor children had become in some part a public responsibility rather than the responsibility of parents or of private philanthropy....Child care facilities may have diminished institutional placement of poor children, but they also shifted significant childrearing responsibilities out of families and away from mothers. The reforms of the progressive era thus consistently expanded the institutions of public responsibility which had emerged in the nineteenth century.

At the same time, however, "the model family remained 'private,' " drastically limiting the public's commitment to "saving" children. Christopher Lasch has taken the most extreme position in this vein, arguing that "public policy, sometimes conceived quite deliberately not as a defense of the family at all but as an invasion of it, contributed to the deterioration of domestic life."[42]

Whether the (essentially middle-class) family was growing or shrinking in importance seems problematical. For Paula S. Fass, "the family no longer mediated between the individual and the society in a direct way. It had become less an institution that was integrated into the mesh of other institutions—work, church, and community. In a rationalized and depersonalized society, the family became an agency of individual nurture and an environment for the development of intimate personal relationships." One thrust of an increasing emphasis on mother-child intimacy, and the role of women generally in child-saving, was the rise of the PTA. Begun in 1897 as the National Congress of Mothers, changing its name in 1908 to the National Congress of Mothers and Parent-Teacher Association, and finally in 1924 to the National Congress of Parents and Teachers, the organization emphasized its members' "duties and obligations, their moral responsibility for the well-being of home and family life in their communities and even throughout the nation." The white middle-class women who dominated the PTA wished to "improve" their own families as well as those of the poor, according to Steven Schlossman. More specifically, as David Pivar has noted, "the Mothers' Congress, in its early years, resolved to cleanse homes, schools, streets, popular amusements, or anything producing evil thoughts or conduct. In brief, its members wanted to control the urban environment. It endorsed a single standard of morality, resolved to raise the age of consent, favored dress reform and advocated physical education for girls." It was part of a broad movement Pivar has termed the *Purity Crusade*, whose central concern was to bolster the family.[43]

In 1885 child-saving was in its infancy, with an institution or two here and a reform movement or charitable crusade there. Within thirty years the landscape would be crowded with theories, organizations, programs (both public and private), institutions, hordes of individual reformers, and the like, all designed to assist and accommodate children to the dizzying pace of social, cultural, economic, and political change. The central battleground was the city, and the target groups were both poor and middle-class youngsters, who, for somewhat different reasons, needed help, guidance, and control. Looking over the situation, Paul Boyer has discerned two rather separate groups of activists, the positive environmentalists and the more traditional coercive moral reformers. The environmentalists believed in a "subtle and complex process of influencing behavior and molding character through a transformed, consciously planned urban environment," while the moral reformers favored overt repression. The increasing environmental thrust marked "a fundamental shift of interest away from the individual to the group." Perhaps this dichotomy helps untangle the confusing nature of Progressive child-saving.[44] Social activists, heavily white, Anglo-Saxon, and Protestant, clung to an older notion of seeing the individual as the key to social change and betterment; yet, simultaneously they categorized children in groups—the poor, delinquents, orphans, genetic inferiors, immigrants. Thus perceived, they could be more easily handled and helped. To be sure, this is but one more example of the organization-building nature of American society at that time. Children were divided into groups and subgroups, each with its own organization—schools, juvenile courts, reformatories, playgrounds, kindergartens, Boy Scouts—and professionally trained staffs—teachers, social workers, playground directors, juvenile probation officers, and youth workers.

This shift from reforming the individual to working with groups mirrored broader trends in American society in the few decades preceding World War I. The general terms "urbanization," "industrialization," and "immigration," used for so long to focus attention on the three major areas of change, serve little purpose, however, unless we fully understand their more specific nature and interaction. Recent scholarship has emphasized not only that the period was marked by extremely rapid growth in these three areas, but also that profound structural and ideological transformations were taking place. People were becoming both more and less able to control their lives and environment. The workplace, for example, was becoming more segmented and fragmented, grouping workers in the factory and office as they were being separated in neighborhoods and organizations. Seemingly, everyone was grasping for control; some, such as middle-class whites, were more successful than others, for example, poor blacks. And all were concerned about the present and future of children—were they surviving, were they under control, were they being properly prepared for the future, were they (and the country) going to conform or rebel? And how would these concerns become transformed into concrete action? What, specifically, was the role of the family in a society that was building institutions and organizations to replace some of its functions because of necessity or distrust?

Whatever was necessary was done on the local level, however, by public or private means. On the eve of World War I, the federal government's role in child-saving was minimal. The National Child Labor Committee had only fleeting success with the passage of the Keating-Owen bill in 1916. More significant was the establishment of the U.S. Children's Bureau in 1912 after a heated struggle. Placed in the Department of Commerce and Labor, the Bureau had the power to investigate and report "upon all matters pertaining to the welfare of children and child life among all classes of our people." Under the able leadership of Julia Lathrop (1912–1921), the Children's Bureau investigated and reported, but it had no power to directly change the lives of children. The federal government's most specific involvement concerned vocational education. The Smith-Hughes Act, passed in 1917, which provided federal money to school districts to improve and expand their vocational course offerings, was an anomaly, however. The government otherwise stayed out of local school affairs.[45]

To understand child-saving during the Progressive Era, it is necessary to focus on personalities, organizations, and institutions on the local level.

Despite the growth of a national corporate economy and impersonal technology, most people still thought in terms of personal interaction and responsibility. The organizational revolution concerned means, not ends, as society was unable to recognize fully what was occurring. Only a few had more radical answers. That a widespread concern for and about children existed during this era of rapid change and immense turmoil should not be surprising, given the country's long-standing concern about the family and its future. That altruism was not the only motive among child-savers should also be remembered, for American society has continued to be a mix of concern, fear, manipulation, and confusion. Progressive reformers were groping for answers to problems they only dimly understood, and their contradictory attitudes and answers must be probed further, while seen in the context of a swiftly changing economic and social milieu. They were, significantly, the bridge between the local world of the nineteenth century and the corporate-technological society of the twentieth.

NOTES

1. Margaret F. Byington, "The Family in a Typical Mill Town," *American Journal of Sociology* 14 (1909), Robert H. Bremner, et al., *Children and Youth in America: A Documentary History*, 3 vols. (Cambridge, Mass.: Harvard University Press, 1970–1971), 2: 75. See, in general, Alan Trachtenberg, *The Incorporation of America: Culture and Society in the Gilded Age* (New York: Hill & Wang, 1982).

2. All figures are from *The Statistical History of the United States from Colonial Times to the Present* (Stamford, Conn.: Fairfield Publishers, 1965); James T. Patterson, *America's Struggle Against Poverty, 1900–1980* (Cambridge, Mass.: Harvard University Press, 1981), 15.

3. Richard Hofstadter, *The Age of Reform* (New York: Alfred A. Knopf, 1955); Gabriel Kolko, *The Triumph of Conservatism: A Reinterpretation of American History, 1900–1916* (New York: Free Press, 1963); Robert H. Wiebe, *The Search for Order, 1877–1920* (New York: Hill & Wang, 1967); Samuel P. Hays, *The Response to Industrialism, 1885–1914* (Chicago: University of Chicago Press, 1957); Melvin G. Holli, *Reform in Detroit: Hazen S. Pingree and Urban Politics* (New York: Oxford University Press, 1969); Otis L. Graham, *An Encore for Reform: The Old Progressives and the New Deal* (New York: Oxford University Press, 1967); Christopher Lasch, *The New Radicalism in America, 1889–1963* (New York: Vintage Books, 1965); T. J. Jackson Lears, *No Place of Grace: Antimodernism and the Transformation of American Culture, 1880–1920* (New York: Pantheon Books, 1981). See also Daniel T. Rodgers, "In Search of Progressivism," *Reviews in American History* 10 (December 1982): 113–132.

4. Allen F. Davis, *Spearheads for Reform: The Social Settlements and the Progressive Movement, 1890–1914* (New York: Oxford University Press, 1967), xi. See, most recently, Robert M. Crunden, *Ministers of Reform: The Progressives' Achievement in American Civilization, 1889–1920* (New York: Basic Books, 1982).

5. Grace Abbott, *The Child and the State*, 2 vols. (Chicago: University of Chicago Press, 1938); Homer Folks, *Care of Destitute, Neglected, and Delinquent Children* (New York: Macmillan Co., 1902); William J. Shultz, "The Humane Movement in the United States, 1910–1922," *Columbia University Studies in History, Economics, and Public Law* 63 No. 1 (1924): 1–320; Susan Tiffin, *In Whose Best Interest? Child Welfare Reform in the Progressive Era* (Westport, Conn.: Greenwood Press, 1982), 285; Robert H. Bremner, *From the Depths: The Discovery of Poverty in the United States* (New York: New York University Press, 1956); Walter Trattner, *From Poor Law to Welfare State: A History of Social Welfare in America* (2d ed., New York: Free Press, 1979), xii.

6. Lasch, *New Radicalism in America*, 146; Michael B. Katz, Michael Doucet, and Mark Stern, *The Social Organization of Early Industrial Capitalism* (Cambridge, Mass.: Harvard University Press, 1982), 390.

7. Robert M. Mennel, *Thorns and Thistles: Juvenile Delinquents in the United States, 1825–1940* (Hanover, N.H.: University Press of New England, 1973), 48–70; Lawrence M. Friedman and Robert V. Percival, *The Roots of Justice: Crime and Punishment in Alameda County, California, 1870–1910* (Chapel Hill: University of North Carolina Press, 1981), 218–221.

8. Joseph M. Hawes, *Children in Urban Society: Juvenile Delinquency in Nineteenth-Century America* (New York: Oxford University Press, 1971), xii, 190; Charles Larsen, *The Good Fight: The Life and Times of Ben B. Lindsey* (Chicago: Quadrangle Books, 1972).

9. Anthony Platt, *The Child Savers: The Invention of Delinquency* (Chicago: University of Chicago Press, 1969), 4, 176; Mennel, *Thorns and Thistles*, 142, 144.

10. Steven L. Schlossman, *Love and the American Delinquent: The Theory and Practice of "Progressive" Juvenile Justice, 1825–1920* (Chicago: University of Chicago Press, 1977), 58, 188; Ellen Ryerson, *The Best-Laid Plans: America's Juvenile Court Experiment* (New York: Hill & Wang, 1978), 97.

11. David J. Rothman, *The Discovery of the Asylum: Social Order and Disorder in the New Republic* (Boston: Little, Brown & Co., 1971); David J. Rothman, *Conscience and Convenience: The Asylum and Its Alternatives in Progressive America* (Boston: Little, Brown, & Co., 1980), 9, 257, 275. For a critical review, see Steven L. Schlossman, "Equity, Education, and Individual Justice: The Origins of the Juvenile Court," *Harvard Educational Review* 52 (February 1982): 77–83.

12. Steven Schlossman and Stephanie Wallach, "The Crime of Precocious Sexuality: Female Juvenile Delinquency in the Progressive Era," *Harvard Educational Review* 48 (February 1978): 71, 76. And see, in general, a work that does not cover juveniles, Estelle B. Freedman, *Their Sisters' Keepers: Women's Prison Reform in America, 1830–1930* (Ann Arbor: University of Michigan Press, 1981).

13. Jack M. Holl, *Juvenile Reform in the Progressive Era: William R. George and the Junior Republic Movement* (Ithaca, N.Y.: Cornell University Press, 1971), 173; Steven Schlossman and Ronald L. Cohen, "The Music Man in Gary: Willis Brown and Child-Saving in the Progressive Era," *Societas* 7 (Winter 1977): 1–17.

14. Laurence A. Cremin, *The Transformation of the School: Progressivism in American Education, 1876–1957* (New York: Alfred Knopf, 1961), viii; Laurence A. Cremin, *Traditions of American Education* (New York: Basic Books, 1977), 124.

15. Patricia A. Graham, *Community and Class in American Education, 1865–1918* (New York: John Wiley & Sons, 1974), 25.

16. David B. Tyack, *The One Best System: A History of American Urban Education* (Cambridge, Mass.: Harvard University Press, 1974), 7; David B. Tyack and Elisabeth Hansot, *Managers of Virtue: Public School Leadership in America, 1820–1980* (New York: Basic Books, 1982), 107. On the demise of the rural school, see Wayne E. Fuller, *The Old Country School: The Story of Rural Education in the Middle West* (Chicago: University of Chicago Press, 1982). An influential earlier study is Raymond E. Callahan, *Education and the Cult of Efficiency: A Study of the Social Forces That Have Shaped the Administration of the Public Schools* (Chicago: University of Chicago Press, 1962).

17. Edward Krug, *The Shaping of the American High School, 1880–1920* (New York: Harper & Row, 1964). See also his followup, *The Shaping of the American High School, Vol. 2: 1920–1941* (Madison: University of Wisconsin Press, 1972).

18. Marvin Lazerson, *Origins of the Urban School: Public Education in Massachusetts, 1870–1915* (Cambridge, Mass.: Harvard University Press, 1971), xi; Joel Spring, *Education and the Rise of the Corporate State* (Boston: Beacon Press, 1972), xiii. A less critical interpretation can be found in Selwyn K. Troen, *The Public and the Schools: Shaping the St. Louis System, 1838–1920* (Columbia: University of Missouri Press, 1975).

19. Walter Feinberg, *Reason and Rhetoric: The Intellectual Foundations of 20th Century Liberal Educational Policy* (New York: John Wiley & Sons, 1975), 20; Samuel Bowles and Herbert Gintis, *Schooling in Capitalist America: Educational Reform and the Contradictions of Economic Life* (New York: Basic Books, 1976), 199. See also Walter Feinberg and Henry Rosemont, Jr., eds., *Work, Technology, and Education: Dissenting Essays in the Intellectual Foundations of American Education* (Urbana: University of Illinois Press, 1975).

20. Paul Violas, *The Training of the Urban Working Class: A History of Twentieth Century American Education* (Chicago: Rand McNally College Pub. Co., 1978), xii, 231.

21. Harvey Kantor and David B. Tyack, eds., *Work, Youth, and Schooling: Historical Perspectives on Vocationalism in American Education* (Stanford, Calif.: Stanford University Press, 1982), 7–8, 123. On jobs for youth, see Selwyn K. Troen, "The Discovery of the Adolescent by American Educational Reformers, 1900–1920: An Economic Perspective," in Lawrence Stone, ed., *Schooling and Society: Studies in the History of Education* (Baltimore: Johns Hopkins University Press, 1976), 239–250; W. Norton Grubb and Marvin Lazerson, "Education and the Labor Market," in Kantor and Tyack, eds., *Work, Youth, and Schooling*, 110–141.

22. Julia Wrigley, *Class, Politics and Public Schools: Chicago, 1900–1950* (New Brunswick, N.J.: Rutgers University Press, 1982), ch. 3; Ronald D. Cohen and Raymond A. Mohl, *The Paradox of Progressive Education: The Gary Plan and Urban Schooling* (Port Washington, N.Y.: Kennikat Press, 1979), 64. See also Marvin Lazerson and W. Norton Grubb, eds., *American Education and Vocationalism: A Documentary History, 1870–1970* (New York: Teachers College Press, 1974); Kantor and Tyack, eds., *Work, Youth, and Schooling*, 27–28; Ira Katznelson, et al., "Public Schooling and Working-Class Formation: The Case of the United States," *American Journal of Education* 90 (February 1982): 125, argue: "Workers did not

act in the school arena as a class. Instead, they selectively attended to educational issues, sometimes as labor, at other times as ethnics."

23. William J. Reese, " 'Partisans of the Proletariat': The Socialist Working Class and the Milwaukee Schools, 1890–1920," *History of Education Quarterly* 21 (Spring 1981): 3; William J. Reese, *Progressivism and the Grass Roots: Social Change and Urban Schooling, 1840–1920* (London and Boston: Routledge, Kegan Paul, forthcoming).

24. David Hogan, "Education and the Making of the Chicago Working Class, 1880–1930," *History of Education Quarterly* 18 (Fall 1978): 231–232; Cohen and Mohl, *Paradox of Progressive Education*, 87; Miriam Cohen, "Changing Education Strategies Among Immigrant Generations: New York Italians in Comparative Perspective," *Journal of Social History* 15 (Spring 1982): 443–466. See also William J. Reese, "Neither Victims Nor Masters: Ethnic and Minority Study," in John Best, ed., *Historical Inquiry in Education: A Research Agenda* (Washington, D.C.: American Educational Research Association, 1983). On parochial schooling, see James W. Sanders, *The Education of an Urban Minority: Catholics in Chicago, 1833–1965* (New York: Oxford University Press, 1977).

25. Mary F. Berry and John Blassingame, *Long Memory: The Black Experience in America* (New York: Oxford University Press, 1982), 265; J. Morgan Kousser, "Progressivism—For Middle-Class Whites Only: North Carolina Education, 1880–1910," *Journal of Southern History* 45 (May 1980): 169–194. See also Louis R. Harlan, *Separate and Unequal: Public School Campaigns and Racism in the Southern Seaboard States, 1901–1915* (Chapel Hill: University of North Carolina Press, 1958).

26. Carleton Mabee, *Black Education in New York State: From Colonial to Modern Times* (Syracuse: Syracuse University Press, 1979), 243–246; Cohen and Mohl, *Paradox of Progressive Education*, 110–116; Judy Jolley Mohraz, *The Separate Problem: Case Studies of Black Education in the North, 1900–1930* (Westport, Conn.: Greenwood Press, 1979), 95, and 97–104 for the Chicago situation; Vincent P. Franklin, *The Education of Black Philadelphia: The Social and Educational History of a Minority Community, 1900–1950* (Philadelphia: University of Pennsylvania Press, 1979), 59.

27. Geraldine J. Clifford, " 'Marry, Stitch, Die, or Do Worse': Educating Women for Work," in Kantor and Tyack, eds., *Work, Youth, and Schooling*, 242.

28. Walter Trattner, *Crusade for the Children: A History of the National Child Labor Committee and Child Labor Reform in America* (Chicago: Quadrangle Books, 1970); Jeremy Felt, *Hostages of Fortune: Child Labor Reform in New York State* (Syracuse, N.Y.: Syracuse University Press, 1965), 222; Eugene F. Provenzo, Jr., "The Photographer as Educator: The Child Labor Photo-Stories of Lewis Hine," *Teachers College Record* 83 (Summer 1982): 593–612; James B. Lane, *Jacob A. Riis and the American City* (Port Washington, N.Y.: Kennikat Press, 1974).

29. Miriam Cohen, "Changing Education Strategies Among Immigrant Generations," 449; Kantor and Tyack eds., *Work, Youth, and Schooling*, 280–281; Daniel T. Rodgers, *The Work Ethic in Industrial America, 1850–1920* (Chicago: University of Chicago Press, 1978).

30. Hamilton Cravens, *The Triumph of Evolution: American Scientists and the Hereditary-Environment Controversy, 1900–1941* (Philadelphia: University of Penn-

sylvania Press, 1978), 40; Mark H. Haller, *Eugenics: Hereditarian Attitudes in American Thought* (New Brunswick, N.J.: Rutgers University Press, 1963), 3.

31. Stephen Jay Gould, *The Mismeasure of Man* (New York: W. W. Norton, 1981), 157–158; Ryerson, *Best-Laid Plans*, 106. See also Allan Chase, *The Legacy of Malthus: The Social Costs of the New Scientific Racism* (New York: Alfred A. Knopf, 1977); Paula S. Fass, "The IQ: A Cultural and Historical Framework," *American Journal of Education* 88 (August 1980): 431–458; Paul Davis Chapman, "Schools as Sorters: Testing and Tracking in California, 1910–1925," *Journal of Social History* 14 (Fall 1980): 701–717; Russell Marks, *The Idea of I.Q.* (Washington, D.C.: University Press of America, 1981).

32. Dorothy Ross, *G. Stanley Hall: The Psychologist as Prophet* (Chicago: University of Chicago Press, 1972), 297.

33. Lears, *No Place of Grace*, 38; David Tyack and Michael Berkowitz, "The Man Nobody Liked: Toward a Social History of the Truant Office, 1840–1940," *American Quarterly* 29 (Spring 1977): 44; Roy Lubove, *The Professional Altruist: The Emergence of Social Work as a Career, 1880–1930* (Cambridge, Mass.: Harvard University Press, 1965), 48. See also Nathan Irvin Huggins, *Protestants Against Poverty: Boston's Charities, 1870–1900* (Westport, Conn.: Greenwood Pub. Corp., 1971), ch. 5; Cravens, *The Triumph of Evolution*, ch. 2.

34. Joseph F. Kett, *Rites of Passage: Adolescence in America, 1790 to the Present* (New York: Basic Books, 1977), 217; John Modell, Frank F. Furstenberg, Jr., and Theodore Hershberg, "Social Change and Transitions to Adulthood in Historical Perspective," in Michael Gordon, ed., *The American Family in Social-Historical Perspective* (2d ed., New York: St. Martin's Press, 1978), 192–219.

35. Kett, *Rites of Passage*, 223–224; David I. Macleod, "Act Your Age: Boyhood, Adolescence, and the Rise of the Boy Scouts of America," *Journal of Social History* 16 (Winter 1982): 9–10, 14; Peter G. Filene, *Him/Her/Self: Sex Roles in Modern America* (New York: Harcourt Brace Jovanovich, 1974), ch. 3; Joe L. Dubbert, *A Man's Place: Masculinity in Transition* (Englewood Cliffs, N.J.: Prentice-Hall, 1979), chs. 5–6; Anita Clair Fellman and Michael Fellman, *Making Sense of Self: Medical Advice Literature in Late Nineteenth-Century America* (Philadelphia: University of Pennsylvania Press, 1981).

36. Cary Goodman, *Choosing Sides: Playground and Street Life on the Lower East Side* (New York: Schocken Books, 1979), xi-xii, 80; Dominick Cavallo, *Muscles and Morals: Organized Playgrounds and Urban Reform, 1880–1920* (Philadelphia: University of Pennsylvania Press, 1981), 3–4, 7–8.

37. Kett, *Rites of Passage*, 244; Cavallo, "Politics of Latency: Kindergarten Pedagogy, 1860–1930," in Barbara Finkelstein, ed., *Regulated Children/Liberated Children: Education in Psychohistorical Perspective* (New York: Psychohistory Press, 1979), 169, 179; Lazerson, *Origins of the Urban School*, 65, 72–73. See also, in general, Evelyn Weber, *The Kindergarten* (New York: Teachers College Press, 1969); Elizabeth Dale Ross, *The Kindergarten Crusade: The Establishment of Preschool Education in the United States* (Athens, Ohio: Ohio University Press, 1976).

38. Tiffin, *In Whose Best Interest?*, 55.

39. Peter Romanofsky, "Saving the Lives of the City's Foundlings: The Joint Committee and New York City Child Care Methods, 1860–1907," *New-York Historical Society Quarterly* 16 (January-April 1977): 68. On foster care, see Tiffin, *In Whose Best Interest?*, ch. 4. For insight into another child-saving issue, see N.

Ray Hiner, "Children's Rights, Corporal Punishment, and Child Abuse: Changing American Attitudes, 1870–1920," *Bulletin of the Menninger Clinic* 43 (1979): 233–248.

40. Andrew Billingsley and Jeanne Giovannoni, *Children of the Storm: Black Children and American Child Welfare* (New York: Harcourt Brace Jovanovich, 1972), 72.

41. Tiffin, *In Whose Best Interest?*, 112; Margaret O'Brien Steinfels, *Who's Minding the Children? The History and Politics of Day Care in America* (New York: Simon & Schuster, 1973), 41; Sheila M. Rothman, *Woman's Proper Place: A History of Changing Ideals and Practices, 1870 to the Present* (New York: Basic Books, 1978), 90.

42. Carl N. Degler, *At Odds: Women and the Family in America from the Revolution to the Present* (New York: Oxford University Press, 1980), 81; Rothman, *Woman's Proper Place*, 98; W. Norton Grubb and Marvin Lazerson, *Broken Promises: How Americans Fail Their Children* (New York: Basic Books, 1982), 25–27; Christopher Lasch, *Haven in a Heartless World: The Family Besieged* (New York: Basic Books, 1977), 13.

43. Paula S. Fass, *The Damned and the Beautiful: American Youth in the 1920s* (New York: Oxford University Press, 1977), 95; Steven Schllossman, "Before Home Start: Notes Toward a History of Parent Education in America, 1897–1929," *Harvard Educational Review* 46 (August 1976): 452; David Pivar, *Purity Crusade: Sexual Morality and Social Control, 1868–1900* (Westport, Conn.: Greenwood Press, 1973), 229.

44. Paul Boyer, *Urban Masses and Moral Order in America, 1820–1920* (Cambridge, Mass.: Harvard University Press, 1978), 221, 224.

45. Tiffin, *In Whose Best Interest?*, 236, and for an overview of the Bureau's work, 236–247; for a recent brief account of the Smith-Hughes Act, see Larry Cuban, "Enduring Resiliency: Enacting and Implementing Federal Vocational Education Legislation," in Kantor and Tyack, eds., *Work, Youth, and Schooling*, 47–53.

BIBLIOGRAPHY

Abbott, Grace. *The Child and the State*. 2 vols., Chicago, 1938.

Ashby, LeRoy. *Saving the Waifs: Reformers and Dependent Children, 1890–1917*. Philadelphia, 1984.

Berry, Mary F., and Blassingame, John. *Long Memory: The Black Experience in America*. New York, 1982.

Best, John, ed. *Historical Inquiry in Education: A Research Agenda*. Washington, D.C., 1983.

Billingsley, Andrew, and Giovanonni, Jeanne. *Children of the Storm: Black Children and American Child Welfare*. New York, 1972.

Bird, Carolyn. *Born Female: The High Cost of Keeping Women Down*. New York, 1960.

Bodnar, John. "Schooling and the Slavic-American Family, 1900–1940." In *American Education and the European Immigrant*, edited by Bernard Weiss. Urbana, 1982. 78–95.

Bowles, Samuel, and Gintis, Herbert. *Schooling in Capitalist America: Educational Reform and the Contradictions of Economic Life.* New York, 1976.

Boyer, Paul. *Urban Masses and Moral Order in America, 1820–1920.* Cambridge, Mass., 1978.

Bremner, Robert H. *From the Depths: The Discovery of Poverty in the United States.* New York, 1956.

———, et al., eds. *Children and Youth in America: A Documentary History.* 3 vols., Cambridge, Mass., 1970–1971.

Byington, Margaret F. "The Family in a Typical Mill Town." *American Journal of Sociology* 14 (1909).

Callahan, Raymond E. *Education and the Cult of Efficiency: A Study of the Social Forces That Have Shaped the Administration of the Public Schools.* Chicago, 1962.

Cavallo, Dominick. *Muscles and Morals: Organized Playgrounds and Urban Reform, 1880–1920.* Philadelphia, 1981.

———. "The Politics of Latency: Kindergarten Pedagogy, 1860–1930." In *Regulated Children/Liberated Children: Education in Psychohistorical Perspective*, edited by Barbara Finkelstein. New York, 1979. 158–183.

Chapman, Paul Davis. "Schools as Sorters: Testing and Tracking in California, 1910–1925." *Journal of Social History* 14 (Fall 1980): 701–717.

Clifford, Geraldine. " 'Marry, Stitch, Die, or Do Worse': Educating Women for Work." In *Work, Youth, and Schooling*, edited by Harvey Kantor and David B. Tyack. Stanford, Calif., 1982: 223-268.

Cohen, Ronald D. "Schooling in Early Nineteenth Century Boston and New York," *Journal of Urban History* (1974): 116–123.

———. "Urban Schooling in the Gilded Age and After." *Journal of Urban History* (1976): 499–506.

———, and Mohl, Raymond A. *The Paradox of Progressive Education: The Gary Plan and Urban Schooling.* Port Washington, N.Y., 1979.

Cravens, Hamilton. *The Triumph of Evolution: American Scientists and the Heredity-Environment Controversy 1900–1941.* Philadelphia, 1978.

Cremin, Lawrence A. *American Education, The Colonial Experience, 1607–1782.* New York, 1970.

———. *American Education, The National Experience, 1783–1876.* New York, 1980.

Crunden, Robert M. *Ministers of Reform: The Progressives' Achievement in American Civilization, 1889–1920.* New York, 1982.

Cuban, Larry. "Enduring Resiliency: Enacting and Implementing Federal Vocational Education Legislation." In *Work, Youth, and Schooling*, edited by Harvey Kantor and David B. Tyack. Stanford, Calif., 1982: 47–53.

———. *How Teachers Taught: Constancy and Change in American Classrooms, 1890–1980.* New York, 1984.

Davis, Allen F. *Spearheads for Reform: The Social Settlements and the Progressive Movement, 1890–1914.* New York, 1967.

Degler, Carl. *At Odds: Women and the Family in America from the Revolution to the Present.* New York, 1980.

Dubbert, Joe L. *A Man's Place: Masculinity in Transition.* Englewood Cliffs, N.J., 1979.

Fass, Paula S. *The Damned and the Beautiful: American Youth in the 1920s.* New York, 1977.

———. "The IQ: A Cultural and Historical Framework." *American Journal of Education* (August 1980): 431–458.

Feinberg, Walter. *Reason and Rhetoric: The Intellectual Foundations of 20th Century Liberal Educational Policy.* New York, 1975.

———, and Rosemont, Henry, Jr., eds. *Work, Technology, and Education: Dissenting Essays in the Intellectual Foundations of American Education.* Urbana, Ill., 1975.

Fellman, Anita Clair, and Fellman, Michael. *Making Sense of Self: Medical Advice Literature in Late Nineteenth-Century America.* Philadelphia, 1981.

Felt, Jeremy. *Hostages of Fortune: Child Labor Reform in New York State.* Syracuse, N.Y., 1965.

Filene, Peter G. *Him/Her/Self: Sex Roles in Modern America.* New York, 1974.

Finkelstein, Barbara, ed. *Regulated Children/Liberated Children: Education in Psychohistorical Perspective.* New York, 1979.

Franklin, Vincent P. *The Education of Black Philadelphia: The Social and Educational History of a Minority Community, 1900–1950.* Philadelphia, 1979.

Freedman, Estelle B. *Their Sisters' Keepers: Women's Prison Reform in America, 1830–1930.* Ann Arbor, Mich., 1981.

Fuller, Wayne E. *The Old Country School: The Story of Rural Education in the Middle West.* Chicago, 1982.

Goodman, Cary. *Choosing Sides: Playground and Street Life on the Lower East Side.* New York, 1979.

Gordon, Michael, ed. *The American Family in Social-Historical Perspective.* 2d ed., New York, 1978.

Gould, Stephen Jay. *The Mismeasure of Man.* New York, 1981.

Graham, Otis L. *An Encore for Reform: The Old Progressives and the New Deal.* New York, 1967.

Graham, Patricia A. *Community and Class in American Education, 1865–1918.* New York, 1974.

Grubb, W. Norton, and Lazerson, Marvin. *Broken Promises: How Americans Fail Their Children.* New York, 1982.

Haller, Mark H. *Eugenics: Hereditarian Attitudes in American Thought.* New Brunswick, N.J., 1963.

Harlan, Louis R. *Separate and Unequal: Public School Campaigns and Racism in the Southern Seaboard States, 1901–1915.* Chapel Hill, 1958.

Hawes, Joseph M. *Children in Urban Society: Juvenile Delinquency in Nineteenth-Century America.* New York, 1971.

Hays, Samuel P. *The Response to Industrialism, 1885–1914.* Chicago, 1957.

Hiner, N. Ray. "Children's Rights, Corporal Punishment, and Child Abuse: Changing American Attitudes, 1870–1920." *Bulletin of the Menninger Clinic* 43 (1979): 233–248.

Hofstader, Richard. *The Age of Reform.* New York, 1955.

Hogan, David. "Education and the Making of the Chicago Working Class, 1880–1930," *History of Education Quarterly* 18 (Fall 1978): 231–232.

Holl, Jack M. *Juvenile Reform in the Progressive Era: William R. George and the Junior Republic Movement.* Ithaca, N.Y., 1971.

Holli, Melvin G. *Reform in Detroit: Hazen S. Pingree and Urban Politics.* New York, 1969.

Huggins, Nathan Irvin. *Protestants Against Poverty: Boston's Charities, 1870–1900.* Westport, Conn., 1971.

Kantor, Harvey, and Tyack, David B., eds. *Work, Youth, and Schooling: Historical Perspectives on Vocationalism in American Education.* Stanford, Calif., 1982.

Katz, Michael B.; Doucet, Michael; and Stern, Mark. *The Social Organization of Early Industrial Capitalism.* Cambridge, Mass., 1982.

Katznelson, Ira, et al. "Public Schooling and Working Class Formation: The Case of the United States." *American Journal of Education* (February 1982).

Kett, Joseph. *Rites of Passage: Adolescence in America, 1790 to the Present.* New York, 1977.

Kolko, Gabriel. *The Triumph of Conservatism: A Reinterpretation of American History, 1900–1916.* New York, 1963.

Kousser, J. Morgan. "Progressivism—For Middle-Class Whites Only." *Journal of Southern History* 45 (May 1980): 169–194.

Krug, Edward. *The Shaping of the American High School, 1880–1920.* New York, 1964.

Lane, James B. *Jacob Riis and the American City.* Port Washington, N.Y., 1974.

Larsen, Charles. *The Good Fight: The Life and Times of Ben B. Lindsey.* Chicago, 1972.

Lasch, Christopher. *The New Radicalism in America, 1889–1963.* New York, 1965.

Lazerson, Marvin. *Origins of the Urban School: Public Education in Massachusetts, 1870–1915.* Cambridge, Mass., 1971.

———, and Grubb, W. Norton, eds. *American Education and Vocationalism: A Documentary History, 1870–1970.* New York, 1974.

Lears, T. J. Jackson. *No Place of Grace: Antimodernism and the Transformation of American Culture, 1880–1920.* New York, 1981.

Lubove, Roy. *The Professional Altruist: The Emergence of Social Work as a Career, 1880–1930.* Cambridge, Mass., 1965.

Mabee, Carleton. *Black Education in New York State: From Colonial to Modern Times.* Syracuse, N.Y., 1979.

Macleod, David I. "Act Your Age: Boyhood, Adolescence, and the Rise of the Boy Scouts of America." *Journal of Social History* 16 (Winter 1982).

———. *Building Character in the American Boy: The Boy Scouts, YMCA, and Their Forerunners, 1870–1920.* Madison, 1983.

Marks, Russell. *The Idea of I.Q.* Washington, D.C., 1981.

Mennel, Robert M. *Thorns and Thistles: Juvenile Delinquents in the United States, 1825–1940.* Hanover, N.H., 1973.

Modell, John; Furstenberg, Frank F., Jr.; and Hershberg, Theodore. "Social Change and Transitions to Adulthood in Historical Perspective." In *The American Family in Social-Historical Perspective,* edited by Michael Gordon. 2d ed., New York, 1978. 192–219.

Mohraz, Judy Jolley. *The Separate Problem: Case Studies of Black Education in the North, 1900–1930.* Westport, Conn., 1979.

Patterson, James T. *America's Struggle Against Poverty, 1900–1980.* Cambridge, Mass., 1981.

Pivar, David. *Purity Crusade: Sexual Morality and Social Control, 1868–1900*. West-
    port, Conn., 1973.

Platt, Anthony. *The Child Savers: The Invention of Delinquency*. Chicago, 1969.

Provenzo, Eugene F., Jr. "The Photographer as Educator: The Child-Labor
    Photo-Stories of Lewis Hine." *Teachers College Record* 83 (Summer 1982):
    593–612.

Reese, William J. "Neither Victims Nor Masters: Ethnic and Minority Study."
    In *Historical Inquiry in Education: A Research Agenda*, edited by John Best.
    Washington, D.C., 1983.

————. "Partisans of the Proletariat: The Socialist Working Class and the Mil-
    waukee Schools, 1890–1920." *History of Education Quarterly* 21 (Spring
    1981): 3.

————. *The Politics of School Reform: Grass Roots Movements During the Progressive
    Era*. London and Boston, forthcoming.

Rodgers, Daniel T. "In Search of Progressivism." *Reviews in American History* 10
    (December 1982): 113–132.

————. *The Work Ethic in Industrial America, 1850–1920*. Chicago, 1978.

Romanofsky, Peter. "Saving the Lives of the City's Foundlings: The Joint Com-
    mittee and New York City Child Care Methods, 1860–1907." *New York
    Historical Society Quarterly* 16 (January–April 1977).

Ross, Dorothy. *G. Stanley Hall: The Psychologist as Prophet*. Chicago, 1972.

Ross, Elizabeth Dale. *The Kindergarten Crusade: The Establishment of Preschool Ed-
    ucation in the United States*. Athens, Ohio, 1976.

Rothman, David J. *Conscience and Convenience: The Asylum and Its Alternatives in
    Progressive America*. Boston, 1980.

————. *The Discovery of the Asylum: Social Order and Disorder in the New Republic*.
    Boston, 1971.

Rothman, Sheila M. *Woman's Proper Place: A History of Changing Ideals and Practices,
    1870 to the Present*. New York, 1978.

Ryerson, Ellen. *The Best-Laid Plans: America's Juvenile Court Experiment*. New York,
    1978.

Sanders, James W. *The Education of an Urban Minority: Catholics in Chicago, 1833–
    1965*. New York, 1977.

Schlossman, Steven L. "Before Home Start: Notes Toward a History of Parent
    Education in America, 1897–1929." *Harvard Educational Review* 46 (Au-
    gust 1976).

————. "Equity, Education, and Individual Justice: The Origins of the Juvenile
    Court." *Harvard Educational Review* 52 (February 1982): 77–83.

————. *Love and the American Delinquent: The Theory and Practice of "Progressive"
    Juvenile Justice, 1825–1920*. Chicago, 1977.

————, and Cohen, Ronald D. "The Music Man in Gary: Willis Brown and Child-
    Saving in the Progressive Era." *Societas* 7 (Winter 1977): 1–17.

————, and Wallach, Stephanie. "The Crime of Precocious Sexuality: Female
    Juvenile Delinquency in the Progressive Era." *Harvard Educational Review*
    48 (February 1978): 71,76.

Shapiro, Michael S. *Child's Garden: The Kindergarten Movement from Froebel to
    Dewey*. University Park and London, 1983.

Shultz, William J. "The Humane Movement in the United States, 1910–1922," *Columbia University Studies in History, Economics, and Public Law* 63, no. 1 (1924): 1–320.

Spring, Joel. *Education and the Rise of the Corporate State.* Boston, 1972.

The Statistical History of the United States from Colonial Times to the Present. Stamford, Conn., 1965.

Steinfels, Margaret O'Brien. *Who's Minding the Children? The History and Politics of Day Care in America.* New York, 1973.

Stone, Lawrence, ed. *Schooling and Society: Studies in the History of Education.* Baltimore, 1976.

Tiffin, Susan. *In Whose Best Interest? Child Welfare Reform in the Progressive Era.* Westport, Conn., 1982.

Trachtenberg, Alan. *The Incorporation of America: Culture and Society in the Gilded Age.* New York, 1982.

Trattner, Walter. *Crusade for the Children: A History of the National Child Labor Committee and Child Labor Reform in America.* Chicago, 1970.

————. *From Poor Law to Welfare State: A History of Social Welfare in America.* New York, 1979.

Troen, Selwyn K. "The Discovery of the Adolescent by American Educational Reformers, 1900–1920: An Economic Perspective." In *Schooling and Society: Studies in the History of Education,* edited by Laurence Stone. Baltimore, 1976: 239–250.

————. *The Public and the Schools: Shaping the St. Louis System, 1838–1920.* Columbia, Mo., 1975.

Tyack, David B. *The One Best System: A History of American Urban Education.* Cambridge, Mass., 1974.

————, and Berkowitz, Michael. "The Man Nobody Liked: Toward a Social History of the Truant Office, 1840–1940." *American Quarterly* 29 (Spring 1977).

————, and Hansot, Elisabeth. *Managers of Virtue: Public School Leadership in America 1820–1980.* New York, 1982.

Violas, Paul. *The Training of the Urban Working Class: A History of Twentieth-Century American Education.* Chicago, 1978.

Weber, Evelyn. *The Kindergarten.* New York, 1969.

Wiebe, Robert H. *The Search for Order, 1877–1920.* New York, 1967.

Wrigley, Julia. *Class, Politics and Public Schools: Chicago, 1900–1950.* New Brunswick, N.J., 1982.

8

Native American Children

Margaret Connell Szasz

Margaret Mead once wrote that "every people has a quite definite image of what a child is at birth." Native Americans were no exception. Iroquois parents, for example, viewed babies as "barely separated from the spirit world." They cut a hole in the moccasins of those infants on the cradle board, to discourage them from following unseen spirits lurking behind the mother on the forest path. The Iroquois said that "an infant's life is as the thinness of a maple leaf."[1]

During the long history of Indian-white relations in this country, non-Indians have generally known little and understood even less about childhood among native Americans. Consequently, when Charles Eastman, the well-known Santee Sioux medical doctor, wrote of his own mid-nineteenth-century boyhood, he noted: "It is commonly supposed that there is no systematic education of their children among the aboriginees of this country. Nothing could be farther from the truth." Eastman suggested further that the educational institutions of the native people "were scrupulously adhered to and transmitted from one generation to another."[2]

Over thirty years later, the pioneering anthropologist, Edward Sapir, reiterated Eastman's observation. "It is strange," Sapir mused, "how little ethnology has concerned itself with . . . the acquirement of culture by a child . . . culture dynamics seems to be almost entirely a matter of adult definition and adult transmission. . . . The humble child . . . is somehow left out of the account.[3]

In the mid-1940s, the University of California published a little noted anthropological study on this subject by George A. Pettitt. Entitled *Primitive Education in North America*, Pettitt's monograph served in part as a response to Sapir's criticism, but it also reflected contemporary educational theory. Using the framework of Progressive education as a springboard, Pettitt articulated the ideas propounded in the late 1920s and 1930s by W. Carson Ryan, John Collier, and Willard Walcott Beatty. Like these Indian Service reformers, Pettitt saw in traditional native American childhood the concept of community which was so visibly absent from contemporary American schooling. By clarifying the attributes of traditional native American education, Pettitt sought to aid both educators and anthropologists in their understanding of the acculturative process of childhood. But it is doubtful if the study exerted any influence. Largely ignored by both scholarly and popular journals, it was relegated to the anonymity of college library shelves.

This was unfortunate because Pettitt had some important things to say. Delineating several themes common to native American childrearing, he supported these with the findings of almost all of the major ethnological studies on Indians and Eskimos that had appeared before the 1940s. Since most ethnological studies published in recent decades have dealt with partially acculturated peoples, they have contributed less to our knowledge of traditional childrearing practices. Hence, Pettitt's synthesis remains the single most important ethnological contribution to the study of traditional native American childhood. It emerges as the *sine qua non* of bibliographical essays in this field.

Before dealing with Pettitt's themes, however, it is important to look at further bibliographical sources on traditional childhood. Native American autobiographies and biographies provide another major source for accounts of traditional childhood, offering, as it were, a reverse image for treatment by ethnologists. Basic bibliographies for these accounts are: Peter Murdock and Timothy J. O'Leary, *Ethnographic Bibliography of North America* (1973); Jack W. Marken, ed., *The Indians and Eskimos of North America* (1973); and Francis Paul Prucha, S.J., *A Bibliographical Guide to the History of Indian-White Relations in the United States* (1977), and its supplement, Prucha, *Indian-White Relations in the United States* (1982).

Even more useful are the annotated bibliographies that have appeared in the last decade. Arlene B. Hirschfelder compiled the earliest of these: *American Indian and Eskimo Authors* (1975). More recently (1981), Daniel Littlefield, Jr., and James W. Parins edited *A Biobibliography of Native American Writers, 1772–1924*. Although this work is somewhat limited, both geographically and chronologically, its chief value lies in its compilation of titles by native authors and its biographical sketches of those authors. A further valuable source is by H. David Brumble III, *An Annotated Bibliography of American Indian and Eskimo Autobiographies* (1981). Following an insightful introduction, Brumble contributes individual descriptions and analyses for each of the 577 entries. The annotated bibliographies serve as a major research tool for students of native American writers, as well as ethnologists and ethnohistorians.

Further sources for traditional native American childhood include the

journals of explorers and travelers, such as the Florentine, John Ver-
arzanus, or the Swedish naturalist Peter Kalm; captivity accounts, typified
by James Everett Seaver's work, *A Narrative of the Life of Mrs. Mary Jamison,
who was taken captive by the Indians in 1775....* (1824); the papers of traders
and missionaries who lived among the Indians during the formative
years of contact, such as the well-known Southeastern trader, James
Adair, who wrote *The History of the American Indians, particularly those
nations adjoining to the Mississippi....* (1775), or the Moravian missionary
John Heckewelder, who wrote *An Account of the History, Manners, and
Customs of the Indian Nations who once inhabited Pennsylvania and the Neighboring States* (1961, [1819; reprint]). Finally, further source material may
be found in the numerous accounts recorded by miscellaneous early
writers whose interest in native Americans antedated the inception of
professional anthropology. These range from Daniel Gookins (Massachusetts Bay colony) and Roger Williams to Henry Rowe Schoolcraft,
George Catlin, and Henry David Thoreau.

In the late fifteenth and early sixteenth centuries, the European no-
menclature for the native American—*los Indios*, the Indian, *les Indien*,
die Indianer—referred to a people who existed only in the imagination
of Europeans. Rather than a single culture, the Indian—hundreds of
different groups living in a dozen or so distinct culture areas—resided
across the continent. In the Southwest lived bands of Dineh (Navajo),
villages of Hopi, and other farming peoples. In the Southeast some of
the varied groups included villages of Muskogee (Creek) and mountain-
eering bands of Yun wi ya (Cherokee). In the Columbia River Plateau
lived bands of Nu mi pu (Nez Perce). In the Northeast some settlements
were Munsee and Unami (Delaware); others were Wampanoag or Nar-
ragansett. Each group retained its own identity and its own culture. None
knew themselves as "Indians."[4]

Generalizations about traditional native American childhood should
bear in mind this multiplicity of cultures. Nonetheless, despite the diversity that characterized groups—both between and within the major
culture areas—several common themes of traditional childhood have
emerged. As described here, these themes generally follow the pioneering work of George A. Pettitt.

In the prehistoric period, most native American groups retained a
degree of insularity that is difficult for us to comprehend. Modern communication and transportation have opened at least superficial windows
to cultural barriers. We no longer live in isolated groupings. By contrast,
native American groups retained separate identities. For example, when
men from the Tewa pueblo *Oke-oweenge* (San Juan) returned from their
fall buffalo hunt on the Southern Plains, they subjected themselves to
ritual precautions designed to reintegrate them fully into the Tewa world.

They viewed their hunting sojourn as a visit "among people [Plains Indians] whom the Tewa did not recognize as people."[5] Like many native groups, they saw themselves as "the people." This sense of insularity and cultural autonomy was once described by an Odawa, who wrote: "our way of life was total, nothing was outside of it, everything was within."[6]

Although native groups exchanged material goods as well as some nonmaterial culture through raiding and warfare, and, more importantly, through the strong trade networks that criss-crossed the continent in the prehistoric era, by and large theirs was a separate and insular world. A child, therefore, was immersed in a homogeneous atmosphere wherein everyone spoke a common language, everyone shared a common spiritual outlook, a common past, and a common set of customs. As Robert K. Thomas noted, life was "integrated and consistent from one sphere to another."[7] This meant that whether survival depended on an abundance of natural resources, such as on the Northwest Coast, or on a paucity of them, such as in the Great Basin, everyone was traveling in the ship together. They would survive or falter through the shared wisdom and heritage of the group.

Within this group children were surrounded by expanding concentric circles of people who cared for them. The immediate family assumed basic guidance, but others were equally important. Within the extended family this included grandparents, maternal uncles or paternal aunts, and cousins. Beyond the family, and depending on the complexity of the society, the child was influenced by clan or lineage groupings, by secret societies, by societal leaders, and, finally, by the community as a whole. Thus, as Pettitt noted, "education was not consciously institutionalized." Rather, it was "a community project in which all reputable elders participated at the instigation of individual family."[8]

Every native American group required that certain skills be mastered before a youth was accepted as a mature member of society. These generally fell into three areas: economic skills, knowledge of cultural heritage, and spiritual awareness. A Tuscarora man once described the prehistoric training of native children as consisting of "three basic courses": "Survival," "Religion," and "Ethics." "They were, of course, interwoven," he added, "and were taught primarily by families, clans and leaders of sub-societies, religious and secular, within the tribe."[9]

Training for survival lay at the core of a child's growing years. Because of the tremendous variation in economic base for native groups, survival training was specifically geared to available resources. The extensive maps that accompany Harold E. Driver's reference volume, *Indians of North America* (1961), graphically illustrate the variations, which range from sedentary horticulturalists of the Southwestern deserts to hunters and gatherers of the Subarctic. A sharply defined ecological boundary limited the raising of the native trilogy of maize, beans, and squash to latitudes roughly south of the Great Lakes. This differentiation was not consistent across the continent, however, for many groups living in these more temperate latitudes and with sufficient water—such as in the Columbia River Plateau or California—failed to cultivate maize.

Regardless of the differences, all children learned at an early age that survival depended on well-tested knowledge of skills, accompanied by proper attitudes toward the earth and all life—animate and inanimate—upon it. As a Cree hunter advised:

The man who earns his subsistence from hunting, who survives, as the Indians say, from the land, depends on knowing where he must stand in the strangely efficient and mysterious balance that is arranged for the propagation of all life. . . . In this scheme of things the man is not dominant; he is a mere survivor, like every other form of life.[10]

A counterpart for this hunter-oriented economy existed in the maize-oriented society of the Hopi. Here, on farming plots below their stark mesas, the Hopis relied on horticultural skills combined with a complex ceremonial cycle. Hopi ceremonial leaders were regarded as possessing extraordinary powers. But not all figures of power were ceremonial leaders. Thus, an exceptionally able farmer, particularly one who had the "ability to manipulate the natural environment with its correlated supernatural forces," might also be called a *pavansino* (a powerful man).[11] The Hopi, too, acknowledged the need for a dual mastery, combining economic skills with a proper attitude toward the universe.

Knowledge of cultural heritage marked the second aspect of childhood among native peoples of North America. One of the strongest means of imparting the culture to children was through storytelling. An ancient, universal art, storytelling remained a familiar part of the European heritage until the late seventeenth century.[12] Cultures without a written language depended totally on oral tradition. Thus, all that was retained of their past was held in the memories of the oldest living generation. Theirs was the responsibility for maintaining this store of knowledge and transmitting it to the younger generations, who then became the teachers.

The Swampy Cree related the story of the porcupine to describe the need to learn of the past in order to inform the generations of the future. Seeking to explain the intentions of the porcupine as he backs into a rock crevice, they noted: "The porcupine consciously goes backward in order to speculate safely on the future, allowing him to look out at his enemy or just the new day." For the Cree, this was "an instructive act of self-preservation." The art of storytelling thus invited the listener to " 'go backward, look forward, as the porcupine does.' "[13]

As the transmitter of the cultural heritage, the storyteller had a sig-

nificant influence on native American children. Pablita Velarde, renowned artist of Santa Clara Pueblo, portrays the storyteller of her Tewa
people in her illustrated narrative, *Old Father, the Story Teller* (1960).
Opening her account with the legend of "The Stars," she writes:

Many stars made bright holes in the clear, cold autumn sky. In the village plaza
a fire danced and children danced around it. They were happy and excited
because Old Father was in the village and would begin tonight to tell them the
winter's stories.

"Tell us a story, tell us a story." They loved Old Father and he loved them
and understood them. His kindness made a warmth like the fire. He laughed
and asked: "What kind of a story?", and a tiny voice came tumbling, "Why are
some stars brighter than all the others? And why don't they ever fall where we
can find them?"

The children settled around the fire as Old Father gazed up at the stars with
a faraway smile. Pointing first toward Orion in the east, he said: That is "Long
Sash."[14]

Storytelling taught in many ways. First, the tales reinforced cultural
ideals learned in more mundane lessons. Moral instruction punctuated
the daily lives of native youth. Thus, Kiowa children learned that only
those who developed courage, generosity, and kindness could become
leaders.[15] Winnebago girls were told: "When you are bringing up children. . . . Let them see what love is by observing you give things away to
the poor."[16] A Hopi child was taught to listen to the old people, obey
his parents, and to "work hard and treat everyone right."[17] An Arapaho
child was instructed to be kind: those without pity for others were told
" 'You have no heart.' "[18] These daily reminders of ethical guidelines
took on new meaning in the context of a story. Storytellers often masked
the moral instruction in the enjoyment of the tales themselves, which,
as Victor Barnouw points out, "is one of the main reasons, after all, why
they are told."[19] In his autobiography, *Guests Never Leave Hungry*, James
Sewid, a Kwakiutl, recalled winter evenings in the big community house
at Village Island. Each family lived in one corner of the house, where
they had their own fire and did most of their cooking. But at night they
built a fire in the middle, and Sewid remembered that when it was time
for sleep, "we would all sit around the fire and some of the older people
would be telling the stories. It was a big open fire and we were all little
kids sitting around it. I remember best the stories about Tlisliglia which
means little Mink, child of the sun."[20] For Sewid, and for countless other
native children in numerous groups across the continent, the winter
evenings of storytelling became a cumulative experience. When these
evenings were repeated winter season upon winter season, they ce-

mented the cultural ideals in the minds of the young. This was particularly true for those who were to become the future storytellers.

In almost every group a certain number stood out as potential storytellers, medicine men, and ritual leaders. These youth displayed unusually keen memories, as well as a strong interest in the significance of
these positions of prestige. A clear memory was imperative. As Pablita
Velarde notes with regards to storytelling: "small details are likely to
carry much meaning."[21] From the training of the universal storytellers
to the discipline endured by Hopi ceremonial leaders, Navajo medicine
men, holy men of the Teton Sioux, or ritual leaders of the Seneca, the
education of these bearers of culture was a life-long process, and one
of crucial importance for each group.[22] Childhood training for these
individuals marked just the beginning of a long apprenticeship.

The difficult path toward spiritual awareness—yet another facet of
native American childhood—was not limited to those who were to become shamans, priests, or medicine men. Indeed, this aspect of childhood permeated all others and was as significant a sign of maturity as
knowing how to cast a harpoon, to scrape a buffalo or moose hide, or
to leach acorns properly to rid them of tannic acid. Moreover, it applied
to all youth within the group, male and female, wealthy and poor.

Spiritual awareness provided the matrix for native American groups.
It pervaded their cultures and gave shape to them. Some groups wor-
shipped a creator or Great Spirit (such as the *Taiowa* of the Hopi); others
saw a supernatural power, single and all powerful (such as *Wakan Tanka*
of the Teton Sioux); most acknowledged an awareness of the creative
force in all things on earth, which suggests that they did not separate
the spiritual and the material, the natural and the supernatural, the
human and the animal. When anthropologist George Spindler spoke
with the Menominee about visions, he recalled later that he was "often,
but gently corrected." " 'A white man might say that' " the Menominee
said, " 'but this was no "vision," this happened.' "[23]

The path toward spiritual awareness began early. Youth absorbed
spiritual attitudes through family and older members of the group, and
through ritual and ceremony, which provided an important dimension
for all native cultures. The intensity of training increased dramatically,
however, about the time of puberty. At this stage, some groups initiated
their youth into secret societies responsible for some aspect of the community's ceremonial life; others sent them on their guardian spirit quest.
While certain groups incorporated both of these rituals, most adopted
just one. As Pettit suggests, the presence of one tended "to minimize
the need for or acceptability of the other."[24]

Training for initiation into a secret society was a group-oriented process. Among the eastern or Rio Grande Pueblos, the length of initiation

varied. At San Juan, for example, it lasted four days, while at Taos the boys' training spanned a period of a year and a half. During this time boys were separated from their home and lived in the kiva. There they were trained by spiritual leaders.[25]

Preparation for the guardian spirit quest spanned a period of several years before the actual event. Among some groups of the Columbia River Plateau, the quest represented the culmination of years of fasting, cold morning baths, food taboos, and less strenuous physical hardship. Thus, when the moment came, the youth was prepared. Many authors have stressed the physical discomfort of the quest, but in so doing they fail to observe that this was an integral part of maturing. The goal of the quest was to have hardened oneself sufficiently to overcome the physical discomfort in order to obtain a guardian spirit—whether in the form of animal or other living creature—which would aid and guide the youth for the remainder of his or her life. Among the Nez Perce and Yakimas, for example, both boys and girls went on the quests. The finding of the spirit was crucial, for it determined the direction of the youth's life. Moreover, it would serve as a presence in that life. Thus, a favorable guardian spirit quest was one of the main keys to success in these cultures.[26]

Spiritual awareness, then, ranked high within the integrated learning patterns for native American children. When E. Adamson Hoebel described the challenges faced by the Cheyenne, he synthesized conditions for many native groups:

The land of the Cheyenne is not a paradise. . . . It is a land where people must hold together, or perish; . . . where the Cheyennes have come to rely not only on technical skill but on mystique and compulsive ritual to bolster their sense of security and give them a faith which will engender courage.[27]

Thus, youth faced these challenges from early childhood, and it was their training—in economic skills, cultural heritage, and spiritual awareness—that taught them to meet such hardship.

Of equal importance, however, were the ingenious methods used by family and community for rearing children. Beyond the substance of what children learned was the means by which these skills were taught. In native American cultures these methods evolved largely around two extremes, which, while seemingly polarized, worked harmoniously toward the same goal. They were discipline and incentive.

As Pettitt, Anthony F.C. Wallace, and others have pointed out, no trait of native American childrearing evoked more criticism than the apparent lack of discipline. In 1657 a Jesuit wrote of the Iroquois: "There is nothing for which these peoples have a greater horror than restraint.

The very children cannot endure it, and live as they please in the houses of their parents, without fear of reprimand or chastisement."[28] In the context of the European or American observer, discipline was often seen as synonymous with corporal punishment. The observer assumed that lack of corporal punishment meant lack of discipline.

Here again, the tremendous diversity of native cultures comes into play. On the one hand, some groups avoided all corporal punishment. Aleš Hrdlička noted that "corporal punishment with sticks did not exist among the Aleut."[29] William W. Newcomb wrote that Delaware children were seldom if ever physically punished.[30] Thomas Wildcat Alford recalled that among his people, the Shawnee, "force seldom was used to enforce good conduct."[31] Dan George said of his Salishan group of British Columbia: "it is not among our people to lick a child or scold harshly."[32] Some tribes, however, did use corporal punishment. Anthropologist Erna Gunther learned that when Klallam youth refused to go on their guardian spirit quest, they were whipped with a digging stick.[33] East of the Cascades, the Sanpoil and Nespelem carried punishment a step further. If one child disobeyed a rule, an old man was brought in to whip not only the offender but all of the children among the several families in the community.[34] Edward Goodbird recalled from his own youth yet another punishment meted out to Hidatsa children. A "very naughty" Hidatsa boy was "sometimes punished by rolling him in a snow bank or ducking him in water."[35]

A total absence of corporal punishment was, therefore, not an accurate assessment. Even the Iroquois resorted to throwing water in the faces of children when it was deemed necessary.[36] But by and large, physical punishment for misbehavior was not imposed frequently, as in the case of some other cultures. The underlying reason for this behavior pattern lay in the attitude held by native groups toward pain. Most native cultures idealized the ability to withstand pain. Thus, they wove this societal ideal into their patterns for childrearing. A youth's ability to endure pain and suffering without flinching was almost universally touted as a sign of maturity.

Native autobiographies and reports of early ethnological field studies are replete with accounts of childhood training in physical endurance. Hrdlička reported that the Aleuts "had a habit of bathing the children in cold water, or in the sea, at all times of the year, with the object of strengthening their body."[37] Newcomb observed of Delaware children that as they grew older they were more and more "exposed to a toughening program."[38] In like fashion, the Eskimo trained their youth to be in excellent physical condition so that they were able "to withstand physical discomfort" and "to perform difficult tasks over long periods of time."[39] Nuligak, an Inuit born in the 1890s, recalled one childhood hunting trip when he and his companions "had difficulty in getting back home." "None of us," he remembered, "had had anything to eat since the day before, when we left."[40]

One of the seldom-noted forms of childhood training for endurance was the use of the ubiquitous cradleboard. The Iroquois attitude toward infants, noted earlier, suggests a general feeling shared by native peoples toward very young children. Infants were believed to be closely linked to the supernatural world. In Taos Pueblo, if an infant were left alone before it was "old enough to eat," it was felt that a spirit might "come and thereafter the child always 'sees things.' "[41] What better place for this fragile being than in a cradleboard, where it was held securely and could be closely watched. But the cradleboard also provided the infant's introduction to discipline. In societies vulnerable to enemy attack, infants were a liability. Under these conditions the cradleboard was ideal: it could be moved quickly, and it was well-suited to teaching the merits of quiet behavior. Groups adopted varying methods to deal with infant crying. When Arapaho children cried, they were "firmly but gently pinched on the nose and mouths, so that their sounds could not give away the village's location to an enemy."[42] When a Cheyenne infant cried, it was taken away from the camp and its cradleboard hung on a bush until it cried itself out. A few such experiences taught that it was preferable to behave, for the "good baby" was "cuddled and constantly loved."[43] In the 1630s William Wood praised the behavior of Massachusetts infants. The mothers' "musick," he noted, "is lullabies to quiet their children, who generally are as quiet as if they had neither spleene or lungs."[44] Wood was probably not aware of the training taught by the Massachusetts to produce this remarkable result.

In native cultures, therefore, where toughness of body and spirit were esteemed, frequent or excessive corporal punishment would have been contrary to a predominant feature of childrearing. One did not physically abuse a child who had been taught to withstand pain. The alternative, however, was not the apparent absence of total restraint. Rather, native cultures chose to rely on other forms of control, most, if not all of them, emanating from outside the nuclear family.

Parents in native societies deliberately avoided the unpleasant duties that might lead to conflict with the child "by projecting the blame upon outside agencies."[45] Sometimes a relative assumed this chore. The Hidatsa Goodbird recalled that his uncle "Flies Low, a clan brother of my father, punished me when I was bad." One evening when Goodbird refused to go to bed, his mother turned to Flies Low and cried, "A patip. duck him." Goodbird was promptly ducked head first into a bucket of water several times, until he promised to obey.[46]

This type of discipline was augmented by an even more powerful form of behavioral control: the use of ridicule. As an incentive for individual reform, no more effective weapon was wielded by the community. Among the Blackfeet if a youth committed an ill-advised act, the incident became the subject of community verbal abuse. Shouted from one tipi at night, the story was picked up and repeated by a chorus of voices until the night reverberated with the sound. The youth was compelled to remain hidden until he had accomplished some great deed to erase the memory of his disgrace.[47] In most cases, however, joking cousins or other relatives identified as "the joking relationship," performed this task of sanctioned societal control.[48] Whether the subject of derisive laughter by one's own sex, or the victim of taunts by the opposite one, in either case the individual took prompt action to remove the focus of derogatory attention. Half a century ago Clark Wissler concluded that among native Americans "the whole control of the local group . . . seems to have been exercised by admonition and mild ridicule instead of by force and punishment."[49]

Ridicule served not only as a means of censure. Like many forms of sanctioned behavior among native societies, it effected a dual purpose: while it controlled unacceptable actions, it also served as a goad toward praiseworthy behavior. Yet another facet of societal control that profoundly affected children was the use of the supernatural. In some instances, the impact of the supernatural overlapped with that of ridicule. For example, masked clowns among the Hopi, Zuni, and other pueblos provided sharply aimed barbs of ridicule for festivals in the annual ceremonial cycle of these peoples. But the supernatural played on still another human emotion very real to children—that of fear. Again, like ridicule, threats of supernatural intervention or punishment served both as censure of unacceptable behavior and as an incentive for good behavior.

Reliance on the supernatural as a means of controlling the behavior of children was universal among native cultures. Frequently, threats called on the power of evil spirits that took on the form of some animal, bird, or reptile. The owl, for example, was probably the most ubiquitous of the bad spirits, feared in many groups not only by children but also by adults. Wissler reported that the Choctaw believed different varieties of owls caused different kinds of malevolence. Hence, the screech owl was harmful to children because in size it was seen as a "baby owl." For the Choctaw, the sound of a screech owl presaged the death of a child under seven years of age.[50] The grandmother of the Santee Sioux, Charles Eastman, who raised him as a young child, also warned of the owl. "It was one of her legends," Eastman wrote, "that a little boy was once standing outside the tepee . . . crying vigorously for his mother, when Hinakaga swooped down in the darkness and carried the poor little fellow up into the trees."[51] Other creatures also reputedly carried away naughty children, but a more immediate threat appeared in the form of masked beings, such as "Living Solid Face" of the Delaware, or the hideous "Spotted Face" of the Flathead, both of whom were said to harm disobedient children.

Ridicule, discipline, and use of the supernatural served, then, as the negative incentives for children to conform. But, as astute judges of human nature, native people also provided clear-cut positive incentives that encouraged children to work toward the goals of maturity: spiritual, economic, and cultural.

Pettitt suggests that native American cultures are unusually perceptive in their "attention to praise, privilege, and prestige on a community basis, as a reward of achievement for culture pattern ideals."[52] Through these methods, the community offered the child well-defined steps of progress. Each accomplishment was worthy of praise and perhaps also some form of reward. Since economic skills were the most visible, so, too, were those rewards. A Yakima boy was given a feast in honor of his first deer; a Wishram girl gave away her first significant gathering of huckleberries to the old women of the community, who were called together for the occasion. "This gave her good luck in picking berries and made her a rapid picker."[53] With maturity came privileges long denied to youth. Among the Blood, a proven warrior no longer had to carry wood and water and tend the fire as a boy had to on his first war party.[54] In many groups marriage was prohibited until the youth had met certain tests—the killing of the first seal, the proven proficiency as a hunter, the preparation of skins. Often these accomplishments signalled the moment for bestowing a new name on the youth. Among many native cultures, names played an important role in determining one's direction in life. Frequently, names were bestowed at high points in life—at birth, when names were given by special relatives, following a successful war party, after a favorable guardian spirit quest, or upon an unusually fortunate escape from danger—and one individual might bear a number of names during a lifetime, as well as many names simultaneously. A name often held a spiritual power, sometimes acquired as an inheritance, passed down through generations as an heirloom. Thus, the bestowing of a new name was both an honor and an incentive.

In all groups, therefore, the child could look forward to maturity. Although it meant increased responsibilities in all realms—spiritual, economic, and cultural heritage—the child had been trained to understand and to accept these responsibilities as a prerequisite of maturity. Moreover, there were compensations. Maturity offered rewards and privileges denied to the young and the untested.

Childhood, then, to a large degree, was a time of learning and a time of testing. As the mother of a young Fox girl explained: " 'That is why I treat you like that.... No one continues to be taken care of forever. The time soon comes when we lose sight of the one who takes care of us.' "[55] Responsibility for the education of youth was, therefore, a duty.

Rearing of children was everyone's concern. The lifeblood of the community itself depended on the strength of its future generations: on their ability to bear the burdens of survival, to maintain the traditions, and to uphold the pride of the people. Thus, children held an integral position in the community, and the portrayal of them as undisciplined children of the forest does not withstand close scrutiny.

On the other hand, play was an important part of early childhood for native youth. Autobiographies recount numerous descriptions of general play—from winter tobogganing and games of tag and wrestling to many kinds of ball games and swimming—as well as play that centered on imitation of adult life. A Cheyenne woman recalled, for example,

In my girlhood days we played what we girls called "tiny play." This play imitated the customs and ways of grown-up people.... After a time as I became a little older we played what we called "large play." The boys would go out hunting. ... We girls would pitch our tipis and make ready everything as if it were a real camp life.... Some of the boys would go on the warpath, and always came home victorious.[56]

Imitative play, then, served both as recreation and reinforcement for the education of native youth.

The complex structure of native childhood was to be severely tested with the arrival of Europeans, for the greatest inroads upon native culture were made through their youth. Native Americans were not blind to the dangers inherent in this threat. Many of them shrewdly assessed the potential damage to their cultural integrity and their identity as a people. Often, however, they had no recourse.

Bibliographical sources for native American childhood in the historic period suggest greater reliance on biographies and autobiographies of native people, and on ethnohistorical accounts of individual groups that describe modifications of their traditional cultures through historical contact. For an excellent example of this type of monograph, see Bruce G. Trigger, *The Children of Aetaentsic* (1976). Since relatively few ethnohistorians have focused on this type of change in the field of native American childhood, biographical material and oral history collections, such as the Doris Duke Indian Oral History collections, remain more useful.[57] However, a number of ethnologies, such as those published by the Smithsonian Institution or various universities, also deal with native childhood in the transitional stages.

The dramatic changes affecting traditional native childhood during a period of more than four centuries may be seen as a microcosm of the vast cultural and biological exchange between Western and Eastern Hemispheres.[58] From the late fifteenth century to the present, peoples of both the Old and the New World have witnessed profound changes in their lives because of this contact. The effects have not been one-sided, and, while the emphasis here will be on the impact of this exchange on native North Americans, it must be borne in mind that the immigrants who settled here, as well as those who remained in the Old World, were also affected.[59]

When the Spanish began their *entradas* into the Borderlands in the early sixteenth century, they initiated the exchange with North American natives. Later in the century the French joined the fray, and, finally, the Dutch, the Swedes, the British, and the Russians. As the international rivalry erupted in earnest, nations began nibbling off chunks of native territory like so many mice surrounding a slab of cheese. They attacked from the Caribbean, the Atlantic, and the Pacific, almost as if they were practicing a mock reconnoiter of the frontier movement of the young republic that claimed the continent between 1783 and 1890, when the frontier of the continental United States officially closed.

This was not merely an allegorical accomplishment: by the end of the nineteenth century, almost all native Americans (excepting only Alaskan) had been restricted to comparatively small parcels of land. These, too, were shrinking rapidly as lands were allotted to native Americans under the Dawes Act of 1887.

By the opening of the twentieth century, therefore, immigrants from the Old World and their descendants had acquired, through one means or another, most of the native land base. This was a visible loss, and it has continued to have a powerful effect on the lives of native people. Other visible changes bore equally devastating results. The twin disasters of disease and alcohol have demanded a heavy toll in pain, suffering, and loss of life. Henry F. Dobyns estimated recently that the prehistoric native population north of the Rio Grande may once have been as high as 10 to 12 million people.[60] Currently, the combined native population of North America is almost 2 million people. If Dobyn's figures are reliable, we can estimate a population loss of as many as 8 million people. What caused the decline? Contrary to popular opinion, disease, and especially smallpox, was the greatest killer, accounting for the virtual decimation of entire groups of people. Francis Jennings wrote that the "American land was more like a widow than a virgin," and Wilbur R. Jacobs notes that the decline of native population after 1492 was "a demographic disaster with no known parallel in world history."[61]

In terms of major visible changes, then, the arrival of Euro-Americans meant epidemics, drastic population decline, and loss of land. But long before direct encounters with these foreign people, most natives became acquainted with their trade goods and other innovations. Moving inland from the coastlines and north from Meso-America, foreign innovations reached into native cultures. The time span for initial cultural exchanges was vast. Rio Grande pueblos met mounted Spaniards in the 1540s; 350 years later, in the 1890s, the Inuit of the Mackenzie River delta greeted international whaling ships.

The material possessions and technology of these foreigners had a powerful impact on native cultures. In the seventeenth century, metal tools supplied by the French to Iroquoian and Algonquian-speaking peoples of the Northeastern Woodlands provided greater leisure and thus led to a "cultural fluorescence" among these groups.[62] In the late sixteenth-early seventeenth centuries, the Spaniards' unwitting introduction of the horse to the Southwestern Borderlands revolutionized the native cultures of the Southwest, Plains, Prairie, Columbia River Plateau, and parts of the Great Basin. By the late 1700s, most of these cultures had adapted the horse and all of its ramifications in such a way as to suggest it had always been a part of their heritage.[63] For native youth in these areas, horses were a significant aspect of childhood. As a Cheyenne woman recalled, "I was taught to ride horseback alone when I was 4 years old."[64]

As native groups adopted these innovations, they incorporated them into their traditional culture patterns. Often this required extensive revision in modes of transportation, societal structure, hunting and warfare, foods, clothing, and an awareness of luxuries. As each group responded to the new, the changes were sufficiently traumatic to provide vivid memories for native children. An Inuit whose boyhood spanned such a period of cultural change remembered that in his earliest years "even flour and sugar were unknown to us. Tea, tobacco, gunpowder and lead for cartridges were the only things we borrowed from the white man." But less than a decade later, in 1908, when a two-masted schooner sailed in, he traded for fifty pounds of flour "and some tobacco for my grandmother." These items he remembered well because they were his "first purchases."[65] A Shawnee educated at Hampton Institute in Virginia recalled the impact of such changes on his people:

Our needs had multiplied, and even then living expenses had begun to mount. Our people were no longer satisfied with the meager necessities of existence that formerly had seemed sufficient. With the advent of traders' stores there were so many things to tempt one to buy.... It seemed that civilization was nothing more or less than a multiplication of man's needs and wants.[66]

It was one thing for traditional native childhood to absorb the impact of epidemics, loss of land, and the disruptive influence of alcohol; and to incorporate into the patterns of maturing the addition of metal tools and firearms, wheat, flour, and tea, and horses, cattle, and sheep. These merged with traditional cultures, were absorbed into legends and stories, and blended with the boundaries of their worlds. It was another matter

when the foreigners—the "Wasichus," the "Bahanas," the "Boston men"—
came to the people and asked to have their children.

In essence, what the foreigners said was that their civilization had
developed many alternatives—many beliefs, customs, and ways of doing
things—that were not only different from native ways and beliefs but
were also superior. In two of these areas—the rearing of children and
religion—the foreigners showed the greatest concern. While they offered
to teach adults, clearly they believed that native children had the greatest
potential to learn. Some children might live at home and attend school
during the day, but those who were taken from home "out of reach of
their Parents, and out of the way of *Indian* examples, and . . . kept to
School under good Government and constant Instruction," would be far
more successful in adopting all of the advantages of white civilization.[67]

For as long as anyone could remember, native childrearing had always
met the needs of the people. Through all of the instruction and methods
described earlier, children had learned to become mature adults and
responsible members of their own community, as well as the larger community of all natural life. Integral to this training had been their guidance
toward spiritual awareness, both as individuals and as participants in
group ceremonies. Now these foreigners brought a new dimension. They
claimed that native children must have further education and that they
must acquire another view of spiritual awareness. Native children had
always learned by word of mouth, through oral tradition; the whites
taught their children through a written heritage, some of which was
sacred and some not.

This, then, became the dilemma that faced native peoples from the
Hispanic *entradas* to the off-reservation boarding schools of the late nineteenth century. It was a dilemma of long duration and one that was
repeated thousands of times. On countless occasions, for hundreds of
different native groups throughout the continent, the question arose.
Should the children be taught by white teachers and spiritual leaders,
or should they remain true to the traditional education of the people?
Sometimes a conscious decision had to be made. Sometimes there was
little choice. A Hopi woman recalled how her husband had been taken
away to school at age five:

. . . he was sleeping with his little brothers on the second floor terrace of his home
in Old Oraibi. One September morning, early, without his mother's knowledge,
the school police took little Emory, still asleep, wrapped in a brand new blanket
that his grandfather had made for him. . . . The "catch" that day was Emory,
another six-year-old boy, and six girls who had not gone back to school after
the summer vacation. . . . They were soon loaded into a wagon for the thirty-
mile trip to Keems Canyon.

Emory remembered that the next morning his beautiful new blanket with colored stripes was gone. "I saw it later," he noted, "in the possession of the wife of the superintendent."[68]

Formal schooling for native Americans has followed many routes during the centuries of contact. More often than not it has been a one-sided affair, with emphasis on white culture. On occasion, however, native cultures have been acknowledged. Pueblo children, especially after the Pueblo Revolt of 1680, learned both Catholic and traditional Pueblo beliefs.[69] In seventeenth-century Virginia, colonists took native youth into their homes to teach them their Anglo-American knowledge. On Martha's Vineyard, the well-known Mayhew family hired a colonial schoolmaster to teach the Pawkunnakut children to read and write. Two of them—Joel Hiscoomes and Caleb Cheeshahteaumauk—did so well they later attended Harvard's Indian College in the 1660s. John Eliot of Massachusetts, the Mayhews, and, later, Eleazar Wheelock of Connecticut employed native people as schoolmasters or assistants to teach their own groups, and sometimes other Indians as well. While the nineteenth century saw a flood of missionary-schoolmasters, who followed the frontier, it also witnessed the establishment of schools by the Five Civilized Tribes. They began schools in the Southeast and reopened them after removal to Indian Territory in the 1830s and 1840s. Despite the fact that their schools provided a better education than those of non-Indians, they were closed by the Federal Government when Oklahoma became a territory.

Until the late nineteenth century, the churches dominated the movement to educate native peoples. By the early twentieth century, however, the Federal Government and the public schools had entered the scene. The pioneering work of Captain Richard Henry Pratt, who enrolled the first Indian students in Hampton Institute and founded Carlisle Indian School in 1879, led the Federal Government to step on the bandwagon. During the assimilationist milieu of the late-nineteenth and early-twentieth centuries, the Federal Government opened boarding schools—both on- and off-reservation—as well as day schools. As early as the 1920s, however, the enrollment of native children in public schools already exceeded the number attending federal schools. The early federal schools taught in an ethnocentric framework. During the years when John Collier was commissioner of Indian Affairs (1933–1945), however, the Bureau of Indian Affairs responded to the 1920s reform movement and the Meriam Report of 1928 by seeking to reorient its Indian schools toward the needs and concerns of native groups. But this change was cut short by World War II and the postwar shift in federal Indian policy which encouraged termination of tribes and relocation of native peoples to urban areas. In the ethnically conscious 1960s and 1970s, however, the movement for Indian self-determination reintroduced the idea of native involvement in education. The Indian-controlled schooling that emerged took many forms, including contract schools, tribally controlled public school districts, native school boards for all types of schools attended by native children, and, finally, native institutions of higher education. All of these have come to rely on federal funds along with some private funding. Clearly, this recent shift in Indian education is more than temporary, but the responsibility for its fulfillment remains with the native groups.

Indian education in the historical period has thus emerged as a complex process characterized by many dimensions. These range from the obvious chronological thrusts—missionaries, federal involvement, public schooling, and the movement for Indian self-determination—to the more subtle spectrum of responses by native peoples. Publications on the main thrusts of Indian education have increased in recent years, but within the dimension of Indian responses, the literature is sparse. Some studies have appeared, but they tend to be narrowly focused. Ferreting out the native view is difficult, and again, biographies and autobiographies probably remain the best published sources, although these are very limited prior to the nineteenth century. The following is a selective description of publications in the field.

The only published survey of Indian education is a slim volume by Evelyn C. Adams: *American Indian Education* (1971 [reprint]). However, several dissertations survey the subject: Theodore Fischbacher, "A Study of the Role of the Federal Government in the Education of the American Indian" (1967); Martha Elizabeth Layman, "A History of Indian Education in the United States" (1942); and Harold W. Morris, "A History of Indian Education in the United States" (1954).

A comprehensive account of the colonial period is "Indian Education in the American Colonies: 1606–1776," by Margaret Connell Szasz (forthcoming). Probably the best brief synthesis of colonial Virginia is "Indian Education and Missions in Colonial Virginia," by W. Stitt Robinson, Jr. (1952). On early New England, see: Francis Jennings: "Goals and Functions of Puritan Missions to the Indians" (1971) and *The Invasion of America*; Neal Emerson Salisbury: "Conquest of the 'Savage'" (1972), and "Red Puritans" (1974); and James P. Ronda, "Generations of Faith" (1981). Two recent articles have appeared on the eighteenth-century New England educator Eleazar Wheelock: James Axtell, "Dr. Wheelock's Little Red School"; and Margaret Connell Szasz, " 'Poor Richard' Meets the Native American" (1980). Probably the best bibliographical source on missionaries for both colonial and national periods is: James P. Ronda and James Axtell, *Indian Missions* (1978).

There is no single, comprehensive study of Indian education in the nineteenth century. Descriptions of schooling within the Five Civilized Tribes are limited to articles and dissertations. See, for example: Caroline

Davis, "Education of the Chickasaw, 1856–1907" (1937); Carolyn Thomas Foreman, "Education Among the Chickasaw Indians" (1937); Abraham E. Knepler, "The Education of the Cherokee Indians" (1939); "Education in the Cherokee Nation" (1943); and Grayson B. Noley, "The History of Education in the Choctaw Nation from Precolonial Times to 1830" (1979).

Federal involvement in Indian education in the late nineteenth century has attracted more attention. Elaine Goodale Eastman's biography of Pratt, *Pratt* (1935), should be supplemented with Richard Henry Pratt's memoirs, *Battlefield and Classroom* (1964). The most recent dissertations on this subject are: Everett Arthur Gilcreast, "Richard Henry Pratt and American Indian Policy, 1877–1906" (1967), and Pearl Lee Walker-MacNeal, "The Carlisle Indian School" (1979). On the tumultuous demise of contract schooling at this time, see Francis Paul Prucha, *The Churches and the Indian Schools* (1979). Other authors on this period include: David Wallace Adams, "The Federal Indian Boarding School" (1975); Frederick E. Hoxie, "Beyond Savagery" (1977); and Robert A. Trennert, "Peaceably If They Will, Forcibly If They Must" (1979); "Educating Indian Girls at Non-Reservation Boarding Schools, 1878-1920" (1982).[70]

There is one historical synthesis for the twentieth century: Margaret Connell Szasz, *Education and the American Indian* (1977). A survey of the 1960s which stresses Indian response in the recent self-determination period is Estelle Fuchs and Robert J. Havighurst, *To Live on This Earth: American Indian Education* (1972; reprint, 1983). One of the first tribal education histories written from a native point of view is: Henrietta Whiteman, "Cheyenne-Arapaho Education, 1871–1982" (1982).

Native peoples responded in a variety of ways to the demands of these insistent foreigners. Their reaction to white schooling typified the wide spectrum of their responses to Euro-Americans. Decisions on schooling varied from group to group, but even more common was the lack of a unified decision within the single group. Like other dilemmas posed by whites, schooling decisions encouraged factionalism.[71] Within just one band or community, the range of divisive opinion might extend from those who encouraged learning about the white world to those who opposed all white ways, and especially schooling. Individuals who favored white ways were generally called progressives; those who opposed them were known as traditionalists (although each term is vastly oversimplified). Often, though not always, the traditionalists were the full bloods. These two positions represented only the extremes. Many people chose not to side with either camp, preferring to remain in the middle.

While the responses varied, therefore, the spectrum of responses was universal. From a Massachusetts child of the 1660s who was tempted by *The Indian Bible* (1663) or *The Indian Primer* (1669), both written in his own language, to a Flathead youth of the early 1900s who hid under the train platform to avoid going to an off-reservation boarding school, the range of choices has been an integral part of the dilemma. The most poignant record of this historical phenomenon emerges through native accounts, in journals, autobiographies, and fictionalized autobiographies.[72] A few excerpts may illustrate the diversity of situations in which the native youth has encountered white schooling.

An eighteenth-century Mohegan who was later ordained as a Presbyterian minister remembered the threatening nature of his first encounter with whites and their books:

And when I was about 10 Years of age there was a man who went about among the Indian Wigwams, and wherever he Could find the Indian Children, would make them read; but the Children Used to take Care to keep out of his Way: and he used to Catch me Some times and make me Say over my Letters.[73]

By contrast, shortly after the Civil War a Shawnee who had already attended a small day school looked forward to further schooling. Thomas Wildcat Alford remembered:

Those long days that I spent with the cattle, riding my pony back and forth to keep them within their own grazing ground...were days of deep thought. I pondered in my mind the things I had been told, and had read about civilization, and daily the conviction grew upon me that there was a better way to live than my people knew. All my visits with the teachers, my talks with the missionary, fired my ambition and strengthened my determination to make something of myself. I had a keen desire to see other parts of the country which I read about ...but above all I wished to see the wonders of a large city.[74]

A negative recollection of schooling came from a Hopi after he had returned from Sherman Institute, a federal boarding school in California. Many native students were able to serve their people after they attended the white men's schools, but Don Talayesva discovered that his schooling also had its shortcomings:

With marriage I began a life of toil and discovered that education had spoiled me for making a living in the desert. I was not hardened to heavy work in the heat and dust and I did not know how to get rain, control winds, or even predict good and bad weather. I could not grow young plants in dry, wind-beaten, and worm-infested sand drifts; nor could I shepherd a flock of sheep through storm, drought, and disease. I might even lead my family into starvation and be known as the poorest man in Oraibi—able-bodied but unable to support a wife.

Talayesva's elders counseled him further: " 'Talayesva, ... Modern ways help a little; but the Whites come and go, while we Hopi stay on forever.' "[75] In the 1920s a northern Athabaskan echoed Talayesva's words. When Jim Huntington left school at the age of twelve, he concluded: "that was the end of my education. I'd gone through the third reader, which is more than most kids do in this part of the world, and now I was ready to start the learning that was going to keep me going for the rest of my life; how to use what the land had to give you."[76]

Throughout the historic period, then, Euro-Americans and native Americans were well aware of the significance of education. Both knew it to be one of the most effective methods for imparting a world-view. Moreover, of all the varieties of schools introduced by whites, both sides recognized the boarding school as the most successful tool of assimilation. It had a virtual monopoly over the native child for up to nine months in a single year, and sometimes for several years without break. With no competition from home and community, the boarding school was able to instill in its pupils Euro-American patterns of thought and a value system based on some variety of Christianity. Equally important, the school was conducted exclusively through the medium of the English language, which, by definition, reflected and reiterated the culture taught.

Under these circumstances, the boarding schools were not unrealistic in setting as their goals the replacement of their pupils' native culture with that of Euro-Americans. Youths who were away from their people for successive winters missed out on the long evenings of storytelling. Their absence also meant they were unable to train mind and body for physical survival or for the spiritual awareness necessary for maturity. Others found themselves unable to prepare for a guardian spirit quest, and still others, for initiation into a secret society.[77] Moreover, as virtual captive audiences, they were taught values that often contradicted the teachings of their own people. They learned, for example, to stress the importance of the individual rather than the concerns of the extended family or community; they were taught that an agricultural people, such as the Euro-Americans, were on the highest rung of civilization and that all other forms of survival were less civilized; they learned that human beings are superior to all else in nature, and that Euro-American civilization would strive to control this land of theirs and to improve it for the goals of progress.[78] All this and more the native pupils learned at school. Had their teachers been more successful, or had all native youth attended these schools, perhaps the native American cultures might have been erased.

Over the centuries of historic contact, however, native peoples have demonstrated a remarkable elasticity and resilience that have enabled them to incorporate into their cultures the direct challenges of white schooling and religion. Over four centuries, native cultures have changed extensively, but they have not disappeared, and in many surprising ways,

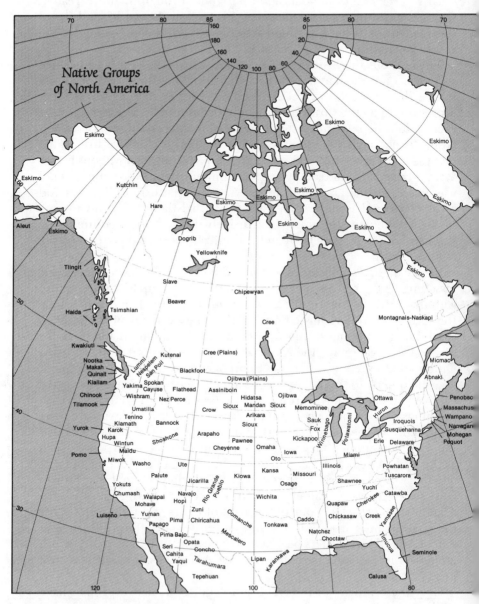

Native Groups
of North America

Prepared by Carol Cooperrider.

they have retained their traditions. They have continued to teach their youth through traditional ways: through storytelling; through instruction and guidance by relatives and elders; and through community gatherings. Many native peoples have also incorporated parts of Christianity through various revitalization movements, such as the Iroquois Longhouse Religion founded in the early nineteenth century by the Seneca prophet, Handsome Lake, or the Native American Church, which entered the United States in the late nineteenth century in the form of peyote rituals introduced to Lipan Apaches by native groups of Mexico, where the use of peyote predated the arrival of Hispanic peoples.[79]

Today the degree of persistence and change in native American childhood varies widely, for in America of the late twentieth century, as in America before the fifteenth century, it remains impossible to generalize about native peoples. At the time of contact, natives lived in widely divergent culture areas and spoke about 250 different languages. Today, while fewer than 150 separate languages are still spoken north of Mexico, native Americans remain a varied people. Some live in remote areas—in regions of the Navajo reservation, or in parts of Canada and Alaska—where they survive without the changes introduced by modern technology. Still others live on the edge of reservations in bordertowns like Gallup, New Mexico, or Toppenish, Washington. A significant percentage live in urban areas, where increasing numbers have emigrated since World War II. Yet, many urban Indians return to their reservations at least once or twice a year, and sometimes more often, for reasons that are difficult to define but, nonetheless, compelling. Still others return to their people when they retire from urban jobs.[80]

Native people, therefore, cannot be described as a single, generalized unit. They are probably as diverse now, though in different ways, as they were when Coronado rode north in 1540 in search of the wealth reputedly held by the Seven Cities of Cibola. Like many who followed him, Coronado had eyes only for material wealth; others, such as the priests and religious figures who joined the front ranks of explorers and colonizers, were concerned primarily with the souls of the natives. Still others voiced concern solely for the "civilized" status of the native Americans. It is history's loss that so few Euro-Americans had eyes for the unique qualities of these many indigenous cultures and for their integrated means for rearing children. After more than four centuries of contact, some of these traditional ways for teaching youth remain strong, attesting through sheer endurance to their proven wisdom.

NOTES

1. William N. Fenton, "Northern Iroquoian Culture Patterns," in Bruce G. Trigger ed., *Handbook of North American Indians, Northeast*, Vol. 15 (Washington, D.C.: Smithsonian Institution, 1978), 314.

2. Charles Alexander Eastman, *Indian Boyhood* (N.p.: Fenwyn Press Books [1902] 1980, reprint), 49.

3. Edward Sapir, "The Emergence of the Concept of Personality in a Study of Culture," *Journal of Social Psychology* 5 (1934): 413, as cited in George A. Pettitt, *Primitive Education in North America*, University of California Publications in American Archaeology and Ethnology, Vol. 43 (Berkeley, Calif., 1946) (cited as *Primitive Education*), 163.

4. See Robert F. Berkhofer, Jr., *The White Man's Indian* (New York: Alfred A. Knopf, 1978), 3–22, and Roy Harvey Pearce, *The Savages of America* (Baltimore: [1953] Johns Hopkins University Press, 1965), 1–49.

5. Alfonso Ortiz, *The Tewa World* (Chicago: University of Chicago Press, 1971), 172–173.

6. Wilfred Pelletier, et al., *for every north American Indian who begins to disappear I also begin to disappear* (Toronto: Neewin Publishing Co., 1971), 8.

7. Robert K. Thomas, "The Role of the Church in Indian Adjustment," in Pelletier, et al., *for every north American*, 88.

8. Pettitt, *Primitive Education*, 5, 22.

9. Myron Jones, "Indian Education Overview," National Institute of Education (unpublished monograph in author's collection, 1977).

10. Boyce Richardson, *Strangers Devour the Land* (New York: Alfred A. Knopf, 1976), 7.

11. Peter Whiteley, "Third Mesa Hopi Social Structural Dynamics and Sociocultural Change: The View from Bacavi" (Ph.D. dissertation, University of New Mexico, 1982), ch. 3.

12. See Philippe Aries, *Centuries of Childhood: A Social History of Family Life* (New York: Alfred A. Knopf, 1962), 96–98.

13. Howard A. Norman, trans., *The Wishing Bone Cycle, Narrative Poems from the Swampy Cree Indians* (New York: Stonehill Publishing Co., 1976), 4.

14. Pablita Velarde, *Old Father, the Story Teller* (Globe, Ariz.: Dale Stuart King, 1960), 25.

15. Allen Quetone (Kiowa), in Sylvester M. Morey, ed., *Can the Red Man Help the White Man? A Denver Conference with the Indian Elders* (New York: Gilbert Church, 1970), 49.

16. Paul Radin, *Crashing Thunder* (New York: D. Appleton & Co., 1926), 71.

17. Leo W. Simmons, *Sun Chief: The Autobiography of a Hopi Indian* (New Haven: Yale University Press, 1971), 51.

18. Sherman Sage (Arapaho), as quoted by Sister M. Inez Hilyer in "Arapaho Child Life and Its Cultural Background," Bureau of American Ethnology (Cited as BAE), *Bulletin* No. 148 (Washington, D.C.: U.S. Government Printing Office, 1952), 100.

19. Victor Barnouw, *Wisconsin Chippewa Myths and Tales and Their Relation to Chippewa Life: Based on Folktales Collected by Victor Barnouw, et al.* (Madison: University of Wisconsin Press, 1977), 4.

20. James P. Spradley, *Guests Never Leave Hungry, the Autobiography of James Sewid, A Kwakiutl Indian* (New Haven: Yale University Press, 1969), 24.

21. Velarde, *Old Father, the Story Teller*, 17.

22. See, for example, Frank James Newcomb, *Hosteen Klah, Navajo Medicine Man and Sand Painter* (Norman: University of Oklahoma Press, 1964); Simmons,

Sun Chief; Anthony F.C. Wallace, *The Death and Rebirth of the Seneca* (New York: Vintage Books, 1972); John C. Neihardt, *Black Elk Speaks* (Lincoln: University of Nebraska Press, 1970).

23. George Spindler, "Personality, Sociocultural System, and Education Among the Menominee," in George Spindler, ed., *Education and Cultural Process: Toward an Anthropology of Education* (New York: Holt, Rinehart & Winston, 1974), 372.

24. Pettitt mentions that Southeastern groups retained both: *Primitive Education*, 38.

25. See Elsie Clew Parsons, "The Social Organization of the Tewa of New Mexico," *American Anthropological Association Memoirs*, No. 36 (Menasha, Wis., 1929), 151; Parsons, "Taos Pueblo," *General Series in Anthropology*, No. 2 (Menasha, Wis.: George Banta Publishing Co., 1936), 46–47.

26. Parts of the guardian spirit quest account are based on interviews with Yakima Indians, 1964–1967. Also see Verne F. Ray, "Native Villages and Groupings of the Columbia River Basin," *Pacific Northwest Quarterly* 27 (April 1936): 99–152.

27. E. Adamson Hoebel, *The Cheyennes, Indians of the Great Plains* (New York: Holt, Rinehart & Winston, 1960), 59.

28. Edna Kenton, ed., *The Indians of North America*, 2 vols. (New York: Harcourt, Brace, 1927), 1: 90, as quoted in Wallace, *Death and Rebirth of the Seneca*, 38. Also see Pettitt, *Primitive Education*, 6.

29. Aleš Hrdlička, *The Aleutian and Commander Islands and Their Inhabitants* (Philadelphia: Wistar Institute of Anatomy, 1945), 72.

30. William W. Newcomb, "The Culture and Acculturation of the Delaware Indians," *Anthropological Papers*, No. 10 (Ann Arbor: Museum of Anthropology, University of Michigan, 1956), 34.

31. Thomas Wildcat Alford, as told to Florence Drake, *Civilization* (Norman: University of Oklahoma Press, 1936), 19.

32. Hilda Mortimer with Chief Dan George, *You Call Me Chief* (Toronto: Doubleday Canada Mtd., 1981), 76.

33. Erna Gunther, "Klallam Ethnography," University of Washington *Publications in Anthropology* (Seattle, 1927), 1: 289.

34. Verne F. Ray, "The San Poil and Nespelem: Salishan People of Northeast Washington," University of Washington *Publications in Anthropology* (Seattle, 1932), 5: 131.

35. Edward Goodbird, *Goodbird. The Indian: His Story*, Gilbert L. Wilson, ed. (New York: Fleming H. Revell Co., 1914), 24.

36. B. H. Quain, "The Iroquois," in Margaret Mead, ed., *Cooperation and Competition Among Primitive Peoples* (New York: McGraw-Hill Book Co., 1937), 272.

37. Hrdlička, *Aleutian and Commander Islands*, 171.

38. Newcomb, "Culture and Acculturation of the Delaware Indians," 34.

39. Richard K. Nelson, *Hunters of the Northern Forest, Designs for Survival Among the Alaskan Kutchin* (Chicago: University of Chicago Press, 1973), 375.

40. Nuligak, *I, Nuligak* (Toronto: Peter Martin Associates, 1968), 57.

41. Parsons, "Taos Pueblo," 40.

42. Margaret Coel, *Chief Left Hand: Southern Arapaho* (Norman: University of Oklahoma Press, 1981), 8–9.

43. Hoebel, *Cheyennes*, 92.

44. William Wood, "New England's Prospect" (1631), in Samuel Eliot Morison, *The Founding of Harvard College* (Cambridge, Mass.: Harvard University Press, 1936), 108.

45. Pettitt, *Primitive Education*, 19.

46. Goodbird, *Goodbird, the Indian*, 24.

47. Clark Wissler, "Social Life of the Blackfoot Indians," American Museum of Natural History, *Anthropological Papers* (New York, 1911), 7: 24, as quoted in Pettitt, *Primitive Education*, 51.

48. On this phenomenon among the Hopi, see Simmons, *Sun Chief*; and Wayne Dennis, *The Hopi Child* (New York: John Wiley & Sons, 1967 reprint), 65–66.

49. Clark Wissler, *The American Indian* (New York: Oxford University Press, 1922), as cited in Pettitt, *Primitive Education*, 50.

50. John A. Swanton, "Source Material for the Social and Ceremonial Life of the Choctaw Indians," BAE *Bulletin* No. 103 (Washington, D.C.: Smithsonian Institution, 1931), 198–199.

51. Eastman, *Indian Boyhood*, 9–10.

52. Pettitt, *Primitive Education*, 48.

53. Leslie Spier and Edward Sapir, "Wishram Ethnography," University of Washington *Publications in Anthropology*, Vol. 3, 1929–1930 (Seattle, 1931), 261.

54. Hugh A. Dempsey, *Red Crow, Warrior Chief* (Lincoln: University of Nebraska Press, 1980), 17.

55. Truman Michelson, ed., "The Autobiography of a Fox Woman," BAE, Fortieth *Annual Report* (Washington, D.C.: Smithsonian Institution, 1925), 299.

56. Truman Michelson, ed., "Narrative of a Southern Cheyenne Woman," Smithsonian *Miscellaneous Collections*, Vol. 87, No. 5 (Washington, D.C.: Smithsonian Institution, 1932), 3.

57. Doris Duke collections are located at the following universities: Arizona, Florida, Illinois, New Mexico, Oklahoma, and Utah.

58. See Alfred W. Crosby, Jr., *The Columbian Exchange, Biological and Cultural Consequences of 1492* (Westport, Conn.: Greenwood Press, 1972).

59. See James Axtell, *The European and the Indian, Essays in the Ethnohistory of Colonial America* (New York: Oxford University Press, 1981).

60. See Henry F. Dobyns, "Estimating Aboriginal American Population: An Appraisal of Techniques with a new Hemispheric Estimate," *Current Anthropology* 7 (October 1966): 395–416. Also useful is Dobyns, *Native American Historical Demography: A Critical Bibliography*, Newberry Library American Indian Bibliographical Series (Bloomington: University of Indiana, 1976).

61. Francis Jennings, *The Invasion of America, Indians, Colonialism, and the Cant of Conquest* (New York: Norton Library and University of North Carolina Press, 1976), 30. Wilbur R. Jacobs, "The Tip of an Iceberg: Pre-Columbian Indian Demography and Some Implications for Revisionism," *William and Mary Quarterly*, 3d ser., 31 (January 1974): 128.

62. Bruce G. Trigger, "Ontario Native People and the Epidemics of 1634–1640," in Shepard Krech III, ed., *Indians, Animals, and the Fur Trade, A Critique of Keepers of the Game* (Athens: University of Georgia Press, 1981), 24–26.

63. See, for example, John C. Ewers, "The Horse in Blackfoot Indian Culture, with Comparative Material from Other Western Tribes," BAE *Bulletin* No. 59

(Washington, D.C.: U.S. Government Printing Office, 1955); Laverne Harrell Clark, *They Sang for Horses: The Impact of the Horse on Navajo and Apache Folklore* (Tucson: University of Arizona Press, 1966).

64. Michelson, ed., "Narrative of a Southern Cheyenne Woman," 1.

65. Nuligak, *I, Nuligak*, 14, 53.

66. Alford, *Civilization*, 82.

67. Eleazar Wheelock, *A Plain and Faithful Narrative of the Original Design, Rise, Progress and Present State of the Indian Charity-School at Lebanon, in Connecticut* ([1763]; Rochester Reprint, Rochester, New York, n.d.), 21.

68. Helen Sekaquaptewa, *Me and Mine, The Life Story of Helen Sekaquaptewa as Told to Louise Udall* (Tucson: University of Arizona Press, 1969), 31–32.

69. Elizabeth A. John, *Storms Brewed in Other Men's Worlds* (College Station: Texas A and M Press, 1975), see ch. 3, esp. 148–150.

70. See also David Wallace Adams, "Education in Hues: Red and Black at Hampton Institute, 1878–1893," *South Atlantic Quarterly* 76 (Spring 1977): 159–176; and Frederick E. Hoxie, "Redefining Indian Education: Thomas J. Morgan's Program in Disarray," *Arizona and the West* 24 (Spring 1982): 5–18.

71. For the Hopi response, see David Wallace Adams, "Schooling the Hopi: The Federal Indian Policy Writ Small, 1887–1917," *Pacific Historical Review* 48 (August 1979): 335–356; Whiteley, "Third Mesa Hopi Social Structural Dynamics," ch. 4; Sekaquaptewa, *Me and Mine*, 63–131; and Edmund Nequatewa, *Truth of a Hopi* (Flagstaff: Museum of Northern Arizona (1936) (1967), chs. 12–14.

72. See, for example, D'Arcy McNickle, *The Surrounded* (1936; Albuquerque: University of New Mexico Press, 1978).

73. Harold Blodgett, *Samson Occom* (Hanover, N.H.: Dartmouth College, 1935), 29.

74. Alford, *Civilization*, 85–86.

75. Simmons, *Sun Chief*, 224.

76. James Huntington, as told to Lawrence Elliott, *On the Edge of Nowhere* (New York: Crown Publishers, 1966), 57.

77. According to Morris Edward Opler in his *Apache Life Way* (New York: Cooper Square Publishers, 1965), the Chiracahua Apache relate many of their important myths only in winter (34–35). Thus, the boarding school interrupted this training. At Taos Pueblo, however, even day schools interfered with the lengthy initiation. See Parsons, "Taos Pueblo," 46.

78. See Brian W. Dippie, *The Vanishing American* (Middletown, Conn.: Wesleyan University, 1982), 29–31; Pearce, *Savages of America*, 155–160.

79. See Anthony F.C. Wallace, "Revitalization Movements," *American Anthropologist* 58 (1956): 264–281; Wallace, "Origins of the Longhouse Religion," in Trigger, ed., *Handbook of North American Indians, Northeast*, 15: 442–448; and G. A. Moses and Margaret Connell Szasz, " 'My Father, Have Pity on Me': Indian Revitalization Movements of the Late Nineteenth Century," *Journal of the West* 23 (January 1985): 5–15.

80. See Whiteley, "Third Mesa Hopi Social Structural Dynamics," ch. 5 (Table 11).

BIBLIOGRAPHY

Adair, James. *The History of the American Indians, particularly those nations adjoining to the Mississippi*... London: E. & C. Dilly, 1775.

Adams, David Wallace. "Education in Hues: Red and Black at Hampton Institute, 1878–1893." *South Atlantic Quarterly* 76 (Spring 1977): 159–176.

———. "The Federal Indian Boarding School: A Study of Environment and Response, 1879–1918." Ed.D. dissertation, Indiana University, 1975.

———. "Schooling the Hopi: The Federal Indian Policy Writ Small, 1887–1917." *Pacific Historical Review* 48 (August 1979): 335–356.

Adams, Evelyn C. *American Indian Education: Government Schools and Economic Progress.* New York: Arno, 1971 (reprint).

Alford, Thomas Wildcat, as told to Florence Drake. *Civilization.* Norman: University of Oklahoma Press, 1936.

Aries, Philippe. *Centuries of Childhood: A Social History of Family Life.* New York: Alfred A. Knopf, 1962.

Axtell, James. *The European and the Indian, Essays in the Ethnohistory of Colonial America.* New York: Oxford University Press, 1981.

Barnouw, Victor. *Wisconsin Chippewa Myths and Tales and Their Relation to Chippewa Life: Based on Folktales Collected by Victor Barnouw, et al.* Madison: University of Wisconsin Press, 1977.

Berkhofer, Robert F., Jr. *The White Man's Indian.* New York: Alfred A. Knopf, 1978.

Blodgett, Harold. *Samson Occom.* Hanover, N.H.: Dartmouth College, 1935.

Brumble, H. David, III. *An Annotated Bibliography of American Indian and Eskimo Autobiographies.* Lincoln: University of Nebraska Press, 1981.

Clark, Laverne Harrell. *They Sang for Horses: The Impact of the Horse on Navaho and Apache Folklore.* Tucson: University of Arizona Press, 1966.

Coel, Margaret. *Chief Left Hand: Southern Arapaho.* Norman: University of Oklahoma Press, 1981.

Crosby, Alfred W., Jr. *The Columbian Exchange, Biological and Cultural Consequences of 1492.* Westport, Conn.: Greenwood Press, 1972.

Davis, Caroline. "Education of the Chickasaw, 1856–1907." *Chronicles of Oklahoma* 15 (December 1937): 415–448.

Dempsey, Hugh A. *Red Crow, Warrior Chief.* Lincoln: University of Nebraska Press, 1980.

Dennis, Wayne. *The Hopi Child.* New York: John Wiley & Sons, 1967 (reprint).

Dippie, Brian W. *The Vanishing American.* Middletown, Conn.: Wesleyan University Press, 1982.

Dobyns, Henry F. "Estimating Aboriginal American Population: An Appraisal of Techniques with a New Hemispheric Estimate." *Current Anthropology* 7 (October 1966): 395–416.

———. *Native American Historical Demography: A Critical Bibliography.* Newberry Library American Indian Bibliographical Series. Bloomington: University of Indiana, 1976.

Driver, Harold E. *Indians of North America.* Chicago: University of Chicago Press, 1961.

Eastman, Charles Alexander. *Indian Boyhood.* N.p.: Fenwyn Press Books, 1980 (reprint).

Eastman, Elaine Goodale. *Pratt: The Red Man's Moses.* Norman: University of Oklahoma Press, 1935.

Ewers, John C. "The Horse in Blackfoot Indian Culture, with Comparative

Material from Other Western Tribes." BAE *Bulletin* No. 59. Washington, D.C.: U.S. Government Printing Office, 1955.

Fenton, William N. "Northern Iroquoian Culture Patterns." In *Handbook of North American Indians, Northeast,* edited by Bruce G. Trigger, pp. 296–321. Vol. 15.

Fischbacher, Theodore. "A Study of the Role of the Federal Government in the Education of the American Indian." Ph.D. dissertation, Arizona State University, 1967.

Foreman, Carolyn Thomas. "Education Among the Chickasaw Indians." *Chronicles of Oklahoma* 15 (June 1937): 139–165.

Fuchs, Estelle, and Havighurst, Robert J. *To Live on This Earth: American Indian Education.* Albuquerque: University of New Mexico Press, 1983 (reprint).

Gilcreast, Everett Arthur. "Richard Henry Pratt and American Indian Policy, 1887–1906: A Study of the Assimilation Movement." Ph.D. dissertation, Yale University, 1967.

Goodbird, Edward. *Goodbird. The Indian: His Story.* Edited by Gilbert L. Wilson. New York: Fleming H. Revell Co., 1914.

Gunther, Erna. "Klallam Ethnography." University of Washington *Publications in Anthropology.* Vol. 1, Seattle, 1927.

Heckewelder, John. *An Account of the History, Manners and Customs of the Indian Nations Who once Inhabited Pennsylvania and the Neighboring States.* New Haven: Human Area Relation Files, 1961 (reprint).

Hilyer, Sister M. Inez. "Arapaho Child Life and Its Cultural Background." BAE *Bulletin* No. 148. Washington, D.C.: U.S. Government Printing Office, 1952.

Hirschfelder, Arlene B., ed. *American Indian and Eskimo Authors.* New York: Association on American Indian Affairs, 1975.

Hoebel, E. Adamson. *The Cheyennes, Indians of the Great Plains.* New York: Holt, Rinehart & Winston, 1960.

Hoxie, Frederick E. "Beyond Savagery: The Campaign to Assimilate the American Indian, 1880–1920." Ph.D. dissertation, Brandeis University, 1977.

———. "Redefining Indian Education: Thomas J. Morgan's Program in Disarray." *Arizona and the West* 24 (Spring 1982): 5–18.

Hrdlička, Aleš. *The Aleutian and Commander Islands and Their Inhabitants.* Philadelphia: Wistar Institute of Anatomy, 1945.

Huntington, James, as told to Lawrence Elliott. *On the Edge of Nowhere.* New York: Crown Publishers, 1966.

Jacobs, Wilbur F. "The Tip of an Iceberg: Pre-Columbian Indian Demography and Some Implications for Revisionism." *William and Mary Quarterly,* 3d ser., 31 (January 1974): 123–132.

Jennings, Francis. "Goals and Functions of Puritan Missions to the Indians." *Ethnohistory* 18 (Summer 1971): 197–212.

John, Elizabeth A. *Storms Brewed in Other Men's Worlds.* College Station: Texas A and M Press, 1975.

Jones, Myron. "Indian Education Overview." National Institute of Education, 1977. (Unpublished monograph in author's collection.)

Knepler, Abraham E. "Education in the Cherokee Nation." *Chronicles of Oklahoma* 21 (December 1943): 378–401.

──────. "The Education of the Cherokee Indians." Ph.D. dissertation, Yale University, 1939.

Layman, Martha Elizabeth. "A History of Indian Education in the United States." Ph.D. dissertation, University of Minnesota, 1942.

Littlefield, Daniel, Jr., and Parins, James W., eds. *A Biobibliography of Native American Writers, 1772–1924*. Metuchen, N.J.: Scarecrow Press, 1981.

McNickle, D'Arcy. *The Surrounded*. Albuquerque: University of New Mexico Press, 1978 (reprint).

Marken, Jack W., ed. *The Indians and Eskimos of North America: A Bibliography of Books in Print through 1972*. Vermillion, S.D.: Dakota Press, 1973.

Michelson, Truman, ed. "The Autobiography of a Fox Woman." BAE, Fortieth *Annual Report*. Washington, D.C.: Smithsonian Institution, 1925, pp. 291–345.

──────. "Narrative of a Southern Cheyenne Woman." Smithsonian *Miscellaneous Collections*. Vol. 87, No. 5. Washington, D.C.: Smithsonian Institution, 1932.

Morey, Sylvester M., ed. *Can the Red Man Help the White Man? A Denver Conference with the Indian Elders*. New York: Gilbert Church, 1970.

Morris, Edward Opler. *An Apache Life Way*. New York: Cooper Square Publishers, 1965.

Morris, Harold W. "A History of Indian Education in the United States." Ph.D. dissertation, Oregon State University, 1954.

Mortimer, Hilda, with Chief Dan George. *You Call Me Chief*. Toronto: Doubleday Canada Mtd., 1981.

Moses, G.A., and Margaret Connell Szasz. " 'My Father Have Pity on Me': Indian Revitalization Movements of the Late Nineteenth Century." *Journal of the West* 23 (January 1985): 5–15.

Murdock, Peter, and O'Leary, Timothy J. *Ethnographic Bibliography of North America*. 4th ed., 5 vols., New Haven: Human Area Relations Files Press, 1973.

Neihardt, John C. *Black Elk Speaks*. Lincoln: University of Nebraska Press, 1970 (reprint).

Nelson, Richard K. *Hunters of the Northern Forest, Designs for Survival Among the Alaskan Kutchin*. Chicago: University of Chicago Press, 1973.

Nequatewa, Edmund. *Truth of a Hopi*. Flagstaff: Museum of Northern Arizona, 1967 (reprint).

Newcomb, Frank James. *Hosteen Klah, Navajo Medicine Man and Sand Painter*. Norman: University of Oklahoma Press, 1964.

Newcomb, William W. "The Culture and Acculturation of the Delaware Indians." *Anthropological Papers*, No. 10. Ann Arbor: Museum of Anthropology, University of Michigan, 1956.

Noley, Grayson B. "The History of Education in the Choctaw Nation from Precolonial Times to 1830." Ph.D. dissertation, Pennsylvania State University, 1979.

Norman, Howard A., trans. *The Wishing Bone Cycle, Narrative Poems from the Swampy Cree Indians*. New York: Stonehill Publishing Co., 1976.

Nuligak. *I, Nuligak*. Toronto: Peter Martin Associates, 1968.

──────. *Childhood and Youth in Jicarilla Apache Society*. Los Angeles: Papers of the Southwest Museum, 1946.

Ortiz, Alfonso. *The Tewa World*. Chicago: University of Chicago Press, 1971.

Parsons, Elsie Clew. "The Social Organization of the Tewa of New Mexico." *American Anthropological Association Memoirs*, No. 36. Menasha, Wis., 1929.

Pearce, Roy Harvey. *The Savages of America*. Baltimore: Johns Hopkins University Press, 1965 (reprint).

Pelletier, Wilfred, et al. *for every north American Indian who begins to disappear I also begin to disappear*. Toronto: Neewin Publishing Co., 1971.

Pettitt, George A. *Primitive Education in North America*. University of California Publications in American Archaeology and Ethnology. Vol. 43, Berkeley, Calif., 1946.

Pratt, Richard Henry. *Battlefield and Classroom: Four Decades with the American Indian, 1867–1904*. Edited by Robert M. Utley. New Haven: Yale University Press, 1964.

Prucha, Francis Paul, S.J. *A Bibliographical Guide to the History of Indian-White Relations in the United States*. Chicago: University of Chicago Press, 1977.

———. *The Churches and the Indian Schools*. Lincoln: University of Nebraska Press, 1979.

———. *Indian-White Relations in the United States: A Bibliography of Works Published, 1975–1980*. Lincoln: University of Nebraska Press, 1982.

Quain, B. H. "The Iroquois." In *Cooperation and Competition Among Primitive Peoples*, edited by Margaret Mead. New York: McGraw-Hill Book Co., 1937.

Radin, Paul. *Crashing Thunder*. New York: D. Appleton & Co., 1926.

Ray, Verne F. "Native Villages and Groupings of the Columbia River Basin." *Pacific Northwest Quarterly* 27 (April 1936): 99–152.

———. "The San Poil and Nespelem: Salishan People of Northeast Washington." University of Washington *Publications in Anthropology*. Vol. 5, Seattle, 1932.

Richardson, Boyce. *Strangers Devour the Land*. New York: Alfred A. Knopf, 1976.

Robinson, W. Stitt, Jr. "Indian Education and Missions in Colonial Virginia. *Journal of Southern History* 18 (May 1952): 152–168.

Ronda, James P. "Generations of Faith: The Christian Indians of Martha's Vineyard." *William and Mary Quarterly*, 3d ser., 38 (July 1981): 369–394.

———, and Axtell, James. *Indian Missions: A Critical Biography*. Newberry Library American Indian Bibliographical Series. Bloomington: Indiana University Press, 1978.

Salisbury, Neal Emerson. "Conquest of the 'Savage': Puritans, Puritan Missionaries, and Indians, 1620–1680." Ph.D. dissertation, University of California at Los Angeles, 1972.

———. "Red Puritans: The 'Praying Indians' of Massachusetts Bay and John Eliot." *William and Mary Quarterly*, 3d ser., 31 (January 1974): 27–54.

Seaver, James Everett. *A Narrative of the Life of Mrs. Mary Jamison, who was taken captive by the Indians in 1775 . . .* Canadaigua, N.Y.: J. D. Bemis & Co., 1824.

Sekaquaptewa, Helen. *Me and Mine, The Life Story of Helen Sekaquaptewa as Told to Louise Udall*. Tucson: University of Arizona Press, 1969.

Simmons, Leo W. *Sun Chief: The Autobiography of a Hopi*. New Haven: Yale University Press, 1971.

Spier, Leslie, and Sapir, Edward. "Wishram Ethnography." University of Washington *Publications in Anthropology*. Vol. 3, 1929–1930, Seattle, 1931.

Spindler, George. "Personality, Sociocultural System, and Education Among the

Menominee." In *Education and Cultural Process: Toward an Anthropology of Education*, edited by George Spindler. New York: Holt, Rinehart & Winston, 1974.

Spradley, James P. *Guests Never Leave Hungry, the Autobiography of James Sewid, A Kwakiutl Indian*. New Haven: Yale University Press, 1969.

Swanton, John A. "Source Material for the Social and Ceremonial Life of the Choctaw Indians." BAE *Bulletin* No. 103. Washington, D.C.: Smithsonian Institution, 1931.

Szasz, Margaret Connell. *Education and the American Indian: The Road to Self-Determination Since 1928*. Albuquerque: University of New Mexico Press, 1977.

——. " 'Poor Richard' Meets the Native American Schooling for Young Indian women in Eighteenth-Century Connecticut." *Pacific Historical Review* 49 (May 1980): 215–235.

Thomas, Robert K. "The Role of the Church in Indian Adjustment." In *for every north American Indian who begins to disappear I also begin to disappear*, by Wilfred Pelletier, pp. 87–108.

Trennert, Robert A. "Educating Indian Girls at Non-Reservation Boarding Schools, 1878–1920." *Western Historical Quarterly* 13 (July 1982): 271–290.

——. "Peaceably If They Will, Forcibly If They Must: The Phoenix Indian School, 1890–1901." *Journal of Arizona History* 20 (Autumn 1979): 314–317.

Trigger, Bruce G. *The Children of Aetaentsic: A History of the Huron People to 1660*. 2 vols., Montreal: McGill-Queen University Press, 1976.

——. *Handbook of North American Indians, Northeast*. Vol. 15, Washington, D.C.: Smithsonian Institution, 1978.

——. "Ontario Native Peoples and the Epidemics of 1634–1640." In *Indians, Animals, and the Fur Trade, A Critique of Keepers of the Game*, edited by Sheperd Krech III, pp. 19–38. Athens: University of Georgia Press, 1981.

Velarde, Pablita. *Old Father, the Story Teller*. Globe, Ariz.: Dale Stuart King, 1960.

Walker-MacNeal, Pearl Lee. "The Carlisle Indian School: A Study of Acculturation." Ph.D. dissertation, American University, 1979.

Wallace, Anthony F.C. *The Death and Rebirth of the Seneca*. New York: Vintage Books, 1972.

——. "Origins of the Longhouse Religion." In *Handbook of North American Indians, Northeast*, edited by Bruce G. Trigger, pp. 442–448. Vol. 15.

——. "Revitalization Movements." *American Anthropologist* 58 (1956): 264–281.

Wheelock, Eleazar. *A Plain and Faithful Narrative of the Original Design, Rise, Progress and Present State of the Indian Charity-School at Lebanon, in Connecticut, 1763*: Rochester Reprint. Rochester, N.Y., n.d.

Whiteley, Peter. "Third Mesa Hopi Social Structural Dynamics and Sociocultural Change: The View from Bacavi." Ph.D. dissertation, University of New Mexico, 1982.

Whiteman, Henrietta. "Cheyenne-Arapaho Education, 1871–1982." Ph.D. dissertation, University of New Mexico, 1982.

Wissler, Clark. *The American Indian*. New York: Oxford University Press, 1922.

9

Ethnicity and American Children

Selma Berrol

This chapter deals with the ethnic factor in American childhood. That such a factor exists should be clear; in a pluralistic society such as ours, the experience of growing up American was strongly affected by the process of fitting the customs, traditions, and culture of one's own group into those of the majority. The child of immigrants and those whose ancestors had come as slaves had problems Yankee children did not. Finding their place in the mainstream was not easy because they had barriers of law, custom, bigotry, and economics to overcome. In any case, the life of such a child was likely to be quite different from the childhood of many white, native-born Americans whose parents had been here for many years.

Ethnicity, of course, is only one of many forces affecting childhood. Ethnic groups are composed of individuals, and the children of these individuals were as much shaped by the differences in their gender, personality, parentage, and upbringing as by their ethnic background. Time is another factor. Even for children of the same ethnic heritage, when they were born affected their chances of basic survival as well as the nature of the opportunities that would be available to them. Geography is also a modifier. Children of diverse ethnic backgrounds living in rural areas often had more in common with each other than with their city cousins. Conditions in the larger society, such as child labor laws and the availability of formal education, were of the greatest significance, transcending ethnic differences.

But even after considering all the caveats, it is clear that ethnicity, either in combination with these factors or standing alone, *did* make a difference in children's lives. This seems to be particularly true of the physical conditions under which they were raised, their relationships to their parents, their school and work experiences, and the ways in which they dealt with the process of assimilation. Consequently, these topics provide a framework within which the influence of ethnicity on American childhood can be examined. This cannot be a comprehensive study; the diversity of the groups that have peopled America does not permit it. It will, rather, be a selective discussion, dwelling on the most suitable evidence available, regardless of the group. Sometimes comparisons will be appropriate, but given the problems of chronology and diversity, most often this will not be a viable approach. In such cases, the experiences of one group must stand alone, none the less significant, however, for being unique.

A great deal has been written about the physical conditions under which immigrants and their children lived. Much of this material comes to us by way of memoirs, and some through the eyes of observers who were often appalled by what they saw.[1] Both sources are somewhat suspect. The first because it is often filtered through a cloud of nostalgia and the latter colored by the reformer's zeal. Still, used with care, memories and exposés can be very useful when we attempt to reconstruct the daily lives of the "little aliens." Recent work has provided similar information about black children under slavery, some of it drawn from the recollections of elderly blacks interviewed for a Works Progress Administration (WPA) project in the 1930s and some stimulated by controversies over the physical treatment of slaves and their children.[2]

The chance of survival, since it was basic to anything else that happened to the child, seems like the best place to start a discussion of the physical aspects of the ethnic child's experience. In his now classic work on immigrant life in mid-nineteenth-century New York City, Robert Ernst says that two-thirds of all the deaths recorded in the city were of children under five years old, the majority of whom had been born to Irish immigrant families.[3] Virginia Yans-McLoughlin presents an equally grim picture of Italian child mortality in Buffalo, New York, some years later. One-third of all the Italian children born there died at an early age due to unsanitary conditions in their overcrowded homes as well as diseases such as cholera, tuberculosis, and infant diarrhea. Partly as a result of incompetent handling by midwives, many never survived the process of birth. Poor diet, sometimes the result of parental desire to save every penny and buy a house, also contributed to infant deaths.[4]

The matter of diet seems to have much to do with the much lower mortality figures for children born to East European Jewish families during a comparable period. In New York City, between 1911 and 1916, the death rate for children born to East European Jewish mothers was only 54 per every 1,000 births, while for other foreign-born white mothers it was 127 and for native-born whites it was 94. Neonatal rates are even more startling: for East European Jews, 28 per 1,000, other foreign-born whites, 46, and native-born whites, 42. The author of this study, Jacob J. Lindenthal, attributes the survival of more East European Jewish babies and children largely to a better diet, both for nursing mothers who weaned their children late and for the children themselves. Alfred Kazin reinforces this when he says that he and his playmates in the working-class Jewish community of Brownsville, Brooklyn, were never given a chance to find out what hunger meant. Mothers were constantly offering sweets, soda, halavah, and chocolate milk, and urging their children to "fix themselves" by eating.[5]

Diet is also a central theme in a most interesting recent article on slave child mortality. Kenneth and Virginia Kiple state that in the mid-nineteenth century, three out of every ten slave babies died before their first birthday and 50 percent died before they were ten years old, a rate more than double that of their white contemporaries. The cause was inappropriate diet, high in carbohydrates and low in protein and calcium. Black infants were weaned early and were unable to benefit from cow's milk because of a genetic lactose intolerance. The Kiples explain this condition by reference to the tsetse fly problem in the West African territories from which most of the slaves came. The insect made cattle raising impossible, and over generations, therefore, children in this part of the world did without cow's milk. They did not develop diseases like rickets, however, because of the "abundant African sun." In the United States, black children needed additional calcium but did not receive it.

Except for saying that the planter owners believed that slave children should eat lots of fat meat and corn in order to become "plump and shiny," the Kiples do not think deliberate mistreatment was to blame for the nutritional deficiencies of black children. Instead, they believe that their susceptibility to infectious diseases, cavities, and bone and skin defects were the result of a mismatch of their African biological heritage and conditions found in North America, exacerbated by ignorance.[6]

In spite of Lindenthal's food-centered explanation of low East European Jewish infant mortality rates, the settlement workers and teachers who worked on the Lower East Side of New York City at the height of the Jewish and Italian immigration believed that the children from both groups were inadequately fed. John Spargo's *The Bitter Cry of the Children* (1906) blamed low wages and consequent poverty for the problem and urged that the schools provide free meals for the children of the poor. Other Progressives joined his campaign, and the result was the formation of a committee that provided cheap (three-penny) and nutritious, although not altogether free, school lunches.

At its start the program was a failure. Reflecting their first-generation tastes, the children hated the bland, American-style food presented to them and preferred to spend their pennies on pickles and soft drinks from the pushcarts that clustered around each school. Dismayed, because pickles were considered a dangerous stimulant leading to eventual alcoholism, the committee began to provide ethnically differentiated lunches. They served kosher food in the schools east of the Bowery, where the population was overwhelmingly Jewish, and offered pasta on the west side, in Little Italy. These changes attracted many more children, and the program became a formal part of the public school budget in 1919.[7]

The urban ethnic child who survived infancy and the perils of an inadequate diet was also endangered by the terrible housing in which he or she lived. Oscar Handlin has written movingly of the cellar apartments and back alleys in which the Boston Irish lived in the mid-nineteenth century, and a variety of observers have told us of the crowded tenements that were homes to the immigrant groups that came to New York City later.[8] One of the most complete reports on immigrant housing was provided by Jeremiah Jencks, who summarized many of the findings of the U.S. Immigration Commission report of 1911 in his book, *The Immigration Problem.*

Jencks pointed out that there was much more congestion in foreign than in native-born households, both white and black. The Commission had found that Italians, Poles, and Russian Jews lived under the most crowded conditions. Thirty-two percent of the immigrant families had three persons sleeping in each bedroom, as opposed to only 18 percent of native-born households. Almost a fourth of the Italians included in the report had made all of their rooms into sleeping rooms. Jencks went on to describe a typical tenement apartment: four rooms of which the rear room was the kitchen, dining room, and living room, containing a stove, table, chairs, and laundry tub. Many such apartments lacked running water or toilet facilities, which made the families dependent on a privy in the back yard and a pump in the basement.[9]

Jacob Riis described the housing of Mulberry Bend in New York's Little Italy as consisting of tiny, dark, dank rooms. He singled out a building called the Mott Street Barracks which was home to 360 families, including 40 babies, living under the worst imaginable conditions. There is a strong resemblance between his description of this building and what Robert Ernst has told us of a pesthole called the Old Brewery located in the same general area of Manhattan some fifty years earlier. The immigrant poor, whether Irish or Italian, endured terrible housing.[10]

A most vivid description of the apartments that were home to millions of ethnic children comes from Samuel Chotzinoff's memoirs. He remembers that, in 1899, his family of eight lived in a three-room "railroad" flat in lower Manhattan. His parents slept in the only real bed, located in the windowless middle room, his sisters slept on improvised beds on the floor of the front room, and he, the only son, slept on four kitchen chairs, arranged for him each night and taken apart for breakfast. Harry Roskolenko's family, living at the same time and in the same place, found a different solution. All their rooms except the kitchen were filled with tiers of beds, fun to climb into, bad when one fell out.

Dr. Morris Fishberg practiced on the lower East Side in the first decade of the twentieth century and has left us his recollections of the tenements he visited. Called "double deckers" or "dumbells," they were six or seven stories high and built on a lot of 25 by 100 feet. Each floor held four apartments, two with four rooms each in the front and two with three rooms in the rear. There were two water closets to a floor but no bathing facilities other than the kitchen sink. Fishberg was most critical of the airshafts that were supposed to provide light and air to the middle room of each flat but instead were usually sources of noise and foul smells. Fishberg also describes crowding worse than Chotzinoff and Roskolenko remember. The apartments he visited rented for $10 to $18 a month, and most families needed to take in boarders in order to manage. In his own words:

A family consisting of husband, wife and six to eight children whose ages ranged from one to twenty-five years slept as follows: The parents occupy the small bedroom together with two, three or even four of the younger children. In the kitchen, on cots and on the floor, are the older children; in the front room two or more . . . lodgers sleep on the lounge, on the floor and on cots.[11]

Another version of immigrant housing was common to those families who were petty entrepreneurs. Jade Snow Wong grew up in San Francisco in the 1930s. Her parents operated a small clothing factory in which the entire family worked. The six of them lived either in a room behind the shop or, if business was brisk and that space was needed for work, in a storeroom above.[12]

There was almost no time for play in Jade Wong's life, but other ethnic children widened their physical horizons by outdoor activities. Jewish immigrant parents viewed such pursuits with a somewhat jaundiced eye. Street play, with good reason, was seen as dangerous. The congestion and traffic on urban slum streets made ball playing and kite flying difficult and risky. But organized sports, played in a more protected setting, were equally in disfavor. They were considered a waste of time that could be spent studying or working and a threat to the child's physical well-being. Baseball, basketball, and handball, after all, could result in bodily injury.

The issue was important enough to come before Abraham Cahan, the editor of the well-known Yiddish newspaper, the *Forward*. Cahan came down hard on the side of athletics, telling the concerned parents who wrote to him that, contrary to their fears, sports were healthy. Outdoor physical activities, he said, would build the size and strength of small and hollow-chested ghetto boys. Even more important, sports were the American way, and learning how to play baseball, for example, was sure proof that an immigrant child had entered the mainstream. To help acculturation proceed, the *Forward* printed a long article, complete with a glossary of terms, describing the American national game.[13]

In spite of Cahan's exhortations, relatively few East European Jewish children became successful athletes. Like Jade Snow Wong, their days were too filled with school and chores to allow much time for sports. Play seems to have occupied a larger part of the slave child's life. According to David K. Wiggins's article on this subject, few demands were placed on slave children until they were twelve or older. As a result, they had plenty of time for simple games like marbles, as well as more energetic athletic activities. Their play was often imitative of events that took place on the plantation such as religious services, funerals, auctions, and whippings.

Both Wiggins and Eugene Genovese suggest that games organized around the two latter activities represented attempts on the part of the children to neutralize and exorcise their fears. Carrying psychological theorizing further, Wiggins says that the children did not play games that revolved around the elimination of one of the contestants; indeed, they avoided games of chance in general and preferred those where skill was important. He suggests that the fear of losing a relative by forced sale and the uncertainties of their real life, dependent as they were on the whims and wishes of their owners, led slave children to prefer games that could be won solely by their own efforts, without any element of chance involved.[14]

Whatever the reason behind the games slave children played, it would seem that since they neither worked nor went to school, they had more time for play than most immigrant children did. The latter were often burdened with school (sometimes two schools, public and religious or cultural) *and* work. In general, school experiences differed widely, and many immigrant children, like almost all slave children, received no education at all. If he came to the United States before his tenth birthday, an immigrant boy was more likely to spend his time in school; if he came at a later age, he was more likely to go to work. This was true even if his family settled in a state with compulsory education laws because during the nineteenth century and for a good portion of the twentieth, these laws were erratically enforced. Girls, regardless of their age on arrival, were even less likely to go to school for any length of time.

For either sex, however, freedom from the classroom did not mean freedom to play. The girl who did not go to school was usually her mother's assistant, or, if the mother worked outside the home, a mother surrogate. Boys who did not attend school did unskilled work and, in the cities, plied different street trades. They were newsboys, wood gatherers, bootblacks, peddlers, and messengers. Children of both sexes worked *after* school, many times at home work on garments or artificial flowers. Jacob Riis reported on backyard "factories" in which tiny Italian children worked at pulling basting threads, while slightly older ones covered buttons with silk to be sold at four cents a gross.[15]

According to a survey done by two opponents of child labor in 1905, foreign-born white children constituted the largest proportion of the national child labor force. Most of them were at least twelve years old, but about one-fifth of the total was younger.[16] The provisions of the 1903 New York Child Labor Law demonstrates how this could occur. Full-time factory work was permissible for children of fourteen; part-time employment was legal for those between twelve and fourteen. Unfortunately, poor enforcement allowed even these minimum rules to be violated. In spite of the fact that working papers were required for children under sixteen and factories were to be regularly inspected, parents often tried to pass off a large and sturdy child as older than he really was, and neither the Board of Health nor the employer would question the parents' statement. Even with better enforcement, the absence of birth certificates for children born abroad made it very difficult to prevent a child who *looked* old enough from working.[17]

Eva McDonald Valesh, who did an article on child labor for the *American Federationist* in 1907, claimed that it was ignorance, not greed, that made immigrant parents want to put their children into factory work at an early age. Because they came from rural, pre-industrialized societies, Valesh thought that they equated factory labor with the work children in rural societies had always done. Consequently, they underestimated the harm that could come to young bodies in an industrial environment.

To modern eyes, this explanation seems rather patronizing; common sense dictates that adult immigrants would know that, even for themselves, working in mines and factories was much more dangerous than doing farm labor. Why then would they not see this to be true for their weaker children? It seems far more likely that most illegal child labor was the result of the employers' desire to pay lower wages and the desperate need of many immigrant families for additional income.[18]

Fred Hall, a long-time member of the New York Child Labor Committee, was delighted with the 1913 law that prohibited home work for children under fourteen. Many immigrant parents, however, were not. Hall deplored their opposition but understood the economic realities that lay behind it. He reserved most of his anger for the greedy manufacturers who supplied the materials to the families. The law itself was basically unenforceable because it allowed the suppliers to treat all home workers as subcontractors about whose labor practices they did not have to be concerned.[19]

Virginia Yans-McLoughlin found that both economic need and the

South Italian view of the child as part of the family unit rather than as an individual led to widespread child labor among the members of this group who lived in Buffalo. Each summer entire families encamped on the Niagara Frontier to pick and can the farm produce of the region. The child never received anything for this work; everything he or she was paid became part of the family's resources. This same focus on the family's needs also led to year-round child labor for some. Buffalo's Italian children went onto the streets and into candy and box factories at an early age.[20]

Some Italian boys suffered an even worse fate. Although the numbers were probably exaggerated, almost every American city had young Italian boys working as street musicians under the control of padrones. Most had been recruited in Italy where in exchange for transportation to America, parents had entrusted their sons to the care of an older man. These boys, like their Greek counterparts who usually worked as bootblacks, were badly exploited and often abused, but the practice was difficult to eliminate. The padrone, or more likely a stand-in he hired, would pretend to be the father of a newly arrived boy, and nothing much could be done to prevent his entry.[21]

Every immigrant group, although not every family in the group, depended on their children's labor in their early years in America. In New York, first-generation Irish and German children worked as fruit, nut, and candy peddlers and in the infant garment industry. Chinese children were especially useful if their parents were operating laundries. They sorted the soiled articles, folded the clean, ironed, and were the interpreters between their parents and English-speaking customers. Technological changes and the upward mobility of earlier Chinese immigrants have decreased the number of Chinese hand laundries, but even in 1979, Betty Lee Sung found that a significant number of the children of recent Chinese immigrants worked at various jobs for long hours after school was over. Some of them were only in elementary school, that is, less than twelve years old.[22]

The school experiences of immigrant children have been of considerable interest to sociologists, historians, and psychologists. As indicated earlier, generalizations are dangerous because so much of the child's interaction with formal education depended on personal factors, timing, and location. On the other hand, ethnicity, directly or indirectly, did play an important role. The background and economic position of the various groups strongly influenced the extent to which their children went to school and the uses they made of their education.

A number of factors accounted for differences in school usage and performance. One set can be grouped under the general heading of attitudes. Children of ethnic groups who valued education as a road to upward mobility were likely to attend school for more years and have more success as measured by grades, promotion, and teacher approval. Those from a group whose prior experience with formal education had proved destructive (for example, Poles who had attended Russified schools) or useless were much less likely to remain in school more than a few years or to do very well while they were there. This would also be true for children from a group who disagreed with the values and procedures of the American public school. Italian parents, for example, disliked the emphasis on individualism and self-expression fostered by some teachers.

Perhaps even more important, since they limited school usage even among children from groups with a very positive attitude toward formal education, were economic factors. Until an immigrant family achieved some economic security, the children in that family had to go to work and not to school. In practice, this usually meant that younger children received more schooling than their older siblings. Indeed, it was often the earning power of older sisters and brothers that enabled the younger ones to remain in school or go on to higher education. Poverty was a block to school success in many ways. Children from poor families became sick more often and fell behind in their studies; sometimes they were too tired or hungry to concentrate. Their families often moved around a great deal, forcing the child to adjust to a new school and a new teacher at frequent intervals. Poor clothing often made them ashamed to go to school at all.

A third set of factors that greatly influenced an immigrant child's education was the school itself. At the turn of the century, in many communities non-English-speaking children, regardless of age, were placed in the first grade when they entered school. The ten- or twelve-year-old boy forced to sit in a seat built for a six year old and assigned books on that level often gave up in disgust and left at the first opportunity. Other school districts arranged for ungraded "vestibule" classes in which the non-English-speaking child was given a five-months cram course in the new language and then sent to the grade level appropriate to his or her age. Some survived such Darwinistic treatment; most did not.

None of the big immigrant-receiving cities was ready for the millions of children who came streaming into their classes at the turn of the century. Shortages of seats led to part-time schooling and classes of 60 to 100 taught by an exhausted young woman who might see as many as 200 children a day. Partly in response to her burdens but more likely as a result of her training, the teacher was likely to disparage the native language, culture, and traditions of the immigrant children in her care. During Julia Richman's tenure as district superintendent on the Lower East Side of New York, the use of Yiddish was forbidden anywhere on school property, and teachers were authorized to use soap (albeit kosher

soap) to wash out the mouths of offenders! All the children got the
message the schools were sending—shed your Old World culture if you
want to succeed in school. Most did, at least to a point, but others rebelled
and abandoned school entirely.[23]

One of the few generalizations that can safely be made regarding
education and ethnicity is that East European Jewish children went to
school longer, and, to a greater extent than any other ethnic group, used
formal education as a route to white-collar work and the professions.
Having said this, however, it is essential to realize that this generalization
did not apply to the first generation and, in many cases, not to the second
either. Limitations of poverty and of the urban schools themselves prevented most East European Jewish children from going beyond a primary school education until 1910 or later. New York City, for example,
did not have any high schools until 1897 and had only five as late as
1914. Many second-generation East European Jews were also unable to
use schooling in the ways usually attributed to all Jews. CCNY, for example, did not have a majority of East European Jewish graduates until
1916 or later. Even then, graduating classes of 200 or less demonstrate
that until the 1930s, the "proletarian Harvard" could not have produced
very many East European Jewish professionals. In reality, for the first
two generations, as Thomas Kessner has quantitatively demonstrated,
Jewish mobility rested on entrepreneurial success much more than on
extended education.[24]

Nonetheless, Jews as a group did utilize the schools to a greater extent
than other immigrants. Why was this so? Leonard Dinnerstein has provided several different answers: family pressure to do well, and, even
more important, the attractiveness of the professions to an ethnic group
that had often experienced discrimination or worse. As a self-employed
professional, with his knowledge in his head and skills at his fingers, a
Jew could make his own future and be able to use his training wherever
it was necessary for him to settle. To reach this position, however, he
had to acquire an extensive education and demonstrate his ability in
competition with his peers.[25]

Was Jewish school success motivated only by crass materialism? Yes,
says Alfred Kazin. In his memoir, A Walker in the City, he states: "It was
never learning that I associated with school; only the necessity to succeed,
to get ahead of others in the daily struggle." He also echoes Dinnerstein's
point about parental pressure. "It was not for myself alone that I was
expected to shine but for [my parents]—to redeem the constant anxiety
of their existence."[26]

But others who have examined the Jewish school experience have
come to a different conclusion. Mark Zborowski has written of Jewish
education in the *shetl* culture from which so many of them came and has
concluded that the Jews, as "people of the book," came to venerate study

for religious reasons. As a result, the community respected a learned man, and theological knowledge conferred high status. This attitude was transmuted in the secular American environment into admiration for any educated man. The professional man, says Zborowski, took the place of the Talmudic expert, and in the United States Jews have blended the American success pattern with an older emphasis on book learning so as to use education for material success.[27]

Still others have remarked on the practical importance of the East European Jewish background. Educational methods in the *cheder*—learning by rote, obedience to the teacher, long hours of sitting still—were traits that helped Jewish children adjust to American schools where the same qualities were required. Furthermore, the petty entrepreneurial and urban background of many East European Jews made them acquainted with numbers and the printed page. Most important, as a group they came with skills that could be used immediately in the United States and thus were able to acquire, most quickly than other immigrants, the economic base that made it possible for their children to use free public education.[28]

Other children who arrived in the United States at the same time brought another kind of practical and cultural baggage. Their school experience, as a result, was quite different. Although there were great individual differences—Jewish dullards plagued their teachers and Italian high achievers such as Leonard Covello were far from unknown—in general, the Slavic and Italian immigrants who came to the United States at the same time as the Jews did not fare as well in the schools.

John Bodnar sees the Slavic struggle for existence in industrial America as the basic explanation for their limited use of the schools. Because many Slavic families needed their earnings as soon as possible, boys were told that it was more important to acquire job skills than to go to school. Girls were taken out very early, either to do factory work or to free their mothers to do so. Certain cultural factors were also operative. Slavic families, like Italians, emphasized sharing and work for the common good, not for individual success. As a result, the family's needs took precedence over the wishes of any child in it. Children, as a matter of course, gave their earnings to the family and kept little or nothing for themselves.

According to Joseph Barton, the connection between economics and education was also true for the Cleveland Slavic community. Among all the groups he studied, there was a strong link between family prosperity and the use of education for further advancement. It was, he concluded, fathers who had accumulated $3,000 worth of property who were most likely to send their sons to college. Since few Slavic fathers were able to accumulate such sizeable sums, most of the children of this group went to work at an early age. When industrial accidents led to disability or

early death for the breadwinner (not an infrequent occurrence in any
working-class community), their children, no matter how well they were
doing, had to abandon the classroom. Barton agrees that the low educational achievement of Slavic children as a group was primarily the
result of the low economic status of their families. Schooling was deemphasized, not because Slavic parents undervalued education but because
for many years it was inappropriate to their needs.[29]

This was also true for the first few generations of American-Italian
children. According to Robert Woods, writing in 1902, the majority of
the pupils in the schools of the heavily Italian North End district of
Boston left at fourteen. Attrition was particularly heavy after the sixth
grade.[30] Woods blamed poverty and lack of interest for limited Italian
school usage, but a modern observer, sociologist Miriam Cohen, believes
that the sole cause was poverty. In her interesting article on "Changing
Education Strategies Among Immigrant Generations," she shows how
Italian families came to send their children to high school when the
economic realities in their lives made it possible.

Most of her emphasis is on Italian mortality and fertility patterns.
Although fewer of their children died in the United States, Italian birth
rates remained as high as they had been in Italy where infant deaths
were very frequent. The result was very large families in the immigrant
and first generation and the consequent need for their children to earn
money as soon as possible. "Time spent in school had negative consequences for the entire family." What made the Italian family game plan
possible was the fact that in the early twentieth century, jobs were available for the young and poorly educated. A 1905 study of Italian boys
of fourteen and fifteen who were not in school showed that 88 percent
of them were working.

By the 1930s, however, Italian birth rates declined, jobs for unskilled
adolescents were harder to get, the abolition of tenement home work
made it less profitable to keep girls home, and truancy laws were better
enforced. All these factors meant that more Italian children, especially
girls, stayed in school longer. Boys could get on-the-job training from
their fathers and enter well-paid blue-collar trades, and so they often
left high school before completing the entire course of study. Girls,
however, took a commercial course and remained to graduate because
a diploma provided entree into the expanding clerical field.[31]

Cohen stresses demographic and economic factors rather than cultural
values as the explanation for limited Italian school usage. She believes
that Italian children, as soon as their earnings could be spared, were
encouraged to stay in school as long as possible. Others have seen the
matter differently and have emphasized cultural factors. Allan Kraut,
for example, cites a Southern Italian proverb "Stupid and contemptible
is he who makes his children better than himself" as evidence for the

fact that Italians had no desire to use formal education as a road to upward mobility.[32]

Leonard Covello's massive study of the Italo-American schoolchild makes the same point but links it to conditions in the devastated *Mezzogiorno* from which the largest number of Italian-Americans came. Although John Briggs found evidence that more schools existed in Southern Italy than was formerly believed to be the case, it is still a fact that life in that region had little connection with anything the schools could teach. That is Covello's theme. The great majority of the Southern Italians who settled in the United States saw no value in extended schooling because there was nothing in their life experience to indicate that it would be anything but a waste of time.[33]

Most recently, Salvatore La Gumina, like Covello a child of Italian immigrants, has suggested some additional reasons for the lukewarm Italian response to American education. Southern Italians, he says, were hostile to formal schooling in the United States because in Italy it was associated with the elite ruling groups who were their exploiters. It was also feared that education might undermine a boy's masculinity because it would prevent him from doing manual labor, the only kind of employment considered to be work. At bottom, however, La Gumina says that for Italians as well as Slavs, family centeredness was the most important cause of limited Italian school usage. He does not, however, stress the economic need that others see as the cause of this attitude, and thus he places himself with those who see cultural factors as being more important than poverty as the explanation for the Italian school experience.[34]

Although the recency of their immigration makes it difficult to be sure, in the case of the Chinese a cultural disposition toward education seems to have overridden economic need. Betty Lee Sung's study, *Transplanted Chinese Children*, describes the successful school adjustment of the thousands of Chinese children who have entered the New York City schools since 1970. Their teachers describe them as earnest, well-disciplined, and hard-working. They earn high marks in spite of language problems and the need to do part-time work. Sung believes that rigorous training in Taiwan and Hong Kong and the fact that education and scholastic achievement are very highly valued among all Chinese account for their school success. Poverty, rather than acting as a barrier, becomes their spur because they see education as the best road to upward mobility.

Sung is certainly correct about the poverty of the newest Chinese families and probably right about their motivation, but she neglects to show why it is possible for them to make the decision for schooling and not work. The reason is largely a matter of timing. Immigrants who have come to the United States in the past two decades have entered a society that has long since abandoned Social Darwinism. Thanks to the

New Deal and Great Society, there are cushions and safety nets for all who have entered legally and probably for many undocumented immigrants as well. It is this protection, unknown to the groups who came earlier, that makes it possible for Chinese parents to avoid the choice between eating or education faced by the families who came before the guarantor state was established. This, as well as the all-important fact that unskilled jobs are now very hard to find and that as a group their children do exceedingly well in the quantitative fields that are so important today, explains why the Chinese school experience differs from that of most earlier groups.[35]

Although there is more certainty that they will attend, getting used to American schools is as much a part of the adjustment process of Chinese children as it was for youngsters from other ethnic groups in years past. Another aspect of their experience is perhaps even more important, and in this regard as well, they resemble the immigrants who came before them. In varying degrees, all immigrant children are "marginal men" with one foot in their parents' world and the other in American society. They are usually secure in neither. As with everything else in immigrant history, the intensity with which this was felt varied with both the individual child and/or his peer group, but to some extent, it was a problem to all. The roots of the difficulty are obvious: even if for a limited time, the child went to school and was exposed to a culture foreign to that of his parents.

At school, in the settlement house, and from their peers in the streets, immigrant children got a clear message to throw off their "backward" Old World language, customs, and dress and become Americans. At the same time, their parents, insecure and homesick, clung to older customs and often insisted that the children do the same. Clearly, the stage was set for conflict. Harry Roskolenko, the son of East European immigrants, says, "We lived between bits and pieces of two countries, the mixture serving to fuse and confuse us all the more." Outside his home he and his siblings saw themselves as Americans, but to their parents they were only Jews. Who was the child to believe?[36]

From a similar background, Samuel Ornitz speaks of his embarrassment when his mother called him "*ziegalle*" (little goat). To her it was a term of endearment, but to him it was a source of pain. He and his friends "lived several kinds of lives, traveling from planet to planet." For example, there was the queer relationship of American street games to "what our old world parents remembered of their childhood." They could not understand what gave him great pleasure—"indeed, an ocean separated us," and the distance created misunderstanding and intolerance on both sides.[37]

Anzia Yezierska wrote a famous book on this theme. *The Children of*

Loneliness of the title were the millions of immigrant youth "wandering between worlds that are at once too old and too new to live in." One of her stories centered around the Cornell-educated daughter of poor Jewish parents who was unable to accept their crude table manners, European mode of dress, and lack of English. She leaves them only to find that she cannot be comfortable in the Gentile world either. At the end of the story she says, "I don't belong with those who gave me birth or to those with whom I was educated."[38]

Margaret Mead believed that the presence of grandparents in an immigrant household exacerbated the problems of marginality because the child's parents found it harder to move away from Old World customs and language while their own parents were alive and present in the home. Their American-born or -raised children resented this and sometimes reacted by pretending not to understand their grandparents even when they really did know the language.[39] Mead is probably correct about the difficulties of a three-generation household, but even without such complications, marginality was a serious problem to millions of ethnic children. I well remember the shame I felt at my mother's poor English and my consequent desire to keep her away from friends and teachers. At the same time I felt enormous guilt because I knew full well why she didn't speak like a "Yankee." Married at sixteen, right off the ship that brought her from her native Lithuania, she was almost immediately involved in the work of bringing up four little girls and managing a household.

Feelings such as mine are common among first-generation immigrant children, and nowhere have they been better expressed than in Maxine Hong Kingston's memoir, *The Woman Warrior*. She was the eldest child of Chinese immigrants who were very much attached to their native traditions and who feared and mistrusted the non-Chinese, whom they called "ghosts." In her home, a child's silence was highly valued, but in school teachers demanded that she speak out. Unable to accommodate herself to these conflicting demands, she remained silent and "flunked" kindergarten. All the Chinese girls in her class were initially speechless, but Kingston's difficulties lasted longer than most. Unable to respond to the school's demands, so different from those at home, she expressed her depression by painting totally black pictures.

Jade Snow Wong was given the same directive at home. Her father told her "to think three times before saying anything and if I said nothing, no one would think I was stupid." In general, Kingston had many more difficulties than Wong. Her mother was very superstitious, and when the neighborhood drugstore delivered medicine to the family by mistake, she feared that a curse had been placed on them. To remedy this, she sent her oldest child to go to the store and exact "reparations," that is, candy to take away the possibility of disaster. Kingston suffered agonies before the drugstore proprietor, more to get rid of her than because he understood, gave her lollipops and she was able to flee.[40]

Chinese children continue to have difficulty assimilating. Betty Sung, writing about the post-1965 arrivals, says that they are brought up to refrain from aggressive behavior, whereas the masculine image in the United States stresses a "macho" style. Chinese boys are much troubled by this contradiction. Differing views on sports add to their difficulties: sports are unimportant in China, very important in America. Sexual attractiveness is valued in both cultures, but in China it is achieved by subtle means and in the United States by more obvious ones. This is usually more of a problem to girls, but other cultural conflicts are common to both sexes. Chinese children are taught to report the misbehavior of others, but "tattling" is a serious offense among American children. Chinese families, in general, discourage early socialization, but most American parents are proud when their children have many friends.[41]

Sung may be quite right about the difficulties faced by these new immigrant children. The growth of gangs and other antisocial behavior in New York's Chinatown today indicate that the children of the more recently arrived Chinese are taking a different road from the one followed by those who came earlier. Marginal children from other ethnic groups have also taken an antisocial path. In Chicago in 1890, Joseph Hawes tells us, "gangs of immigrant youth whose contempt for their parents found expression in defiant and anti-social activities, roamed the streets."[42] Ten years later, Chicago court records showed that nearly 75 percent of the male juvenile delinquents and 70 percent of the females were foreign-born or the children of foreign-born parents.[43] Progressive social workers in all cities found these statistics to be extremely alarming. Much of their literature is filled with theories on the parent-child conflict which they saw as the primary cause of delinquency, as well as with recommendations for prevention.

With the gift of hindsight, we can see that resolution of the "marginal man" problem was mostly a matter of time, but the testimony of those who lived through the experience makes it clear that immigrant parents and their first-generation children were often in a state of war. A successful son took his father to a fashionable shop to buy him new clothes and wrote to the *Forward* of what ensued. His father, accustomed to shopping on the Lower East Side, assumed that the clerk would speak Yiddish and addressed him in that language. The clerk, of course, did not understand him and made it clear that his patronage was not welcome. Totally humiliated, the son vented his rage at his father and not at the bigoted clerk. He told the *Forward* editor that he would never again accompany his father outside the ghetto.[44]

The behavior of this particular son conformed to one of sociologist

Irwin Childs's theories on intergenerational conflicts in immigrant families. Childs pointed out that first-generation children had three choices: apathy, identification, and rebellion. In the first instance, appropriate to a passive personality, the child was able to go along with his parents' ways when he was with them and act like a "Yankee" when he was not. In the second, he would speak the family's native tongue, follow their traditions, and generally isolate himself from the mainstream of American life. In the last case, he would refuse to associate himself with his parents' culture and cast off as much of the relationship as he could. In reality, none of Childs's scenarios was as likely to be as clear-cut as he stated them. Most immigrant children married people from their own group, spoke Italian, Yiddish, or German to their parents, observed traditional holidays, and kept their foreign-sounding names but, at the same time, participated in the larger society as Americans.[45]

Two writers who were the sons of Italian immigrants, Jerre Mangione and Mario Puzo, have written of the conflicts that erupted within their families. Mangione tells of his mother's absolute insistence that only Italian be spoken in their home. There was only one exception to her rule: she overlooked her daughter's tendency to speak English in her sleep! When confronted with her children's opposition, Mangione's mother gave a perfectly logical reason for the rule. She could not speak or understand English very well and was unlikely to learn it. Unless her children spoke Italian, they could not communicate with her, and what was the good of having children if they couldn't talk to each other?[46]

Puzo's quarrels were also with his mother, but on a different issue. He describes the adults in the Hell's Kitchen Italian community in which he grew up as "coarse, vulgar and insulting," and early in his life he decided to escape from them by becoming a writer. To his mother it was incomprehensible that he could succeed. Her highest ambition was for him to become a clerk for the New York Central Railroad whose tracks ran through the neighborhood. Many of the Italian men who lived in Hell's Kitchen worked as manual laborers for the railroad. Mrs. Puzo was willing to accept her son's aspirations for something better, at least up to the point of a white-collar job, but to her a writer was an artist and that was a status leap she could not envision. As a result, Puzo tells us that he "like all the children in the ghettos of America, became locked in a bitter struggle with the adults responsible for me."[47]

Lincoln Steffens has left a vivid picture of the gulf that could emerge between immigrant children and their parents. In many Jewish families, first-generation rebellion resulted in rejection of religious orthodoxy. Steffens described a scene outside a Lower East Side synagogue in which traditionally garbed and bearded fathers ran a gauntlet of their sons who lounged near the synagogue on the Sabbath, smoking and jeering at those who entered to pray. The fathers responded by going through the procedures normally reserved for the dead—tearing their clothes and "shivah"—mourning their sons who although living were to them as dead.[48]

Every child found a different way out of the dilemma posed by marginality. For many, the rebellion that is inherent in the maturation process of all children became self-hatred and resulted in a total rejection of their ethnic identity. Robert Ernst quotes some Irish youths who refused to participate in the community enterprises of their elders, saying, "I am ashamed to go; they will end in some quarrel or another and I don't want to be called Irish." Rose Mary Prosen, daughter of Slovenian immigrants, recalls similar feelings.

As a young child, she was content to speak Slovenian at home and learn English in her parochial school classes. When she entered a public high school, however, her classmates told her that she "talked funny," and she was terribly ashamed. Wanting to remove the stigma, she spent a hard-to-come-by twenty-five cents on a self-improvement pamphlet, locked herself in the bathroom and practiced English pronunciation in secret. Criticism of her speech reinforced her shame at other things she saw as Slovenian: that her mother cooked and served their meals but never sat down to eat with the family, that her father drank heavily, and that the furniture and linens in her home were made from scrap wood and feed bags. Her goal was to remove herself from her parents' environment as soon as possible.[49]

William V. D'Antonio became hostile to the pattern of his earlier life when he won a scholarship to Yale and left the extended Italian family in which he had grown up. As a "Yalie," he totally embraced assimilation and became "ashamed of the ethnic concerns of his elders." Harriet Polowska believed that a Pole would never be hired to teach in an American school and attempted to change her name to something more American. Her father, however, saw this as her rejection of their common ethnic heritage and not merely as an accommodation to the demands of a bigoted society.[50] But Polowska's desire to prevent ethnic identification via her name was mild indeed when compared to the extreme self-hatred of John Fante.

In his "Odyssey of a Wop," he says that even as a young child he was aware that it was not desirable to be Italian. When he entered school, therefore, he was afraid of being identified as such and told the other children that he was French. He avoided other Italian boys and chose friends with Anglo-Saxon names. He brought them to his house only when it was essential, and on those occasions, he was very nervous because "the place [his home] looked so Italian. The cut pitcher of wine, the pictures of King Victor Emmanuel and of the Milan Cathedral all testified to the fact that his was not an American household." At one point he lost control and told his father to stop being a wop and become an American!

Fante apparently saw no value at all in his Italian background, and this justified his rejection of it. But Jade Snow Wong, who did value her dual heritage, also harbored doubts. Whenever she experienced bigotry she wondered if the Chinese were perhaps as inferior as the larger society implied. Thomas Napierkowski, on the other hand, found that a Polish parochial school education and strong identification with his ethnic church did not hinder his assimilation but rather minimized any conflicts he might have suffered.[51]

Few of the professionals who worked with the immigrant families who arrived in the decades surrounding the turn of the century did as much thinking about them as social worker Sophonisba Breckenridge. To begin with, she isolated the various conflict areas that emerged in immigrant homes. Basic differences in childrearing ideas, she thought, underlay all the problems. "Modernized" parents, that is, those who had lived in the United States for many years, believed that a child must be allowed the freedom to "develop his own personality." European parents, on the other hand, thought that the child must be trained for subservience. Although there was no doubt where she stood—"early placing of the responsibility for his acts on the child himself will better train citizens for democracy"—Breckenridge did seem to understand why it was difficult for Old World parents to accept New World practices.[52]

Serious quarrels erupted over the disposition of the child's wages because "maintenance of parental authority seems to be tied up with control of their children's earnings." Using evidence from Slavic families, she found that the great majority required the child to contribute his or her entire salary to the parents, sometimes giving the child a small portion back as an allowance. One Slovak girl of sixteen who earned $13 a week received less than a dollar to spend on herself. With characteristic understatement, Breckenridge observed that "It is not surprising that a boy or girl would chafe under such a system"[53]

Although the families wanted their children to work outside the home, when their daughters did so it caused great difficulties. Old World traditions required that a girl be closely supervised until she married, but it was not possible to do this when she worked away from home. Even worse, if she was "on her own" during working hours, how could her parents deny her the right of unsupervised recreation after her work was done? Slovak parents, Breckenridge observed, were more likely to waive the old rules, but Italians would not, saying, "If a daughter could not be trusted alone or unchaperoned in a village in which they knew most of the people, and all of the places of amusement, is she any more safe in a city in which [parents] don't know what is around the corner?"

When parents were unwilling to relax the rules at all, children often ran away. Family breakup was certainly not a desirable outcome of parent-child hostility, but Breckenridge thought that the child in such a scenario was better off than some because he or she would at least have learned what his or her parents' values were. Not so the child whose parents gave up the fight. Those who abandoned the attempt to shape their children's behavior into traditional forms were setting them adrift with no training or values at all. This, she believed, was the most damaging step a parent could take. Without learning the importance of rules, even if the rules were inappropriate to American society, the child would never be able to judge right from wrong and act accordingly.[54]

But some parents were simply not strong enough to carry on the battle indefinitely. One way out was for them to accept their child's interpretation of what was American. After all, their son or daughter understood English when they did not and went daily to work in a world they did not know. Carried far enough, such an attitude resulted in "role reversal" in which the child assumed the position of leader and the parents followed behind. Jane Addams found this "pathetic dependence of the family upon the child to be deplorable" and placed some of the blame on the settlement house and the schools. In both institutions, immigrant children were taught the American way to perform practical tasks and were encouraged to teach these ways to their parents.

This was an integral part of the Americanization process, not a mere by-product. As Julia Richman, superintendent of the Lower East Side public schools, told the National Education Association in 1904, the immigrant child was to be the instrument by which his or her parents would learn to be good Americans. Other educators, like Addams, had some doubts about the process. Frank Thompson, superintendent of the Cleveland, Ohio, schools in an era of heavy immigration, wondered if the costs of "instant Americanization" were not too high. "Children of foreign parentage," he feared, "might turn in contempt against [their] parents' speech and ways." Undoubtedly, this often happened, leading to great conflict if the parents fought back or to role reversal if they did not.[55]

Joseph Lopereato, writing much later, points out another way in which the schools weakened parental authority. Immigrant children, like all children, learned from Dick and Jane type books which portrayed a middle-class environment totally different from the one they knew. This could lead them to question why they were poor and eventually blame their fathers for not providing them with a Dick and Jane life. By building a false image of American life, the schools made it harder for poor children (and few first-generation children were middle class) to respect their fathers. One of the earliest sociologists to concern himself with the immigrant family, Arthur Calhoun, pointed out something else in the American environment that led to loss of respect.

In Europe, sons often learned their trade by working with their fathers. In this case, the parent was very much respected. He knew a great deal, and, furthermore, what he knew was of direct practical value to his son. This would be less true in America because fewer sons were likely to follow their father's trade; indeed, they often wanted to leave it behind entirely and rise into a white-collar job if they possibly could.[56] What led the son to scorn his father's occupation (often with his father's encouragement) is that it produced few tangible rewards. It did not take very long for a child to discover that in America a poor man was not much respected. What often followed was contempt for the "old man" and a determination to do otherwise. This was not a recipe for family harmony.

Betty Sung reminds us that this matter of loss of respect transcends both culture and chronology. She has found the same reversal of parent-child roles in the Chinese families of today. The child learns English first, and the parent turns to them for help. This is particularly true in those cases where the parents have had little education themselves. Sung's comments are interesting in light of the fact that the schools today no longer try to deracinate the immigrant child. Dick and Jane are long since gone, ethnic pride and bilingualism are "in." Nevertheless, older attitudes reappear, and marginality remains a problem. Human nature, it seems, is stronger than educational trends.[57]

Individual immigrant fathers, although they might never become financially successful and continued to follow the traditions, religious and otherwise, of their homelands, *were* able to gain the respect of their children. These men exhibited strength and determination that would brook no opposition. Individual mothers, although usually less Americanized than their husbands, were also able to dominate their children because they were so close to them in their most dependent years. Children became accustomed to turning to their mother for practical advice, and this continued into adulthood. The classic example is the Jewish mother, celebrated in song, story, and on the stage. She has also been a subject of intense interest to psychologists, sociologists, and professors of literature. Irving Howe, for example, points out that the Jewish mother "is assaulted with a venom that testifies to her continuing moral and emotional power"[58]

But she also has not lacked for defenders. Psychologist Matthew Besdine, for example, set out to answer the question of why Jews have produced a disproportionate number of high achievers and found the answer in Jewish mothering. Because they are deeply involved and dedicated, he says, Jewish mothers spend more time than the average coddling, playing, and communicating with their offspring. As a result, their children develop an unusual capacity for "achievement, intellectual and creative growth." But other, less desirable results can also occur.

Another psychologist, Martha Wolfenstein, found that the intensive care so characteristic of the stereotypical Jewish mother caused her children to be insecure and full of self-doubt. If Mama is constantly hovering over me and fulfilling my every wish even before I clearly express it, reasons the child, there must be something wrong with me. Overprotection also delays maturity, and Wolfenstein thought that this was the *real* motivation of the Jewish mother, that is, to keep the child an infant. In Europe, mothers were a strong influence only in their sons' earliest years because once he went to *cheder*, usually at five, his education became the most important part of his life. Mothers played no role at all in that. In secular America, relatively few Jewish boys went to all-day religious schools, and thus their mothers were able to continue the closeness and protectiveness of their earliest years.[59]

Sociologist Zena Smith Blau has written a very strong defense of the Jewish mother, crediting her with providing valuable information on the road to upward mobility in America, data she gathered from the vast "information exchange" maintained by all Jewish mothers. Along with her guidance, she told her children that a Jew had to be twice as qualified as a Gentile in order to receive the same rewards, and this "hard-headed" realism led her children to increase their efforts. Her unquestioning love, says Blau, meant that the Jewish child developed a close, trusting, free, and fearless relationship with his or her mother, and this was one of the greatest sources of the child's strength in later life.

Blau is a good defense attorney, but even she speaks of the guilt that is another part of such a child's inheritance. Jewish mothers typically did not use corporal punishment to discipline their children (although given the circumstances in which millions of immigrant families lived, this is hard to believe). They relied instead on nagging and trying to arouse feelings of guilt if the child misbehaved. Blau says, "It was the discomfort and anxiety of guilt that parental disapproval induced... that led Jewish children to internalize [certain] norms of behavior." Some of these behavior patterns, however, might be quite harmful and may explain much of the hostility that required Blau to speak so strongly for the defense.[60]

The Jewish mother has been a subject of investigation for many years, but it is the black family and the role of the mother in it that has been of great interest in recent decades. Although the black sociologist Franklin Frazier published *The Negro Family* in 1939 and Stanley Elkins included it in his 1959 work, *Slavery*, it was the 1970s that produced the largest number of works on the subject. Eugene Genovese, John Blassingame, and Herbert Gutman each published a widely read book, and Elizabeth Pleck contributed a significant article on the free black family in nineteenth-century Boston. Most recently, Thomas Webber has written about *Education in the Slave Community* and included important material on the slave family.

Herbert Gutman was the first historian to say that the black family in slavery and freedom and in the North and in the South was neither "unorganized or disorganized." During slavery, long monogamous relationships were well known, most of the fieldhands maintained two-parent households, and family ties were very strong. This pattern, says Gutman, continued well into the twentieth century, even in the urban North. It was the Depression of the 1930s that caused a change. Devastating unemployment, especially severe for black males, led to family breakup and the emergence of the single-parent matriarchal family that is characteristic of many black households today.[61]

Webber's book, concentrating as it does on the educational role of slave parents, finds that they did a great deal in this regard. Mothers, he says, taught household skills, religious beliefs, folklore, and literacy whenever possible. Fathers were a strong influence even when they lived on a different plantation. In such cases, they would come to where their sons were living and take them hunting (actually poaching) and fishing, teaching them the practical skills needed to expand the basic diet supplied by the master.[62] Genovese agrees that slave fathers did what they could to protect and support their family, including supplying them with fresh meat and game whenever possible. As a result, he does not think the slave father was emasculated, although he does believe that black women were strong figures. Genovese denies the widely held idea that the slave family was matriarchal; indeed, he suggests that there was considerable equality between the sexes.

Elizabeth Pleck studied the family life of blacks who came North during the Gilded Age and Progressive Era and found that during those years 82 percent of all the black households in Boston contained two parents. Seven out of every ten Boston black children lived with both a mother and a father. To demonstrate the Boston experience was not unique, Pleck cites similar conclusions reached by Theodore Hershberg in his study of Philadelphia black families. Both she and Hershberg, like Gutman, attribute problems of the modern black family to the hardships of their ghetto lives, and not to anything they brought with them or the dislocations of the migration itself. John Blassingame seems less certain. When masters permitted slave families to remain intact, they were indeed an important mechanism for survival. But when fathers lived on different plantations, they were not present very much while their children were growing up. Unlike Webber, he does not stress the educational role of the visiting father; he finds that while monogamy was present on many plantations, promiscuity was even more widespread. Blassin-game, then, finds that modern black family disorganization has at least some of its roots in the patterns developed under slavery.[63]

Stanley Elkins carries the point further. The capitalist nature of the plantation economy made it impossible to treat slave liaisons as per-manent because "any restrictions on the separate sale of slaves would have been reflected immediately on the market; their price would have dropped considerably." He concludes that "a father, among slaves, was legally unknown" and that it was the slave owner who took the father's role for the slave child. Two-parent slave households, therefore, were neither as permanent nor as prominent as Gutman and Genovese in-dicated. Elkins wrote in 1959, echoing ideas expressed twenty years earlier by Franklin Frazier who had found that only when the black father was able to obtain his freedom, acquire property, and purchase his wife and children could he really be the head of the household. This was certainly not possible for most blacks before the Civil War, and, as a result, slave society was heavily matriarchal with grandmothers often at the head. Frazier, much concerned with the high delinquency rate among urban black children at the time he was writing, found that family disorganization originating under slavery was the cause.[64]

The diversity of opinion discussed above may well represent the times in which the various scholars lived. Frazier and Elkins, writing after the black family was well established in the urban North but before the modern Civil Rights Movement had taken hold, wrote from a perspective that made slavery the source of the problem. Gutman, Genovese, Pleck, and Webber, on the other hand, while equally cognizant of modern black family problems, were writing at a time when black activism was very strong and therefore found the fault to lie in more recent societal fail-ures. Although neither group blamed the blacks per se, the older reports of sexual promiscuity and emasculated black men cast the black family in a poor light. Gutman, et al., were very anxious to do the opposite and have thus stressed the tradition of a strong black family, weakened in the twentieth century by economic injustice.

The influence of the times in which they live has also led scholars who study the white ethnic child to revise older views of immigrant family disorganization. Carol Groneman's dissertation, "The Bloody Ould Sixth," was one of the first to do this. Her work strongly contradicts the earlier findings of Oscar Handlin. She emphasizes the continuities and strengths of Irish family life, rather than dwelling on the dislocations and discon-tinuities that Handlin found in Boston. Irish families in the Sixth Ward of New York City in the mid-nineteenth century, Groneman finds, were poor and had severe problems born of poverty but were nonetheless strong and stable units.

Another Gutman student, Virginia Yans-McLoughlin, came to similar conclusions in her study of Italian families who arrived in the United States a half-century after the famine Irish. Her work contradicts the views of the Progressive social workers and the themes expressed in the classic study of Polish immigrants authored by Thomas and Florian Znaniecki. The trans-Atlantic journey, she finds, did not uproot Italians and cause severe family disorganization. Life in America was very different, but she argues that, as a group, Italians adjusted to their new environment by retaining the most useful of the traditions they brought with them, modifying others, and discarding very few.[65] John Briggs's recent study of the same group makes a similar point. Most of his evidence lies in the communities from which the Italians came. In the church and municipal records of these small towns, he found evidence of behavior continued in Italian-American communities here. Like Yans-McLoughlin, he thinks there was little dislocation, more continuity, and consequent stability.[66]

Why did teachers and settlement personnel who observed the immigrant families directly and scholars who wrote prior to the 1960s see disorganization when modern students of these same families see stability? Because the former, assuming the superiority of their own culture, disliked and disapproved of immigrant life-styles and sought to change them. Indeed, they believed it was their duty to do so. Unlike most social workers today, they saw ignorance and superstition where present-day writers see traditions as worthy as any of those in the host society. Spurred by the ideas of the Civil Rights Movement, ethnicity is celebrated, and there is more recognition that cultural differences do not imply inferiority or superiority. Starting with this point of view, the trend in recent scholarship has been to avoid WASP biases and to look at immigrant family life through friendly eyes. Seen in this light, there are fewer marginal men and less intergenerational conflict.

Revision of earlier scholarship usually produces more accurate history, but in this case there is simply too much evidence to deny the serious adjustment problems faced by immigrant parents and children. Undoubtedly, the zeal to Americanize led many to exaggerate the deficiencies of the immigrant family, but an equal zeal to rectify the value judgments of an earlier generation should not be allowed to blind historians to the reality. Most immigrants were not uprooted, and all families assimilated some of what they took from the American environment into what they had brought with them, but this was not done without pain and difficulty. How much pain and difficulty depended on a number of factors.

From what Napierkowski indicates, one way to ease the assimilation of the immigrant child was to provide him with a sturdy ethnic base. As he says, "All the important institutions in my life—family, school and church—reinforced my identity." Other views on what affects the process of assimilation stress different factors. Maxine Seller thinks that it was easier for younger children in a family to adopt American ways because older siblings had done the painful groundwork. Helen S. Zand points out that in many cases immigrant parents were themselves somewhat separated from Old World customs by the time they came to the United States.

Immigration, she points out, was often a multistep process, and many of the new arrivals had been away from the tightly knit rural villages that were their places of origin for some years. By the time they had children in the United States, their Old World customs had been greatly weakened. A team of Canadian sociologists whose own background is Indian and Pakistani believe that when the first members of a group met considerable hostility in the United States, later arrivals were less likely to strive for assimilation. This theory was also expressed by their fellow sociologist Harvey Zorbaugh, who offered the Chinese, surely the objects of such hostility, as an example.[67]

At this point, it is perhaps pertinent to restate one of the caveats discussed at the start of this chapter, namely, that the story of the ethnic child in America is a highly individualized one and that even the most valid generalizations are inappropriate for some members of every ethnic group. This is particularly true for the process of Americanization where there were great differences between groups as well as between individuals in them. When we allow for both these individual and group differences, it is at first hard to see what, if anything, ethnic children had in common. But, as this essay has tried to show, they often shared a great deal. After all, poverty and consequent early entry into the workplace, school adjustments, conflicts with parents, and the need to become part of the mainstream were in some degree part of every ethnic child's experience. This set him or her apart from those who faced only the ordinary problems of childhood. Growing up to be an American, therefore, was different from just growing up *in* America, and the story of the ethnic child in American society is therefore worth recording.

NOTES

1. Mary Antin, *The Promised Land* (Boston: Houghton Mifflin, 1969); Samuel B. Ornitz, *Haunch, Paunch and Jowl* (New York: Boni & Livewright, 1923); Samuel Chotzinoff, *A Lost Paradise* (New York: Alfred A. Knopf, 1955); Alfred Kazin, *A Walker in the City* (New York: Harcourt, Brace, 1951); Jacob Riis, *Children of the Poor* (New York: Charles Scribner's Sons, 1892); Hutchins Hapgood, *Spirit of the Ghetto* (New York: Funk & Wagnalls, 1902).

2. Thomas Webber, *Deep Like the Rivers: Education in the Slave Quarter Community, 1831–1865* (New York: W. W. Norton, 1978); John Blassingame, *The Slave Community: Plantation Life in the Ante-Bellum South* (New York: Oxford University Press, 1972).

3. Robert Ernst, *Immigrant Life in New York* (Port Washington, N.Y.: Ira J. Friedman, 1948), 53.

4. Virginia Yans-McLoughlin, *Family and Community* (Urbana: University of Illinois Press, 1982), 106.

5. Jacob J. Lindenthal, "Health and the East European Immigrant," *American Jewish History* 70 (June 1981): 433; Kazin, *Walker in the City*, 32.

6. Kenneth and Virginia Kiple, "Slave Child Mortality: Some Nutritional Answers to a Perennial Puzzle," *Journal of Social History* 10 (March 1977), 290, 296, 299, 286, 287.

7. Selma Berrol, *Immigrants at School: New York City, 1898–1914* (New York: Arno Press, 1978), 174, 177, 178.

8. Oscar Handlin, *Boston's Immigrants* (Boston: Atheneum, 1968); Lawrence Veiller and Robert DeForest, *The Tenement House Problem* (New York: Macmillan Co., 1903).

9. Jeremiah Jencks, *The Immigration Problem: A Study of American Immigrant Conditions and Needs* (New York: Funk & Wagnalls, 1912), 119, 120, 133.

10. Riis, *Children of the Poor*, 134; Ernst, *Immigrant Life in New York*, 39.

11. Chotzinoff, *Lost Paradise*, 122; Harry Roskolenko, "America the Thief," in Thomas Wheeler, ed., *The Immigrant Experience* (New York: Dial Press, 1971), 151–152; Abraham Karp, *Golden Door to America* (New York: Penguin Books, 1977), 128.

12. Jade Snow Wong, "Puritans from the Orient," in Wheeler, ed., *Immigrant Experience*, 112.

13. Alan M. Kraut, *The Huddled Masses: The Immigrant in American Society, 1880–1921* (Arlington, Ill.: Harlan Davidson, 1981), 136; Irving Howe, *World of Our Fathers* (New York: Harcourt Brace Jovanovich, 1976), 182; J. C. Rich, *The Jewish Daily Forward* (New York: Forward Association, 1967), 31.

14. David K. Wiggins, "The Play of Slave Children in the Plantation Communities of the Old South, 1820–1860," *Journal of Sport History* 7 (Summer 1980): 25, 26, 29, 33.

15. Riis, *Children of the Poor*, 184.

16. Thomas S. Adams and Helen L. Sumner, *Labor Problems* (New York: Macmillan Co., 1905), 50, 58.

17. Eva McDonald Valesh, "Child Labor," *American Federationist* 14 (March 1907): 157; Riis, *Children of the Poor*, 180–181.

18. Valesh, "Child Labor," 173.

19. Fred S. Hall, *Forty Years: The Work of the New York Child Labor Committee* (New York: New York Child Labor Committee, 1942), 85, 83.

20. Yans-McLoughlin, *Family and Community*, 195, 196.

21. "The Greek Padrone System in the United States," *Report of the United States Immigration Commission*, Vol. 2, Washington, D.C., 1911; Stanley Feldstein and Lawrence Costello, eds., *The Ordeal of Assimilation* (Garden City, N.Y.: Anchor Books, 1974), 258; Joseph M. Hawes, *Children in Urban Society: Juvenile Delinquency in Nineteenth Century Urban America* (New York: Oxford University Press, 1971), 141.

22. Ernst, *Immigrant Life in New York*, 53, 77; Diane Mei Lin, Mark and Ginger Chih, *A Place Called Chinese America* (San Francisco: Organization of Chinese

Americans, 1982), 70; Betty Lee Sung, *Transplanted Chinese Children* (Washington, D.C.: U.S. Government Printing Office, 1979), 104.

23. Maxine S. Seller, *To Seek America* (New York: Jerome Ozer, 1977), 131, 140; Selma Berrol, "Education and Economic Mobility: The Jewish Experience in New York City, 1880–1920," *American Jewish History* 65 (March 1976): 260; Selma Berrol, "Julia Richman, Agent of Change in the Urban School," *Urban Education* 11 (January 1977): 368.

24. Berrol, "Education and Economic Mobility," 261; Thomas Kessner, *The Golden Door* (New York: Oxford University Press, 1977), 65.

25. Leonard Dinnerstein, "Education and the Advancement of American Jews," in Bernard Weiss, ed., *American Education and the European Immigrant* (Urbana, Ill.: University of Illinois Press, 1982), 46.

26. Kazin, *Walker in the City*, 17, 21.

27. Mark Zborowski, "The Place of Book Learning in Traditional Jewish Culture," in Margaret Mead and Martha Wolfenstein, eds., *Childhood in Contemporary Culture* (Chicago: University of Chicago Press, 1955), 118, 140.

28. Berrol, *Immigrants at School*, 68, 70; Samuel Joseph, *History of the Baron De Hirsch Fund* (Philadelphia: Jewish Publication Society, 1935), 256.

29. John Bodnar, "Schooling and the Slavic American Family, 1900–1940," in Weiss, ed., *American Education and the European Immigrant*, 81–83; Joseph Barton, *Peasants and Strangers* (Cambridge, Mass.: Harvard University Press, 1975), 123.

30. Robert Woods, *Americans in Process* (Boston: Houghton Mifflin, 1902), 297.

31. Miriam Cohen, "Changing Education Strategies Among Immigrant Generations: New York's Italians in Comparative Perspective," *Journal of Social History* 15 (Spring 1982), 443, 447, 451, 453; Mary Fabian Matthews, "Role of the Public School in the Assimilation of Italian Immigrant Children in New York City, 1900–1914" (Ph.D. dissertation, Fordham University, 1966), 282.

32. Kraut, *Huddled Masses*, 138.

33. John Briggs, *An Italian Passage* (New Haven: Yale University Press, 1978), xx–xxi; Leonard Covello, "Social Background of the Italo-American School Child," Vol. 2 (Ph.D. dissertation, New York University, 1944), 405, 412, 455, 457, 467, 473, 488, 511.

34. Salvatore La Gumina, "American Education and the Italian Immigrant Response," in Weiss, ed., *American Education and the European Immigrant*, 63, 69, 71.

35. Sung, *Transplanted Chinese Children*, 74, 104.

36. Lawrence Brown, *Immigration* (New York: Longmans, Green & Co., 1933), 254; Roskolenko, "America the Thief," in Wheeler, ed., *Immigrant Experience*, 258.

37. Ornitz, *Haunch, Paunch and Jowl*, 30.

38. Anzia Yezierska, *The Children of Loneliness* (New York: Funk & Wagnalls, 1923), 101, 103.

39. Margaret Mead, "Grandparents As Educators," *Teachers College Record* 76 (December 1974): 242.

40. Maxine Hong Kingston, "A Song for a Barbarian Reed Pipe," in Maxine S. Seller, ed., *Immigrant Women* (Philadelphia: Temple University Press, 1981), 290–297; Wong, "Puritans from the Orient," in Wheeler, ed., *Immigrant Experience*, 120.

41. Sung, *Transplanted Chinese Children*, 104.

42. Hawes, *Children in Urban Society*, 160.

43. Sophonisba Breckenridge and Grace Abbott, *The Delinquent Child and the Home* (New York: Survey Associates, 1916), 57.

44. Kraut, *Huddled Masses*, 125–126.

45. Joseph Lopereato, *Italian Americans* (New York: Random House, 1970), 69.

46. Jerre Mangione, "Talking American," in Oscar Handlin, ed., *Children of the Uprooted* (New York: Grosset & Dunlap, 1968), 355, 356.

47. Mario Puzo, "Choosing a Dream," in Wheeler, ed., *Immigrant Experience*, 35, 36.

48. Karp, *Golden Door to America*, 129.

49. Ernst, *Immigrant Life in New York*, 180; Rose Mary Prosen, "Looking Back," in Michael Novak, ed., *Growing Up Slavic in America* (EMPAC!: 1976), 3, 4–5.

50. William V. D'Antonio, "Confessions of a Third Generation Italian-American," *Society* 13 (November-December 1975): 57; Harriet Powlowska, "The Education of Harriet Powlowska," in Novak, ed., *Growing Up Slavic in America*, 22.

51. John Fante, "The Odyssey of a Wop," in Handlin, ed., *Children of the Uprooted*, 391, 393; Wong, "Puritans from the Orient," in Wheeler, ed., *Immigrant Experience*, 120; Thomas Napierkowski, "Growing Up Polish," in Novak, ed., *Growing Up Slavic in America*, 14.

52. Sophonisba Breckenridge, *New Homes for Old* (New York: Harper Bros., 1921), 151.

53. Ibid., 170, 171.

54. Ibid., 175, 154.

55. Yans-McLoughlin, *Family and Community*, 148; Jane Addams, "Democracy and Social Ethics," in Robert Bremner, ed., *Children and Youth in America: A Documentary History* (Cambridge, Mass.: Harvard University Press, 1971), 2: 1322.

56. Lopereato, *Italian Americans*, 65; Arthur Calhoun, *A Social History of the American Family* (Cleveland: Arthur H. Clark Co., 1917), 3: 132.

57. Sung, *Transplanted Chinese Children*, 154.

58. Howe, *World of Our Fathers*, 177.

59. Matthew Besdine, "Jewish Mothering," *Jewish Spectator* 35 (February 1970), 7, 10; Martha Wolfenstein, "Two Types of Jewish Mother," in Mead and Wolfenstein, eds., *Childhood in Contemporary Culture*, 420.

60. Zena Smith Blau, "In Defense of the Jewish Mother," in Peter Rose, ed., *The Ghetto and Beyond* (New York: Random House, 1969), 59, 65, 60, 61.

61. Herbert Gutman, *The Black Family in Slavery and Freedom* (New York: Pantheon, 1976), 43, 13.

62. Webber, *Deep Like the Rivers*, 160–164, 167–174; Eugene Genovese, *Roll, Jordan, Roll* (New York: Pantheon, 1974), 491, 500.

63. Elizabeth Pleck, "The Two Parent Household: Black Family Structure in Late Nineteenth Century Boston," in Michael Gordon, ed., *The American Family in Social-Historical Perspective* (New York: St. Martin's Press, 1973), 166–167; Blassingame, *Slave Community*, 77–103, passim.

64. Stanley Elkins, *Slavery* (Chicago: University of Chicago Press, 1959), 53; E. Franklin Frazier, *The Negro Family in the United States* (Chicago: University of Chicago Press, 1939), 119, 128, 140.

65. Carol Groneman, "The Bloody Ould Sixth: A Social Analysis of a New York City Working Class Community in the Mid-Nineteenth Century" (Ph.D. dissertation, University of Rochester, 1973), v, vii; Yans-McLoughlin, *Family and Community*, 18.

66. Briggs, *Italian Passage*, xix-xxi.

67. Napierkowski, "Growing Up Polish," in Novak, ed., *Growing Up Slavic in America*, 14; Seller, *To Seek America*, 131; Helen S. Zand, "Polish Folkways in the United States," *Polish-American Studies* 13 (July-August 1955): 66; S. Parviz Walkil, C. M. Siddique, and F. A. Walkil, "Between Two Cultures: A Study in the Socialization of the Children of Immigrants," *Journal of Marriage and the Family* 43 (November 1981): 931; Harvey Zorbaugh, *The Gold Coast and the Slum* (Chicago: University of Chicago Press, 1929), 187–189.

BIBLIOGRAPHY

Adams, Thomas S., and Sumner, Helen L. *Labor Problems*. New York, 1905.

Addams, Jane. "Democracy and Social Ethics," In *Children and Youth in America: A Documentary History*, edited by Robert Bremner, et al. Vol. 2, Cambridge, Mass., 1971, 1322–1324.

Antin, Mary. *The Promised Land*. Boston, 1969 (reprint).

Barton, Joseph. *Peasants and Strangers*. Cambridge, Mass., 1975.

Berrol, Selma. "Education and Economic Mobility: The Jewish Experience in New York City, 1880–1920." *American Jewish History* 65 (March 1976): 257–271.

———. *Immigrants at School: New York City, 1898–1914*. New York, 1978.

———. "Julia Richman, Agent of Change in the Urban School." *Urban Education* 11 (January 1977): 357–374.

Besdine, Matthew. "Jewish Mothering." *Jewish Spectator* 35 (February 1970): 7–10.

Blassingame, John. *The Slave Community: Plantation Life in the Ante-Bellum South*. New York, 1972.

Blau, Zena Smith. "In Defense of the Jewish Mother." In *The Ghetto and Beyond*, edited by Peter Rose. New York, 1969, 57–68.

Breckinridge, Sophonisba P. "Government's Role in Child Welfare." *Annals of the American Academy of Political and Social Science* (November 1940), 42–50.

———. *New Homes for Old*. New York, 1921.

Briggs, John. *An Italian Passage*. New Haven, 1978.

Brown, Lawrence. *Immigration*. New York, 1933.

Calhoun, Arthur. *A Social History of the American Family*. 5 vols., Cleveland, 1917.

Chotzinoff, Samuel. *A Lost Paradise*. New York, 1955.

Cohen, Miriam. "Changing Education Strategies Among Immigrant Generations: New York's Italians in Comparative Perspective." *Journal of Social History* 15 (Spring 1982): 443–466.

Covello, Leonard. "Social Background of the Italo-American School Child." Ph.D. dissertation, New York University, 1944.

D'Antonio, William V. "Confessions of a Third Generation Italian-American." *Society* 13 (November-December 1975): 57–63.

Dinnerstein, Leonard. "Education and the Advancement of American Jews." In *American Education and the European Immigrant*, edited by Bernard Weiss. Urbana, 1982, 44–60.

Elkins, Stanley. *Slavery*. Chicago, 1959.

Ernst, Robert. *Immigrant Life in New York*. Port Washington, N.Y., 1948.

Fante, John. "The Odyssey of a Wop." In *Children of the Uprooted*, edited by Oscar Handlin. New York, 1968, 387–401.

Frazier, E. Franklin. *Negro Youth at the Crossways: Their Personality Development in the Middle States*. Washington, D.C., 1940.

Genovese, Eugene. *Roll, Jordan, Roll*. New York, 1974.

Gordon, Michael, ed. *The American Family in Social-Historical Perspective*. New York, 1973.

"The Greek Padrone System in the United States." In U.S. Immigration Commission. *Report of the United States Immigration Commission*. Washington, D.C., 1911.

Groneman, Carol. "The Bloody Ould Sixth: A Social Analysis of a New York City Working Class Community in Mid-Nineteenth Century." Ph.D. dissertation, University of Rochester, 1973.

Gutman, Herbert. *The Black Family in Slavery and Freedom*. New York, 1976.

Hall, Fred S. *Forty Years: The Work of the New York Child Labor Committee*. New York, 1942.

Handlin, Oscar. *Boston's Immigrants*. Boston, 1968.

———, ed. *Children of the Uprooted*. New York, 1968.

Hapgood, Hutchins. *Spirit of the Ghetto*. New York, 1902.

Hawes, Joseph M. *Children in Urban Society: Juvenile Delinquency in Nineteenth Century Urban America*. New York, 1971.

Howe, Irving. *World of Our Fathers*. New York, 1976.

Jencks, Jeremiah. *The Immigration Problem: A Study of American Immigrant Conditions and Needs*. New York, 1912.

Joseph, Samuel. *History of the Baron De Hirsch Fund*. Philadelphia, 1935.

Karp, Abraham. *Golden Door to America*. New York, 1977.

Kazin, Alfred. *A Walker in the City*. New York, 1951.

Kingston, Maxine Hong. "A Song for a Barbarian Reed Pipe." In *Immigrant Women*, edited by Maxine S. Seller. Philadelphia, 1981, 290–297.

Kiple, Kenneth, and Kiple, Virginia. "Slave Child Mortality: Some Nutritional Answers to a Perennial Puzzle." *Journal of Social History* 10 (March 1977): 284–309.

Kraut, Alan M. *The Huddled Masses: The Immigrant in American Society, 1880–1921*. Arlington, Ill., 1981.

La Gumina, Salvatore. "American Education and the Italian Immigrant Response." In *American Education and the European Immigrant*, edited by Bernard Weiss. Urbana, 1982, 61–77.

Lindenthal, Jacob J. "Health and the East European Immigrant." *American Jewish History* 70 (June 1981). 420–441.

Lopereato, Joseph. *Italian Americans*. New York, 1970.

Mangione, Jerre. "Talking American." In *Children of the Uprooted*, edited by Oscar Handlin. New York, 1968, 355–369.

Mark, Diane Mei Lin, and Chih, Ginger. *A Place Called Chinese America*. San Francisco, 1982.

Matthews, Mary Fabian. "Role of the Public School in the Assimilation of Italian Immigrant Children in New York City, 1900–1914." Ph.D. dissertation, Fordham University, 1966.

Mead, Margaret. "Grandparents as Educators," *Teachers College Record* 76 (December 1974): 240–249.

———, and Wolfenstein, Martha, eds. *Childhood in Contemporary Culture*. Chicago, 1955.

Napierkowski, Thomas. "Growing Up Polish." In *Growing Up Slavic in America*, edited by Michael Novak. Boyville, N.Y.: EMPAC!, 1976, 9–20.

Novak, Michael, ed. *Growing Up Slavic in America*. N.p., 1976.

Ornitz, Samuel. *Haunch, Paunch and Jowl*. New York, 1923.

Pleck, Elizabeth. "The Two-Parent Household: Black Family Structure in Late Nineteenth Century Boston." In *The American Family in Social-Historical Perspective*, edited by Michael Gordon. New York, 1973, 152–177.

Powlowska, Harriet. "The Education of Harriet Powlowska." In *Growing Up Slavic in America*, edited by Michael Novak. N.p., 1976, 21–27.

Prosen, Rose Mary. "Looking Back." In *Growing Up Slavic in America*, edited by Michael Novak. N.p., 1976, 1–8.

Puzo, Mario. "Choosing a Dream." In *The Immigrant Experience*, edited by Thomas Wheeler. New York, 1971, 35–49.

Rich, J. C. *The Jewish Daily Forward*. New York, 1967.

Riis, Jacob. *Children of the Poor*. New York, 1892.

Roskolenko, Harry. "America the Thief." In *The Immigrant Experience*, edited by Thomas Wheeler. New York, 1971, 151–178.

Seller, Maxine S. *To Seek America*. New York, 1977.

Sung, Betty Lee. *Transplanted Chinese Children*. Washington, D.C., 1979.

U.S. Immigration Commission. *Report of the United States Immigration Commission*. Washington, D.C., 1911.

Valesh, Eva McDonald. "Child Labor." *American Federationist* 14 (March 1907): 157–173.

Veiller, Lawrence, and De Forest, Robert. *The Tenement House Problem*. New York, 1903.

Walkil, S. Parviz; Siddique, C. M.; and Walkil, F. A. "Between Two Cultures: A Study in the Socialization of the Children of Immigrants." *Journal of Marriage and the Family* 43 (November 1981): 929–940.

Weiss, Bernard, ed. *American Education and the European Immigrant*. Urbana, 1982.

Webber, Thomas. *Deep Like the Rivers: Education in the Slave Quarter Community, 1831–1865*. New York, 1978.

Wheeler, Thomas, ed. *The Immigrant Experience*. New York, 1971.

Wiggins, David K. "The Play of Slave Children in the Plantation Communities of the Old South, 1820–1860." *Journal of Sport History* 7 (Summer 1980): 21–39.

Wolfenstein, Martha. "Two Types of Jewish Mother." In *Childhood in Contemporary Culture*, edited by Margaret Mead and Martha Wolfenstein. Chicago, 1955.

Wong, Jade Snow. "Puritans from the Orient." In *The Immigrant Experience*, edited by Thomas Wheeler. New York, 1971, 107–131.

Woods, Robert. *Americans in Process*. Boston, 1902.

Yans-McLoughlin, Virginia. *Family and Community*. Urbana, 1982.

Yezierska, Anzia. *The Children of Loneliness*. New York, 1923.

Zand, Helen S. "Polish Folkways in the United States." *Polish-American Studies* 13 (July-August 1955), 77–88.

Zborowski, Mark. "The Place of Book Learning in Traditional Jewish Culture." In *Childhood in Contemporary Culture*, edited by Margaret Mead and Martha Wolfenstein. Chicago, 1955.

Zorbaugh, Harvey. *The Gold Coast and the Slum*. Chicago, 1929.

10

American Children's Literature, 1880–Present

Sally Allen McNall

INTRODUCTION: GROWING UP IN FICTION

Books written for children, perhaps more than any class of literature, reveal a society's values and contradictions. American children's literature, for the past 100 years, has presented a remarkably consistent picture of the American child as naturally good and capable of realizing all our national dreams, from the sublime to the trivial. This literature has also steadily reflected the idea, supported by a more and more securely established network of schools, libraries, publishing houses, and periodicals, that it should teach those dreams to its readers. Like other forms of mass art in the twentieth century, it has become increasingly responsive to the trends of the moment. Yet the effect produced by a story for a young person has not changed much since 1880. The effect is produced by a double image: children's writers imagine a *reader* who will be encouraged to hold on to his or her youthful dreams by identifying with a *fictional character* who manages the trick.

Many of the most popular products of American children's literature, and most of the better ones, have been about older children, children on the brink of, or dealing with, the issues of adulthood. In the years between the Civil War and World War I, while American social scientists were discovering adolescence, children were already reading about it. In the years that followed, adolescence was institutionalized: between 1900 and 1930, high school attendance increased from 11 to 51 percent; by 1979 it was figured as 94 percent.[1] Over that span of time, the interest of younger children in the adolescent experience increased, and began at an earlier and earlier age. Beginning in the 1950s and booming in the 1960s, a new category, "young adult" fiction, entered the scene. Since before the turn of the century, then, American writers for children have appeared to be fascinated with the burdens and prerogatives of achieving

identity. Like American childrearing practices, and the theory (if not
the practice) of our educational system, children's literature has continued to imagine our youngsters as capable of early autonomy. Even stories
that have seemed to speak in favor of submission to authority carry
another potent message. In these books, American young people have
been told that their desire for the freedom to be themselves is right and
good—and that they can achieve it. So this chapter emphasizes themes
that concern the passage to adulthood in children's literature and, therefore, deals exclusively with fiction.

There is another good reason for this choice of genre, which is more
literary than cultural. Most critics and teachers of children's literature
state as dogma that during the years in question our books for young
people have become more and more "realistic" in content and in style.
(In fact, this idea acquired the value of doctrine in some quarters. The
1920s and 1930s saw an extended debate over whether or not children
should read "unrealistic" fairy tales.) Certainly, it is a long way from the
language and milieu of *Little Women* (1868) to those of *Dinky Hocker Shoots
Smack* (1972). Yet there are deep similarities. Both follow the same plot
formula, in which the heroine gains insight and with it maturity, and
this is a happy ending. Even more importantly, heroines in both stories
invite reader identification. This is a seeming requirement of American
children's fiction. Literary realism is rightly thought of as including details that an earlier, more sentimental and didactic mode excluded. There
is "progress," if you will, along those lines. But plots make didactic statements, and reader identification makes sentimental reader responses.
Louisa May Alcott spoke in her own voice to point a moral now and
then; contemporary writers do this by a distribution of rewards and
punishments. Since these matters are handled dramatically and symbolically, they seem more subtle, at first glance. And the naturalistic detail
often functions as a sort of smokescreen for the manipulations of plot
and feeling. For these reasons, "realistic" novels for children and young
people bear more watching than any other literary form, and this chapter
focuses on them accordingly.

American childhood is portrayed, in these books, as a time of serious
and often painful preparation for life. This attitude, a legacy of the
genteel tradition, predominates in children's stories from 1880 through
the period of World War I.[2] By the 1920s, as Dora V. Smith puts it,
"real children became the subject of fiction."[3] The implication is that
their own interests, rather than those of their solemn elders, now held
center stage. At this time, and through the 1950s, it is true that the
central characters of children's fiction were no longer divided into mel-
odramatically good and bad boys and girls, in the nineteenth-century
style, nor were the things that happened to them as improbable as they
had been. Until the end of World War II, they were often described as

ordinary children having ordinary troubles and hard times—but troubles and hard times in a society that was viewed as benign. A happy ending was always provided for the protagonists, who were good-hearted and true. In books of the 1960s, and after, the central characters definitely have problems, and they do not live in a benign world. Yet the upbeat ending remains, and, inseparable from it, the vision of the young person as morally clear-sighted.

THE SYSTEM

The task of making generalizations about American children's literature in the twentieth century is made easier by the fact that it has been supervised and shaped by certain literary and extra literary agencies. While children's books were reviewed in the years before 1880,[4] in the 1910s and 1920s this practice spread, under the influence of a new professionalism, and periodicals about children's books (for example, *Booklist*, *The Horn Book Magazine*, and *Elementary English*) came into being. The professional influence in question was that of children's librarians, in particular Caroline M. Hewins and Anne Carroll Moore of the New York Public Library. In the 1890s, Miss Hewins's work had helped to instigate an interest in library work with children, and by 1904 there were children's rooms in all Carnegie libraries, as well as in many others. In 1898 a training course for children's librarians was started at the Pratt Institute, and others followed.

Also in the 1890s and the first decade of this century, school libraries began to be planned for and brought into being, although the greatest growth in this area resulted from 1950s legislation. Special divisions of several professional organizations oversaw this development from its earliest days; the National Education Association, the American Library Association (then as now the most influential), and the National Council of Teachers of English, which also began publishing reading guides in this period. Hewins's *Books for Boys and Girls* (1915) is an example of the typical approach of the time. The concerted efforts of librarians and educators were directed, in the period before World War I, toward getting children to read the "classics." After the war, the development of intelligence tests and the use of surveys of children's abilities and interests broadened the field. The "child-centered" curriculum advocated by Progressive educators had its influence here as well, in that it seemed to advise placing the child's interests before adult standards of literary excellence.

In the 1920s and 1930s, guides, library purchases, and publishers began the creation of a genuine mass literature for children. After 1919, when Macmillan hired the first children's book editor (Louise Bechtel, like many who soon followed her in the field, a former librarian), the

consolidation of the literary establishment was aided in other ways. One
has been professional conventions, attended by editors, and another the
National Children's Book Week. The Book Week was established in 1919
by Franklin K. Mathiews, librarian of the Boy Scouts of America, together with Frederic G. Melcher, at the convention of the American
Booksellers' Association. With the American Library Association and
children's editors participating, National Book Week is still celebrated
annually in many schools and libraries. A second means of setting standards and disseminating the works that satisfy them has been the institution of awards. The first and still most prestigious was the American
Library Association's Newberry Award, first given in 1922. Other examples of awards are the Caldecott Medal, for picture books, which
followed in 1938, and, in the 1940s, the Child Study Association of
America's establishment of an award for books that "deal realistically
with problems in [the] contemporary world." Many other special awards,
publisher's special series and/or reprint series, and children's book club
selections achieve similar ends. In 1940 the Children's Series Division of
the American Library Association began publishing its still very influential annual list of "notable" books. *Booklist* and *The School Library Journal*
(since 1954) remain influential publications. Since the 1950s, guides and
lists have proliferated, stimulated in part by elaborated age-grading systems, book clubs, and, in the 1960s, the upgrading of school libraries so
that books needed to be chosen and purchased for them. Also in the
middle-to-late 1940s and in the 1950s, sales boomed. Despite cultural
competition from other media, the boom lasted well into the 1970s,
helped considerably by the advent of paperbacks. Even these developments, however, failed to create a climate in which publishers could or
would offer "what the public wants," if by public we mean readers. The
reason for this is very simple.

By far the largest number of buyers of "approved" children's literature
has been and continues to be adults—librarians, in particular, who account for nine out of ten children's books purchased. Books from earlier
periods remain on library shelves at the discretion of librarians who
judge them to be "classics," so that girls may read *Little Women* and
Seventeenth Summer who are at the same time reading *You Would If You
Loved Me* and *Are You in the House Alone?* These and other imponderables
make it very difficult to say just what is being done to American children
by their books. What the books are *meant* to do will be a little easier to
describe.[5]

The question of how, and how much, the establishment standards
have changed since the 1920s is fairly easy to answer: hardly at all, until
the mid-1960s. About then, in books for older children at least, an apparently enormous change in possible subject matter took place. As we
will see, however, the appearance of change is greater than the reality.

For the rest of it, in 1920, most of the "child-centered" standards were in place: that is to say, certain educational aims were clearly defined in publishing, library work, or teaching. The question of literary form, then as now, took second place to the question of the values to be illustrated; even the drive toward "realism" must be seen in part as an expression of the value America places on "facing the facts" as part of growing up. In the pages that follow, certain eras in modern American children's literature are categorized according to the cluster of values they emphasize.

DEMOCRATIC IDEALISM, 1880–1920

Americans have never ceased to feel the anxiety that accompanies life in a rapidly changing society. This quality of American experiences is always brought into discussions of nineteenth-century children's literature[6] and applies just as well to that of later periods. What, after all, can make us more uneasy about our uncertain future than the thought that our children may be going to lead lives very different from our own?

Writers for children have always exhibited mixed motives. One of the most persistent themes in the literature throughout the twentieth century is as follows: the past was better than the present; hold fast to the values of the past. This theme exists in contradiction with another—the suggestion that children are actually better able to deal with contemporary reality than adults are—but this scary idea surfaces briefly in any book and very slowly in the literature as a whole. In stories written for children between 1880 and 1920 it is almost nonexistent. Despite what R. Gordon Kelly has called the "new antididacticism" of the latter decades of the nineteenth century, children's "natural goodness" was appealed to during that period in a conservative context. The moral discoveries of the child heroines and heroes of the period are sanctioned by the approval of the most respectable segment of the adult world.

The reasons for this penchant are not hard to find. Many scholars see the years in question as decisive in the process of "modernization"; in any case, they saw the transition to an urban-industrial, technologically oriented society, with accompanying features such as mass immigration and world war. By the end of World War I, the personal childhood experience of many of the best writers of this period lay in an irrecoverable past. Dislocated men and women tried to shape the values of their own, often rural and simpler childhoods to fit the present actualities, with varying success.[7] The boys and girls they wrote about are typically members of small, peaceful communities, where value consensus is essential but democratic. These settings are also invested with the nostalgia of a lost time.

For the women who wrote for girls (and frequently for other adults) during these years, the problem had one major aspect, the redefinition of womanhood. Prominent in this enterprise, because of her position as co-editor of one of the important new magazines for children, was Lucy Larcom. Her *A New England Girlhood* (1889) is autobiography with a good deal of moralizing along the way. Larcom speaks with conviction of "useful lesson of doing without," of the need to live a life that is both useful and independent. The meaning of life, she says, "is education . . . growth, the development of our best possibilities from within outward." Reading, religion, the beauties of nature, but most of all work allow a girl to "cultivate and make use of her individual powers." She remarks that American girls were already being encouraged to do so in her youth. "God sent [girls] into the world full of power and will to be helpers," she claims, but the emphasis is on the power and will, and on how, while being a helper, she supported herself.

This sounds much like Louisa May Alcott's archetypal heroine, Jo March, in *Little Women*. Her fierce youthful independence is turned, in the series of books in which she appears, toward the use and purposes of others' lives. In *Jo's Boys* (1886), one of her charges is another "restless, wilful" child grown into a "woman full of the energy and promise that suddenly blossoms when the ambitious seeker finds the work she is fitted to do well [in this case, the medical profession]." Jo firmly states that the young woman "shall earn her place first and prove that she can fill it; then she may marry if she likes." Strong stuff, and—as we will see—to be diluted in a long line of American stories about "restless, wilful" girls.

The angelic girl-child of mid-nineteenth century, in fact, has all but disappeared. (*Pollyanna* [1913] is a sort of exception but far too unlady-like to fit the mold). In her place, we have the Little Colonel (series beginning 1895), the heroines of Laura E. Richards, as well as *Rebecca of Sunny Brook Farm* (1903) and *Anne of Green Gables* (series beginning 1908). Several of this group of fictional heroines play the familiar role of reawakening the hard hearts of bitter old people. Yet the Little Colonel begins by offending her aristocratic grandfather by appearing barefoot and playing with "niggahs." Her likeness to the Big Colonel is her "vile tempah," and he comes to admire her for her spirit, so she can win his forgiveness for her mother's imprudent marriage. In Richard's *Captain January* (1890), "Star," too, has a temper. When the crusty old sea captain who has raised her claims he wants her to go with the *real* (rich) family that has just found her, she does not behave angelically. *"You lie!"* she cries, throwing his cap in the fire, " 'You lie to me, and you lie to God; and you *know* you lie!' . . . her great eyes flashing fire that fell like a burning torch on every heart."

Rebecca also has astonishing eyes—"like faith,—'the substance of things hoped for, the evidence of things not seen.' . . . Their glance was eager and full of interest, yet never satisfied." Two points are being made here and by other similar heroines. One is that, although a willful, imaginative nature *will* get a girl in trouble, it is very attractive. Another is that, at the worst, a vivid imagination is a solace in adversity. This conclusion is a constant in Kate Wiggins's fiction, as well as in that of L. M. Montgomery. Anne, whose temper matches her red hair, survives the necessity of giving up college because "nothing could rob her of her birthright of fancy or her ideal world of dreams. And there was always the bend in the road!"

Thus, the new girl heroine of the period, in a pattern that does not change until the 1920s, is allowed to exhibit all the "power and will" she likes, until the story's end, when she must store it away in the realm of "things not seen."

In stories for boys, the same values are enshrined but with significant differences. In the first place, with the early exception of Tom Sawyer, hardly any boys in the popular books of the time have much of an imagination. The ordeal survived by a boy hero of this period is typically entered into out of pride, which forbids him to ask for any help, when it would seem sensible to do so. In the second place, boy's stories have different settings. Typically, the young hero faces his conflict away from home, and it is resolved in a burst of violent action. The act, rather than the imaginative transcendence of circumstance, validates his courage and determination. A girl grows up when she renounces some dreams in order to realize others. A boy becomes a man when he can *show* it and thus transforms his lonely pride into a becoming modesty among his admiring peers.

This formula is worked out in a seemingly endless series of sports, school, outdoor, scouting, and war stories, including historical adventure novels. During this period, there was a critical revulsion from the story that rewarded its hero or heroine by a wholly fortuitous acquisition or recovery of wealth or social position. This caused many writers to concentrate on the description of dogged courage and application. To this extent, writers seem to have been expecting as difficult a time for boys as for girls. Pure adventure stories for boys, following in the tradition of "Oliver Optic" and Horatio Alger, gave only lip service to the social ideal of steady, sober advance, but in other series novels a boy must undergo a rigorous training. In a school sports story, he might spend a year learning how to "play the game" before he made the winning touchdown and stopped a runaway team (R. H. Barbour, *Weatherby's Inning*, 1903). In an historical novel, he might spend arduous, if rebellious, years of training to be a knight, before he could fight the trial by battle to clear his father's name (Howard Pyle, *Men of Iron*, 1891).

Daniel T. Rodgers offers two explanations for the popularity of the boy's story formula just described.[8] In the first place, the old forms of masculine responsibility were obviously losing some of their meaning. The work world had changed, and hence there was a "retreat to anachronistic settings"—Medieval Europe, the woods, the West. Another related value change was that from self-reliance to teamwork. The boy who struggled in lonely pride in the early part of the story has learned the value of "fitting in" by the last page, and, moreover, he has learned not to flout authority. Never mind that we do not see much actual teamwork on those last exciting pages; we hear about it from the boys. The hero of *For the Honor of the School* (1900) at first wants to refuse the honor of being the next season's team captain, because he almost lost the meet by not listening to his coach and teammates. And so on.

In 1896 William Patten wrote the first dime novel for boys, *Frank Merriwell*, and in 1906 Edward Stratemeyer founded the Stratemeyer Syndicate, which subsequently turned out the Rover Boys, Motor Boys, Outdoor Girls, Tom Swift, Motor Girls, Hardy Boys, Bobbesey Twins, and other books, including, of course, Nancy Drew.[9] In the pages of these popular books, there is no time to learn anything. True, characters are sketched in as sensible or else frivolous manner as possible so that the reader can tell them apart, but they all engage in such a whirlwind of "scrapes," detective efforts, practical jokes, trips, picnics, parties, shipwrecks, treasure hunts, games, righting of wrongs, and more practical jokes that the reader need not stop to observe that no possible combination of human qualities could support such an activity level.

Yet these books were not the only ones that did not stress the "test of manhood" or "true womanhood" theme. During the earlier years of the period, there was also a vogue for "bad boy" books. Stimulated by Thomas Bailey Aldrich's *Story of a Bad Boy* (1869) and *The Adventures of Tom Sawyer* (1876), American writers went to work to produce *Peck's Bad Boy* (1883) and its five sequels, Henry A. Shulte's *The Real Diary of a Real Boy* (1903), Booth Tarkington's Penrod books (beginning in 1913), and a number of similar books. Somewhat like the girls in their domestic novels, these boys are basically middle-class conformists trying to liven it all up a bit. Yet their salient characteristic is ingenuity rather than imagination, and this ingenuity issues in prank after harmless prank. Their families are often (though privately) amused and sympathetic, from Tom's Aunt Polly: "*He* never meant any harm and he was the best-hearted boy that ever was," to the fathers of Penrod and his friend Sam, who give the boys a quarter each for getting up a "show" that temporarily tarnishes the reputation of a virulently snobbish family.

The Adventures of Huckleberry Finn (1885), as others have pointed out,[10] belongs to none of these genres, for Huck is a genuine rebel against respectability. In fact, the discomfort many readers feel at the end of the book stems largely from the intrusion, into a world where real freedom seems a possibility, of Tom's "harmless," contained fantasy of it. *Huckleberry Finn*, however, shares more than one prejudice with other books of its day; its very raft and shore structure defines the terms of a persistently illustrated paradox. Nature, Americans have believed, is somehow superior to civilization—and if not exactly nature, certainly the small town as opposed to the city, that symbolic locus of all the new unmanageable forces that were changing the American landscape and character. Not only stories of adventure in the wilds reflect this theme. Ernest Thompson Seton's books about animals and woodcrafts were part of a wave of such stories. Some were fanciful, like Thornton Waldo Burgess's *Old Mother East Wing* (1910), some sentimental, like *Black Beauty* (published in America in 1890) and *Beautiful Joe* (1894), and some realistic, like those of Jack London and Alfred Ollivant's *Bob, Son of Battle* (1895). A series of best-sellers as popular with adults as with young people had inspired amateur naturalists as central characters: in Gene Stratton-Porter's *Freckles* (1904), *The Girl of the Limberlost* (1909), and *Laddie* (1913), we know the young heroes and heroines are good and true because they love nature. This makes them instinctively noble. Nature, in *Freckles* and *Michael O'Halloran* (1915), is life-giving. So it is in Frances Hodgson Burnett's *The Secret Garden* (1910) and Dorothy Canfield's *Understood Betsy* (1916). This last book illustrates the virtues of a common sense upcountry childrearing, in which chores and an ungraded school rid a city-bred child of a nervous, self-pitying disposition. Although the unlimited fresh milk and fresh air are not unimportant, the real emphasis falls on Betsy's developing ability to take care of herself. Here as elsewhere in children's fiction we learn the value of what Kelly describes as "the unpretentious home in the small classless village."[11] Nothing the city had to offer carried the same weight of symbolism for American writers of the period, for the village setting neatly combined the romantic vision with democratic ideals and a promise of security. (Besides, it was where most of these writers had grown up.) When it came right down to it, even Dorothy gladly left the Emerald City for home in Kansas, to find Uncle Henry milking the cows there (*The Wonderful Wizard of Oz*, 1900).[12]

The other major current in children's literature that appealed to the national nostalgia for small town or rural life was the regionalism for children which followed shortly on the regionalist movement in American literature in general. The new interest in American folk literature, local color, and local humor satisfied two impulses. In the first place, it presented what Fred Erisman[13] has called an idealized vision of rural America, in which frontier optimism always prevails. On the other hand, it expresses a more present-oriented enthusiasm for the variety of American life. Joel Chandler Harris's Uncle Remus collections began to be published in 1881, while other writers, such as Wiggins and Pyle, were collecting and retelling folk tales. Wiggins was also the author of *Summer in a Canon* (1889) which, like *Rebecca of Sunny Brook Farm* (1903), presents the sort of colorful local characters who epitomize the qualities of a region. Eggleston's *Hoosier School Boy* (1883), Hamlin Garland's realistic

Boy Life on the Prairie (1889), and many of the "bad boy" books contain such types. F. C. Baylor's *Juan and Juanita* (1888), set in the Southwest, makes the explicit point that if the boy and girl had not learned fortitude and self-discipline from their Comanche captors, they could not have survived their journey home after the escape. The detail in this novel is in the same style as Ernest Thompson Seton's *Two Little Savages* (1903), in which two boys learn to live like Indians. Indeed, the theme of being on one's own in nature, popular since *Robinson Crusoe*, received a new impetus in America from this period's fascination with Indian lore. James Willard Schultz, for example, beginning in the second decade of the new century, wrote a series of children's novels depicting American Indian life. Although regionalism was a turn-of-the-century movement in American literature, it was to remain a staple of children's literature well into the 1950s, for the sake of its built-in messages of tolerance and equality.

At the same time, the American writers for children were busily at work recording the manners and customs of the near-past and the out-of-the-way corners of the country. They also took a new interest in the European past and in early American experiences. This trend in children's fiction, like the trend in regionalism, followed a wider cultural movement. The romantic escapism of the period's historical novel appealed to an enormous number of adult readers, well through World War I.[14] Even the critics who condemned the melodramatic unreality of the genre were not entirely out of sympathy with the state of mind of its readers. When William Dean Howells attempted to define realism in 1891, he found himself speaking of a "large, cheerful average of health and success."[15] This was not a position any critic could maintain for long; yet in a society ever more sharply and confusingly divided in terms of class and opportunity, it was powerfully seductive. Certainly it was maintained as a hope for the future. It also sheds some light on the period's vision of the past, for, feudalism and all, the past was imagined by writers for adults and children as a world in which a hero's or heroine's intrinsic quality was invariably recognized. (This even happens in Twain's otherwise grim satire, *A Connecticut Yankee in King Arthur's Court*.)

The most popular historical writer for children in the period was Joseph Altsheler, whose books about the earlier nineteenth century were widely read through the 1920s and even after. Like the stories of the English master of the genre, G. R. Henty, Altsheler's adventure stories take place in a fairly well-detailed context, but an extremely simple one, morally speaking. The ultimate victory of the hero is never for a moment in doubt. Howard Pyle published four Arthurian books between 1903 and 1910, as well as *Otto of the Silver Hand* (1888) and *Men of Iron* (1892). Mark Twain's *The Prince and the Pauper* (1881) is, of course, an extended exploration of the democratic dogma that one boy is as good as any other.

Literary romanticism was, among other things, a protest against the emerging values of a bourgeois, capitalist society. A literature that persistently looks back to an earlier period, or that persistently has for hero or heroine a character who is in reaction against the "getting and spending" that offended Wordsworth, is a romantic literature. Yes, Tom Sawyer, entrepreneur, arranges to have the fence whitewashed for him; Jo March sells potboilers; Penrod charges admission to his "shows"; the girl of the Limberlost sells her moth collection to go to school. Yet the young heroes and heroines of these books, so many of which were popular with adult readers as well, are freed by their very youth from the full weight of routine or compromise. The serious lessons they may learn are still the lessons of a romantic idealism; they do not tarnish the bloom of youth.

DEMOCRATIC REALISM, 1920–1945

Those who have written about the period in children's literature between the two world wars have agreed to agree that it was a very good time. Some of the structural reasons for an upsurge in the quantity and supposed quality of books published have been discussed in the second section of this chapter. In the 1920s, in America, moreover, literature in general flourished. Fairy tales and fantasies for children rose again in popularity (as they were to do again in the similarly prosperous decade of the 1960s). The Oz book, the Dr. Dolittle books, and Carl Sandburg's *Rootabaga Stories* (1922) are some American products of the decade of Winnie the Pooh.

This, however, was hardly the dominant trend of the period, which by the 1930s was very clearly toward "realism." This tendency, as already indicated, was encouraged by the literary trend of the times as well as the arbitrators of the world of children's literature, who took the explicitly moral position that realism was good for children. Indeed, one observer, not far off the mark, has called their attitude a "fetish for realism."[16] The trend does not seem, however, to be merely a reaction against the romantic idealism of the earlier period, any more than the naturalism on the larger literary scene was only a reaction against the genteel tradition. At work also is a democratization of experience, sometimes genuine and sometimes forced.

In both adult and children's fiction, throughout the 1930s and 1940s, there is a new fascination with the "stuff" of all sorts of daily life. Both contemporary fascination with science as a method and the simultaneous shedding of inhibitions about a materialistic ethos are reflected in a style that imitates or gives the impression of objectivity and completeness. Two quite different books will illustrate this change in tone. *Black Beauty* (1890) is told from the horse's point of view, and the reader responds to such passages as "my life was now so utterly wretched, that I wished I might...drop down dead at my work, and be out of my misery." Moreover, Beauty's life story is arranged to permit us a glimpse of every sort of abusive treatment that could be meted out to horses in Victorian England. Will James's *Smoky the Cow Horse* (1926), however, is not only told in the third person, but it also makes its point without moralistic or evaluative comment. James tells precisely how a good owner trains and cares for his or her horse, and allows the contrast with bad owners and riders to speak for itself. Both tales have happy endings, but when Smoky is found and brought back to health by his original owner, the difficult process is not glossed over; it is no miracle.

This new attempt to offer the child reader the facts was given impetus by the inescapable facts and effects of the Great Depression and World War II. Yet the new realism avoided such topics. As Cornelia Meigs puts it, "little attempt was made during and after the Second World War to thrust upon the very young and happily unaware American children... the experiences of children devastated by the war."[17] Stories depicting either of the world wars in this period were adventures, removed from scenes of devastation. They did not often portray serious contemporary problems, let alone personal human tragedies. The works of Carolyn Haywood and Robert McCloskey illustrate this point, for both Haywood and McCloskey, like many other writers, set their stories in "typical" small towns (McCloskey's Lentil and Homer Price live in Ohio), and their characters' problems are chiefly funny ones. *Homer Price* (1943) continues the bad boy tradition, with the new twist of a scientific bent which, more than any simple ingenuity, causes the problems in question. Elizabeth Enright's Melendy family and Eleanor Estes's Moffats (both begin their sagas in 1941) are similarly jolly in tone.

Yet these writers for the 1930s and 1940s are not trying to reduce experience. Consciously, at least, they are trying to make the lives of all sorts of children accessible to their readers. American realism's vision of democratic action is a vision of "the primacy of what ordinary people, living under recognizable pressures, *try to do*."[18] This works reasonably well in stories of "ordinary" children read by "ordinary" children, even though children's writers of this period sidestepped realistic portrayal of the actual limitations of human action. It does not work at all when the writer attempts to give a sense of the "ordinariness" of a character very different from the prospective reader. When fiction of this sort is produced, it is simply a romance in period or regional dress.

The genres of regional and "faraway lands" and historical fiction grew enormously in the period. These romantic adventures gain in both accuracy and verisimilitude, and the values now emphasized are those of tolerance and understanding. As late as 1928, Eric P. Kelly's *Trumpeter of Krakow*, set in fifteenth-century Poland, eulogizes self-sacrificial loyalty and portrays characters in black and white, involving—on the dark side— brutal Cossacks and evil alchemists who "practised dark ways simply to frighten superstitious folk into giving them money." Yet here, in fact, from Charles Boardman Hawes's *The Dark Frigate* (1923) through Elizabeth Janet Gray's *Adam of the Road* (1942) and Esther Forbes's *Johnny Tremain* (1943), the central character is typically on his own and accomplishes his quest without needing to learn obedience to any authority. Stories of faraway lands exhibit the same shift, beginning in the 1920s: the rites of passage depicted take place outside the context of the adult world. A good example of this is Armstrong Sperry's *Call It Courage* (1940) in which Mafatu is deposited by a storm on a cannibal island, with only his dog for company, and learns to conquer his fears. The rite of passage story is used a number of times in the increasingly popular stories of Indian life. In *Waterless Mountain* (1931), by Laura Armer, a boy learns to become a medicine man.[19] The attempt made by these stories and others like them to show that people are really pretty much alike is in part an attempt to get young readers to identify with the fictional heroines and heroes. From the rise of a "child-centered" ideology among those who work with children, such identification is assumed to be the necessary approach. However, characters with whom the reader can easily identify tend to be stereotyped or—worse—empty.

A fair share of the period's books for girls are set in the American past. These heroines contrast with those of the earlier period in at least two ways. While they are still the daughters of Jo March, in the sense that a quirky imagination and a distaste for ladylike behavior characterizes them—for example, *Caddie Woodlawn* (1935), the Laura of Wilder's Little House series, beginning in 1932, Ruth Sawyer's Lucinda in *Roller Skates* (1936), and *The Year of Jubilo* (1940)—they are not encouraged to take refuge in their imaginations. Quite another sort of advice and solace is proffered to these girls. "It is the sisters and wives and mothers," Caddie's father tells her, "who keep the world sweet and beautiful. What a rough world it would be if there were only men and boys in it, doing things in their rough way! A woman's task is to teach them gentleness and courtesy and love and kindness. . . . I don't want you to be the silly, affected person with fine clothes and manners whom folks sometimes call a lady . . . I want you to be a woman with a wise and understanding heart, healthy in body and honest in mind." And here is Lucinda's elder brother on the subject: "You've reached the point where the poet says childhood and womanhood meet. Lots of things can happen to you. . . . You can stay a fighting, disagreeable hoyden, or you can grow in understanding, in lovely ways, in a gentle giving-in that won't hurt you." Written in 1943, Doris Gates's *Sensible Kate* is set in contemporary time. Kate (orphaned, but no pathos here, only a matter of fact acceptance) learns to value being a sensible, responsible, helpful girl. She gets to go to college where she trains to become a home economics teacher. The heroines of this period learn maturity when they learn to see their social context for what it is, and what it requires of them; unlike the extomboys of an earlier day, they will take no refuge in unrealistic dreaming.

The 1930s and 1940s were not, then, a time when writers of children's books encouraged girls to be dreamers. But they did not encourage boys to be dreamers either. *My Friend Flicka* (1941), an extremely popular novel about life on a Wyoming ranch, is, in fact, the story of how a fifth grade boy is cured of the habit of daydreaming when he is given a wild filly to train. "He's learning to face facts," remarks his mother, while the issue is still in doubt. The filly turns out well, Ken makes up his schoolwork and is admitted to sixth grade, his father and he achieve a better understanding of each other. Yet the reader is told quite clearly (by the family doctor) that "the great experiences of life: falling in love, bliss, despair, sacrifice, death," and *not* Ken's dreams, have made him a useful member of society. The sacrifice of a pet for the sake of the family is also a part of the maturing process for Jody, in another regional novel, Marjorie Kinnan Rawlings's *The Yearling* (1938), which details day-to-day life in the Florida scrub forests. Death—and not just the death of pets—is also encountered by Lucinda in *Roller Skates* and by Laura Wilder, who survives and learns from a number of vividly portrayed hardships and misfortunes. Caddie Woodlawn, in the historical novel of that name, also "faces up" to an ugly reality: some hotheaded settlers are planning retaliation for Indian atrocities, against her innocent Indian friends. She rides to warn them; this is her last adventure as a tomboy, an acceptable mission of tolerance and peace. (This emphasis on tolerance is also regularly found in a relatively domestic setting: in one of her early Betsy books, *Betsy Tacy and Tib* [1941], Maud Hart Lovelace's trio of girls are a Baptist, an Episcopalian, and a Catholic.)

One of the most notable, and certainly the most prolific, of those who have written explicitly to increase American children's understanding of each other has been Lois Lenski. Her books, authentic in detail, range from historical fiction for older children to regional stories for all ages. *Strawberry Girl* (1945), about the life of Florida "crackers," is the best known. Children, Lenski felt, "have never learned to put themselves in the other person's place," and she made an extraordinary effort to do this. "It is all these racial and regional differences that make our country unique. Our country has always stood for the widest kind of cosmopolitanism," she claimed.[20] Yet like others she gave strongest emphasis to the message that "the strange person's thoughts, emotions, motives and intentions . . . *are not very different from the reader's own*" (emphasis in the original). She has also written a kind of story for younger children which first became popular in the 1930s: instead of talking animals, the central characters are humanized cars, boats, airplanes, and so forth. Other examples in this vein are *The Little Engine That Could* (1929) and Virginia Lee Burton's *The Little House: Her Story* (1942), which is a different sort of attempt to deal with the results of technology. From the early pages of this book, the little house smiles in a pastoral landscape of apple orchards, but the following pages see her idyll destroyed by the encroachments of the highway, the suburbs, and the black dirty city itself. Her smile vanishes when the El goes up, but reappears when she is moved back out to the country. "Never again would she be curious about the city.... Never again would she want to live there." Nostalgia, in other words, reaches into the work of the period despite its best efforts to face reality. The continuing preeminence of fiction set in a past where moral decisions are clear and right action possible is complemented by the emphasis on similar societies, in stories of children in other lands. Thus, Kate Seredy's best-selling and award-winning *The Good Master* (1935), while realistic in some respects, depicts an idyllic master-worker relationship in the Hungarian countryside of her youth, and Hilda Van Stockum's *The Cottage at Bantry Bay* (1938) is an Irish family idyll.

In 1934 Annie E. Moore wrote: "Stories of good literary quality suited to the age-span under discussion (five to ten years) appear always to be written with a certain degree of idealism and with an imaginative treatment which lifts them out of the crass circumstances and unmitigated hardness of much of modern life."[21] In 1943, Margaret Scoggins, writing for the *Horn Book*, claimed that young Americans were "untouched by bitterness and pessimism ... [were] idealistic, hopeful and impressionable." She still finds them "fresh, energetic, and optimistic" in 1959. She is surely not anticipating all the results, in the decade to follow, of youthful idealism and energy fostered in part by a tradition in children's writing which made plausible a picture of a world in which the dreams of tolerance and social equality could be achieved.

The salient exception to the one-world concept of these years occurred in the Stratemeyer series books. In these books there is no realistic outer world and no question of personal problems for Nancy Drew or the Hardy boys. The appeal of these characters lies in the aplomb with which they court their adventures and avoid the interference of the adult world. In addition, they have unlimited time, money, and their own cars and—in the case of Nancy Drew—tame male help if she really needs it. Set against these WASP protagonists is a vague cast of undesirable and criminal characters, all from the lower classes and usually looking like members of one minority group or another. This flat opposition to the trend in "approved" children's literature was characteristic of all Stratemeyer books: a Bobbesey twin claims blithely of the poor, "They like to live that way." (All the books have at this point been reissued in new, impeccably nondiscriminatory editions. In the new *Shore Road Mystery*, originally 1928, the Hardy boys' good friends are named Phil Cohen and Tony Prito!)[22]

Work and money are far more frequently integral to the plots of these books than they had been before World War I. The Alger or Burnett (*Sara Crewe*, *Little Lord Fauntleroy*) story line, in which a child is rescued from poverty by a wealthy adult, is no longer in evidence. Gertrude Warner's *The Boxcar Children* (1942) is an exception, but the portrayal of the four children's ability to work and be loyal and to contrive to keep themselves is the real emotional focus and interest of the story.[23] In other books, children learn the value of money the hard way (*My Friend Flicka*, *The Yearling*), or else it is a usual concern. In Eleanor Estes's first Moffat book, poverty is so cheerily borne that the reader is hardly aware of it—but the heroine is overcome with guilt at having spent all her nickel on herself, instead of sharing. In Elizabeth Enright's *The Saturdays*, the four Melendy children, city-dwellers, share their weekly allowances in order to have one really good time each. However, adult work, when it is described, is almost never white collar or otherwise dull. In the late 1930s and early 1940s, the girl's "career" book series appeared. Here Sue Barton, Cherry Ames, and others glamorized the jobs open to women at the time. Like Stratemeyer books, they neglected detail for action, and the action almost never had anything to do with the job in question.

In the period in question, the central characters of American children's literature from all walks of life, all periods in history, and many lands illustrate over and over again the proposition that if they are given the opportunity, they will show good sense and a sense of common humanity. These characters acquire knowledge from experience without having to forfeit their idealism, which, however, they practice without preaching. The American dream of social mobility is the heart and soul of the fiction of the period, which reiterates the hope for dissolution of class and ethnic barriers. Moreover, the fiction of the period portrays a new sort of American family. Often, especially in the adventure fiction, writers have taken the notorious editorial advice to "get rid of the parents." But when they have not, no parents or parent figures illustrate the values of the democratic family: like their children—but not *quite* as good at it—they are tolerant, accepting, sensible, kind. Bad parents are virtually unknown.

As suggested earlier, high school life became increasingly interesting to young Americans throughout the period. In 1942 and 1951, respectively, two novels appeared which described the world of the American adolescent from inside. In Maureen Daly's *Seventeenth Summer* and J. D. Salinger's *Catcher in the Rye* (parts of which had been published in 1945), the difficulties and penalties of growing up in the 1940s in America are very fully detailed. Holden Caulfield is alienated from nearly everything, as his little sister points out, while Angie is only very insecure and unable (but who can blame her?) to grasp the principles of dating. Yet the two share a basic preoccupation. "Sex is something I just don't understand," says Holden, who only "wants to" with girls he likes. "It really screws up my sex life," he tells another boy. (He also stops when girls say to.) Holden's sensitivity to the personal pain that "phoniness" can cause doesn't prevent him from telling a girl that he loves her—"a lie of course, but the thing is I meant it when I said it." Angie's concern is also the dilemma of role playing and still "being yourself." She is appalled at having allowed a kiss on the third date. She describes at length her (largely unpleasant) discovery that "going with a boy gives you a whole new identity," and observes not only how her older sister prepares for a date "as if she were dressing up a paper doll," but also how the older girl—unlike Angie; Angie is *really in love*—"necks" and justifies it, just to keep a boyfriend.

Both Angie and Holden find another source of discomfort in their awareness of class differences. Angie is horribly embarrassed by her boyfriend's table manners; she knows all along that she will go to college rather than marry him. Holden sums up the problem: "It's really hard to be roommates with people if your suitcases are much better than theirs." Here, as with the relationship between the sexes, the awareness of contradictions is important, but here too neither young protagonist has any idea of what to do about the situation.

The problem of the changing relationship between the sexes functions as an issue that allows Holden and Angie to demonstrate innocence and sincerity. For the girl, it is *the* way; for the boy, it is one of several ways. Holden and Angie are alike, in that they are far from possessing the comfortable optimism illustrated in books for younger children. Yet they are determined, against odds, to *hold on to* their innocence and sincerity. This was to make them prototypes for characters in American fiction for young people for the next forty years.

In the 1930s and 1940s, then, American books for children continued to depict an idealized version of the world. Despite the greater realism of their settings, these books showed problems being solved with ease by boys and girls of common sense and good will. The material and social constraints so carefully detailed are then transcended by the heroes and heroines of the fiction. Between 1880 and the end of World War II, in adult fiction, naturalism drew a different picture: nature and society combined to crush or warp the individual. Yet even in such fiction, an obdurate strain of primitivism often used a child to symbolize hope. It was taken for granted that children and young people would be more idealistic and hopeful than their elders, and those who tampered with these qualities were antagonists, in both adults' and children's fiction. During Depression and war, a considerable price was paid for the continuance of the national dream of prosperity and freedom. The future—

the children—had to justify that price. So, in all American fiction, they did.

REALISM AND THE NORM, 1945–1960

In the postwar period, children's literature, like many other products that were supposed to occupy the leisure time of Americans, became big business. This did not, of course, mean that the agencies that kept watch over its standards relaxed their vigilance or even particularly lost their efficacy. It did mean, however, that a new competitiveness in the field resulted in an increased responsiveness to contemporary trends and issues. (This tendency was, of course, to increase.) In the years following World War II, nostalgia was still an important theme, and the central characters of the fiction still regularly exhibited qualities of innocence and sympathy that endowed them with unique abilities for right action. Yet they were very much more children of their times than ever before. What had seemed, in the 1930s and early 1940s, merely the counsels of prudence became the "way of the world." The basic formula was the same: if you take a risk because your heart says you must, you may be punished for it, but not more than you deserve. Yet after the war, the punishment—now, not being *part* of "the world"—seemed more intolerable, and protagonists began to work harder in order to avoid it.

Even in the stories that take place outside the context of contemporary American society, there is a tendency for the hero or heroine to pay greater attention to the social sanctions they flout in the name of sincerity or idealism. Stories written about life at home in the United States are, over and over again, stories about learning to accept the standards and values of the community, and community is often defined quite narrowly. The difference has, in part, to do with the postwar flight from the world into the home, and one could have predicted that writers for children would have some trouble making the direction of this flight an appealing one.

In the earliest years covered by this study, community and family were often at odds. Now, with the exception of some stories about immigrants or minority group members, the two categories overlap. Parents are at once more present and less important. Mothers and fathers are usually even more reasonable and understanding than ever, but they are, overwhelmingly, conformists. Moreover, they are almost never interesting characters. Their lives are shown almost exclusively on the stage of the household. Father is shadowy; Mother cooks. The other theme that dominates in the domestic realism of the period is a new and equally dull pragmatism about the central characters' career choices. In a time when adolescents were supposed to have been busy creating a "subculture"[24] or at least having their period of dependency extended, stories often show a quite young boy or girl busily preparing for adulthood in the most practical way by pursuing hobbies related to an eventual career goal. Moreover, the central characters of these stories are very interested in acquiring status symbols. In book after book the plot hinges on the acquisition of a bike, a certain dress, a car. (The days of "making do" are over.)

Not too surprisingly, the acceptance—and the exhibiting—of community standards and values is seen as girl's work. By the late 1940s, M. H. Lovelace's Betsy is in high school. Her story is set at the turn of the century, but her concerns are strictly contemporary. "When there are boys around . . . it's a strain," she comments. And sure enough, she puts on airs in order to captivate sophisticated Phil, who has a car, when she really cares for the iconoclastic Joe. The fantasy act with Phil breaks down, but two developments in the story undercut the supposed message of "Be yourself." One is that Joe apparently couldn't afford to "keep up with the crowd" anyway. The other is that Betsy's big sister, at story's end, advises her that, after all, "a little play acting has its place . . . with a woman, that is."

Conformity is invested with larger implications by Madelaine L'Engle in her 1960 *Meet the Austins*. Maggy, an unloved and orphaned child, comes to stay with the normal, happy Austin family and under their benign influence changes into someone they can love. Leonora Weber's 1950 "Beany" book, *Leave it to Beany* is, on the other hand, a comedy of well meant errors, in which the heroine determines to begin a "career of helping," and proceeds to meddle. The novel is filled with details of dances and dates and dresses; a charm bracelet figures importantly in the plot. Beany's ostensible lesson—leave people alone—is undercut by the resolution of the most important subplot. The Irish immigrant girl whom Beany has offended with her efforts at remolding does, on her own, learn to fulfill Beany's stereotypes for a nice American girl. This book is typical of the flood of "junior novels" that came from the presses in the 1950s; whether or not they have much psychological insight, their scope is narrowed to that of the "teenage world."[25]

Virginia Sorensen, in *Plain Girl* (1955), deals with the problem of conformity by creating a heroine who is an Amish girl. The moral issue here is, shall Esther, aged ten, now in public school, *trade dresses* with a classmate? The implications are clear enough. Esther's father claims that people who dress differently all the time "don't know who they are," and Esther's brother (who has run away from the Amish community) comes back with tales of the fickle and untrustworthy outsiders. A compromise is achieved, when Esther realizes that her friend Mary's parents have rules for her, too, and that Mary, like Esther, has secrets from her parents. "It was only being young and being old," Esther consoles herself—while her big brother returns to the fold as an adult. Here, as elsewhere in the fiction of the period, a young person is seen breaking social rules and escaping consequences—but only if he or she agrees, in the end, to start playing by them again.

Mary Stolz's 1957 novel for girls, *Because of Madelaine*, confronts the issues directly. Again, as in the case of Esther's brother, there are male characters who rebel against conformity in a way the central girl character cannot match. "If you want to get along with people, you have to observe mores and social laws and ... go to ... dancing classes," says she, and "besides being a conformist, I'm an escapist, so I try not to think about" the threat of nuclear war. She does achieve some measure of insight, but only after the chance for stepping outside her small world has passed.

Jessie Bernard has observed that the childrearing practices of the late 1940s and 1950s aimed to develop types comfortable in bureaucratic work situations—more complaisant, more "feminine."[26] This observation would seem to be borne out by the themes and plots of novels for children and young people in this period, but it is clear that the way in which boys are complaisant is still quite different from the way girls are.

The picture drawn holds substantially in stories about life in the United States for much younger children. In Beverly Cleary's books for younger girls, "getting along with others" is the usual lesson to be learned, and when she writes for older children (*Jean and Johnny*, 1959), an explicitly ordinary girl briefly dates an unconventional boy and will *remember him* gratefully. In Cleary's Henry Huggins series (*Henry Huggins*, 1950, *Henry and Beezus*, 1952, and so on), she recasts a bad boy formula: how to combat the boredom of being a suburban third grader? In finding answers to this question, Henry regularly gets into mild trouble but always manages to get what he wants, however ludicrous the means to his end. Cleary's bad boy is all boy, too—in *Henry and Beezus*, besides remarking "she's just a girl" and "girls thought of the dumbest things," he is devoured with embarrassment at winning a girl's bike and beauty parlor coupons at a supermarket opening.

A new note is sounded in the bad boy genre when the boys are no longer merely ingenious at having a good time or getting what they want, but are also budding scientific or technological geniuses. A rash of such heroes followed the "skills crisis" in the American schools in the late 1950s.[27] Keith Robertson's *Henry Reed* (1958) joins Robert McCloskey's Homer Price, whose career continues into the 1950s, as an experimenter, while in Losi Slobodkin's Spaceship books, the American boy befriended by the young Martian is a technological wizard—he could "fix anything." The books themselves are dreams of safe, controlled technology. In such stories, the tension between the values of conformity and antiauthoritarianism is contained by plots that allow for one certain kind of originality. It is okay to exercise your ingenuity to its full capacity in RESEARCH, as Henry Reed's workshop sign announces. However, in books for older children and young people, the scientifically or mechanically gifted hero is not so free.

In Archie Binn's *Sea Pup* (1954), we have another example of the pet sacrifice theme, when the central character must give up his pet seal in order to go to the right high school and prepare for his career in marine biology. Similarly, in one of the period's many stories about a boy and his car, the central character of *Drag Strip* (1959) learns about long-term goals, as well as community spirit. Of the drag strip that he and his friends work to acquire, he comments that it is the "laboratory and training ground for the engineers who are to inherit this civilization." He gives up his youthful idea of freedom in this endeavor.

Sports novels for boys continue in much the same vein as at the turn of the century. In fact, the plot formula previously outlined becomes even more explicit. The characters in these books are not allowed to be "loners" for more than a few pages, if at all.[28] Two prolific writers in this genre, John R. Tunis and Jackson Scholz, routinely punish overconfidence, which destroys real team spirit, quite severely. Their cocky heroes undergo some real humiliations, both voluntary and involuntary, before they are allowed the reward of the final big win. In all of these boys' books (as in most of those for girls), family and community are present to applaud. As James Coleman observed, it is adults who fix the activities of the school, "for example, by using high school sports as community entertainment, and as contests between communities." This is exactly the pattern of Tunis's *Go, Team Go* (1954) in which the fathers are vitally concerned. "School forces a scholar to choose," Coleman concludes, "between being *selfish* by studying hard, and being *unselfish* by working for the glory of the school in its interscholastic games."[29] The only acceptable form of scholastic excellence, according to his study and in the fiction of the period, is the brilliant nonstudious protoscientist, and he is a late development of the period.

When there is painful conflict between generations in the books of this decade and a half, the family portrayed is usually the highly traditional one—the nonassimilated one—of a minority group. This was the case in *Plain Girl*, and the story in Joseph Krumgold's *... And now Miguel* (1953) is that of a boy who must struggle very hard to be accepted as a sheepherder like the rest of the men in his Mexican-American community. He learns that an adult must give up wishes and accept God's will. In these two stories and others like them, as well as a number of historical novels of the period, the insularity of a community within the larger community is an important discovery of the central character. *... (A)nd now Miguel* touches on another theme that is made much of in the postwar years. Miguel finally gets to go to the mountains with the herd because his older brother has been drafted, and nobody is happy about this at all. Without exception, books for children and young people in the 1950s are more pacifist, even retreatist, than ever. At the end of the period, in Elizabeth George Spear's historical novel, *The Bronze Bow* (1961), a first-century Galilean boy learns to overcome his hatred of the Roman oppressors. After he meets Jesus, he gives up his revolutionary aims. Yet the idea of universal brotherhood implied here remains remote and, as already suggested, when potential "brothers" (or sisters) are also Americans, differentiated by ethnic origin or class, the story is about their assimilation. This continues to be true of stories about black children, right through the early years of school integration. Marguerite de Angeli's *Bright April* (1946) and Jesse Jackson's *Charley Starts from Scratch* (1958) are representative. In Dorothy Sterling's *Mary Jane* (1959), the (sheltered, upper-middle-class) protagonist is shocked by the ugliness of pro-segregation demonstrations, but eventually differences among the students smooth out in an atmosphere of acceptance.

In Krumgold's 1959 novel, *Onion John*, the differences in question are ineradicable. Onion John is a peasant from Central Europe with a speech impediment. In some unexplained way, however, the central character can understand him. This boy attempts to prevent his father and the other Rotarians from bringing John "out of the fourteenth century" by building him a new house in which he may live "decently." Andy also resists his father's attempts to make his career choice for him—*he* doesn't *want* to realize his father's dream of going to MIT and being an industrial chemist. Onion John leaves town, telling Andy he can't come along because he is grown up now (beyond John's Medieval belief system), and sure enough, Andy maturely compromises with his father—he will try college. Onion John can't be assimilated, and, like all surrogates for childish rebellion, or symbols of eccentricity, he is removed from the scene. (Something of the kind even goes on in *Charlotte's Web*, for the pig protagonist learns to love the very different spider, only to lose her.) This plot device is a staple of fiction for young people.

Through the 1950s, adventure stories with exotic or historical settings grant protagonists somewhat greater freedom than they enjoy at home. The hero of *Old Yeller* (1956), a story about frontier days, is left to care for his mother and small brother while his father makes the Long Drive with the cattle. However, in still another sacrifice-for-the-family, the boy must shoot his dog after it has fought and saved them from a rabid wolf. (Like Onion John and Flicka, moreover, Old Yeller was "bad.") Elizabeth Speare's heroine of Puritan days in Connecticut, Kit, in *The Witch of Blackbird Pond* (1958), also manages to dispose of a surrogate for "different" behavior. Ostensibly, the story tells of the grim repressiveness of that frontier community and allows Kit to reject it by marrying a dashing ship's captain's son, rather than the tedious bore the Puritan community has marked out for her. In fact, she and her lover conspire to rescue the old woman whom the town suspects of witchcraft, spiriting her away to a permanent home on board his new ship. The townspeople clear Kit of the charge of witchcraft. The solution is not as drastic as in the death of Old Yeller, but the result is the same: the troublesome young person may remain an "insider," because someone else assumes— and suffers—the "outsider" role for him or her. In another plot formula characteristic of adventure stories during these years, an outsider may fight his or her way *in*. In de Angeli's *The Door in the Wall* (1949), set in thirteenth-century England, young Robin de Bureford seizes the opportunity to save a castle from the Welsh. He helps to rout them as well, proving to his father that he can be useful to the family even though he is crippled.

There are numerous examples of the survivor, or Robinson Crusoe, story in the postwar period; here, too, the young protagonist can leave society behind. In *The Black Fox of Lorne* (1956), de Angeli writes of twin Norse boys shipwrecked on the coast of Scotland, and in *The Big Wave* (1948), Pearl Buck writes of a Japanese boy whose village is swept away. The decade's outstanding book of this type is Scott O'Dell's *The Island of the Blue Dolphins* (1960), based on the true story of an Indian girl who lived alone on an island for eighteen years. O'Dell's heroine is happy with her animal friends, and when missionaries finally take her off the island, she dons their clothing with reluctance, putting away her shirt of cormorant feathers to wear "sometimes when the men were not around." In Jean George's *My Side of the Mountain* (1959) the theme undergoes a change. In the first place, the father encourages his son to live alone in the woods for a year. The story provides the usual amount of detail: in this case a good deal of woodcraft and some native American lore. *This* hero comments that he doesn't like to be dependent on "electricity, rails, steam, oil, coal, machines and all those things that can go wrong"—quite a switch on the young inventor theme. The results are the same, however, for his experiment in survival ends when his entire family moves up to the woods to live with him. "You can't live in America today and be quietly different," he is firmly told. People will find you out. "And that ended it."

Yet other popular books of the 1950s allow boys the opportunity for extrasuburban adventure: they climb mountains, rescue other boys, find ancient jungle roads, and tame wild horses. In these stories, the protagonist defies family or tribal advice or precedent, but somehow, in doing what he sets out to do, each achieves a very acceptable triumph.

As observed earlier, books for boys and girls in this period are pacifist. Historical fiction very often works the theme of the reconciliation of differences; the English and American civil wars are popular topics. Examples are Harold Keith's *Rifles for Watie* and William O'Steele's *The Perilous Road*, both published in 1958. This second story is set in Ten-

nessee. The strong regional flavor of the book, believable conflict between generations, and realistic battle scene are subverted by the way
the story ends. Chris believes he has aided in a Rebel attack, while his
brother, enlisted on the Union side, is in the camp. He finds he is guiltless,
and, safe at home, he submits gratefully to his father's lecture on not
getting involved. Irene Hunt's *Across Five Aprils* (1964), a book for older
readers, makes the same point about the pointless horror of war.

In the late 1940s and 1950s, science fiction provided the only reliable
models for self-determining, "unsocialized" character. Two examples
from Robert Heinlein's very popular series for young people will suffice.
In *Between Planets* (1951) Don learns that he cannot maintain neutrality
when Venus is at war (despite his birth in space). He is a Venusian, and
his best friends are Venusians. He will make his own decision to fight.
In *The Star Beast* (1954) John has acquired the Star Beast as a pet, from
outer space. This pet is *not sacrificed*—although John's mother and the
community badly want it to be disposed of. "The deuce with common
sense!" decides John. "His ancestors hadn't used common sense, any of
'em!" John earns the right to go home with the Star Beast to her planet,
who turns out to be the Imperial Princess of her enormously advanced
and powerful race, and thus he preserves interstellar peace. Science
fiction stories for the next three decades are not only openly admiring
of rebellion, but they are often about the dangers of social stasis, the
wonders of social change.

In the 1950s, then, books for children and young people reflected
contemporary ideas about the needs of children. A reaction from early
permissive theory appears to have occurred. Daniel R. Miller and Guy
E. Swanson summarize one set of assumptions underlying the children's
fiction of the late 1940s and 1950s:

The world does not change as rapidly as was supposed. Some things persist for
long periods if not forever. The fundamental relations the child must expect to
establish with other people, if they are to tolerate him, are much the same as
they ever were in human history.... He [*sic*] must be a good member of the
groups in which he participates.

With the exception of a few adventure stories and science fiction, the
books just reviewed assume the sort of social world for which Miller and
Swanson say the children in their 1958 study are being reared: one
"closely knit and moral ... in which ... their behavior will be guided and
supervised."[30] In *The Lonely Crowd* (1950), David Reisman analyzes a story
for very young children, "Tootle," in which a young engine learns to
stop at a red flag and "always stay on the track, no matter what." Reisman
was not quite alone in questioning whether or not "other-directedness"
really lifted a moral burden from young shoulders, even in a supposedly

secure environment. Where psychological realism occurs in the stories of the 1950s, the characters depicted are hardly anxiety-free. They are, rather, somewhat confused and cautious—despite all the signals they are getting. In any case, confidence in a secure, let alone closely knit and moral, society was misplaced. This was to become clear during the next decade, in which a generation of adolescents behaved as if the moral burden of the ages was their unique prerogative.

In the postwar period, then, the world portrayed in children's books and books for young people is safer but more limited than it has ever seemed. The adult world is portrayed as harder to escape, but at the same time more elusive; young protagonists prepare to enter it, but that is about all. Above all, the values of tolerance and understanding undergo a change into the value of conformity; the achievement of understanding presupposes that people will become like one another.

THE 1960S AND AFTER: REALISM AND THE INDIVIDUAL

Before the 1960s, the approved formula for a children's novel went something like this: create a character with heroic potential but do not allow it to be fully realized, if that will entail an open, possibly tragic, conflict between youthful idealism and social constraints. A happy ending, in which these differences are reconciled (or discovered to be illusory), is obligatory. The 1960s changed the formula.

Since the latter half of the 1960s, and regularly since then, children's fiction has thrived on the theme of open conflict between generations. On the evidence of the literature, moreover, this conflict is experienced by children at an earlier and earlier age. In books for the "preteen" (grades five through seven), there are as many issues of autonomy raised as there are in books for the "young adult" or high-school-aged reader. The protagonists of these books are no longer sheltered. Parents, in sharp contrast to those portrayed in the preceding years, may be drawn as insensitive, bigoted, ineffectual, and selfish, not to speak of mentally ill, alcoholic, or criminal.

The conflict of generations is dealt with, in books for all ages, as part of the wider conflicts or dislocations in American society that seemed to surface in the 1960s. Civil rights, the women's movement, the "sexual revolution," the peace movement, and a louder and more pervasive criticism of the American dream of success—all get time in books of the late 1960s and 1970s. In part, of course, this is an effect of the field's ever-greater responsiveness to the market. But it may also reflect a change of approach on the part of librarians, publishers, and writers which parallels a shift in parents' attitudes toward their offspring. Glenn Davis speaks persuasively of what he terms the "delegated release" mode of childrearing current after 1940. It is characterized in part by the vision of the child as "containing potentialities which could be distorted through improper child care." Here, parents' delegations begin to be concerned with missions of the id (rather than the ego, or superego, as in earlier periods), so that children are expected to act out the repressed infantile wishes of the parents.[31] As Philip Slater puts it, "Spockian parents feel that it is their responsibility to make their child into the most all-around perfect adult possible, which means paying a great deal of attention to his [*sic*] inner states and latent characteristics." As he points out, Spock's work epitomizes the long-standing American tradition of the uniqueness of the individual, as well as our long-standing "permissiveness."[32] However, there was at least a shift of emphasis in the years in question.

Seen from this perspective, the children's literature of the postwar period looks like a temporary reaction *against* the shift: the forces of children's literature putting forth their best efforts at denying the old American anxiety over social change and social differences of all kinds, as represented by children. Yet the very intensity of the effort betrayed it for what it was. Children in the books of the postwar period were held in check, despite (perhaps because of ?) their potential. However, it would appear that writers of American children's books and those who judge, publish, and buy the books want something more than an image of sensible, secure childhood and youth. The hold on our imaginations of a more romantic image, despite its dangers, has proved stronger. Whatever other values we have doubted, we have gone on believing in self-confidence and love—"id involved" though these powers may be. Surely, they will be applicable in the insecure present, the uncertain future?

A generation of writers has tried to imagine what a generation of creative, loving, autonomous children thinks and feels. It has not been possible for them to prevent a standoff between youthful idealism and contemporary society's invitations to cynicism. Far from it. In book after book, racial prejudice, sexism, sexual hypocrisy, war, and the empty materialism of the middle class threaten the potential of the young heroine or hero. The attempt to depict a safe and beautiful world, outside of fantasy, to anyone over the age of seven, is quite abandoned. The family, which lost its function as a boundary between child and world sometime in the 1940s, is now seen as fatally involved with the wrongs of that world. Only those parents who assume the role of friends, taking as well as giving advice and support, are portrayed as good adults. No one can pretend these kids are innocent! But they can be loving and strong—and often are stronger than adults.

So radical a reorganization of an entire popular genre, plot formula, character stereotypes and all, is surprising. In the course of examining some relevant texts we will discover, some continuities, however.

Stories about minority children and families provide an especially intriguing glimpse at the "new realism".[33] Before the 1960s, they typically focused on a process of assimilation or else described "a different way of life" in virtual isolation from the larger society, often with the aid of historical displacement. Now even historical fiction, for example, stories about native Americans, tends to focus on the conflict between groups: Scott O'Dell's 1970 *Sing Down the Moon* documents the Navahos' "Long Walk" from Canyon de Chelly to Fort Sumner. In Judy Blume's story for preadolescent girls, *Are You There, God? It's Me, Margaret* (1970), an ugly struggle between her grandparents (Christian) and her parents (her father is Jewish) temporarily causes Margaret to quit praying to the God *she* knows—although from neither church nor temple. Emily Cheney Neville's *Berries Goodman* (1965) also portrays adult anti-Semitism. The working mother, a realtor, steers Jews away from the restricted neighborhood. The children in the story resist parental efforts to break up their friendship. In the 1960s and 1970s, predictably, stories about American blacks proliferated. Natalie Savage Carlson's *The Empty Schoolhouse* (1965) is a story of integration in a Southern town and involves imported agitators and violence. Yet this early story still portrays white and black children, despite the efforts of their parents, as friends. By 1967, in Paula Fox's *How Many Miles to Babylon?* the focus sharpens. The streets where James lives are a fearful chaos, against which he sets his aunts' memories of rural childhood. He also daydreams that his absent mother has gone to Africa to "fix everything" so he'll be an African prince. James learns not only that his daydreams are just daydreams—as we would expect—but also that he can be himself however the environment threatens him, and finally, when his mother returns, that she is "hardly any bigger than he is." In 1968 and 1972, Frank Bonham's *The Nitty Gritty* and *Hey, Big Spender* continue the documentation of black urban ghetto realities, both material and social. In *The Nitty Gritty*, we again encounter a central character given to nonproductive daydreaming. Yet here, as in Fox's novel, the dreams are a necessary bridge to his eventual discovery of inner strength. His parents are janitor and maid, and they put down his high hopes as "just stupid." He must learn that his irresponsible uncle is just irresponsible—but he will not be another janitor. In *Hey, Big Spender*, young blacks learn to work hard in the hope of change.

Stories of other disadvantaged young people follow a similar pattern. Robert Burch's *Queenie Peavy* (1966), for example, is about a girl in rural Georgia whose father returns home from the penitentiary, gets in trouble again, and goes back. Queenie's inner strength, discovered in the course of the story, is self-control—in particular how to control her anger. Virginia and Bill Cleaver's character Mary Call in *Where the Lilies Bloom* (1969) and *Trial Valley* (1977) is simply a strong, independent young woman able to run a family after her parents are gone. (This discovery of strength in girls and young women as well as their male counterparts occurs in all sorts of contexts: in the very different *Did You Hear What Happened to Andrea?* (1979), a fifteen-year-old survivor of rape deals with the trauma with far greater courage and insight than her mother can.)

The message of hope is also the usual last word in feminist stories of girls, which also proliferated in the period.[34] Louise Fitzhugh's *Harriet the Spy* (1964) and *Nobody's Family Is Going to Change* (1974) offer two unconventional heroines. Harriet, a rich city child, is also brilliant, with an insatiable need for knowledge. She keeps notebooks in which she records everything she observes, with complete candor. This is discovered by her schoolmates, with predictably disastrous results. The ending, which shows her learning tact and sublimating her oddness by editing the school paper, is a disappointment, but Fitzhugh's gallery of characters—independent and competent children, ineffectual and useless women, an older woman who tells Harriet that "people who love their work love life"—almost make up for that. In *Nobody's Family Is Going to Change*, the heroine is a fat, ugly black girl, although again well off and brilliant—her lawyer father can afford to hire a white maid. Here, however, the advantage is stood on its head, for the father won't let his son follow his talent to become a dancer because *he* has fought all his life to overcome those stereotypes! And the mother wants Emma to *marry* a lawyer, not *be* one. Emma confronts her father: "You don't even know us!" and wears him down. Her little brother Willie is allowed his dancing lessons, and she can plan a career in law. But the real discovery for Emma is that her father won't love her for this, so she needn't try to please him any more. *She* can change, however. Once again, social change (represented in this story by a secret Children's Army which Emma must reject as male-dominated, like families) is transmuted into a concern for personal growth.

Norma Klein's books for girls also portray nontraditional roles for women and some for men. In *Mom, the Wolf Man and Me* (1972), an eleven year old lives with her unmarried mother, a photographer, and is very much her own person. This is contrasted with the total empty conventionality of a friend's mother (who attempts suicide). Moreover, the "wolf man," Brett's mother's lover, bakes bread. Brett says of her mother, "for her to have a husband, I guess I imagine she would have *to...do* more regular things." But the marriage takes place without any such apparent consequences. In *It's Not What You Expect* (1973) the father of Carla, who is fourteen, has gone to live in New York during his midlife crisis. Carla and her twin brother, who cooks, successfully open and run a restaurant. The older brother's girl has an abortion; when Carla tells her mother, her mother tells about *her* abortion. "She must think I'm fairly mature.... That made me feel good...she felt she could trust me." Carla's mother also trusts her with an explanation of her father's behavior—his drive, his unrealistic expectations, his disappointments. The twist on this is that Carla is like her father and not her more present-oriented mother and brother. Father returns, so that the novel's warning against ambition and perfectionism is somewhat muted.

Novels aimed at the feminine audience among young adults seem less feminist than many written for younger girls. This is because they are likely to deal with sexual roles and stereotypes as if they were one part of the larger problem of whether or when to have sex. Thus, social conformity, rather than sexism, is the problem—not so different a picture from that painted in *Catcher in the Rye* or *Seventeenth Summer*. Madelaine L'Engle, in *Camilla* (first published in 1951, revised for a 1965 edition), creates a heroine who must learn to balance the values of sexual attractiveness and strength. Her mother is weak, and Camilla despises her for having an affair. Like Angie in *Seventeenth Summer*, she loses her love, but being an aspiring astronomer is a consolation. In Mary Stolz's *Leap Before You Look* (1972), the heroine says women are forced to be "devious, even schizophrenic" and is none too sure that feminist ideas can apply to her experience. Norma Stirling's *You Would If You Loved Me* (1969) is one of many novels illustrating a change in sexual mores since the 1940s, since the question for her character, Trudy, is "how long will Tom date me if I don't have sex with him?" Trudy's mother is no help to her. Her decision *not to* is presented as a moral victory; it is also rewarded by the discovery that Tom is really a dreadful person in several ways, and good riddance. Yet Stirling does attempt to depict the very different attitude the two sexes take toward the whole issue. (There are many more stories about sex for young women than for young men, with the interesting exception of stories about homosexuality. Attempts are M. E. Kerr's *If I Love You, Am I Trapped Forever?* [1973] and Jerome Brooks's *The Testing of Charlie Hammelman* [1977]. The "devious and schizophrenic" behavior enjoined upon young men with respect to the opposite sex deserves better treatment than it has gotten so far.)

In Zena Sutherland's *The Best in Children's Books 1973–1978*[35] there is a "developmental values" index, in which interpersonal relations easily outnumber all other categories. This categorization seems to reflect fairly accurately one obsessive concern in American books for children and young people in the latter half of this century. Despite a new willingness to admit social insecurity and social differences, as well as the infinite fallibility of families, American children are still being taught, through their fiction, how to get along with each other. The emphasis does not now fall, however, on similarities and how to achieve them. On the contrary, rather than finding a place in society, the protagonist becomes his or her own person and finds one or two other oddballs to appreciate it. Peculiar friends (often older eccentrics) with wisdom to impart are a time-honored convention in children's literature, indeed, in all romances. (This is related to the convention of the lovable, noble, but impossible pet.) This former convention is overworked in the 1960s and 1970s.

In Alice Low's *Kallie's Corner* (1966), the older person is an Italian puppeteer, who helps to teach two preadolescent girls that they can "make something happen all by [themselves]"—art. "I never really *had* it," Kallie says of one of her creations, "and yet I'll always have it." Her friend Jane, a far more timid and conventional child, has learned that social acceptance (represented by a club at her private school) is less important than creativity. Yet this knowledge is presented as a way to compromise—Jane gets both; art is a sort of safety valve for the social pressure. In Barbara Wersba's *The Dream Watcher* (1969) a 1960s Holden named Albert becomes fond of an elderly alcoholic woman who helps him to accept himself as he is, not the "popular, successful and rich" person his parents want him to be. But old Mrs. Woodfin also tells him that the only way to be unconventional is to fulfill conventional obligations first. In Emily Nevill's *It's Like This, Cat* (1963), there are two eccentrics who help the hero cope with an unhappy home life. This pattern recurs in E. L. Konigburg's *From the Mixed-Up Files of Mrs. Basil E. Frankenweiler* (1967). In John Ney's *Ox Goes North* an aging ex-actress sides with the youngsters against a pair of rich and powerful sadists who are driving a boy crazy so as to get his inheritance. She can only help them by dynamiting herself together with the evil couple, in the most dramatic image of sacrifice in the literature.

But this is not the only image: in these stories, the strange old people go the way of the "bad" pets of earlier children's fiction. Mrs. Woodfin dies, the Pigman in Paul Zindel's *The Pigman* (1977) dies, and so does the very strange adult, Lloyd, in Zindel's *The Confessions of a Teenage Baboon* (1977). In such stories, bright and sensitive young people learn about life and themselves by befriending the oldsters, whose subsequent deaths are seen as "a merciless warning and command to grow" (*Confessions*). Of course, the warning not to be *too* different comes across a little more strongly than the command to grow, but it is true that the "wake up, dreamer" theme has changed. Now the dream is a precious and rare discovery, fostered on the margins of existence, and as fragile as the hope of change. The ability to face reality is translated as "our life would be what we made of it" (*The Pigman*).

The theme of facing up to facts is by no means a large item on the agenda of children's writers during and after the 1960s; rather, they appear to assume that their readers need assistance in building personal definitions and defenses against its encroachments. "If you don't have dreams, what do you have?" asks Danny, in Blume's *Tiger Eyes* (1981).

It is adults who do not face reality, and parental characters are regularly preoccupied with fantasy, or meaningless trivia, or worse. In *It's Not What You Expect*, while the father goes to New York to find himself, another family copes with a mother who is in and out of mental hospitals. Albert, in *The Dream Watcher*, has a mother who lives in the pages of her movie magazines. In *Camilla*, not only is the mother infantile, but the father is emotionally remote enough to excuse the fact that she looks elsewhere for warmth and attention. Other parents escape into alcohol, as in Zindel's *My Darling, My Hamburger* (1969) and Ney's Ox books, where the preteen and later teenaged hero matter of factly helps the houseboy bring father in off the lawn most mornings. Ox is more than strong enough to face the fact that "everything can always get worse for a kid."

A new subcategory of books for children and young adults deals explicitly with the death of a parent. In the books for older readers, the plot reveals the consequent family realignments—in which, of course, the children become stronger. Wersba's *Run Softly, Go Fast* (1970) belongs here, as does Blume's *Tiger Eyes*, in which mother and daughter adjust separately, without being able to help each other, to the father's death. Of course, it is the daughter who makes the better, earlier adjustment. This is yet another novel about the importance of making changes inside yourself. One more subgenre carrying this message is the story about overcoming handicaps—deafness, autism, scoliosis, dyslexia, and the results of sports and traffic accidents. John Neufeld has dealt with mental illness in *Lisa, Bright and Dark* (1969) and cerebral palsy in *Touching* (1970).

Of course, there are young adult novels, as there are books for younger readers, in which the readers' desires for wish fulfillment and excitement are answered—stories in which hero or heroine achieves or finds what he or she had dreamed of, whether this is a sports-victory,[36] love relationship, or adult status. The standby genres of adventure fiction (with the exception of science fiction) decline somewhat in popularity, despite a rash of stories about American history celebrating the bicentennial. The Old West provides scope for younger protagonists, both male and female, particularly in the work of Betty Baker and Patricia Beatty. The popular Great Brain stories (1967–) by John D. Fitzgerald belong in this category, since they are set in turn-of-the-century Utah. These stories of a bad boy with a brain and "money loving heart" are told by a younger brother who despairs of making "a true Christian out of my brother." When he *is* reformed, life is "so dull there is no more to tell." This split message, at any rate, has remained constant since Tom Sawyer. A favorite location for historical fiction continues to be England, but other locales are explored. A trend toward turn-of-the-century and earlier twentieth-century settings is new in the 1970s, celebrating old-fashioned values, accurate in detail, soaked in the period's nostalgia. The greatest number of "intercultural" stories are of the "roots" variety, including a large number about African children, but there are also a number of Holocaust and World War II stories.

The widest scope for adventure and the only opportunities to get right outside contemporary social value structures—or else to highlight their conflicts starkly and dramatically—are provided by fantasy and science fiction. A high proportion of science fiction stories involve a conflict between a group or a mysterious force that is *against* all change. In Josephine Rector Stone's *Praise All the Winds of Morning* (1979), the heroine must struggle against programming that is meant to insure a society "free of war, crime and interpersonal conflict" as well as aliens who believe "what always has been, must always be." A similar mind control theme pervades William Sleator's *House of Stairs* (1974) and John Christopher's *The Lotus Caves* (1969), while in Zilpha Keatley Snyder's *Below the Root* (1975) and *And All Between* (1976), young people rebel against the received wisdom of a highly ordered society, in order to include all human potential. Ben Bova's *End of Exile* (1975) has a similar theme, as does Christopher's Wild Jack trilogy (1974–). The science fiction of this period illustrates the same development as the field as a whole: a movement toward the soft, or social, sciences for the conceptual interest. Technological wonders are replaced by the insights of the anthropologists. This trend is also at the source of the flourishing fantasy of the 1960s and 1970s. While teenagers were reading of Tolkien's alternate world, younger readers found Lloyd Alexander's *Chronicals of Prydain* and Ursula Le Guin's Earthsea trilogy, among many other such series, in which the cultures described are very different from our own, usually in the direction of greater simplicity. In fantasy, the passage to maturity is a triumph rather than a diminishment, however serious the protagonist's trials on the way. In both science fiction and fantasy, moreover, the protagonist is often female (even Heinlein, in this period, invents a heroine, Podkayne of Mars), sometimes even a heroine in a nonsexist society.

During and since the 1960s, then, American fiction for children and young people began to portray painful and destructive conflicts between individuals and American society. The central characters in this "new realism" are not innocent any more, but they are always able to detect hypocrisy, self-deception, and other weaknesses among the adult members of the society. The most persistent flaw of adults as they are portrayed in this fiction is a desire to impose their own empty, repressive, or oppressive value system on the young. The young, however, discover that they are strong enough to resist such pressures—to be (with some qualifications) themselves.

CONCLUSION

American children's literature, despite the naturalistic trappings, remains very much a romantic literature. Moreover, though the endings of these stories are often less neatly happy than those of earlier stories, more open, even sadder—they still offer, almost without exception, better hopes for the future. Adult fiction of the postwar period to the present portrays the achievement of insight *without* hope. We clearly don't want to face our children with that.

Happy endings "work" in popular genres where readers expect them, where they are part of the formula. American children have been thoroughly conditioned to expect them in their books. The central character of *The Dream Watcher* comments of his English class: "if we ever read a book in which youth went to pieces at the end, I would be more interested."[37] The problem novel for young adults, he is saying, is a copout. Like any reader, real or imaginary, he wants to identify with the protagonist of the story he reads, and he can't at the moment imagine a happy ending for himself. (Mrs. Woodfin has yet to die for his craziness.) In all formula fiction, in other words, heroes and heroines are there *to be identified with*. Such stories cannot be complicated into an imitation of life of an "other." On the contrary, in these stories actual human differences are melted together into a composite metaphor for the uniqueness of the individual reader.

Now, as fifty years ago, the most commonly mentioned criterion of excellence in a children's book appears to be the "plausibility" or "believability" of its young characters. This is another way of saying that readers can imagine themselves in the characters' places, can join the mass dream life of the cultural establishment. Before the 1930s, this dream life consisted largely of an inability to abandon the romantic ideal of a simple, open, and morally intelligible society, in which everyone knew how to prove himself or herself worthy of happiness. The central characters of children's fiction illustrated this principle by being natural, but at the same time able to know their places. During the Depression and World War II, the dream enlarged to attribute worthiness to everyone, in an upsurge of conviction in the myth of social mobility, and in the value of tolerance. In children's literature, even the image of the American family became more democratic, while children became simultaneously more daring and more sensible.

For a while, in the postwar years, the democratic family, children and all, appeared to be absorbed by a society that believed itself to be both moral and secure. Only in the science fiction of the 1950s were there characters who could not be assimilated to community—or even high school—standards. To be an insider was all important. Yet these years

appear now to have been an aberration. With the 1960s, children's fiction
returned overwhelmingly to a portrayal of children and young people
who illustrate and symbolize America's hope for the future by the fresh-
ness of their vision and by their toughness. In problem novels and science
fiction and fantasy, they struggle against control and to be themselves.
More individualistic than ever, these fictional boys and girls of the 1960s
and after legitimate every variety of personal pain and estrangement—
up to a point, for before the story ends, hope must resolve the conflicts.
Undoubtedly, this series of paradoxes has proved as "plausible" and
"believable" to readers as those in any romantic literature. Four generations of publishers and librarians have been able to keep the dream
alive.

NOTES

1. James S. Coleman, *The Adolescent Society: The Social Life of the Teenager and
Its Impact on Education* (New York: Free Press, 1961), 4, and the Autumn 1979
Digest of Educational Statistics (Washington, D.C.: National Center for Educational
Statistics, 1979).
2. Daniel T. Rodgers, *The Work Ethic in Industrial America, 1850–1920* (Chicago: University of Chicago Press, 1979), ch. 5.
3. Dora V. Smith, *Fifty Years of Children's Books* (Champaign, Ill.: National
Council of Teachers of English, 1963), 20.
4. See Richard L. Darling, *The Rise of Children's Book Reviewing in America.
1865–1881* (New York: R. R. Bowker, 1968).
5. The books described have been selected from approved guides for their
periods, and Newberry and other award winners have frequently been included.
Best-sellers have also been included. See, for example, Jean Spealman Kujoth,
Best Selling Children's Books (Metuchen, N.J.: Scarecrow Press, 1973).
6. See, for example, R. Gordon Kelly, *Mother Was a Lady: Self and Society in
Selected American Children's Periodicals, 1865–1890* (Westport, Conn.: Greenwood
Press, 1974), v; Rodgers, *Work Ethic in Industrial America*, 125.
7. Kelly, *Mother Was a Lady*, ch. 5.
8. Rodgers, *Work Ethic in Industrial America*, 126, 136, 145.
9. Dierdre Johnson, *Stratemeyer Pseudonyms and Series Books: An Annotated
Checklist of Stratemeyer and Stratemeyer Syndicate Publications* (Westport, Conn.:
Greenwood, 1982) is invaluable for sorting out such matters.
10. See, for example, Anne Trensky, "The Bad Boy in Nineteenth Century
American Fiction," *Georgia Review* 27 (1973): 503–517.
11. Kelly, *Mother Was a Lady*, 124.
12. L. Frank Baum's fables are, of course, not that simple. Oz was a highly
individualistic society with a barter economy, where "everyone worked half of
the time and played half of the time, and the people enjoyed the work as much
as they did the play" (*The Emerald City of Oz*). Baum's utopia shows our pastoral
ideal and our passion for invention, though he was troubled by the latter. In
The Master Key: An Electrical Fairy Tale (1901), science and technology get out of

hand when the bad boy hero accidentally summons the Demon of Electricity. The boy ends by refusing the Demon's gifts, because man is not ready for them. "You forgot to be a slave," he admonishes the Demon. No wonder the Oz books were more popular.

13. Fred Erisman, "American Regional Juvenile Literature 1870–1910: An Annotated Bibliography," *American Realism, 1870–1910* (Spring 1973): 109.

14. James D. Hart entitles the relevant chapter of *The Popular Book: A History of America's Literary Taste* (New York: Oxford University Press, 1950) "When Knighthood Was in Flower," after a novel of the time.

15. William Dean Howells, *Criticism and Fiction* (New York: Harper & Brothers, 1891).

16. Bess Porter Adams, *About Books and Children: An Historical Survey of Children's Literature* (New York: Henry Holt & Co., 1953), 109.

17. Ruth Hill Viguers, "Golden Years and Time of Tumult 1920–1967" in Cornelia Meigs, Elizabeth Nesbit, Anne Thaxter Eaton, and Ruth Hill Viguers, eds., *A Critical History of Children's Literature: A Survey of Children's Books in English* (rev. ed.) (Toronto, Ontario: Macmillan Co., 1969), 506.

18. Alfred Habegger, *Gender, Fantasy and Realism in American Literature* (New York: Columbia University Press, 1982), 111.

19. In the 1940s, a few books about Negroes were published; for example, Jesse Jackson's *Call Me Charley* (1945). This book, typically for the period, follows a different pattern from the one I have been describing, in being more concerned with the Negro boy's problems of acceptance by whites than by any other sort of self-definition. In Arna Bontemps's *The Sad Faced Boy* (Boston: Houghton Mifflin, 1937), some boys from Alabama try to make it into the big time in New York but decide they prefer home.

20. Lois Lenski, "Regional Children's Literature," *Wilson Library Bulletin* 21 (December 1946): 290.

21. Annie E. Moore, *Literature Old and New for Children: Materials for a College Course* (New York: Houghton Mifflin, 1943), 388.

22. Johnson documents these revisions.

23. It goes without saying that poverty and/or families in which children contribute labor provide some of the color of regional stories.

24. Coleman describes and attempts to account for the new orientation toward peers.

25. See Richard S. Alm, "The Glitter and the Gold," *The English Journal* 44 (September 1955): 315–322, 350.

26. Jessie Bernard, *The Future of Motherhood* (New York: Dial Press, 1974), 100.

27. Robert H. Bremner, *Children and Youth in America: A Documentary History, Vol. 3: 1933–1973*, 1576, discusses the aftermath of the Soviet launching of Sputnik.

28. Daniel R. Miller and Guy E. Swanson, *The Changing American Parent: A Study in the Detroit Area* (New York: John Wiley & Sons, 1955) drew a picture of friendship as team spirit: "The child increasingly meets his *[sic]* peers as colleagues whose favors he must court and whose respect he must win.... He must learn to fit in smoothly with all of them" (202–203).

29. Coleman, *Adolescent Society*, 305, 310.

30. Miller and Swanson, *Changing American Parent*, 22, 56.

31. Glen Davis, *Childhood and History in America* (New York: Psychohistory Press, 1976), 153–154.

32. Philip Slater, *The Pursuit of Loneliness: American Culture at the Breaking Point* (Boston: Beacon Press, 1970), 57, 63. Miller and Swanson add that "A method of handling life's problems, not a preconstructed set of solutions for them, is [seen as] the heritage each generation should pass to the next" (20–21).

33. Kenneth L. Donelson and Alleen Pace Nilsen, *Literature for Today's Young Adults* (Glenview, Ill.: Scott, Foresman & Co., 1980), ch. 6.

34. With feminist guides, for example, Judith Adell and Hilary Dole Klein, *A Guide to Non-Sexist Children's Books* (Chicago: Academy Press, 1976), and feminist analyses, for example, Lenore Weitzman, et al., "Sex Role Socialization in Picture Books for Pre School Children," *American Journal of Sociology* 77 (May 1972): 1125–1150. This article demonstrates the overwhelming sex bias of the Caldecott winners between 1953 and 1971.

35. Sutherland is children's book editor for the *Chicago Tribune* and a professor in the Graduate Library School at the University of Chicago. The book is one of a series, and selections are from those published regularly in the *Bulletin of the Center for Children's Books*. The Center was established at the University in 1945.

36. In the 1970s, sports stories for girls appear.

37. Clearly, he, unlike his creator, has not read Salinger.

BIBLIOGRAPHY

Adams, Bess Porter. *About Books and Children: An Historical Survey of Children's Literature*. New York, 1953.

Adell, Judith, and Klein, Hilary Dole. *A Guide to Non-Sexist Children's Books*. Chicago, 1976.

Alm, Richard S. "The Glitter and the Gold." *The English Journal* 44 (September 1955): 315–322, 350.

Baum, L. Frank. *The Emerald City of Oz*. Chicago, 1910.

———. *The Master Key: An Electrical Fairy Tale*. Indianapolis, 1901.

Bernard, Jessie. *The Future of Motherhood*. New York, 1974.

Bontemps, Arna. *The Sad Faced Boy*. Boston, 1937.

Coleman, James S. *The Adolescent Society: The Social Life of the Teenager and Its Impact on Education*. New York, 1961.

Darling, Richard L. *The Rise of Children's Book Reviewing in America, 1865–1881*. New York, 1968.

Davis, Glen. *Children and History in America*. New York, 1976.

Erisman, Fred. "American Regional Juvenile Literature 1870–1910: An Annotated Bibliography." *American Realism, 1870–1910* (Spring 1973).

Habegger, Alfred. *Gender, Fantasy and Realism in American Literature*. New York, 1982.

Hart, James D. *The Popular Book: A History of America's Literary Taste*. New York, 1950.

Howells, William Dean. *Criticism and Fiction*. New York, 1891.

Jackson, Jesse. *Call Me Charley*. New York, 1945.

Johnson, Dierdre. *Stratemeyer Pseudonyms and Series Books: An Annotated Checklist of Stratemeyer and Stratemeyer Syndicate Publications.* Westport, Conn., 1982.

Kelly, R. Gordon. *Mother Was a Lady: Self and Society in Selected American Children's Periodicals, 1865–1890.* Westport, Conn., 1974.

Kuhoth, Jean Spealman. *Best Selling Children's Books.* Metuchen, N.J., 1973.

Lenski, Lois. "Regional Children's Literature." *Wilson Library Bulletin* 21 (December 1946).

Meigs, Cornelia, et al., eds. *A Critical History of Children's Literature: A Survey of Children's Books in English.* Rev. ed., Toronto, 1969.

Miller, Daniel R., and Swanson, Guy E. *The Changing American Parent: A Study in the Detroit Area.* New York, 1955.

Moore, Annie E. *Literature Old and New for Children: Materials for a College Course.* New York, 1943.

Rodgers, Daniel T. *The Work Ethic in Industrial America, 1850–1920.* Chicago, 1979.

Slater, Philip. *The Pursuit of Loneliness: American Culture at the Breaking Point.* Boston, 1970.

Smith, Dora V. *Fifty Years of Children's Books.* Champaign, Ill., 1963.

Trensky, Anne. "The Bad Boy in Nineteenth Century American Fiction," *Georgia Review* 27 (1973): 503–517.

Viguers, Ruth Hill. "Golden Years and Time of Tumult 1920–1967." In *A Critical History of Children's Literature: A Survey of Children's Books in English*, edited by Cornelia Meigs, Elizabeth Nesbit, Anne Thaxter Eaton, and Ruth Hill Viguers. Rev. ed., Toronto, 1969.

Weitzman, Lenore, et al. "Sex Role Socialization in Picture Books for Pre School Children." *American Journal of Sociology* (May 1972): 1125–1150.

11

Child-Saving in the Age of Professionalism, 1915–1930

Hamilton Cravens

In the American experience this century has witnessed the rise of a new perception of children and childhood. Perceptions of children, like those of adults, have always been integrally related to perceptions and definitions of the national population and culture, and of the relative utility of interpreting members of the national population as individuals or as members of groups in the larger national population. After the mid-nineteenth century, children (and adults) were defined as individuals who belonged to particular groups because of their moral or religious characteristics. Therefore, the problems children experienced were attributed to their moral or religious flaws. They could transcend their unfortunate group identifications by appropriate homiletic and pietistic efforts. And public policy proceeded from that assumption. It occurred to no one, for example, to explain children, or adults, with the methods and conceptions of scientific determinism.

By the 1890s, a new perception of children and of the national population had emerged as the basis for public policy action and interven-

I would like to thank the following institutions for support of much of the research for this chapter: Faculty Improvement Leave Program and Graduate College, Iowa State University; the Rockefeller Archive Center and Rockefeller University; and History and Philosophy of Science Program, National Science Foundation, for grants SES 78–06709 and SES 79–08514. I would also like to thank the following scholars for comments and helpful suggestions: Achilles Avraamides, John C. Burnham, Merle Curti, James B. Gilbert, Richard S. Kirkendall, Richard Lowitt, Alan I Marcus, George T. McJimsey, Robert M. Mennel, Zane L. Miller, Stow Persons, Steven L. Schlossman, Robert E. Schofield, Robert R. Sears, Henry D. Shapiro, Alice B. Smuts, and William Tuttle. My editors, Joseph M. Hawes and N. Ray Hiner, made helpful suggestions and provided invaluable moral support, for which I am grateful. I would also like to thank Margo Horn of the University of California at San Diego for sharing the results of her work on the child guidance movement, and especially on the Philadelphia Child Guidance Clinic, all part of a larger book in progress.

tion. It was in fact a new conception of social reality. Children constituted a distinct group within the national population. This new perception was part of the new view of the national population and culture as comprised of rigidly defined groups, or races, or types, to which individuals perforce belonged, not as individuals who could by certain kinds of exertions change their group identity if they took action in time. This view had been gaining momentum for perhaps two decades, as in the crystallization of nativist sentiment in public politics, in the growth of the color line in national culture, and in the revival and reconstitution of the old doctrine of the separate spheres of male and female activity. This new conception of the population as comprised of groups, arranged in a hierarchy of superior and inferior ranks, was thoroughly materialistic and naturalistic. It spoke the language of contemporary positivistic scientific materialism. Following from that level of explanatory discourse, the new perception of children assumed that children, like all other groups of the national population, were legitimate objects of scientific study. Before the 1890s, a handful of Americans saw elements of the new point of view. In that decade the new perspective crystallized and gained the kind of acceptance that would permit new departures in thought and action.

In the early 1900s, the new conception of children, child science, and child-oriented public policy came into its own as a central element of the Progressive reform movement and, in this way, gained widespread public attention throughout national culture. In many states child welfare reformers agitated for legislation that would define and protect children and women in many aspects of existence. Often the child welfare reformers worked for similar goals. Laws for compulsory education, child labor, delinquent boys, and wayward girls, for the feeble-minded, for pure milk, for public health, for mothers' pensions, and for prevention of the sale of such harmful substances as tobacco and alcoholic substances to minors were only some of the more prominent examples. Professional educators began to advocate new ways of teaching children and new curricula to train teachers. The child welfare reform campaigns counted as the most numerous and energetic of their leaders and followers middle- and upper-class women who belonged to the newly minted national women's organizations, such as the National Congress of Mothers, the Woman's Christian Temperance Union, and the General Federation of Women's Clubs. Women's organizations in many states and localities organized child study organizations whose purposes and intentions emphasized the amelioration of child life and welfare. Within women's organizations child welfare was less controversial than, for example, suffrage. Child welfare reformers helped organize the first federal White House Conference on Children in 1909, which was chiefly devoted to matters of health. In 1912 they also successfully pushed for the establishment of the Children's Bureau, which became, among other things, a centralized clearinghouse for the distribution of information about the proper nurture of children.

In the 1880s pediatrics, the medical specialty devoted to children, established a distinct professional identity in American public health. Previously, of course, doctors had treated children, and, since the 1840s, most medical schools had taught a course in the diseases of women and children. The 1880s and 1890s was an age of disciplinary and subdisciplinary separation in medicine as it was in science, engineering, and other fields of culture. Probably the most notable teacher of pediatrics after the late 1880s was Luther Emmett Holt, professor at the College of Physicians and Surgeons of Columbia University. Barely had he returned from study in Europe in the mid-1880s than he threw himself into helping create both a journal, the *Archives of Pediatrics*, and a professional society, the American Pediatric Society. He worked closely with that pioneer of pediatrics, Abraham Jacobi, in these efforts. In 1894 Holt published *The Care and Feeding of Children: A Catechism for the Use of Mothers and Children's Nurses*, the first such manual that sought to distill the knowledge of child science and technology and to present soothing answers to the practical questions of those who raised the nation's children. By 1915 Holt's little tome had passed through seven editions, constantly revised and expanded, and it had a growing number of imitators. Pediatrics was now a recognized specialization in American medicine, testimony that American doctors implicitly understood that childhood was a distinct phase of life apart from adulthood. Furthermore, within the public health movement, much attention was paid to questions and problems of children, as, for example, nutrition, physical growth, and sanitation.[1]

Between 1890 and 1930 organized child-saving can be divided into two distinct phases. To 1915 or so, the dominant theme was reform, that is, Progressive child-saving, the manipulation of the circumstances of child life through public policy. From about 1915 to the 1930s, the emphasis changed dramatically, to professional activities, to the use of the human sciences and technologies to investigate children, or, more precisely, the so-called normal child, as the necessary precondition of further public action. Throughout the entire period, Progressive and professional child-savers believed that science could unlock the secrets of human life, that professional expertise was the highest authority in organized child-saving, and that the many different groups in the American population had to be brought up to national standards of health, nutrition, education, and socialization. Furthermore, Progressive and professional child-savers were active throughout the entire period. Many of the Progressives' institutional innovations, such as the juvenile court, the organized municipal playground, the reformatory, and the public

school, endured long after 1915. Professional child-savers were active
before 1915. Yet the intellectual and ideological emphases of each period
were distinct.

In the Progressive Era, reformers made three basic assumptions about
society which were rooted in the new, late-nineteenth-century, perception of national culture. First, national culture was constituted of groups
of the population arranged in a hierarchical pyramid; some groups were
superior to others, although the whole of national culture comprised
more than the mere sum of its parts. This perception of America guided
reformers, whether they were interested in child welfare, industrial enterprises, or popular participation and legitimacy in politics.

Progressive reformers assumed that only a hierarchical, centralized
authority could achieve the public good; only it could stand above the
various groups of society and mediate among them. Progressives working
for many seemingly different ends sought precisely that goal, sometimes
by agitating for the invention of a new popular will through the perfection of democratic institutions and other times by advocating stronger
federal powers at the expense of the states, or, more commonly, cham-
pioning the powers of statehouse over courthouse or city hall. The successful campaign for the direct primary in the South most tellingly
demonstrated this new notion of national culture as consisting of superior and inferior groups, for it effectively created a lily-white public
will. But that notion of national culture also fueled other reform efforts
elsewhere in Progressive America, as, for example, in the attacks on
"boss politics," or in the creation of public school curricula with nation-
alistic emphases such as American history and English literature, all of
which were based on the new conception of groups in the national
population.

Second, the Progressives believed that human behavior and conduct
should be measured by nationally defined standards. Regulation of industry, elimination of corrupt, undemocratic politics, restructuring and
standardization of education, Americanization of the immigrants, and
sobering up of the besotted masses were obvious examples of the Progressives' penchant for standardizing American national culture and the
groups that made up the national population. They also reflected the
Progressives' hierarchical perceptions of society and culture.

Third, the Progressives assumed that the wellsprings of man's actions
and ideas were rather simple to decipher, indeed virtually possessed of
a mechanical simplicity. Human nature seemed astonishingly easy to
understand. Some Progressives invoked environmental explanations, such
as poverty, poor health, inadequate nutrition, or insufficient education,
whereas others employed the language of contemporary natural science
and attributed conduct to Mendelian unit characters, racial traits, instincts, or other evidences of original human nature. In either case Pro-

gressives appealed to the authority of science, that is, science as they understood it as materialists and positivists.

The Progressive child-savers easily embraced the larger Progressive vision of national culture as comprised of groups of different levels of capability, and the concomitant Progressive solutions of expertise, standardization, and scientific positivism. As they organized their activities, the Progressive child-savers usually dealt with children as members of groups, as, in other words, types, within the larger national population—for example, white or nonwhite, male or female, intelligent or dull, American or foreign born, well behaved or delinquent, prosperous or dependent, healthy or sickly, normal or degenerate, and so on. Believing that these types or categories of children were derived from science, or what they took for science, Progressive child-savers devoted their energies to applying the known facts of science to social problems involving children. Often the result of their actions was institutional, as in the invention of the juvenile court or in the reformulation of public education. Research as such was distinctly a secondary enterprise; science had already defined the categories upon which social action should be based. Institutional innovation and reform mattered more, especially if said institutions were public, and therefore, part of national culture. In that way professional expertise could help uplift various groups to the national standards science had established.

The professional child-savers inverted the Progressives' priorities. They insisted that research must precede social innovation and application. They were far more conscious than were the Progressive child-savers that the scientific and medical conceptions of children were beginning to change in the 1910s. The sources of human conduct suddenly appeared more complex and perplexing than before. The human body was redefined as as intricate machine about which there was much to learn, as, for example, about the function and effect of such newly discovered substances as "vitamines." Within a decade the child became the object of new levels of sustained research, often interdisciplinary in character.

In many respects, scientific professionalism came later to the child sciences and technologies than to the more traditional sciences. Scientific professionalism got underway in the 1890s with the emergence of the modern graduate university as a new kind of institution in national culture, and, indeed, as a reflection of the new perception of groups in the national culture. The presidents and trustees who organized and managed this new type of institution acted on the premises of the new conception of national culture. They created the university as a pyramid, with the undergraduate college of letters and sciences at the base, the elective and major systems at the middle, and the graduate and professional schools positioned at the apex. As in all such questions, it is pointless to speculate whether specialization and professionalism originated as an intellectual or a social construct. What was involved was a new cultural dynamic. Scientists and scholars now redefined themselves as professionals, or, more precisely, as *academic* professionals, who identified with specific disciplines. Specialized expertise became a major cultural distinction between professionals and amateurs in such widely disparate fields as astronomy, entomology, history, literature, and civil engineering. The new professionals invented the trappings of the modern professional academic subculture. They identified clients and constituents for their professional services. They erected professional standards, based on the new notion of groups, for admission into their castes. They founded societies and journals for their disciplines. They also established a prestige system, supposedly to differentiate among levels of competence and distinction which celebrated national and cosmopolitan standards of judgment, not local ones, thus facilitating their tacit goals of enhancing professional autonomy and weakening popular criticism and censure. In these ways the new professionals established a new politics of power in culture, knowledge, and science that neatly complemented the new perception of national culture and population.

In the 1910s, this new idea of professional expertise began to redefine child-saving as specialists in the human sciences and the social or human technologies came to the fore and began to think of themselves as different from, if nevertheless dependent on, their lay constituents and clients. In the 1920s, the professional development of child science and technology proceeded rapidly, sometimes well in advance of scientific research and ideas. Child research institutes were founded, often with lavish foundation support; these institutes stressed research before child-saving. Even with the new child-saving institutions of that decade, the child guidance clinics, the research ethos was so pervasive among child-savers that social application took a back seat to specialized investigation. By the 1930s, the professional institutional revolution had virtually run its course. The die was cast; the context was entirely different than it had been in the age of reform.

Another distinguishing feature of professional child-saving after 1915 was the angle of vision which the professionals employed in research and application. Increasingly, the professionals abandoned the Progressives' simple, mechanical notions about human thought and conduct. The new professional view stressed, not forces external to the individual, but inner conflicts within the individual or the group, deep-seated emotional conflicts, various problems of adjustment which, it was assumed, described, classified, and explained the child. The professionals' perspective was psychological and owed much to the evolutionary natural and behavioral sciences. They insisted that a psychological level of description and interpretation was superior to the Progressives' mechanical notions of thought and conduct. Drawing upon what they regarded as their common Darwinian intellectual heritage, professional child scientists and technologists stressed the importance of facilitating the individual's adjustment to the standards of national culture. Research was more important than reform to the professionals. They considered themselves professional investigators, and they had persuaded themselves that little was yet known about the processes and structures of adjustment to society. If the causes of human behavior were psychological, then obviously professional expertise and research took precedence over mere politics and legislation.

The Progressives and the professionals differed in their conception of the child in national culture. Influenced by late-nineteenth-century biological determinism, the Progressives divided children into superior, normal, and subnormal categories, assumed that the gaps among them were indelible and permanent, and developed distinctive strategies and tactics for dealing with each. The Progressives were primarily interested in fitting individual children into preconceived pigeonholes. If the categories were generally known and understood, then research was merely a matter of mopping up the details. The professionals were also interested in facilitating the child's adjustment to national standards but went about that task in a different manner. They did not arrange children in a linear progression from subnormal to superior, that is, in a pyramid. On the contrary, the professionals' cultural geometry assumed a continuum, a juxtaposing of different types of children cheek by jowl according to their adjustment, or lack thereof, to the norms of national culture. Put another way, the Progressives believed in a hierarchy of different types of children, whereas the professionals believed that there was essentially only one kind of child, the normal child, and that the purpose of child science and technology was to uncover that child's characteristics and propensities. If there was but a normal child in national culture, with, to be sure, variations which specialists could identify and remedy, then it made sense to the professional child-savers to have as their ultimate goal the adjustment of the individual to the standards of the larger national culture.[2]

The evolutionary natural and behavioral sciences became the intellectual foundation of child-saving and technology and, therefore, of professional child-saving. Especially crucial was the new physiological psychology, but important also were psychiatry, nutrition, physical anthropology, pediatrics, and educational psychology. These sciences were recast as developmental in intellectual orientation, as disciplines of applied science whose practitioners explained the unfolding development of the child from fertilization through adolescence. Modern naturalistic psychology owed much to British evolutionary biology and German psychology which after mid-century emphasized the actions of the nervous system and brain, thus pointing out the biological basis of mind. British evolutionary biologists insisted that mind, like body, had evolved.[3] Among others Charles Darwin made this argument, insisting that patterns of thought and action, as well as the organic structures undergirding mental life, had evolved from the lowest animals to man. Increasingly, psychologists took up Darwin's theory and speculated on the relationships between the minds of men and of brutes.[4]

In the 1880s and 1890s the new psychology emerged in American culture. It rapidly acquired a distinctive American identity and focus; within two generations it differed substantially from European psychology. Thus, the German psychologists, pioneers as they were in psychophysics, insisted that psychology's proper study was of the conscious mental processes in the normal adult human mind.[5] Darwin's ideas about the origins of mind, or, more precisely, of minds, which in turn suggested the mental life of animals or differences in human intelligence as research topics, held relatively little appeal to the Germans. In the 1890s American psychologists turned to investigation of individual and group differences in intelligence. This was evidence, if such were needed, of the influence of the new conception of national culture on the structures and processes of science. Yet the full Americanization of psychology was not completed in that generation. American psychologists, especially those who were well established, accepted the Germans' focus on the normal adult mind. Animal and child psychology were neither respected nor popular research focuses among mainstream American psychologists until after 1915.

Squarely within the intellectual mainstream of American psychology was James McKeen Cattell. He had studied psychology in Germany with Wilhelm Wundt at Leipzig, as many Americans of his generation had, and then with Francis Galton in England, one of the founders of the modern eugenics movement. In the 1890s Cattell conducted an ambitious research program to investigate the relationships between physical and mental characteristics in college students at Columbia, where he taught. He assumed that he could prove that individual intellectual differences had a basis in physical characteristics. Unfortunately for him, the data he laboriously collected could not be correlated statistically. Yet Cattell's interest in individual differences and in mental measurement was representative of American psychology.[6]

By the early twentieth century, American psychologists had developed two major approaches to psychology, which in turn reflected the new perception of national culture. Many were interested, as Cattell was, in mental measurement. After the introduction of the Binet test in 1910, this psychology of capacity, or psychometrics, became a widespread interest among psychologists. They thought mental tests were socially useful for classifying and sorting individuals and groups in the national population, and they were able to persuade many institutional clients of the values of their services, including the U.S. Army.[7] American psychologists worked out a psychology of conduct. This social psychology of individual behavior was inspired by Darwin's suggestion that instincts were the major phylogenetic survival instruments. Their didactic interest in the dynamics of human behavior persisted well into the twentieth century, and included preoccupation with various theories of instincts, drives, and human personality.[8]

Until the 1920s, most academic psychologists believed that psychology was, and should remain, the study of the normal adult mind. Few thought or cared very much about child psychology, or about the origins of minds more generally. For these prissy academics child psychology meant child study. They associated child study with ladies' child study clubs or, perhaps, lowly professors of pedagogy. American psychology had not yet become what it would be by the 1930s, a thoroughly developmental, evolutionary psychology linking all sentient species in a kind of mental great chain of being. Yet the science and profession of American psychology were sufficiently large and diverse to include those who marched to a different drummer than the majority. By 1915 there were clear signs that a new psychology was crystallizing, a developmental or genetic psychology, whose advocates would emphasize stages of growth, their differentness from one another, the origins of minds, and, above all, the importance of child psychology.

Between the 1890s and the 1920s, Granville Stanley Hall did more than any other founder of American psychology to develop the new genetic and child psychology.[9] Born in 1846, he finished his doctorate in philosophy at Harvard with William James at the age of thirty-two. Hall's dissertation was psychological rather than philosophical in orientation. To further prepare himself he studied psychology in Europe. After teaching psychology for part of the 1880s, he became president and professor of psychology at the new Clark University in Worcester, Massachusetts, in 1888, where he remained for the rest of his career. He founded two journals, the *American Journal of Psychology* and the *Pedagogical Seminary and Journal of Genetic Psychology*; played an important role in founding the American Psychological Association; and, under his intellectual leadership, Clark became a leading center of the new psychology, granting about one-fourth of all American doctorates in psychology as of the early 1920s.[10]

Hall's contributions to child and genetic psychology were intellectual and professional. He insisted that mind had to be understood from a thoroughly evolutionary or genetic point of view, thus distinguishing himself from the German psychologists' definition of psychology as merely the study of the normal adult mind. Mind, or minds, Hall argued, had evolved from one-celled animals to man. To buttess his view, he borrowed the recapitulation doctrine, that ontogeny recapitulates phylogeny, from nineteenth-century embryology. He insisted that the development of the individual as embryo, child, and adult, passed through the stages of evolution from the lowest to the highest species. Hall's specific use of recapitulation won relatively little credence, but his more general typological framework, which paralleled the new conception of national culture, and his biological thought on speciation, resonated widely among his various lay and professional constituencies. In time, it came to provide form and configuration to genetic psychology as American psychologists worked it out in the second and later decades of the twentieth century. For Hall, it was just as important to study the mind of the lowly cockroach, or the horse's comparatively mightier intellect, as it was the mind of the child, or the mental defective, for all shed light on how the minds of normal adult humans functioned. In a very real sense, Hall legitimated child psychology and the larger pursuit of genetic psychology by arguing that the child was father to the man.

Hall argued further that individual development followed a sequence of stages. Here and elsewhere he was thoroughly evolutionary in the sense that biological structure caused cultural function. He used the idea that the life cycle had stages of unfolding development, all based in biological structure, to impose thematic unity on his most important publication, *Adolescence: Its Psychology and Its Relation to Physiology, Anthropology, Sociology, Sex, Crime, Religion, and Education* (1904). Hall's conception of stages of development became one of the controlling and organizing assumptions of child and human psychology in the twentieth century.[11]

Hall promoted genetic and child psychology in other ways. He drew popular attention to child study and interested many women's organizations, as, for example, the National Congress of Mothers, later known as the National Congress of Parents and Teachers. Leaders of these organizations thus became involved in the child welfare reform crusades. Hall's message that child study mattered for the reconstitution and reform of national culture and institutions made good sense to them. Upon occasion Hall's influence was astonishing. Cora Bussey Hillis, a wealthy and prominent Des Moines, Iowa, matron, heard him speak only once on child study. This experience helped inspire her to become a life-long worker for child welfare. Almost singlehandedly, she led the movement for the juvenile court in Iowa, organized the state Congress of Mothers, and made other contributions as well.[12] Yet Hall's personality was sufficiently difficult that it was sometimes hard for him to maintain systematic intellectual and institutional linkages with his feminine constituents and, thus, to transmit to them any fully developed catechism of child study and child welfare. Therefore, they were usually left to their own intellectual devices, at least to create anything more intricate than a slogan or partly developed idea. For the most part they gravitated to the Progressive, not the professional, version of organized child-saving. They stressed such issues as health, education, and protective legislation. Often they declared that the object of child study and child welfare was the abnormal or subnormal child, the dependent, delinquent, or defective youngsters not born into the white middle class and who by definition were in dire need of social uplift.

Thus, child welfare and child study became associated, in the eyes of academic psychologists, with social reform, which merely convinced the mental professoriate that child study was unscientific. Psychology as an academic, let alone scientific, enterprise, was too new, and psychologists in the academy were too worried about their prestige with their brethren in better established sciences for self-conscious psychologists to welcome child study with open arms.

Hall trained many students as child psychologists. Indeed, with the exception of a handful of individuals, most notably Lightner Witmer of the University of Pennsylvania, who ran a psychological clinic in which he occasionally examined children, it was Hall's students who comprised the corporal's guard of child psychologists before 1915. His students landed professional positions in what academic psychologists condescendingly regarded as marginal institutions, chiefly teachers' colleges and institutions for the mentally abnormal or deficient. Nor did it help child psychology as a field that Hall's relationships with other major figures in psychology were often difficult and brittle. Yet Hall did train many students. In addition, he contributed new and large ideas to his science, as, for example, when he sponsored a major conference in 1909 at which Sigmund Freud first spoke to an American audience. After 1915 Hall began to win major recognition for genetic psychology. This was due, not to Hall, but to the changing conceptions of natural and social reality which were sweeping both American culture and American psychology. Older binary and mechanistic models of nature and society were being replaced by new notions of infinite dimensions and inter-relationships, of variations among many varieties of types, and of a new sense of the relativity of things to one another. In turn, these more general currents in American civilization had their manifestations among growing numbers of psychologists. Younger psychologists moved toward a genetic approach. His students were making their mark on the discipline.

As Hall's students began to enter the profession in the early 1900s, one, Henry Herbert Goddard, stood out in particular. In the 1910s Goddard rapidly became a well-known, respected authority on mental deficiency. Born to Quaker parents on a Maine farm the year after Appomattox, when it came time for him to choose a career, he decided on teaching. He graduated from Haverford College in 1888. Then he taught school, chiefly psychology and mathematics, until 1896, when he entered Clark. He wrote his thesis on an aspect of applied psychology and won his doctorate in 1899. For the next seven years he taught psychology and pedagogy at a Pennsylvania normal school. Neither the school's atmosphere nor its working conditions were congruent with Goddard's professional ambitions. In 1901 he met E. R. Johnstone, superintendent of the Vineland Training School for feeble-minded boys and girls, located in the southern New Jersey hamlet of Vineland. This chance circumstance altered Goddard's whole life. Johnstone recruited Goddard into the newly developed field of mental deficiency. Over the next several years Goddard published several articles and took postdoctoral work in Europe.[13] Johnstone admired his protege, and by 1906 he had been able to raise enough funds for the school's endowment to appoint Goddard as the school's first director of psychological research.[14]

The Vineland Training School was a distinguished institution of its type. Founded in 1890, it was chartered under state law as a private eleemosynary and custodial institution. It housed approximately 400 mentally deficient persons from New Jersey and surrounding states. The Vineland Association, a not-for-profit private corporation, owned the school. The association had about 250 shareholders. Most had relatives in the school. The stockholders elected thirteen men to the board of directors, for staggered terms. The stockholders helped raise money and promoted favorable publicity for the school. The directors worked with Johnstone to establish policy. On a daily basis Johnstone ran the institution. Since Johnstone admired Goddard, Goddard had much time and freedom for research, with a minimum of distraction and interference. He edited the school's journal, *The Training School Bulletin*; he ran a summer institute for teachers of the mentally deficient; and he consulted for many institutions, including the U.S. Children's Bureau and the Immigration and Naturalization Service.[15] The school did not have a large research budget, especially in the early years.[16] Yet few professional psychologists had Goddard's professional advantages, including an accessible research population, free time, a journal, and some research funds. He rapidly published much on the psychology of mental deficiency and became well known in the United States and Europe.

Goddard's work bore his master's imprint. Hall always insisted that the key to psychology was inheritance; mind was innate. Goddard agreed. As he wrote in his application to the Carnegie Institute of Washington for a large grant to expand Vineland's research program, the overriding question of contemporary science was the relationship of structure to function, how biological structure determined psychological function.[17] Through his work with the New Jersey Commission on Charities and Corrections, Goddard discovered the problem of the social evils, that is, dependency, delinquency, and other manifestations of deviant conduct and how they could be solved through his science. He rapidly concluded that low intelligence caused low morals. Individuals so afflicted were, he believed, aberrant types in the national population. It was relatively easy for Charles B. Davenport, a prominent geneticist and eugenics advocate, to convince Goddard that mind was inherited according to the Mendelian ratios and to recruit him into the eugenics movement.[18] Indeed, the idea that mind was innate, not acquired, was conventional wisdom among contemporary natural scientists.[19] Goddard turned to sounding the alarm over the menace of the feeble-minded.[20]

Goddard soon discovered Alfred Binet's scaled mental test. In 1910 he published his revision and translation of the French psychologist's 1908 examination, modified for American children. He insisted it was capable of discriminating among normal mental levels up to twelve years in mental age. Goddard wanted to use the test to diagnose the mentally deficient, especially the Vineland inmates, and to arrange them in different mental levels. With this social technology he worked out a hierarchy of mental defect by mental age or level. Idiots tested below three, imbeciles between three and seven, and morons between eight and twelve in mental age. He explained that the idiots and imbeciles presented no real danger to society. They were so obviously deficient that they could not escape institutionalization. The morons, however, were another matter entirely. They were sufficiently intelligent to appear normal unless an expert examined them, or they got into trouble. Goddard believed that the morons, of all three types of mental defectives, presented the greatest danger to society, for they were intelligent enough to get into trouble but lacked the intelligence required for moral judgment.[21]

For the next several years Goddard devoted much time publicizing the social dangers of innate mental defect. His best known effort, *The Kallikak Family* (1912), was a melodramatic monograph in which he traced "good" and "bad" heredity in two family lines of Martin Kallikak, Sr., since the American Revolution. The "bad" Kallikaks resulted from Martin's casual, ill-advised liaison with a wench of unquestionable mental and moral defect, begetting 480 persons including degenerates, bastards, alcoholics, criminals, paupers, epileptics, prostitutes, and feeble-minded persons. The "good" Kallikaks resulted from Martin's marriage to an upstanding Christian lady, some 496 worthwhile, moral citizens.[22] Goddard argued here and elsewhere that an unbridgeable gulf separated normal and subnormal types of persons. Each type had inherited that condition. Thus, for Goddard the primary cause of immorality and degeneracy was bad mental inheritance, and psychology was ultimately a typological science.

After 1913 Goddard turned increasingly from propaganda to working out practical solutions for retraining the mentally deficient—the morons—to live in civilian society outside the institution. He knew that institutions such as Vineland could not house all mental defectives and that putting as many of the morons on "parole" (as he thought of it) as possible would ease overcrowding. Over the next several years, as he tried to figure out ways to integrate the high-grade defectives into society as hewers of wood and haulers of water, he began to change his notions about the mentally defective, and, in particular, became skeptical of the mental typology he had done so much, if not to create, then certainly to legitimize.[23] This was not obvious to any save his closest professional associates much before the 1920s.

In the 1910s most people who worked professionally with the problems of delinquency or mental problems assumed, as Goddard did, that there were types of minds and that a sharp line separated the normal from the subnormal mind. This was even true of Dr. William Healy, whose views are usually considered to have differed radically from Goddard's. Certainly, they regarded one another as intellectual rivals.[24] There were intellectual differences between them, especially in their assessments of the causes of social evils. Born in England in 1869, Healy gravitated to the field of juvenile delinquency as a specialist in mental disease and psychiatry. He studied at Harvard, took his M.D. from Rush Medical School in 1900, and studied in Vienna, Berlin, and London. In 1909 he was appointed director of the Juvenile Psychopathic Institute of Chicago, the research and diagnostic clinic of Chicago's juvenile court system. Healy and Goddard explained the causes of delinquency differently. Thus, Healy abandoned a narrowly biological framework rather quickly, whereas Goddard emphasized heredity until the later 1910s. As long as they were preoccupied with explaining the causes of delinquency, they seemed at odds. The divergent populations they initially studied explained in large measure their differences. Healy studied juveniles of varying mental abilities who had run afoul of the law. Goddard's experience was with persons of undeniably low mental ability but widely varying temperaments. Yet even in their analyses they were similar. Healy was a psychiatric determinist; he insisted that mental and emotional conflicts caused delinquency if not caught early. Goddard was a biological determinist; he argued that the roll of the Mendelian dice determined social behavior. After 1915, as each came to prescribe therapies, they increasingly emphasized that behavior could be modified if expertly diagnosed.[25] Obviously, the field was changing intellectually, if Healy and Goddard could now agree on the importance of professional expertise and research, and on the efficacy of therapeutic technique.

Another of Hall's students, Arnold L. Gesell, joined the field of child study in the 1910s. Eventually, he became one of America's most recognized pediatricians with a developmentalist perspective. Born in a Wisconsin village in 1880, Gesell finished his doctorate with Hall in 1906. He taught educational psychology for several years at Los Angeles State

Normal School. In 1911 he took a similar appointment at Yale. There he established the first psychological clinic for children associated with an American university. He also graduated from medical school in 1915. Besides creating the example of a clinic for children in an academic context, Gesell's major contribution to the field of child science and technology before the 1920s was intellectual. His most important publication in the 1910s, *The Normal Child and Primary Education* (1912), projected the maturation hypothesis for which he was to become world renowned, and it redefined child psychology as the study of the normal child. As a developmentalist, Gesell argued that mind was innate, that individuals differed in mental capacity, that mind and body developed in a succession of unfolding stages.

Gesell's definition of the normal child deserves further comment, if for no other reason than it anticipated an important intellectual element of professional child-saving. He insisted that the normal child was not merely the average child in reality. The normal child was ideal in the sense that, under proper expert supervision, he or she could develop to the utmost of his or her physical, physiological, mental, and moral abilities. Thus, almost all children—save the afflicted—could become normal, that is, live up to the fullest of their hereditary potential. The challenge of professional child science and technology, insisted Gesell, was to bring out the fullest development or maturation in each individual.[26] In this Gesell went beyond the Progressive notions of the child and of children. In 1912 he was somewhat ahead of workers in his field.

In the 1910s a more important child-saving organization than Gesell's psychoclinic was the Ohio Bureau of Juvenile Research. Indeed, the bureau's development from 1913, when it was founded, to 1918, when it took on a different role, reflected the transformation in national culture from Progressive to professional child-saving. In the early twentieth century, Ohio was fertile ground for progressivism. Progressives won many victories, including the adoption of a new state constitution in 1912. With regard to child-saving, Progressives in the legislature created a juvenile court system in 1906 and five years later established a new state Board of Administration in order to centralize the management of Ohio's custodial and eleemosynary institutions. The board took control of these twenty-two institutions, created a unified budget and budgetary control, revised job classifications according to new standards, and gave much discretionary authority to the board's directors. While centralization, rationalization, and expertise were not as firmly established in the board over the formerly autonomous institutions as Ohio Progressives wished, nevertheless the context was now very different. In 1913 the legislature, following the lead of James B. Cox, the new reform Democratic governor, and Goddard, who advised Cox on such matters, created the Bureau of Juvenile Research as the board's diagnostic agency.

The bureau administered medical and psychological examinations to all juveniles sent to the board by the juvenile courts and was given the further power to recommend the placement of juveniles in particular institutions. Hence, the board and its bureau were at the apex of this new institutional pyramid, and the custodial and eleemosynary institutions at the base. Initially, however, the legislature kept the bureau on a tight fiscal leash and only appropriated enough funds to appoint a director of research to examine the state's current inmates.[27]

Thomas H. Haines became the bureau's director of research. A Harvard-trained animal psychologist, Haines had taught psychology at Ohio State University since 1901. From his Harvard professors he had learned the new genetic psychology, the evolution of types of minds from one-celled animals to man, which became increasingly accepted by the younger psychologists after the early 1910s. In order to do more research, Haines shifted from animal to abnormal psychology. In 1912 he became an M.D., and then he studied nervous diseases and psychiatry abroad, chiefly in Munich and Vienna.[28] Just before coming to the bureau, he published several papers on mental abnormality in which he assumed that there were many different types of mental diseases and that they had many different causes.[29] At the bureau he usually explained mental defect as the primary cause of antisocial conduct in ways strongly reminiscent of Goddard's *The Kallikak Family*. Once he even suggested that each state sponsor a survey of its population "so as to map out the tainted stocks."[30] Initially impressed by that instrument of social technology, the mental test, he tried out various ones to see which was the most precise for determining an individual's mental level. At first, at least, he believed there were normal and subnormal minds, and that heredity explained mind. Increasingly, Haines became skeptical of the assumption that the mentally deficient were *ipso facto* a danger to society. As he shifted his attention from analyzing the feeble-minded as an apparent problem in scientific explanation to devising practical solutions for their placement in institutions in civilian society, he underwent the same kind of intellectual shift that Goddard was experiencing at about the same time. "Great injury is done to the individual, to society, and to the field of practical psychology, by calling feeble-minded any individual who later proves himself capable of earning his own living, and managing himself in an inoffensive manner," Haines wrote in 1916.[31]

In the later 1910s, many workers in the tightly knit field of mental deficiency were making the same kind of intellectual turnabout as Haines and Goddard. It was not a matter of intellectual influence, as usually conceived, in which one or two in the group infected the others. Rather, this represented a shift in the kind of activities pursued and in the questions that arose as the consequence of new activities. These specialists did not abandon their belief in the reality of mental deficiency, in the inheritance of mind, or in levels of intelligence. The new perception, that the high-grade mental defectives were not necessarily a threat to established society, arose from the necessities of social technology, of devising solutions to the problems of severe institutional crowding and the realization that the public would never pay for the institutionalization of all who were mentally substandard. The more workers studied the high-grade defectives, the more they came to see that such persons could usually be retrained to take their place in society. Goddard came to this conclusion by 1916 or 1917. So did several other former Hall students, who, like Goddard, had devoted themselves to this field, including Frederick Kuhlmann, superintendent of Minnesota's school for the mentally deficient in Faribault and editor of the *Journal of Psycho-Asthenics*, the field's major journal, and John E. W. Wallin, who peregrinated from one institution to another and wrote several state surveys on mental deficiency. Perhaps Walter E. Fernald, superintendent of the Massachusetts institution for the "feeble-minded," in Waverley, and his brilliant associate, Florence Mateer, did most to work out a *theory* of rehabilitation for the so-called morons. Mateer had just finished her doctorate at Clark in 1914. She was very taken with John B. Watson's work in behavioral conditioning. She borrowed, lock, stock, and barrel, Watson's technique of the conditioned reflex to break down and to reconstitute behavior patterns in the Waverly inmates. Thus, she worked out a systematic program of reeducation as a solution to the problem of "paroling" the morons. Having worked out a theory and a social technology that owed much to behaviorist psychology, which was itself an intellectual offshoot of rapidly crystallizing genetic psychology, Mateer and Fernald now insisted that the vast majority of the mentally deficient presented no danger to society, that they could be retrained to be upstanding citizens, and that low intelligence by itself did not cause immoral or disruptive conduct. In effect, mental deficiency was becoming redefined as a specialized matter in education, not a vast and horrific social problem in criminology and the social evils. Furthermore, the distinction between the normal and subnormal mind became blurred. The practical reasons for making the distinction had virtually evaporated. For that matter, as workers in the field assessed the incidence of mental deficiency in the national population, they recognized that only a tiny fraction—between 1 and 2 percent at the most—was so afflicted. Yet a more important explanation for this shift is that specialists shifted from structural to functional analysis, from taxonomizing types to retraining individuals, and therefore came to think of the problem of mental deficiency in terms of the adjustment of the individual to the norms of society. In the main, then, they had concluded that there was a normal mind, and, therefore, a normal child, an individual who could be trained to adjust to society and its rules.[32] They had embraced a new conception of the national population as well, which was based on a new conception of social reality.

Academic psychologists were beginning to shift toward genetic or developmental conceptions of their science after 1915. This was especially true of the younger and more professionally restive sort, who started working out various facets of the new genetic psychology. It was William McDougall, an English psychologist, who lent considerable legitimacy to the new genetic psychology. His *An Introduction to Social Psychology* (1908) popularized the genetic model of psychology. It was an astonishingly popular book in the United States; it went through many printings and was easily the most widely cited single book of the more than 600 American books and articles that argued that humankind's social conduct was attributable to innate instincts. The instinct theory was a literary convention of American psychology. What McDougall contributed to the American formulation was the genetic model of evolution of instincts as the basis of human social behavior. In reality, there were considerable logical and technical problems with McDougall's theory, but so great was the interest in both human instincts among the public and in the genetic and animal explanations among the younger psychologists that it was not until the early 1920s that McDougall's theories, and those of the instinct theorists more generally, came under attack.[33]

Probably a more enduring contribution to the genetic model from academic psychologists came from the small group of animal or comparative psychologists who, at least, had enough experimental rigor to satisfy even the most arrogant academic colleague. In 1911 several comparative psychologists started the *Journal of Animal Behavior*, an austerely technical journal. The two most important editors and, in reality, theoreticians of the field, were Robert M. Yerkes of Harvard University and John B. Watson of Johns Hopkins University. In his many publications, Yerkes worked out a brilliant interpretation of the evolution of mind in which the complexity of neurological structure was directly correlated with the complexity of the organism's mental life.[34] Watson agreed with this general proposition but sharply dissented from Yerkes's belief that consciousness—the "stuff of mental life"—actually existed. For Watson it was an undefinable term as well as a nonphenomenon. Watson preferred to define mental life as behavior, as Yerkes did, but to leave consciousness, with its philosophical implications, out of the picture. Watson soon founded the behaviorist movement in psychology or, at least, articulated its premises, insisting that the key to psychology was stimulus and response. By 1914 he was trying out his ideas by working with newborn infants at the university hospital. He soon found evidence that there were no definite instincts and that at birth human nature was relatively plastic.[35] Rapidly, other psychologists picked up Watson's arguments or arrived at similar conclusions. One immediate casualty in the later 1910s and early 1920s was the human instinct theory, another example of late-nineteenth-century typological and hierarchical thinking. The behaviorist psychologists were soon joined in their assaults on the instinct theory by the recently professionalized social scientists.[36] Unfortunately for Watson and, most probably, child psychology, he was forced to resign his professorship, for personal reasons, and, in losing professional caste, was not able to confer prestige upon child psychology in the 1920s.[37]

Yerkes made an equally important contribution to genetic psychology. During the war he organized the army's mental testing program for recruits. The mental testing movement had gained much ground even before the war with psychologists, educators, and social workers. By 1917 a new and more useful version of the Binet test was available. Indeed, Lewis M. Terman, another Hall student, had worked out a more technically successful version of the Binet—it could measure ages above twelve—by standardizing it for small town California school children of Northwestern European ancestry.[38] Yerkes and his colleagues used Terman's version as a control on the tests they developed for the army. By 1921, when the results of the army tests became known, they suggested a hierarchy of races or nativity groups according to presumed innate endowment. For a few years, this interpretation of racial mental superiority and inferiority, which Yerkes embraced, and Watson strongly opposed, was very popular. It was even used by immigration restrictionists to push restrictionist legislation through the Congress. Yet, rather rapidly the race differences hypothesis came under vigorous counterattack from a variety of scientific quarters, including social scientists, statisticians, psychological testers, behaviorists, and geneticists. The restrictionists accomplished their objectives in 1924 with the passage of the National Origins Act. Thereafter, many scientists abandoned the race differences hypothesis, agreeing that it was difficult technically, and unpopular politically, to maintain the theory. What remained was the assumption that many races might well be potentially equal and that some individual differences were innate. Interestingly, the notion that psychology should be the study of the genetic development of minds was now taken in all seriousness in the academy, even by the prissiest academic psychologist.[39] Yet if genetic, and, therefore, child, psychology won some credibility as a field of psychological *science* in the later 1910s and early 1920s, nevertheless child psychology was still applied psychology within the *profession* of psychology, still identified with reform crusades, and with the notion of Progressive child welfare. It also became clear in the later 1910s and early 1920s that, if child psychology was to have an institutional and professional future, that would have to take place not in state or other public agencies, but within the context of American colleges and universities. Why this was so, why the institutional possibilities of child psychology rested with higher education, can be grasped by examining the contrasting experiences of the Ohio Bureau of Juvenile Research and the Iowa Child Welfare Research Station.

In 1917 Haines resigned because he thought the Bureau of Juvenile Research had been immobilized by fractious state politics.[40] Appointed his successor was Henry H. Goddard. Goddard still believed low intellect caused low morals when he arrived in Columbus in 1918, even though he had become very skeptical of that view in recent years. His new chief psychologist, Florence Mateer, whom he had hired from the Massachusetts school, agreed with him.[41] For the first year and a half, all Goddard, Mateer, and the staff could do was administer mental and physical examinations, often under hurried circumstances, usually with insufficient resources. Most children they examined, whether brought from the juvenile courts or by anxious relatives, spent little time at the bureau's crowded temporary quarters.[42] In early 1920 the bureau moved to its permanent campus, which included residential cottages for long-term observation of the most intractable offenders. Mateer supervised this work. Within another year her research convinced her and Goddard that their former view of the causes of delinquency, essentially the Progressive view, was wrong. It was not feeble-mindedness but mental psychopathy that caused individuals to misbehave. Psychopathy was caused by emotional and mental conflicts which the child acquired in his life circumstances. This was a condition that could be cured by the application of psychological technology and therapy.[43] By the early 1920s Goddard and Mateer had completed their intellectual shift from the Progressive to the professional point of view on children in society. They had closed the gap considerably between "normal" and "subnormal" or "abnormal" minds, first, by insisting that high-grade mental defectives—the overwhelming majority of mental defectives—could be integrated into society, and, now, by insisting that most offenders, if caught early enough, could be retrained to be wholesome citizens. In a popular book he published in 1921, Goddard attacked the entire custodial ideology as punitive and self-defeating, and he extolled his new methods and point of view as those that would cure delinquency and the social evils more generally.[44] Obviously, Goddard, Mateer, and the bureau had come to represent aspects of the professional conception of organized child-saving.

Consequently, the bureau's political fortunes deteriorated. Key personnel in the custodial institutions resented the bureau and its sudden new visibility as well as its ideology. Many institutional officials regarded the old custodial approach, with its smattering of medical science and its militaristic discipline, as vastly superior to what they perceived as the unscientific psychologizing of Goddard and Mateer and their apparent permissiveness in proposing to retrain and parole juvenile offenders. Indeed, a majority of the bureau's staff shared this view. In the spring of 1921, the new Republican governor decided to upgrade the budgets of board and bureau and to begin implementation of Governor Cox's grand ambitions over the next few years. New institutions would be built. The bureau would become in fact as well as in name the scientific head of the new system, and the board's powers would be clarified and amplified. A group of bureau employees leaked unfounded rumors to several influential legislators who attacked the bureau's budget and functions. Once the governor's impetus had been blunted, he retreated to other issues and left the bureau dangling. The bureau was shorn of its potential and became reduced to a mere examining agency for those board custodial institutions that desired its services. Goddard soon left the bureau for a professorship at Ohio State University. By the Progressives' original expectations, the bureau failed because it became too enmeshed in state politics, and also because state government and its politics could not easily absorb the new professional child-saving mentality that Goddard and Mateer now insisted was appropriate.[45]

The Iowa Child Welfare Research Station escaped problems of political strangulation, but for a while it might have become an outpost of the Progressive notion of child-saving as child welfare. Conceived of as a public health and educational research institute after the model of an agricultural experiment station, for a number of years it was no more than the idea of Des Moines matron Cora Bussey Hillis, an important child welfare worker and power broker in the affairs of the Iowa Woman's Christian Temperance Union (WCTU) and the Iowa Federation of Women's Clubs. In 1901 she broached the idea of a child welfare station with officials of nearby Iowa State College; when told that the college's mission was pigs, not people, she shelved the idea until 1909, when she discussed it with Carl E. Seashore, professor of psychology and graduate dean at Iowa University, whom she knew through the Iowa Child Study Association. Seashore was receptive, but nothing could be done until 1915 when a new research-oriented university president had been appointed, and when the women's organizations she dominated now agreed to lobby for the idea with the legislature. The effort failed narrowly that year and succeeded at the next session; the bill passed in 1917 provided an annual appropriation of $25,000 and established the Iowa Child Welfare Research Station as an autonomous institute within the university.

Hillis believed the research station's purpose was immediate practical demonstrations of child therapy and welfare. University officials were able to deflect her and to insist on research as the primary activity. Appointed director was Bird T. Baldwin, a psychologist interested in physical and mental growth. He was able to keep Hillis's enthusiasms for amelioration harnessed, as when he turned a $50,000 grant she won from the National Women's Christian Temperance Union for an eugenics professorship into a fund to support the station's research activities in child growth, physical stature, intelligence, and nutrition. By 1922 the station's state appropriation had increased to $35,700, and this, combined with the WCTU grant, permitted the station to expand its activities and create the first preschool nursery for research purposes in a university environment, as well as a monograph series and other manifestations of a full academic identity.

Even more important was the intellectual reorientation of child psychology and science which the station effected. Baldwin's research had increasingly shifted toward the new conception of the normal child which other specialists were also formulating. By the early 1920s, he too deemphasized the problem of feeble-mindedness and its typological implications. Thus, he concluded that the minds of most children could be arranged on a continuum from low to high intelligence within a larger rubric of normal intelligence. Even more importantly, he created the idea of the different ages of child growth—chronological, physical, educational, social, and moral. At any point in a child's life, all of these had to be in balance for the child to be well adjusted. Obviously, this was not the Progressive point of view. Baldwin and his associates had provided a fresh model of child psychology, a deftly drawn portrait that took account of the many aspects of child life and that could be, and was, used to attack both biological determinism and the kind of mental testing determinism that such leaders of the psychometric movement as Lewis M. Terman championed.

Now the normal child emerged as a multifaceted person, of considerable complexity, regardless of the angle of vision employed. Dentistry, nutrition, familial relations, school environment, play, disease, intelligence, physical growth, and other factors had to be considered in assessing the normal child. Mere psychometrics were inadequate, as were other yardsticks of simple psychobiological determinism. If the mentally disadvantaged comprised but a tiny fraction of the population, this was a liberating perception for child scientists such as Baldwin and, for that matter, for Goddard. In effect, child science could be studied with reference to virtually all children and their parents as well. Even before Hillis died in 1924, her Progressive ideas on child welfare had been superseded by the new professional conception of the normal child which the station did so much to establish and articulate in the early 1920s.[46]

This holistic redefinition of the normal child, so much fuller and more multifaceted than Arnold Gesell's formulation in 1912, had been suggested even before Gesell, by John Dewey, as early as 1899 in *The School and Society*. Yet, however much academic psychologists and psychometricians might have paid Dewey homage in the early twentieth century, apparently the period of his greatest influence was yet to come.[47] Even at the University of Iowa, which had one of the most recognized research departments of psychology of any state university in the country, Dean

Seashore made sure that the Child Welfare Research Station was not meshed, intellectually or administratively, with the psychology department. To academic psychologists, child welfare smacked of reform crusades managed by giddy females bent on civic uplift.

A concrete illustration of this prejudice arose with the attempt of the California Congress of Parents and Teachers, an organization which, under the determined leadership of Mrs. Josephine Rand Rogers, an influential San Jose clubwoman, tried to create an institute of child welfare at the University in Berkeley. The California Congress had lobbied for child welfare causes for years, including compulsory school attendance, public health, playgrounds, and "Americanization" courses that would instruct minorities and immigrants in citizenship according to the American standard. In 1923 Mrs. Rogers founded a special statewide organization to lobby for a child research institute, patterned after what she thought was the example of the Iowa Station. She enlisted thousands of citizens and members from the PTAs and other organizations. So powerful was her political coalition that the legislature voted an appropriation of half a million dollars for the proposed institute. Clearly, the Berkeley faculty wanted this budgetary bonanza, but not for child welfare as Rogers and the legislature understood the term. The majority of the faculty did not value child research.[48] And the few faculty who wanted a child study institute were women without political power in the university and were chiefly interested in a preschool for teaching, not for research. The legislature cheerfully rescinded the appropriation.[49]

Something more than the lonely example of the Iowa Child Welfare Research Station was necessary for the establishment of professional child-saving. Certainly, by the later 1910s and early 1920s, the context had substantially changed. New perceptions and opportunities had been created. Child scientists shifted their focus from the subnormal to the normal child, thus creating the possibility that the idea of the normal child was capable of considerable scientific expansion and elaboration. At the same time, this shift was part of the larger transformation of the notion of the national population and of the groups that comprised it which crystallized in the years following 1915. More than ideas about groups of the population in national culture were required; large-scale philanthropic intervention was also necessary. Philanthropic intervention meant the infusion of relatively large funds to professional child-saving and thus led to the rapid development of the new scientific profession of the normal child, as well as the new applied professional subcultures of parent education and child guidance. By the early 1930s, the intellectual and institutional development of professional child-saving had been completed.

Both the popular and scientific focus on the child and the child's relationship to the larger national culture was changing, then, in the

years following 1915 and especially after 1920. To some extent there
were changes within the structures and processes of the human sciences
themselves. By the early 1920s, applied psychologists had done much to
undermine to the Progressive child-savers' notions of subnormal and
normal children, and, by inference, the whole taxonomy of the national
population and culture. The passage of immigration restriction legislation in 1924 robbed scientific racism and eugenics—one of the clearer
manifestations of the post-1890 notion of the national culture and population—not perhaps of its popular credibility, but clearly of its mass
appeal and *raison d'etre*. Many scientists distanced themselves from scientific racism, not because they had changed their minds on racial superiority, but simply because they feared being identified with a now
controversial and perhaps unseemly scientific ideology that could damage their relations with scientific colleagues and foundation officials.[50]

Presumably popular attitudes had not absorbed or digested all of the
ramifications of the idea of the normal child. Nevertheless, it took relatively little intellectual acumen to grasp a darker, or, at least, more
threatening, implication of the notion of the normal child. If most children were normal, if, in other words, there was no wide gap separating
the children of the white middle class from those of other groups in the
national population, then possibly the sons and daughters of the white
middle class might go astray if care were not taken that they were correctly and carefully reared. Normality, in other words, could be a two-
edged sword. Within the child-saving organizations the shift to the normal child meant that the Progressive preoccupation with the subnormal
child was a luxury, and a marginal one at that. If the normal child was
mere plastic protoplasm at birth, as such popularizers of behaviorism as
John B. Watson and others urged in the 1920s, then it was the normal
child which child-savers should pay attention to.[51]

The shift from the Progressives' interest in the subnormal child to the
professional focus on the normal child has been, and could be, understood as a transformation from humanitarian to conservative impulses,
from prewar reform to postwar "normalcy." More likely, however, this
interpretation rests on a simplistic and not very useful model of national
history, the so-called presidential synthesis of American history. A more
helpful and compelling explanation of the shift from prewar to postwar
American culture would stress changes from one conception of national
culture to another, rather than cycles of "reform" and "reaction." The
earlier conception of national culture arose in the 1890s. It assumed a
hierarchy of inferior and superior groups, with the white Anglo-Saxon
Protestant culture at the apex, or the norm by which all other groups
in the national population were to be judged. Within this model of
national culture, it was perfectly reasonable to invent the subnormal
child and attribute to it most of society's social evils. Especially after the

early 1920s, postwar thought assumed a different relationship between the parts and the sum of the whole. The new perception tended to blend distinctions among various groups, to juxtapose them on a continuous line, and to assume that from many could come one. Perhaps this is how the new cultural relativism and cultural pluralism of the mid- and later 1920s should be understood, not as an end to racism and nativism as such, but as a subtle redefinition in which each group (*nee'* race) became identified as American, albeit as hyphenated American. For that matter, other intellectual trends of the decade, such as the concepts of indeterminancy and equilibrium in science, the reorganization and divisional decentralization of large corporations, the sudden discovery of regionalism within the larger context of the national culture, the new notions of form and function in the arts and sciences, and the new interest in interdisciplinary studies and in international relations might well have been parallel to this new conception of the relationship of the parts to one another in the whole.[52]

In the 1920s the Laura Spelman Rockefeller Memorial drastically altered the possibilities and circumstances of professional child-saving. It created the institutional and financial framework for a national professional subculture of child science and parent education. The memorial was founded in 1918 by John D. Rockefeller in his wife's memory, with a mandate to improve the conditions of women and children the world over. This hardly gave the trustees a crisply defined program. For several years they marked time, appropriating large sums for immediate purposes, as, for example, almost $3.5 million to social welfare organizations and about $700,000 to public health organizations in the New York environs. Between 1919 and 1922, they gave away more than $13 million, $50,000 of which went to scientific research. They knew theirs was but a holding operation. They wanted a large plan that would implement the memorial's mandate by creating new departures in social and public policy.

In 1922 the memorial's trustees took steps to carry out their grand ideas. They appointed a brilliant young psychologist, Beardsley Ruml, as director of programs to take charge. As an applied psychologist, Ruml considered child psychology a legitimate field, but he was far more interested in large-scale cooperative research projects in the social sciences. Hence, he appointed Lawrence K. Frank as associate director of programs to take charge of child study. Ruml had already worked out some ideas for a national program in child study and parent education, which Frank eventually modified considerably. When appointed to the memorial in the spring of 1923, Frank was thirty-three years old. He already had many ideas about child study, parent education, and the ways in which science could reform and reconstruct society. A graduate of Columbia in economics, Frank had been influenced by the ideas of Thorstein Veblen, John Dewey, and Wesley Clair Mitchell, the distinguished expert on the business cycle. Frank had worked for local reform organizations and, as an economist for the New York Telephone Company, had learned the intricacies of the application of social science methods to social reality. From Lucy Sprague Mitchell, Wesley's wife, and the founder of the Bank Street College of Education, Frank imbibed the yeastier pronouncements of left-liberal Progressive education, an intellectual and ideological posture that in most respects was akin to professional, not Progressive, child-saving.

Frank thought of child study as the basic science from which the twin applications of that science, Progressive education and parent education, should naturally flow. He was entirely convinced that science was positive truth. Its application to social problems would eliminate social errors. Progressive education was the reconstitution of public education to prepare the younger generation for public life. Parent education he considered the parallel to Progressive education in the home, the reform that would make people wholesome, healthy persons and upgrade the condition of family life in America. Assured that Progressive education was converting the nation's public schools, at the memorial he assumed he could establish a national program of parent education. He believed that child science would rescue the American family from the problems of industrialization and urbanization. Yet child science was so poorly organized and accurate knowledge was so lacking that the first priority must be to support the development of child science. Parent education could not be elaborated on an unscientific basis. This new child science must be interdisciplinary and holistic. Its practitioners must understand that there was only the normal child in all of its complexities and that it made no more sense, at least as far as Frank was concerned, to insist that there were different types of children in national culture than it did to study children from narrow, single-disciplinary points of view. The prewar notion of national culture as divided into superior and inferior groups—including the ideology of scientific racism—was alien to Frank's way of thinking.[53]

If Frank wanted to invent an interdisciplinary social technology and science with which to reconstruct society, he nevertheless fell back on the hierarchical assumptions and models of contemporary scientific professionalism. His first priority, understandably, was to create more child research centers, patterned after the Iowa Child Welfare Research Station, so that the new interdisciplinary science could be established on a firm basis. He wanted these centers to be strategically located throughout the country and to incorporate parent training and experiments in parent training with their research work on children. From these centers would radiate the new knowledge concerning child study and parent education, and, it was hoped that other centers devoted to parent training alone would become further points of contact between the new social technologists and the public. The methods of diffusion would vary. They would include the preparation of curricula for parent study groups, the publication of various pamphlets and bibliographies, the initiation of evening study classes in parent education, and the like. In most cases, parent training centers would be attached to state universities and colleges, which, as the leaders of public opinion and education in their states, would help generate public support for parent education and, in time, Frank hoped, take over complete responsibility for child study and parent education. In some instances they would be assisted by federal matching grants to extension programs in land grant institutions of higher learning.

Frank was well aware that academic psychologists were cool toward, if not contemptuous of, child study and psychology. Much missionary work, and, perhaps some hard negotiations as well, were needed to establish the centers and to attract competent scientists to the field. He also knew that the possibilities for parent education in the 1920s were considerable. By the early 1920s, there were both mass and professional constituencies for parent training. The National Congress of Parents and Teachers (NCPT), for example, had more than trebled its membership from 1915 to 1920; by 1930 the NCPT enrolled 1.5 million members. While this reflected several factors, the NCPT was receptive toward parent training, and a number of state affiliates, as, for example, those of California, Iowa, Texas, and Georgia, were vigorously committed to child study and parent education. Furthermore, there was much interest in childhood and "youth" in national culture, interest that went far beyond Greenwich Village literati. As Paula Fass has perceptively pointed out, the 1920s marked the beginnings of the perception and the social reality of a "youth" culture, especially among college students. Perhaps an even more revealing indication of the potential interest in parental information is that when *Parents' Magazine* began publication in the late 1920s, publisher George Hecht was astonished to discover that sales reached 100,000 copies a month within a year, a figure he initially thought was a decade away.[54]

When Frank started at the memorial, the trustees had already given small grants to the Iowa Child Welfare Research Station, for a study of rural children, and to Arnold Gesell's psychoclinic, for his studies of maturation in infants.[55] Over the next year and a half Frank spent most of his time investigating the possibilities for a national program in child study and parent education. In 1924 he presented his proposals to the trustees on several occasions. By the fall of 1924 they gave him full authority to negotiate with various institutions to elicit proposals from those he deemed the most promising and could thus recommend to them for examination and approval.[56] In the 1920s the memorial ap-

propriated $5,760,000 for child study and parent education, except for
$24,350 in awards which Frank sponsored. This was certainly not as
much as Ruml won for the social sciences, and it paled by comparison
with the funds available to workers in traditional scientific fields in that
decade. Nevertheless, the memorial's largess alone, without consideration of the actions of other philanthropies, did much to alter the possibilities and circumstances of child science, parent training, and,
therefore, professional child-saving.[57]

While Frank served as institutional midwife of child science and parent
education, this jaunty positivist and reformer discovered that the relations between the person who paid the piper and the person who played
the tune were not as simple and direct as that aphorism might imply.
Thus, it is questionable how much influence he exerted on the research
centers. He was virtually required to underwrite research institutes at
Columbia and Yale, for example, under circumstances he found dissat-
isfying, if not galling, and over which he had relatively little control.
Negotiations with Teachers' College were probably inevitable. Teachers'
College was the most important institutional center of Progressive education in America in the 1920s. In addition, there were many ties,
formal and informal, between Columbia University and the Rockefeller
Foundation. Frank initiated the discussions with the dean with less care
than he was to employ later. The dean was cool; Teachers' College was
not, in his opinion, organized to handle either large research projects
or, for that matter, public service programs outside Gotham. The dean
agreed when he discovered that his most productive researchers strongly
wanted the institute and that Frank would permit the institute to be
organized as an adjunct to Teachers' College rather than integrated
within it. Hence, the dean defined the Institute of Child Welfare, established in 1924, as a training institution for teachers of parent and preschool education that would not be administratively meshed with Teachers'
College. Its staff could not be tenured. The institute's administrative
history was chaotic in the early years. It sponsored very little significant
research, save for the work of William I. and Dorothy Swaine Thomas.
Furthermore, the institute turned out to be very costly because of the
high cost of living in New York. In any event, as Frank put it ruefully
in recommending yet another emergency appropriation to the trustees,
the dean and his faculty believed that "Teachers' College is running this
Institute for the Memorial."[58] A new director was appointed in 1930,
but she could never overcome the obstacles and difficulties created by
the initial agreements or effect the institute's integration into Teachers'
College. When the memorial's appropriations lapsed in 1936, the institute was closed.

The institute that developed at Yale never suffered from a low rate
of scholarly productivity. But from Frank's perspective it was probably

a disappointment for different reasons. It was hardly the plastic institutional substance he supposed it would be. For several years Ruml had discussed the possibility of a major psychological research institute with Yale's president (and Ruml's former teacher) James Rowland Angell. In 1924 they concluded negotiations for the Institute of Psychology, to last five years. The research professors were Robert M. Yerkes, in animal psychology; Raymond Dodge, in physiological psychology; and Clark Wissler, in anthropology. No one at Yale, including Gesell, thought to include Gesell and his Psycho-Clinic. By their lights—and Ruml's—psychology and child science were not the same. When Gesell applied to the memorial for new funds in 1925, Frank intervened and forced placement of Gesell's operation within the institute. None of the four research professors wished to work together as an interdisciplinary research team, and it took a little while before Gesell's colleagues even thought of his work as administratively related to their own. From Frank's point of view, the institute remained a one-man show in child study.[59]

Frank's successes with the two state universities besides Iowa where he helped wetnurse a child research institute, California and Minnesota, were closer to his plans, though perhaps not institutional accomplishments in which he could dominate or control as he wished. Twice he tried to interest faculty at Berkeley in an institute, but he retreated when he discovered that the Berkeley faculty had no conception of what he meant by child science and parent education. Those who wanted child research looked at it from a single-disciplinary point of view, and those who supported parent education had little interest in research. It was not until 1927 that he could complete his missionary work and his negotiations with Berkeley. In 1923 he opened discussions for a child research institute with Lotus D. Coffman, a former classmate and president of the University of Minnesota. Minnesota's students and faculty had already shown considerable interest in child study and parent education. And Coffman was receptive. Initially, however, several members of the recently established psychology department objected. It took slightly more than a year for President Coffman, through a faculty study committee, to reeducate the opponents and to marshall enough enthusiasm among the supporters so as to engineer a favorable faculty endorsement for the institute. Coffman was perhaps wiser than he knew in insisting that the new Institute of Child Welfare be organized as a regular department of the university, on the Iowa model, for this helped resolve problems of faculty status and recognition. He also created incentives for faculty in established departments to participate in the institute, chiefly by awarding research time and funds in return for teaching courses at the institute. Frank suggested parent education as an integral part of the institute's functions, primarily because parent education had much support from administrators, faculty, and even students. Frank could not resist the temptation to suggest a director, which Coffman deftly ignored. Frank could not comprehend the difficulties of parent education beyond the Twin Cities in the outlying areas of the state.

The Minnesota Institute of Child Welfare, which began operations in 1925 with a grant of $245,000 to last five years, soon functioned like clockwork, at least from the perspective of those involved in the university. John E. Anderson, a comparative psychologist and protégé of Robert M. Yerkes, was appointed director. Anderson was an effective administrator, a productive researcher, and a man entirely confident to surround himself with the ablest colleagues he could find. The core faculty included Richard Scammon, a brilliant anatomist, who specialized in infancy; Edith Boyd, a perceptive, thoughtful pediatrician; and Florence Goodenough, a brilliant, rigorous, and highly productive researcher in mental testing. The institute faculty cooperated with one another on research projects and rapidly became oversubscribed. The preschool laboratory was used for research by 500 students a year. If the parent training centers located throughout the state did not attract the many thousands of enrollees Frank blithely assumed they would, nevertheless their resources were stretched to the limit.[60]

Frank conducted negotiations for research institutes and parent training centers simultaneously. He tried out a few small experiments in parent training before solidifying his plans. Perhaps the most spectacular of his early interventions was with the Federation of Child Study, founded in 1888 as the Society for the Study in Child Nature, one of the earliest child study associations in America. Based in New York City, the federation had a heavily middle- and upper-middle-class Jewish membership. It was entirely secular in its approach to child study. Through a grant in 1923, Frank engineered the metamorphosis of the federation into a national organization, the Child Study Association of America. This bold strategy helped disguise the ethnicity of its membership and, at the same time, implied that Jews were an integral part of national culture. Thus, the association could disseminate its rather sophisticated curricula and publications on child study to a national constituency, and Frank could refer to it as a national institution in his negotiations and missionary work with others.[61] Frank also sponsored awards for the Maternity Center Association of Brooklyn, an organization that served working-class and indigent mothers, so that women of that social status could receive at least the rudiments of infant and child care; and for the Monmouth County Organization for Social Service in northern New Jersey to assist its child guidance clinic for rural problem children. The New Jersey organization was in turn receiving most of its funding from the Commonwealth Fund of New York, which supported child guidance clinics in a number of locations throughout the country.[62] In 1924, satisfied that he had learned enough from these experiments, he presented his overall plans for parent training to the trustees, who approved them forthwith.[63]

An unseemly squabble in Iowa over the politics of child welfare and higher education gave Frank the chance to craft the first statewide parent education program. The Iowa Child Welfare Research Station was unpopular with certain figures in the Iowa women's organizations, who resented the influence of Mrs. Hillis, the station's founder, and with certain constituencies of the Iowa State College, who were jealous that the state university had the station at all. The station's small grant from the memorial to study rural child welfare struck these individuals—correctly—as scientific investigation, not social uplift.[64] In the 1923 legislature, they combined forces to embarrass the station, the state university, and Hillis. By 1924 the situation worsened. As a gambit to impose his and the station's legitimacy in the politics of child welfare and higher education, the director, Bird Baldwin, accepted Frank's overtures to submit a parent training application. Frank acutely sized up the situation, encouraged Baldwin to prepare a more ambitious proposal, and, when Baldwin did, used the opportunity to impose his own ideas on Baldwin for a statewide program. Frank wanted the station (and Baldwin) at the head, experimental projects in various localities, and the involvement of Iowa State College and the State Teachers' College. The revised proposal gave the station another $100,000 for five years for its own research enterprises, involved the other state institutions in parent education, and anointed Baldwin as the chief administrator of organized professional child-saving in Iowa.[65]

Frank understood that the memorial's resources could only establish a few pilot programs in parent education. The memorial's hope was that in time local authorities would assume full financial responsibility for them. If a parent training program in Iowa appealed to Frank because the station was the pioneer institute and because he thought Iowa representative of Middle Western culture, he also understood that he had to plant seeds in larger states commonly regarded as trend-setters. California was the leading Western state. It had cities, large and small, rural communities, a rather cosmopolitan mixture of whites, nonwhites, and immigrants, a progressive reputation in education and social welfare, and a powerful state PTA organization. When in 1925 he had to postpone negotiations with officials at the University of California for a child research institute, he opened discussions for a parent education program run by the California Department of Public Instruction. Will C. Wood and his staff were very interested, and promised to integrate it into the entire state curriculum if the memorial could provide sufficient seed money. In November 1925 the trustees agreed to support an experimental program in Berkeley and Oakland. The Berkeley Institute of Child Welfare was created in 1927, after protracted negotiations. Herbert Stolz, who had run the Department of Education's program, became director of the new institute, thus uniting parent education and child study.[66]

Frank also moved to create parent education centers in New York. It had already become apparent that the Institute of Child Welfare at Teachers' College would have to focus on parent training. Yet Frank wanted a statewide program, a goal that Teachers' College could not fulfill. In late 1924 he opened discussions with home economists at Cornell University to discover that they were already teaching courses in child study. They wanted more funds to expand the courses and to offer new ones in parent training. Starting in February 1925, the memorial awarded Cornell enough funds to create a Department of Family Life, Child Development, and Parent Education, to appoint a professor of parent training, the staff for a nursery school, a pediatrician's services, and field organizers in the extension division. The university put up matching funds. All involved hoped that the legislature would assume financial responsibility within a few years.[67] The 1927 legislature refused. Yet Frank was not deterred. He was determined to have a statewide program in child study and parent education in New York. In 1929 he succeeded. He persuaded officials in the New York Department of Education to lead and coordinate an expanded program, in which Cornell would train professionals, offer residential courses, carry on some research, and continue its efficient extension work; the Regents of the State University of New York would provide for the training of nursery school teachers at Albany State Teachers College and Buffalo State Teachers College; and the Albany Board of Education would run an experimental nursery school. This complex program started in 1930 and was to last five years. There was little guarantee that any of the participants, except Cornell, would be able to continue the program when the memorial's contributions lapsed, but Frank did not quibble. He had his program.[68]

Of the other parent education programs Frank established outside the university research centers, perhaps the most interesting was at the University of Georgia. Frank wished to carry the gospel of child study and parent education to the South. He honestly believed that the South desperately needed the benefits of modernity. Nor was he blind to the opportunity to combine, in one program, the memorial's commitments to child study and parent education with its long-standing interests (and those of other Rockefeller philanthropies) in the "improvement" of race relations. The improvement of race relations, in the Rockefeller understanding, meant the same kind of joining of hands between "modern" Northerners and Southerners on matters of science, public health, and social technology. The "New South" industrialists had worked out such a strategy with Northern captains of industry in the Republican party in the generation after the Civil War.[69]

The local situation in Georgia struck Frank as promising. The women's and child welfare groups were well organized and had political influence. They were committed to child study and parent education, as were Governor Clifford Walker and his wife, who had many ties to Atlanta's business elite and who were willing to sponsor projects that included participation by blacks as well as whites. University President Andrew Soule was similarly inclined, and he also was influential in Georgia politics. Frank had concluded that there was no university in the South ready to handle a research institute. After initial discussions, the memorial awarded a small three-year grant to underwrite costs of a demonstration nursery school in the university's State Agricultural College.[70] Barely had the program begun operations when President Soule inquired about a much expanded program. Frank could not argue for new proposals until a committee of the trustees favorably reviewed the memorial's program in child study and parent education. Frank had made sure that officials at the memorial and the larger Rockefeller Foundation were aware that there would be full participation and planning for the inclusion of blacks in the expanded Georgia proposal. The new program was centered chiefly in Athens, not Atlanta or Savannah or elsewhere in Georgia. It included funds for a nursery school, for graduate student and professional training, and for extension work, even a weekly radio program.[71]

Another parent education experiment involving blacks as well as whites which Frank orchestrated was at the University of Cincinnati. Frank hoped that this project would provide different possibilities, for he had no illusions that the color line would be violated in Deep South Georgia. At the most "separate" might in time approximate "equal," but he was none too sanguine about that possibility. Cincinnati was a border city with Eastern ties, a well-established local gentry, many of whose members were quite sophisticated, and a heterogeneous population that included a reasonably large black population. Furthermore, as a municipal institution, the university had different traditions and constituencies than the University of Georgia. In 1928 Ada Hart Arlitt, professor and head of the university's Department of Child Care and Training, made the initial overture to the memorial. By profession an educational psychologist, Arlitt was a vigorous, perceptive researcher and, ultimately, a nationally recognized authority in parent education.[72] As a city university, Cincinnati had a well-developed conception of public service. Arlitt had already initiated a full-fledged child research program and had organized twenty-five parent discussion groups. Of particular notice was the close alliance between Arlitt's programs and the medical and nursing schools. Arlitt had also been able to raise funds from local service agencies for equipment in hospitals and day nurseries. On the basis of these developments, the memorial awarded a small three-year grant for $15,000 to initiate a parent training program for blacks which would include a demonstration nursery school, parent groups, and educational literature. The emphasis in the program was on the dissemination of basic information regarding health and conduct throughout the black community. Ten parent groups were started, and, in the first year or so, enthusiasm among the parents was quite high. Physical examinations were given. Full cooperation between the university and the black groups was achieved, with blacks being trained at the university to become child study and parent education professionals within the black community.[73] Yet the color line existed in Cincinnati as well.

Frank was also aware of the need to invent institutional mechanisms to attract workers into the profession he was doing so much to build. In time he was able to effect a series of changes within the National Research Council which led to the first national child science and technology conferences. These conferences promoted professional awareness among the leading researchers. As a further stimulus, Frank devised a fellowship program to encourage men and women to enter the field. Created in 1916 as an arm of the National Academy of Sciences, the Council's original purpose was to advise the president on scientific and technical matters regarding mobilization and war. In 1919 the council was reorganized on a peacetime basis. Those scientists and engineers who served in its disciplinary divisions, usually on loan from prestigious universities, attempted to raise funds from private foundations for research topics they considered important, first, by recommending certain lines of investigation, and, second, by using the imprimatur of the council as leverage with philanthropic foundations. In a sense, this provided something like the peer review and broker functions which the federal scientific foundations and institutes were to provide after World War II. Since the early 1920s, there had been a Committee on Child Welfare within the council's Division of Anthropology and Psychology, and, thus, at least a rhetorical commitment to legitimating research funding in child science and technology. But even the presence of Carl Seashore of Iowa University as divisional chairman—who, after all, had welcomed the establishment of the Iowa Child Welfare Research Station—had produced no more than the recommendation that the committee have a display at the Philadelphia Exhibition. The division's members were far more interested in professionalizing psychology and in winning support for studies in racial psychology.[74]

It was not until 1925, when Robert S. Woodworth, a Columbia psychologist, became division chairman that matters moved off dead center. Woodworth was interested in what might be called dynamic psychology, in the sources of social conduct. He found it intellectually easy to embrace child psychology as a part of that larger intellectual construct, and he waxed enthusiastic about the crystallizing concept of the normal child. In time he became one of the most important sponsors and promoters of child psychology, science, and technology among academic psychologists.[75] In early 1925 Woodworth told Frank he was sending out a questionnaire to 1,200 scientists to find out who was interested in child research. His respondents included all members of the American Psychological Association (the bastion of academic psychology) and specialists in the other related disciplines, including the natural and social sciences and even animal husbandry. Slightly more than a quarter responded; 129 declared they were actively working in genetic psychology, with children or animals. Of the several score laboratories Woodworth sampled, the vast majority were medical, not psychological or developmental in orientation.[76] In effect, Woodworth challenged Frank and the memorial to fund the National Research Council's (NRC's) Committee on Child Development, as he had rechristened it, so as to help organize a national professional subculture. In time that was precisely what happened. That fall the memorial sponsored the first "national" conference on child development, which all of the important researchers in the field attended. They exchanged ideas and, more importantly, solidified their conceptions of the field and, of course, of the normal child.[77] The memorial appropriated funds to appoint an executive secretary for the committee, who handled many functions that helped solidify the committee as a national clearinghouse and agent of professionalization, including conducting surveys of researchers, preparing bibliographies, and coordinating other matters. The national fellowship program began in 1926. Researchers nominated candidates for training in child study or parent education at specific institutions, and the memorial made the final selections. The next year *Child Development Abstracts and Bibliography* began publication, supported by the memorial's largess. In these and other efforts Woodworth acted as the organizing genius. By the early 1930s the field was attracting professionals and was growing. By a complicated process, the Committee on Child Development became the Society for Research in Child Development by resolution in 1933. A new journal, *Child Development*, began publication three years before.[78] In effect, the memorial, through the NRC, had created an institutional structure for a national professional scientific subculture.

The work with the NRC Committee was intended to integrate child research and parent training. To insure that child research—the means— would not dominate the end—parent training—Frank engaged in several other forays to solidify parent training institutions and to add to its constituencies. Mindful of the social influence of graduates of prestigious women's colleges, he encouraged the establishment of curricula in which undergraduates would learn about parenthood long before marriage. Perhaps he did not realize that, in promoting what amounted to the professionalization of motherhood and domesticity, he was positioning himself squarely against these colleges' sense of identity and purpose of providing well-born women with a liberal arts education comparable to that which men received at prestigious institutions such as Harvard or Yale. He remained optimistic, in the face of considerable contrary evidence. Only at Mills College did his missionary work achieve the expectations he had defined.[79]

Frank had more success with national women's organizations than with women's colleges, probably because they were more amenable to new external overtures. He was able to interest the American Association of University Women in starting a parent education program through the association's auspices. The program began in 1924 and rapidly reached a large constituency. The director was the very capable young psychologist Lois Hayden Meek, who had studied with Woodworth at Columbia.[80] Frank insisted that Meek's job was to interpret the findings of child development research to college women who, in Frank's judgment, would serve on boards of day care centers and therefore needed to learn about scientific child care. Meek wrote several pamphlets and spoke at meetings all over the country. What interested Frank most, at least as Meek remembered it decades later, was family life education, not science per se.[81] Frank also worked out a similar kind of program with the American Home Economics Association in the mid-1920s. The person appointed to carry on the work was Anna E. Richardson, dean of home economics at Iowa State College. In the program's early phases, Richardson was not to encourage research, or even study groups, "but a more general program of contacts, help, guidance, and advice."[82] In particular, Richardson's mission came to focus on preschool education, parent education, and all other aspects of activities that would support homemaking, because, as she put it, "over 80 percent of the women who take home economics go into their homes and . . . the major vocational objective of home economics is homemaking."[83] Frank's purpose with the American Association of University Women was to reach a potential leadership; with the American Home Economics Association his purpose was to firm up collateral ideological and professional impulses of domesticity among an influential group of potential followers, or, in some instances, even leaders.[84]

Frank then made a series of moves designed to provide solidity to his entire venture. He was aware that the child study and parent education program was under some discussion among the trustees. Once their review committee had given the program a ringing endorsement in 1927, he entered into a new round of complex negotiations with the research institutes. In each case the current appropriations were to lapse, and the new ones were to last a decade on a declining base. Teachers' College received $500,000, Minnesota, $715,000, and Iowa, $834,000. Parent education and child study were to be wedded, bonded so strongly, Frank hoped, that as the universities took over complete financial responsibility for the institutes, this intellectual and institutional marriage would remain secure. The University of California's appropriation did not lapse until 1933; therefore, Frank did not negotiate it at this time. Another measure of Frank's blithe optimism—or, perhaps, his stark realism, depending on one's point of view—came with the Yale Institute, whose appropriation was to end in 1929. Frank knew that Arnold Gesell's work had never been integrated into the Yale Institute for professional and intellectual reasons. Again Frank was outmaneuvered. In 1928 Yale President James Rowland Angell asked Ruml about a new grant for a new center, at least in name, an Institute of Human Relations, whose purpose would be to unify all the behavioral sciences and bring together a multidisciplinary perspective to bear on problems of human relations. Psychology, medicine, biology, psychiatry, law, and other fields would be represented. There was skepticism among Rockefeller Foundation officials as to whether the proposed institute would be interdisciplinary. After complex negotiations in which Frank found it necessary to support the larger proposals to win funding for Gesell, the new Institute of Human Relations was created. The substantive change, at least in the early years, was the addition of psychologist Clark Hull to the institute. Eventually, Hull became the major theoretician and leader of a reformulated behaviorism which led into new theories of personality and culture. But the immediate result seemed to be the same Yale Institute, with the same lack of integration, as before. Frank also engineered a complex scheme, with Ruml's full approval, whereby the memorial purchased stock in *Parents' Magazine*. The stock was given to Teachers' College, Yale, Minnesota, and Iowa, with the expectation that the dividends would fund research at each of these institutions. In January 1929 the Rockefeller Foundation abolished the memorial and created a new philanthropy, the Spelman Fund of New York, with $10 million to carry on the memorial's work in child study and parent education and in the social sciences.[85]

In less than a decade, then, the memorial had wrought a revolution in child study and parent education. What it had created by 1930 could not have been imagined, let alone predicted, from the prospects of child study and parent education in 1915. The memorial's investment of approximately $10 million in direct and future commitments rapidly developed the institutional structure for a new national profession. The research centers, the professional organizations, the arrangements for recruiting future professionals, the experiments in parent training, and the mechanisms designed to forge a symbiosis between investigation and

popularization—all constituted interrelated elements of a larger institutional and conceptual whole. Nor was this all. So compelling and powerful was the memorial's professionalization campaign that it preempted
the prewar Progressive movement, extracted its leaders and organizations from their former affiliations, and integrated them smoothly into
the new professional structure. Thus, the memorial's professionalization
campaign did much to push organized child-saving from its Progressive
to its professional phase. Whether the memorial's campaign would also
achieve the larger social policy goal of rescuing the American family, so
cherished by Frank and the trustees, was, of course, a different
consideration.

The intellectual consequences of the memorial's efforts to profession-
alize child-saving mattered as well. Frank always insisted that child science was interdisciplinary and that its professionals should view children
as a whole, as persons of many attributes, facets, and characteristics, to
be studied in the entire context in which they lived. He made that point
of view, and the future assertion that the normal child was the subject
of child science, a condition of serious negotiations with any potential
recipient of the memorial's support—whenever he had the leverage to
do so. In so doing he provided demonstrable incentives for the conception of the normal child which was taking shape as a theoretical artifact
among workers in the field. His motive, of course, was that it was only
in this way that the larger purposes of parent education and the reconstruction of American family life could be achieved. He understood
academic culture well enough to realize that specialists would only be
interested in children from their disciplinary point of view and that only
a holistic, interdisciplinary child science would become the stable basis
of parent education and social policy more generally.

While Frank always insisted on this particular intellectual definition
of child study in his dealings with professionals, it remains an open
question as to how much intellectual influence he actually exerted on
them. Because he constantly interjected his views on scientific matters
into his discussions with professionals, asked researchers about their
projects, often in some technical detail, and enthusiastically participated
in professional intercourse with them, the impression has been left in
some quarters that he served as the field's intellectual midwife and, by
controlling appropriations, perhaps helped promote certain lines of investigation at the expense of others.

In actuality, the situation was rather different. Many workers in the
field have remembered him as a stimulating, even charismatic, and always sympathetic foundation official who took a deep interest in their
careers, who often brought them together for conferences and discussions, and who did not hesitate to express his views on large and small
issues in the field. He was not a routine foundation bureaucrat preoc-

cupied with mere administrative regulations and details. Yet his intellectual influence was circumscribed by the structural limitations of his social role as a foundation officer. He was self-trained in the field. He was not and could not be a researcher. In retrospect, he could only be a gadfly, a man who could raise questions and make suggestions but not intervene further in the culture of science, in its structures and processes. Furthermore, it is arguable whether there was any *particular* intellectual, technical, or ideological coherence to the totality of research programs he supported, except that they focused on the many attributes of the normal child. Nor could he act with complete freedom as a negotiator or broker between the trustees and the scientists. It was true that the trustees usually accepted his recommendations in particular cases. Yet within the politics of the memorial and the larger parent organization, the Rockefeller Foundation, he had to negotiate with some institutions, notably Columbia and Yale, which had close ties to Rockefeller philanthropy. He had little influence over the results. Once Rockefeller money had been invested in an institution, for all practical purposes, no errors could be admitted and no penalties imposed. He certainly could and did influence proposals; the projects, the results, were a different matter. He was the trustees' go-between. As they did not possess even the pastiche of technical expertise he possessed to oversee the projects, their influence was in many respects even less than his. Most importantly, while Frank believed strongly in the new idea of the normal child, and, although undeniably he helped promote the idea, in fact he learned the idea of the normal child from intellectuals and workers in the field, especially Lucy Sprague Mitchell, John Dewey, and other Progressive educators. The idea of the normal child was a complex cultural and ideological artifact which he but diffused and workers in the field devised. To a very large extent, the professionals, not the memorial or Frank, defined the field's intellectual horizons, at least in a direct, concrete sense. By institutionalizing professional child-saving, and, therefore, its idea of the normal child, Frank and the memorial did influence the field.

The other major foundation that intervened heavily in organized child-saving in the 1920s was the Commonwealth Fund of New York. Officers and trustees of the Commonwealth Fund engineered a professional institutional revolution in child psychiatry, parallel in its structural aspects to the transformation of child study and parent education, with perhaps one-fifth the financial investment of the memorial. The revolution uprooted child psychiatry from its prewar reform and professional context and recast it as another national child-saving profession, known as child guidance. Like their brethren at the memorial, officers and trustees at the Commonwealth Fund believed that their benefactions would accomplish more than mere remedial philanthropy; they would identify innovative, long-range strategies for solving social problems of great significance. The major social problem to which the Commonwealth Fund's officers and trustees addressed themselves was juvenile delinquency. Initially, they defined the problem and their manner of procedure from a Progressive, not a professional, point of view. They assumed that they were to underwrite reforms in social policy and psychiatric technique. They defined the juvenile delinquent as a type of individual who possessed a diseased or abnormal mind—a common enough description in the late 1910s. Therefore, they solicited assistance and cooperation from professionals with the requisite expertise. The plans they initially approved seemed cut from Progressive cloth. Yet within a few years the program they supported veered from a Progressive to a professional basis, almost in midair, as it were, from the idea that there were different types of children to the notion that all children were normal but often had incipient symptoms of larger problems and were thus in need of professional ministration.[86]

The National Committee for Mental Hygiene and its staff of professional psychiatrists were the experts whose labors were recruited by the Commonwealth Fund for the juvenile delinquency program. The National Committee for Mental Hygiene had organized and run the mental hygiene movement in prewar America. This was clearly a Progressive campaign. The man who served as the catalyst of the mental hygiene movement, Clifford W. Beers, was a former mental patient. His widely read memoir of his harrowing experiences in an institution, *A Mind That Found Itself* (1908), became the era's haunting indictment of the institutional treatment of mental patients. Beers helped found the National Committee in 1909 and functioned as an effective symbol for the movement. The movement soon attracted much support from influential scientists, educators, and philanthropists.[87] In the 1910s the National Committee directed the mental hygiene movement as a typical Progressive reform. It attempted to awaken public interest in practices in mental hospitals. It also broadcast claims, not unlike Henry Goddard's in his famous *The Kallikak Family*, that the mentally ill and deficient caused most social problems. Perhaps mental hygiene's leading apostle, Adolf A. Meyer, a Johns Hopkins psychiatrist, taught that the individual's mental hygiene should be understood holistically. Original nature and social milieu were part of the individual's process of continual adjustment to society and its expectations. Meyer insisted that mental hygiene would enable each individual to achieve a healthy adjustment to society's norms. Thus, the purpose of mental hygiene was better mental health; it was parallel to public health, which was intended to bring each individual to a predetermined standard of physical well-being. Meyer certainly thought of the problem from a Progressive point of view; he believed that the mentally ill or deficient were responsible for most of society's problems, as was implicit in his notion of the necessity of adjustment. He was enough of a professional in the 1910s, however, to believe that expertise would solve social problems.[88]

By the later 1910s, leaders in the mental hygiene movement were seeing larger social uses for mental hygiene than helping the relatively few of their fellow citizens who were mentally diseased or deficient. In 1920, for example, George K. Pratt, a prominent National Committee official, broadened the application of mental hygiene almost to infinite proportions. Mental hygiene, he insisted, meant the application of "psychiatric knowledge to social problems in which mental factors seem to be fundamentally important." Like other mental hygienists, Pratt believed that American society had evolved to a stage of complexity and interdependency in which mental factors were involved in all pressing social issues. From the standpoint of enhancing the opportunities of mental hygiene, this was a happy thought indeed. There was virtually no issue in which mental hygienists should not intervene. Thus, the National Committee for Mental Hygiene suddenly had an enlarged agenda. No longer should it content itself with the campaign to upgrade the circumstances of the mentally unfortunate. It should embrace all social problems, such as those associated with childhood, crime and delinquency, and industry. Pratt urged that with the committee's new responsibility came the necessity to work for the improvement of professional training of specialists, medical and nonmedical alike, and to further investigation as well. If mental hygiene had begun as a crusade to reform the conditions of the mentally afflicted, by 1920 it had become transformed into a professional movement with the all-encompassing license to promote the adjustment of every American citizen to the standards of contemporary civilization.[89]

Ever since the Commonwealth Fund had been founded in 1918, its officers and trustees had become increasingly entranced with the potentialities of mental hygiene as a solution to fundamental social questions. An early indication of their fascination was their decision to contribute to the publication of *Mental Hygiene*, the National Committee's journal. Certainly in the later 1910s, it was becoming fashionable in many circles to propose that juvenile delinquency be prevented by scientific means. This heightened interest was suggested, for example, by the creation of state bureaus of juvenile research in California and Ohio, and the founding of the Judge Baker Clinic in Boston. In this sense, the Commonwealth Fund and the National Committee simply followed suit in their discussions in the summer of 1920 of the possibilities of a special cooperative campaign for the scientific prevention of juvenile delinquency. The Commonwealth Fund would provide the financial means; the National Committee would supply the experts and the plan. Their discussions continued the next January at Lakewood, New Jersey, where they worked out most of the particulars for the proposed effort. The campaign's intellectual focus was "the individual delinquent child" and what science could do for that type of child. The conferees believed that mental deficiency and abnormality caused delinquency. They formulated the problem from a recognizably Progressive perspective. Yet they also assumed that the problem would be solved by professional means.[90] The Lakewood conference, and the complex resolutions adopted at it, combined both Progressive and professional perspectives. The shift to professional child-saving was in process. That November the Commonwealth Fund's directors approved the new plan, known as the Program for the Prevention of Juvenile Delinquency. It was to run for five years as a demonstration effort. To those involved, it would illustrate the fruitful possibilities of professional science for preventing delinquency.

The demonstration program assumed a fully professional posture with respect to political and public processes. It was not a hypothesis to be tested and verified by Francis Bacon's methods. Nor was it a bathetic plebiscitary appeal to the laity for their suggestions and collective wisdom. Rather, it would illuminate the wonders of professional science to a grateful populace. The program as adopted supported the professional training of psychiatrists, psychiatric social workers, and other nonmedical professionals, various public relations and advisory efforts, and, finally, so-called child guidance demonstration clinics. Presumably, the seeds sown would in time yield a rich harvest.

Initially, the program was a mixture of Progressive and professional child-saving ideas. Its central object of attention—the juvenile delinquent—belonged, as an intellectual artifact, to the Progressive mentality and to the post-1890 hierarchical conception of the national population and culture. Yet as an early report of the Commonwealth Fund put it, "the decision as to what is the best thing to do for him [the juvenile delinquent] [is to] be based on a thoroughgoing knowledge."[91] Thus, the program's definition of professionalism cleary belonged to the post-1920 cultural epoch. It owed little to the idea of professionalism dominant between 1890 and 1920. Officials of the Commonwealth Fund and the National Committee assumed that scientific professionalism involved a congeries of disciplines, and, therefore, of professions, whose practitioners would work in harmony, balance, and proportion as a team, as discrete but interrelated partners in a larger, holistic institutional and intellectual enterprise, that of tackling the multicausal problems of child behavior understood within the context of the child's multidimensional relationships with its relatives, peers, and acquaintances. On the other hand, the earlier period's idea of scientific professionalism assumed a hierarchy of disciplines and discriminated among superior and inferior ones, in a kind of "single-disciplinary-mindedness." In the same way, its conception of national population was predicated on a hierarchy of superior and inferior groups, with just one group at the pryamid's apex.

Quite obviously, the post-1920 notion of professionalism shared by fund and committee leaders paralleled the interdisciplinary, holistic vision which Lawrence K. Frank was simultaneously promoting in child study and parent education. What has been called the modern temper, the world-view that assumed indeterminacy, fluctuation, relativism, multiple or n dimensions, and the interrelatedness of the parts to the larger whole, was crystallizing in this as in other aspects of American civilization in the early 1920s.[92]

In the final analysis, the program's strongest ingredient was its professionalism. Commonwealth Fund officers also supported an ambitious scheme in child health, which they thought of as a companion to the delinquency effort, all within the rubric of the fund's efforts in "child welfare"—a customary term for Progressive child-saving. Yet the child health program, complete with demonstration clinics in selected rural areas, was intended to show country folk the virtues of physical health and, perhaps not incidentally, to create or even restore the confidence rural communities should have in the medical profession. For the Commonwealth Fund, child welfare may have been a term borrowed from reform language, but it was freighted with different implications and connotations. By focusing on prevention, not cure, and on the virtues of specialization, the Commonwealth Fund was underwriting the expansion of professional operation and legitimacy.

It was not long before the professionals associated with the Commonwealth Fund's delinquency program began to speak about their problems from a different point of view. Less and less did they refer to delinquents as such. Binary distinctions between "good" and "bad" children became less common. Increasingly, they declared that all children were essentially normal, except for the handful of afflicted ones. Each child differed from every other in many respects. Each child also was an element in a larger psychosocial whole, discrete but interrelated to be sure; the whole included kin, peers, and acquaintances. Children were not divisible into different types. Children could not be depicted apart from their larger context. Those who required professional care usually suffered from various emotional maladjustments, usually induced by the immediate social milieu. These were usually mild behavior problems, such as bedwetting or temper tantrums, but might also include unfortunate sex habits, most commonly masturbation. The professionals working at the demonstration clinics began redefining the program as they proceeded, and, as happened at the Ohio Bureau of Juvenile Research in Goddard's tenure, they quickly discovered that juvenile delinquents were not a type and were few and far between. The Commonwealth Fund's annual report published in February 1925 noted that the delinquency program's orientation "has been broadened somewhat during the three years of operation ... the administrators ... have come to view the ... work as a positive and constructive effort, not alone to prevent delinquency, but to establish sound and effective methods for the well-rounded development of the child."[93]

By the mid-1920s, the juvenile delinquent was rapidly vanishing from the vocabularies of child guidance workers, certainly as an etyomological phenomenon, but, more importantly, as a working category of ideological and intellectual analysis. A new conception of the relationship of the parts to one another and to the larger whole was forming in child guidance—and all across American culture and civilization. Two distinguished professionals, Smiley and Margaret Gray Blanton, explained the new point of view in *Child Guidance* (1927). While the proximate causes of behavior problems in the normal child might appear miniscule, even trivial, when understood in their larger context they were important. The child was always related to the other active human elements of his or her larger psychosocial environment. Something as small as a grain of sand in the shoe might be a character determiner of the gravest sort, and psychological causes might be smaller still. The "causes of behavior are often obscure because they are small and because they are nearly always multiple... the minuteness, the inevitableness, and the multiplicity of causes of all behavior point at once to the earliest years as the most vital to training," the Blantons wrote.[94] Child guidance was no longer primarily concerned, then, with juvenile delinquents as such. Rather, it sought to prevent juvenile delinquency, or its potential, among normal children and to promote the happy adjustment of every individual to society. In the catchwords of another distinguished child guidance worker, they were now interested in the everyday problems of the everyday child. Fortunately for those involved in the new profession, the reformulated rationale for the program was predicated upon the new, post-1920 conceptions of social reality which dictated a different picture of the relationships among the parts and the whole. The reconstituted gospel of child guidance also simultaneously enlarged the profession's claims of suzerainty and license.

Of all the elements of the delinquency program, probably the child guidance demonstration clinics had the largest impact, or, at least, the greatest visibility, at the time. Demonstration child guidance clinics were started as part of the Commonwealth Fund's program in St. Louis, Missouri, Monmouth County, New Jersey, Norfolk, Virginia, Dallas, Texas, Minneapolis and St. Paul, Minnesota, Los Angeles, California, Cleveland, Ohio, and Philadelphia, Pennsylvania. The demonstration clinics were ostensibly temporary, although clearly Commonwealth Fund officials hoped that most would take root permanently. The demonstrations lasted for periods ranging between six and twenty-four months. The clinics were to be thoroughly professional and interdisciplinary in character. Their professional staff was to have specialists in psychiatry, psychology, and psychiatric social work in that ratio as the correct blend for the most successful operation. In reality, the clinics' staff members were at least as involved in nontherapeutic activities, notably, training future professionals and cultivating public support, as they were in ministering to patients. Permanent clinics arose in St. Louis, Dallas, Los Angeles, Cleveland, and Philadelphia, largely as the result of local circumstances. These were all relatively populous cities that had well-organized professionals, sympathetic lay constitutents, wealthy patrons, and receptive social welfare agencies. Eventually, families became as important a source of patients as institutions. By the early 1930s, there were forty-two child guidance clinics scattered across the country; most of them had been inspired or helped into existence by the program's consultation field service or the demonstration program. Their sources of financial support by then were chiefly patient fees, private donations, and grants from confederated local charities.[95]

Some understanding of the clinics can be grasped from the development of the Philadelphia Child Guidance Clinic. Established as the last of the Commonwealth Fund's demonstrations in 1925, it enjoyed perhaps more local professional and lay support than any other Commonwealth Fund demonstration clinic. During the two-year demonstration period, members of the clinic's staff accepted a total of 744 patients, almost half referred by social welfare agencies, indicating good relations with those institutions. Indeed, staff professionals worked closely with professionals at local social welfare agencies. The clinic's staff members did a lot of public relations work. They gave evening lectures, offered short courses, and published popular bulletins in addition to techical treatises. They also facilitated the training of fellows in psychiatry and psychiatric social work in a cooperative program with the University of Pennsylvania. When the demonstration period concluded in 1927, the staff elicited sufficient support from patrons and clients to launch the clinic on a permanent basis. Two and a half years later, the city's Welfare Federation officially made the clinic a financial beneficiary.[96]

Historian Margo Horn has explained how therapeutic practices and procedures at the clinic actually functioned. In turn, these reflected changing intellectual and theoretical currents in child psychiatry and psychology and in the national culture as well. From the clinic's massive patient records, Horn selected 240 cases spanning the years 1925–1945, or about one a month. She described the relations between the clinic's social workers, on the one hand, and the children and their parents (almost always the mothers), on the other. In the clinic's early years, to about 1931, that is, the psychiatric social workers sought to intervene in the parent-child relationship and to instruct parents on correct behavior—parents and children alike. The social workers thought of the children as troublesome and as a type apart from other children, which was clearly a Progressive assumption. Yet the social workers also recognized that children, even obnoxious ones, were part of a larger psychosocial milieu, as their stern admonitions to the parents indicated—an assumption that was definitely part of the new, post-1920 conceptions of social reality. If the social workers' intervention represented a moralistic, directive attitude, and if they catalogued "bad habits" and "faulty training" in conferences with parents, nevertheless they also thought of the children as discrete but interrelated elements of a larger psychosocial unity. In reality, the social workers combined Progressive and professional child-saving notions in their actual practices. Their attitudes were clearly transitional. From the early 1930s on, however, their therapeutic strategies became increasingly congruent with their analytical framework for depicting social reality. These procedures and strategies changed, first, to a passive mode of emotional support and reassurance for the parents, and, then, in the 1940s, to a new emphasis on technical diagnosis of the children's inner emotional stresses and psychodynamics within the larger whole of family, kin, and acquaintances.[97] Horn's work amply illustrates the shift from Progressive to professional child-saving and the resulting diffusion of those ideas from the articulate leaders to the field workers in child guidance. If on one level the social workers were responding to situations in which they devised new techniques that they deemed more efficacious than traditional ones, on another level they were caught up in a larger cultural transformation of world-views, of which child guidance was simply one element.

There was more to the Commonwealth Fund's program than the child guidance clinics, to be sure. Its field consultation service consisted of a team of professionals who would respond to communities that were interested in child guidance but that were not, for one reason or another, ready insofar as the Commonwealth Fund was concerned to start a clinic. The Commonwealth Fund's program also supported systematic training of professionals in child guidance. It established the Bureau of Child Guidance within the New York School of Social Work as a training center. The first director was Dr. Bernard Glueck who for many years had been psychiatrist at Sing Sing prison. The bureau's purpose was "to give students the best possible training and to demonstrate the maximum possibilities of psychiatric treatment."[98] Fifteen fellowships, on an annual basis, were made available for those who wished to prepare themselves for careers as nonmedical child guidance professionals, that is, as psychiatric social workers, probation officers, or visiting teachers. Visiting teachers would assist the public schools in identifying potentially troublesome children and in developing child guidance programs. Soon fund and committee officials realized that the demand for personnel in child guidance, especially at the lower and middle echelons, far outstripped the available supply. Accordingly, in the bureau's last two years, they arranged for students from the Smith College School of Social Work, itself organized in 1921, to enroll for training and for several to receive fellowships. By 1927, when the Commonwealth Fund closed its demonstration program, 190 persons had completed training at the Bureau of Child Guidance.[99]

The year 1927 was indeed a pivotal year for for the Commonwealth Fund, the National Committee, and the child guidance movement. The demonstration program concluded; new mechanisms were invented to carry forth child guidance permanently; and the Bureau of Child Guidance was transformed into the Institute for Child Guidance where child guidance workers would be trained. As a field and training center, the institute had close ties with the New York School of Social Work, the Smith College School of Social Work, and the National Committee. Glueck's successor, psychiatrist Lawson Lowrey, became the institute's director. In its early years the institute had space for as many as fifty-four students at any given time. Five fellows in psychiatry and three in psychology spent a year in residence, participating in clinic work and in seminars in human behavior, theory and practice of social work, and clinic administration. Twenty students from the Smith College School of Social Work attended nine months of training, and as many as thirty-six neophyte social workers from the New York School were assigned for varying periods of time, depending on their interests. The institute had its own child guidance clinic, which its professional staff directed and in which the fellows and the students learned their various roles. In the institute's first year, the clinic served 627 children, slightly less than two-thirds intensively.

Nor was this all. The Commonwealth Fund also supported the National Committee's new Division on Community Clinics. Staffed by a psychiatrist, a psychiatric social worker, and a researcher, the division functioned as an advisory and educational body. Its members offered advice to communities where local leaders had expressed interest in founding child guidance clinics. Often the division's staff perceived their responsibilities as warning against "premature developments in communities where interest has outrun sound preparation. The initiatory phase of the child guidance movement . . . is past, and the present need is for training, not only of staff workers, but of communities." The division's staff believed, in short, that clinics would depend on the context of the communities in which they were located, or, in other words, that the clinics were discrete but interrelated elements of their local communities. The division's staff also assisted the established clinics select personnel and decide on "major problems of policy and procedure." In addition, the Commonwealth Fund supported fellowships in psychiatry at the University of Pennsylvania, in conjunction with the Philadelphia Child Guidance Clinic, at the Henry Phipps Psychiatric Clinic in Balti-

more, at the Boston Psychopathic Hospital, and at the University of
Colorado Medical School in Denver. It also increased its support for
training visiting teachers in New York and Chicago, and created a program to train public school teachers in the subject of visiting teaching
at the State Teachers College, Oshkosh, Wisconsin, and the University
of North Carolina. Finally, the fund established a Child Guidance Council in Great Britain in 1927, so as to launch the child guidance movement
in the British Isles and perhaps throughout the British Empire.[100] Apparently, the Commonwealth Fund's officers considered their plans and
programs as international, if not precisely imperial, in their impact. Quite
clearly, they did make a difference. Like Frank and the memorial, they,
too, were able to create a national child-saving profession and, in so
doing, helped effect the transition from Progressive to professional child-
saving. The fund's officers, even more than their colleagues at the memorial, had implemented the professionals' ideas and ideologies. Whether
their actions could solve the larger public and social policy questions
they had originally addressed was yet unclear.

By the early 1930s, the professionalization of organized child-saving
was completed. If the memorial and the fund did not touch every aspect
of organized child-saving in the 1920s, nevertheless their contributions
were absolutely fundamental.[101] They established professional child-saving in academic culture, they provided legitimacy for professional child-
saving, and they incorporated Progressive child-saving into the new
structure. They were able to do so primarily because the Federal Government and the states, the only other institutions that might have been
able to carry out this professional revolution, were in no position to offer
assistance or leadership. The Federal Government could do, and did,
less than the states. The White House Conferences on children, held in
1909, 1919, and 1930, could only publish the delegates' views on child
welfare and life. The federal Children's Bureau, created in 1912, had
only a small staff. The bureau could merely investigate and report on
the conditions of child life.[102] Even the Sheppard-Towner Maternity and
Infancy Protection Act, enacted in 1921 and touted in some quarters as
the Federal Government's shining accomplishment in child-saving in the
1920s, only provided matching funds to the states to establish their own
programs for disseminating hygienic information to mothers. Congress
allowed the law to expire in 1929.[103] As if to underline the Federal
Government's lack of activity in child-saving, the 1930 White House
Conference resolutions merely reflected the new ideas of professional
child-saving, as those from earlier conferences had endorsed those of
Progressive child-saving.[104] As a whole, the states appropriated more
funds and were more active than the Federal Government in child-
saving. But in so doing the states simply furthered the institutionalization

of protective laws regarding children which, as group-specific legislation, perpetuated the Progressive child-saving mentality.[105] Little could be expected from government, then, as a patron, constituent, leader, or institutional home of organized child-saving, especially professional child-saving.

Higher education, in tandem with philanthropy, thus offered more prospects to professional child-saving. Institutions of higher learning, however, insisted that the new child-saving would have to conform to the folkways and mores of university culture. Furthermore, the politics of academic disciplines within university culture probably made large-scale philanthropic intervention indispensable. The professionalization of disciplines in American university culture did not proceed from lofty Platonic ideals. The disciplines that experienced the most rapid growth had profited from the market demands for their services off campus and on. Thus, chemistry and physics benefited from the organization of the electrical, chemical, and automotive industries around the turn of the century. Technically based corporations often financed research. By insisting on technically trained personnel, they created a demand for courses in those sciences. The biological disciplines drew many students in such applied fields as forestry, agriculture, and the health professions. Constituencies mattered even for the development of the liberal arts. Although a field such as history was notoriously lacking in industrial clients or commercial application, the age's fascination with questions of nationalism, ethnicity, progress, and citizenship guaranteed it mushrooming enrollments.

In this context, the professionalization of child-saving in university culture was blocked, at least temporarily, by the firm establishment of psychology as a discipline and profession within academe. Intellectually, psychology was related to child-saving, and psychologists had already provided some of the elements of child study for their most powerful constituency, the public schools. The elaboration of professional child study within university culture triggered resentment and opposition among traditional psychologists, thus necessitating massive philanthropic intervention. Without that child study would probably not have been established in the 1920s.[106]

It was precisely the establishment of professional child-saving in university culture that resulted from philanthropic intervention, no less and no more. The memorial's research institutes quickly made complex contributions to the science of the normal child. Researchers at the Berkeley Institute, for example, initiated three longitudinal studies, two of Berkeley infants and one of Oakland adolescents. The studies were predicated on the idea of the normal child, and, beyond that, on the new worldview of multiple factors infinite or n dimensions, as well as on the idea that the elements were but interrelated parts of the larger whole. In-

vestigators at the Iowa Child Welfare Research Station developed research programs in physical growth, rural children, the inconstancy of
the intelligence quotient, and small-group social psychology which was
based on the idea of the normal child and the new relativistic multicausal
and n-dimensional world-view from which that idea sprang. At Yale's
Institute of Human Relations, Clark Hull's seminar pioneered in the
creation of behavioral personality and drive theories and, like Arnold
Gesell's work and that of workers in the field generally, incorporated
the new idea of reality as well.[107] The Commonwealth Fund's program
certainly accomplished the professionalization of child guidance. Child
psychiatrists founded the American Orthopsychiatric Association (AOA)
in 1924, and social workers followed suit two years later with the American Association of Psychiatric Social Workers. Apparently, the fund's
interest in their work encouraged them to establish these professional
organizations. Starting in 1930, the AOA's *American Journal of Orthopsychiatry* provided new opportunities for professional, theoretical, and
therapeutic discourse which the annual meetings by definition could
not.[108] The Commonwealth Fund continued to support child guidance
as a field and the National Committee as an organization in various ways.
Intellectually, of course, child guidance professionals took as their central
idea the normal child and his or her adjustment to society.[109]

In neither case, it should be noted, were the foundations' larger public
policy goals accomplished, at least by their own expectations. The American family was not reconstructed as Frank had immoderately hoped.
By the criteria of the National Committee and the fund, many American
children remained maladjusted years after the demonstration program
had concluded. More importantly, neither program touched the numbers of persons their creators had hoped. Doubtless, the Depression's
harsh economic realities were partly to blame; for example, they made
it difficult for those institutions that had accepted grants from the memorial or the fund to assume full responsibility for the programs they had
initiated. Yet the more important reason why the foundations' programs
never achieved their creators' public policy expectations was the serious
discrepancy between the problems they perceived and the solutions they
devised. So smitten were they with their naive positivistic faith that science would conquer all problems—a belief very common to the era—
they assumed that scientific professionals would easily transcend the
limitations of their social roles as professionals and participate in a new
golden age of social reform and experimentation.[110] Parent education
devised as a series of evening or extension courses could not reach many
middle-class people who were interested, let alone the impoverished
whom Frank thought would benefit the most. Such daring experiments
as the Cincinnati and Georgia programs fizzled, not because those involved had no commitment to parent education, but because they were

not addressed to the social realities of the situation. Even in California, where parent education was conducted with considerable energy and talent, it was difficult to attract many enrollees. By the 1930s, it was painfully apparent that the mass media, notably *Parents' Magazine*, could easily preempt the demand for parent education far more efficiently and effectively.[111] Nor did child guidance ever live up to the National Committee's expectations. It became established in many privately financed clinics, located only in certain major cities but not in public clinics or facilities, especially those outside large metropolitan centers. Part of the reason was that the large centers had been developed earlier and had acquired their own ideological, bureaucratic, and therapeutic identities. Another reason was that the National Committee had made such public institutions the object of their reform criticisms and calls for improvement. Little more could have been expected under the circumstances.[112]

Furthermore, it was highly dubious whether the memorial or the fund was able to exert much intellectual influence on the professions they created or on organized child-saving. They attracted workers to the field, and their interests were reflected in the proposals they funded. But there their influence essentially ceased. Foundation officials were not scientific investigators. They could not intervene in the complex projects which the professionals executed. Even Lawrence K. Frank was less influential than otherwise might appear. The social role of the scientist was different from that of the foundation executive or trustee. The investigators, once having received their support, proceeded according to what they believed were their own intellectual lights. This was most obvious in the case of the Commonwealth Fund, which allowed the professionals to change the delinquency program in midstream in a highly significant way. Nor did a consistent ideological theme arise from the two programs. Parent education seemed predicated on Deweyite premises of Progressive education, on liberating parents, children, and the family from the dead hand of past social convention, whereas child guidance appeared oriented toward equating mental health with conventionality. In actual practice professionals in each field held and communicated divergent, often conflicting, social policy recommendations.

In a finite sense, of course, workers in the field devised and elaborated their own ideas. Only they could develop their ideas as complex and technical cultural constructs. Yet to leave the assessment at that point prevents deeper analysis of the historical context. Ultimately, workers in child study and child guidance were members of and participants in American culture as well as their own professional subcultures. There is much evidence that they applied their tacitly held general perceptions of reality to the particular problems and issues at hand. The Progressives' view of children as a special group, with an array of types, seemed to have been derived from the larger world-view common in American culture and civilization between the later nineteenth century and the 1920s. As long as that conception of reality and, therefore, of the national population and culture prevailed, so did Progressive child-saving and its ideological, organizational, and behavioral manifestations.

This materialistic, hierarchical, mechanical, binary, and three-dimensional perception of how reality actually worked, with its distinctive formula of the relations between the whole and its parts, began to disintegrate in many aspects of American life and culture in the 1920s. The new perception took shape in those years. It was predicated on relativism, pluralism, multiple factors, and infinite dimensions. It achieved solidity in the structures and processes of American civilization before the 1940s. While this would appear to be a view of reality restricted to the arts and sciences, actually it was pervasive in many facets of American life.

Consider, for example, the practical worlds of business and government. In industry, many large manufacturing corporations created decentralized divisions within their larger organizational structures to handle the manifold functions and seemingly endless aspects of business enterprise which their central executive committees could no longer manage efficiently. In commerce, the 1920s witnessed the massive elaboration of retail chain franchises, and, in advertising, the invention of a "national" consumer market. Both notions were based on a new conception of the relationships between the whole and its distinct but related parts. Even corporate mergers, as in the banking and electrical industries, followed the new pattern. Politics and government underwent parallel changes as well. The Federal Government, for example, redefined its role in the national economy as ally and broker of the many distinct but interrelated sectors of economic enterprise. Partisan differences remained between the two major political parties. These largely reflected their different constituencies. Yet the overall conception of the Federal Government's role in the national political economy outlasted the second Roosevelt's four administrations. The principles and processes defining the relations between the Federal Government and the states, and, for that matter, the states to their counties, underwent similar redefinitions in the interwar years. In urban politics and government, zoning, first tried in New York City in 1915, swept the nation in less than two decades, thus defining new relationships of zones of the city to one another and to the city as a whole. Even urban planning suddenly became reoriented on similar lines.

In social action and thought, a new conception of the national population and culture took shape in the 1920s. The National Origins Act, passed in 1924, settled the "racial" composition of American culture, and so both reflected and furthered the new notion of the national population. In this new idea, which the National Origins Act mirrored, the many distinct white immigrant groups suddenly appeared as distinct but interrelated elements of a larger national culture. By the 1940s, the mass media legitimated the new idea of a nation of nations unified by an overarching cultural identity as American first. Related to this phenomenon was the sudden discovery, after 1920, of America as a culture with its own past. Literature now meant American as well as English literature. American history became increasingly fashionable, whether the sentimental frontier version of Frederick Jackson Turner or the seemingly hard-bitten dualistic schema of the privileged few versus the common folk which Charles and Mary Beard, among others, worked out. In mass culture, novels, films, radio programs, art, and music, all celebrated the American past and its newfound legitimacy—in short, their roots of American cultural identity. In these and other cultural discussions in the interwar years, everyone assumed that there were many factors and incalculable aspects to any situations, but as long as Americans were unified as a people, they could roll up their sleeves and tackle any problem.

The culture of science in America developed parallel perceptual and behavioral constructs predicated on the new concept of how reality was organized. New ideas of relativity, indeterminacy, randomness, multiple factors, and infinite or n dimensions emerged almost simultaneously in such distinct sciences as physics, chemistry, medicine, engineering, and the biological disciplines. Major ideas in science changed drastically between 1910 or 1915 and the 1930s, including how species were formed, the behavior of subatomic particles, the structure of chemical atoms, the relationships between culture and personality, and fundamental notions of causation. Theories of nature predicated on polarities yielded to those stressing interrelatedness, as, for example, the shift from heredity *versus* environment to heredity *and* environment. More pertinently, the earlier conception of species as a fixed type changed to a new idea, that of a fluctuating, interbreeding population. Within this context, it was to be expected that there would be a transformation of organized child-saving in American civilization in the years 1915 to 1930. As the earlier perception of the national population and culture formed the basis for the major assumptions of Progressive child-saving, so the new view of reality as applied to the national population and culture defined the broad horizons of professional child-saving as a cultural enterprise. Similarly, just as the Progressive child-savers' assumption that there were many types of children owed much to larger cultural constructs, so the professional child-savers' belief with regard to the normal child in its many dimensions and interrelationships was a product of its age. Those involved in the multiple transformations of American culture believed that they were responding to specific, concrete situations. On a finite level, perhaps they were. That they could not perceive the forest for the trees was certainly understandable. But then such is the nature of "progress" in science as in all human affairs.

NOTES

1. The literature on children and child-saving is enormous, and no attempt is made to provide a comprehensive bibliography. The following works have been especially useful, however. For an important study of the colonial period, see Ross W. Beales, Jr., "In Search of the Historical Child: Miniature Adulthood and Youth in Colonial New England," *American Quarterly* 27 (1975): 379–398. Important studies of ideas of children and childhood in the nineteenth century include Bernard Wishy, *The Child and the Republic* (Philadelphia: University of Pennsylvania Press, 1968) and Joseph F. Kett, *Rites of Passage: Adolescence in America, 1790 to the Present* (New York: Basic Books, 1977). A suggestive account that focuses on changing notions of social reality in nineteenth-century American social thought is Alan I Marcus, "In Sickness and In Health: The Marriage of the Municipal Corporation to The Public Interest and the Problem of Public Health, 1820–1870. The Case of Cincinnati" (Ph.D. dissertation, University of Cincinnati, 1979). There is much valuable source material in Grace Abbott, *The Child and the State*, 2 vols. (New York: Greenwood Press, 1968 [1938]), esp. Vol. 2; Robert H. Bremner, et al., eds., *Children and Youth in America: A Documentary History*, 3 vols. (Cambridge, Mass.: Harvard University Press, 1970–1971). An interesting interpretation of the emergence of "youth" as a social phenomenon in the 1920s is Paula S. Fass, *The Damned and the Beautiful: American Youth in the 1920s* (New York: Oxford University Press, 1977). Joseph M. Hawes, *Children in Urban Society: Juvenile Delinquency in Nineteenth-Century America* (New York: Oxford University Press, 1971) treats developments from the nineteenth to the early twentieth century. Standard accounts of child-saving include Robert H. Bremner, *From the Depths: The Discovery of Poverty in the United States* (New York: New York University Press, 1956); Clarke A. Chambers, *Seedtime of Reform* (Minneapolis: University of Minnesota Press 1963); Chambers, *Paul Kellogg and the Survey* (Minneapolis: University of Minnesota Press, 1971); Walter I. Trattner, *Homer Folks: Pioneer in Social Welfare* (New York: Columbia University Press, 1968); Trattner, *Crusade for the Children: A History of the National Child Labor Committee and Child Labor Reform in America* (Chicago: Quadrangle, 1970); Trattner, *From Poor Law to Welfare State: A History of Social Welfare in America* (New York: Free Press, 1974). An interesting account is Dominick Cavallo, *Muscles and Morals: Organized Playgrounds and Urban Reform, 1880–1920* (Philadelphia: University of Pennsylvania Press, 1981). Revisionist accounts include David J. Rothman, *Conscience and Convenience: The Asylum and Its Alternatives in Progressive America* (Boston: Little, Brown, & Co., 1980) and, less successfully, Susan Tiffin, *In Whose Best Interest? Child Welfare Reform in the Progressive Era* (Westport, Conn.: Greenwood Press, 1982). Valuable accounts on professional child-saving include Roy Lubove, *The Professional Altruist: The Emergence of Social Work As a Career* (Cambridge, Mass.: Harvard University Press, 1965); Robert R. Sears, *Your Ancients Revisited: A History of Child Development* (Chicago: University of Chicago Press for the Society for Research in Child Development, 1975).

2. My discussion of the Progressive and professional child-saving outlooks

was stimulated in part by several of the above secondary accounts, notably Abbott, ed., *Child and the State*, Vol. 2, Sears, *Your Ancients Revisited*, Bremner, et al., eds., *Children and Youth in America*, esp. Vol. 2, and Rothman, *Conscience and Convenience*. Helpful too has been the research I have done with respect to "reform" in the early twentieth century in the states of Washington, Ohio, and Iowa (see, for example, Hamilton Cravens, "The Emergence of the Farmer-Labor Party in Washington Politics, 1918–1920," *Pacific Northwest Quarterly* 57 [1966]: 148–157) and my work over the last several years on the Iowa Child Welfare Research Station and the Rockefeller programs in child study and parent education.

3.   There is no modern account of the history of experimental psychology, but E. G. Boring, *A History of Experimental Psychology* (2d ed., New York: Appleton-Century-Crofts, 1950), easily transcends the usual pitfalls of "insider" history of science and treats scientific ideas in historicist, not presentist, terms. Other secondary accounts include John C. Burnham, "Psychiatry, Psychology, and the Progressive Movement," *American Quarterly* 12 (1960): 457–465; and Burnham, "The New Psychology: From Narcissism to Social Control," in Robert H. Bremner, John Braeman, and David Brody, eds., *Change and Continuity in Twentieth Century America: The 1920s* (Columbus: Ohio State University Press, 1966), 351–308. See also Hamilton Cravens, *The Triumph of Evolution: American Scientists and the Heredity-Environment Controversy 1900–1941* (Philadelphia: University of Pennsylvania Press, 1978); Cravens and Burnham, "Psychology and Evolutionary Naturalism in American Thought, 1890–1940," *American Quarterly* 23 (1971): 635–657.

4.   Charles R. Darwin, *The Descent of Man and Selection in Relation to Sex*, 2 vols. (New York: D. Appleton & Co., 1898 [1871]); Darwin, *Expression of the Emotions in Man and Animals* (London: J. Murray, 1872). Probably the most widely accepted versions of psychological evolution in the late nineteenth century were George J. Romanes, *Mental Evolution in Man; Origin of Human Faculty* (New York: D. Appleton & Co., 1889), Edward Drinker Cope, *Origin of the Fittest* (New York: D. Appleton & Co., 1887 [1886]) and William James, *The Principles of Psychology*, 2 vols. (New York: Henry Holt & Co., 1890). The reductionist and ultimately behaviorist reaction to these late-nineteenth-century theories were represented by C. Lloyd Morgan, *Animal Life and Intelligence* (Boston: Ginn, 1895 [1890–1891]; Edward Lee Thorndike, *Animal Intelligence* (New York: Macmillan Co., 1911 [1898]; John B. Watson, "Psychology As the Behaviorist Views It," *Psychological Review* 20 (1913): 158–177. See also John C. Burnham, "On the Origins of Behaviorism," *Journal of the History of the Behavioral Sciences* 2 (1968): 143–151. An interesting discussion of the whole problem—as well as a seminal contemporary critique—is Luther Lee Bernard, *Instinct: A Problem in Social Psychology* (New York: Henry Holt & Co., 1924).

5.   See Boring, *History of Experimental Psychology*, esp. 505–578, for much information on Americans who studied the new psychology in Europe and brought it home; a thorough case study is Michael M. Sokal, ed., *An Education in Psychology: James McKeen Cattell's Journal and Letters from Germany and England, 1880–1888* (Cambridge, Mass.: MIT Press, 1981).

6.   Sokal, ed., *Education in Psychology*, 333–338; Cravens, *Triumph of Evolution*, 67–69.

7.   Cravens, *Triumph of Evolution*, chs. 2, 5, and 7. See also Stephen J. Gould, *The Mismeasure of Man* (New York: W. W. Norton, 1981), 146–321, which is not,

despite the author's intention, a work of history, but merely an effort at retrospective criticism of scientific method. Both works have extensive bibliographies of other secondary accounts and of many primary sources on the history of mental testing.

8. See, for example, James, *Principles of Psychology* and the most famous of the instinct theorists, William McDougall, *An Introduction to Social Psychology* (Boston: J. W. Luce & Co., 1911 [1908]). A good example of the social and public policy uses of instinct and social psychology, written from a liberal point of view, is Ordway Tead, *Instincts in Industry* (Boston: Houghton Mifflin, 1918). Several discussions of the instinct movement can be found in Cravens and Burnham, "Psychology and Evolutionary Naturalism in American Thought, 1890–1940," passim, Cravens, *Triumph of Evolution*, chs. 2 and 6, and Bernard, *Instinct*.

9. The definitive biography of Hall is Dorothy Ross's superlative account, *G. Stanley Hall: The Psychologist as Prophet* (Chicago: University of Chicago Press, 1972).

10. Robert S. Harper, "Tables of American Doctorates in Psychology," *American Journal of Psychology* 62 (1949): 580–581.

11. G. Stanley Hall, *Adolescence. Its Psychology and Its Relations to Physiology, Anthropology, Sociology, Sex, Crime, Religion, and Education*, 2 vols. (New York: D. Appleton & Co., 1905 [1904]). On Hall and his ideas, see especially Ross, *G. Stanley Hall*; Cravens, *Triumph of Evolution*, 63–66; Cravens and Burnham, "Psychology and Evolutionary Naturalism in American Thought, 1890–1940," 645. On the history of child development theories, see Sears, *Your Ancients Revisited*.

12. On the Iowa Congress of Mothers, see Hazel Hillis, *The First Fifty Years: The Iowa Congress of Parents and Teachers* (n.p., n.d.), 1–30 and passim.; see also the many clippings concerning Hillis and the ICM in Box 2, folders 1 and 2, Cora Bussey Hillis Papers, State Historical Society of Iowa, Iowa City; *First Iowa State Congress of Mothers, January 28th to 31st, 1902* (n.p., 1902). Hillis's activities can be followed in her Papers. On Hillis and the juvenile court issue, see also Cora B. Hillis to Benjamin B. Lindsey, November [?] 1904, Feb. 7, 1908, Benjamin B. Lindsey Papers, Library of Congress.

13. Goddard's thesis was published as Henry H. Goddard, "The Effect of Mind on Body as Evidenced by Faith Cures," *American Journal of Psychiatry* 10 (1899): 431–502. On Goddard's pre-Vineland career, see Henry H. Goddard, "Anniversary Address," in Edgar A. Doll, ed., *Twenty-Five Years: A Memorial Volume in Commemoration of the Twenty-Fifth Anniversary of the Vineland Laboratory, 1906–1931* (Vineland, N.J.: Publication of the Training School at Vineland, New Jersey, Department of Research, 1932): 55–57; [flyer] "New Jersey Association for the Study of Children and Youth... March 31, 1900... Program...., one page, folder 5, Box M37, Henry H. Goddard Papers, Archives of the History of American Psychology, University of Akron, Akron, Ohio: hereafter cited as *HHG*: Henry H. Goddard to G. Stanley Hall, Jan. 14, Oct. 19, 1901. G. Stanley Hall Papers, Clark University Archives, Clark University, Worcester, Massachusetts; hereafter cited as *GSH*.

14. E. C. Sanford to Henry H. Goddard, Feb. 9, 1906, folder AA2, Box M33, *HHG*.

15. On the history of the Vineland School, see Bird T. Baldwin, "The Psychology of Mental Deficiency," *Popular Science Monthly* 79 (1901): 82–93; Doll, ed., *Twenty-Five Years*, passim; Lucy Chamberlain, "The Spirit of Vineland," *The*

Training School Bulletin 19 (1922–1923): 113–120; Joseph B. Byers, *The Village of Happiness: The Story of the Training School* (Vineland, N.J.: Smith Printing House, 1934), 1–90. Much of the history of the school can be followed in its publication, *The Training School Bulletin*. A good scholarly history of this important institution is sorely needed.

16. See, for example, Henry H. Goddard to J. [*sic*], S. Woodward and Members of the Board of Trustees of the Carnegie Institution of Washington, June 1, 1908, folder AA2, Box M33, *HHG*. A competent portrait of the Carnegie Institution is in Howard S. Miller, *Dollars for Research: Science and Its Patrons in Nineteenth-Century America* (Seattle: University of Washington Press, 1970), 166–181.

17. Henry H. Goddard, "Ideals of a Group of German Children," *Pedagogical Seminary and Journal of Genetic Psychology* 13 (1906): 208–220.

18. Henry H. Goddard to Charles B. Davenport, Mar. 15, May 5, May 27, July 18, July 26, July 31, Oct. 1, Oct. 18, Oct. 25, Nov. 21, Dec. 9, 1909, Charles B. Davenport to Henry H. Goddard, Mar. 18, Apr. 19, May 7, May 24, July 9, July 21, July 24, July 28, Aug. 5, Aug. 14, Sept. 7, Oct. 2, Oct. 26, Nov. 26, 1909, Henry H. Goddard File, Charles B. Davenport Papers, Library of the American Philosophical Society, Philadelphia: hereafter cited as *CBD*.

19. Cravens, *Triumph of Evolution*, chs. 1 and 2.

20. Henry H. Goddard to Charles B. Davenport, May 5, July 18, 1909. Charles B. Davenport to Henry H. Goddard, May 7, 1909, *CBD*; Henry H. Goddard, "Heredity of Feeble-Mindedness," *American Breeders' Magazine* 1 (1910): 165–178.

21. Henry H. Goddard, "A Measuring Scale of Intelligence," *The Training School* 6 (1910): 146–154; Goddard, "Four Hundred Feeble-Minded Children Classified by the Binet Method," *Pedagogical Seminary and Journal of Genetic Psychology* 17 (1910): 388–397; Goddard and Helen F. Hill, "Delinquent Girls Tested by the Binet Scale," *The Training School Bulletin* 8 (1911): 50–56.

22. Henry H. Goddard, *The Kallikak Family: A Study in the Heredity of Feeble-Mindedness* (New York: Macmillan Co., 1939 [1912]).

23. Henry H. Goddard, "Educational Treatment of the Feeble-Minded," in William A. White and Smith E. Jelliffe, eds., *Modern Treatment of Nervous and Mental Diseases*, 2 vols. (Philadelphia: Lea & Febiger, 1913), 1: 143–194; Goddard, *School Training of Defective Children* (Yonkers-on-Hudson, N.Y.: World Book Co., 1915); Goddard, *Feeble-Mindedness: Its Cause and Consequences* (New York: Macmillan Co., 1914).

24. See, for example, Florence Mateer to Henry H. Goddard, Apr. 24, 1918, folder AA2, Box M33, *HHG*.

25. William Healy, *The Individual Delinquent: A Textbook* (Boston: Little, Brown & Co., 1915). Indeed, after 1915, Goddard and Healy came to similar conclusions concerning public policy toward juveniles. Compare, for example, William Healy and Augusta Bronner, *Delinquents and Criminals, Their Making and Unmaking* (New York: Macmillan Co., 1926) and Henry H. Goddard, *Juvenile Delinquency* (New York: Dodd & Mead, 1921).

26. Arnold L. and B. C. Gesell, *The Normal Child and Primary Education* (Boston: Ginn & Co., 1912).

27. Hoyt Landon Warner, *Progressivism in Ohio, 1897–1917* (Columbus: Ohio State University Press for the Ohio Historical Society, 1964), 312–421, esp. 391, 406–407, 419 n.52 and n.54, 432–433; a printed copy of the bill, "House Bill No.

214 AN ACT, To Supplement Section 1841 by the enactment of supplemental sections 1841–1, 1842–2, 1842–3, 1842–4, 1842–5, 1841–6, 1841–7, and relating to the Ohio Board of Administration," is in folder 5, Box M37, *HHG*; Thomas H. Haines, "The Ohio Plan for the Study of Delinquency," *Popular Science Monthly* 86 (1915): 576–580 summarizes the law's provisions.

28. An excellent understanding of Haines's record, ambitions, and ideas can be gleaned from his correspondence with his graduate teacher, Robert M. Yerkes, in Author Folder 200 [Thomas H. Haines], Robert M. Yerkes Papers, Sterling Library, Yale University Libraries; hereafter cited as *RMY*.

29. Thomas H. Haines, "High-Grade Mental Defectives at the Psychopathic Hospital During 1913," *Boston Medical and Surgical Journal* 171 (December 3, 1914): 854–856; Haines, "Analysis of Recoveries at the Psychopathic Hospital, Boston II. A Second Series of One Hundred Cases, Considered Especially from the Standpoint of Psychopathic Nursing of Brief Manic-Depressive Excitements and of Hysterical and Other Deliria," *Boston Medical and Surgical Journal* 171 (December 31, 1914): 1002–1008.

30. Haines, "Ohio Plan for the Study of Delinquency," 580.

31. Thomas H. Haines, "Relative Values of Point-Scale and Year-Scale Measurements of One Thousand Minor Delinquents," *Journal of Experimental Psychology* 1 (1916): 51–82, quote at 70–71.

32. Thomas H. Haines, "The Feeble-Minded Situation in Ohio," *Ohio Bulletin of Charities and Corrections* 23 (1917): 29–36; Lightner Witmer, "Two Feeble-Minded Maidens—A Clinical Lecture," *Psychological Clinic* 10 (1917): 224–234; J. E. Wallace Wallin, "The Problem of the Feeble-Minded and Its Educational and Social Bearings," *School and Society* 2 (1915): 115–121; Florence Mateer, *Child Behavior: A Critical and Experimental Study of Young Children in the Method of Conditioned Reflexes* (Boston: Badger & Co., 1918); Frederick Kuhlmann, "Part Played by the State Institutions in the Care of the Feeble-Minded," *Journal of Psycho-Asthenics* 21 (1916): 3–24; Goddard, *School Training of Defective Children*, 51–75, passim; Goddard, "Schools and Classes for Exceptional Children," *Journal of Educational Psychology* 7 (1916): 287–294; Walter E. Fernald, "A State Program for the Care of the Mentally Defective," *Mental Hygiene* 3 (1919): 566–574; Florence Mateer, "The Future of Clinical Psychology," *Journal of Delinquency* 6 (1921): 283–293.

33. McDougall, *Introduction to Social Psychology*; Cravens, *Triumph of Evolution*, 76–78, 219–223; Cravens and Burnham, "Psychology and Evolutionary Naturalism in American Thought, 1890–1940"; Boring, *History of Experimental Psychology* 692–729; an excellent review of the technical literature is Charles M. Diserens and James Vaugh, "The Experimental Psychology of Motivation," *Psychological Bulletin* 28 (1931): 15–65.

34. Much of this discussion is based on the correspondence between John B. Watson and Robert M. Yerkes, and Robert M. Yerkes, "The Scientific Way," typescript autobiography, *RMY*; see also Cravens, *Triumph of Evolution*, 204–210.

35. Watson's initial statement on instinct and personality is in Herbert Spencer Jennings, et al., *Suggestions of Modern Science Concerning Education* (New York: Macmillan Co., 1918).

36. See Bernard, *Instinct*, for a full discussion and citations.

37. See, for example, John B. Watson, *Behaviorism* (New York: People's Insti-

tute Publishing Co., 1925); Watson, *The Ways of Behaviorism* (New York: Harper & Bros., 1928).

38. Lewis M. Terman, "The Stanford Revision of the Binet-Simon Scale, Results from Its Application to One Thousand Non-Selected Children," *Journal of Educational Psychology* 6 (1915): 551–562; Terman, *The Measurement of Intelligence: An Explanation of and a Complete Guide for the Use of the Stanford Revision and Extension of the Binet-Simon Intelligence Scale* (Boston: Houghton Mifflin, 1916).

39. Robert M. Yerkes, ed., *Psychological Examining in the United States Army*, Memoirs of the National Academy of Science, Vol. 15 (Washington, D.C., 1921) is the full official report. Popularization of the army test results which emphasized innate racial superiority include Robert M. Yerkes, "Testing the Human Mind," *Atlantic Monthly* 131 (1923): 364–365; Lothrop Stoddard, *The Revolt Against Civilization: The Menace of the Under Man* (New York: Charles Scribner's Sons, 1922). Secondary accounts include: Lawrence A. Cremin, *The Transformation of the School Progressivism in American Education, 1876–1957* (New York: Alfred A. Knopf, 1961), 185–192; Daniel J. Kevles, "Testing the Army's Intelligence: Psychologists and the Military in World War I," *Journal of American History* 55 (1968): 565–581; Cravens, *Triumph of Evolution*, 224–265.

40. Thomas H. Haines to Robert M. Yerkes, Jan. 5, 1917, Author Folder 200, *RMY*.

41. Goddard's negotiations with the Ohio Board of Administration over the Bureau of Juvenile Research can be followed in Henry H. Goddard to Ohio Board of Administration, Jan. 3, 1918, folder "Correspondence No. 2," Box M31.1, Henry H. Goddard to Dr. S[tanley] D. Porteus, Apr. 17, 1918, folder "Correspondence PQR," Box M615, Henry H. Goddard to H. S. Riddle, Feb. 21, 1918, folder "AA3," D. S. Creamer to Henry H. Goddard, Feb. 27, 1918, folder "AA2," H. S. Riddle to Henry H. Goddard, Feb. 27, 1918, folder "AA1," Box M33, *HHG*: Henry H. Goddard to Charles B. Davenport, Mar. 25, 1918, Goddard file, *CBD*. Goddard's intellectual position can be grasped in Henry H. Goddard, *Human Efficiency and Levels of Intelligence* (Princeton: Princeton University Press, 1920). Florence Mateer, *The Unstable Child* (New York: Appleton, 1924) contains thinly disguised autobiographical reminiscences.

42. For example, Henry H. Goddard, "First Report of the Bureau of Juvenile Research. The Ohio Board of Administration," Oct. 17, 1918, folder "Correspondence No. 2," Box M31.1, *HHG*: Henry H. Goddard, et al., *The Bureau of Juvenile Research. Review of the Work, 1918–1920*, Ohio Board of Administration, Publication No. 19, Feb. 1921 (Mansfield, Ohio: Press of the Ohio State Reformatory, 1921).

43. See, for example, Mateer, "Future of Clinical Psychology," 283–293; Henry H. Goddard, "The Problem of the Psychopathic Child," *American Journal of Insanity* 57 (1920): 511–516; Goddard, "Feeble-Mindedness and Delinquency," *Journal of Psycho Asthenics* 25 (1920): 168–176; Goddard, "The Sub-Normal Mind Versus the Abnormal," *Journal of Abnormal Psychology* 16 (1921): 47–54; a full explanation for the shift Goddard and Mateer made from "feeble-mindedness" to "psychopathy" is beyond the scope of this essay. But, suffice it to say, that at Vineland and Waverley, each dealt with a population whose distinguishing characteristic was mental defect. What defined the cottage children was not mental defect but recidivism.

44. Goddard, *Juvenile Delinquency*, passim.

45. An example of the resentment the Bureau of Juvenile Research created among the superintendants of the custodial institutions is R. U. Hastings to Henry H. Goddard, Sept. 5, 1919, folder "Bureau of Juvenile Research," Box M31, *HHG*. The affair can be followed in folder "Bureau of Juvenile Research," Box M31, and folder "Some Clippings *re* the BJR Affair," Box M31.1, *HHG*. The Columbus newspapers carried many stories on the bureau's political problems. See, for example, Columbus [Ohio] *Dispatch*, 3/7/21, 2, 12; 3/8/21, 2, 5; 3/10/21, 2; 3/11/21, 1-2; 3/13/21, 2; 3/15/21, 6; 3/16/21, 1-3; 3/25/21, 3; 3/27/21, 7, 15; 3/28/21, 6; 3/30/21, 23; 4/1/21, 1-2; 4/3/21, 3; 4/4/21, 1; 4/7/21, 1; microfilm edition, roll 170, Ohio Historical Society, Columbus, Ohio. An excellent picture of the bureau's reduced functions and purposes can be gleaned from Dr. E. J. Emerick, *The Bureau of Juvenile Research*, State of Ohio Departments of Public Welfare, Publication No. 27 (Columbus: Department of Public Welfare, September 1927), passim.

46. This sketch is based on my research on the Iowa Station. A good document that illustrates the station's definition of child development is Bird T. Baldwin, Eva Fillmore, and Lora Hadley, *Farm Children: An Investigation of Farm Children in Selected Areas of Iowa* (New York: Appleton, 1930); see also Dorothy Bradbury and George D. Stoddard, *Pioneering in Child Welfare: A History of the Iowa Child Welfare Research Station, 1917–1933* (Iowa City: University of Iowa, 1933).

47. See, for example, Cravens, *Triumph of Evolution*, 15–153, passim.

48. [clipping] *The Mercury Herald* [Oakland, California], May 10, 1923, Lawrence K. Frank memorandum of interview with Faculty and Officers, University of California, Berkeley, Mar. 6-12, 1925, Series III, Subseries 5, Box 43, Laura Spelman Rockefeller Memorial Papers, Rockefeller Archive Center, Pocantico Hills, New York; hereafter cited as *LSRM*.

49. Mary Cover Jones, Oral History Number 35, 6–7; Jean Walker Macfarlane, Oral History Interview Number 45, 2–4; Milton J.E. Senn Oral History Interviews in Child Development, History of Medicine Division, National Library of Medicine, Bethesda, Md.; hereafter cited as *SOHICD*.

50. See, for example, Gilman M. Ostrander, *American Civilization in the First Machine Age: 1890–1940* (New York: Harper & Row, 1970), 277–361; John Higham, *Strangers in the Land. Patterns of American Nativism, 1860–1925* (New Brunswick: Rutgers University Press, 1955), 300–330; Cravens, *Triumph of Evolution*, 157–190, 224–241.

51. For example, Watson, *Behaviorism*, passim. See also Elizabeth M.R. Lomax, *Science and Patterns of Child Care* (San Francisco: W. H. Freeman & Co., 1978), 113–142.

52. A brilliant discussion of social theory with far broader implications than might be imagined is Henry D. Shapiro, *Appalachia on Our Mind: The Southern Mountains and Mountaineers in the American Consciousness* (Chapel Hill: University of North Carolina Press, 1978). A helpful discussion of corporate reorganization in the 1920s is Alfred D. Chandler, Jr., "The Large Industrial Corporation and the Making of the Modern American Economy," in Stephen G. Ambrose, ed., *Institutions in Modern America. Innovations in Structure and Process* (Baltimore: Johns Hopkins University Press, 1967), 71–102.

53. The various annual reports of the memorial are helpful; for example, Laura Spelman Rockefeller Memorial, *Report of the Laura Spelman Rockefeller Mem-*

orial (New York: n.p., 1919–   ). See also Sears, *Your Ancients Revisited*, 18–20; Steven L. Schlossman, "Philanthropy and the Gospel of Child Development," *History of Education Quarterly* 21 (Fall 1981): 275–299; Stanley Coben, "Foundation Officials and Fellowships: Innovation in the Patronage of Science," *Minerva* 14 (1976): 225–240; Milton Senn, *Insights on the Child Development Movement in the United States*, Monographs of the Society for Research in Child Development, Vol. 40, No. 161 (Chicago: University of Chicago Press, 1975), 11–24; Lawrence K. Frank, Oral History Interview Number 22, *SOHICD*; Lawrence K. Frank, "Two Tasks of Education," *School and Society* 15 (June 17, 1922): 655–659. A biography of Frank is sorely needed.

54. Steven L. Schlossman, "Before Home Start: Notes Toward a History of Parent Education in America, 1897–1929," *Harvard Educational Review* 46 (1976): 452–454; G. M. Whipple, ed., *The Twenty-Eighth Yearbook of the National Society for the Study of Education. Preschool and Parental Education* (Bloomington, Ill.: School Publishing Co., 1929), 7–43, 275–353; National Congress of Parents and Teachers, *Parents and Teachers* (Boston, 1928); the entire issue of *Child Study*, Vol. 6, November 1928, is devoted to the history of the most important child study and parent education organization, the Child Study Association of America; Fass, *Damned and the Beautiful*, passim; the circulation figures for *Parents' Magazine* are in George Hecht, Oral History Interview Number 27, 4, *SOHICD*.

55. Laura Spelman Rockefeller Memorial, *Report of the Laura Spelman Rockefeller Memorial* (New York: n.p., 1923), 12–19; ibid., *Report for 1923* (New York: n.p., 1924), 7–11.

56. Lawrence K. Frank, untitled thirty-eight page memorandum, 9–10, passim, October 1922, Series 2, Box 3, folder "Policy LSRM," Spelman Fund Papers, Rockefeller Archive Center, Pocantico Hills, N.Y.; hereafter cited as *SF*; Beardsley Ruml to Raymond B. Fosdick, Sept. 5, 1922, Series 2, Box 2, folder "Policy 1921–1929," *LSRM*; Lawrence K. Frank, "Memorandum: Child Study and Parent Training," six-page manuscript, May 23, 1924, Lawrence K. Frank, "Child Study and Parent Training," twenty-three page memorandum, Oct. 1924, Series III, Subseries 5, Box 31, *LSRM*.

57. Figures calculated from: Laura Spelman Rockefeller Memorial, *Report for 1924* (New York: n.p., 1924), 7–11; Laura Spelman Rockefeller Memorial, *Report for 1925* (New York: n.p., 1926), 8–13; Laura Spelman Rockefeller Memorial, *Report for 1926* (New York: n.p., 1927), 7–12; Laura Spelman Rockefeller Memorial, *Report for 1927 and 1928* (New York: n.p., 1929), 7–14. Excellent secondary accounts on philanthropy and science include: Stanley Coben, "The Scientific Establishment and the Transmission of Quantum Mechanics to the United States, 1919–1932," *American Historical Review* 76 (1971): 442–466; Coben, "American Foundations as Patrons of Science: The Commitment to Individual Research," in Nathan Reingold, ed., *The Sciences in the American Context: New Perspectives* (Washington, D.C.: Smithsonian Institution Press, 1979), 229–248; Robert E. Kohler, Jr., "Warren Weaver and the Rockefeller Foundation Program in Molecular Biology: A Case Study in the Management of Science," in Reingold, ed., *Sciences in the American Context*, 249–294; Nathan Reingold, "National Science Policy in a Private Foundation: The Carnegie Institution of Washington," in Alexandra Oleson and John Voss, eds., *The Organization of Knowledge in Modern America, 1860–1920* (Baltimore: Johns Hopkins University Press, 1979), 313–341; Daniel J. Kevles,

The Physicists: The History of a Scientific Community in Modern America (New York: Alfred A. Knopf, 1978).

58. Lawrence K. Frank, memorandum of interview with Dean [James E.] Russell, June 15, 1926, Series III, Subseries 5, Box 42, *LSRM*: Schlossman, "Philanthropy and the Gospel of Child Development," 282–283.

59. See, for example, Yerkes, "Scientific Way," 251–257, *RMY*; Lawrence K. Frank, memorandum of interview with Arnold Gesell, Jan. 20, 1925, Series III, Subseries 5, Box 47, *LSRM*, and the entire folders on the Yale negotiations contained therein.

60. Lawrence K. Frank, "The University of Minnesota," three-page memorandum, Feb. 18, 1925; Frank, memorandum of interview with L. D. Coffman, Feb. 27, 1925; [L. D. Coffman], "Revised Proposal for an Institute of Child Welfare, answering the questions raised by Mr. Lawrence K. Frank, March 6, 1925," and seven attached memoranda; Arthur Woods to L. D. Coffman, Apr. 14, 1925; John E. Anderson to Dorothea Davis, Apr. 13, 1927, and eight attached documents, Box 45, Series III, Subseries 5, *LSRM*; Marian R. Yarrow, Oral History Number 79, 6; Dale B. Harris, Oral History Interview Number 26, 2–4; Willard Olson, Oral History Interview Number 52, 1–2; Edith Boyd, Oral History Interview Number 10, 20–30, 42–55; Myrtle McGraw, Oral History Interview Number 48, 2; *SOHICD*.

61. Laura Spelman Rockefeller Memorial, *Report for 1923* (New York: n.p., 1924), 11, 17. Frank was not anti-Semitic; he had been a member of the Ethical Culture Society. He simply believed that making the federation into a "national" organization would make it more "useful."

62. Laura Spelman Rockefeller Memorial, *Report for 1923*, 11, 17; the Commonwealth Fund, *Fourth Annual Report for the Year 1921–1922* (New York: n.p., 1923), 15–16.

63. Lawrence K. Frank, "Memorandum. Child Study and Parent Training," May 23, 1924, six-page typescript memorandum, "Child Study and Parent Training," Oct. 1924, twenty-three page typescript memorandum, *LSRM*, Series III, Subseries 5, Box 31.

64. Walter A. Jessup to Beardsley Ruml, July 21, 1922, Bird T. Baldwin to Walter A. Jessup [telegram], Nov. 22, 1922, Bird T. Baldwin to Walter A. Jessup, Mar. 9, 1923, and attached "Conversation of the Rural Child in Iowa," three typescript pages with the notation "Corrected copy," Papers of the Presidents of the University of Iowa, Department of Special Collections, University of Iowa Libraries, Iowa City, hereafter cited as *IP*.

65. Beardsley Ruml to Bird T. Baldwin, Dec. 20, 1924, Lawrence K. Frank to Bird T. Baldwin, Jan. 12, 1925, Lawrence K. Frank, memorandum of interview, with group in Des Moines, Iowa, Mar. 25, 1925, Series III, Subseries 5, Box 40, *LSRM*; Anna E. Richardson to Lawrence K. Frank, Apr. 3, 1925, and attached "Recommended Development in Child Care and Training at Iowa State College," Apr. 3, 1925, two typescript pages, Arthur Woods to Raymond A. Pearson, Apr. 14, 1925, Series III, Subseries 5, Box 32, *LSRM*; Arthur Woods to Walter A. Jessup, Apr. 14, 1925, Walter A. Jessup to Arthur Woods, May 6, 1925, *IP*.

66. Lawrence K. Frank, memorandum of interview with Will C. Wood, Ethel Richardson, Grace Stanley, and Herbert R. Stolz, Mar. 17–20, 1925, Lawrence K. Frank, memorandum of interview with Will C. Wood, Nov. 2, 1925, Lawrence K.

Frank, memorandum of interview with Ethel Richardson, Mar. 29, 1926, Beardsley Ruml to Will C. Wood, Series III, Subseries 5, Box 27, *LSRM*.

67. Lawrence K. Frank, memorandum of interview with Flora Rose and Martha Van Rensselaer, Oct. 30, 1924, Lawrence K. Frank to Flora Rose, Dec. 20, 1924, Jan. 3, 1925, Beardsley Ruml to Dr. Livingston Farrand, Feb. 25, May 28, 1925, Series III, Subseries 5, Box 31, *LSRM*.

68. Lawrence K. Frank, memorandum of interview with Dean A. R. Mann, Flora Rose, and Martha Van Rensselaer, Nov. 14, 1929, Lawrence K. Frank, memorandum of interview with Commissioner J. Cayce Morrison, Nov. 26, 1929 [two interviews], Paul J. Kruse to Lawrence K. Frank, Mar. 22, 1930, Dorothea Davis, memorandum of interview with J. Cayce Morrison, Mar. 16, 1928, Series III, Subseries 5, Box 38, *LSRM*: [Catherine Hill Taylor], "Regents of the University of the State of New York, New York State College for Teachers, Progress Report," Dec. 9, 1932, Series III, Subseries 5, Box 26, *LSRM*.

69. See [Lawrence K. Frank], "Policy in Child Study and Parent Education, Extracts from Various Memoranda and Dockets," n.d. [circa 1930], Series 2, Box 3, *SF*.

70. Pauline Park Knapp, Oral History Interview Number 38, 5, *SOHICD*; Sydnor H. Walker, memorandum of interview with Mrs. Clifford H. Walker, Feb. 26, 1925, Sydnor H. Walker, memorandum of interview with Mary Cresswell, Feb. 27, 1925, Sydnor H. Walker, memorandum of interview with Andrew M. Soule, Feb. 27, 1925, T. F. Abercrombie to Laura Spelman Rockefeller Memorial, Mar. 5, 1925, Beardsley Ruml to Andrew M. Soule, Mar. 28, 1925, Series III, Subseries 5, Box 44, *LSRM*.

71. Andrew M. Soule to Lawrence K. Frank, Jan. 15, 1927, Lawrence K. Frank, memorandum with Andrew M. Soule, Mary Cresswell, Martha McAlpine, and various members of the faculty, Mar. 9, 1927, Lawrence K. Frank, memorandum of interview with Mrs. Clifford Walker and Rhoda Kaufman, Mar. 11, 1927, Mrs. Clifford Walker to Lawrence K. Frank, May 18, 1927, Andrew M. Soule to Lawrence K. Frank, Oct. 15, 1927, Beardsley Ruml to Andrew M. Soule, Series III, Subseries 5, Box 44, *LSRM*.

72. The Ada Hart Arlitt Papers, Department of Special Collections, University of Cincinnati Archives, contain biographical information and materials concerning her work in 1933–1934 as national chairman of Parent Education.

73. Ada Hart Arlitt to Beardsley Ruml, Jan. 10, 1928, Beardsley Ruml to Herman Schneider, Mar. 3, 1928, Dorothea Davis, memorandum of interview with Ada Hart Arlitt, Afton Smith, Miss Deyer, Ellen Kleppe, Miss Babcock, May 15, 1928, Sydnor H. Walker, memorandum of interview with Ada Arlitt, Nov. 20, 1928, Ada Hart Arlitt to Marian Knight, Sept. 18, 1929, and attached "Report to the Laura Spelman Rockefeller Foundation [*sic*] 1928–1928," three typescript pages, Marian A. Knight, "Progress Report University of Cincinnati," Sept. 27, 1929, Series III, Subseries 5, Box 44, *LSRM*.

74. Carl E. Seashore, "Report of the Division of Anthropology and Psychology for the Year Ending June 30, 1922," June 30, 1922, thirteen typescript pages [multilith copy], p. 3, Series II, Subseries 5, Box 30, *LSRM*.

75. See the following testimonials, for example: John A. Clausen, Oral History Interview Number 13, 25; Wayne Dennis, Oral History Interview Number 15, 22; Charles Gershenson, Oral History Interview Number 23, 12; Arthur Jer-

sild, Oral History Interview Number 33, 3, 5, 20, 24; Mary Cover Jones, Oral History Interview Number 34, 1–2; Lois B. and Gardner Murphy, Oral History Interview Number 51, 1–2, 3, 7; Willard Olson, Oral History Interview Number 52, 3–4; George D. Stoddard, Oral History Interview Number 69, 7–8; Lois Hayden Meek Stolz, Oral History Interview Number 71, 2; *SOHICD*; Sears, *Your Ancients Revisited*, 18.

76. Robert S. Woodworth to Lawrence K. Frank, Feb. 18, 1925, Apr. 21, 1925, and attachment, Series III, Subseries 5, Box 30, *LSRM*.

77. National Research Council, Committee on Child Development, *Conference on Research in Child Development, Gramatan Hotel, Bronxville, New York, October 23 to 25, 1925* (n.p.; n.d., 1925), passim.

78. Lawrence K. Frank to George M. Stratton, Nov. 9, 1925, Lawrence K. Frank, memorandum of interview with Dr. [George M.] Stratton of the National Research Council, Dec. 2, 1925, George M. Stratton to Bird T. Baldwin, Dec. 3, 1925, Lawrence K. Frank to Arnold Gesell, Dec. 12, 1925, Lawrence K. Frank Memorandum Child Study Fellowships, to Beardsley Ruml, Jan. [?], 1926, Beardsley Ruml to Vernon Kellogg, Mar. 3, 1926, Bird T. Baldwin, "Report of the Committee on Child Development of the Division of Anthropology and Psychology of the National Research Council, July 1, 1925 to June 30, 1926, Leslie Ray Marston, "Report of the Committee on Child Development of the Division of Anthropology and Psychology of the National Research Council (For the Year 1926–1927)," Beardsley Ruml to Bird T. Baldwin, Jan. 31, 1928, Mervin A. Durea, "Report of the Executive Secretary, Committee on Child Development, Division of Anthropology and Psychology, National Research Council, Sept. 8, 1929," Revell McCallum to Vernon Kellogg, Jan. 30, 1930, Series III, Subseries 5, Box 30, *LSRM*. See also Sears, *Your Ancients Revisited*, 18–19.

79. See, for example, Lawrence K. Frank, "Child Study Work in the Women's Colleges," Apr. 1927, Series III, Subseries 5, Box 30, *LSRM*; Herbert R. Stolz to Lawrence K. Frank, Mar. 28, 1927, Lawrence K. Frank to Will C. Wood, Apr. 4, 1927, Dorothea Day to Aurelia Reinhardt, Sept. 29, 1927, Beardsley Ruml to Aurelia Reinhardt, Dec. 2, 1927, Aurelia Reinhardt, "Report by the President of Mills College to the Spelman Fund of New York, Concerning Appropriation No. 40," Aug. 15, 1931, Series III, Subseries 5, Box 33, *LSRM*.

80. Helen Thompson Woolley, "Grant from the Laura Spelman Rockefeller Memorial for the Educational Program," *Journal of the American Association of University Women* 17 (May 1924): 14; Lawrence K. Frank, memorandum of interview with Mrs. Frank Fenton Bernard, Educational Secretary [AAUW], Dec. 3, 1923, Helen T. Woolley to Lawrence K. Frank, Feb. 4, 1924, Lawrence K. Frank to Frances Fenton Bernard, Mar. 1, 1924, Series III, Subseries 5, Box 26, *LSRM*.

81. Lois Hayden Meek Stolz, Oral History Interview Number 71, 8–20, *SOHICD*. On Meek's program as it developed, see Lois Hayden Meek, "Department of Pre-School and Elementary Education: General Survey of Educational Programs," *Journal of the American Association of University Women* 18 (October 1924): 22–23; Helen Thompson Woolley, "Educational Policies," *Journal of the American Association of University Women* 18 (May 1925): 14; Lois Hayden Meek, "Our Educational Program (Including the Report of the Educational Secretary) April 1, 1925," *Journal of the American Association of University Women* 19 (June 1926): 15–17; Lois Hayden Meek, "A Pre-School Project for University Women," *Progressive*

Education 2 (1925): 38–41; Lois Hayden Meek, "New Ventures in Education for University Women," *Journal of the American Association of University Women* 20 (October 1926): 17–19.

82. Anna E. Richardson, "The Association's Program for Child Study and Parent Education," *Journal of Home Economics* 18 (October 1926): 23.

83. Anna E. Richardson, "Standards of Home Economics in Colleges," *Bulletin American Home Economics Association*, Ser. 9 (October 1926): 23.

84. Richardson's reports can be followed consecutively in *Bulletin American Home Economics Association*, complete with the printing of the official correspondence with the memorial.

85. Laura Spelman Rockefeller Memorial, *Report for 1927 and 1928* (New York: n.p., 1929), 5, 7–14.

86. Still the best and most perceptive published account of psychiatric social work, mental hygiene, and child guidance is Lubove, *Professional Altruist*, 85–117, passim. I am indebted to Dr. Margo Horn, of the University of California at San Diego, for sharing her perceptive insights with me on the Commonwealth Fund and the child guidance program. Figures on the Commonwealth Fund's disbursements can be found in Commonwealth Fund, *Annual Report*, after 1921.

87. An outstanding study of Beers and the mental hygiene movement is Norman Dain, *Clifford W. Beers. Advocate for the Insane* (Pittsburgh: University of Pittsburgh Press, 1980). For a revisionist point of view, see Rothman, *Conscience and Convenience*, 293–323; see also Christine Mary Shea, "The Ideology of Mental Health and the Emergence of the Therapeutic Liberal State: The American Mental Hygiene Movement, 1900–1930" (Ph.D. dissertation, University of Illinois, Urbana-Champaign, 1980: University Microfilms International, Order Number 8026596), 33–353.

88. See, for example, Lewellys F. Barker, "The First Ten Years of the National Committee for Mental Hygiene, With Some Comments on Its Future," *Mental Hygiene* 2 (1918): 557–581; many of the documents of the movement are reprinted in National Committee for Mental Hygiene, *Twenty Years of Mental Hygiene 1909–1929, First Distributed at the Twentieth Anniversary Dinner Held at Hotel Biltmore, New York City, Evening of November Fourteenth Nineteen Hundred Twenty-Nine, Under the Auspices of the National Committee for Mental Hygiene and of the American Foundation for Mental Hygiene*, (n.p., 1929), passim. An interesting assessment of Meyer is in Helen L. Witmer, *Psychiatric Clinics for Children with Special Reference to State Programs* (New York: Commonwealth Fund, 1940), 9–27.

89. See George K. Pratt, "Twenty Years of the National Committee for Mental Hygiene," *Mental Hygiene* 14 (1930): 399–428, esp. 417–419. According to some interpretations, the first child guidance clinic was founded by William Healy as an adjunct to the Chicago juvenile court in 1909. Yet Healy's clinic was thoroughly part of the Progressive child-saving mentality. Conceived of as a clinic whose practitioners could advise the court by diagnosing offenders, it was entirely oriented toward the question of juvenile delinquency; Healy assumed that there were types of minds. This was not a professional but a generalized scientific clinic in aid of social reform; Healy himself recognized the differences between his essentially Progressive outlook at Chicago and his later professional operation at the Judge Baker Clinic in Boston. See William Healy and Augusta F. Bronner, "The Child Guidance Clinic: Birth and Growth of an Idea," in Lawson G. Lowrey and Vic-

toria Sloane, eds., *Orthopsychiatry 1923–1948. Retrospect and Prospect* (New York: American Orthopsychiatric Association, 1948), 14–45.

90. George S. Stevenson, "Child Guidance and the National Committee for Mental Hygiene," in Lowrey and Sloane, eds., *Orthopsychiatry*, 50–82, details on the Lakewood conference at 53–56. Together with George S. Stevenson and Geddes Smith, *Child Guidance Clinics: A Quarter Century of Development* (New York: Commonwealth Fund, 1934), one can gain a reasonably clear discussion of the program's genesis and execution. On the other hand, Dr. George S. Stevenson, Oral History Interview Number 55, Milton J.E. Senn Oral History Interviews in Child Guidance, National Library of Medicine, Bethesda, Maryland, is essentially useless.

91. Commonwealth Fund, *Fourth Annual Report for the Year 1921–1922* (New York, 1923), 9–10.

92. There is considerable evidence that this shift in the notion of what constituted social reality, and of the relationship of the parts to the whole, was generalized in the culture, and was not simply a peculiarity of the psychiatric and child guidance workers. In a very real sense, for example, the heredity-environment controversy in the natural and social sciences began as a series of single-disciplinary (and professional) conflicts and concluded with interdisciplinary notions of intellectual and professional collaboration; see Cravens, *Triumph of Evolution*, passim. A brilliant and suggestive work that treats this level of social theory is Shapiro, *Appalachia on Our Mind*, passim. See also Hamilton Cravens, "The Child Research Movement in the Depression Decade, 1928–1941," paper presented at meeting of Society for Research in Child Development, Apr. 1983, and Cravens, "The Wandering IQ: American Culture and Mental Testing," *Human Development* (in press).

93. Commonwealth Fund, *Sixth Annual Report for the Year 1923–1924* (New York, 1925), 24.

94. Smiley and Margaret Gray Blanton, *Child Guidance* (New York: Century Co., 1927), 6.

95. See the Commonwealth Fund's *Annual Report* after 1921 for further information. Other accounts of the child guidance clinics include Stevenson and Smith, *Child Guidance Clinics*, 20–24, passim; Forest N. Anderson and Staff, "Six Years of Child Guidance," *Journal of Juvenile Research* 15 (1931): 73–100; and the following accounts in Lowrey and Sloane, eds., *Orthopsychiatry*: William Healy and Augusta F. Bronner, "The Child Guidance Clinic: Birth and Growth of an Idea," 14–19; Henry C. Schumacher, "The Cleveland Guidance Center," 377–393; Frederick H. Allen, "The Philadelphia Child Guidance Clinic," 394–413. See also Lubove, *Professional Altruist*, 85–117, for a perceptive account.

96. Stevenson and Smith, *Child Guidance Clinics*, 44–47.

97. Dr. Margo Horn, "The Moral Message of Child Guidance 1925–1945," *Journal of Social History* 18 (Fall 1984): 25–36. This pathbreaking work is based on systematic examination of the patient records of the Philadelphia Child Guidance Clinic. Her work is of unusual importance, not merely because of its interpretive contribution but also because the Philadelphia Clinic's records constitute by far the only extant primary sources of the major child guidance clinics. Dr. Horn is finishing what promises to be an important monograph on the child guidance movement.

98. Commonwealth Fund, *Fifth Annual Report for the Year 1922–1923* (New York, 1924), 32.

99. Commonwealth Fund, *Eighth Annual Report for the Year 1925–1926* (New York, 1927), 44–45. Not all of these persons received fellowships, of course. Much information on this program can be found in Porter R. Lee and Marian E. Kenworthy, eds., *Mental Hygiene and Social Work* (New York: Commonwealth Fund, 1929), passim.

100. Commonwealth Fund, *Tenth Annual Report for the Year Ending September 30, 1928* (New York, 1929), 48–66; Sarah H. Swift, *Training in Psychiatric Social Work at the Institute for Child Guidance 1927–1933* (New York: Commonwealth Fund, 1934), passim, provides some of the institute's history and rationale from the participants' point of view; Lawson G. Lowrey, ed., *Institute for Child Guidance Studies. Selected Reprints* (New York: Commonwealth Fund, 1931), passim, provides convenient access to technical papers written by institute staff. Lubove, *Professional Altruist* has an excellent bibliography.

101. Sears, *Your Ancients Revisited*, 13–21, and Witmer, *Psychiatric Clinics for Children*, 41–243, treat developments in the field not directly influenced by the memorial and the fund.

102. Abbott, ed., *Child and the State*, 2: 621–622, reprints the law establishing the bureau in its entirety.

103. J. Stanley Lemons, *The Woman Citizen: Social Feminism in the 1920s* (Urbana: University of Illinois Press, 1973), 153–180, covers the Sheppard-Towner Act, especially in the nonadministrative aspects, very well indeed. See also Lemons, "The Sheppard-Towner Act: Progressivism in the 1920s," *Journal of American History* 65 (1969): 776–786.

104. See Bremner, et al., *Children and Youth in America* 2: 799–789, for a convenient summary of the plenary resolutions.

105. Abbott, *Child and the State*, Vol. 2, reprints many of these laws; Tiffin, *In Whose Best Interest?*, has useful information.

106. On academic professionalization the following are useful: Barry D. Karl, "The Power of Intellect and the Politics of Ideas," *Daedalus* 86 (1968): 1002–1035; Coben, "The Scientific Establishment and the Transmission of Quantum Mechanics to the United States, 1919–1932," a seminal article that suggests fascinating parallels; Edward H. Beardsley, *The Rise of the American Chemistry Profession, 1850–1900* (Gainesville: University of Florida Press, 1964); Kevles, *Physicists*; Cravens, *Triumph of Evolution*, 15–153; Robert E. Kohler, *From Medical Chemistry to Biochemistry: The Making of a Biomedical Discipline* (Cambridge: Cambridge University Press, 1982). Still the best general account of the rise of university culture is Laurence Veysey, *The Emergence of The American University* (Chicago: University of Chicago Press, 1965), but an excellent history of a major university is Merle Curti and Vernon Carstensen, *The University of Wisconsin. A History 1848–1924*, 2 vols. (Madison: University of Wisconsin Press, 1948).

107. An excellent and succinct discussion of these intellectual developments may be found in Sears, *Your Ancients Revisited*, 22–55.

108. Lawson G. Lowrey, "The Birth of Orthopsychiatry," in Lowrey and Sloane, eds., *Orthopsychiatry*, 190–208.

109. See, for example, the several technical and theoretical essays in Lowrey and Sloane, eds., *Orthopsychiatry*, 100–189, 231–247, 287–309, 524–549; Steven-

son and Smith, *Child Guidance Clinics*, 53–169; Lee and Kenworthy, eds., *Mental Hygiene and Social Work*, passim.

110. On social role theory as it applies to science, see Joseph Ben-David, *The Scientist's Role in Society* (Englewood Cliffs, N.J.: Prentice-Hall, 1971). Specific applications to historical contexts include Mary O. Furner, *Advocacy and Objectivity: A Crisis in the Professionalization of American Social Science, 1865–1905* (Lexington: University Press of Kentucky, 1975); Hamilton Cravens, "American Science Comes of Age: An Institutional Perspective, 1850–1930," *American Studies* 17 (Fall 1976): 49–70.

111. This can be readily ascertained by reading the voluminous reports in the appropriate files in *LSRM*. See, for example, Janet Arnold, "A History of the Organization of Negro Groups in Cincinnati," 16 typescript pages, n.d., attached to Ada Hart Arlitt to Lawrence K. Frank, Nov. 27, 1929, Series III, Subseries 5, Box 44, *LSRM*. See also the lengthy assessment of the effects, or lack thereof, of the parent education program of the National Congress of Parents and Teachers, Mrs. Verplanck B. Magdsick to Mrs. Max Meyer and Mrs. M. P. Summers, Dec. 16, 1932, 12 typescript pages, Ada Hart Arlitt Papers, Department of Special Collections, University of Cincinnati. By the early 1930s, the California program had reached a point of stagnation, even though it was developed with much enthusiasm and expertise. See Vierling Kersey [California Superintendent of Public Instruction] to the Secretary, Spelman Fund, Dec. 17, 1931, and attached 19 typescript page reprint, Series III, Subseries 5, Box 27, *LSRM*.

112. Witmer, *Psychiatric Clinics for Children*, 54–62. Witmer's study was commissioned by the Commonwealth Fund to examine the prospects of the penetration of child guidance as a profession into public clinics and similar facilities. She argued essentially that this could not happen until many communities were educated—an admission, if such were needed, that the gospel of child guidance had fallen on deaf ears outside of its special network.

BIBLIOGRAPHY

Abbott, Grace. *The Child and the State*. 2 vols., Chicago, 1938.
Allen, Frederick H. "The Philadelphia Child Guidance Clinic." In *Orthopsychiatry, 1923–1948, Retrospect and Prospect*, edited by Lawson G. Lowrey and Victoria Sloane. New York, 1948.
Baldwin, Bird T.; Fillmore, Eva; and Hadley, Lora. *Farm Children: An Investigation of Farm Children in Selected Areas of Iowa*. New York, 1930.
Barker, Lewellys F. "The First Ten Years of the National Committee for Mental Hygiene, With Some Comments on Its Future." *Mental Hygiene* 2 (1918): 557–581.
Beales, Ross W., Jr. "In Search of the Historical Child: Miniature Adulthood and Youth in Colonial New England." *American Quarterly* 27 (1975): 379–398.
Beardsley, Edward H. *The Rise of the American Chemistry Profession, 1850–1900*. Gainesville, Fla., 1964.
Ben-David, Joseph. *The Scientist's Role in Society*. Englewood Cliffs, N.J., 1971.
Bernard, Luther Lee. *Instinct: A Problem in Social Psychology*. New York, 1924.
Boring, E. G. *A History of Experimental Psychology*. New York, 1950.

Bradbury, Dorothy, and Stoddard, George D. *Pioneering in Child Welfare: A History of the Iowa Child Welfare Research Station, 1917–1933*. Iowa City, 1933.

Bremner, Robert. *From the Depths: The Discovery of Poverty in the United States*. New York, 1956.

———, et al., eds. *Children and Youth in America: A Documentary History*. 3 vols. Cambridge, Mass., 1970–1971.

Burnham, John C. "The New Psychology: From Narcissism to Social Control." In *Change and Continuity in Twentieth Century America: The 1920s*, edited by Robert Bremner. Columbus, Ohio, 1966.

———. "On the Origins of Behaviorism." *Journal of the History of the Behavioral Sciences* 2 (1968): 143–151.

———. "Psychiatry, Psychology, and the Progressive Movement." *American Quarterly* 12 (1960): 457–465.

Byers, Joseph B. *The Village of Happiness: The Story of the Training School*. Vineland, N.J., 1934.

Cavallo, Dominick. *Muscles and Morals: Organized Playgrounds and Urban Reform, 1880–1920*. Philadelphia, 1981.

Chamberlain, Lucy. "The Spirit of Vineland." *The Training School Bulletin* 19 (1922–1923): 113–120.

Chambers, Clarke A. *Paul Kellogg and the Survey*. Minneapolis, 1971.

———. *Seedtime of Reform*. Minneapolis, 1963.

Chandler, Alfred D., Jr. "The Large Industrial Corporation in the Making of the Modern American Economy." In *Institutions in Modern America. Innovations in Structure and Process*, edited by Stephen Ambrose. Baltimore, 1967.

Child Study. (November 1928). (Entire issue is devoted to a history of the Child Study Association of America.)

Coben, Stanley. "American Foundations as Patrons of Science: The Commitment to Individual Research." In *The Sciences in the American Context: New Perspectives*, edited by Nathan Reingold. Washington, D.C., 1979.

———. "Foundation Officials and Fellowships: Innovations in the Patronage of Science." *Minerva* 14 (1976): 225–240.

———. "The Scientific Establishment and the Transmission of Quantum Mechanics to the United States, 1919–1932." *American Historical Review* 76 (1971): 442–466.

Cope, Edward Drinker. *Origin of the Fittest*. New York, 1887.

Cravens, Hamilton. "American Science Comes of Age: An Institutional Perspective, 1850–1930." *American Studies* 17 (Fall 1976): 49–70.

———. "The Child Research Movement in the Depression Decade, 1928–1941." Unpublished paper presented at Society for Research in Child Development Meeting, April 1983.

———. "The Emergence of the Farmer-Labor Party in Washington Politics, 1918–1920." *Pacific Northwest Quarterly* 57 (1966): 148–157.

———. *The Triumph of Evolution: American Scientists and the Heredity-Environment Controversy, 1900–1941*. Philadelphia, 1978.

———, and Burnham, John C. "Psychology and Evolutionary Naturalism in American Thought, 1890–1940." *American Quarterly* 23 (1971): 635–657.

Cremin, Lawrence A. *The Transformation of the School: Progressivism in American Education, 1876–1957*. New York, 1961.

Curti, Merle, and Carstensen, Vernon. *The University of Wisconsin: A History, 1848–1924.* 2 vols., Madison, Wis., 1948.

Dain, Norman. *Clifford W. Beers: Advocate for the Insane.* Pittsburgh, 1980.

Darwin, Charles R. *The Descent of Man and Selection in Relation to Sex.* 2 vols., New York, 1898.

———. *Expression of the Emotions in Man and Animals.* London, 1872.

Diserens, Charles M., and Vaugh, James. "The Experimental Psychology of Motivation." *Psychological Bulletin* 28 (1931): 15–65.

Emerick, E. J. *The Bureau of Juvenile Research.* State of Ohio Department of Public Welfare, Publication No. 27. Columbus, 1927.

Fass, Paula S. *The Damned and the Beautiful: American Youth in the 1920s.* New York, 1977.

Fernald, Walter. "A State Program for the Care of the Mentally Defective." *Mental Hygiene* 3 (1919): 566–574.

First Iowa State Congress of Mothers, January 28th to 31st, 1902. N.p., 1902.

Frank, Lawrence K. "Two Tasks of Education." *School and Society* 15 (June 1922): 655–659.

Furner, Mary O. *Advocacy and Objectivity: A Crisis in the Professionalization of American Social Science, 1865–1905.* Lexington, Ky., 1975.

Gesell, Arnold, and Gesell, B. C. *The Normal Child and Primary Education.* Boston, 1912.

Goddard, Henry H. "Anniversary Address." In *Twenty-Five years: A Memorial Volume in Commemoration of the Twenty-Fifth Anniversary of the Vineland Laboratory, 1906–1931,* edited by Edgar A. Doll. Vineland, N.J., 1932.

———. "Educational Treatment of the Feeble-Minded." In *Modern Treatment of Nervous and Mental Diseases,* edited by William A. White and Smith E. Jelliffe. 2 vols., Philadelphia, 1915.

———. "The Effect of Mind on Body as Evidenced by Faith Cures." *American Journal of Psychiatry* 10 (1899): 431–502.

———. "Feeble-Mindedness and Delinquency." *Journal of Psycho Asthenics* 25 (1920): 168–176.

———. *Feeble-Mindedness: Its Cause and Consequences.* New York, 1914.

———. "Four Hundred Feeble-Minded Children Classified by the Binet Method." *Pedagogical Seminary and Journal of Genetic Psychology* (1910): 388–397.

———. "Heredity of Feeble-Mindedness." *American Breeders' Magazine* 1 (1910): 165–178.

———. "Ideals of a Group of German Children." *Pedagogical Seminary and Journal of Genetic Psychology* 13 (1906): 208–220.

———. *Juvenile Delinquency.* New York, 1921.

———. *The Kallikak Family: A Study in the Heredity of Feeble-Mindedness.* New York, 1912.

———. "A Measuring Scale of Intelligence." *The Training School* 6 (1910): 146–154.

———. "The Problem of the Psychopathic Child." *American Journal of Insanity* 57 (1920): 511–516.

———. "Schools and Classes for Exceptional Children." *Journal of Educational Psychology* 7 (1916): 287–294.

———. *School Training of Defective Children.* New York, 1915.

———. "The Sub-Normal Mind Versus the Abnormal." *Journal of Abnormal Psychology* 16 (1921): 47–54.

———, and Hill, Helen F. "Delinquent Girls Tested by the Binet Scale." *The Training School* 8 (1911): 50–56.

———, et al. *The Bureau of Juvenile Research: Review of the Work, 1918–1920.* Mansfield, Ohio, 1921.

Gould, Stephen J. *The Mismeasure of Man.* New York, 1981.

Haines, Thomas H. "Analysis of Recoveries at the Psychopathic Hospital, Boston II. A Second Series of One Hundred Cases, Considered Especially from the Standpoint of Psychopathic Nursing of Brief Manic-Depressive Excitements and of Hysterical and Other Deliria." *Boston Medical and Surgical Journal* 171 (December 31, 1914): 1002–1008.

———. "The Feeble-Minded Situation in Ohio." *Ohio Bulletin of Charities and Corrections* 23 (1917): 29–36.

———. "High-Grade Mental Defectives at the Psychopathic Hospital During 1913." *Boston Medical and Surgical Journal* 171 (December 3, 1914): 854–856.

———. "The Ohio Plan for the Study of Delinquency." *Popular Science Monthly* 86 (1915): 576–580.

———. "Relative Values of Point-Scale and Year-Scale Measurements of One Thousand Minor Delinquents." *Journal of Experimental Psychology* 1 (1916): 51–82.

Hall, G. Stanley. *Adolescence: Its Psychology and Its Relations to Physiology, Anthropology, Sociology, Sex, Crime, Religion, and Education.* 2 vols., New York, 1905.

Harper, Robert S. "Tables of American Doctorates in Psychology." *American Journal of Psychology* 62 (1949): 580–581.

Hawes, Joseph M. *Children in Urban Society; Juvenile Delinquency in Nineteenth-Century America.* New York, 1971.

Healy, William. *The Individual Delinquent: A Textbook.* Boston, 1915.

———, and Bronner, Augusta F. "The Child Guidance Clinic: Birth and Growth of an Idea." In *Orthopsychiatry, 1923–1948, Retrospect and Prospect*, edited by Lawson G. Lowery and Victoria Sloane. New York, 1948.

———. *Delinquents and Criminals: Their Making and Unmaking.* New York, 1926.

Higham, John. *Strangers in the Land: Patterns of American Nativism, 1860–1925.* New Brunswick, N.J., 1955.

Hillis, Hazel. *The First Fifty Years: The Iowa Congress of Parents and Teachers.* N.p., n.d.

Horn, Margo. "The Moral Message of Child Guidance, 1925–1945." *Journal of Social History* 18 (Fall 1984): 25–36.

James, William. *The Principles of Psychology.* 2 vols., New York, 1890.

Jennings, Herbert Spencer, et al. *Suggestions of Modern Science Concerning Education.* New York, 1918.

Karl, Barry D. "The Power of Intellect and the Politics of Ideas." *Daedalus* 86 (1968): 1002–1035.

Kevles, Daniel J. *The Physicists: The History of a Scientific Community in Modern America.* New York, 1978.

———. "Testing the Army's Intelligence: Psychologists and the Military in World War I." *Journal of American History* 55 (1968): 565–586.

Kohler, Robert E., Jr. *From Medical Chemistry to Biochemistry: The Making of a Biomedical Discipline.* Cambridge, 1982.

———. "Warren Weaver and the Rockefeller Foundation Program in Molecular Biology: A Case Study in the Management of Science." In *The Sciences in the American Context: New Perspectives,* edited by Nathan Reingold. Washington, D.C., 1979.

Kuhlman, Frederick. "The Part Played by the State Institutions in the Care of the Feeble-Minded." *Journal of Psycho-Asthenics* 21 (1916): 3–24.

Laura Spelman Rockefeller Memorial. *Report of the Laura Spelman Rockefeller Memorial.* New York, 1919–.

Lee, Porter R., and Kenworthy, Marian, eds. *Mental Hygiene and Social Work.* New York, 1929.

Lemons, J. Stanley. "The Sheppard-Towner Act: Progressivism in the 1920s." *Journal of American History* 65 (1969): 776–786.

———. *The Woman Citizen: Social Feminism in the 1920s.* Urbana, 1973.

Lomax, Elizabeth M.R. *Science and Patterns of Child Care.* San Francisco, 1978.

Lowrey, Lawson G. "The Birth of Orthopsychiatry." In *Orthopsychiatry, 1923–1948: Retrospect and Prospect,* edited by Lawson G. Lowrey and Victoria Sloane. New York, 1948.

———, ed. *Institute for Child Guidance Studies. Selected Reprints.* New York, 1931.

———, and Sloane, Victoria, eds. *Orthopsychiatry, 1923–1948: Retrospect and Prospect.* New York, 1948.

Lubove, Roy. *The Professional Altruist: The Emergence of Social Work As a Career.* Cambridge, Mass., 1965.

McDougall, William. *An Introduction to Social Psychology.* Boston, 1911.

Mateer, Florence. *Child Behavior: A Critical and Experimental Study of Young Children in the Method of Conditioned Reflexes.* Boston, 1918.

———. "The Future of Clinical Psychology." *Journal of Delinquency* 6 (1921): 283–293.

———. *The Unstable Child.* New York, 1924.

Meek, Lois Hayden. "Department of Pre-School and Elementary Education: General Survey of Educational Programs." *Journal of the American Association of University Women* 18 (October 1924): 22–23.

———. "New Ventures in Education for University Women." *Journal of the American Association of University Women* 20 (October 1926): 17–19.

———."Our Educational Program (Including the Report of the Educational Secretary) April 1, 1925." *Journal of the American Association of University Women* 19 (June 1926): 15–17.

———. "A Pre-School Project for University Women." *Progressive Education* 2 (1925): 38–41.

Miller, Howard S. *Dollars for Research: Science and Its Patrons in Nineteenth Century-America.* Seattle, 1970.

Morgan, C. Lloyd. *Animal Life and Intelligence.* Boston, 1895.

National Committee for Mental Hygiene. *Twenty Years of Mental Hygiene.* N.p., 1929.

National Congress of Parents and Teachers. *Parents and Teachers.* Boston, 1928.

National Research Council, Committee on Child Development. *Conference on Research in Child Development*. N.p., 1925.

Ostrander, Gilman M. *American Civilization in the First Machine Age: 1890–1940*. New York, 1970.

Pratt, George K. "Twenty years of the National Committee for Mental Hygiene." *Mental Hygiene* 14 (1930): 399–428.

Reingold, Nathan. "National Science Policy in a Private Foundation: The Carnegie Institution of Washington." In *The Organization of Knowledge in Modern America, 1860–1920*, edited by Alexandra Oleson and John Voss. Baltimore, 1979.

————, ed. *The Sciences in the American Context: New Perspectives*. Washington, D.C., 1979.

Richardson, Anna E. "The Association's Program for Child Study and Parent Education." *Journal of Home Economics* 18 (October 1926).

————. "Standards of Home Economics in Colleges." *Bulletin American Home Economics Association*, Ser. 9 (October 1926).

Romanes, George J. *Mental Evolution in Man; Origin of Human Faculty*. New York, 1889.

Ross, Dorothy. *G. Stanley Hall: The Psychologist as Prophet*. Chicago, 1972.

Rothman, David J. *Conscience and Convenience: The Asylum and Its Alternatives in Progressive America*. Boston, 1980.

Schlossman, Steven L. "Before Home Start: Notes Toward a History of Parent Education in America, 1897–1929." *Harvard Educational Review* 46 (1976): 452–454.

————. "Philanthropy and the Gospel of Child Development." *History of Education Quarterly* 21 (Fall 1981): 275–299.

Schumacher, Henry C. "The Cleveland Guidance Center." In *Orthopsychiatry, 1923–1948: Retrospect and Prospect*, edited by Lawson G. Lowrey and Victoria Sloane. New York, 1948.

Sears, Robert. *Your Ancients Revisited: A History of Child Development*. Chicago, 1975.

Senn, Milton. *Insights on the Child Development Movement in the United States*. Chicago, 1975.

Shapiro, Henry D. *Appalachia on Our Mind: The Southern Mountains and Mountaineers in the American Consciousness*. Chapel Hill, 1978.

Shea, Christine Mary. "The Ideology of Mental Health and the Emergence of the Therapeutic Liberal State: The American Mental Hygiene Movement, 1900–1930." Ph.D. dissertation, University of Illinois, 1980.

Sokal, Michael M., ed. *An Education in Psychology: James McKeen Cattell's Journal and Letters from Germany and England, 1880–1888*. Cambridge, Mass., 1981.

Stevenson, George S. "Child Guidance and the National Committee for Mental Hygiene." In *Orthopsychiatry, 1923–1948: Retrospect and Prospect*, edited by Lawson G. Lowrey and Victoria Sloane. New York, 1948.

————, and Smith, Geddes. *Child Guidance Clinics: A Quarter Century of Development*. New York, 1934.

Stoddard, Lothrop. *The Revolt Against Civilization: The Menace of the Under Man*. New York, 1922.

Swift, Sarah H. *Training in Psychiatric Social Work at the Institute for Child Guidance, 1927–1933*. New York, 1934.

Tead, Ordway. *Instincts in Industry*. Boston, 1918.

Terman, Lewis M. *The Measurement of Intelligence: An Explanation of and a Complete Guide for the Use of the Stanford Revision and Extension of the Binet-Simon Intelligence Scale*. Boston, 1916.

———. "The Stanford Revision of the Binet-Simon Scale, Results from Its Application to One Thousand Non-Selected Children." *Journal of Educational Psychology* 6 (1915): 551–562.

Thorndike, Edward Lee. *Animal Intelligence*. New York, 1911.

Tiffin, Susan. *In Whose Best Interest? Child Welfare Reform in the Progressive Era*. Westport, Conn., 1982.

Trattner, Walter I. *Crusade for the Children: A History of the National Child Labor Committee and Child Labor Reform in America*. Chicago, 1970.

———. *From Poor Law to Welfare State: A History of Social Welfare in America*. New York, 1974.

———. *Homer Folks: Pioneer in Social Welfare*. New York, 1968.

Veysey, Laurence. *The Emergence of the American University*. Chicago, 1965.

Wallin, J. E. Wallace. "The Problem of the Feeble-Minded and Its Educational and Social Bearings." *School and Society* 2 (1915): 115–121.

Warner, Hoyt Landon. *Progressivism in Ohio, 1897–1917*. Columbus, 1964.

Watson, John B. *Behaviorism*. New York, 1925.

———. "Psychology as the Behaviorist Views It." *Psychological Review* 20 (1913): 158–177.

———. *The Ways of Behaviorism*. New York, 1928.

Whipple, G. M., ed. *The Twenty-Eighth Yearbook of the National Society for the Study of Education Preschool and Parental Education*. Bloomington, Ill., 1929.

Witmer, Helen L. *Psychiatric Clinics for Children with Special Reference to State Programs*. New York, 1940.

Witmer, Lightner. "Two Feeble-Minded Maidens—A Clinical Lecture." *Psychological Clinic* 10 (1917): 224–234.

Woolley, Helen Thompson. "Educational Policies." *Journal of the American Association of University Women* 18 (May 1925).

———. "Grant from the Laura Spelman Rockefeller Memorial for the Educational Program." *Journal of the American Association of University Women* 17 (May 1924): 14.

Yerkes, Robert M. "Testing the Human Mind." *Atlantic Monthly* 131 (1923): 364–365.

———, ed. *Psychological Examining in the United States Army*. Memoirs of the National Academy of Science. Washington, D.C., 1921.

12

Partial Promises and Semi-Visible Youths: The Depression and World War II

In 1940 Katharine Lenroot, long-time advocate of children's rights and chief of the U.S. Children's Bureau, asserted that "the direction of progress" during the previous decade had "been toward a broadened concept of child welfare."[1] She was not engaged in wishful thinking. Considerable evidence existed that during the Depression years public recognition of the special needs, rights, and place of children and youth had expanded. Moreover, during the war years the trend continued. By 1945 a host of cultural and social landmarks attested to this: the formation of the American Academy of Pediatrics in 1930 (defining a medical specialty in terms of the young age of the patient); provisions for dependent and crippled children in the Social Security Act; new child labor laws; the publication in 1938 of a popular childrearing book, *Babies Are Human Beings*, which prepared the way for Dr. Benjamin Spock; the growth of public child care facilities; medical breakthroughs concerning problems such as "blue babies"; public health gains, especially during the war; the popularity of child stars such as Shirley Temple and Mickey Rooney on the motion picture screen; and the discovery of the "teenager," reflected partly in the magazine *Seventeen*, which first appeared in 1944.

Against this backdrop, however, were signs that a children's age had hardly arrived. Insofar as the history of America's public responsibility for young people has been a series of "broken promises,"[2] the era of Depression and war would share part of the blame. From 1930 to 1945, recognition of children's welfare developed haltingly, sometimes reluctantly, often inadvertently, and left a genuinely ambivalent legacy to the postwar period. In most instances, government programs for children were only for emergency purposes and did not reflect long-range expectations. Where long-range entitlements for specific groups took shape—as with Social Security—the legislative interest in aiding children was secondary and peripheral. Concessions to state and local control often limited the effectiveness of federal measures which, in some ways, pointed in new directions. Politics intruded continually at all levels as factions within the government fought for positions, as local and professional interest groups sought to protect or enhance their status, and as traditional attitudes regarding families, parenthood, and the role of the state collided with newer ideas, social trends, and national crises.

In significant ways, children and youth were not only absent from much of the national agenda in the 1930s and early 1940s, but they were also largely hidden from public view except as symbols and abstractions. Then, and later, accounts of children generally revealed far more about the worlds of adults than of young people. Youths have been "studied but neither seen nor heard," according to one scholar,[3] who could easily have used the era from 1930 to 1945 as a prime example. Years later, the texture of children's lives in the Depression and war, and the ways in which young people themselves had perceived their world and tried to deal with it, remained far below the surface of historical understanding.

Such a judgment would undoubtedly have been too harsh for many of the early interpreters of New Deal and wartime child welfare policies. Most shared the view of Emma Octavia Lundberg, who believed that the nation's response to the needs of children manifested "slow but sure progress."[4] Lundberg's exceptionally useful general history of America's child welfare services, *Unto the Least of These* (1947), recognized the weaknesses of existing laws and programs; but the book was essentially a lingering expression of Progressive child-saving, in compassion, mood, and tone. This was hardly surprising, for Lundberg had been an active member of the Children's Bureau since its early years and had also been on the staff of the Child Welfare League of America. Affection for friends such as Julia Lathrop, Katharine Lenroot, Grace Abbott, C. C. Carstens, and other celebrated child-savers suffused Lundberg's book. Her positive assessment of child welfare services during the 1930s and early 1940s (her final chapter was entitled "The Road Leads Forward" and the epigraph was a quotation from Franklin D. Roosevelt) summed up the sentiments of numerous other contemporaries, including Helen Glenn Tyson, Mary Irene Atkinson, and Sophonisba P. Breckinridge— all of whom had worked for the Children's Bureau or other youth agencies.[5] They gave what was in effect the child-savers' version of social change in Depression and war, a version that for many of them marked their last hurrah. During the 1930s, death claimed some of the giants of Progressive child rescue work: Florence Kelley (1932), Julia Lathrop (1932), Hastings H. Hart (1932), Rudolph R. Reeder (1934), Monsignor William J. Kerby (1936), Grace Abbott (1939), and C. C. Carstens (1939).[6]

But to a survivor of the era, such as Emma Lundberg, there were satisfying indications between 1930 and 1945 that her old friends had

not made their earlier sacrifices for children in vain. Renewed public
interest in the needs of young people was evident in various New Deal
programs for general relief, such as the Federal Emergency Relief Association (FERA), the Civilian Work Administration, and the Public Works
Administration. It was apparent in child labor laws, initially within the
National Recovery Administration, and later in the Federal Sugar Act
of 1937 and the 1938 Fair Labor Standards Act. It was clear in the
expanded definition of youth in the National Youth Administration and
the Civilian Conservation Corps, which included people in their late
teens and early twenties. It took the form of limited federal day care
programs during the 1930s, especially through the Works Progress
Administration (WPA), and the considerable enlargement of such programs during the war under the Lanham Act of 1940. There was also
the wartime Emergency Maternal and Infant Care Program, which Dorothy Bradbury of the Children's Bureau has described as "the biggest
public maternity program ever undertaken in the United States."[7] Particularly significant were the sections in the 1935 Social Security Act
providing aid for dependent, rural, and crippled children.

Numerous federal agencies after 1932 aided young people. The FERA
(1933–1937) was important less for specific commitments to children
than for ways in which its philosophy of relief and the grass-roots experiences of its staff influenced child welfare. The basic assumption of
the FERA, which financed state-run employment projects, was that government had a clear-cut responsibility to provide adequate assistance for
"needy unemployed persons and/or their dependents."[8] Mary Irene Atkinson, director in the 1930s of the Child Welfare Division of the Children's Bureau, believed in retrospect that the FERA's definition of relief
had revitalized one of the major recommendations of the 1909 White
House Conference on Dependent Children: namely, that poverty alone
was an insufficient excuse to remove children from families. Instead,
welfare agencies were to provide enough relief to enable poor families
to stay together. Not only had FERA workers breathed new life into this
strategy, but also their duties had brought them face to face with the
plight of needy children, especially in rural areas. They discovered, for
instance, that during one year in one state in the early 1930s, "some
200,000 children (had) never set foot in a schoolhouse."[9]

While New Deal relief agencies, like the FERA, continually encountered the needs of children, several government programs offered direct
aid. This was especially true of the WPA, founded in 1935 as part of
the New Deal effort to tie public relief to work. The WPA programs for
young people, although a relatively minor part of the agency's activities,
established noteworthy precedents. In New York City, for example, the
WPA took over a local school hot lunch program that the city's Board
of Education had instituted early in the Depression. By 1939, two central

kitchens served free lunches daily to more than 100,000 children in 817 public and parochial schools. The Federal Government provided workers while the state and local administrations bore the costs. (By the decade's end, the Federal Surplus Commodities Corporation had expanded free lunch programs elsewhere in the nation to some 3 million undernourished children.)[10] The WPA also enhanced the quality of recreation for young people by building more than 2,000 playgrounds as well as picnic areas, swimming facilities, and athletic fields. In June 1939, almost 2 percent of the WPA workers (41,780) had jobs as recreation leaders.[11] By late 1941, the WPA was employing some 38,000 needy women as housekeeping aides for distressed families having difficulties caring for the elderly, the ill, and the children in their homes. The idea of homemaker services did not originate in the 1930s, but the unprecedented scale of the WPA efforts unquestionably benefited hundreds of children who otherwise would have gone to institutions and foster homes.[12]

As important as the WPA and other New Deal relief programs were, their responses to children's needs were nonetheless piecemeal and usually temporary. Moreover, they bear out the suspicions of historian Ruby Takanishi "that no federal bill on early child care and education has yet been passed without an economic rationale or as a rider on another nonchild-related bill."[13] Edwin E. Witte's inside account of the origins of the Social Security Act confirms, for example, that Congress in 1935 had little interest in the sections pertaining to children. The decision to limit federal matching funds for children to one-third of that spent by state governments—as opposed to one-half for the elderly and the blind—clearly defined Congress's priorities. (Actually, the law was constructed in such a way that federal funding in many states was not even a third.) The section of the act providing federal money to help states launch comprehensive programs for crippled children passed with no serious difficulties, but even it did not stir much enthusiasm. Roosevelt himself, although sympathetic due to his own handicap, "never manifested any greater interest in this particular aid than in any other provision of the social security bill."[14]

While the needs of children were tangential to the Social Security legislation, such was at least partly the case with child labor and school attendance laws as well. According to historian Jeremy P. Felt, the long struggle to raise the school-leaving age to sixteen did not make notable progress until the Depression sharply reduced jobs.[15] True, the renewed interest in 1933 in the child labor amendment was on one level a reaction to shocking revelations about the exploitation of youthful laborers. The "children's strikes" that year in Pennsylvania's Lehigh Valley attracted national attention when the governor's wife joined thirteen- to eighteen-year-old girls who had walked out of the D & D shirt factory. "Our ancestors fought their revolution," she said. "We must fight our economic revolution now." Such emotions helped to explain why fourteen new states ratified the child labor amendment in 1933, suddenly making final ratification a real possibility. The ultimate result, however, was not passage of the amendment but, instead, the Fair Labor Standards Act of 1938, which included sections barring from interstate commerce goods made by persons under age sixteen in occupations "hazardous" to health and well-being.[16]

Child labor legislation from the Progressive Era through the New Deal may have owed far less to reformers than to economic conditions and technological innovations that rendered unnecessary or unacceptable the employment of youths. By the end of the 1930s, the great underside of child labor—in agriculture, street trades, and mercantile jobs—remained free of regulation. The 1933 National Recovery Act's codes overlooked perhaps as many as 80 percent of working children under sixteen. Although many child labor reformers considered the Fair Labor Standards Act a triumph, it was actually, according to historian Robert W. McAhren, "a Pyrrhic victory," coming too late and applying "to only a few industries where other processes were already eliminating the child worker." McAhren and Felt have concluded that child labor laws were mainly symbolic, giving the public a sense of settling a problem while arming politicians with rhetorical weapons for other causes. Franklin Roosevelt's endorsement of the child labor section of the Fair Labor Standards Act was, from Felt's view, largely a tactical maneuver to rally support for the larger goal of wages and hours legislation. Montana's Senator Burton K. Wheeler may, in turn, have proposed his own version of child labor reform primarily to outflank advocates of the president's Supreme Court "packing plan" who were arguing that only by remodeling the Court could social change occur. As Felt puts it, "The child labor provisions became a political football."[17] Moreover, America's entry into World War II quickly brought about what one advisor to the Children's Bureau described as an "unprecedented increase in the employment of adolescent youth," along with sharply reduced public school enrollments.[18]

Despite disappointments that such reversals stirred among child rescue workers, the war provided an opportunity for major advances in maternity and infant care. For years the Children's Bureau in particular had battled for public services to reduce risks in childbearing and infancy. For a while in the 1920s, the Sheppard-Towner Act, America's first federally funded health care program, had provided educational services for expectant mothers; but in 1929 the medical profession had mobilized sufficient opposition to kill the act.[19] Not until World War II did Congress reconsider subsidizing health care for mothers and their babies. In 1943 the Federal Government inaugurated the Emergency Maternal and Infant Care program (EMIC), which until the 1960s was "the most extensive single public medical care program ever undertaken in this country."[20] Until the program ended in 1949, it provided free medical and hospital care to wives and babies (up to one year) of servicemen in the four lowest pay grades. Financial need was not a requirement for such aid. Over a five-year period, the Federal Government appropriated more than $133 million to care for 1.5 million maternity and infant cases. Especially notable was a marked drop in the maternal and infant mortality rates. Maternal death rates plunged nearly 38 percent, from 37.6 per 10,000 live births in 1940 to 20.7 in 1945, while infant deaths dropped from 47 per 1,000 live births to 38.3.[21]

From the outset, however, Congress was obviously uneasy about EMIC's "socialistic" precedents and defended the program entirely on the basis of wartime emergency. Legislators hoped that the temporary measure would boost the morale of soldiers who were worried about the health of wives and babies. And there was no doubt about the program's popularity. Support for it was broadly based, coming from the press, veterans' organizations, and soldiers' families (who signed up in numbers far greater than anyone had anticipated). Most skeptics, not wishing to appear unpatriotic or ungrateful to soldiers, grudgingly accepted it as "a form of distasteful war medicine." Representative Butler B. Hare of South Carolina, for example, backed down on the need for a means test on the grounds that EMIC was "a contribution to the family as an expression of gratitude to those in the armed forces who are actually offering their lives in the service." "This is a war program," Katharine Lenroot reminded one congressman who fretted about the drift toward "socialized medicine." Significantly, EMIC administrators themselves voluntarily asked for a reduction in funds following the surrender of Japan. One surprised congressman asked: "Do you mean to say that somebody has come up here voluntarily and said that their agency was a wartime agency and need not be continued in peacetime? It is most unusual."[22]

One of the striking innovations during the 1930s and early 1940s was that of federally funded day care which, like EMIC, ended shortly after the war. For awhile, the WPA operated some preschool and day care programs. (In one month in 1937, 1,500 WPA nursery schools served some 40,000 children.) Like the Social Security Act and EMIC, however, such government activity reflected only marginal concerns with children. The WPA moved almost accidentally into child care work—it lacked specific authorization to do so—and sought primarily to create jobs for unemployed teachers, nurses, nutritionists, and janitors.[23]

In 1942, as the WPA closed down, the government channeled funds to day care only because vital wartime production demanded it. Working mothers, caught between staying home with their children and reporting to defense jobs, sent government and industry scrambling for solutions.

The Roosevelt administration reluctantly decided to fund day care centers through the Community Facilities Act (Lanham Act), which Congress had established in 1940 to aid areas feeling the stress of the national defense buildup. Ironically, Texas Congressman Fritz G. Lanham opposed interpreting his act for such purposes. Because the act required local governments to provide half of the costs, and because towns had to provide need (and had to reimburse the government if later investigations proved that such claims were false), public day care during World War II proved woefully inadequate. Probably only 10 percent of children needing supervision received it. At their peak, Lanhan Act centers cared for only around 105,000 children.[24] As Gilbert Steiner of the Brookings Institution has written, the Lanham funds underwrote "a win-the-war program, not a save-the-children program."[25] Dorothy Bradbury, in her history of the Children's Bureau, after describing the limits of the wartime child care programs, speculated hopefully that at some point the problem of day care might "be considered in terms of the welfare of children."[26]

The problem was more complex than Bradbury suggested—a point evident in the history of the Children's Bureau itself (although not in Bradbury's version). "The welfare of children" has always been anything but a neutral concept; as a social ideal it has resembled a mine field in a war zone. And the war zone has involved not only children, but nothing less than deeply held feelings about the nature of the American family—a subject that historically, as Norton Grubb and Marvin Lazerson point out, "has proved to be a catchall for every social problem and every ideological position."[27]

Predictably, the issue of child welfare during the 1930s and 1940s was ideologically loaded, as a host of private and public groups struggled to define the division of responsibilities for children. Again and again traditional views of motherhood, home, and poverty received legislative endorsements. Some of the most important developments concerning child care—including the Social Security Act and federal day care offerings—bore the stamp of an earlier era.

Aid for dependent children (ADC) under the Social Security Act was in many respects a "logical conclusion" to the fight for widows' pension (or mothers' aid) laws, a fight that originated during the Progressive Era in order to allow needy children to receive care at home rather than in institutions.[28] Between 1911 and 1931, forty-five states had established mothers' aid programs; but the programs tended to be permissive rather than mandatory, miniscule in coverage, and at the mercy of local politics. Moreover, the coming of the Depression forced dozens of counties to discontinue payments. The Progressive rationale and strategies for mothers' pensions nonetheless continued to appeal strongly to many

Americans. This was abundantly clear when child rescue workers and legislators in the mid-1930s considered possible solutions to the growing needs of dependent children.[29]

One option was inherent in the philosophy of the Federal Emergency Relief Administration. It defined need broadly and, according to Josephine Brown, "would have provided aid within the limits of available funds to practically every family in need in which there was a child under sixteen." Another option rested on an important premise of the mothers' aid programs: rehabilitation of families was more important than economic assistance. From the start of the widows' pension drive, the "moral fitness" of mothers had largely determined who received aid. When Congress in 1935 awarded the Children's Bureau administrative responsibility for grants-in-aid to families of dependent children, it affirmed the rationale of mothers' aid. To members of the Children's Bureau, the victory over FERA was a blow for hard-won standards of child care. From the bureau's view, the FERA represented a throwback to the inadequacies and stigma of local poor relief.[30]

But the mothers' aid legacy was itself in important respects a prisoner of "the spirit of the poor laws," as Roy Lubove has shown. By failing, in Lubove's words, "to defend economic assistance as a legitimate constructive end in itself," Congress saddled ADC with the unenviable task of combining "economic and behavioral objectives in a single welfare program." Consequently, "vague moralistic imperatives competed with objective economic needs," undercutting any claims that dependent children had a right to public assistance.[31]

A striking example of such moralistic concern, as Winifred Bell has effectively demonstrated, was the "suitable home" eligibility requirement that characterized much of the ADC program. Although the federal law itself (Title IV of the Social Security Act) did not require the eligibility condition for aid, it permitted states to do so. At the state and local levels, the "suitable home" requirement flowed naturally from mothers' pension schemes, under which mothers had typically lost their pensions or failed to qualify for a variety of reasons, ranging from breaking the law to "moral unfitness," dishonesty, drunkenness, inadequate discipline, having a "poor history," or, often in the South, being black. By the 1930s, pressure for judging the "fitness" of homes remained overpowering despite the paltry amount of funding for widows' pensions. Across the nation in 1931, perhaps less than 0.7 percent of all children under age 14 may have benefited from such aid; payments ranged as low as $4.33 per month in Arkansas. Given this background, the chances were small indeed that Congress in 1935 would have approved an aid program for families of dependent children without some kind of "fitness" eligibility requirement. Any hopes that ADC would benefit all needy children were overwhelmingly doomed in such a setting. States predictably adopted various kinds of "suitable home" conditions for aid. In the South, these requirements grossly discriminated against black families, and federal efforts in the late 1930s to remedy this proved largely ineffectual. Although after World War II some states began to drop the "suitable home" requirements, as late as 1960 twenty-three states still had them and Louisiana suddenly terminated aid to 22,000 impoverished children (95 percent of whom were black) because their mothers had allegedly misbehaved.[32]

From the beginning, ADC thus had trouble setting priorities: whether to meet the economic needs of dependent children or judge the morals and values of adults. The highly limited coverage of the program was hardly surprising. According to the first executive director of the Social Security Board, Frank Bane, "The ADC example we always thought about was the poor lady in West Virginia whose husband was killed in a mining accident, and the problem of how she could feed those kids." The problems of deserted or unwed mothers, also struggling to support themselves and their children, lay outside ADC. Whatever the program's benefits for some, it did not tie the goal of reasonable subsistence, as a principle, to public welfare.[33]

While older attitudes concerning the moral fitness of families marked the Social Security plan from the outset, so too did deeply rooted assumptions about poverty and working mothers shape day care in the 1930s and 1940s. Day care, since its origins in day nurseries just before the Civil War, had tended to offer a broadly based range of services cloaked in the rhetoric of moral uplift for poor families and children. But by the 1920s the public and professional view of day care had narrowed considerably, making it a custodial place of last resort for needy, pathological families.[34]

In this context, the WPA and Lanham Act programs of the 1930s and 1940s pointed in new directions. However inadvertently, they at least for a while redefined somewhat the nature of day care. Because the Depression adversely affected so many Americans, children of middle class as well as poor backgrounds attended the WPA nursery schools. Moreover, the schools had a strong educational bent. This was partly because the WPA hired unemployed teachers to operate them and also because the programs were usually attached to public or college laboratory schools. Because the WPA preschools were open all day, five days a week, all year, they easily became support agencies for working parents. In addition, Lanham Act day care facilities were suffused with patriotic necessity, aiding not disturbed families but Rosie the Riveters in their nation's service. This further eroded the assumption that day care existed primarily for poor, aberrant families. Ultimately, however, the WPA-Lanham experience was only a brief and abruptly forgotten detour from the traditional skepticism regarding a broad application of day care services. Not until the 1960s would the Federal Government specifically authorize funds for day care, and then only on the premise that it was a relief program for the destitute.[35]

Ideology, not merely short memories, accounted for tendencies to overlook the WPA-Lanham precedents. Although the emergency nature of the Depression and war weakened the impression that day care was relief-oriented and class-based, the WPA-Lanham programs had never left open the possibility of universal day care. The norm of the home-centered mother remained intact. Even during the war, no less notable a reformer than New York City's Mayor Fiorello LaGuardia discouraged maternal employment. "Apparently even in wartime," Bernard Greenblatt has written, "LaGuardia believed the interest of the state must be secondary to the well-ordering of the family."[36] LaGuardia's sentiments echoed dominant wartime opinion. "The 'at home as usual' champions" (as reporter Susan B. Anthony II described individuals who wanted women to remain at home) carefully scrutinized the Lanham centers. After the war, they successfully thwarted the efforts of several groups, most notably the women's auxiliaries of the Congress of Industrial Organizations, which lobbied to continue federal day care. Postwar arguments that working women should relinquish jobs to returning veterans further damaged the cause of day care advocates. And with the coming of the Cold War, day care became a prime target for politicians and citizens fighting "creeping socialism."[37] Hence, after 1945, in states such as New York, women who pressed for day care were allegedly Communists—or so claimed none other than Governor Thomas E. Dewey.[38]

Suspicions about day care were not confined to politicians and policymakers, however. Even during the war, families themselves were often unreceptive to child care available under the Lanham plan. In some cases, working mothers boycotted available facilities. One government official believed that working women had "a positive aversion to group care of children" because it seemed to conflict "with the traditional idea of the American home," smacked of socialism, or suggested "an inability to care for one's own."[39]

Alongside such perceptions of motherhood and family that sharply curtailed public responsibility for children was another limiting factor that haunted virtually every aspect of the Roosevelt administration: the tensions between local, state, and national governments.[40] Individuals who tried, for example, to expand the coverage of ADC continually had to deal with what James Patterson has described as "the pervasive curse of localism." Patterson, in his important overview of America's battle against poverty in the twentieth century, discusses a prime example: Virginia Senator Harry Byrd's amendment enlarging local discretion over aid to dependent children. Byrd successfully removed from the original bill a proviso that, to qualify for federal funds, states had to

guarantee "reasonable subsistence compatible to decency and health."
White Southerners in particular opposed any federal control over state
affairs, especially regarding race. (In Louisiana in 1937, for instance,
two-thirds of the 20,192 children receiving ADC money were black.) But
Patterson insists that more than racism accounted for the Byrd amendment. "States rights in 1935 was a vital ideology," he writes, "not a
functional cover for racism. . . . In this sense the ADC program testified
to the enduring vitality of pre-Depression notions—among them the
equation of democracy with local control." One result was that ADC
lacked consistency of coverage or standards, and states moved in dozens
of directions at different paces. Some states did not move at all; by 1939,
ten still had not joined the categorical assistance plans.[41]

Protective services for neglected and abused children hardly fared any
better. Although Title V of the Social Security Act provided federal
grants-in-aid to states "for the protection and care of homeless, dependent, and neglected children," the actual expansion of child protective services may have been negligible. In fact, in California from 1935
to 1937, services declined despite increased federal funds. Without explicit statutory authorization from the state legislature, such programs
could only flounder. Even California's wartime boom—along with federal support for day care, recreational facilities, and other kinds of aid
for children of families working in defense-related industries—did not
boost available protective services. Wartime priorities, the shortage of
trained social workers, and the reluctance of the Federal Government
to require county welfare agencies to develop protective programs ex-
acted a price. Between mid-1942 and mid-1944, the total number of
children in California who received child welfare services decreased.[42]

In Mississippi as well, the gaps between federal and state programs
were often great, and in some cases shifts in federal policies left cracks
through which needy children easily slipped. The transition in 1935
from the FERA to Social Security actually hurt dependent children.
Direct relief under the FERA had produced a broad variety of aid: for
example, sewing rooms so that mothers and unemployed women could
make clothes for dependent children; home-canning programs for school
lunch programs; and provisions of shoes and clothing for many school-
age children. (In 1934 an estimated 30,000 children in the state had no
shoes, and more than 11,000 avoided school because they lacked adequate clothing.) But in the mid-1930s, as FERA's direct relief gave way
to work relief and Social Security programs, substantial numbers of
needy children faced even more precarious conditions. The Mississippi
legislature quickly implemented the old age pension part of the Social
Security Act, but chose to wait until federal financing for ADC was more
favorable. Until 1941, when Mississippi started an ADC program, dependent children in the state were left in a void.[43]

Even when the Mississippi legislature recognized children's needs—when in 1936, for example, it established a Division of Child Welfare, or when that same year it consented to participate in the Social Security Act's program for crippled children—it failed to supply necessary funds. Invariably, the state's priorities reflected the racial and moral biases of the white majority. Until 1942 there was no institution, public or private, for black delinquents or dependents; even then, females were not admitted due to overcrowding. Wartime trends forced the state's Welfare Department and Board of Health to expand children's services, and the EMIC aided 25,000 applicants. Overall, however, Mississippi's Depression and wartime response to child welfare was sadly deficient.[44]

The situation was similar in states such as North Carolina, Virginia, Kentucky, and Tennessee. Federal assistance under ADC made some difference, but child welfare programs, however expanded, remained woefully inadequate. (Kentucky, although quick to establish Old Age Assistance through the Social Security Act, did not inaugurate an ADC program until 1943.) The importance of local contexts, backgrounds, and traditions—which the Federal Government challenged in some respects, built upon in others, and deferred to time and again—was indisputable in each state.[45]

From one angle, the Federal Government's sensitivity to the power of local mores and priorities was less a betrayal of children's needs than it was a realistic assessment of American politics. An extremely vulnerable federal agency administered the ADC program in a setting that resembled a can of worms. As Winifred Bell has noted, administrators of ADC were "well aware of the limited interest in ADC, the absence of any national commitment to eradicate family poverty, the long indifference to the income status of Negroes, and the strong Mothers' Pension preference for 'elite' families."[46]

From another angle, however, localism was more than a bastion of established privilege. Its proponents were not all myopic opponents of social justice. Jeremy Felt makes clear, for example, the extent to which deeply felt fears and values shaped opposition in the 1930s to the proposed national child labor amendment. In their unwillingness to assume that the Federal Government would not exploit its powers, the amendment's foes drew on a well-established and honored American tradition.[47] Nor did defenders of an enlarged federal role always tactfully present their case. For instance, in the face of local critics of the Civilian Conservation Corps' (CCC) educational programs, some CCC advisors compounded the problem by accusing public schools of teaching "twaddle and detail," and by making claims for the CCC as "the first step toward a school without diploma and credits."[48]

In this context, perhaps the surprising thing about federal child welfare programs in the 1930s and 1940s was that they developed as extensively as they did. However limited and imprecise the Social Security provisions were for children, they nonetheless represented a milestone. Earlier, the mothers' pension movement had dissolved the old welfare dichotomy between public and private relief, and had thus been "a liberating, innovating force in American social welfare."[49] But the Social Security Act had accelerated this development considerably in terms of federal responsibility for children, as well as other groups. Similarly, despite the temporary and emergency nature of the WPA-Lanham Act funds for children, they nonetheless established "the first federally supported preschool programs in the nation's history"—major precedents for the idea of "social parenthood."[50] As Walter Trattner has said, however ineffective child labor laws were, they did not signal "many backward steps; most bills, once passed, remained on the books."[51] Certainly not all needy children had reason to appreciate the New Deal; but in 1939 a rural black schoolchild probably spoke for more than himself when he finished his lunch, courtesy of the Farm Security Administration, with a prayer: "Say, my Lord just knows we've been fed. If it weren't for the President, we'd all be dead."[52]

While government, especially at the federal level, increasingly affected the lives of American children, so too did a growing number of specialists—doctors, counselors, and educators among them. Sometimes the results were tangible. This was especially so concerning where children were born and under what conditions. An important transformation in birth practice between 1900 and 1939 meant that more and more babies were born in hospitals and under circumstances that were manipulative and interventionist. Whereas in 1900 less than 5 percent of deliveries took place in hospitals, by 1939 half of all women (and 75 percent of urban women) gave birth in hospitals and in ways that reflected the growing role of doctors. Automatic preventive treatment for babies (such as eyedrops to combat gonococcal blindness) became routine.[53]

Throughout the 1930s, infant mortality rates dropped—from 69 per 1,000 live births in 1928 to 51 in 1938.[54] This decline resulted partly from medical advances that were even more notable in the next decade. By 1945, the dreaded disease pellagra, two-thirds of whose victims were aged two to fifteen, was finally becoming "an echo of the past." Moreover, during the early 1940s, Doctors Helen B. Taussig and Alfred Blalock pioneered the treatment of "blue babies." And although the battle against poliomyelitis virus did not achieve victory until the 1950s, notable research breakthroughs occurred as early as 1931 when an Australian and two Yale physicians identified more than one strain of the virus.[55]

Improved health care may also have resulted from several decades of parent education. A study in the mid-1930s of some eighty families with at least one child of school age in Grinnell, Iowa, was illuminating in this respect. Advice from various childrearing experts over at least the previous few years had apparently succeeded all too well in shaping parents' expectations and perceptions. After receiving instructions about children's needs for milk, meat, vegetables, and dental care, many parents felt guilty because the Depression made it difficult for them to meet prescribed standards.[56]

Insofar as parents accepted the advice of childrearing experts, they must have felt both a greater burden of responsibility and encouragement to follow their instincts. The 1930s and war years marked a significant alteration in the prescriptive literature regarding child development.[57] The appearance in 1930 of the journal *Child Development* ("concerned with exploring the whole realm of childhood"), the publication a year later of the first *Handbook of Child Psychology*, and the formation in 1933 of the Society for Research in Child Development attested to vigor in the field. University of Pennsylvania sociologist J. P. Shalloo observed at the end of the decade that several dominant theories of psychiatric diagnosis vied for attention. They all represented a shift "away from a psycho-genetic explanation" of child behavior "toward a broader total personality, total-situation approach." This meant that the larger world in which children acted—the world of parents, siblings, teachers, and others—was receiving more attention. "To put it bluntly," wrote Shalloo, "problem children have problem parents"; moreover, parents mirrored community changes. In order to understand children, it was imperative to know more about their parents.[58]

In turn, parents learned from the changing literature on childrearing that they should openly demonstrate affection for their children and respect their needs. This signalled a movement away from John B. Watson's behaviorist theories which had dominated the 1920s. Watson had emphasized strict schedules; parents, like army sergeants, were supposed to enforce acceptable conduct. Rather than indulge their offspring, they were to follow closely the rules of scientific upbringing. During the 1930s and 1940s, however, childrearing advice conceded more to the emotions and "natural" development of children. Parents needed to be no less vigilant than before, but they were to watch more closely for cues which the children offered.[59]

As Daniel Beekman has said, in his overview of Western theories of childrearing, "The hope was that the child would still end up as regular as clockwork—but the tendency was towards less mechanical methods to achieve that goal." Psychologists, who in the 1920s had given parents rigid rules to follow, allowed for more parental discretion. As economic and international crises decimated old certainties, there was a resurgence of sympathy for "the basic emotional interaction of parent and child." The shift in tone was evident in 1938 when C. Andrews Aldrich, professor of pediatrics at the University of Minnesota, and Mary M. Aldrich published an important book, *Babies Are Human Beings: An Interpretation of Growth*. In a world slipping from Depression into war, the Aldriches offered parents what Beekman has described as "the promise of the 'secure' child in a 'world of change.' " The book emphasized the needs of children and urged parents to respond warmly to those needs. In the words of the Aldriches, "most spoiled children are those who, as babies, have been denied essential gratifications in a mistaken attempt to fit them into a rigid regime." The child who insisted on attention was one who had not received it. "A satisfied baby does not need to develop those methods of wresting his comforts from an unresponsive world. It is axiomatic that satisfied people never start a revolution."[60]

Childrearing advice in favor of loving care and individual attention became even more conspicuous during World War II. This was abundantly true with C. Madelaine Dixon's *Keep Them Human* (1942), Dorothy Baruch's *You, Your Children, and War* (1944), and especially Dr. Dorothy Whipple's *Our American Babies* (1944), "certainly the best of the wartime books," according to Beekman. These early 1940s' books generally ignored or played down the matter of discipline. Dr. Arnold Gesell's *Infant and Child in the Culture of Today* (1943), by one of the giants in the child care field, advised parents to follow—not force—the child's progress. "If one can judge a time from its books," Beekman has concluded, "the 1940s during the war and in the years immediately afterwards may be described as the most permissive time in child care." The pre-1930s' belief that young people should adapt to adult desires and schedules gave way bit by bit to an awareness of the child's own physical and mental processes.[61]

If adult images of children softened in the childrearing literature of the era, so too did the mass media portray youths sympathetically. This was especially true with the movies. Granted, in the 1930s' films there were *Wild Boys of the Road* (1933) and *Dead End Kids* (1937). But the movies of the Depression usually showed the tough street boys as products of dreary, poverty-stricken environments; deep down the youths were supposedly decent: *Angels with Dirty Faces* (1938). Sometimes, as in *Angels Wash Their Faces* (1939), they even battled corruption. More familiar on the theater screen were lovable youngsters such as Shirley Temple, Jackie Cooper, Judy Garland, and Mickey Rooney—representatives not of wretched slums but of Main Street, U.S.A. In the 1930s, Warner Brothers produced the Penrod series, based on Booth Tarkington's celebration of growing up in small town Indiana. Even more influential were the seventeen Andy Hardy pictures, starring Mickey Rooney, between 1937 and 1946. (In 1942 the Hardy family series received a special Academy Award for "furthering the American way of life.") By the end of the 1930s, as film historian David Considine has pointed out, "the top box office draws across the country were juveniles." In 1939 Mickey Rooney was the leading male star at the box office.

Indeed, the Andy Hardy image was so important to the film industry that an MGM employee kept careful watch on Rooney to make sure that, off screen, he did not sully his movie character's image as an all-American youth. Other pictures, such as *Barefoot Boy* (1938) and *Tom Boy* (1940) with Jackie Moran, also honored wholesome, village youths.[62]

Nor did the war transform Hollywood's stereotypical boys and girls. The narrator of *Janie* (1944) told audiences that the protagonist was from "an average homely little town like yours and mine." And in 1945 came *Junior Miss*, which *Life* magazine featured as its film of the week. If adolescence had a darker, painful side, it was virtually missing from the era's movies. Hollywood, rather than dealing seriously with the realities of being young in America, seized upon a popular (and profitable) formula to propagandize an idealized version of American life. That version suggested much about national culture—anxieties, values, aspirations—but told little about the flesh-and-blood youngsters who were supposed to model themselves after Andy Hardy or Dorothy in *The Wizard of Oz*. Even the redoubtable Rooney conceded to a reporter, "It isn't worth it. . . . It's all work and no play." His father sadly reminisced, "Mickey didn't actually have much childhood."[63]

Just as American movies about youth have ironically been most informative about grown-ups and their perceptions of young people, so have most analyses of education and delinquency focused on adults. This is defensible up to a point. Historians can no more ignore adult attitudes toward children than they can study the lives of convicts while overlooking the guards, wardens, state legislators, and the physical limits of the walls (however misleading the prison analogy may be in terms of, say, family life or public education).

During the 1930s and, to a lesser extent, the war years, American education was full of debate regarding curricula, teachers' responsibilities for social change, and the Federal Government's role in public schools. Such debates were hardly new, but now they intensified because of the era's social and economic disorder. Arguments from business organizations such as the Chamber of Commerce that schools needed to retrench, by cutting teachers' salaries and educational programs, may have encouraged at least some educators to be more skeptical than before about the business community.[64] Prominent educators divided over the extent to which teachers should direct student thinking. Some argued that teachers should seize the opportunity to recruit students for a new social order. Others responded that instructors, as servants of society, needed to defend and reinforce existing values. John Dewey and his followers advocated a middle route: not molding student opinions, but stimulating critical and independent thinking.[65]

According to historian Lawrence Cremin, the 1930s completed "an age of reform in American education." By the end of the decade, Progressive theories marked the classrooms in substantial ways: reorganized curricula, expanded extracurricular activities, more varied and flexible student groupings, the decline of recitation as a pedagogical technique, larger guidance programs, more attractive textbooks, better trained teachers, modified school architecture (with gymnasiums, laboratories, athletic fields, and furniture that reflected wide-ranging educational goals), and a burgeoning administrative bureaucracy that was increasingly separate from the teachers. Progressive education had become "conventional wisdom," and phrases about "recognizing individual differences," "the whole child," and "teaching children, not subjects," were now cliches.[66]

Edward A. Krug has described the triumph of the idea by World War II that the American high school, no less than its counterpart, should be essentially "an institution of custodianship" for all youths. Focusing strictly on the top levels of secondary schooling, Krug discusses the "great variety of ideas and events" that bombarded educators during the Depression as they forged the modern high school—comprehensive, nonselective, and sometimes anti-academic. "Stand by the schools" was a rallying cry against individuals who wished to reduce educational budgets. Other conflicts swirled around whether education should be primarily general or vocational.[67]

Krug, Cremin, and other historians agree that, even before America entered World War II, the debate over American education had shifted. By 1940, says Cremin, opposition against Progressive theories was well established. Criticism of alleged Progressive permissiveness ("Lollypops versus Learning," according to one observer) hardened during the war as themes of patriotism, training for citizenship, and modified vocational education dominated.[68] "Education for Victory" suddenly received priority, although there was still some disagreement over how schools could best serve this function. "Our one objective?" asked the Massachusetts commissioner of education rhetorically: "To do as well as we can in making soldiers." None other than Harry Hopkins, one of Franklin Roosevelt's closest advisors, attacked "*non*essentials, such as Chaucer and Latin," when he urged some students to "quit high school entirely. . . . a diploma can only be framed and hung on the wall. A shell that a boy or girl helps to make can kill a lot of Japs." And Toledo's superintendent introduced premilitary training into the public schools by saying that English and history had to "take a back seat" in order to produce "a future soldier." There was no doubt about it: "Toledo school children are to become completely war-minded and war-educated."[69]

Surprisingly, traditional liberal arts or academic courses were remarkably resilient, despite the considerable push to subsume them under a vocational curriculum. For one thing, many of the students who remained in school, rather than enlist early or enter the job market, were those who planned to attend college. For another, social studies teachers scrambled to adapt their courses to wartime needs, no doubt opening the door to propaganda but helping to protect their disciplines.[70] Thus, some high school English classes wrote essays on the value of air power; history students dealt with themes of democracy and wars for freedom; and art classes produced war bond posters.[71]

World War II, by forcing schools into many roles and by pushing national needs to the top of the educational agenda, refueled old arguments about federal versus local authority.[72] This also helped set the stage for the Cold War. According to Ronald Lora, "the normal functioning of educational institutions was impossible. . . . Attitudes forged in the grueling experience of total war proved difficult to eradicate and continued into the postwar period with scarcely a hitch."[73]

While such discussions of educational debates and trends between 1930 and 1945 are useful, the connections between what educators said and what happened in the nation's classrooms are tenuous.[74] Most superintendents and school officials were generally conservative and ill-informed, so arguments in educational publications probably had little impact even on them. (One study showed, for example, that 84 percent of superintendents believed that history texts should eliminate information that might raise doubts about the United States.)[75] Perhaps more representative of teachers' attitudes than all the writings of Progressive educators put together was a word association test that 200 white teachers in Cleveland took around 1930. The teachers, all of whom taught in predominantly black schools, were supposed to describe their first thoughts when they heard the word "Negro." Pejorative or negative associations were abundant—including 43 who thought of slavery and 39 who expressed feelings of antipathy.[76] A few years later, Malcolm Little—later known as Malcolm X—listened to a white English teacher in the Lansing, Michigan, public schools advise him to forget about being a lawyer because he needed "to be realistic about being a nigger."[77]

What struck journalists Ernest and Betty Lindley, as they criss-crossed the nation in the late 1930s, was the sterility of American education. "Why," they wondered, "do so many children and young people in school have distrust, even hate, for the place where they spend so many hours of their lives?" "I don't know," one youth told them. "It's just so dead."[78]

Robert S. Lynd and Helen Merrell Lynd, in their classic study of *Middletown in Transition* (1937), probed as effectively as anyone into a major part of the problem. Although the setting of Muncie, Indiana, was special—a Midwestern city of about 50,000—the Lynds sketched out dilemmas that undoubtedly plagued many, if not all, American communities. "One sees Middletown attempting to move in two opposed directions at once," wrote the Lynds. Residents were torn between meeting the needs of individual students and those of the community, between encouraging young people to think and forcing on them the cultural value system of the larger society, and between offering the best educational opportunities and working within tight economic restrictions. In Muncie, discussions of education quickly slipped from the abstract to specific classroom matters. When, for example, parents objected to a high school sociology course that discussed sexual problems, the course disappeared from the curriculum. Teachers, not wanting to take risks, tended to be cautious, trying to offend no one. "I have an uneasy furtive sense about it all," commented one instructor. In terms of publicizing their ideas across the country, teachers perhaps enjoyed unprecedented academic freedom, but at the local level they were, as the Lynds put it, "dangerously in jeopardy." Educational debates and theories were thus far removed from the lives of most students. Teachers sought the safe middle ground. Parents alternately celebrated education and worried about its effects. Even guidance counseling, one of the era's much-heralded administrative strategies, may have received more attention than it deserved. Although Muncie adopted a guidance program, the counselor in the mid-1930s saw each student from the seventh through the twelfth grade only for about ten minutes each semester. The uneven counseling system stirred parental concerns about wasting money and teacher complaints about wasting time. Guidance may have "arrived," but for most students it probably made little difference.[79]

The gap between theory and reality may have been equally as great in the juvenile justice system. Historians of the Depression and war era desperately need studies that are comparable to Steven Schlossman's regarding the actual workings of the Milwaukee juvenile court during the Progressive Era, Peter Prescott's about the proceedings within New York City's Family Court in the 1970s, or David Rothman's concerning the Norfolk, Massachusetts, penitentiary in 1932 or 1933.[80] In terms of sociological and psychological theory, at least, important trends were clearly evident by the 1930s. According to one observer, the juvenile court system was concerned more and more with preventing problems; it therefore dealt increasingly with pre-delinquency cases while elevating the importance of child guidance as a strategy.[81] Ironically, the juvenile courts themselves—once bright spots on the Progressive landscape—lost some of their earlier luster. As the belief grew that delinquency's roots were largely emotional, and thus susceptible to psychological treatment, the courts faded from public view.[82]

Perhaps one sign of the juvenile court's declining prestige by the mid-1930s was the emergence of organizations known as "coordinating councils." In these councils, citizens from various children's and law enforcement agencies formed "adjustment" committees in which they heard cases of youths who seemed destined for trouble. Such unofficial proceedings were supposed to place potential delinquents under appropriate supervision and thereby to discourage unacceptable conduct. Over 350 of these coordinating councils existed in mid-1938, primarily in the Pacific Coast states.[83]

In some instances, a small but influential minority of people began to question the earlier Progressive faith in the juvenile court system as an answer to delinquency. By the 1930s it was difficult to ignore the Freudian challenge to assumptions of childhood innocence. An emerging view in the early part of the decade posited a subculture of delinquency with distinct behavior patterns, social organization, values, and norms. Following the war, this interpretation flourished, leading the eminent child psychologist Bruno Bettelheim to observe in 1959 that "love is not enough" for a problem child. As this assumption took shape in the 1930s, the juvenile court seemed far less useful than before as a rehabilitative agency. Some observers wanted to separate judicial and therapeutic functions, keeping youths out of courts as much as possible and leaving matters of prevention and rehabilitation to agencies such as the schools. But the critique of the juvenile court system, although powerful, never developed into a coherent argument in the years prior to 1945. National and international crises were simply too distracting for any major reform of the court structure. Nonetheless, the juvenile court, once a bastion of reformers' hopes, no longer stirred great support. Suspicions grew that it was in fact doing more harm than good. One sociologist contended in 1930 that "a boy cannot be a delinquent without thinking of himself as a delinquent.... Appearance in court places a stigma on the child and gives him a pernicious definition of himself." Significantly, in 1943 the National Council on Crime and Delinquency removed the "delinquent" label altogether from its revised Standard Juvenile Court Act.[84]

This hardly attested to a belief that delinquency was less of a problem, however. Throughout the Depression, and especially the war, adults anxiously fretted over the increase in juvenile crime and socially unacceptable conduct. In a 1946 poll, 42 percent of the adult respondents were convinced that teenagers behaved worse than their parents' generation; only 9 percent thought that youthful behavior had improved.[85] Moreover, statistics seemed to confirm the negative judgment. The percentage of juvenile court cases not only grew, but also leaped alarmingly during the war years.[86] Delinquency may in fact have been the most disturbing social issue of the period. In Indianapolis during the last nine months of the war, for example, juveniles comprised 64 percent of all arrests. Historian Richard Ugland has speculated that by 1945 the delinquency "problem had expanded to perhaps unprecedented dimensions." Young females in particular seemed more willing to defy social conventions, especially regarding sex. A newspaper advertisement for one wartime movie asked hysterically, "Where is your daughter tonight? In some joint...lapping up liquor...petting...going mad?"[87]

Despite such panic, wartime delinquency rates deserved calmer scrutiny. Although juvenile crime generally increased in urban areas, it declined in some rural locales.[88] In a war-boom community such as Seneca, Illinois, the war's impact was ambiguous. On one hand, easy money, lack of community roots, and overcrowding encouraged crime. On the other hand, recreation and a watchful attitude kept the town from being "wide-open." Consequently, Seneca did not confront serious problems of law-breaking delinquency.[89]

Sociologist Francis E. Merrill concluded that, across the country, the changing social definition of delinquency was basic to the heightened public sense of the problem. Merrill had no doubts that wartime conditions encouraged delinquency in numerous ways. A dislocated population, broken community and family relationships, understaffed schools, more spending money, and lack of supervision prepared the way for youthful misconduct. For girls especially, the chances of finding socially approved outlets through war-related activities were considerably less than were those of boys. But none of these facts meant that juvenile delinquency swept across the nation. "The courts were busier during the war," Merrill conceded, "but it is not clear to what extent their activity reflected actual changes in adolescent behavior and to what extent changes in the definitions of this behavior. Social problems rest upon social values," and such values were definitely in flux as the nation became more sensitive to the problems of wartime mobilization.[90]

To some adult observers, the perceived spread of misbehavior among young people was due to wartime passions. Families under stress reportedly set a tone "of restlessness and excitability." Movies, comic strips, and radio serials—filled with stories of battles and spies—were supposedly "overstimulating" children. One junior high school teacher claimed that an incessant " 'day-before-Christmas-vacation fever' " kept the students continually on edge. Younger boys were particularly disorderly in such a setting.[91]

At least a few adults saw deeper signs of social malaise affecting America's youth. Some blamed modern music for corrupting adolescent morals. Earlier in the century, ragtime and jazz had stirred anxieties about the perversion of social values; by the late 1930s and early 1940s, swing music had become a source of worry for some nervous citizens. In 1938 one psychologist charged that swing's rhythms unleashed nothing less than a "mental epidemic" causing "moral weakness." Six years later, the conductor of the New York Philharmonic contended that boogie woogie was "the greatest single contributing factor to juvenile delinquency among American youth today." It was producing "war degeneracy." Violinist Fritz Kreisler believed that jitterbugging was the "same old stuff that mating animals have used far down the zoological line."[92] Young people themselves were probably more in agreement with the interpretation that swing music simply demonstrated "the immortal right of adolescence to assert itself." As a letter to the *New York Times* asserted, "Swing is the voice of youth striving to be heard in this fast-moving world of ours.... Give us a slow-moving era if you want to see the minuet."[93]

Actually, if historian Gilman M. Ostrander is correct, the chances were slim during the Depression and war years that adults would be attentive to "the voice of youth." Ostrander's provocative thesis is that American society, especially in the twentieth century, has undergone "a comprehensive reorientation—from a patriarchal faith in the wisdom of age and experience to a filiarchal faith in the promise of youth and innovation." The rise of a "filiarchy"—or "rule by the young"—has been part of the nations's adjustment to an increasingly technological world where experience and traditional wisdom are apparent liabilities. In this context, young people—relatively free of the useless baggage of outdated ways—have a special flexibility and capacity to adapt to the new. According to Ostrander, the 1920s were particularly conducive to "the technological filiarchy." Striking symbols of this were evident in the flapper fashions, which celebrated girlish figures, and the youthful Charles Lindbergh's popularity. The flapper style was notably harsh on older women. Advice columnist Dorothy Dix urged them not to adopt the new fashions lest they resemble "old mutton," which "never seems so old, and tough, and stringy as when it is dressed as spring lamb." The drop in hemlines during the troubled 1930s may have been one of many signals of diminished filiarchal influence. Across society there was evidence of a search for old certainties. As Robert and Helen Lynd observed in Muncie, Indiana, "the parents' world" had struck back. For such reasons Gilman Ostrander has concluded that the Great Depression "proved unfavorable to filiarchy." So did the war, "which imposed the absolute patriarchy of the military system on the youth of the nation."[94]

"The voice of youth" may have been hard to hear during the Depression and war years, but historians have subsequently not listened very carefully for it either. As a result, children have been relatively silent in most historical interpretations of the era. Understandably, of course, the larger tumult of that crisis-torn period has attracted the most scholarly attention. Another problem, however, is determining in retrospect what sounds were really those of children.

Some scholars have attempted to infer from demographic statistics certain conclusions about childhood and growing up. Journalist Landon Jones, in his popular summary of a rich and growing literature on the subject, has shown very effectively that a particular generation's size can profoundly influence its history. Although Jones focuses mainly on the post-World War II baby boom, he has suggested that the relatively small Depression-era birth rate would in itself be of major consequence. For many children, the Depression and war provided unpleasant experiences, but in the long run the small size of their generation proved an advantage. When they became adults there were few enough of them that they did not continually bump into each other searching for education and jobs. Ironically, from this view, children born in the 1930s and early 1940s comprised the "Good Times Generation" of the 1950s.[95]

As children grew up in the turbulent period from 1930 to 1945, however, many of them knew anything but good times. Schools that were overcrowded and understaffed (due to declining revenues or, during the war, to a lack of teachers); family tensions due to hard times, mobility, and loss; worries, especially for high school students, about finding jobs in the 1930s and, in the early 1940s, about the draft and postponed goals—such were the facts of life for hundreds of thousands of young people. But the ways in which age, gender, ethnic, racial, and class differences filtered out or molded such facts remain largely uncharted.[96]

Glen H. Elder, Jr.'s *Children of the Great Depression* offers a rare glimpse into the impact of the 1930s economic crisis on one group of children. The source materials for Elder's major study are unique. In 1931 a team of child psychologists started gathering data on 167 preadolescents who lived in Oakland, California. The psychologists collected massive amounts of information through testing, interviews, and observations, but, most importantly, they and their successors in the project conducted periodic checks on the subsequent lives of the children. The youths, who were just entering junior high school when the project began, came from working-class, lower-middle-class, and middle-class backgrounds. Most were white Protestants whose parents were native born. None had known either extreme poverty or great wealth. But between 1929 and 1933 "family income in the Oakland sample declined approximately 40 percent."[97]

Elder's primary objective is to discover what impact this sudden economic loss had on the lives of the children. He focuses on a variety of themes: gender, class, self-worth, and the division of child labor. "Both in the middle and the working class," he says, "economic losses increased the involvement of children in household affairs, emphasized the centrality of mother in family matters and children's sentiments, and expanded the social world of children beyond the family in desire if not in activity." There was a marked growth of children's responsibilities within families. Boys, far more than girls, took part-time jobs outside the home. Although boys assumed more household chores than previously, domestic duties expanded largely for girls. This division of work roles tended to free boys from traditional parental restraints; girls gained little independence. In fact, the females were further "oriented toward a domestic future."[98]

Class background, according to Elder, was an important factor. Lower-class children were better prepared for economic adversity, but middle-class offspring drew on "a wider range of problem-solving experience and skills," and responded more adaptively to social change. For poorer children, early acquaintance with hard times had left a legacy of distrust, fear, limited experiences, and inclinations toward fatalism. In contrast, although children of the middle class suddenly faced economic deprivation, they "rated higher on ego strength . . . utilization of personal resources . . . capacity for growth. They were . . . more resilient, more self confident, and less defensive." In terms of values, however, children of both classes eschewed any desire to break from the past or explore new ground. Indeed, *signs of family change among the offspring of deprived families are consistently in a conservative direction, toward traditional values and relationships.*" The shared crises of Depression, and later of war, tended to strengthen community ties and to inspire feelings of civic duty.[99]

Elder's book, as valuable as it is, nonetheless focuses so much on the impact of temporary economic loss on Depression children that it downplays other childhood experiences. Formative experiences prior to adolescence, for example, receive little attention.[100] Elder himself warns about "generalizing across cohorts on the Depression experience."[101] His study may be as useful as any in understanding some consequences of temporary economic crisis for children. Because of the nature of the Oakland sample, however, it tells little about children whose deprivation was virtually permanent—as, say, with many rural blacks, Mexican-Americans in the Southwest, Appalachian whites, reservation Indians, or urban alley children.[102]

A related problem for historians is how to recognize and interpret children's perceptions of the world. During the 1930s and 1940s, many young people clearly enjoyed Walt Disney movies, novels about adventuresome youths such as the Hardy boys and Nancy Drew, and the afternoon radio serials.[103] But when historians attempt to explain the meaning of such entertainment forms to youngsters, they may once again end up learning more about the expectations and values of adults.

James Borchert's examination of *Alley Life in Washington* is provocative in this respect. Although Borchert deals only briefly with black alley children in the 1930s, he shows that mass culture influenced them in different ways than adults expected. During the Depression, the young alley residents certainly liked Disney's movie *Snow White* and the "Dick Tracy" comic strip. Their personal backgrounds, however, provided a very special lens through which they filtered meanings of what they saw. Specific scenes from *Snow White*, and not the plot or the aesthetics of the film, appealed to them. "The culture of the alley (and black experience generally) strongly influenced what they saw, liked and remembered," writes Borchert. "In spite of claims that the mass media are making a mass audience, not everyone sees the same thing. . . . If alley residents were being increasingly bombarded by the mass media, the media could have reinforced alley culture, rather than breaking it down."[104]

From the perspective of mainstream attitudes and values, alley culture in the 1930s (and later) may have seemed pathologic. But Borchert insists that, from the viewpoint of the alley children, their culture was adaptive, realistic, and sensible. Because they were more familiar with an oral than a written culture, education in the public schools was often irrelevant. Unlike the individualistic pedagogical strategies of the schools, "alley culture was communal, corporate, and cooperative." Teachers, except in areas such as athletics, generally discouraged collaborative efforts; where teachers saw plagiarism, the children drew naturally on an oral folk tradition that encouraged repetition and sharing. Similarly, physically rough alley play was far better preparation than schoolroom assignments in terms of the employment that probably awaited most blacks as day laborers or domestics. Stuffed toys, or commercially packaged games, were generally alien to the street children who, again and again, adapted their activities to the alley community. Borchert, in a relatively few pages, is very insightful regarding the relativity of socializing patterns and the importance of "selective perception" for the worlds of children.[105]

The world for high school students during the early 1940s was that of a new social type—the "teenager." This is a point that historian Richard M. Ugland has argued persuasively in his case study of Indianapolis youth during the war years. While Ugland realizes that adults helped to invent the "teenager," he uses sources such as high school newspapers to reveal the roles of the youths themselves. His conclusions, in part, contradict wartime speculation that young people directly participated in the defense effort and thereby encountered the realities of the adult world.[106] According to Ugland, teenagers more often interpreted their assignments as peripheral and even useless. Adults urged sacrifice, responsibilities, and public activity, but typically gave youths only hollow assignments and patriotic slogans. Student response to the war was not especially enthusiastic or cohesive. Substantial numbers of high school youths were in fact confused, indifferent, ill-informed about the nature of the conflict, and bored. "At the root of the morale problem," says Ugland, "was the peculiar position adolescents held in American society. ...they were trapped in an age group that society had come to expect little of."[107]

None of this occurred in a vacuum, of course. The invention of adolescence as a social grouping had been underway for some time and helped to isolate youths, reducing them to marginal status. The war further removed them from participating fully in society. Teenagers, regardless of class or race, increasingly saw themselves as part of a cultural subgroup—a group that adults and the mass media also recognized.

Two cultural landmarks of the era were the teenage "canteens," some 3,000 of which flourished as recreation centers during the war, and the appearance in 1944 of the monthly magazine, *Seventeen*. The new journal's goal was not to mold youths into adults, but instead to show them how to be teenagers. "You buy loafer moccasins because your friends do," the magazine advised. "You go to Joe's grill...or Doc's for cokes not because these places are charming, or the food good—but because the crowd goes."[108]

One of the strengths of Ugland's work is his conviction "that youth has its own history, a history closely linked yet undistinguishable from the history of the family, school, and other institutions." By drawing on a wide variety of evidence, he captures more successfully than most studies the actual world of youth. Although his focus is on one city, he keeps sight of the larger national context. Alan Clive's examination of wartime Michigan is also illuminating. He briefly describes the hardships that children of Southern rural white families encountered when they moved from Tennessee's mountain country to Detroit. For such transplanted youths, the freedom from farm chores and rural poverty came at a substantial emotional price, as they tried to cope with fragmented family units, poor educational backgrounds, and the taunts of other students who perceived them as "Hillbillies" and hicks. According to one story, children at a Willow Run school refused one day to sing "Michigan, My Michigan," on the grounds that the state was not really their home.[109] Similar case studies may ultimately open the door on the lives of children and finally reveal more about the texture of their experiences.

In the meantime, a few biographies, autobiographies, and oral histories suggest something about the varied backgrounds from which children emerged in the 1930s and 1940s. Robert J. Hastings's delightful recollection, based partly on childhood diaries, evokes a fond sense of growing up in the small southern Illinois coal town of Marion. He describes his grade school years from 1930 to 1938, a period during which his father lost a job in the local mines and the family's neighborhood grocery store went bankrupt. Despite the economically harsh times, Hastings's boyhood was overall a pleasant period. An admitted "sentimentalist," Hastings recalled fondly the joys of listening to the annual "Lum and Abner" Christmas show on the family's Atwater-Kent radio; the elation at having a new pair of Oshkosh B'Gosh bibbed overalls; the pleasure of munching a Powerhouse candy bar or playing marbles or "Cops'n'Robbers"; the excitement of reading newspaper comic strips such as "Flash Gordon"; the enjoyment of "the biggest Depression bargain in town"—the Saturday afternoon movie matinees; and the fun of attending the county fair, sitting contentedly in the dusty stands believing that "someone up there...must surely be looking after me." As Hastings prepared to enter high school in the late 1930s, he was optimistic about his future: "There were no storm clouds on my horizon."[110]

Memories of childhood innocence also dominated satirist Russell Baker's recollections of growing up in Baltimore. Baker knew economic hard times firsthand, and he also felt the emotional strain of his parents' unhappy marriage. But, despite brushes with the adult world, he always sensed that being a child kept him at least somewhat apart from the vicissitudes of the larger world. His innocence grew, then, out of assumptions that adults would protect him.[111]

Such was assuredly not the case for the young Malcolm X, Maya Angelou, or Cesar Chavez. For Malcolm X, the 1930s were "nightmare" years. In 1931, when Malcolm was six, his father was killed in what appeared to be a brutal racial incident. His mother struggled to keep the family together, sometimes boiling a pot of dandelion greens to eat. "We would be so hungry we were dizzy," Malcolm remembered. In his opinion, the state welfare agency, the courts, and medical doctors destroyed his family, driving his mother into a mental institution and splitting the children apart. The welfare people "were as vicious as vultures," lacking "feelings, understanding, compassion, or respect."[112] (Even the ebullient Hastings had bad thoughts about the Depression era welfare agencies: "At a time when we needed help most, we were made to feel undeserving, lazy, and shiftless.")[113]

Maya Angelou, growing up in the cotton country around Stamps, Arkansas, faced a rigidly segregated society. The few times when she and her brother crossed the railroad tracks into "whitefolksville," they felt like "explorers walking without weapons into man-eating animals' territory." Once when the "powhitetrash children" cruelly taunted her grandmother, Angelou, age ten, angrily contemplated blowing them away with the rifle behind the door. Yet she also often dreamed of being "one of the sweet little white girls who were everybody's dream." Always, it seemed, there was the terrible sense of being an outsider, even in the black community: "If growing up is painful for the Southern Black girl, being aware of her displacement is the rust on the razor that threatens the throat."[114]

In 1934, when Cesar Chavez was six years old, his family lost a little piece of land north of Yuma, Arizona, due to a bank foreclosure. For several years the parents and their five children bumped along in their battered Chevrolet as migrant workers in California. From the first to the eighth grade, Cesar Chavez was in thirty-seven different schools. The standard academic year was nine months, but he was actually in class about half that time because of working the crops. In California towns such as Indio and Brawley, he felt the sharp sting of prejudice and discrimination. Waitresses refused to serve him or his family on grounds that the restaurants did not "sell to Mexicans." Chavez later guessed that one of the waitresses "never knew how much she was hurting us. But it stayed with us." Looking back years later, he said, "This is the truth, you know. History."[115]

It is precisely this kind of history—incredibly complex and diverse—that nags at the edges of the remembered record of the Depression and war years. In important respects, those years marked a turning point in terms of federal policies toward children. Aid for Dependent Children, whatever its limits, set a major precedent regarding federal responsibilities for young people. If the actual implementation of the program too often amounted to a broken promise, at least the promise—direct or implied—was there. Promises, like much-stated ideals, take on lives of their own. Once made, they remain—as reminders, if nothing else. The 1930s and early 1940s set down, however unintentionally and unenthusiastically, a number of precedents regarding day care and other programs that promised more children healthier, longer lives. From another angle, of course, many needy children had little to show for such developments; indeed, in some cases, shifts in government policy came at their expense.

And certainly for millions of children, evolving government programs, changing educational theories, and related matters were generally far removed from their daily lives. They marched to the many drums of their own personal neighborhood, family, and peer group experiences. If some wondered on occasion why "the inexorable THE END" flashed across the motion picture screen at the Saturday matinee, others—like the little alley girl in Washington, D.C.—sometimes had other memories: "When I was a little girl about six or three/My father took a stick and beated me."[116]

NOTES

1. Katharine F. Lenroot, "Child Welfare, 1930–40," *Annals of the American Academy of Political and Social Science* 212 (November 1940): 11.

2. W. Norton Grubb and Marvin Lazerson, *Broken Promises: How Americans Fail Their Children* (New York: Basic Books, 1982).

3. Valerie Polakow Suransky, "A Tyranny of Experts," *Wilson Quarterly* 6 (Autumn 1982): 60.

4. Emma Octavia Lundberg, *Unto the Least of These: Social Services for Children* (New York: Appleton-Century-Crofts, 1947), 384.

5. See, for example, Sophonisba P. Breckinridge, "Government's Role in Child Welfare"; Helen Glenn Tyson, "Care of Dependent Children"; and Mary Irene Atkinson, "Child Welfare Work in Rural Communities," *Annals of the American Academy of Political and Social Science* 212 (November 1940): 42–50; 168–178; 209–215.

6. Lundberg, *Unto the Least of These*, 206–264, contains a memorable tribute to these and other "Pathfinders of the Middle Years" of child-saving.

7. Dorothy E. Bradbury, *Five Decades of Action for Children: A History of the Children's Bureau* (Washington, D.C.: U.S. Government Printing Office, 1962), 68.

8. "Rules and Regulations No. 3, issued July 11, 1933, by the FERA," in Edith Abbott, ed., *Public Assistance: American Principles and Policies* (Chicago: University of Chicago Press, 1940), 1:780. Abbott's collection of documents is invaluable. For the philosophic importance of the FERA, see Dorothy Zeitz, *Child Welfare, Principles and Methods* (New York: John Wiley & Sons, 1959), 155–158.

9. Atkinson, "Child Welfare Work in Rural Communities," 212.

10. Theodore L. Reller, "The School and Child Welfare," *Annals of the American Academy of Political and Social Science* 212 (November 1940): 56.

11. Weaver W. Pangburn, "Play and Recreation," *Annals of the American Academy of Political and Social Science* 212 (November 1940): 123–125.

12. Maud Morlock, *Homemaker Services, History and Bibliography* (Washington, D.C.: U.S. Government Printing Office, 1964), 1–6. See also Alfred Kadushin, *Child Welfare Services*, (2d ed., New York: Macmillan Co., 1974), 293–294.

13. Ruby Takanishi, "Federal Involvement in Early Education (1933–1973): The Need for Historical Perspectives," in Lilian G. Katz, ed., *Current Topics in Early Childhood Education* (Norwood, N.J.: Ablex Publishing Corp., 1977), 1:158. Ironically, even the organization of the American Academy of Pediatrics in 1930 may have been due more to changes in the medical profession than to developments in children's medicine. Rosemary Stevens, *American Medicine and the Public Interest* (New Haven: Yale University Press, 1971), 219–222, argues that "the specialty had a social rather than a scientific rationale." It grew out of the increasing specialization within the profession. Indeed, "pediatrics flourished in part because of a lack of interest or qualification on the part of general practitioners" in treating children. For medical graduates, pediatrics offered "a relatively uncomplicated specialty as an alternative to general practice."

14. Edwin E. Witte, *The Development of the Social Security Act* (Madison, Wis.: University of Wisconsin Press, 1962). See also Winifred Bell, *Aid to Dependent Children* (New York: Columbia University Press, 1965), 22–23, regarding the general apathy about children's assistance.

15. Jeremy P. Felt, *Hostages of Fortune: Child Labor Reform in New York State* (Syracuse: Syracuse University Press, 1965), 223.

16. Robert W. McAhren, "Making the Nation Safe for Childhood: A History of the Movement for Federal Regulation of Child Labor, 1900–1938" (Ph.D. dissertation, University of Texas, 1967), 192–193; Raymond G. Fuller, "Child Labor—Continued," *Annals of the American Academy of Political and Social Science* 212 (November 1940): 149.

17. McAhren, "Making the Nation Safe for Childhood," v, 192–239, 259–262; Felt, *Hostages of Fortune*, 210–224; Jeremy P. Felt, "The Child Labor Provisions of the Fair Labor Standards Act," *Labor History* 11 (Fall 1970): 467–481. Walter I. Trattner, *Crusade for the Children: A History of the National Child Labor Committee and Child Labor Reform in America* (Chicago: Quadrangle Books, 1970), 205–206, also discusses the weaknesses of the 1938 legislation.

18. Between 1930 and 1940, public high school enrollment increased 50

percent; between 1941 and 1944, high school enrollment fell some 24 percent. Not only did child labor rebound during the war, but also the federal and state governments loosened standards. Elizabeth S. Magee, "Impact of the War on Child Labor," *Annals of the American Academy of Political and Social Science* 236 (November 1944): 101, has excellent information on this. See also Gertrude Folks Zimand, "The Changing Picture of Child Labor" and Beatrice McConnell, "Child Labor in Agriculture," *Annals of the American Academy of Political and Social Science* 236 (November 1944): 86–87; 74–100.

19. See, for example, Sheila Rothman, *Woman's Proper Place: A History of Changing Ideals and Practices, 1870 to the Present* (New York: Basic Books, 1978), 136–153.

20. Bradbury, *Five Decades of Action for Children*, 68.

21. Robert H. Bremner, "Families, Children, and the State," in Bremner and Gary W. Reichard, eds., *Reshaping America: Society and Institutions, 1945–1960* (Columbus: Ohio State University Press, 1982), 18, 31; Nathan Sinai and Odin W. Anderson, *EMIC (Emergency Maternity and Infant Care): A Study of Administrative Experience* (Ann Arbor: School of Public Health, University of Michigan, 1948), esp. 1–88; Bradbury, *Five Decades of Action for Children*, 64–65. According to Sinai and Anderson, 54, $130.5 million was appropriated between March 1943 and July 26, 1946.

22. Sinai and Anderson, *EMIC*, are especially useful regarding the debate over socialized medicine and concerns about federal intervention in state health matters. Although their book is an administrative history, not social or cultural, it conveys quite well the ideological battlelines. On the emergency aspects of the program, see pages 30, 35–36, 47–48, 176. See also Bradbury, *Five Decades of Action for Children*, 68, and Charles P. Taft, "Public Health and the Family in World War II," *Annals of the American Academy of Political and Social Science* 229 (September 1943): 148–149.

23. Bernard Greenblatt, *Responsibility for Child Care* (San Francisco: Jossey-Bass Publishers, 1977), 54–57; Margaret O'Brien Steinfels, *Who's Minding the Children? The History and Politics of Day Care in America* (New York: Simon & Schuster, 1973), 66–67; Sheila M. Rothman, "Other People's Children: The Day Care Experience in America," *The Public Interest* 30 (Winter 1973): 19–20. According to Mary Cable, *The Little Darlings, A History of Child Rearing in America* (New York: Charles Scribner's Sons, 1975), 190, "Day care legislation has been passed when its main purpose was to help adults, as during the Depression, when it created jobs, or as during World War II, when it freed mothers to work in factories." See also Kadushin, *Child Welfare Services*, 338–341.

24. William H. Chafe, *The American Woman, Her Changing Social, Economic, and Political Roles, 1920–1970* (New York: Oxford University Press, 1972), 162–170; Howard Dratch, "The Politics of Child Care in the 1940s," *Science and Society* 38 (Summer 1974): 167–204; Rothman, "Other People's Children," 20–21; Greenblatt, *Responsibility for Child Care*, 233–234; Takanishi, "Federal Involvement in Early Education," 142, 146–148. Although some figures show that Lanham Act centers cared for over 1.5 million children, Gilbert Y. Steiner, *The Children's Cause* (Washington, D.C.: Brookings Institution, 1976), 17, says that such a number is "inflated." The estimate of 105,000 children at the height of the program comes from Steiner. Several highly publicized day care programs

operated under the sponsorship of defense industries. Those of the Curtiss-Wright Corporation and Kaiser Industries were particularly important. But Dratch points out, pages 195–200, that these programs were actually quite small and sometimes more expensive than the Lanham facilities. Moreover, they were "privately" sponsored only in a very special sense—the funds coming, in effect, through profits from government contracts and tax write-offs. "In short," argues Dratch, "Henry J. Kaiser's world-famous showcase child care centers were entirely funded at public expense." Excellent on the Kaiser centers is Karen Beck Skold, "Women Workers and Child Care During World War II: A Case Study of the Portland, Oregon, Shipyards" (Ph.D. dissertation, University of Oregon, 1981), 116–214. Skold gives the centers high marks as innovative, well-designed, and clearly deserving "a place in the history of child care as a unique experiment."

25. Steiner, *Children's Crusade*, 16.

26. Bradbury, *Five Decades of Action for Children*, 62.

27. Grubb and Lazerson, *Broken Promises*, 3. The authors, on pages 3–40, offer a fine overview of the politics of the family.

28. Walter I. Trattner, *From Poor Law to Welfare State: A History of Social Welfare in America* (2d ed., New York: Free Press, 1979), 187.

29. Josephine C. Brown, *Public Relief, 1929–1939* (New York: Henry Holt & Co., 1940), 26–28, 308–309. Although only small sections of Brown's important study deal with children, the material is excellent. On the growth of mothers' pension laws, see Brown, *Public Relief*, 47–49; Roy Lubove, *The Struggle for Social Security, 1900–1935* (Cambridge, Mass.: Harvard University Press, 1968), 91–112; Bell, *Aid to Dependent Children*, 3–19; Mark H. Leff, "Consensus for Reform: The Mothers'-Pension Movement in the Progressive Era," *Social Service Review* 47 (September 1973): 397–417.

30. Brown, *Public Relief*, 308–312.

31. Lubove, *Struggle for Social Security*, 91–112.

32. Bell, *Aid to Dependent Children*, esp. vi, 1–19, 29–39, 51–59, 137–138, 175, 188.

33. Gilbert Y. Steiner, *Social Insecurity: The Politics of Welfare* (Chicago: Rand McNally, 1966), 257–260.

34. Rothman, "Other People's Children," 13–16, and especially Steinfels, *Who's Minding the Children*, 35–52, show that early day care was not merely custodial but was remarkably adaptive and innovative. Steinfels insists, for example, that Progressive reformers were "genuinely responsive to the needs of working mothers," while dealing with matters of children's health and even education. Not until the 1920s, she writes, did professional social workers gain control and transform the day nursery into "a marginal and limited agent of social welfare," defining day care as a temporary aid to troubled and poor families, and generally ignoring what working mothers needed. Rothman and Greenblatt, *Responsibility for Child Care*, 31–54, may be less inclined than Steinfels to see the Progressive period as a "modest Golden Age" for day care, but all agree that by the 1920s day care labored under the stigma of being simply a source of temporary relief for a deeply troubled clientele.

35. Rothman, "Other People's Children," 19–20; Steinfels, *Who's Minding the Children*, 66–68; Greenblatt, *Responsibility for Child Care*, 41–64, 98, 102–104, 120, 270.

36. Greenblatt, *Responsibility for Child Care*, 85–86.

37. Chafe, *American Woman*, 164–170, and Dratch, "Politics of Child Care in the 1940's," 177–203, stress that the home-as-usual advocates were persistent and ultimately triumphant. But they offer differing opinions about the bureaucratic factions that struggled for control of the Lanham centers. Chafe sees the Federal Security Administration (FSA)—"an amalgam of social-welfare departments including the Office of Education and Children's Bureau"—as more open than the Federal Works Administration (FWA)—which administered the Lanham Act's funds—to the long-range interests of children. According to Chafe, the FSA "envisioned day-care centers as a permanent addition to the nation's social-welfare institutions." In contrast, the FWA was concerned only with temporary, emergency care that did not emphasize education. Dratch, on the other hand, believes that the FSA (with the strong support of the Children's Bureau) had a narrower and much more restrictive view of child care than did the FWA. Hence, the FSA "power play" in 1943 to move the FWA to the sidelines was largely a product of preserving states' rights and undercutting publicly supported child care.

38. Greenblatt, *Responsibility for Child Care*, 64. See also Skold, "Women Workers and Child Care During World War II," 122, 210.

39. Richard Polenberg, *War and Society: The United States, 1941–1945* (Philadelphia: Lippincott, 1972), 149. See also Skold, "Women Workers and Child Care During World War II," 169–170, 210.

40. Indeed, according to Gilbert Steiner, as late as 1962 the states' rights philosophy was dominant, thus "providing federal support for categorical programs drawn by and tailored to the interests of the individual states with an absolute minimum of insistence upon uniformity." Steiner, *Social Insecurity*, 46.

41. James T. Patterson, *America's Struggle Against Poverty, 1900–1980* (Cambridge, Mass.: Harvard University Press, 1981), 67–71. Byrd's amendment required states to fund ADC programs only "as far as practicable under the conditions in such states." In 1939 Arkansas paid to families under ADC an average of $8.10 per month; Massachusetts paid $61.07. The statistics re Louisiana are in Robert E. Moran, "The History of Child Welfare in Louisiana, 1850–1960" (Ph.D. dissertation, Ohio State University, 1968), 90.

42. Rino J. Patti, "Child Protection in California 1850–1966: An Analysis of Public Policy" (Ph.D. dissertation, University of Southern California, 1967), 209–210, 220–223, 237, 342.

43. Thomas E. Williams, "The Dependent Children in Mississippi: A Social History, 1900–1972" (Ph.D. dissertation, Ohio State University, 1976), 49–67, 93.

44. Ibid., 45–113, 273–287. EMIC in Mississippi was "an unqualified success," according to Williams.

45. William F. Lisenby, "An Administrative History of Public Programs for Dependent Children in North Carolina, Virginia, Tennessee, and Kentucky, 1900–1942" (Ph.D. dissertation, Vanderbilt University, 1962).

46. Bell, *Aid to Dependent Children*, 38. Witte, *Development of the Social Security Act*, 167–170, shows, for instance, that the decision to provide matching federal funds to develop state and local child welfare services came about only through compromise. Private child welfare organizations, especially those of the Catholic

Church, feared federal incursions into charitable work. The limiting of federal funds to rural areas reflected a significant fact: most Catholic and private welfare work focused on metropolitan areas. Catholic leaders endorsed the Social Security measure only after its boundaries were certain. As Steiner, *The Children's Cause*, 7–8, puts it, "The rural emphasis was a tag that said 'Think small' "—an axiom that confined federal funds to rural areas until 1958, even though by that time 60 percent of America's children lived in urban settings.

47. Felt, *Hostages of Fortune*, 210–216.

48. Calvin W. Gower, "The Civilian Conservation Corps and American Education: Threat to Local Control?" *History of Education Quarterly* 7 (Spring 1967): 58–70. The educational aspect of the CCC, a New Deal program from 1933 to 1942 that provided jobs in reforestation and related projects for males, ages eighteen to twenty-five, was, of course, a small part of the larger work relief goals of the program. See also Kenneth E. Hendrickson, Jr., "Relief for Youth: The Civilian Conservation Corps and the National Youth Administration in North Dakota," *North Dakota History* 48 (Fall 1981): esp. 17–22, an interesting case study.

49. Lubove, *Struggle for Social Security*, 106.

50. Greenblatt, *Responsibility for Child Care*, 61–64.

51. Trattner, *Crusade for the Children*, 233.

52. Quoted in Sidney Baldwin, *Poverty and Politics: The Rise and Decline of the Farm Security Administration* (Chapel Hill: University of North Carolina Press, 1968).

53. Richard Wertz and Dorothy Wertz, *Lying-In: A History of Childbirth in America* (New York: Free Press, 1977), esp. 133, 136–143.

54. Richard A. Bolt, "Progress in Saving Maternal and Child Life," *Annals of the American Academy of Political and Social Science* 212 (November 1940): 98.

55. Elizabeth W. Etheridge, *The Butterfly Caste, A Social History of Pellagra in The South* (Westport, Conn.: Greenwood Press, 1972), 131, 206–217; James Bordley III and A. McGehee Harvey, *Two Centuries of American Medicine, 1776–1976* (Philadelphia: W. B. Saunders, 1976), 505–507, 646–653. Also useful regarding the spread of children's health care is William C. Richards and William J. Norton, *Biography of a Foundation: The Story of the Children's Fund of Michigan, 1929–1954* (Detroit: Children's Fund of Michigan, 1957). The book discusses such examples as pediatric clinics and oral hygiene programs that grew out of the Children's Fund, established by Michigan Senator James Couzens "to promote the health, welfare, happiness and development of the children of the state of Michigan primarily, and elsewhere in the world." James N. Giglio, "Voluntarism and Public Policy Between World War I and the New Deal: Herbert Hoover and the American Child Health Association," *Presidential Studies Quarterly* 13 (Summer 1983): esp. 443–448, assesses the limits and contributions of Hoover's efforts in behalf of child health.

56. Laetitia M. Conrad, "Some Effects of Depression on Family Life," *Social Forces* 15 (1936–1937): 76–79.

57. Curiously, Mary Cable's readable, popularly written book, *The Little Darlings*, virtually skips over the era, jumping from John Watson to Benjamin Spock with only brief mention of a subject such as day care.

58. John E. Anderson, "Child Development: An Historical Perspective," *Child*

Development 27 (June 1956): 187; J. P. Shalloo, "Understanding Behavior Problems of Children," *Annals of the American Academy of Political and Social Science* 212 (November 1940): 194–201.

59. Nancy Pottishman Weiss, "Mother, The Invention of Necessity: Dr. Benjamin Spock's *Baby and Child Care*," *American Quarterly* 29 (Winter 1977): 529–531.

60. Daniel Beekman, *The Mechanical Baby: A Popular History of the Theory and Practice of Child Raising* (Westport, Conn.: Lawrence Hill & Co., 1977), 163–165, 189; Aldriches quoted in Bremner, "Families, Children, and the State," 12. (Bremner notes that Aldrich advised Benjamin Spock.) Beekman, a nonspecialist writing for a popular audience, has read widely in primary materials, is attentive to changing historical contexts, and in several chapters provides a very useful discussion of the Depression and war years.

61. Beekman, *Mechanical Baby*, 167–189.

62. David M. Considine, "The Cinema of Adolescence," *Journal of Popular Film and Television* 9 (Fall 1981): 123–126, 128. For a readable discussion of Rooney, Garland, and company, see Norman J. Zierold, *The Child Stars* (New York: Coward-McCann, 1965). The book is not a scholarly effort, but does show through photos and narrative the extensive number of child stars in the 1930s and early 1940s, their film images, and the industry's efforts to hold them up as youthful role models. Somewhat helpful regarding specific films is Ruth M. Goldstein and Edith Zornos, *The Screen Image of Youth: Movies About Children and Adolescents* (Metuchen, N.J.: Scarecrow Press, 1980).

63. Considine, "Cinema of Adolescence," 127–128; quotes from the Rooneys in Zierold, *Child Stars*, 222, 228. The gaps between the Hollywood image and real life were painfully clear in one screen magazine which reported that "off screen Judy (Garland) and Mickey (Rooney) are normal, happy young people who enjoy the sort of thing that the kid around the corner likes." For Rooney, as Zierold observes (p. 126), "Twenty years later, with the wreckage of half a dozen broken marriages strewn along the road, it didn't look that way." Nor were things much happier for Garland.

64. S. Alexander Rippa, "Retrenchment in a Period of Defensive Opposition to the New Deal: The Business Community and the Public Schools, 1932–1934," *History of Education Quarterly* 2 (June 1962): 76–82.

65. Paul C. Violas, "The Indoctrination Debate and the Great Depression," *The History Teacher* 4 (May 1971): 25–35.

66. Lawrence A. Cremin, *The Transformation of the School: Progressivism in American Education, 1876–1957* (New York: Alfred A. Knopf, 1961), esp. 306–308, 324, 328.

67. Edward A. Krug, *The Shaping of the American High School, 1920–1941* (Madison: University of Wisconsin Press, 1972), esp. xiii–xiv, 201–255, 275.

68. Cremin, *Transformation of the School*, 324–327; also Krug, *Shaping of the American High School*, 340–351, and I. L. Kandel, *The Impact of the War Upon American Education* (Chapel Hill: University of North Carolina Press, 1941; reprinted, Westport, Conn.: Greenwood Press, 1974), 4.

69. Richard M. Ugland, " 'Education for Victory': The High School Victory Corps and Curricular Adaptation During World War II," *History of Education Quarterly* 19 (Winter 1979): 435–451. Hopkins's and Toledo superintendent's

quotes in Thomas C. Connelly, "Education for Victory: Federal Efforts to Promote War-Related Instructional Activities by Public School Systems, 1940–45" (Ph.D. dissertation, University of Maryland, 1982), 168, 173. Connelly is very useful regarding the expanded role of schools during the war. For similar trends in Michigan, see Alan Clive, *State of War: Michigan in World War II* (Ann Arbor: University of Michigan Press, 1979), 203–205.

70. This is Ugland's point in " 'Education for Victory,' " 435–451. Kandel, *Impact of the War Upon American Education*, 78, 93, believes nonetheless that the war "threw the balance in favor of vocational education."

71. Connelly, "Education for Victory," 172.

72. Kandel, *Impact of the War Upon American Education*, esp. 5, 8, 65–66, 75–275. Ugland, " 'Education for Victory,' " is also helpful on this theme.

73. Ronald Lora, "Education: Schools as Crucible in Cold War America," in Bremner and Reichard, eds., *Reshaping America*, 223–226.

74. Violas, "Indoctrination Debate and the Great Depression," 25, admits that "although the debate was heated and seemed important, no one knows whether it had any influence on practices in the schools." In Michigan, for example, according to Clive, *State of War*, 117, "one-sixth of the state's rural school districts closed entirely in 1943 for lack of personnel."

75. Connelly, " 'Education for Victory,' " 14–18, leaves little doubt about the innate conservatism, lack of curiosity, and provincialism of most school officials and teachers during the era.

76. David B. Tyack, *The One Best System: A History of American Urban Education* (Cambridge, Mass.: Harvard University Press, 1974), 228.

77. Malcolm X, *The Autobiography of Malcolm X* (New York: Grove Press, 1965), 35–36.

78. Betty and Ernest K. Lindley, *A New Deal for Youth: The Story of the National Youth Administration* (New York: Viking Press, 1938), 193, 196–199.

79. Robert S. Lynd and Helen Merrell Lynd, *Middletown in Transition: A Study in Cultural Conflicts* (New York: Harcourt, Brace, 1937), 204–241.

80. Steven Schlossman, *Love and the American Delinquent: The Theory and Practice of "Progressive" Juvenile Justice, 1825–1920* (Chicago: University of Chicago Press, 1977); Peter Prescott, *The Child Savers: Juvenile Justice Observed* (New York: Alfred A. Knopf, 1981); David J. Rothman, *Conscience and Convenience: The Asylum and Its Alternatives in Progressive America* (Boston: Little, Brown & Co., 1980), 379–421. In this respect, perhaps the most informative work concerning the Depression years and juvenile justice is Justine Wise Polier, *Everyone's Children, Nobody's Child: A Judge Looks at Underprivileged Children in the United States* (New York: Charles Scribners's Sons, 1941), 81–207. Polier was Children's Court Judge of the Domestic Relations Court of New York at the time, and she offered firsthand observations of actual cases from a viewpoint that was sympathetic to the children.

81. Benedict S. Alper, "Progress in Prevention of Juvenile Delinquency," *Annals of the American Academy of Political and Social Science* 212 (November 1940): 202, 208.

82. See, for example, Michael Gordon, *Juvenile Delinquency in the American Novel, 1905–1965: A Study in the Sociology of Literature* (Bowling Green, Ohio: Bowling Green University Press, 1971), 30–32.

83. Alper, "Progress in Prevention of Juvenile Delinquency," 205–206.

84. Ellen Ryerson, *The Best-Laid Plans: America's Juvenile Court Experiment* (New York: Hill & Wang, 1978), 120–145.

85. Richard M. Ugland, "The Adolescent Experience During World War II: Indianapolis as a Case Study" (Ph.D. dissertation, University of Indiana, 1977), 415.

86. See, for example, Francis E. Merrill, *Social Problems on the Home Front, A Study of War-time Influences* (New York: Harper, 1948), 108–109.

87. Ugland, "Adolescent Experience During World War II," 226, 230, 235, 241.

88. Theodore Sellin, "Child Delinquency," *Annals of the American Academy of Political and Social Science* 229 (September 1943): 157–159.

89. Robert J. Havighurst and H. Gerthon Morgan, *The Social History of a War-Boom Community* (New York: Longman, Green & Co., 1951), 290.

90. Merrill, *Social Problems on the Home Front*, 145–168; also 80–82, 108–109. Ugland, "The Adolescent Experience During World War II," 230, agrees that the delinquency statistics were confusing and "did not justify sweeping generalizations about delinquency." A study of delinquency in Michigan in 1944 concluded, in Alan Clive's words, "that youth crime per capita was no higher in the 1940–43 period than it was during the boom years, 1926–29." Clive, *State of War*, 208–209.

91. Eleanor S. Boll, "The Child," *Annals of the American Academy of Political and Social Science* 229 (September 1943): 70–71, 73.

92. J. Frederick MacDonald, " 'Hot Jazz,' the Jitterbug, and Misunderstanding: The Generation Gap in Swing 1935–1945," *Popular Music and Society* 2 (Fall 1972): 43–49.

93. Ibid., 50–51.

94. Gilman M. Ostrander, *American Civilization in the First Machine Age: 1890–1940* (New York: Harper & Row, 1970), esp. 2, 9–13, 176–196, 237–273, 253–261; Lynd and Lynd, *Middletown in Transition*, 233. Social commentator Roy Helton, writing in 1940, hardly agreed that filiarchal authority had lost ground. Children, he complained, had too much power. "We allow them to direct our taste in amusement, to control our time, and to determine our outlays." Helton, "Are We Doing Too Much for Our Children?" *Annals of the American Academy of Political and Social Science* 212 (November 1940). 233.

95. Landon Jones, *Great Expectations: America and the Baby Boom Generation* (softbound ed., New York: Ballantine Books, 1980), 29–30, 211–212, 372.

96. Oscar and Mary Handlin, *Facing Life: Youth and Family in American History* (Boston: Little, Brown & Co., 1971), is extremely impressionistic and sketchy on the post-1930 era, containing only several paragraphs on the Depression and war. Louis Filler, *Vanguards and Followers: Youth in the American Tradition* (Chicago: Nelson-Hall, 1978), has material on the period but discusses individuals—in their twenties and thirties—who were youthful only in a very special sense. Joseph F. Kett, *Rites of Passage: Adolescence in America 1790 to the Present* (New York: Basic Books, 1977), is illuminating regarding the experiences of young people in earlier eras, but tails off quickly after the 1920s. Kett does stress (265) that "a dramatic change...occurred in the experience of adolescence between 1930

and 1970, for in those decades the age group primarily affected by the institutions and subculture of youth dropped and contracted."

97. Glen H. Elder, Jr., *Children of the Great Depression; Social Change in Life Experience* (Chicago: University of Chicago Press, 1974), xvi–xvii, xxi, 5–6, 275. Some of the families, of course, felt the effects of the Depression far more than others.

98. Ibid., 28, 64–65, 79, 114–115, 278–279.

99. Ibid., 36, 53–54, 281, 286–287, 295. Elder's emphasis.

100. Frank F. Furstenberg's review of Elder's book, *American Journal of Sociology* 81 (November 1975): 647–652.

101. Elder, *Children of the Great Depression*, 16, 284.

102. For helpful insights into one of those groups, see E. Franklin Frazier, *Negro Youth at the Crossways: Their Personality Development in the Middle States* (Washington, D.C.: American Council on Education, 1940), one of several studies of black children sponsored in the 1930s by the American Youth Commission. Frazier's book includes extensive interviews with black youths.

103. Arthur Prager, *Rascals at Large, or, The Clue in the Old Nostalgia* (Garden City, N.Y.: Doubleday, 1971), is a breezy account of the print culture that Prager, "a member of the generation that fell between the sharp pincers of the Depression on one side and World War II on the other," recalls with affection. Good information on children's radio programs is scattered throughout J. Fred MacDonald, *Don't Touch That Dial! Radio Programming in American Life from 1920 to 1960* (Chicago: Nelson-Hall, 1980).

104. James Borchert, *Alley Life in Washington: Family, Community, Religion, and Folklife in the City, 1850–1970* (Urbana: University of Illinois Press), 150–152.

105. Ibid., 152–165.

106. See, for example, Mary M. Shirley, "Children's Part in War," *Smith College Studies in Social Work* 14 (September 1943): 15–23.

107. Richard M. Ugland, "Viewpoints and Morale of Urban High School Students During World War II—Indianapolis as a Case Study," *Indiana Magazine of History* 77 (June 1981): 150–178.

108. Ugland, "Adolescent Experience During World War II," 4, 10, 13–14, 19, 248–249, 288–290, 410; re "canteens," 313–337; re *Seventeen*, 354, 380–391.

109. Ibid., 8–9; Clive, *State of War*, 176–177, 181–182. A notable fictional treatment of a transplanted Kentucky family living in Detroit at the end of World War II, Harriette Arnow's *The Dollmaker* (1954) is provocative in this respect. Author and literary critic Joyce Carol Oates "can think of no other work except Christian Stead's *The Man Who Loved Children* that deals so brilliantly and movingly with the lives of children." Oates's afterword to Arnow, *The Dollmaker* (Softbound ed., New York: Avon Books, 1972), 606.

110. Robert J. Hastings, *A Nickel's Worth of Skim Milk, A Boy's View of the Great Depression* (Carbondale: Southern Illinois University Press, 1972).

111. Russell Baker, *Growing Up* (New York: Congdon & Weed, 1982), 42.

112. Malcolm X, *The Autobiography of Malcolm X*, 9–22.

113. Hastings, *Nickel's Worth of Skim Milk*, 22.

114. Maya Angelou, *I Know Why the Caged Bird Sings* (Softbound ed., New York: Bantam Books, 1969), 1–3, 20–27, 40.

115. Quoted in Studs Terkel, *Hard Times, An Oral History of the Depression* (Softbound ed., New York: Avon Books, 1970), 71–75.

116. Prager, *Rascals at Large*, 8–9; the alley girl's poem quoted in Borchert, *Alley Life in Washington*, 154.

BIBLIOGRAPHY

Abbott, Edith, ed. *Public Assistance: American Principles and Policies.* Vol. 1, Chicago, University of Chicago Press, 1940.

Alper, Benedict S. "Progress in Prevention of Juvenile Delinquency." *Annals of the American Academy of Political and Social Science* 212 (November 1940): 202–208.

Anderson, John E. "Child Development: An Historical Perspective." *Child Development* 27 (June 1956): 181–196.

Angelou, Maya. *I Know Why the Caged Bird Sings.* Softbound ed., New York: Bantam Books, 1969.

Arnow, Harriette. *The Dollmaker.* Softbound ed., New York: Avon Books, 1972.

Atkinson, Mary Irene. "Child Welfare Work in Rural Communities." *Annals of the American Academy of Political and Social Science* 212 (November 1940): 209–215.

Baker, Russell. *Growing Up.* New York: Congdon & Weed, 1982.

Baldwin, Sidney. *Poverty and Politics: The Rise and Decline of the Farm Security Administration.* Chapel Hill: University of North Carolina Press, 1968.

Beekman, Daniel. *The Mechanical Baby: A Popular History of the Theory and Practice of Child Raising.* Westport, Conn.: Lawrence Hill & Co., 1977.

Bell. Winifred. *Aid to Dependent Children.* New York: Columbia University Press, 1965.

Bell, Eleanor S. "The Child." *Annals of the American Academy of Political and Social Science* 229 (September 1943): 69–78.

Bolt, Richard A. "Progress in Saving Maternal and Child Life." *Annals of the American Academy of Political and Social Science* 212 (November 1940): 97–104.

Borchert, James. *Alley Life in Washington: Family, Community, Religion, and Folklife in the City, 1850–1970.* Urbana: University of Illinois Press, 1980.

Bordley, James, III, and Harvey, A. McGehee. *Two Centuries of American Medicine, 1776–1976.* Philadelphia: W. B. Saunders, 1976.

Bradbury, Dorothy E. *Five Decades of Action for Children: A History of the Children's Bureau.* Washington, D.C.: U.S. Government Printing Office, 1962.

Breckinridge, Sophonisba P. "Government's Role in Child Welfare." *Annals of the American Academy of Political and Social Science* 212 (November 1940): 42–50.

Bremner, Robert H. "Families, Children, and the State." In *Reshaping America: Society and Institutions, 1945–1960,* edited by Robert H. Bremner and Gary W. Reichard. Columbus: Ohio State University Press, 1982, 3–32.

Brown, Josephine C. *Public Relief, 1929–1939.* New York: Henry Holt & Co., 1940.

Cable, Mary. *The Little Darlings, A History of Child Rearing in America.* New York: Charles Scribner's Sons, 1975.

Chafe, William H. *The American Woman, Her Changing Social, Economic, and Political Roles, 1920–1970.* New York: Oxford University Press, 1972.

Clive, Alan. *State of War: Michigan in World War II.* Ann Arbor: University of Michigan Press, 1979.

Connelly, Thomas C. "Education for Victory: Federal Efforts to Promote War-Related Instructional Activities by Public School Systems, 1940–45." Ph.D. dissertation, University of Maryland, 1982.

Conrad, Laetitia M. "Some Effects of the Depression on Family Life." *Social Forces* 15 (1936–1937): 76–81.

Considine, David M. "The Cinema of Adolescence." *Journal of Popular Film and Television* 9 (Fall 1981): 123–136.

Cremin, Lawrence A. *The Transformation of the School: Progressivism in American Education, 1876–1957.* New York: Alfred A. Knopf, 1961.

Dratch, Howard. "The Politics of Day Care in the 1940s." *Science and Society* 38 (Summer 1974): 167–204.

Elder, Glen H., Jr. *Children of the Great Depression; Social Change in Life Experience.* Chicago: University of Chicago Press, 1974.

Etheridge, Elizabeth W. *The Butterfly Caste, A Social History of Pellagra in the South.* Westport, Conn.: Greenwood Press, 1972.

Felt, Jeremy. "The Child Labor Provisions of the Fair Labor Standards Act." *Labor History* 11 (Fall 1970): 467–481.

———. *Hostages of Fortune: Child Labor Reform in New York State.* Syracuse: Syracuse University Press, 1965.

Filler, Louis. *Vanguards and Followers: Youth in the American Tradition.* Chicago: Nelson-Hall, 1978.

Frazier, E. Franklin. *Negro Youth at the Crossways: Their Personality Development in the Middle States.* Washington, D.C.: American Council on Education, 1940.

Fuller, Raymond G. "Child Labor—Continued." *Annals of the American Academy of Political and Social Science* 212 (November 1940): 146–152.

Furstenberg, Frank F., Jr. "Review Essay." *American Journal of Sociology* 81 (November 1975): 647–652.

Giglio, James N. "Voluntarism and Public Policy Between World War I and the New Deal: Herbert Hoover and the American Child Health Association." *Presidential Studies Quarterly* 13 (Summer 1983): 430–452.

Goldstein, Ruth M., and Zornos, Edith. *The Screen Image of Youth: Movies About Children and Adolescents.* Metuchen, N.J.: Scarecrow Press, 1980.

Gordon, Michael. *Juvenile Delinquency in the American Novel, 1905–1965: A Study in the Sociology of Literature.* Bowling Green, Ohio: Bowling Green University Press, 1971.

Gower, Calvin W. "The Civilian Conservation Corps and American Education: Threat to Local Control?" *History of Education Quarterly* 7 (Spring 1967): 58–70.

Greenblatt, Bernard. *Responsibility for Child Care.* San Francisco: Jossey-Bass Publishers, 1977.

Grubb, W. Norton, and Marvin Lazerson, *Broken Promises: How Americans Fail Their Children* (New York: Basic Books, 1982).

Handlin, Oscar, and Mary Handlin, *Facing Life: Youth and Family in American History* (Boston: Little, Brown, 1971).

Hastings, Robert J., *A Nickel's Worth of Skim Milk, A Boy's View of the Great Depression* (Carbondale: Southern Illinois Univ. Press, 1972).

Havighurst, Robert J., and H. Gerthon Morgan, *The Social History of a War-Boom Community* (New York: Longman, Green & Co., 1951).

Helton, Roy, "Are We doing Too Much for Our Children?" *The Annals of the American Academy of Political and Social Science*, 212 (November, 1940), 231–40.

Hendrickson, Kenneth E., Jr., "Relief for Youth: The Civilian Conservation Corps and the National Youth Administration in North Dakota," *North Dakota History*, 48 (Fall, 1981), 17–27.

Jones, Landon, *Great Expectations: America and the Baby Boom Generation* (softbound ed., New York: Ballantine Books, 1980).

Kadushin, Alfred, *Child Welfare Services* (2d ed., New York: Macmillan, 1974).

Kandel, I. L., *The Impact of the War Upon American Education* (Chapel Hill: Univ. of North Carolina Press, 1941; reprinted, Westport, CT: Greenwood Press, 1974).

Kett, Joseph F., *Rites of Passage: Adolescence in America 1790 to the Present* (New York: Basic Books, 1977).

Krug, Edward A., *The Shaping of the American High School, 1920–1941* (Madison: Univ. of Wisconsin Press, 1972).

Leff, Mark H., "Consensus for Reform: The Mothers'-Pension Movement in the Progressive Era," *Social Service Review*, 47 (September, 1973), 397–417.

Lenroot, Katharine F., "Child Welfare, 1930–40," *The Annals* of the American Academy of Political and Social Science, 212 (November, 1940), 1–11.

Lindley, Betty, and Ernest K. Lindley, *A New Deal for Youth: The Story of the National Youth Administration* (New York: Viking Press, 1938).

Lisenby, William F., "An Administrative History of Public Programs for Dependent Children in North Carolina, Virginia, Tennessee, and Kentucky, 1900–1942 (Ph.D. dissertation, Vanderbilt Univ., 1962).

Lora, Ronald, "Education: Schools as Crucible in Cold War America," in Robert H. Bremner and Gary W. Reichard (eds.), *Reshaping America: Society and Institutions, 1945–1960* (Columbus: Ohio State Univ. Press, 1982), pp. 223–60.

Lubove, Roy, *The Struggle for Social Security, 1900–1935* (Cambridge: Harvard Univ. Press, 1968).

Lundberg, Emma Octavia, *Unto the Least of These: Social Services for Children* (New York: Appleton-Century-Crofts, Inc., 1947).

Lynd, Robert S., and Helen Merrell Lynd, *Middletown in Transition: A Study in Cultural Conflicts* (New York: Harcourt, Brace, 1937).

MacDonald, J. Fred, *Don't Touch That Dial! Radio Programming in American Life, from 1920 to 1960* (Chicago: Nelson-Hall, 1980).

———, "'Hot Jazz,' the Jitterbug, and Misunderstanding: The Generation Gap in Swing 1935–1945," *Popular Music and Society*, 2 (Fall, 1972), 43–55.

Magee, Elizabeth, S., "Impact of the War on Child Labor," *The Annals* of the American Academy of Political and Social Science, 236 (November, 1944), 101–09.

Malcolm X, *The Autobiography of Malcolm X* (New York: Grove Press, 1965).

McAhren, Robert W., "Making the Nation Safe for Childhood: A History of the

Movement for Federal Regulation of Child Labor" (Ph.D. dissertation, Univ. of Texas, 1967).

McConnell, Beatrice, "Child Labor in Agriculture," *The Annals* of the American Academy of Political and Social Science, 236 (November, 1944), 92–100.

Merrill, Francis E., *Social Problems on the Home Front, A Study of War-time Influences* (New York: Harper, 1948).

Morlock, Maud, *Homemaker Services, History and Bibliography* (Washington D.C.: Government Printing Office, 1964).

Moran, Robert E., "The History of Child Welfare in Louisiana, 1850–1960" (Ph.D. dissertation, Ohio State Univ., 1968).

Ostrander, Gilman M., *American Civilization in the First Machine Age: 1890–1940* (New York: Harper & Row, 1970).

Pangburn, Weaver W., "Play and Recreation," *The Annals* of the American Academy of Political and Social Science, 212 (November, 1940), 121–29.

Patterson, James T., *America's Struggle Against Poverty, 1900–1980* (Cambridge: Harvard Univ. Press, 1981).

Patti, Rino J., "Child Protection in California 1850–1966: An Analysis of Public Policy" (Ph.D. dissertation, Univ. of Southern California, 1967).

Polenberg, Richard, *War and Society: The United States, 1941–1945* (Philadelphia: Lippincott, 1972).

Polier, Justine Wise, *Everyone's Children, Nobody's Child: A Judge Looks at Under-privileged Children in the United States* (New York: Charles Scribner's Sons, 1941).

Prager, Arthur, *Rascals at Large, or, The Clue in the Old Nostalgia* (Garden City, NY: Doubleday, 1971).

Prescott, Peter, *The Child Savers: Juvenile Justice Observed* (New York: Knopf, 1981).

Reller, Theodore L., "The School and Child Welfare," *The Annals* of the American Academy of Political and Social Science, 212 (November, 1940), 51–58.

Richards, William C., and William J. Norton, *Biography of a Foundation: The Story of the Children's Fund of Michigan, 1929–1954* (Children's Fund of Michigan, 1957).

Rippa, S. Alexander, "Retrenchment in a Period of Defensive Opposition to the New Deal: The Business Community and the Public Schools, 1932–1934," *History of Education Quarterly*, 2 (June, 1962), 76–82.

Rothman, David J., *Conscience and Convenience: The Asylum and Its Alternatives in Progressive America* (Boston: Little, Brown, 1980).

Rothman, Sheila, "Other People's Children: The Day Care Experience in America," *The Public Interest*, 30 (Winter, 1973), 11–27.

———, *Woman's Proper Place: A History of Changing Ideals and Practices, 1870 to the Present* (New York: Basic Books, 1978).

Ryerson, Ellen, *The Best-Laid Plans: America's Juvenile Court Experiment* (New York: Hill & Wang, 1978).

Schlossman, Stephen, *Love and the American Delinquent: The Theory and Practice of "Progressive" Juvenile Justice, 1825–1920* (Chicago: Univ. of Chicago Press, 1977).

Sellin, Theodore, "Child Delinquency." *The Annals* of the American Academy of Political and Social Science, 229 (September, 1943), 157–63.

Shalloo, J. P., "Understanding Behavior Problems of Children," *The Annals* of the American Academy of Political and Social Science, 212 (November, 1940), 194–201.

Shirley, Mary M., "Children's Part in War," *Smith College Studies in Social Work*, 14 (September, 1943), 15–23.

Sinai, Nathan, and Anderson, Odin W. *EMIC (Emergency Maternity and Infant Care): A Study of Administrative Experience*. Ann Arbor: School of Public Health, University of Michigan, 1948.

Skold, Karen Beck. "Women Workers and Child Care During World War II: A Case Study of the Portland, Oregon, Shipyard." Ph.D. dissertation, University of Oregon, 1981.

Steiner, Gilbert Y. *The Children's Cause*. Washington, D.C.: Brookings Institution, 1976.

———. *Social Insecurity: The Politics of Welfare*. Chicago: Rand McNally, 1966.

Steinfels, Margaret O'Brien. *Who's Minding the Children? The History and Politics of Day Care in America*. New York: Simon & Schuster, 1973.

Stevens, Rosemary. *American Medicine and the Public Interest*. New Haven: Yale University Press, 1971.

Suransky, Valerie Polakow. "A Tyranny of Experts." *Wilson Quarterly* 6 (Autumn 1982): 53–60.

Taft, Charles P. "Public Health and the Family in World War II." *Annals of the American Academy of Political and Social Science* 229 (September 1943): 145–149.

Takanishi, Ruby. "Federal Involvement in Early Education (1933–1973): The Need for Historical Perspectives." In *Current Topics in Early Childhood Education*. Edited by Lilian G. Katz, pp. 139–163 Vol. 1, Norwood, N.J.: Ablex Publishing Corp., 1977.

Terkel, Studs. *Hard Times, An Oral History of the Depression*. Softbound ed., New York: Avon Books, 1970.

Trattner, Walter I. *Crusade for the Children: A History of the National Child Labor Committee and Child Labor Reform in America*. Chicago: Quadrangle Books, 1970.

———. *From Poor Law to Welfare State: A History of Social Welfare in America*. 2d ed., New York: Free Press, 1979.

Tyack, David B. *The One Best System: A History of American Urban Education*. Cambridge, Mass.: Harvard University Press, 1974.

Tyson, Helen Glenn, "Care of Dependent Children," *The Annals* of the American Academy of Political and Social Science, 212 (November, 1940), 168–78.

Ugland, Richard M., " 'Education for Victory' " The High School Victory Crops and Curricular Adaptation During World War II," *History of Education Quarterly*, 19 (Winter 1979), 435–51.

———, "The Adolescent Experience During World War II: Indianapolis as a Case Study" (Ph.D. dissertation: Indiana Univ., 1977).

———, "Viewpoints and Morale of Urban High School Students During World War II—Indianapolis as a Case Study," *Indiana Magazine of History*, 77 (June, 1981), 150–78.

Violas, Paul C., "The Indoctrination Debate and the Great Depression," *The History Teacher*, 4 (May, 1971), 25–35.

Weiss, Nancy Pottishman, "Mother, The Invention of Necessity: Dr. Benjamin Spock's *Baby and Child Care*," *American Quarterly*, 29 (Winter, 1977), 519–546.

Wertz, Richard, and Dorothy Wertz, *Lying-In: A History of Childbirth in America* (New York: Free Press, 1977).

Williams, Thomas E., "The Dependent Child in Mississippi: A Social History, 1900–1972" (Ph.D. dissertation, Ohio State Univ., 1976).

Witte, Edwin E., *The Development of the Social Security Act* (Madison: Univ. of Wisconsin Press, 1962).

Zeitz, Dorothy, *Child Welfare, Principles and Methods* (New York: John Wiley & Sons, 1959).

Zierold, Norman J., *The Child Stars* (New York: Coward-McCann, 1965).

Zimand, Gertrude Folks, "The Changing Picture of Child Labor," *The Annals* of the American Academy of Political and Social Science, 236 (November, 1944), 83–91.

13

The Baby Boom, Prosperity, and the Changing Worlds of Children, 1945-1963

Charles E. Strickland
Andrew M. Ambrose

THE GENERATION OF THE BABY BOOM

The generation that grew up following World War II was unique in American history, for these were the years of the "baby boom."[1] In just eighteen years after the war, the population had increased more than it had in the fifty years preceding 1946. Most of this increase was due to the phenomenal birth rate. To the surprise of everyone, including the demographic experts, American mothers had reversed an historic trend of downward birth rates, which had reached a low of 18 per 1,000 population in the years 1930–1940. By 1957, the peak year of the baby boom, the rate had soared to 25 per 1,000 population, the highest since 1920.[2]

The sheer size of the baby boom gave a distinctive shape to the experience of the children and youth who made it up, although, as we shall see, there is considerable debate about the exact nature of those consequences. One might argue, for example, that the children of the baby boom were the most favored in the history of the nation.[3] Certainly, with some notable exceptions, they were the most affluent, for they came of age during the most sustained period of prosperity in American history, lasting twenty years after the war, with minor interruptions.[4] What prosperity meant was that by 1955 America, with only 6 percent of the world's population, was producing nearly two-thirds of the world's goods, while consuming one-third of the world's goods and services.[5] One consequence of prosperity was that the children of the postwar era were (again with notable exceptions) the healthiest, best-fed, best-clothed, and best-housed generation the nation had seen. During the postwar period, modern medicine won spectacular victories over disease, the most dramatic being the development of the Salk polio vaccine in 1955.[6]

But if this generation was the healthiest, was it the best reared and the best educated? As this chapter shows, the picture is much more complex and controversial. Families and schools underwent significant changes during the period. In addition, the postwar years witnessed important shifts in the nature of community life, while schools were plagued by problems arising from the Cold War. New forms of mass communication arose, notably television, and it seemed that the peer group was acquiring new power over the lives of the young, especially of teenagers. Scholars are still attempting to sort out the immediate and long-range consequences of these changes in the patterns of childhood and youth during the postwar period. The period might be viewed as the golden age of American childhood, but it seemed that prosperity also held perils for the young. In any event, not all American children and youth enjoyed the benefits of affluence.

However one assesses the impact of postwar society on the young, it should be emphasized that it was not, by any means, a one-way street. If society affected the young, it is also true that children and youth of the baby boom years wielded a powerful influence on society. It fact, it may be that the baby boom generation, because of its sheer size, left a greater mark on the life of the nation than any comparable age group in American history. The young altered in particular the behavior of adults involved in family life, schooling, the mass media, and the industries that catered to their needs and wishes. Moreover, the influence of the baby boom generation did not cease when they left behind childhood and adolescence. As young adults, they contributed to the upheavals of the 1960s; it is difficult to imagine the Civil Rights Movement, the controversy over Vietnam, or the emergence of the "counterculture" without the participation of those who came of age in the period following World War II. Their activities provide particularly dramatic proof of the importance of the history of childhood and youth to an understanding of other events in American history.

What follows, then, is a survey and tentative assessment of the way America shaped its children and youth in these years and how they, in turn, shaped America. Particular attention will be paid to families (both within and without the prosperous "mainstream"), to schools, to the mass media, and to the peer group—those institutions that constituted the worlds of childhood during the period. Throughout, attention will also be paid to the interrelations of these institutions, as the young frequently found themselves the victims or beneficiaries of conflict or cooperation between parents, teachers, peers, and the media.

Of necessity, the picture presented will be not only complex—as benefits the subject—but also incomplete, for historians have only begun to tell the story of the 1950s and the early 1960s, and still fewer historians have fixed their sights on the experience of the young during the period.[7]

Even the few historical accounts available focus on such readily accessible evidence as public policy about children and published advice to parents and teachers, leaving the actual experience of children neglected. Consequently, many of the sources for a history of childhood are still what might be called "primary"—documents left by those who were themselves young during the period or by those adults who witnessed and commented on the treatment of children and youth.[8]

THE SOURCES OF THE BABY BOOM

Understanding the experience of the young requires an understanding of their parents and of their motivation for bringing children into the world. Two centuries of declining fertility rates made it evident that American couples could limit reproduction if they chose to do so, but why did this postwar generation of Americans decide to reverse historic trends? Why, in other words, did these postwar parents create the baby boom?

One obvious explanation is pent-up demand: the soaring birth rate represented the desire of Americans to have babies, after fifteen years of economic deprivation and war.[9] Certainly, it seems that the initial surge of births after 1945 represented in part the determination of returning veterans to embrace the joys and sorrows of family life, for, after all, they had been told repeatedly during the war that they were fighting for a peaceful world of domesticity. Just as Detroit promised these men that "there's a Ford in your future," so did it seem that the entire culture promised them a home populated by wife and children. Women, too, looked to the cessation of hostilities as a chance to realize long-deferred personal goals. From 1940 to 1950, the sharpest gains in fertility were by those women over the age of thirty-five, women who had come of age during the Great Depression, and who had been forced to postpone parenthood.[10] This resurgence of familistic values was anticipated by popular wartime songs that expressed yearning for a domestic world free of turmoil, death, and destruction.[11]

The thesis that Americans were simply having babies long deferred is persuasive, but only to a point. The thesis adequately explains the initial phase of the baby boom, during which births rose in 1946 and subsided in 1948, prompting demographic experts to predict that Americans, having caught up in their urge to reproduce, would now resume historic trends toward fewer and fewer babies.[12] This was, in fact, what happened in Western Europe, which experienced its own boomlet in the immediate postwar years.[13] Americans, on the other hand, revived their boom in 1951 and set it off toward new heights. Clearly, more was at work than pent-up demand. Landon Jones has taken a close look at the demographic data, and what he found was that it was not simply the returning veterans and older women who were choosing parenthood. The baby boom represented rather a more basic shift—involving an increase in the proportion of Americans marrying, a decline in the number of childless marriages, a decline in the age at which women married and bore their first child, and a decline in the number of marriages with only one child.[14] The increased popularity of marriage itself was significant because, in a culture that still condemned illegitimate childbirth, marriage was for most a prerequisite for pregnancy. More important, however, was the fact that women were marrying younger and having children younger. The median age of marriage for women dropped from 21.5 in 1940 to 20.1 in 1956.[15] The interval between marriage and first child dropped to 13 months on the average, while more than half of first-time brides gave birth to their first child before they were 20.[16] These trends shattered historical precedent and set the stage for a higher fertility rate.

But what, precisely, motivated more Americans—both older and younger—to have children? Here the picture is less clear. One factor might have been the lack of convenient methods of birth control, because the contraceptive pill did not appear on the market until 1960. Moreover, the Supreme Court had not yet struck down state laws banning abortion. Obviously, however, the laws and the state of contraceptive technology were only indirectly relevant to the baby boom, because couples lived under the same restrictions during the 1930s. More likely causes were postwar economic prosperity and the resurgence of popular attitudes favoring childbirth. Of all factors singled out by scholars in explaining the boom, prosperity is the most popular. As Landon Jones has argued, prosperity made American couples both more careless in the present and more optimistic about the future.[17] A sense of economic security might have accounted especially for the appearance of third and fourth babies, many of whom were probably not planned for.[18] After all, birth control requires some deliberate effort, and prosperity might have made the effort not really worthwhile.

Still, economic prosperity alone could not explain the baby boom, for how can one account for the fact that the boom cut across all income groups? The highest fertility rates were, in fact, found among poor Indians and Southern blacks.[19] Consequently, any adequate explanation of the baby boom must take into account what men and women valued and the way they perceived their roles. Society's conception of woman's place is critically relevant here, and there seems little doubt that the postwar period witnessed a resurgence of a traditional emphasis on woman's role as a mother. Variously described as "the feminine mystique," "familism," "pro-natalism," and the "procreation ethic," this cluster of values represented a repudiation of feminist ideology.[20] One of the most influential books of the period, *Modern Woman: the Lost Sex*, appeared in

1947 and launched a strident attack on women who placed careers above motherhood. Ferdinand Lundberg, a free-lance writer, and Marynia Farnham, a psychiatrist, drew heavily on Freudian concepts to argue that women who rejected the role of motherhood were suffering from a malady called "penis envy." Only when such women purged themselves of this sickness, and only when society gave motherhood the respect it was due, would women recover their true identity: "It is the difficulty of having children at the same time enjoying the prestige and psychic well-being that goes with having them as other needs are met that is the prime root of women's psychic problems today."[21]

The glorification of motherhood was not confined to the print media. To be sure, the most popular female film stars of the period were neither mothers nor career women.[22] Rather, they were sex goddesses like Marilyn Monroe or sophisticated (and single) socialites like Grace Kelly and Audrey Hepburn. Still, Hollywood did its share to enhance the image of motherhood, providing Joan Crawford an Oscar-winning role in *Mildred Pierce* as a mother who sacrifices her life for the benefit of an ungrateful daughter. The burgeoning television industry was even more enthusiastic about sympathetic portrayals of mothers, providing a seemingly endless parade of domesticated women in series like "The Goldbergs," "I Remember Mama," and "Ozzie and Harriett."[23] Not so often noticed was the manner in which both film and television featured nurturing fathers, in films like *The Yearling* or *Father of the Bride*, and in television series like "Father Knows Best" and "Leave It to Beaver."[24] Familistic values meant good box office and high ratings during the 1940s and 1950s, which suggests that the media were a faithful reflection of popular attitudes during the period as well as a powerful reinforcement of those attitudes.[25]

It should be noted that those who took the trouble during the 1950s to ask women themselves what they thought of pregnancy and child-rearing came back with the report that most women were enthusiastic about motherhood. Robert Sears and his colleagues reported that half of Boston mothers interviewed were "delighted" with their pregnancy, while another 18 percent were "pleased."[26] Two-thirds of the Detroit women interviewed by Daniel Miller and Guy Swanson in 1953 reported that children represented "very pleasant" experiences for them.[27] John and Ann Fischer, in their study of New England mothers, did not quantify their responses but reported that most women welcomed pregnancy and childbirth.[28] The studies reported, however, some sobering dissent. A minority of women were definitely unhappy with the role of motherhood, and there is some evidence that the unhappiness increased with each child born. Sears reported, for example, that the number of women "delighted" with pregnancy decreased from an average of 62 percent for the first pregnancy to 34 percent for later pregnancies.[29] Among this minority, obviously disillusioned with the Procreation Ethic, was born the seed of the movement that was later to be known as women's liberation, but for the moment, at least, they were a minority without a spokeswoman. The baby boom, for better or worse, was a fact.

THE "CHILD-CENTERED" FAMILY

In one of John Updike's stories of the period, a couple reveal to their children that they are contemplating divorce, which prompts one of the children to cry, "What do you care about us? We're just the little things you had." The father then replies, "You're not the little things we had, You're the whole point."[30] Postwar parents seemed ready to give their children everything, whether or not it was precisely what the children wished at the moment. For many parents, everything meant material things; for others, it meant the advantages of an education; for still others, it meant "permissive" upbringing; for most, it meant at the least that they would give a good deal of thought to their children's needs and interests. Postwar parents chose large families and then placed the welfare of the children at the center of family life. It is this high degree of parental preoccupation with the needs and interests of their children that we have in mind when we use the term "child-centered."[31]

The child-centeredness of postwar American parents has attracted a good deal of comment, most of it negative, and a great deal of it directed toward the book believed responsible, Dr. Benjamin Spock's *The Common Sense Book of Baby and Child Care*.[32] Critics might just as well have singled out the U.S. Children's Bureau publication, *Infant Care*, which gave similar advice, but *Baby and Child Care* has come to stand for the period's ethos.[33] Certainly, there is no doubt about the popularity of Spock's book, which had sold more than 4 million copies within the first six years of its appearance in 1946, but that was only the beginning.[34] Within the next fourteen years it had sold another 14 million copies and had gone through fifty-eight printings. By 1976, and several editions later, 28 million copies had been issued, making it the best-selling book in the twentieth century, next to the Bible. Dr. Spock himself has attempted to explain the popularity of the book by pointing out that it was both cheap and "friendly."[35] Pocketbooks, which was just beginning to exploit the growing market for paperbacks, brought out *Baby and Child Care* for only thirty-five cents and kept the price relatively low in subsequent editions. As for its "friendliness," Dr. Spock meant that he attempted to make the book easy to read, to make it easy to understand, and to fill it with many expressions of solace and reassurance. Spock was also gifted with a sense of the irony and comedy of parent-child relations, which prevented the book from becoming merely a dry set of formulas and commands.[36]

In accounting for the popularity of his book, Dr. Spock may have given himself both too little and too much credit—too little credit because the appeal of the book did not lie alone in its cheapness—too much credit because the popularity of the book cannot be traced alone to Spock's writing, however accessible it proved to be. Rather, it appears likely that the sales of the book benefited as well from a fortuitous convergence between the book and the times. Although Spock claims he did not foresee the baby boom, his book appeared just at its onset, when millions of novice mothers badly needed medical advice, and most undoubtedly used *Baby and Child Care* as a ready reference for health problems rather than as a treatise on childrearing. For those mothers who did give attention to Spock's psychological advice, however, there seemed to have been a remarkable congruity between what the doctor was advising mothers to do and what they were ready to hear.

Spock's advice was "child-centered" in a double sense. First, Spock advised permissiveness in the handling of the child, which was not by any means extreme but which was a significant departure from the most influential expert opinion of the past.[37] More importantly, Dr. Spock implied that proper child care required a good deal of thought and time on the part of both mother and child. Although some feminist scholars have complained that Spock's emphasis on the responsibilities of child care placed entirely too large a burden on women, it was Spock's clear intention to relieve mothers of anxiety in their child care tasks. The inspiration for *Baby and Child Care* came out of Spock's experiences as a pediatrician in New York City during the 1930s, when he advised a succession of affluent and well-educated but hyperconscientious mothers. They read all the latest childrearing advice, but it had the effect of leaving them utterly confused and uncertain. Spock resolved to write a book that would give them good advice but also relieve them of their anxiety, for he believed that the mother's anxiety itself could do more harm to the emotional health of the child than any particular strategy of childrearing.[38]

Spock's permissive advice had little in common with the "child-centered anarchy" that some commentators of the period believed reigned in American homes.[39] It was also evident, however, that a mother who followed Spock's advice could easily make childrearing into a full-time job. It was, after all, much easier simply to ignore the child altogether and allow him to do what he wished, thus producing true anarchy. It was also much easier to follow the more traditional norms of "proper" childrearing, according to which a mother could adhere to rigid, pre-conceived schedules of feeding and toilet training, and, later on, lay down a set of inflexible rules for behavior enforced by superior strength. A Spock-trained mother would also have to give considerably more time and thought to child-rearing, carefully monitoring the child's growth and development and seeking, gently and tactfully, to guide him or her toward becoming a cooperative member of a happy family. As Martha Wolfenstein pointed out in her review of childrearing literature, advice for mother to enjoy her child might be taken as additional duty rather than as an invitation.[40] The *leitmotiv* of *Baby and Child Care* was not, after all, permissiveness, but rather, as Michael Zuckerman has pointed out, the avoidance of conflict.[41] To socialize the child and yet avoid confrontation within the intimate context of family life was the formidable task that Dr. Spock laid on American mothers of the postwar generation.

Whatever heavy responsibility Spock placed on mothers was justified, in his mind, at least, by the goal of creating a more democratic society. In a perceptive analysis, William Graebner has described the intellectual heritage that provided the source of Spock's thinking, a heritage compounded by ideas drawn from Freud, John Dewey, Margaret Mead, Erik Erikson, Kurt Lewin, and Lawrence Frank. Although basically Freudian in his psychological orientation, Spock chose, like many Americans, to strain out the pessimistic elements of Freud's thought and to emphasize, instead, the possibilities of creating a democratic person who was at peace with both self and society. The ultimate result would be, as Graebner points out, a society "more cooperative, more consensus oriented, more group conscious, and a society that was more knowable, more consistent and more comforting." Insofar as childrearing was concerned, the objective was to bring up a child in such a way that he or she felt no need either to submit or to dominate; hence, the stress on flexibility and tactful manipulation, rather than on the pulling of rank. In this sense, says Graebner, Spock was something of a social engineer.[42]

Although it is difficult to prove that Dr. Spock directly influenced postwar parents, there is impressive evidence that mothers were acting as if they had taken his advice to heart. The evidence has surfaced from a remarkable series of investigations by American anthropologists, who turned their attention to their native land, and by American psychologists, who moved out of their laboratories to test their theories about personality development in the natural setting of the family. The studies showed a definite trend, especially evident among middle-class parents, toward a moderate permissiveness in childrearing techniques. Urie Bronfenbrenner, summarizing many of the studies, suggested that a massive change had in fact occurred in the practices of middle-class parents after 1945. Before then, he contends, middle-class mothers were more severe in their demands than mothers of the working class. After 1945, however, the social classes exchanged positions, with the working class now more severe than the middle class.[43] Accompanying the greater permissiveness of the middle class was a rising preoccupation of parents with the psychological welfare of the young. As Max Lerner noted in his massive analysis of postwar American culture, "It is evident that in no other culture has there been so pervasive a cultural anxiety about the rearing of children."[44]

The evidence does not prove that middle-class mothers were coddling their children. Rather, it seems that most of them were adopting what Dr. Spock was recommending; namely, a "common sense" avoidance of extremes as they moved gradually away from a strict tradition. Such at least was the picture presented by Robert Sears and a team of investigators, who conducted a study in 1951–1952 in two communities on the outskirts of Boston. On the bases of interviews with 379 working-class and middle-class mothers, the researchers reported that most mothers were child-centered in the sense that they were responsible caretakers and that they kept their attention "rather continuously (and mainly pleasantly) directed toward the child."[45] In summarizing their findings, Sears and his colleagues suggested that most mothers represented a moderate departure from the tradition of strict infant care, with middle-class mothers more permissive than the working class. The researchers concluded that strict mothers "are living in what is essentially an alien culture."[46]

The inroads made by the child-centered family were most noticeable in the new postwar suburbs, which attracted an extraordinary amount of attention from intellectuals, journalists, and scholars, in large part because the growth of these communities on the outskirts of major American cities was both rapid and dramatic during the period after 1945.[47] The same prosperity that fostered the baby boom also made possible the suburbs, but federal policies also encouraged the development of the new communities. Government-guaranteed mortgages and tax deductions for mortgage interest payments made new homes available to millions with little or nothing down and low monthly payments. Americans were discovering that it was cheaper to buy than to rent. Home ownership doubled between 1940 and 1960, and for the first time more Americans owned than rented.[48] Prosperity, easy credit, and a massive road-building program also increased the number of automobiles, and without the auto, the suburbs would be unthinkable.[49]

It is possible now, with the benefit of hindsight, to sort out some of the facts from the falsehood in what proved to be a decade-long jeremiad against the suburbs.[50] There seems to be general agreement among the investigators, for example, that the new suburbs did feature a uniformity in housing design since the low sale prices required such mass production techniques as those practiced by Levittown's builder, Abraham Levit. This architectural uniformity produced convenient symbols for what was undeniably also a more significant demographic uniformity. The new suburbs were relatively homogeneous in income, age, and race. The poor could not qualify, even with government-backed loans, while the very rich seemed content to stay where they were. Neither were the elderly inclined to transplant themselves, while nonwhites were excluded by covenants and other, more informal "agreements." The new suburbs, then, were populated by young white adults with young children—lots of them.

It is also true that the new suburbs were child-centered. Of all reasons given by residents for moving from the city to the suburbs, the most popular explanation was that the move was for the sake of the children. Some parents were literally driven to the suburbs by landlords who refused to rent to couples with children. Wendell Bell also reported in 1956 that most persons he interviewed who had moved from the city had "chosen familism as an important element in their life styles as over against career or consumership."[51] Of 100 respondents, Bell reported that 80 percent gave reasons having to do with bettering conditions for their children. Of these, most cited physical reasons, such as more space inside and outside the house, fresh air and sunshine, less traffic, and no neighbors in the same building. Fewer mentioned "social reasons"— better schools and other children to play with, especially "nice" children.[52] There was also widespread support in suburbia for such child-related organizations as the PTA, Scouts, and Little League.[53] Bennett Berger, in his study of a working-class suburb, reported that *Parents' Magazine* attracted more subscribers than any periodical except *Reader's Digest* and *Life*.[54] In the same community, the PTA was the most popular organization listed by men, ahead of the Moose and the American Legion, and ahead of church organizations and sewing clubs by women.[55] William Whyte found that it was the children who initiated and determined the patterns of friendship among adults in Park View, Illinois. He quoted one resident who said, "we are not really 'kid-centered' here like some people say, but our friendships are often made on the kids' standards, and they are purer standards than ours. When your kids are playing with the other kids, they force you to keep on good terms with everybody."[56] Whyte pointed out that the mother's *Kaffeeklatsch* routes followed the flow of child traffic: "Sight and sound are important; when wives go visiting they gravitate toward the houses within sight of their children and within hearing of the telephone, and these lines of sight crystallize into the court 'checkerboard movement.' "[57] Herbert Gans noted in his study of Levittown, New Jersey, that the stress which Levittowners placed on uniformity of life-style was a product of their child-centeredness. While Levittowners could tolerate a great deal of heterogeneity at the community level, they preferred homogeneity at the block level because it reduced the amount of conflict among neighbors over the disciplining of children.[58] As Gans observed:

Levittowners wanted homogeneity of age and income—or rather, they wanted neighbors and friends with common interests and sufficient consensus of values to make for informal and uninhibited relations. Their reasons were motivated neither by antidemocratic feelings nor by an interest in conformity. Children need playmates of the same age, and because child-rearing problems vary with age, mothers like to be near women who have children of similar age. And because these problems also fluctuate with class, they want some similarity of that factor—not homogeneity of occupation and education so much as agreement on the ends and means of caring for child, husband and home.[59]

If the suburbs were child-centered, they were not necessarily female-dominated. The charge that the suburbs were "sorority houses with babies" seems wide of the mark. Popular celebration of family "togetherness" was a more accurate description.[60] Most men reported that they spent more time at home since they moved to the suburbs, and suburban men seemed readier than other males to take a hand in household tasks. Ernest Mowrer found one of the most striking characteristics of suburban life to be a trend toward a greater flexibility of sex roles and a greater egalitarian pattern: "When the children are young, husbands help with the household tasks, sharing in feeding and sometimes diapering the infants; wives shovel snow from walks and help in caring the yard and garden."[61] Herbert Gans found that 65 percent of Levittown men interviewed said they had moved to the suburbs in order to spend more time with their children. Of that group, 70 percent of them said they had achieved their objective. It would appear, then, that suburban children could count on more contact with their fathers than their urban counterparts.[62]

Although there seems to be general agreement among scholars that suburban parents were much preoccupied with the welfare of their children, there is considerably less agreement that all of them were slavishly following Dr. Spock's recommendations for more permissive childrearing techniques. In summarizing the evidence, Scott Donaldson pointed to general agreement that suburban children were spoiled rotten, but he warned that these opinions were based on little solid evidence, and, even if it were true, it was not a pattern unique to the new suburbs.[63] Herbert Gans, who made his observations while living in Levittown, firmly denied that most of his fellow residents spoiled their children. He asserted that most families in Levittown were "child-centered" only to the extent that "the home is run for both adults and children, and the children are allowed to be themselves and to act as children. At the same time, they are raised strictly, for parents are fearful of spoiling them."[64] A major difficulty in generalizing about the way suburban parents reared their children is that the new suburbs were marked by a great deal more of variety in social-class structure than many critics supposed. Many seemed to assume that all new suburbs were populated by families of upwardly mobile junior executives like those Whyte encountered in Park View, Illinois. Later investigations by scholars such as Gans and Bennett

Berger revealed that the new housing developments were equally attractive to working-class Americans who shared in the general prosperity. These working-class families were not only less likely to be transients than those in the middle class, but they seemed also to have reared their offspring more strictly.[65]

Just as it is difficult to generalize about degrees of strictness or permissiveness in postwar childrearing, so it is difficult to arrive at simple conclusions about the extent to which little boys were reared differently from little girls. Given the emphasis which the postwar popular culture placed on the differences in masculine and feminine roles, it is logical to assume that parental practices simply mirrored and reinforced those distinctions in the rearing of their boys and girls. On the other hand, Dr. Spock's influential *Baby and Child Care* did not make much of sexual differences, except to emphasize the importance of the child achieving a firm sense of sexual identity through identification with the same-sex parent.[66] Even such identification, where it occurred, may not have had the result of exaggerating gender differences, given the observed trend, among middle-class families at least, for an equalization of sex roles during the period. The difficulty of arriving at a judgment was underscored by one of the most reliable surveys of the research on sex-role socialization conducted during the period. Sanford Dornbusch lamented that the research was "meager," and he pointed out that, despite the emphasis which the popular media placed on gender differences, "there is a relatively low level of consensus on sex roles in American society." Dornbusch called attention to the rapidity of social change and to the presence of considerable differences among ethnic groups and social classes. Just as working-class parents tended to be more strict with their children than those of middle class, so working-class parents seemed to place more emphasis on traditional gender roles.[67]

The growing influence of the child-centered ethos attracted a rash of speculation concerning its causes. While not discounting the impact of such books as *Baby and Child Care* and *Infant Care*, most commentators have looked to changes in the economy to account for changes in childrearing during the period. One such economic influence was prosperity. As we have seen, prosperity contributed to parental decisions to have babies in the first place, but affluence may also have influenced the way babies were treated. Surprisingly, it was an historian rather than a psychologist who first called attention to this possibility. In 1954, David Potter cited the ways that an economy of abundance could lead to an alteration of socialization practices. After noting that abundance made possible full-time child care, Potter also pointed out that affluence made possible more privacy and more permissiveness in the treatment of children. Automatic washing machines and diaper services, for example, facilitated later and more relaxed toilet-training. Prosperity was also leading to improvements in heating (central heating, for example), which meant that infants were no longer as dependent on clothing for warmth, which in turn meant an increase in the physical freedom that the young enjoyed. In short, prosperity made it possible for parents to put into practice the childrearing that Dr. Spock was preaching.[68]

A more subtle and profound impact of the economy on childrearing could be traced to changes in the nature of work itself toward large-scale, corporate organization. David Riesman and his colleagues called attention to this possibility in a brilliant, if admittedly impressionist, book, that appeared in 1950.[69] *The Lonely Crowd* argued that social character in America had been marked by a gradual shift from the "inner-directed" type of the nineteenth century to the "other-directed" type of the twentieth. What this shift entailed was a relative decline in the importance of such "production values" as hard work, self-denial, and saving, and a relative increase in the importance of learning the skills of consumption. In addition, the shift entailed changes in the type of conformity, with the "inner-directed" person more inclined to obey an internal "gyroscope," as Riesman termed it, while the "other-directed" person would be more sensitively attuned to signals received from the peer group by the means of a kind of psychological "radar." Moreover, in the stage of other-direction, the importance of parents as agents of socialization receded, giving way gradually to the importance of the mass media and peer group, while techniques of childrearing became more subtly permissive.[70]

Riesman's suggestions prompted investigation in 1953 by Daniel Miller and Guy Swanson, who led a team of researchers in a survey of a carefully selected sample of more than 500 mothers in the Detroit area, both inner city and suburban.[71] They found, as had other investigators, that only a minority of mothers were strict in their childrearing, and they also found that middle-class mothers leaned more toward permissiveness than working-class mothers. What made the Detroit study unique, however, was the discovery of another difference among the mothers. More important than social-class membership was the kind of employment held by the head of the household. Miller and Swanson divided their respondents into those families whose head worked in an "entrepreneurial" setting and those whose head worked in a "bureaucratic" setting. They discovered that entrepreneurial mothers were more likely to emphasize training for self-denial, self-control, and independence, whereas bureaucratic mothers were more likely to encourage children to be accommodating and to follow impulse. Although Miller and Swanson declined to endorse Riesman's model, there was a remarkable resemblance between their "bureaucratic" personality and Riesman's "other-directed" man. Miller and Swanson went on to suggest, as had Riesman, that childrearing had changed and that the changes were related to changes in the nature of work.[72]

OUTSIDE THE MAINSTREAM: CHILDREN IN POOR FAMILIES

Whatever the source of the child-centered model, it proved irrelevant to the children of the poor. David Potter's *People of Plenty* made clear that prosperity was a prerequisite for the new style, and not all American families participated in the postwar affluence. As Nancy Weiss has observed, Spock's advice presumed a household with a full-time breadwinner, a full-time homemaker, ample room for privacy, access to telephones and refrigerators, and freedom from worry about where the next meal was coming from.[73]

The plight of children outside the prosperous mainstream received little attention during the 1950s. The seeming invisibility of the American poor in the 1940s and 1950s was due in part to their dwindling numbers. From 1936 to 1963, the ranks of the impoverished were reduced by two-thirds, while the middle-class rose from 13 percent of all families to a near majority of 47 percent.[74] The primary reason that the poor escaped the attention of most of mainstream America, however, was that they were literally not to be seen. While the growing and prosperous middle class migrated in increasing numbers to suburbs located on the urban periphery (where poverty was scarce), those who did not share as fully in the general affluence of the postwar period were often confined to isolated rural areas, or, when they did move (as large numbers of the rural poor did during the 1940s and 1950s), to decaying sections of the inner city.

Although federal welfare legislation in the 1940s and 1950s and a rapidly expanding postwar economy did serve to reduce the number of poor in America, there was no significant redistribution of wealth during this period as a result of increased national prosperity. In 1947 the poorest fifth of the U.S. population received 3.5 percent of the nation's total personal income; in 1960 the figure had declined to 3.2 percent. At the other end of the wage spectrum, America's richest fifth garnered 45.6 percent of the total personal income of the United States in 1947 and 44 percent thirteen years later.[75] Thus, the postwar poor, though reduced in numbers, continued to draw an incredibly meager slice of the American pie.

In addition, some Federal Government policies and programs actually contributed to a worsening of living conditions for impoverished Americans. The government's decision in 1948 to cut mortgage subsidies for rental-unit construction and to increase subsidies instead for privately owned, single family houses, for example, worked to the disadvantage of low-income groups living in urban areas, as did the Federal Housing Administration (FHA) policy of "red-lining" huge sections of cities threatened by "Negro invasion." In these selected urban areas, the FHA refused to guarantee mortgage loans, claiming that an influx of blacks would make such loans risky, and local banks and savings and loan associations frequently followed the agency's lead.[76] In 1959 Lorraine Hansberry made such discrimination and its impact on black families a theme in her drama, "A Raisin in the Sun."

Discriminatory practices were also evident in the suburbs, where the FHA actively encouraged the use of restrictive covenants to promote homogeneity and prevent declining property values.[77] Even well-intended measures like the 1949 National Housing Act, which was designed to provide decent dwellings and a suitable living environment for the poor by means of "urban redevelopment" (or slum clearance) and the construction within four years of 810,000 public housing units for low-income families, seemed to handicap rather than assist the urban poor. By 1960, fewer than 300,000 of the proposed units had been completed, and low-income families, displaced by massive slum clearance and government-supported highway construction, often found their housing choices little improved.[78]

In the areas of health care, child welfare, and family services, the Federal Government's record was equally spotty. To be sure, important advances in government support for maternal and child care were made in the 1940s. Amendments to the Social Security Act in 1946, for example, nearly doubled authorizations and appropriations for maternal and child health, crippled children, and child welfare service programs. And the Emergency Maternal and Infant Care Program (EMIC), funded by the U.S. Children's Bureau from 1943 to 1949, provided free medical, nursing, hospital, maternity, and infant care to the wives and babies of enlisted men in the four lowest pay grades. At its peak, EMIC coverage was extended to one out of every seven births in the country. These programs, together with advances in the control of infectious diseases and improved care for prematurely born infants, helped bring about a sharp drop in infant and maternal death rates in the 1940s.[79]

As with federal housing programs, however, government health care in the postwar period was inadequately and unevenly extended, and clinic and hospital admission policies based on residency or race continued to work to the particular disadvantage of impoverished blacks and migrant workers. Despite a promising start in the 1940s, little progress was made in the next decade in reducing infant mortality rates, and the nonwhite rate was actually higher in 1960 than in 1950.[80]

Another federal welfare program whose coverage and appropriations were expanded during the 1940s and 1950s was Aid to Dependent Children (ADC). First established under Title IV of the Social Security Act of 1936, ADC extended financial support to needy dependent children deprived of parental support as a result of the death, absence from home, or physical or mental incapacity of a parent. Although the number of people receiving ADC rose during the postwar period, reaching a total of 3,080,000 in 1960, flaws in the implementation of the program limited its effectiveness and at times blocked the extension of its benefits to many of those who needed it the most.[81]

While the Social Security Act laid down general guidelines which all states receiving ADC federal grants-in-aid were to follow, many major decisions regarding the implementation of the program were left up to the individual states. Thus, in the 1950s and early 1960s, while the Federal Government increasingly relaxed restrictions determining who might receive benefits, many states actually tightened eligibility requirements in an effort to eliminate unwed mothers from their rolls and enforce paternal responsibility. In the summer of 1960, for example, Louisiana completely cut off aid to 23,000 children on the grounds that their mothers' sexual promiscuity rendered their homes unfit. The persistent belief that a father should be solely responsible for the support of his children also influenced state application of ADC funds. In 1961 Congress authorized the extension of Aid to Dependent Children to families where the father was present and physically fit but unemployed. Only half of the states, however, took advantage of the option.[82]

The technological advances of the postwar period which contributed so greatly to increased national production and prosperity also worked to the detriment of millions of the American poor. As a result of mechanization and federal subsidies, for example, agricultural production per acre soared following World War II. The major benefactors of this agricultural revolution, however, were not the small farmers but the big corporate farms and agribusinesses. In 1954 some 12 percent of the farm operators controlled more than 40 percent of the land and grossed almost 60 percent of farm sales.[83] At the other end of the spectrum, small independent farmers and sharecroppers unable to increase their acreage or to expend large sums on agricultural machinery saw their profits drop steadily during this period, and many were forced to abandon their farms. Between 1953 and 1964, more than 1.5 million farm jobs were wiped out as a result of agricultural mechanization.[84] Tens of thousands of these displaced farmers joined a vast postwar exodus of the rural poor to the cities. Others remained in agriculture, adopting the harsh nomadic life-style of the migrant farmer.

When Edward R. Murrow's TV documentary, "Harvest of Shame," aired in 1960, there was a moment of intense national shock. For the first time, millions of Americans became aware of the desperate plight of American migrant workers—one of the worst housed, least educated, and most impoverished groups in the United States. In the midst of postwar agricultural abundance, these unskilled laborers traveled from state to state, performing jobs too dirty or delicate for farm machinery to handle, in return for wages insufficient to adequately feed, clothe, or house their families.

The deprivations of this life-style worked particular hardships on children. As most migrant children began work in the fields at age seven or eight, there was often little additional time for schooling, and what little education these children received was likely to be interrupted and inferior. In 1960 only 1 out of 500 migrant children finished grade school and only 1 out of 5,000 finished high school. As a result, migrant worker families had the highest illiteracy rate of any group in America.[85]

This is not to suggest, however, that the life of a migrant child was without any degree of warmth or happiness. In fact, as a 1965 study of ten Eastern Seaboard migrant families by psychiatrist Robert Coles reveals, infants born to migrants received a good deal of continual attention and care from both parents and siblings.[86] Most of the dwellings provided migrant workers were one-room shacks with a minimum of interior divisions—a layout that discouraged or precluded excessive family privacy or modesty. Thus, the migrant infant grew up and became a child in the constant physical presence of others, their smells, noises, and actions, while being touched, held, and observed by all members of his family.

The infants Coles observed were usually breast-fed for a year or more and slept with their mothers for the first few months before being entrusted to the care of older brothers or sisters. As the parents followed the sun in their migratory routes, the growing child was allowed and even encouraged to remain naked much of the time. Toilet-training normally did not begin until the child's second or third year when he or she was able to walk outside to use the bathroom, and was accomplished quickly with a minimum of frustration and self-consciousness.

Although these early years of childhood were often years of happiness and freedom, the majority of migrant children observed by Coles assumed work responsibilities at a very early age and moved quickly into adulthood without ceremony or a lengthy adolescence. As they reached sexual maturity, many of these young migrants began to display greater social and economic independence, and a large number married (many at age fourteen or fifteen) and began having children of their own. (The first baby, Cole notes, was often given to the maternal grandmother as a kind of "present" until the mother was ready to accept greater responsibility for the baby and, with it, for adulthood itself.) By age twenty to twenty-two, these couples had become full-fledged adults, moving about by themselves, with little attachment to their original families or interest in seeing or visiting them even when the groups shared the same migratory route. Although barely in their twenties, most, Coles found, had already lost much of their interest in the possibilities of another kind of life-style and had resigned themselves to the deprivations of a migratory existence.

Also particularly hard hit by inequalities in the distribution of postwar affluence were blacks—51 percent of whom lived in central cities in 1960.[87] Despite promising relative income gains registered between 1940 and 1954, when Negro family median income jumped from 37 percent to 56 percent of the white figure, black income gains quickly leveled off and remained far below those of whites during the 1950s and 1960s.[88] In 1959, for example, the black median family income was only $3,161, or 54 percent of the white family's $5,893.[89]

Although the attention of academia was, for the most part, focused elsewhere during the 1940s and 1950s, those scholars who did examine the black family in the postwar period identified, often in very critical terms, the ways in which nonwhite household structure and childrearing practices differed from those of mainstream society. There is, of course, no denying that important differences did exist. Data from the 1950 and 1960 censuses, for example, revealed that black married couples were 4 to $4^{1}/_{2}$ times more likely than white couples to live in separate domiciles. Similarly, although the majority of black and white families had both husband and wife present, nonwhite families were more likely to be headed by a woman, and black households were more likely than their white counterparts to include "extended" family members.[90] In addition, black families had a lower economic status, a higher percentage of females in the labor force, more workers per family, a higher birth rate, and an earlier average age at marriage.

Investigators also found important differences in childrearing practices and training among black mothers which served to distinguish them from middle-class white America. A study in the early 1960s by Zena Smith Blau of 224 mothers in three Chicago maternity wards revealed that, although black mothers had a much higher opinion of baby experts (and Dr. Spock in particular) than did white mothers interviewed, far fewer black women had had any direct exposure to baby-raising manuals. Among white middle-class mothers, the overwhelming majority (77 percent) in the study had read Spock's *Baby and Child Care*, but in the black middle class the proportion was strikingly smaller (32 percent) and was indeed lower than the white working class (48 percent). The smallest proportion of Spock readers was found among the black working class (12 percent).[91] Given the inappropriateness of Spock's advice to poor families, the indifference seemed sensible.

Other studies conducted in the two decades after World War II concluded that black parents were much more permissive than whites in the feeding and weaning of their children, but were much more rigorous than whites in toilet-training; that black mothers were more likely to use physical punishment in disciplining young children (as opposed to the approaches most commonly adopted by mainstream families which were based on the withdrawal of love or which made parental approval and affection contingent on the child's behavior and accomplishments); and that nonwhite parents were more concerned than white middle-class parents with nudity and preventing masturbation.[92]

The major shortcoming of many of these studies of the black family, however, lay in the adoption of what one scholar has called a "comparative deficit" approach to the subject—an approach that assumed that blacks were culturally deprived and that viewed differences between black families and white mainstream families as deficits.[93] Although research from 1945 to 1965 on low-income and black families succeeded in identifying some legitimate differences between impoverished and mainstream groups in postwar America, the middle-class bias inherent in the comparative deficit interpretational framework frequently invited overgeneralizations by investigators and the stereotyping of black family behavior. One study by Norma Radin and Constance K. Kamii of forty-four culturally deprived black mothers and fifty middle-class white mothers in a Midwestern city, for example, concluded that: "The lower class Negro is usually characterized by great sexual freedom (promiscuity and illegitimacy) and aggressiveness (violence and fighting)."[94] Findings such as these on low-income families, although representative of only a small portion of the black population, increasingly became accepted by the general public as accurate descriptions of the family life of all blacks in America. Greatly contributing to this misconception was the highly publicized and highly influential government-sponsored report by Daniel P. Moynihan, entitled *The Negro Family: The Case for National Action*. This study concluded, in part, that the black ghetto was a "tangle of pathologies" in which domineering "matriarchal" mothers brought about the disintegration of black families—a development that in turn contributed to high rates of delinquency, illegitimacy, and unemployment.[95]

Postwar research such as the Moynihan report often proceeded under the incorrect assumption that low-income blacks were without a culture and that the black family was a pathological variation of a healthier mainstream model. Nevertheless, during this period both scholars and the Federal Government exhibited a growing awareness that unhealthy, impoverished environments, discrimination, and inequalities of opportunity could contribute to increasing frustration and tensions within the family. Poor parents found themselves caught between the ideals of the middle-class, child-centered family and the reality of poverty. The child-centered ideal told poor women, for example, that they should stay home and take care of their children. Yet, the ideal also implied a standard of living above the poverty level, driving many women into the marketplace to seek employment. One of the paradoxes of the postwar period was the persistent rise in the proportion of mothers entering the labor force.[96] Many undoubtedly enjoyed their work or sought ego enhancement through a career, but since most jobs available to unskilled women offered only low pay, low prestige, and low psychic rewards, it is more likely that many mothers were compelled to seek employment either for survival's sake or to keep their families abreast of the rising standard of living most Americans were enjoying. To be poor in a society of the prosperous was to be doubly poor.

SCHOOLS, THE COLD WAR, AND THE GREAT TALENT SEARCH

Schools have frequently been sources of controversy, but they never experienced as much difficulty as in the years after World War II. The baby boom itself created problems of a very practical sort as schools struggled to keep up with expanding enrollments. Moreover, child-centered parents were demanding a higher quality education. To make matters worse, the curricula of the schools were dragged into the Cold War. Some Americans suspected that the schools were harboring Communists and Communist literature. Others became concerned that the schools were not producing trained manpower in the race with the Soviet Union for technological and military superiority. Still others, mostly academicians, charged that the schools were betraying the life of the mind itself. Finally, the Supreme Court of the United States cast the schools in the forefront of the war against racial discrimination. Clearly, a variety of groups had a variety of priorities for the schools, and schools would have to scramble to accommodate these competing claims. The children of the baby boom found themselves in the middle.

Certainly, the parents who had created the baby boom had posed problems for elementary schools during the period, for how were schools to supply classrooms and teachers for the hordes of children that began to descend on them? Although birth rates had been higher in the nineteenth century, they were not accompanied by the widespread expectation that all of the children would attend school. After 1945, however, birth rates and educational expectations combined to push up enrollments steadily until the early 1970s when school enrollment peaked. Schools tried to adjust. From 1950 to 1960, spending on elementary and secondary schools increased from $6.6 billion to $18.6 billion. Expenditures per pupil rose by 370 percent between 1940 and 1960.[97] Prodded by irate parents, school boards ordered the building of 50,000 new classrooms in 1952 alone, but still the classrooms were crowded. Teachers, too, were in short supply, and, by 1959, 100,000 were working with substandard credentials.[98]

To the problems of the baby boom were added the anxieties created by the Cold War. As early as 1948, a battle broke out in Scarsdale, New York, over allegedly subversive books in the school library.[99] States began passing laws requiring teachers to take loyalty oaths. In 1950 a superintendent was fired in Pasadena, California, for his alleged leftist leanings, although it turned out that he had done nothing more radical than to invite William Kilpatrick, one of John Dewey's disciples, to a teacher-training workshop.[100] In the climate of the Cold War, it was easy for some to confuse a mild Socialist with a hard-line Communist.

Soon, a distinguished group of academicians also began to complain about the influence of John Dewey, but not because of his leaning toward socialism. Critics like Arthur Bestor, an historian, asserted that Dewey's followers had created a climate of anti-intellectualism in the schools. Bestor charged that the schools had become an "educational wasteland," and in particular he singled out a movement called "life adjustment," which called for schools to provide a more practical, less academic education for the majority of American children. Bestor countered with the call for a revived emphasis on traditional disciplines—mathematics, science, history, English, and foreign languages.[101]

Bestor was inclined to lay blame on professional educators for the neglect of academic disciplines, but it seemed that some parents themselves preferred courses that would help their children achieve a practical "adjustment" in life. William Whyte reported that both the educators and the parents of Park View agreed on a heavy dose of life-adjustment topics. Whyte found that of the seventy subjects offered in the high school, half were of the nonacademic variety. The course in "family living," for example, included money management, everyday social relationships, care of the sick, nutrition and food management, clothing and housing the family, and preparation for marriage. Like the suburban homes from which the children came, the course emphasized "shared responsibility in building a successful, happy home."[102]

Complaints of the red-baiters and of scholars like Bestor might have left little impact on the schools had it not been for the dramatic achievements of the Soviet Union in launching Sputniks I and II in the fall of 1957. Suddenly, it appeared to Americans that a society they regarded as backward had surged ahead of them in the Space Race. Americans, who prided themselves on their technological know-how, were humiliated. Casting about for a scapegoat, they fastened on the schools. *Life*, always sensitive to currents of popular opinion, launched a series in the spring of 1958 on "The Crisis in Education," which made clear that the schools should be weapons in the Cold War.[103] The series began with a photo essay comparing the education of a Russian high school student, Alexei, and his American counterpart, Stephen. The photos showed Alexei working hard, while Stephen was portrayed as enjoying himself in extracurricular activities. Leaving no doubt about conclusions to be drawn, *Life* published an editorial by Sloan Wilson, author of *The Man in the Gray Flannel Suit*. Wilson declared that America's lag in the Space Race could be traced to the teachings of Dewey and to a misguided emphasis on egalitarianism. "It's time to close our carnival," Wilson asserted.[104] Thus did the critical assault on the suburbs and on the Organization Man establish a connection with the attack on educational Progressivism, all in the name of American defense.

It was not long after Sputnik that the nation's schools received a massive infusion of federal funds, aimed at a transformation of the curriculum and a grim search for the talented young. Within a few weeks after the launching of Sputnik I, President Dwight Eisenhower called for the measures that led to the passage of the National Defense Education Act, which appropriated money for summer institutes to train teachers of science and mathematics, for graduate fellowships in the sciences, for grants to states to improve school programs in testing, guidance, and counseling, and for the teaching of foreign languages, particularly those of the Third World.[105]

In a political climate of anxiety, men like Admiral Hyman Rickover and James Conant acquired influence with the public, and they called for a Great Talent Search. Rickover fused the political anxieties of the red-baiters with the sophisticated intellectual concerns of scholars like Bestor, although he gave "talent" a somewhat narrower definition than Bestor had contemplated. Rickover, the father of America's nuclear navy, charged in 1959 that America was losing the Cold War because it had neglected its most talented youth. He called for a reform of the schools that would make them effective weapons in the Cold War, and he emphasized in particular the training of scientists and engineers.[106] Conant, former president of Harvard, had long perceived the connection between education and national security. He served during World War II on the Manhattan Project and supported the establishment of the National Science Foundation. In 1950 he became chairman of the Committee on the Present Danger, a group dedicated to combatting the spread of communism. After diplomatic service in West Germany, Conant turned his attention to the public schools. His study of the schools led in 1959 to the publication of *The American High School Today*, in which he called for the elimination of small high schools, improvements in guidance and counseling, and a tightening of graduation requirements to include at least four years of English, three or four years of social studies, one year of math, and one of science.[107]

Federal money and public agitation provided the support for a fundamental reform of school curricula, particularly in science and mathematics. The climate of the Cold War made possible the implementation of innovations in subject matter that had long been in the making, including new curricula in physics (PSSC), mathematics (SMSG), biology (BSCS), and chemistry (CHEM). While scholars were putting together new concepts and materials, psychologists like Jerome Bruner were rethinking the psychology of teaching. Bruner's *The Process of Education* called for a new emphasis on teaching the structure of the disciplines rather than inculcating facts. One of the most memorable dicta of the book was the ringing pronouncement that "any subject can be taught effectively in some intellectually honest form to any child at any stage of development."[108] One result of this flurry of educational reform was that by the early 1960s, American children, especially those identified as "academically talented," were encountering learning tasks that baffled their parents, thus contributing to a growing disparity between the experience of the young and the old.[109]

The Cold War emphasis on a talent search was helped by the spread of the testing movement, which held the promise of identifying and encouraging the academically gifted. Again Conant's influence can be detected, for he was one of those instrumental in the formation of the Educational Testing Service (ETS) in 1947. In subsequent years, ETS persuaded most colleges to adopt the Scholastic Aptitude Test as a requirement for admission, and by the late 1950s it was proving difficult for high school graduates to gain admission to more prestigious colleges without the submission of SAT scores. Men like Conant hoped that the SAT would provide a valid estimate of native aptitude and thus serve as a more just measure of talent than teacher recommendations or high school grades. Nevertheless, it proved difficult to devise a test that would not unfairly penalize children of disadvantaged cultural groups, such as blacks. Moreover, the precision with which the SAT identified talent and reduced it to a number could not disguise the fact that there were many kinds of talent, such as the ability to write, that the SAT did not measure.[110]

Even in the midst of the Cold War, there were some who worried about the implications of the Great Talent Search. Among them was the novelist John Hersey, who in 1960 published a novel that raised serious questions about Cold War pressures on schoolchildren. *The Child Buyer*, a science-fiction fantasy, told the story of Wissey Jones, the representative of a corporation with defense contracts who arrives in a small New England town to purchase juvenile geniuses. He discovers ten-year-old Barry Rudd, who clearly fits the category of academically talented. Jones sets out to secure Barry for the corporation and in the process finds that everyone in the little town has his price, including teachers, guidance counselors, superintendents, school board members, and even Barry's parents. Only the school principal, Dr. Gozar, resists Jones's bribes. As she tells an investigating committee: "It's a failure of national vision when you regard children as weapons, and talents as materials you can mine, assay, and fabricate for profit and defense."[111] Ultimately, however, even

Dr. Gozar agrees to the sale of Barry, who goes along with the corrupt bargain, because he perceives that society has no use for him except as a weapon in the Cold War.

Hersey's assessment of the Great Talent Search was a gloomy one, but the movement could be viewed more optimistically, for it seemed to hold out the promise that schools would at last become genuine vehicles for promoting a meritocracy, albeit with a somewhat narrow definition of merit. Looked at in this light, the Great Talent Search fused with the Second Civil Rights Movement, launched in 1954 by the U.S. Supreme Court's historic decision, *Brown* v. *the Topeka Board of Education*. Reversing the "separate but equal" doctrine of *Plessy* v. *Ferguson*, the Court declared that the racial segregation of children in public schools was unconstitutional.[112] Like the Great Talent Search itself, the Civil Rights Movement was a blend of idealism and practical politics, and both bore the stamp of the Cold War. President Harry S Truman had made black civil rights one of his major political objectives because he believed in the promises of the Declaration of Independence and also because he took note that migration northward had made blacks into a more powerful political constituency.[113] Moreover, Truman and other high government officials recognized that racial discrimination was becoming an embarrassment in the American competition with the Soviet Union for the friendship of peoples in the nonwhite Third World. In its brief before the Supreme Court, the National Association for the Advancement of Colored People made the most of this embarrassment, noting the link between security abroad and social justice at home: "Racial discrimination furnishes grist for the Communist propaganda mills, and it raises doubts even among friendly nations as to the intensity of our devotion to the democratic faith."[114]

The Brown decision had little direct impact on most American schoolchildren until the 1960s, because there emerged both massive and passive resistance by local officials to the court orders.[115] Nevertheless, the Court had thrust the schools into the frontline of the battle for social justice, and some children—both black and white—were caught in the conflict even before 1960. One of the first of such confrontations occurred in the fall of 1957 at Little Rock, Arkansas, where black high school students and their parents, with the encouragement of the local board of education, defied mob violence and seized the promises of equality made by the Brown decision.[116] The challenges spread throughout the South, and one of the most lasting contributions of the desegregation movement was the work of psychiatrist Robert Coles. Recognizing that the Second Civil Rights Movement had plunged young people into the thick of controversy, Coles was prompted to study the impact of social crisis on children. Eschewing superficial survey techniques and suspicious of pat psychological explanations of human behavior, Coles spent months visiting and living with the families of children who were caught in the desegregation battle, and he employed the technique of having the children draw pictures as a way of getting at their feelings. The first child Coles interviewed was Ruby, a six-year-old black girl in New Orleans, who braved daily mobs to attend school. Coles discovered, through Ruby's drawings, that she had been deeply affected by racism, always drawing white people large and lifelike, while Negroes were pictured with smaller, mutilated bodies.[117] Subjected to a daily barrage of insults and threats, Ruby lost her appetite, and Coles discovered that the little girl was afraid she would be poisoned.[118] Why would parents put their child through such an ordeal? Coles found, through patient questioning, that Ruby's family was motivated by a combination of courage and naivete. Not expecting the outcry that ensued, Ruby's parents were also "strong and stubborn people—to be alive is an achievement when one grows up in the unspeakable poverty and toil that were theirs—and they managed."[119]

CHILDREN, YOUTH, AND THE MESSAGES OF THE MEDIA

While national debates raged around the schools in the 1950s, less attention was paid to other influences that shaped the lives of children and youth. The mass media—comic books, popular magazines, movies, radio, television, and the recording industry—ultimately would prove more powerful than schools in their impact on postwar youth. It is ironic that both those who defended the schools and those who attacked them fell into the same error of overestimating the role of schooling in the lives of children during the period. While local communities argued over the curriculum of the classroom and the books in the school library, the attention of children and youth was increasingly drawn to the exciting sights and sounds outside the school.

Forms of mass media antedated the postwar period, of course, but they acquired a new power after 1945. First, there was the appearance of television, which surpassed all other media in its ubiquity and intimacy. Second, children and youth found new uses for older media, such as radio and the movies, which were losing their older, more traditional audiences to television. Third, unparalleled prosperity created new markets among the young for goods and services, and the entrepreneurs of the media were not slow in discovering that fact. Prosperity placed spending power in the hands of parents (and of their children) and led the media to court the young with single-minded concentration. The discovery of the children's market began in the immediate postwar period with the explosion of demand for diapers, toys, clothes, and baby food.[120] In 1958 *Life* devoted a cover story to "Kids: Built-in Recession Cure:

How 4,000,000 a Year Make Billions in Business." As Landon Jones has pointed out, the children were creating fads that included Davey Crockett costumes (1955), Hoola Hoops (1958), and Barbie Dolls (1959).[121] By 1964, teenagers were buying 55 percent of the soft drinks, 53 percent of the movie tickets, and 43 percent of musical recordings. In that same year, one in five high school seniors drove his or her own car.[122] Teenagers were also an important factor in the spread of the fast food industry, supplying not only much of the market but also a good deal of the labor behind the counter.[123]

Finally, it should be noted that the media exercised a powerful force on the young because the media suffered neither the division nor the doubt that plagued families and schools during the postwar years. The moguls of the media did not trouble themselves over philosophical debates about patriotism and educational values, nor were they restrained by any concern for the welfare of children and youth. Like any business, the media were intent on making a profit, and to make a profit, it remained only for the media to find out what the customers wanted and then to give it to them. Achieving a psychological sophistication that excelled that of most parents and teachers, the masters of the media were extraordinarily successful in keeping their fingers on the pulse of youth during the period.

The most dramatic media challenge to traditional family life after the war was posed by television. In 1946, only 8000 American households contained a television set; by 1948, there were 100,000; by 1950, the number had risen to 3.9 million and by 1959, to 50 million. In 1952, 46 percent of households contained a set; by 1960, television had entered 90 percent of households, and more homes boasted a set than indoor plumbing, a refrigerator, or a telephone.[124] A study conducted in 1955 revealed that television sets had reduced daily magazine reading time from an average of 17 minutes to 10 minutes per person, reduced newspaper reading from 39 to 32 minutes, and radio from 122 to 52 minutes. The same households reported that their television viewing had increased from 12 minutes to 267 minutes.[125] In fact, television had become so widespread by 1960 that it became difficult for researchers to find nontelevision families as a control group to measure the impact of television viewing.[126]

Despite parental concerns, children became enthralled by television. Wilbur Schramm and his colleagues reported in 1960 that by the age of three, one of three children was watching the tube, and the ratio rose to four out of five at age five, and to nine out of ten by age six. By the sixth grade, American children were watching, on the average, three to four hours of television each day, nearly as much as they spent in school. Moreover, the children did not limit their watching to shows designed for them. Although they might begin with "Howdy Doody" and "Kookla,

Fran, and Ollie," they quickly graduated to adult fare. By 1960, in fact, it was found that most of children's viewing consisted of so-called adult programs—Westerns, adventure, crime, situation comedies, popular music, and variety shows. In the 1950s, "I Love Lucy" was as popular with the children as it was with their parents. Obviously, the children liked television (except for news and public affairs programs), and they told interviewers that of all the media, they would miss television most if it were taken away.[127]

Given the rapid growth of television viewing by American children, it is hardly surprising that a debate erupted about the effect of television on children. While not as furious as that which surrounded the schools in the 1950s, most of the discussion was diverting, if uninformed. Senator Estes Kefauver gave prominent attention in 1956 to an alleged link between televised violence and juvenile delinquency, and popular periodicals joined the fray. Schramm found that most parents he interviewed were, indeed, concerned about the effect of television on their offspring, with highly educated parents more likely to worry about crime and violence, and blue-collar parents more likely to object to sexual content. Some, but not many, complained about the low cultural level of television offerings.[128]

Schramm and his colleagues conducted one of the first comprehensive efforts to provide scientific evidence of television's influence on children. Not surprisingly, they concluded that the issue was too complex for sweeping generalizations. Whether television was harmful depended on the child, the program, and the family context. Some children could be frightened by television, others could be provoked into violence by watching violence on television, and still others could be driven into passivity by the tube. Much depended on the child's family life.[129]

Although it might be difficult to uncover evidence that television was causing definite harm to children in the 1950s, still it seems true that the tube deflected the attention of children from other activities. Schramm and his colleagues admitted that television failed to contribute to a child's cognitive development, and they noted that a "turning point" occurred at the beginning of adolescence when children separated into two groups—those who continued heavy watching and those who tapered off. The latter group was more likely to score higher on academic measures, although the investigators could not sort out causes and effects.[130] Later investigations suggested a high correlation between heavy television watching and low SAT scores.[131] Joyce Maynard, who watched television as a child in the late 1950s and early 1960s at her home in Durham, New Hampshire, later regretted the hours lost.[132]

A more subtle issue—one hardly amenable to scientific proof—had to do with whether television watching encouraged children and youth of the 1950s to grow up too fast. Schramm noted the issue and suggested that "premature aging" might make children fearful of adulthood.[133] Joyce Maynard subtitled her autobiography "A Chronicle of Growing Up Old in the Sixties," and she attributed a major role to television in the process.[134] Likewise, Jeff Greenfield, who grew up during the post-war years, believed that television encouraged what he called "eaves-dropping" on adult secrets and thus contributed to a premature loss of childhood innocence. Greenfield was not speaking of news programs, which the children did not watch anyway. Rather, he was speaking of such family shows as "I Love Lucy" and "My Little Margie," in which much of the comedy hung on dishonesty, fear, and pretense. "If, for example, Ricky Ricardo or Vern Albright called to say he was bringing an important person home to dinner, it was reason to lie—about life styles, wealth, or tastes."[135] Whether or not such sophistication harmed the children, there can be no doubt that the dikes proper parents had erected for generations around the young to protect them and prolong their childhood had developed leaks in the postwar period. The mys-teries of adult life were exposed, for better or worse.

Exposure to cynicism could also be seen in the postwar period in another medium—the comic books. Although less important in the long run than television, the comics were freer of adult control. Comics were cheaper than television sets, and they could be more easily hidden. Wil-liam Gaines, publisher of "Entertaining Comics," set out to experiment with new themes in the 1950s, and he soon discovered that young readers were tired of the patriotic sentiments that had dominated the comics. What they wished instead were blood, gore, and horror. Don Thompson, who was sixteen in 1951, recalled that he was bored with superheroes, but one day he came upon one of Gaines's new horror comics, "Vam-pire," which led him to the discovery of "The Vault of Horror," which featured villains with warts, staring eyes, missing teeth, and mouths dripping slime, all illustrated with considerable artistic skill and an eye for detail. Like many other boys, Thompson became hooked on Enter-taining Comics, which were all the more delicious because they were shocking to parents.[136]

The popularity of the new comics soon prompted complaints from parents and disapproving editorials from newspapers. As with violence on television, a connection was suggested between horror comics and the rising rate of juvenile crime. A psychiatrist, Frederic Wertham, seized on the issue and in 1954 published *The Seduction of the Innocent*, a book which charged that juvenile delinquents had been prompted to a life of crime by reading comic books like those Gaines published. Wertham's charges stimulated an investigation by the Senate Subcommittee on Ju-venile Delinquency, which in turn prompted Gaines's fellow publishers to organize the Comic Magazine Association of America. The association adopted a code prohibiting the glorification of criminals and banning horror themes.[137]

Ironically, one of Gaines's publications escaped the code's restrictions, and it proved to be more subversive of traditional values than the horror comics that were banned. *Mad* magazine, described by Paul Goodman as the "bible of the twelve-year-olds who can read," relied more on satire than on horror, and to *Mad*, nothing was sacred. In well-drawn and well-scripted stories, *Mad* ridiculed any available target, beginning with the patriotic adventure comics themselves and going on to lampoon God, mother, country, and capitalism. *Mad* adhered to no particular party line, however, for left-wing reformers could also be targets for satire. The essential thing was to prick the balloon of authority—whether parents, teachers, or politicians. When a theologian professed to find in *Mad* a hidden moral purpose, Gaines replied, "We reject the insinuation that anything we print is moral."[138] Even in the early 1950s, Gaines was tapping a vein of nihilism among the young that would find other outlets and ultimately contribute to the counterculture of the 1960s.

As postwar American youngsters passed into the adolescent years, they seemed to lose interest in television and the comics, turning instead to other forms of entertainment that their elders were abandoning. The movies suffered a disastrous decline in box office receipts during the 1950s, thanks largely to the competition of television. By 1953, when nearly half of American families owned a television, motion picture attendance had dropped to half of what it had been in 1946.[139] In desperation, Hollywood abandoned the "family movies" that had been its staple product since the early 1930s and cast about for new themes. A Supreme Court decision in 1952 weakened the movie industry's censorship code, ruling that movies were a form of speech and thus entitled to the protections of the First Amendment. Movies were thereafter allowed much more latitude in the selection of themes. Certainly, they labored under no such restrictions as bound television.[140] Teenagers responded and flocked to the cinema, making up to some extent for the desertion of their parents. Since no age classification system had yet appeared to replace the weakened code, it was relatively easy for teenagers to gain admittance to theaters to see films that dealt more frankly with such themes as sex and drugs (*The Moon Is Blue, Baby Doll, The Man with the Golden Arm*). Hollywood was also attracted to the theme of adolescence itself and especially to the growing phenomenon of juvenile delinquency and juvenile alienation. Among the first was *The Wild One* (1954) in which Marlon Brando played a member of a tough motorcycle gang, but middle-class adolescents could identify more readily with the protagonist of *Rebel Without A Cause* (1955). The film portrays a sensitive middle-class boy who becomes involved with a gang of hoodlums. The film left the clear impression that the boy's problems could be traced to a domineering mother and a weak father, thus providing a startling contrast to the positive image of family life that parents and younger children were watching at home on the television screen. The film also made the star, James Dean, into a cult figure and a symbol to disenchanted teenagers.[141]

Hollywood found other themes that appealed to teenagers, especially those dealing with rock music. *Black Board Jungle* (1955) tells the story of a young, idealistic teacher in a ghetto school who is beaten by a gang of hoodlums after he interrupts their rape of a female teacher. What made the movie memorable to teenagers, however, was that the film opened with "Rock Around the Clock," featuring Bill Haley and the Comets. After the movie, the tune sold fifteen million records, setting off a series of rock and roll movies for teenagers, including *Rock Around the Clock, Jailhouse Rock, Don't Knock the Rock,* and *The Girl Can't Help It.*[142]

As these successful rock movies indicated, it was the recording industry that made the most impact on teenagers of the later 1950s. Adolescents turned to the radios abandoned by their parents and their younger siblings, and the teenagers also made use of their parents' prosperity to buy records. Rock music was not their preference during the immediate postwar years for the good reason that it did not exist, at least not in a form that was palatable to mainstream youngsters. During the late 1940s and early 1950s, the most popular music was what one scholar has called "fifties schlock," featuring crooners like Frankie Laine and Eddie Fisher, and tunes like "If I Knew You Were Coming I'd Have Baked a Cake," "I Believe," or "Oh My Papa." Novelty tunes like "The Typewriter" were also popular, as were cute, sentimental ballads like "How Much Is That Doggie in the Window," by Patti Page.[143]

Under this bland surface, however, were hints of musical rebellion. Alan Freed, a disc jockey in Cleveland, noticed in the spring of 1951 that white teenagers were buying recordings by black artists, music then called "race" music, or later "rhythm and blues." He renamed the music "rock and roll," a ghetto euphemism for dancing and sex, and began to play it on his radio show. The favorable response prompted him to sponsor a rock and roll concert, to which 25,000 teenagers, mostly white, showed up. Thereafter, Freed moved to a New York City radio station and became a promoter of rock and roll music. By 1957, white teenagers like Jeff Greenfield would be huddled in lines at six-thirty in the morning to purchase tickets for one of Freed's rock and roll concerts.[144]

Freed had accidentally struck a gold mine, and for the first time black rhythm and blues artists began to receive a hearing from white youngsters. As early as 1952, the Clovers crossed over from race to pop charts with "One Mint Julep." In 1956, white teenagers were buying Little Richard's "Long Tall Sally," and Chuck Berry's "Roll Over Beethoven."

Freed himself actually insisted, during the early 1950s, on featuring only black performers on his radio show and at his rock concerts. Needed, however, was a performer acceptable to the great mass of white teenagers, one who would bring rock into the mainstream of popular music. Elvis Presley proved to be that performer. The Memphis youth was familiar with the sound of black music, and yet he was white and "nice." Sam Phillips, whose Sun Records first recorded Elvis in 1954, once remarked to a friend, "If I could find a white boy who could sing like a nigger, I could make a million dollars." Presley proved to fit the bill, although Phillips did not make a million for his discovery, because he had the bad business judgment to sell Presley's contract for only $25,000. After arousing Memphis teenagers with "That's All Right Mama," and "You Ain't Nothin' But a Hound Dog," Presley went on to make recordings with RCA Victor where, in early 1956, he recorded "Heartbreak Hotel," the first recording in history to be number one on all three charts—country and western, rhythm and blues, and pop.[145]

What was the appeal of rock music to 1950s teenagers? The first explanation and the simplest is that the music's heavy, insistent beat provided something a kid could dance to. The music was rough, loud, and unsophisticated, a music that had not been claimed and certified by the older generation and the show business professionals.[146] Moreover, the music itself, together with its lyrics, was blatantly sensual. If rock was a euphemism for sex, then the message of "Rock Around the Clock," was clear, as was the Elvis ballad, "I want you, I need you," or Little Richard's Sue, who "knows how to love me, yeesiree."[147] The music was, as Jeff Greenfield recalled, "a world of unbearable sexuality and celebration."[148] Beyond the music itself was its association with disreputable subcultures—Southern, black, and delinquent—which proved attractive to teenagers in rebellion against their elders. Elvis was yet another version of James Dean, whom he much admired, although the ducktail, sideburns, and the greasy look derived from the hoodlums, teddy boys, and bikers who appeared in urban working-class neighborhoods after the war.[149]

Some commentators have found even deeper, more ideological meanings in rock music, something that went beyond shifts in musical taste or phases in adolescent rebellion against modesty and propriety. They have argued that rock was a protest against the entire culture of the postwar years. Douglas Miller and Marion Nowak, themselves products of the era, bluntly declared that "We were daydreaming, and rock was one of the forces that woke us up."[150] Chuck Berry's "Too Much Monkey Business" could be interpreted as a complaint about the supposed meaninglessness of work offered by the economy.[151]

Whether the teenagers intended rock to mean rebellion, there is little doubt that many adults took it that way in the 1950s and made their disapproval clear. Many homes were like those of Jeff Greenfield: "My adolescence is a continuing replay: the door swinging open, the dark, furrowed brow, the flash of anger, the sullen retreat. Like a river of troubled water, rock and roll music was the boundary of a house divided."[152]

With the benefit of hindsight, it is possible to say that adults who feared the impact of rock music and other forms of the media because of their supposed subversive tendencies had exaggerated the danger. For one thing, most of the daring innovators had been driven out of the business of rock, to be replaced by such singers as Pat Boone, Frankie Avalon, Fabian, Paul Anka, Connie Stevens, and Ricky Nelson—whites who offered a blander version of rock music.[153] Moreover, those who controlled the mass media had no particular interest in promoting subversion of traditional mores. They were more interested in making money, which involved training the young as consumers. Herein lay the major significance of the development of the mass media after the war. As David Riesman and his colleagues observed in 1950, the mass media served to train the young for the "frontiers of consumption."[154]

A JURY OF THEIR PEERS[155]

The growing power of the media in the lives of the young during the postwar period was intertwined with the growing importance of the peer group. Indeed, as David Riesman and his colleagues pointed out, the media and the peer group seemed to reinforce one another, and, together, they challenged the authority of both parents and schools.[156] It is true, of course, that the young had always been subjected to peer influences, although these peer groups were usually under at least the nominal direction of adults. Schooling itself provided an example of such adult-supervised peer groups of youth, while still another example could be found in the scouting movement, which made significant gains in membership after World War II. Another, newer form of adult-controlled youth activity were the Little League baseball teams which also flourished in the postwar period. The growth of such adult-dominated organizations and the child-centered family made it seem, in fact, as if the informal world of unsupervised children's play was disappearing, to be replaced by suburban mothers chauffering their offspring from activity to activity in wood-paneled station wagons. From this evidence one might conclude that the peer group was losing, rather than gaining, power.[157]

The extension of adult authority over youthful peer groups was, however, confined largely to children in their preadolescent years. After World War II, organizations like scouting, although gaining in enrollment, were losing their attraction for the young who were entering their adolescent years.[158] While younger children might docilely accept the activities arranged for them by their parents, teenagers were expressing increasing dissatisfaction with adult-supervised organizations. Herbert Gans reported, for example, that as suburban youngsters grew into their adolescent years, they became more unhappy with their families and with their communities, complaining bitterly about the lack of transportation and the lack of a place to "hang out." The suburbs, which seemed so ideal for small children, seemed ill-suited to their interests as they grew older, possibly because the suburbs denied them opportunities to operate as an autonomous peer group.[159]

American teenagers, having left behind the adult-dominated world of play, seemed adrift in the postwar period and attempted to fashion a subculture of their own, often in ways that disturbed their elders.[160] As we have seen, rock music provided an occasion for the gathering of the young who celebrated rituals of their own invention and those provided by the media. Indeed, it was as if rock music provided a catalyst uniting youth of divergent backgrounds and setting them apart from their elders.[161] The high school, while officially dedicated to the transmission of adult values, provided yet another arena for the peer group to work its power. James Coleman, a sociologist, called attention to the development of a separate adolescent social system that underlay the official high school culture. After surveying students and teachers in ten high schools in northern Illinois in 1957–1958, Coleman concluded that the teenagers offered "a united front to the overtures made by the adult society." While adults argued about the merits of an "academic" versus a "life adjustment" curriculum, the students themselves seemed indifferent to both. More than the praise of adults, the high school students sought prestige among their peers. For boys, this prestige was secured by athletic ability and possession of an automobile, and for girls, by good looks and popularity with boys.[162]

Most adults who took note of this adolescent behavior were inclined to regard it with a tolerant eye, for they regarded it as only a "phase"— a harmless fling after which youngsters would settle down to adult commitments of job and family. More disturbing, however, were the teenage gangs organized by the urban poor and the rise of the incidence of juvenile delinquency. The number of court cases involving juveniles tripled between 1950 and 1962, while the rate of delinquency increased from thirteen delinquency court cases per 1,000 children in 1948, to more than twenty per 1,000 in 1958. After a slight downturn, the rates of juvenile delinquency began climbing again in 1961.[163] Far from harmless, the sometimes violent acts of delinquent youth seemed harbingers of a life of crime. As a consequence, the issue of youth gangs and juvenile delinquency overshadowed all other adult concerns about youth during the period, provoking Senate hearings, television documentaries, research studies, and government reports, and becoming the subject of Broadway musicals, movies, and best-selling books.[164] The extent of the alarm was indicated in the 1960 White House Conference on Children and Youth, where the subject of juvenile delinquency overshadowed all other topics.[165]

The appearance of so many young people in trouble with the law produced a good deal of "desperate handwringing," as Rochelle Beck has put it, and a search for causes and cures.[166] Two competing theories emerged. In the 1940s and 1950s, juvenile delinquency was linked primarily to the psychological problems and deficiencies of the child and his or her parents, in keeping with the current ideal of the "child-centered family." The 1950 White House Conference on Children and Youth placed heavy emphasis on the "healthy personality development in children and youth" and pointedly called for better parent education.[167] Harrison Salisbury concluded in 1958 that the problem of the juvenile delinquent "begins early in his life. It starts with lack of love and care and attention."[168] Poor families, which postwar America generally ignored, became the focus of attention only when their children violated the law.

In the early 1960s, however, social and environmental interpretations of the origins of delinquent behavior gained greater acceptance and support as a result of programs like the Ford Foundation's "gray areas" project and Mobilization for Youth—a combined municipal and voluntary agency program in New York City. Both of these programs operated under the assumption that high delinquency rates stemmed from the inability or unwillingness of the existing social, economic, and political system to offer impoverished youth a legitimate chance for a decent standard of living. "It is the lack of congruence between aspirations of youth and the opportunities open to them," Mobilization for Youth stated, "that in the main accounts for delinquent adaptations."[169]

In 1961 this theory received the support of the Federal Government with the passage of the Juvenile Delinquency and Youth Control Act. Noting that delinquency occurred disproportionately among "school drop outs, unemployed youth faced with limited opportunities and with employment barriers, and youth in deprived family situations," the act authorized federal grants for the evaluation or demonstration of techniques and practices designed to control juvenile delinquency and for the development or securing of more effective cooperation among public and nonprofit organizations and institutions dedicated to this task.[170]

The lack of economic opportunity might have accounted for much of the rising juvenile crime rate, but many observers noted that more privileged youth of the postwar period were turning their backs on opportunities that were theirs for the asking. They were, as the movie title suggested, "rebels without a cause." This phenomenon, labeled "alienation," was the most unsettling of all postwar expressions of the youth culture, for it implied a severe indictment of society itself, even if the alienated did not run afoul of the law. Among the most celebrated examples of alienation were the "beats," men like Jack Kerouac and Allan Ginsberg, who proclaimed "secession from business civilization." Not content, like William Whyte, to criticize the Organization Man, the beats set out to live a life deliberately at odds with the values of postwar America, renouncing materialistic success and providing models that younger men might emulate.[171] Yet another symptom of alienation was the popularity among elite youth of J. D. Salinger's *Catcher in the Rye*, first published in 1951. Although banned by many school boards in the 1950s because it contained profanity and obscenity, the book proved more subversive in its philosophy. Many young people apparently identified with Holden Caulfield, a privileged teenager, who finds most adults hypocritical and their values "phony." The only person with whom Holden feels comfortable is his kid sister Phoebe, who is not yet corrupted by adult values, and it is to her that he reveals his dreams. When Phoebe presses her brother to say what he'd like to become, he rejects the idea of being a scientist or a lawyer. Lawyers do not save innocent people; instead, they "make a lot of dough and play golf and play bridge and buy cars and drink Martinis and look like a hot-shot." Instead, Holden dreams of helping children:

I keep picturing all these little kids playing some game in this big field of rye and all. Thousands of little kids, and nobody's around—nobody big, I mean—except me. And I'm standing on the edge of some crazy cliff. What I have to do, I have to catch everybody if they start to go over the cliff—I mean if they're running and they don't look where they're going I have to come out from somewhere and catch them. That's all I'd do all day. I'd just be the catcher in the rye and all. I know it's crazy, but that's the only thing I'd really like to be. I know it's crazy.[172]

By the latter 1950s, a number of books appeared that commented on the alienation of elite youth. Writers like Jules Henry, Edgar Z. Friedenberg, Kenneth Keniston, and Paul Goodman declined to explain alienation as the result of psychological problems alone.[173] Nor, unlike most officials and experts, did they believe it could be remedied by the eradication of barriers to opportunity. Indeed, these critics charged that young men did not wish to find a place in the "rat race." The problem, these commentators agreed, lay not with alienated youth but rather with what Keniston called the "alienating society."[174] Goodman, the most provocative and influential of these writers, found much in common among beats, juvenile delinquents, and the alienated youth of privileged background. Echoing writers like Salinger and rock musicians like Chuck

Berry, Goodman argued that youth suffered because postwar America offered them no honorable work to do, no worthy goals toward which to aspire.[175]

Goodman may have overestimated the amount of discontent among Americans coming of age during the postwar period. Certainly, many other observers were complaining because they perceived that elite youth of the 1950s seemed much too at ease in Zion. Far from being alienated, college youth were responding to surveys with expressions of content that could be described as complacent. These young people did not see Corporate America as a threat to their liberty, but rather as their guarantee of material comfort and security.[176]

This complacency might, of course, have provided a cover for cynicism, and, in the end, Goodman and his fellow critics proved more accurate, not perhaps because of their powers of observation but rather because of their powers of prophecy. The alienation they detected among elite youth in the 1950s grew during the next decade as the cultural and political consensus of the postwar period fell apart. The bloody battles over black rights, the "discovery" of poverty, the assassination of American political leaders, the continued threat of nuclear holocaust, and the agony of the war in Vietnam shocked many youth into an early maturity. In their response, many of these youth proved that their experience of growing up in postwar America, whatever may be said about it, had not robbed them of their capacity for moral indignation.[177] Having been reared to take a prosperous society for granted, it seemed that they then expected it to become a humane society as well.

NOTES

1. The only comprehensive treatment of the "baby boom" is Landon Y. Jones, *Great Expectations: America and the Baby Boom Generation* (New York: Coward, McCann & Geoghegan, 1980). See also Paul Glick, *American Families* (New York: John Wiley & Sons, 1957).

2. Jones, *Great Expectations*, 16; U.S. Bureau of the Census, *Current Population Reports*, Series P-25, No. 706, (Washington, D.C.: U.S. Government Printing Office, 1977), 7. See also William Peterson, "The New American Family: Causes and Consequences of the Baby Boom," *Commentary* 21 (January 1956): 1–6.

3. Jones, *Great Expectations*, 1.

4. Godfrey Hodgson, *America in Our Time* (New York: Vintage, 1976), ch. 3.

5. Jones, *Great Expectations*, 20.

6. J. A. Dudgeon, "The Control of Diptheria, Tetanus, Poliomyelitis, Measles, Rubella and Mumps," *The Practitioner* 215 (September 1975): 299–314; American Academy of Pediatrics, *Lengthening Shadows: A Report of the Council on Pediatric Practices of the American Academy of Pediatrics on the Delivery of Health Care to Children* (Evanston, Ill.: American Academy of Pediatrics, 1971), 10–23. Other

crude measures of child health during the period include a continued (though slackening) decline in infant mortality and lower rates of child death by homicide and suicide than in the 1960s and 1970s. See Urie Bronfenbrenner, "Reality and Research in the Ecology of Human Development," *American Philosophical Society Proceedings* 119, No. 6 (December 1975): 455, 457.

7. In addition to Jones, *Great Expectations*, Robert Bremner has provided an excellent review article, "Families, Children and the State," with emphasis on public policy, in Robert Bremner, ed., *Reshaping America: Society and Institutions, 1945–1960* (Columbus: Ohio State University, 1982), 3–31. See also chapters 6, 9, 10, and 11 in Douglas T. Miller and Marion Nowak, *The Fifties: The Way We Really Were* (New York: Doubleday, 1977) for a provocative, if biased, portrait of families, schools, media, and peer groups of the period.

8. Robert Bremner and his colleagues have collected many primary documents of the period in *Children and Youth in America: A Documentary History*, 3 vols. (Cambridge, Mass.: Harvard University Press, 1974), 3: Parts One through Seven.

9. Jones, *Great Expectations*, 24. See also Glen H. Elder, Jr., *Children of the Great Depression: Social Change in Life Experience* (Chicago: University of Chicago Press, 1974), 287, and Peter Filene, *Him/Her Self: Sex Roles in Modern America* (New York: Harcourt, Brace, Jovanovich, 1974), 172.

10. Jones, *Great Expectations*, 24.

11. Titles that convey the sentiment include: "There'll Be Blue Birds Over the White Cliffs of Dover"; "I'll Buy That Dream"; "It's Been a Long, Long Time"; and "When the Lights Go On Again." See Filene, *Him/Her Self*, 172.

12. Jones, *Great Expectations*, 16.

13. Ibid., 21.

14. Ibid., 24–29. See also Glick, *American Families*, ch. 11.

15. Jones, *Great Expectations*, 23.

16. Ibid., 24–25.

17. Ibid., 21 and 30. See also Miller and Nowak, *The Fifties*, 11.

18. Jones, *Great Expectations*, 30. Peter Filene points out, however, that the percentage of white women indicating four children as the ideal number rose from 31 percent in 1945 to 41 percent in 1955: (*Him/Her Self*, 172).

19. Jones, *Great Expectations*, 32–33.

20. Ibid., 28 and Filene, *Him/Her Self*, 172–183. Unsympathetic views of postwar familism include: Miller and Nowak, *The Fifties*, esp. ch. 6, "The Happy Home Corporation and Baby Factory"; Ellen Peck and Judith Senderowitz, eds., *Pronatalism: The Myth of Mom and Apple Pie* (New York: Thomas Y. Crowell, 1974); Jessie Shirley Bernard, *The Future of Motherhood* (New York: Dial Press, 1974); William Henry Chafe, *The American Woman: Her Changing Social, Economic and Political Roles, 1920–1970* (New York: Oxford University Press, 1972), ch. 9; Philip Slater, *The Pursuit of Loneliness: American Culture at the Breaking Point* (Boston: Beacon Press, 1970), 64–76; Betty Friedan, *The Feminine Mystique* (New York: Dell, 1963); Mary Ryan, *Womanhood in America: From Colonial Times to the Present* (New York: New Viewpoints, 1975), 282–286. One of the few favorable estimates of familistic values is found in Urie Bronfenbrenner, "Reality and Research."

21. Ferdinand Lundberg and Marynia Farnham, *Modern Woman: The Lost Sex* (New York: Harper, 1947), 30.

22. For analyses of images of women in the mass media, see Leslie Friedman, *Sex Role Stereotyping in the Mass Media: An Annotated Bibliography* (New York: Garland Publishing, 1977); Molly Haskell, *From Reverence to Rape: The Treatment of Women in the Movies* (New York: Holt, Rinehart & Winston, 1974); and Marjorie Rosen, *Popcorn Venus: Women, Movies and the American Dream* (New York: Coward, McCann & Geoghegan, 1973).

23. Gaye Tuchman, et al., *Hearth and Home: Images of Women in the Mass Media* (New York: Oxford University Press, 1978); Billie Wahlstrom, "Images of the Family in the Mass Media: An American Iconography?" in Virginia Tufte and Barbara Myerbroff, eds., *Changing Images of the Family* (New Haven: Yale University Press, 1979), 193–227; Arlene Skolnick, "Public Images, Private Realities: The American Family in Popular Culture and Social Science," in Tufte and Myerbroff, eds., *Changing Images*, 297–315.

24. Horace Newcomb, *TV: The Most Popular Art* (New York: Doubleday, 1976), 42–45.

25. A survey of popular television programs may be found in Harry Castlemen, *Watching TV: Four Decades of American Television* (New York: McGraw-Hill, 1982).

26. Robert Sears, et al., *Patterns of Child Rearing* (Stanford: Stanford University Press, 1957), 32.

27. Daniel Miller and Guy Swanson, *The Changing American Parent: A Study in the Detroit Area* (New York: John Wiley & Sons, 1958), 216.

28. John and Ann Fischer, "The New Englanders of Orchard Town, U.S.A." in Beatrice Whiting, ed., *Six Cultures: Studies of Child Rearing* (New York: John Wiley & Sons, 1963), 937. Additional perspective is supplied from a mental health survey taken in 1957 of 2,500 adults, which reported that 58 percent of the respondents were positively oriented toward parenthood, compared to 22 percent who were negative and 20 percent who were neutral. A replication of the survey in 1976 revealed 44 percent positive, 28 percent negative, and 28 percent neutral. The authors interpret this trend as a decline since 1957 in the "overinvestment" in the role of parenthood: Joseph Veroff, Elizabeth Douvan, and Richard Kulka, *The Inner American: A Self-Portrait from 1957 to 1976* (New York: Basic Books, 1981), 200, 203.

29. Sears, *Patterns of Child Rearing*, 36.

30. Quoted in Jones, *Great Expectations*, 47.

31. Discussions of "child-centeredness" that equate it solely with permissive childrearing generate confusion, because parents who are preoccupied with the children's welfare may be strict, and because parents who are permissive may sometimes be indifferent to their children. The essential point is to keep in focus orientation toward children rather than techniques.

32. The child-centered family in general, and Spock in particular, have attracted much critical commentary, much of it either feminist in orientation or radical. Feminists have been disturbed by the responsibilities that the child-centered ethos placed on women, while radicals have focused on the alleged fit between permissive childrearing and the corporate economy, and they have expressed alarm that the new style of socialization would produce servile "or-

ganization men." For feminist critiques, see Nancy Pottishman Weiss, "The Mother-Child Dyad Revisited: Perceptions of Mothers and Children in 20th Century Child-Rearing Manuals," *Journal of Social Issues* 34 (1978): 29–45; and "Mother, the Invention of Necessity: Dr. Benjamin Spock's *Baby and Child Care*," *American Quarterly* 29 (Winter 1977): 519–546. See also the citations listed in Note 20 above. Radical critiques include Jules Henry, *Culture Against Man* (New York: Vintage Books, 1963); Michael Zuckerman, "Dr. Spock: The Confidence Man," in Charles Rosenberg, ed., *The Family in History* (Philadelphia: University of Pennsylvania Press, 1975), 179–208; and Christopher Lasch, *Haven in a Heartless World: The Family Besieged* (New York: Basic Books, 1977). Other analyses of the subject of parent education during the period include Mary Jo Bane, "A Review of Child Care Books," *Harvard Educational Review* 43 (November 1973): 669–680; Celia Stendler, "Sixty Years of Child Training," *Journal of Pediatrics* 36, no. 1 (January 1950): 122–134; and A. Michael Sulman, "The Humanization of the American Child: Benjamin Spock as a Popularizer of Psychoanalytic Thought," *Journal of the History of Behavioral Sciences* 9 (1973): 258–265. Dr. Spock himself has been the subject of a book-length study by Lynn Bloom, *Doctor Spock: Biography of a Conservative Radical* (Indianapolis: Bobbs-Merrill, 1972).

33. Martha Wolfenstein, "Fun Morality: An Analysis of Recent American Child-Training Literature," in Margaret Mead and Martha Wolfenstein, eds., *Childhood in Contemporary Cultures* (Chicago: University of Chicago, 1955), 168–178.

34. Jones, *Great Expectations*, 48.

35. Interview by Charles Strickland with Dr. Benjamin Spock, April 15, 1982.

36. For example, in advising a mother how to deal with a two-year-old who wishes to play with a lamp cord, Spock suggests: "Don't say 'No' in a challenging voice from across the room. This gives him a choice. He says to himself, 'Shall I be a mouse and do as she says, or shall I be a man and grab the lamp cord?'" Benjamin Spock, *The Common Sense Book of Baby and Child Care* (New York: Duell, Sloan & Pearce, 1946), 210–211.

37. Zuckerman, "Spock," 202; Spock, *Baby and Child Care*, 19–20, 26, 268–269.

38. Interview, Strickland, April 15, 1982. Spock's child-centered emphasis also anticipated the postwar growth among scholars of a concern about "mother-infant bonding." See John Bowlby, *Maternal Care and Mental Health* (Geneva: World Health Organization, 1951) and Sonya L. Rhodes, "Trends in Child Development Research Important to Day-Care Policy," *Social Service Review* 53 (June 1979): 285–294. Michael Rutter reviews the maternal deprivation literature in "Separation Experiences: A New Look at an Old Topic," *Journal of Pediatrics* 95 (July 1979): 147–154.

39. Max Lerner, *America as a Civilization* (New York: Simon & Schuster, 1957), 568.

40. Wolfenstein, "Fun Morality," 168.

41. Zuckerman, "Spock," 202–203.

42. William Graebner, "The Unstable World of Benjamin Spock: Social Engineering in a Democratic Culture, 1917–1950," *Journal of American History* 67 (December 1980): 612–629. See also William G. Bach, "The Influence of Psychoanalytic Thought on Benjamin Spock's *Baby and Child Care*," *Journal of the*

History of Behavioral Sciences 10 (1974): 91–94 and Sulman, "Humanization of the American Child," 258–265.

43. Urie Bronfenbrenner, "Socialization and Social Class Through Time and Space," in Eleanor Maccoby, Theodore Newcomer, and Eugene Hartley, eds., *Readings in Social Psychology* (New York: Holt, 1958), 400–425. See also Michael Gordon, "Infant Care Revisited," *Journal of Marriage and the Family* 30 (November 1968): 578–583.

44. Lerner, *America as a Civilization*, 562. Miller and Nowak, *The Fifties*, argue (155) "Never before had so little been asked of so many. Child rearing alone had never been a full-time job in any culture." Although the ideal of full-time mothering can be traced to the early nineteenth century, it is true that never before had the ideal been within the practical reach of so many American women as in the period after World War II. See Charles Strickland, "Paths Not Taken: Seminal Models of Early Childhood Education in Jacksonian America," in Bernard Spodek, ed., *Handbook of Research in Early Childhood Education* (New York: Free Press, 1982), 321–340. Reuben Hill supplies further evidence of the trend toward child-centeredness in a study that compares family orientation of couples married in 1907, 1931, and 1953, respectively: *Family Development in Three Generations* (Cambridge, Mass.: Schenkman Publishing Co., 1970).

45. Sears, *Patterns of Child Rearing*, 475.

46. Ibid., 469. See also Fisher, "Orchard Town," 939–946, 954, 975, 963, 957, 965–968, 993, and 970.

47. Scott Donaldson, *The Suburban Myth* (New York: Columbia University Press, 1969), 3–5. See also Daniel Boorstin, *The Americans: The Democratic Experience* (New York: Vintage, 1973), 289.

48. See Mark Gelfand, "Cities, Suburbs and Government Policy," in Bremner, ed., *Reshaping America*, 261–281; Jones, *Great Expectations*, 39.

49. Jones, *Great Expectations*, 139.

50. Donaldson, *Suburban Myth*, reviews the controversy. See also Gwendolyn Wright, *Building the Dream: A Social History of Housing in America* (New York: Pantheon Books, 1981). Another assessment is Bennett Berger, "Suburbia and the American Dream," *Public Interest* 2 (Winter 1966): 80–91. One of the most balanced contemporary surveys of the suburbs was William Dobriner, ed., *The Suburban Community* (New York: G. P. Putnam's Sons, 1958), especially Ernest Mowrer's "The Family in Suburbia," 147–164. See also the excellent bibliography in Joseph Antinoro-Polizzi, *Ghetto and Suburbia: An Urban Guide* (Rochester, N.Y.: Great Lakes Associates, 1973), esp. 250–254.

51. Wendell Bell, "Social Choice, Life Styles and Suburban Residence," in Dobriner, ed., *Suburban Community*, 231.

52. Ibid., 236.

53. Peter Muller, "Everyday Life in Suburbia: A Review of Changing Economic Forces That Shape Daily Rhythms Within the Outer City," *American Quarterly* 34 (1982): 262–277.

54. Bennett Berger, *Working-Class Suburb: A Study of Auto Workers in Suburbia* (Berkeley: University of California Press, 1960), 77.

55. Ibid., 60.

56. William Whyte, *The Organization Man* (New York: Doubleday, 1956), 378.

57. Ibid., 379.

58. Herbert Gans, *The Levittowners: Ways of Life and Politics in a New Suburban Community* (New York: Pantheon, 1967), 172 and 235.

59. Ibid., 167.

60. Filene, *Him/Her Self*, 179.

61. Mowrer, "Family in Suburbia," 156–157. Further evidence of the egalitarian trend has been uncovered by Marilyn Rubin, who argues that the extent to which suburban women were working outside the home has been underestimated: "Debunking the Myth: Working Women in Suburbia," *New York Affairs* 5 (1979): 78–83.

62. Gans, *Levittowners*, 221.

63. Donaldson, *Suburban Myth*, 126–127.

64. Gans, *Levittowners*, 27–28.

65. Ibid., 24–31; Berger, "Suburbia and the American Dream," 18–91. See also Eleanor Maccoby, "Methods of Child-Rearing in Two Social Classes," in William Martin and Celia Stendler, eds., *Readings in Child Development* (New York: Harcourt, Brace, 1954), 380–396.

66. Spock, *Baby and Child Care*, 254–255. Feminist historians have made much of Spock's use of "he" in reference to the infant (Ryan, *Womanhood in America*, 351–352), but Spock made clear that this usage was only conventional and that he intended his advice to apply equally to boys and girls, unless he specifically stated otherwise (*Baby and Child Care*, 2). Spock later made clear his conservatism on the issue of sex-role socialization in *Decent and Indecent: Our Personal and Political Behavior* (Cleveland: McCall Books, 1969), but these extreme views were not evident in *Baby and Child Care*. See also "Women and Children: Male Chauvinist Spock Recants—Almost," in Louise Howe, ed., *The Future of the Family* (New York: Simon and Schuster, 1972), 151–158.

67. Sanford Dornbusch, "Afterword," in Eleanor Maccoby, ed., *The Development of Sex Differences* (Stanford: Stanford University Press, 1966), 208–216. By 1974, researchers were reporting that parents were not differentiating significantly in rearing boys and girls: see Eleanor Maccoby and Carol Jacklin, *The Psychology of Sex Differences* (Stanford: University of Stanford Press, 1974), 360–362. See also Mirra Komarovsky, *Blue-Collar Marriage* (New York: Random House, 1962).

68. David Potter, *People of Plenty: Economic Abundance and the American Character* (Chicago: University of Chicago, 1954), ch. 9.

69. David Riesman, with Nathan Glazer and Reuel Denney, *The Lonely Crowd* (New Haven: Yale University Press, 1961 ed.).

70. Ibid., 47.

71. Miller and Swanson, *Changing American Parent*.

72. Ibid., 55, 57–58. See also 109–114.

73. Weiss, "Mother: The Invention of Necessity."

74. Dwight MacDonald, "Our Invisible Poor," in Louis A. Ferman, Joyce Kornbluh, and Alan Haber, eds., *Poverty in America: A Book of Readings* (Ann Arbor, Mich.: University of Michigan Press, 1965), 15.

75. U.S. Bureau of the Census, *Historical Statistics of the United States, Colonial Times to 1970* (Washington, D.C.: U.S. Government Printing Office, 1973), 292.

76. Wright, *Building the Dream*, 247.

77. Although the Supreme Court ruled against restrictive covenants in 1948,

FHA officials continued to accept unwritten agreements and existing "traditions" of segregation until 1968.

78. Robert H. Bremner, "Families, Children, and the State," in Bremner, ed., *Reshaping America*, 16. See also Anthony Downs, "The Impact of Housing Policies on Family Life in the United States Since World War II," *Daedalus* 106 (Spring 1977): 163–180.

79. Bremner, "Families, Children, and the State," 18–20.

80. Ibid.

81. Ibid., 23.

82. Ibid.

83. Michael Harrington, *The Other America: Poverty in the United States* (Rev. ed., Baltimore: Penguin Books, 1971), 46.

84. Tom Kahn, "The Economics of Equality," in Ferman, Kornbluh, and Haber, eds., *Poverty in America*, 247.

85. CBS, "Harvest of Shame," 1960, produced by Edward R. Murrow.

86. Robert Coles, *The Migrant Farmer: A Psychiatric Study* (Atlanta: Southern Regional Council, 1965).

87. Ben J. Wattenberg, *This U.S.A.* (Garden City, N.Y.: Doubleday & Co., 1965), 81.

88. Kahn, "Economics of Equality," 241.

89. G. Franklin Edwards, "Marriage and Family Life Among Negroes," *Journal of Negro Education* 32 (Fall 1963): 464.

90. In 1950, the number of black families headed by women was about 11.6 percent, as opposed to 8.3 percent for white families. Ten years later, female-headed households accounted for 21 percent of all black families and 9 percent of all white families. For a more detailed discussion of this and other characteristics linked to black marriages and family life, see two articles by Howard University sociologist G. Franklin Edwards: "Marital Status and General Family Characteristics of the Nonwhite Population of the United States," *Journal of Negro Education* 22 (Summer 1953): 280–296 and "Marriage and Family Life Among Negroes," 451–465.

91. Zena Smith Blau, "Exposure to Child Rearing Experts: A Structural Interpretation of Class-Color Differences," in Robert Staples, ed., *The Black Family: Essays and Studies* (Belmont, Calif.: Wadsworth Publishing Co., 1971), 222–235.

92. See, for example, Allison Davis and Robert J. Havighurst, "Social Class and Color Differences in Child-Rearing," *American Sociological Review* 11 (December 1946): 698–710; Norma Radin and Constance K. Kamii, "The Child-Rearing Attitudes of Disadvantaged Negro Mothers and Some Educational Implications," *Journal of Negro Education* 34 (Spring 1965): 138–146; and Frank Riessman, *The Culturally Deprived Child* (New York: Harper & Row, 1962), esp. ch. 5, 36–48.

93. Marie F. Peters, "Parenting in Black Families with Young Children: A Historical Perspective," in Harriette Pipes McAddoo, ed., *Black Families* (Beverly Hills: Sage Publications, 1981), 214.

94. Radin and Kamii, "Child Rearing Attitudes," 143.

95. Daniel Patrick Moynihan, *The Negro Family: A Case for National Action* (Washington, D.C.: U.S. Government Printing Office, 1965). For a more bal-

anced description of what it meant to be poor and black in the 1940s and 1950s, see Claude Brown's *Manchild in the Promised Land* (New York: Macmillan Co., 1965) and Anne Moody's *Coming of Age in Mississippi* (New York: Dial Press, 1968). Other autobiographies written by blacks growing up in the postwar period include: Eldridge Cleaver, *Soul on Ice* (New York: McGraw-Hill, 1967); Angela Davis, *Angela Davis—An Autobiography* (New York: Random House, 1974); Huey P. Newton, *Revolutionary Suicide* (New York: Harcourt Brace Jovanovich, 1973); and Bobby Seale, *A Lonely Rage: The Autobiography of Bobby Seale* (New York: Times Books, 1978). For an historical perspective on the Moynihan report, see Herbert Gutman, *The Black Family in Slavery and Freedom, 1750–1925* (New York: Pantheon Books, 1976).

96. Valerie Oppenheimer, *The Female Labor Force in the United States* (Westport, Conn.: Greenwood Press, 1976), 3–14. See also Carl Degler, *At Odds: Women and the Family in America from the Revolution to the Present* (New York: Oxford University Press, 1980), ch. 17.

97. Ronald Lora, "Education: Schools as Crucible in Cold War America," in Bremner, ed., *Reshaping America*, 223–260. See also Jones, *Great Expectations*, 49–51; Miller and Nowak, *The Fifties*, ch. 9; and Bremner, et al., *Children in America*, 3: Part Seven, 1573–1906.

98. Jones, *Great Expectations*, 51.

99. Joel Spring, *The Sorting Machine: National Educational Policy Since 1945* (New York: David McKay, 1976), 13 and Lora, "Schools as Crucible," 226–228.

100. Spring, *Sorting Machine*, 9 and Lora, "Schools as Crucible," 229.

101. Spring, *Sorting Machine*, 21.

102. Whyte, *Organization Man*, 428–432.

103. "The Crisis in Education," *Life* 44 (March 24, March 31, April 7, April 14, and April 21, 1958).

104. Ibid., 44 (March 24, 1958): 35.

105. Spring, *Sorting Machine*, 98–101.

106. H. G. Rickover, *Education and Freedom* (New York: E. P. Dutton, 1959).

107. Lora, "Schools as Crucible," 242–245; James B. Conant, *The American High School Today* (New York: Signet, 1959).

108. Spring, *Sorting Machine*, 128–129.

109. Joyce Maynard provides a wry description of these reforms from a child's view in *Looking Back: A Chronicle of Growing Up Old in the Sixties* (New York: Doubleday, 1973), 18–19.

110. Spring, *Sorting Machine*, 42–43.

111. John Hersey, *The Child Buyer* (New York: Bantam, 1960), 56.

112. Richard Kluger has supplied the definitive history of the Brown decision in *Simple Justice* (New York: Alfred A. Knopf, 1976).

113. Ibid., 249–251. For another perspective, see William Chafe, "The Civil Rights Revolution, 1945–1960: The Gods Bring Threads to Webs Begun," in Bremner, ed., *Reshaping America*, 67–100.

114. Spring, *Sorting Machine*, 147–148.

115. Kluger, *Simple Justice*, ch. 27.

116. Chafe, "Civil Rights Revolution," 86–87.

117. Robert Coles, *Children of Crisis: A Study of Courage and Fear* (Boston: Little, Brown & Co., 1967), 46–47.

118. Ibid., 78–79.

119. Ibid., 76.

120. Jones, *Great Expectations*, 37–38.

121. Ibid., 44–45.

122. Ibid., 73.

123. Ibid., 74.

124. James C. Williams, "Television—Reflection of Modern America," in Gerald R. Baydo, ed., *The Evolution of Mass Culture in America—1877 to the Present* (St. Louis: Forum Press, 1982), 160. An excellent bibliographic review of the literature on radio and television is J. Fred MacDonald, et al., "Radio and Television Studies and American Culture," *American Quarterly* 32 (1980): 301–317. See also Erik Barnouw, *Tube of Plenty: The Evolution of American Television* (New York: Oxford University Press, 1975), ch. 3.

125. Thomas E. Coffin, "Television's Impact on Society," *American Psychologist* 10 (October 1955): 633. See also Wilbur Schramm, et al., *Television in the Lives of Our Children* (Stanford: Stanford University Press, 1961), 169.

126. Jeff Greenfield recalls the excitement when the first TV set appeared: *No Peace, No Place: Excavations Along the Generational Fault* (Garden City, N.Y.: Doubleday, 1973), 107.

127. Schramm, *Television in the Lives of Our Children*, 169–170, 309.

128. Erik Barnouw, *The Image Empire* (New York: Oxford University Press, 1970), 83 and Schramm, *Television in the Lives of Our Children*, 55–56. See also Lerner, *America as a Civilization*, 842–843.

129. "In short, although we are not trying to excuse the sins of television, whether of omission or commission, it seems to us quite a remarkable thing that if a child has security and love, interests, friendships, and healthful activities in his non-television hours, there is little chance that anything very bad is going to happen to him as a result of television." Schramm, *Television in the Lives of Our Children*, 175.

130. Jones, *Great Expectations*, 130–136.

131. Ibid.

132. "If I had spent at the piano the hours I gave to television, on those afternoons when I came home from school, I would be an accomplished pianist now. Or if I'd danced, or read, or painted . . . But I turned on the set instead, everyday, almost, every year, and sank into an old green easy chair, smothered in quilts, with a bag of Fritos beside me and a glass of milk to wash them down, facing life and death with Dr. Kildare, laughing at Danny Thomas, whispering the answers—out loud sometimes—with 'Password' and 'To Tell the Truth.' Looking back over all those afternoons, I try to convince myself they weren't wasted." Joyce Maynard, "An 18-Year-Old Looks Back on Life," in Jim Watts and Allen F. Davis, eds., *Generations: Your Family in Modern American History* (New York: Alfred A. Knopf, 1978), 20.

133. Schramm, *Television in the Lives of Our Children*, 174.

134. Maynard, *Looking Back*, esp. 51–52.

135. Greenfield, *No Peace, No Place*, 114–116.

136. Frank Jacobs, *The Mad World of William M. Gaines* (Secaucus, N.J.: Lyle Stuart, 1972) and Don Thompson, "The Spawn of the Son of M. C. Gaines," in

Don Thompson and Dick Lupoff, eds., *The Comic-Book Book* (New Rochelle, N.Y.: Arlington House, 1973), 294–297.

137. Jacobs, *Mad World of William M. Gaines*, 99–113; Lerner, *America as a Civilization*, 799.

138. Jacobs, *Mad World of William M. Gaines*, 114, 198–199; Paul Goodman, *Growing Up Absurd* (New York: Random House, 1959), 26.

139. Robert Sklar, *Movie-Made America: A Cultural History of American Movies* (New York: Vintage, 1975), 272.

140. Richard S. Randall, *Censorship of the Movies* (Madison: University of Wisconsin, 1968), 25–70.

141. David Pichaske, *A Generation in Motion: Popular Music and Culture in the Sixties* (New York: Schirmer Books, 1979), 17–18. See also Miller and Nowak, *The Fifties*, 299–300.

142. Pichaske, *Generation in Motion*, 33–34.

143. Ibid., 7–8; Miller and Nowak, *The Fifties*, 294.

144. Greenfield, *No Peace, No Place*, 35. See also Pichaske, *Generation in Motion*, 36, and Miller and Nowak, *The Fifties*, 295–296.

145. Albert Goldman, *Elvis* (New York: McGraw-Hill, 1981), 110 and 175. See also Pichaske, *Generation in Motion*, 33, 39–41, 43, 45, 93, 156–157, 165–168, and Miller and Nowak, *The Fifties*, 299–309.

146. Pichaske, in his history of rock, has explained: "Any number of things distinguish rock-n-roll from commercial shlock. Most obviously, it is rougher, simpler, more homemade, less professional. In a lot of cases, it's just plain off-key.... Roughness in the quality of music slightly out of control, eager, impatient, urgent, setting out, young." Pichaske, *Generation in Motion*, 41. See also Greenfield, *No Peace, No Place*, 48.

147. Pichaske, *Generation in Motion*, 44–45.

148. Greenfield, *No Peace, No Place*, 53.

149. Goldman, *Elvis*, 81–82.

150. Miller and Nowak, *The Fifties*, 312.

151. Pichaske, *Generation in Motion*, 48.

152. Greenfield, *No Peace, No Place*, 55.

153. Pichaske, *Generation in Motion*, 37–39; Miller and Nowak, *The Fifties*, 302–303; Goldman, *Elvis*, 177, 181.

154. Riesman, *Lonely Crowd*, 164.

155. This title is borrowed from Chapter III of *The Lonely Crowd*, with grateful acknowledgment.

156. Riesman, *Lonely Crowd*, 70, 76.

157. Joseph Kett, *Rites of Passage: Adolescence in America, 1790 to the Present* (New York: Basic Books, 1977), 245–266; Jones, *Great Expectations*, 56; Mary and Herbert Knapp, *One Potato, Two Potato: The Secret Education of American Children* (New York: W. W. Norton, 1976), 265.

158. Kett, *Rites of Passage*, 266.

159. Gans, *Levittowners*, 206–208.

160. Kett, *Rites of Passage*, 269.

161. Jeff Greenfield, *No Peace, No Place*, 56. Greenfield recalls the feeling of teenagers that rock music *belonged* to them and that adults were not supposed to listen to it.

162. James Coleman, *The Adolescent Society: The Social Life of the Teenager and Its Impact on Education* (New York: Free Press of Glencoe, 1961), esp. chs. I and II.

163. John Janeway Conger and Wilbur C. Miller, *Personality, Social Class and Delinquency* (New York: John Wiley & Sons, 1966), 4.

164. Barnouw, *Image Empire*, 83; Lerner, *America as a Civilization*, 799; Bremner, *Children and Youth*, 3: Part Five, 1003–1145; Harrison Salisbury, *The Shook-Up Generation* (Greenwich, Conn.: Fawcett, 1958); Miller and Nowak, *The Fifties*, 280–287, 299–300.

165. Rochelle Beck, "The White House Conferences on Children: An Historical Perspective," *Harvard Educational Review* 43 (November 1973), 96.

166. Ibid.

167. "Recommendations of the White House Conference on Children and Youth," *Social Security Bulletin* 14 (February 1951): 10. See also Bremner, et al., *Children and Youth*, 3: 1109.

168. Salisbury, *Shook-Up Generation*, 166.

169. Bremner, et al., *Children and Youth*, 3: 1100.

170. Ibid., 1127. For an authoritative survey of juvenile delinquency, see Conger and Miller, *Personality, Social Class and Delinquency*, which concluded that neither sociological nor psychological explanations were alone adequate. See also Robert Havighurst, et al., *Growing Up in River City* (New York: John Wiley & Sons, 1962), for a discussion of juvenile delinquency outside major urban areas.

171. Lawrence Lipton, *The Holy Barbarians* (New York: Julian Messner, 1959), 292.

172. J. D. Salinger, *The Catcher in the Rye* (New York: Signet, 1951), 155–156.

173. Henry, *Culture Against Man*; Edgar Z. Friedenberg, *The Vanishing Adolescent* (New York: Dell, 1959); Kenneth Keniston, *The Uncommitted: Alienated Youth in American Society* (New York: Harcourt, Brace & World, 1960); Goodman, *Growing Up Absurd*.

174. Keniston, *The Uncommitted*, esp. Section II.

175. Goodman, *Growing Up Absurd*, 12.

176. David Riesman, "The Found Generation," in David Riesman, ed., *Abundance for What? and Other Essays* (Garden City, N.Y.: Doubleday & Co., 1964), 320.

177. In contrast to radical historians who have argued that middle-class, permissive childrearing made children acquiescent, Kenneth Keniston conducted interviews with young antiwar activists during the 1960s, most of whom reported a childhood experience consistent with the features of a child-centered family: *Young Radicals: Notes on Committed Youth* (New York: Harcourt, Brace & World, 1968), esp. ch. 2.

BIBLIOGRAPHY

American Academy of Pediatrics. *Lengthening Shadows: A Report of the Council on Pediatric Practices of the American Academy of Pediatrics on the Delivery of Health Care to Children.* Evanston, Ill.: American Academy of Pediatrics, 1971.

Antinoro-Polizzi, Joseph. *Ghetto and Suburbia: An Urban Guide.* Rochester, N.Y.: Great Lakes Associates, 1973.

Bach, William G. "The Influence of Psychoanalytic Thought on Benjamin Spock's *Baby and Child Care.*" *Journal of the History of Behavioral Sciences* 10 (1974): 91–94.

Bane, Mary Jo. "A Review of Child Care Books." *Harvard Educational Review* 43 (November 1973): 669–680.

Barnouw, Erik. *The Image Empire.* New York: Oxford University Press, 1970.

———. *Tube of Plenty: The Evolution of American Television.* New York: Oxford University Press, 1975.

Beck, Rochelle. "The White House Conferences on Children: An Historical Perspective." *Harvard Educational Review* 43 (November 1973): 653–668.

Bell, Wendell. "Social Choice, Life Styles and Suburban Residence." In *The Suburban Community*, pp. 225–247. Edited by William Dobriner. New York: G. P. Putnam, 1958.

Berger, Bennett. "Suburbia and the American Dream." *Public Interest* 2 (Winter 1966): 80–91.

———. *Working-Class Suburb: A Study of Auto Workers in Suburbia.* Berkeley: University of California Press, 1960.

Bernard, Jessie Shirley. *The Future of Motherhood.* New York: Dial Press, 1974.

Blau, Zena Smith. "Exposure to Child Rearing Experts: A Structural Interpretation of Class-Color Differences." In *The Black Family: Essays and Studies*, pp. 222–235. Edited by Robert Staples. Belmont, California: Wadsworth Publishing Company, Inc., 1971.

Bloom, Lynn. *Doctor Spock: Biography of a Conservative Radical.* Indianapolis: Bobbs-Merrill, 1972.

Boorstin, Daniel. *The Americans: The Democratic Experience.* New York: Vintage, 1973.

Bowlby, John. *Maternal Care and Mental Health.* Geneva: World Health Organization, 1951.

Bremner, Robert, ed. *Children and Youth in America: A Documentary History.* 3 vols. Cambridge, Mass.: Harvard University Press, 1970–1974.

———. "Families, Children and the State." In *Reshaping America: Society and Institutions, 1945–1960*, pp. 3–31. Edited by Robert Bremner. Columbus, Ohio: Ohio State University, 1982.

Bronfenbrenner, Urie. "Reality and Research in the Ecology of Human Development." *American Philosophical Society Proceedings* 119 No. 6 (December 1975): 439–469.

———. "Socialization and Social Class Through Time and Space." In *Readings in Social Psychology*, pp. 400–425. Edited by Eleanor Maccoby, Theodore Newcomer and Eugene Hartley. New York: Holt, Inc., 1958.

Brown, Claude. *Manchild in the Promised Land.* New York: Macmillan, 1965.

Castleman, Harry. *Watching TV—Four Decades of American Television.* New York: McGraw-Hill, 1982.

Chafe, William Henry. *The American Woman: Her Changing Social, Economic, and Political Roles, 1920–1970.* New York: Oxford University Press, 1972.

———. "The Civil Rights Revolution, 1945–1960: The Gods Bring Threads to Webs Begun." In *Reshaping America: Society and Institutions, 1945–1960*, pp. 67–100. Edited by Robert Bremner. Columbus, Ohio: Ohio State University, 1982.

Cleaver, Eldridge. *Soul on Ice.* New York: McGraw-Hill, 1967.

Coffin, Thomas E. "Television's Impact on Society." *The American Psychologist* 10 (October 1955): 630–641.

Coleman, James. *The Adolescent Society: The Social Life of the Teenager and Its Impact on Education.* New York: Free Press of Glencoe, 1961.

Coles, Robert. *Children of Crisis: A Study of Courage and Fear.* Boston: Little, Brown, 1967.

———. *The Migrant Farmer: A Psychiatric Study.* Atlanta: Southern Regional Council, 1965.

Conant, James B. *The American High School Today.* New York: Signet, 1959.

Conger, John Janeway and Miller, Wilbur C. *Personality, Social Class and Delinquency.* New York: John Wiley and Sons, 1966.

"Crisis in Education." *Life* 44 (24, 31 March; 7, 14, 21 April 1950).

Davis, Angela. *Angela Davis—An Autobiography.* New York: Random House, 1974.

Davis, Allison and Havighurst, Robert J. "Social Class and Color Differences in Child Rearing." *American Sociological Review* 11 (December 1946): 698–710.

Degler, Carl. *At Odds: Women and the Family from the Revolution to the Present.* New York: Oxford University Press, 1980.

Dobriner, William Mann, ed. *The Suburban Community.* New York: G. P. Putnam, 1958.

Donaldson, Scott. *The Suburban Myth.* New York: Columbia University Press, 1969.

Dornbusch, Sanford. "After Word." In *The Development of Sex Differences,* pp. 203–219. Edited by Eleanor Maccoby. Stanford: Stanford University Press, 1966.

Downs, Anthony. "The Impact of Housing Policies on Family Life in the United States since World War II." *Daedalus* 106 (Spring 1977): 163–180.

Dudgeon, J. A. "The Control of Diptheria, Tetanus, Polio Myelitlis, Measles, Rubella and Mumps." *The Practitioner* 215 (September 1975): 299–314.

Edwards, G. Franklin. "Marital Status and General Family Characteristics of the Nonwhite Population of the United States." *Journal of Negro Education* 22 (Summer 1953): 280–296.

———. "Marriage and Family Life Among Negroes." *Journal of Negro Education* 32 (Fall 1963): 451–465.

Elder, Glen H. *Children of the Great Depression: Social Changes in Life Experience.* Chicago: University of Chicago Press, 1974.

Filene, Peter. *Him/Her Self: Sex Roles in Modern America.* New York: Harcourt, Brace Jovanovich, 1974.

Fischer, John and Fischer, Ann. "The New Englanders of Orchard Town, U.S.A." In *Six Cultures: Studies of Child Rearing,* pp. 869–1010. Edited by Beatrice Whiting. New York: John Wiley and Sons, 1963.

Friedan, Betty. *The Feminine Mystique.* New York: Dell, 1963.

Friedenberg, Edgar Zodiag. *The Vanishing Adolescent.* New York: Dell, 1959.

Friedman, Leslie. *Sex Role Stereotyping in the Mass Media: An Annotated Bibliography.* New York: Garland Publishing, 1977.

Gans, Herbert J. *The Levittowners: Ways of Life and Politics in a New Suburban Community.* New York: Pantheon Books, 1967.

Gelfand, Mark. "Cities, Suburbs and Government Policy." In *Reshaping America: Society and Institutions, 1945–1960*, pp. 261–282. Edited by Robert Bremner. Columbus, Ohio: Ohio State University, 1982.

Glick, Paul. *American Families*. New York: John Wiley and Sons, Inc., 1957.

Goldman, Albert. *Elvis*. New York: McGraw-Hill, 1981.

Goodman, Paul. *Growing Up Absurd: Problems of Youth in the Organized System*. New York: Random House, 1959.

Gordon, Michael. "Infant Care Revisited." *The Journal of Marriage and Family* 30 (November 1968): 578–583.

Graebner, William. "The Unstable World of Benjamin Spock: Social Engineering in a Democratic Culture, 1917–1950." *Journal of American History* 67 (December 1980): 612–629.

Greenfield, Jeff. *No Peace, No Place: Excavations Along the Generational Fault*. Garden City, New York: Doubleday, 1973.

Gutman, Herbert. *The Black Family in Slavery and Freedom, 1750–1925*. New York: Pantheon Books, 1976.

Harrington, Michael. *The Other America: Poverty in the United States*. Revised edition. Baltimore: Penguin Books, Inc., 1971.

Haskell, Molly. *From Reverence to Rape: The Treatment of Women in the Movies*. New York: Holt, Rinehart & Winston, 1974.

Havighurst, Robert and the Committee on Human Development. *Growing Up in River City*. New York: John Wiley and Sons, 1962.

Henry, Jules. *Culture Against Man*. New York: Vintage Books, 1963.

Hersey, John Richard. *The Child Buyer*. New York: Bantam, 1960.

Hill, Reuben. *Family Development in Three Generations*. Cambridge, Mass.: Schenkman Publishing Co., 1970.

Hodgson, Godfrey. *America in Our Time*. New York: Vintage, 1976.

Howe, Louise. "Women and Children: Male Chauvinist Spock Recants—Almost." In *The Future of the Family*, pp. 151–158. Edited by Louise Howe. New York: Simon and Schuster, 1972.

Jacobs, Frank. *The Mad World of William M. Gaines*. Secaucus, New Jersey: Lyle Stuart, 1972.

Jones, Landon Y. *Great Expectations: America and the Baby Boom Generation*. New York: Coward, McCann and Geoghegan, 1980.

Kahn, Tom. "The Economics of Equality." In *Poverty in America: A Book of Readings*, pp. 240–259. Edited by Louis A. Ferman, Joyce Kornbluh, and Alan Haber. Ann Arbor: University of Michigan Press, 1965.

Keniston, Kenneth. *The Uncommitted: Alienated Youth in American Society*. New York: Harcourt, Brace and World, 1960.

———. *Young Radicals: Notes on Committed Youth*. New York: Harcourt, Brace and World, 1968.

Kett, Joseph F. *Rites of Passage: Adolescence in America, 1790 to the Present*. New York: Basic Books, 1977.

Kluger, Richard. *Simple Justice: The Story of Brown v. Board of Education and Black America's Struggle for Equality*. New York: Alfred A. Knopf, 1976.

Knapp, Mary and Knapp, Herbert. *One Potato, Two Potato . . . : The Secret Education of American Children*. New York: W. W. Norton, 1976.

Komarovsky, Mirra with the collaboration of Jane H. Philips. *Blue-Collar Marriage*. New York: Random House, 1962.

Lasch, Christopher. *Haven in a Heartless World: The Family Besieged*. New York: Basic Books, 1977.

Lerner, Max. *America as a Civilization: Life and Thought in the United States Today*. New York: Simon and Schuster, 1957.

Lipton, Lawrence. *The Holy Barbarians*. New York: Julian Messner, 1959.

Lora, Ronald. "Education: Schools as Crucible in Cold War America." In *Reshaping America: Society and Institutions, 1945–1960*, pp. 223–260. Edited by Robert Bremner. Columbus, Ohio: Ohio State University, 1982.

Lundberg, Ferdinand and Farnham, Marynia. *Modern Woman: The Lost Sex*. New York: Harper & Brothers, 1947.

Maccoby, Eleanor. "Methods of Child-Rearing in Two Social Classes." In *Readings in Child Development*, pp. 380–396. Edited by William Martin and Celia Stendler. New York: Harcourt, Brace, 1954.

Maccoby, Eleanor and Jacklin, Carol. *The Psychology of Sex Differences*. Stanford: Stanford University Press, 1974.

MacDonald, Dwight. "Our Invisible Poor." In *Poverty in America: A Book of Readings*, pp. 7–24. Edited by Louis A. Ferman, Joyce Kornbluh, and Alan Haber. Ann Arbor: University of Michigan Press, 1965.

MacDonald, J. Fred; Marsden, Michael T.; and Geist, Christopher O. "Radio and Television Studies and American Culture." *American Quarterly* 32 (1980): 301–317.

Maynard, Joyce. "An 18–Year-Old Looks Back on Life." In *Generations: Your Family in Modern American History*, pp. 18–24. Edited by Jim Watts and Allen A. Davis. New York: Alfred Knopf, 1978.

———. *Looking Back: A Chronicle of Growing Up Old in the Sixties*. New York: Doubleday, 1973.

Miller, Daniel R. and Swanson, Guy. *The Changing American Parent: A Study in the Detroit Area*. New York: John Wiley and Sons, 1958.

Miller, Douglas T. and Nowak, Marion. *The Fifties: The Way We Really Were*. Garden City, New York: Doubleday, 1977.

Moody, Anne. *Coming of Age in Mississippi*. New York: Dell Publications, 1968.

Mowrer, Ernest. "The Family in Suburbia." In *The Suburban Community*, pp. 147–164. Edited by William Dobriner. New York: G. P. Putnam's Sons, 1958.

Moynihan, Daniel Patrick. *The Negro Family: A Case for National Action*. Washington: U.S. Government Printing Office, 1965.

Muller, Peter. "Everyday Life in Suburbia: A Review of Changing Economic Forces that Shape Daily Rhythms within the Outer City." *American Quarterly* 35 (1982): 262–277.

Newcomb, Horace. *TV: The Most Popular Art*. New York: Doubleday, 1976.

Newton, Huey P. *Revolutionary Suicide*. New York: Harcourt Brace Jovanovich, 1973.

Oppenheimer, Valerie. *The Female Labor Force in the Demographic and Economic Factors Governing its Growth and Changing Composition*. Westport, Conn.: Greenwood Press, 1976.

Peck, Ellen and Senderowitz, Judith, eds. *Pronatalism: the Myth of Mom and Apple Pie*. New York: Thomas Y. Crowell, 1974.

Peters, Marie F. "Parenting in Black Families with Young Children: A Historical Perspective." In *Black Families*, pp. 211–224. Edited by Harriette Pipes McAddoo. Beverly Hills: Sage Publications, 1981.

Peterson, William. "The New American Family: Causes and Consequences of the Baby Boom." *Commentary* 21 (January 1956): 1–6.

Pichaske, David. *A Generation in Motion: Popular Music and Culture in the Sixties.* New York: Schirmer Books, 1979.

Potter, David Morris. *People of Plenty: Economic Abundance and the American Character.* Chicago: University of Chicago, 1954.

Radin, Norma and Kamii, Constance K. "The Child-rearing Attitudes of Disadvantaged Negro Mothers and Some Educational Implications." *Journal of Negro Education* 34 (Spring 1965): 138–146.

Randall, Richard S. *Censorship of the Movies: The Social and Political Control of a Mass Medium.* Madison: University of Wisconsin, 1968.

"Recommendations of the White House Conference on Children and Youth." *Social Security Bulletin* 14 (February 1951): 10–14.

Rhodes, Sonya L. "Trends in Child Development Research Important to Day-Care Policy." *Social Service Review* 53 (June 1979): 285–294.

Rickover, Hyman George. *Education and Freedom.* New York: E. P. Dutton, 1959.

Riesman, David. "The Found Generation." In *Abundance for What? and Other Essays*, pp. 309–323. Garden City, New York: Doubleday and Company, Inc., 1964.

———. In collaboration with Glazer, Nathan and Denney, Revel. *The Lonely Crowd.* New Haven: Yale University Press, 1961 ed. (1950).

Riessman, Frank. *The Culturally Deprived Child.* New York: Harper and Row, 1962.

Rosen, Marjorie. *Popcorn Venus: Women, Movies and The American Dream.* New York: Coward, McCann & Geoghegan, 1973.

Rubin, Marilyn. "Debunking the Myth: Working Women in Suburbia." *New York Affairs* 5 (1979): 78–83.

Rutter, Michael. "Separation Experiences: A New Look at an Old Topic." *Journal of Pediatrics* 95 (July 1979): 147–154.

Ryan, Mary P. *Womanhood in America: From Colonial Times to the Present.* New York: New Viewpoints, 1975.

Salinger, J. D. *The Catcher in the Rye.* New York: Signet, 1951.

Salisbury, Harrison Evans. *The Shook-Up Generation.* Greenwich, Conn.: Fawcett, 1958.

Schramm, Wilbur; Lyle, Jack; and Parker, Edwin B. *Television in the Lives of Our Children.* Stanford: Stanford University Press, 1961.

Seale, Bobby. *A Lonely Rage: The Autobiography of Bobby Seale.* New York: Times Books, 1978.

Sears, Robert; Maccoby, Eleanor; Levin, Harry. *Patterns of Child Rearing.* Stanford: Stanford University Press, 1957.

Sklar, Robert. *Movie-Made America: A Social History of American Movies.* New York: Vintage, 1975.

Skolnick, Arlene. "Public Images, Private Realities: The American Family in Popular Culture and Social Science." In *Changing Images of the Family*, pp.

297–315. Edited by Virginia Tufte and Barbara Myerbroff. New Haven: Yale 1979.

Slater, Philip E. *The Pursuit of Loneliness: American Culture at the Breaking Point.* Boston: Beacon Press, 1970.

Spock, Benjamin. *The Common Sense Book of Baby and Child Care.* New York: Duell, Sloan and Pearce, 1946.

———. *Decent and Indecent: Our Personal and Political Behavior.* Cleveland: McCall Books, 1969.

Spring, Joel. *The Sorting Machine: National Educational Policy Since 1945.* New York: David McKay, 1976.

Stendler, Celia. "Sixty Years of Child Training." *Journal of Pediatrics* 36:1 (January 1950): 122–134.

Strickland, Charles. "Paths Not Taken: Seminal Models of Early Childhood Education in Jacksonian America." In *Handbook of Research in Early Childhood Education*, pp. 321–340. Edited by Bernard Spodek. New York: Free Press, 1982.

Sulman, Michael A. "The Humanization of the American Child: Benjamin Spock as a Popularizer of Psychoanalytic Thought." *The Journal of the History of Behavioral Sciences* 9 (1973): 258–265.

Thompson, Don. "The Spawn of the Son of M. C. Gaines." In *The Comic-Book Book*, pp. 290–316. Edited by Don Thompson and Dick Lupoff. New Rochelle, N.Y.: Arlington House, 1973.

Tuchman, Gaye; Daniels, Arlene Kaplan; and Benet, James, eds. *Hearth and Home: Images of Women in the Mass Media.* New York: Oxford University Press, 1978.

U.S. Bureau of the Census. *Historical Statistics of the United States, Colonial Times to 1970.* Washington: U.S. Government Printing Office, 1973.

Veroff, Joseph; Douvan, Elizabeth; and Kulka, Richard A. *The Inner American: A Self-Portrait from 1957 to 1976.* New York: Basic Books, 1981.

Wahlstrom, Billie. "Images of the Family in the Mass Media: An American Iconography?" In *Changing Images of the Family*, pp. 193–227. Edited by Virginia Tufte and Barbara Myerbroff. New Haven: Yale, 1979.

Wattenberg, Ben J. In collaboration with Richard M. Scammon. *This U.S.A.: An Unexpected Family Portrait of 194,067,296 Americans Drawn from the Census.* Garden City, N.Y.: Doubleday and Company, Inc., 1965.

Weiss, Nancy Pottishman. "The Mother-Child Dyad Revisited: Perceptions of Mothers and Children in 20th Century Child-Rearing Manuals." *Journal of Social Issues* 34, No. 2 (1978): 29–45.

———. "Mother, the Invention of Necessity: Dr. Benjamin Spock's *Baby and Child Care*." *American Quarterly* 29 (Winter 1977): 519–546.

Whyte, William Hollingsworth. *The Organization Man.* New York: Doubleday, 1956.

Williams, James C. "Television—Reflection of Modern America." In *The Evolution of Mass Culture in America—1877 to the Present*, pp. 159–178. Edited by Gerald R. Baydo. St. Louis: Forum Press, 1982.

Wolfenstein, Martha. "Fun Morality: An Analysis of Recent American Child-Training Literature." In *Childhood in Contemporary Cultures*, pp. 168–178.

Edited by Margaret Mead and Martha Wolfenstein. Chicago: University of Chicago, 1955.

Wright, Gwendolyn. *Building the Dream: A Social History of Housing in America.* New York: Pantheon Books, 1981.

Zuckerman, Michael. "Dr. Spock: The Confidence Man." In *The Family in History,* pp. 179–208. Edited by Charles Rosenberg. Philadelphia: University of Pennsylvania Press, 1975.

14

The Age of Narcissism, 1963–1982

Elizabeth Douvan

In the 1980s, we continue to hear about spoiled children, the need for greater discipline, the absurd extent to which American parents cater to and fear their children. But we hear more ominous hints and other messages: child abuse, latch-key children who go home to empty houses and need special instruction in how to handle strangers who call or knock at the door, kiddie porn, and the surfacing of a political group whose purpose is to legitimize "cross-generational" sex. The most recent addition to the warnings about the situation of our children is a growing literature on the "disappearance of childhood," the trend toward deemphasizing developmental differences and including children in aspects of parents' lives from which they had been excluded and protected in the idealized suburban postwar family.[1]

Can all of these views be valid? Is it possible that we both overprotect our children and burden them with parents' problems? Do we both overindulge them and deny them the gift of parental protection? Do we both idealize childhood and deny it to our own children by exposing them prematurely to the hardest realities and problems for which they have no developmental preparation? Do we disguise rejection and abandonment as permissiveness?

If we recognize at the outset that childhood in the United States is extremely variable, that race and social class and religion and ethnicity all affect the experience of childhood and the conditions under which children are raised, we come to see that apparently contradictory statements about childhood may all carry some parcel of truth. It is simply a matter of needing to be clear and explicit about the part of the culture, the particular group we are looking at and describing.

Children in single-parent, female-headed households may have to "grow

up a little sooner" and may be denied the privilege of protection against
harsh realities. They may be latch-key children. The child of divorce
may be the only source of emotional support to a parent devastated by
desertion. Children in upper-middle-class families may be overindulged
but also pressured for early, continuous, and self-conscious achievement
and may feel that love is always contingent on compliance with parental
standards. Some rural and small town families still raise children in
highly traditional ways and in coherent communities of kin, church members, and neighbors. There is no single experience of childhood in the
United States. When we speak of changes in that experience over time,
we are simplifying and to a certain extent distorting reality. We need to
remind ourselves at intervals that the reality is always more complex and
variable than our presentation of it can reasonably be.

In 1963 Betty Friedan's book, *The Feminine Mystique*, was published.[2]
Thus was signalled the beginning of the end of a period of focused and
intense turning inward, of privatized and isolated family life dominated
by an ideal of the large family, sufficient unto itself, headed by an adult
couple who shared a life-long, monogamous, loving relationship and
divided spheres. The male wrested a livelihood for the family in the
outside world and represented ultimate authority in the family because
of his position between two worlds. The woman devoted herself to the
raising of the next generation and to all of those functions that provide
adhesive and grace to group life, to the family, the neighborhood, the
community.

This ideal, the dream of returning to an earlier, simpler, more manageable life, to "the classic family of Western nostalgia," failed after a
strong eighteen-year try.[3] Educated women, isolated in the suburbs with
preschool children and faced with the task of finding meaning and satisfaction exclusively in the spheres of home and child care, were an
audience ripe for Friedan's message. The flight to the suburbs strained
men's resources as well. Although the ideal of "togetherness" and sharing
family rites and pleasures was promoted by the women's magazines, the
struggle to wrest a living in the city and manage the Little League in
the suburbs put unrealistic demands on the husband/father. When the
strain became too intense, as novels of the period as well as social
science document, it was the job that won out in the competition for
time for most men.[4] The wife/mother was thus left more isolated and
alone in handling the tasks and crises of child care than she had ever
been before.

Women began to look around for ways out of their isolation and their
radical loss of self. Friedan's analysis reads like a revelation to many of
these women: the discovery that their unhappiness and sense of entrap-
ment were not unique inventions, or the product of their individual
neuroses or personal failures, was often the thing that allowed women

release from depression and the possibility of moving out of isolation and into the world. The movement for women's equality in the world was once again resurgent.

Married women began to move into the work force in unprecedented numbers and to define themselves in more clearly individual terms. Patterns of authority in the family were bound to shift in response to women's entry into the paid labor force, creating strains and requiring changes in the structure and function of family members. Divorce increased at a brisk pace.[5]

Many forces contributed to the breakdown of pro-marriage and pro-natal norms and to the suburban idyll's coming apart at the seams. Depending on the disciplinary and ideological allegiances of the particular social analyst, various causal factors have been emphasized. Demographic factors have been adduced: for example, the disproportion of females in the society at the end of World War II. The presence of large numbers of single females demands the legitimation of roles for women other than wife and mother, thus offering at least a vision of alternative life paths. Demographers have pointed to the fact that each renewal of feminism has occurred at a time when women were overrepresented in the population of marriageable age.[6]

Other demographic factors have been offered to account for the younger generation's postponing marriage and childbearing and thus reducing overall fertility. Richard Easterlin's hypothesis is that whenever a large cohort enters adulthood to replace a smaller cohort, competition for jobs and resources is strong and the young will not be as optimistic or bouncy about their prospects. When, on the other hand, a small cohort follows a large one (for example, the Depression generation who came to adulthood during World War II and produced the baby boom immediately after the war), members of the small cohort will be optimistic about their future and will reflect that optimism in early decisions to marry and have children.[7]

The ecology movement and the recognition of population pressures—the costs and potential disaster that impend if population growth is not controlled in recognition of the limited nature of world resources—was another critical demographic factor that began to erode familistic values.

Some social critics saw the decline of religious values and their replacement by secular "egocentric" values playing a crucial role in the turn away from family. The new birth control technology and changes in sexual morality—changes that had been underway since the turn of the century but that acquired greater impetus and publicity in the 1960s' "sexual revolution"—were blamed for the shift.[8] Conservative critics have seen the women's movement as the source of family breakdown. Others think that social scientists, the experts, robbed parents of their legitimate authority and security in the parent role, thus causing it to become an anxious, problematic role that the young were afraid to take on.[9] Dr. Spock and his child-centered, permissive advice are blamed by conservative critics for the breakdown in parental authority and the youth rebellion of the late 1960s that has challenged and eroded still further our grounding in traditional values and forms. Philip Slater and many feminist theorists hold, on the other hand, that the whole familistic ideology became so slavish and joyless that it alienated the younger generation by its own weight.[10]

CHANGING NORMS

Whatever the source or sources of change—and in all likelihood several of the factors alluded to in the preceding paragraphs played a part—there can be no doubt that profound change has occurred in the norms and values surrounding marriage, childbearing, and childrearing over the course of the last twenty years. These norms and values undergird the way in which young adults look at parenthood, how they define and measure its satisfactions, how they conceive the commitment involved in becoming a parent, how they make the choice whether to have children. When the undergirding norms and values change, the experience of childhood itself must also change.

This chapter describes changes in familistic values and norms that occurred during this period.[11] The description of these changes is followed by a discussion of other aspects of the culture's values and ideology that affect children; presentation of evidence about ways in which childhood has changed; and an argument for a certain ordering of causal forces in the production of such changes.

To begin with the most obvious reflection of change in family values: over the course of the last twenty years, we have seen a drop in the birth rate from its postwar high of 3 to 4 children per family and have achieved the goal of zero population growth.[12] In 1976 5 percent of a sample of college women, when asked their ideal family size, now say they think childlessness is ideal. This represented a substantial change from a similar survey in 1957. Young people are marrying later and are postponing the decision to have children.

In 1957 pro-marriage and pro-natal norms were strong, rigid, and monolithic. It was difficult or even impossible for a woman to say she would rather be single or rather not have children. Most adults, asked what they would think of a young person who decided never to marry (or never to have children), gave answers that indicated they would see such choices as deviant, reflecting either moral or psychological flaws in the young person.[13] Even unmarried and childless women gave such answers, and unmarried women presented particularly idealized concepts of marriage and parenthood. If the culture thought that a person who chose not to marry was sick or immoral, the single individual wanted to make it clear that his or her marital status did not reflect a personal rejection of marriage!

By 1976 the normative climate had changed radically. Most people then said that the choice not to marry or not to have children was a choice like any other, involving costs and benefits and made for a wide variety of reasons. The tone of the answers was now quite neutral and in great contrast to the moral tone of 1957. Unmarried women have changed most dramatically, giving up their idealized concepts of marriage and parenthood and viewing these as choices to be made among a variety of ways to spend a life, no one of which guarantees truth or beauty or perfect happiness.

The difference in climate between 1957 and 1976 is striking. In 1957 marriage and parenthood were part of a given pattern of life, roles to be assumed as part of adult life and as indicators of both adulthood and "maturity" (with all of the psychiatric and mental health judgments implied by the term). The assumption of the spouse and parent roles was used as a criterion of adjustment, maturity, and health. By 1976, on the other hand, the criterion by which experience and roles and actions were judged had shifted from maturity and adjustment to a concept of personal fulfillment and happiness. Now the question was not whether a person was mature and "healthy" enough to have managed all of the crucial adult roles ("to love and to work") but whether any or all of the roles brought personal "fulfillment" and pleasure to the person involved. Traditionally, we judged the individual by the way he or she managed social roles; now we measure roles by the rewards they hold for the individual. The individual who is in a role and does *not* find it fulfilling or pleasurable is thought to be foolish or strange for remaining in it. Young people must *choose* to become parents with a degree of deliberation that previous generations did not know. And since it is a personal choice, young people may feel they must justify it with their happiness-in-role.

Despite the softening of norms, family roles continue to hold a central position in the values and life satisfactions of most people. We have become more tolerant of a variety of life choices, including the choice to forego the spouse and/or parent role(s). But for most of us, marriage and parenthood remain the most important goals to be achieved. Both marriage and parenthood have become more problematic: Many more people in 1976 said that at some time they had faced serious problems in marriage and in raising their children. Nonetheless, family roles remain the central sources of satisfaction for both men and women.

CHANGING FAMILY PATTERNS

In the last twenty years, two major changes have radically affected family structure in the United States and our ideas about what a family is. These are the mass entry of women into the labor force and the increasing number of households headed by a single adult. Women's movement into the labor force has meant that two-earner families have become more common than the traditional nuclear family in which the male head earned the money that supported the family and the wife/mother worked in the home, raising the children and managing non-market productive work in the household.

The other development—the increase in single-parent households—occurred as more and more families broke up through divorce or desertion. It also increased because changes in sexual morality and practice led to an increasing incidence of never-married women bearing children and raising them rather than giving them up for adoption. Both of the new family forms—the two-earner family and the single-parent family—have affected the experience of childhood profoundly.

Divorce and Single-Parent Families

Nearly one out of every three marriages in the United States ends in divorce. Mary Jo Bane and others who have analyzed divorce statistics estimate that four out of every ten children born in the 1970s will spend a part of their childhood in a one-parent family.[14] For most of these children the experience will be temporary since, within three or four years, they will become part of a reconstituted or blended family when the single parent remarries.

We know that the breakup of a family creates problems and pain for children, though our information on the extent and nature of the crisis is based on relatively small studies and limited samples.[15] Depending on the age of the child and the extent to which contact with both parents (and other similar conditions) are exempt from serious disruption, the effects will be more or less drastic. Children mourn the loss of relationships, often feel that they have participated in the family breakup and must be at fault, and sometimes experience a degree of disturbance—school problems, or depression, or acting out in delinquent or difficult behavior—that requires professional intervention. The first year following divorce is the period of most acute problems, though some children continue to suffer the trauma long after the fact. Children who show the most serious effects are often youngsters who had preexisting problems that were intensified by the family crisis.

Aside from psychological problems, divorce and family dissolution have other serious consequences. In a very high proportion of cases, children of divorce and their mothers who have custody are plunged into poverty, or at least experience a drastic reduction in standard of living as a result of the divorce. The poverty rate for women and children in female-headed families is three to four times as high as for those living in other family forms. The large proportion of women who head households with dependent children and also work outside the home suffer the double burden of trying to carry two full-time roles and having minimum resources with which to buy supplementary help. If the mother in the two-earner family has a hard time fulfilling her parent role in a way that satisfies her and meets her own standards, the woman who is raising children alone and working full time to support them has the same problems but in double measure.[16]

The problems of single parents affect their interaction with their children. A mother who is constantly beset with basic issues of survival, who must work outside the home full time and still has overwhelming financial problems because of wage discrimination and inadequate social policies and supports, suffers from chronic overload and worry. She feels guilty leaving her children in inadequate day care situations or alone to fend for themselves. The effects of strain are almost certain to leave their mark on her interaction with her children.[17]

Two relatively positive (or at least not wholly negative) effects of divorce on children have surfaced in recent research findings. Robert Weiss has reported that many children in single-parent families "grow up a little sooner" because of the very real contributions they make to family chores and tasks and because they are required by their life circumstances to develop greater self-reliance and autonomy than children from intact two-parent families.[18]

The other effect—less positive, yet not unrelievedly negative either— is a special case of this precocious self-reliance. This is the situation in which the child becomes a source of support and a confidante for the strained and perhaps distraught parent. A number of observers have simultaneously noted this new development and have seen it as a denial of protection and a lack of sensitivity to the developmental status of the child, an equating of children with adults that effectively denies the child the right to childhood.[19]

In its most extreme forms, the failure of a parent or any adult to recognize and credit the difference between childhood and adulthood can, of course, be destructive to the child. It would mean, for example, assuming that a small child had the same judgment and background of information that an adult has and thus failing to interfere with the three year old's decision to cross a busy street. Or to cite an example that has actually been raised by certain fringe elements in our society, denial of the fact that sexual intercourse between an adult and a child necessarily carries a power asymmetry that makes it by definition nonvoluntary and different in kind from intercourse between consenting adults.

In less extreme forms, a parent's inclusion of children in some of the harsh realities of life and in the human experience of mutual support is not necessarily harmful to the child or her/his development.[20] In fact,

the extreme protectiveness that characterized middle-class child-raising
in the post-World War II period—the determination of parents to create
for their children a perfect environment insulated from problems, conflicts, "undesirable elements" of society, and all the other complexities
and varieties that comprise urban life—is probably in the long run more
harmful to children. Richard Sennett, for example, has developed strong
support for the position that the earlier form of this overprotective
family, the fortress middle-class family of the nineteenth century, was
disastrously inept as a form of adaptation and as a socialization setting
for the young. In its determination to protect its members from the
dangers of the city, the family became a hothouse of emotion and conflict
that the father/husband often deserted, and it failed to provide children
the training they would need to adapt to their world.[21]

Children need experience with reality, and they need varied models
of human behavior from which they can fashion a personal integration
that has meaning, fits comfortably with their own tastes and history, and
allows them to live in the world. Farm children and children in simpler
societies know reality from their earliest days. Only the strange, artificial,
overcultivated isolation of the Victorian nuclear family (and its imitation
in suburban United States in the 1940s and 1950s) promulgated the idea
that children should know nothing of the real world. We now know from
biographies of Virginia Woolf and other figures that, as with much of
Victorian ideology, the goal of protecting childhood innocence was more
purely ideology than a directive for action. Nevertheless, ideology is
important in itself and in the anxiety and guilt it imposes on parents
who are unable fully to meet the dreams and ideals it encourages.[22]

The Two-Earner Family

The most widespread change in family form over the last twenty years
has been from the traditional family consisting of a male head who works
outside the home and supports his homemaker wife and dependent
children to the family in which both adults work outside the home. The
new two-earner form accounts for more than half of all families headed
by a husband-wife pair. The movement of married women into the labor
force has been underway since World War II and has had two phases.
Between 1940 and 1960 the most rapid acceleration in labor force participation occurred among women who were between thirty-five and fifty
years old, but since 1960 the greatest rate increase has been among
younger women, those who have children under school age.[23]

Although the effects of a mother going to work outside the home are
not as drastic as the effects of divorce, they are similar in many ways
and they are much more widespread. Most people who become parents
today grew up with nonemployed mothers. Many of their images and

concepts of family life are set and colored by these early experiences. Yet their lives as parents with their own children will not duplicate those experiences.

The central problem for the two-earner family is child care. Who will take care of the children while the parents work? Our society, unlike most European societies, has been both slow and reluctant about assuming a communal responsibility for child care. Part of our extreme allegiance to individualistic beliefs is our defensive attitude toward the entry of government into realms held to be "private," particularly anything to do with family. We will discuss the broader effects of this ideology at a later point in this chapter. Suffice it here to say that the American concept of family has been dominated by the beliefs that children belong to parents and that what parents do with their children is their own business and is neither a legitimate concern nor a responsibility of the community except when the family shows clear signs of failure and dissolution. Such beliefs have led to a particularly nonsupportive climate for two-earner families in their struggles to manage both work outside the home and family life.[24] Day care, family allowances, paternity leaves, part-time work, flextime—all of the arrangements that can make life reasonable and manageable for two-earner families have been much slower and more difficult to realize in the United States than in most industrialized countries. What gains have been made have been won only through the considerable political efforts of the women's movement.[25]

Hence, child care for most families has been a matter of catch-as-catch-can. Since communities do not provide day care and since many day care facilities run for profit provide poor quality environments, most families depend on kin, older children, or the nonoverlapping schedules of the two adults and their own resilience to handle the taxing work of tending infants and toddlers. School-aged children can—and in many cases are left to—take care of themselves when they are not in school, although, obviously, relying on the judgment, responsibility, and courage of a seven year old does not greatly ease a parent's mind.

Television has become a major form of child care. American children spend more time watching television than they spend at school or in interpersonal interactions. For the child who is home alone because of sickness or school holidays, television is the major source of stimulation and company and can also reassure the parent that at least the child is likely to be quiet and immobile. This passivity may not be ideal compared to active play, but it is better than playing with matches or being out on the streets.[26]

Even when working parents are at home, tired parents are likely to use television as a substitute for active interaction. Unless a parent is very well organized and has the children integrated into a cooperative family work force, it is a lot easier at the end of the work day to prepare a meal if one is not faced with constant interruptions and interaction with tired children. So television plays a large role in the socialization of even middle-class children from two-parent families.

Husbands and children have come to play a somewhat larger role in child and home care as married mothers have entered the work force for wages. The change has been slow: large-scale studies before 1978 consistently showed that, when a woman worked full time outside the home, she added that job to her full responsibilities at home. Although men whose wives held full-time jobs were slightly more likely to spend a very limited amount of time in child care than men whose wives were full-time homemakers, they did not increase their share of household tasks at all. Around 1978 this finding began to change, and, significantly, it changed most among the youngest cohorts.[27] Young husbands and fathers showed significant increases in time spent in home and child care. Although we are a long way from the feminist ideal of equal sharing between husbands and wives (especially equality in parenting), the trend is clearly in the direction of greater sharing, and is thus a hopeful sign. Findings from a number of recent studies indicate that the male's as-suming a larger role has salutary effects on marital and life satisfaction for both wives and husbands.[28] Clearly, expectations and attitudes have changed more than behavior, but in many cases we can take attitudinal changes as precursors of behavioral change. Around 1960 we entered a period of profound change in the norms governing family life and our expectations about sex roles and family roles. We have seen fluc-tuations in the pace and direction of these changes, and the final outcome is by no means a foregone conclusion. We are still in the process of shifting from traditional patterns and stabilizing around new norms and roles. It seems probable, however, that, overall, the transition will be toward greater equality between the sexes.

We have some evidence that recent changes in family structure and functioning have been more unsettling to men than to women. These changes have caused strain in men's lives at the same time that they have opened up opportunities for fulfillment and satisfaction for women. When women enter the labor force, they realize many gains, including a certain amount of power in family decision-making. This, in turn, unhinges traditional authority relations in the family. When men worked in the labor force and women took care of home and family, men were assured a unique authority simply because they held the roles of hus-band, father, and breadwinner. When women took over part of family support, this automatic association of power with the male "head of household" role declined. Many studies have found that, when a wife goes to work outside the home, she gains power in the family.[29]

At the same time that his power in the family has been reduced, the man is also reminded daily that a woman can fill his role at work as women (and other minority groups) press for equal employment opportunities at all occupational levels.

Men have experienced a reduction in authority, and they feel stressed by it. When asked to interpret a picture that shows a man talking to children at the breakfast table, men who participated in 1976 differed from their 1957 counterparts in two ways: they more often saw the child as an active initiator of exchange, and they were more strongly concerned with controlling the child. Their preoccupation with control again seemed to testify to their concern about their authority, their apprehension that it would not prevail. In 1957 a greater number of men saw the child as a passive recipient of parental instruction, neither questioning nor challenging the father's authority.[30]

Similar signs of men's increased concern about parenting come from direct questions: How does having children change a person's life? What are the nicest things about having children? What are the hardest things about parenthood? What problems have arisen in their own parenting? In what ways do they think or wish they could have been better parents?

The problems men allude to and their self-criticism about their own parenting indicate that they no longer feel the same confidence about their ability to control their children as they did in the previous generation. Many men express the wish that they had closer, warmer relationships with their children.[31] It seems that the old style of parenting, in which the child was passive and the father had automatic authority, does not work as well for men today. They know and can articulate what they want in its stead—authority based on warm interaction with a child whose needs and wishes are respected—but they have problems achieving this new relationship.

Early in the women's movement, feminists decried the fact that women lived vicariously through their husbands and children and realized no ambitions or achievements on their own. Overlooked in these claims was the fact that men also lived vicariously through their wives. It was a two-way exchange in which women achieved through their husbands' achievements, and men realized their emotional needs through the intervention of their wives. In the traditional division of tasks, the wife/mother maintained the emotional relationships in the family, interpreted the children to their father, and sustained daily exchange. She wrote to and maintained social contact with her husband's family as well as her own. She arranged social life with friends. Her husband realized social and emotional satisfactions through her good offices.[32] When women went into the labor force, they adapted quickly to finding achievement pleasures on their own. It was simply a matter of shifting arenas for expressing their achievement needs. But for husbands, the transition has not been as simple. As their wives become more committed to outside work, they also have less time and energy to serve the emotional needs of others, to provide the emotional glue for daily life in the family. The husband is more often thrown on his own to interact with the children directly; yet his socialization has not prepared him for such interaction. He has not been taught how to be close to other people, how to express his feelings and disclose the personal thoughts and responses that build warm relationships.

Striking evidence that men are less able than women to build and maintain relationships and that they are dependent on their wives comes from questions about friendships and supportive relationships. When asked to whom they can talk about things that trouble or bother them, women reveal extensive networks of helping relationships. They talk over their problems with their husbands, but they also talk to their mothers, sisters, and friends. Men, on the other hand, rely mainly on their wives for expression of intimacy and obtaining support. Most married men list *only* their wives when asked to whom they talk about worries and troubles.[33]

With new roles developing, with wives committed more strongly to work, men's exclusive reliance on their wives for emotional expression may put too great a burden on the wives and create strain in marriage. One of the most striking changes from 1957 to 1976 is an increase in men's recognition of problems in their marriages. While their marriages were happy (more so than in 1957!), men were much more likely in 1976 to say that they had had serious marital problems at some point.[34]

In addition, men whose wives work show more signs of strain than do those whose wives are full-time homemakers.[35] It seems clear that the distress men are experiencing is at least in part the result of sex-role transitions that are occurring in our culture. The conclusion that it is *transition*—the fact that things are in process of change—that creates stress is supported by the fact that younger men show less strain as a result of their wives' working. Younger men enter marriage with the expectation that their wives will work, and they do not feel unsettled by it. Many middle-aged or older men, on the other hand, began marriage with one set of expectations and now find that the conditions of their lives demand other expectations. It is the shift that causes strain and problems in adaptation.

IDEOLOGICAL ISSUES

The 1960s and 1970s witnessed extraordinary changes in the world-view and self-definition of Americans—extraordinary in their radicalism as well as in the speed with which they have spread through the population. Among the profound changes have been a loss of religious faith and the decline of religious authority in daily life. Between 1957 and

1976 church membership and attendance and, more importantly, the belief in the efficacy of prayer dropped dramatically in the general population. By 1976 religion as a dominant belief system was no longer the norm. Most people no longer attend church or use prayer in their daily lives.[36]

As religion declined in importance, new beliefs and concepts came into play to define values and help people construct meaning. Whereas religious believers guide their behavior by moral concepts and belief in an afterlife, secularization brings with it a shift in values, a movement toward more palpable criteria and bases for judgment that exist in the present and in life rather than in an afterlife. Humanistic values and internal criteria (satisfaction, maturity, mental health, richness of experience, love, and community) have come to play a larger role in directing behavior and judgments—larger than fear of hell or the search for redemption.

Clearly, such a shift has critical importance in ideologies and beliefs about child-raising. If you believe in original sin and see the infant's impulsivity not as part of nature but as a direct manifestation of inherent evil, monitoring and controlling the infant's action and growth take on a more critical tone than a less Calvinistic view inspires. And in judging actions or choosing among alternatives, ideas of right and wrong and "oughtness" come to be replaced by human or social criteria (the greatest good for the greatest number, happiness, or "whatever turns you on"). We have seen this effect in the changes in norms about marriage and parenthood described earlier: In 1957 the choice to marry and have children was supported by strong norms backed with moral force. The common view was that one "ought" to marry and parent, that choosing not to do so was a sign of a flaw. The individual who failed to fill these crucial roles was judged to be immature and/or selfish. In 1976 the moralistic tone and moral judgmental quality had dropped out of the discourse, and the role of spouse or parent was now judged by whether or not it could provide pleasure, satisfaction, and fulfillment to the individual. Once one gives up the idea of divine authority and the existence of one "right" way to live and behave to which all must adhere, the way is opened for softer, more flexible, more contextual, and more internal guides to frame decisions and choices.

In our own society in the last two decades, the shift to internal criteria has been accompanied and encouraged by a growing psychological orientation. Under the influence of psychoanalytic ideology which burgeoned in the decades 1940 to 1960, "maturity" and "mental health" came into ascendance as criteria for judging action. With the counterculture came a broadening tolerance for varied choice and action, but the internal, human base for judgment had been firmly established. The dilution of external absolute authority and the shift to internal bases for choice and action underlaid all of the great ideological movements of the 1960s and 1970s.[37]

IDEOLOGICAL MOVEMENTS: FEMINISM, THE COUNTERCULTURE, AND PEACE

A fresh and enspiriting egalitarianism began to develop in the United States in the period we are considering. This new spirit began with the court cases and political activities that led to the Brown decision in 1954 and reached a crescendo in the late 1960s, with the Civil Rights Movement. The determined struggle of American blacks for recognition and their rightful share in American society and its resources radically altered American consciousness. A number of important developments in one way or another stemmed directly from the Civil Rights Movement: a new and penetrating critique of the dominant values of the culture spread broadly in the younger generation (most clearly and dramatically represented in the counterculture and the peace movement), and the movement for women's rights gained stimulus, momentum, and political insight.

The black action movement, the women's movement, the counterculture, the personal growth movement, and the peace movement were all based on a sharp critique of existing dominant values and established power arrangements. Women asked why the materialistic productive system was valued so much more than the human realm of reproduction and the rearing of the next generation. Why were market values the only values that counted while women's crucial nonmarket labor in the home was omitted from calculations of gross national product and other measures of value? Why did men have all the power, recognition, and rewards in the system? Why were women's wages and women's labor subjected to segregation and discrimination? Why, in other words, was our society constructed in a way that systematically ignored or deemphasized human needs in the interest of power and the market?

Youth of the counterculture asked similar questions, and were specific and personal in their indictments: what good did it do their fathers to run the rat race, to work eighty hours a week, and accumulate wealth, possessions, and power when in the final analysis they lost their own children and destroyed their marriages? Life could be lived according to different, simpler, less material values: loving, sharing, being, experiencing. Many sons of the affluent middle class and of industrial leaders chose mind expansion through drugs and Eastern religion, and rejected the joyless work ethic of their fathers. Even those who stayed in the mainstream were sensitive to the importance of keeping their lives open to more than work. They intended and tried hard to construct lives that included work but left room for the arts, nature, love, and important relationships. Having been abandoned by their own fathers, many of these men were candidates for persuasion into more active parenting. They married women influenced by the feminist movement, and they now make up the growing group of couples who are trying to share parenting equally.[38]

The peace movement and the war that inspired it threw into sharp relief the limitations of a dominant system whose methods of "saving" a people included destruction of them and their land. Betrayal of democratic principles, President Lyndon Johnson's secret usurping of power, and the attempts to subvert the legal structure of the democratic system exposed in the Watergate scandals, combined with hysterical and brutal use of force to put down protesting youth in Washington and Kent State—all of these facets of the existing power structure came under explicit and dramatic analysis and led to a large measure of both protest and alienation in the younger generation. If these were the methods and "goods" of democratic capitalism, many youth decided they wanted no part of such a system.

The critique was mounted, the troops assembled, and an organized assault on the established system was underway. The coalition of blacks, women, and youth at the 1972 Democratic Convention represented the highwater mark of the movement for reform, the effort to reorganize and reconstruct government and society on principles of life and peace rather than on objects, profits, and war.

The growth and success of the coalition have not gone unattended by those who hold power and see in it a major threat to existing arrangements. Right wing forces in government, business, and the churches have drawn a bead on the reform coalition and have poured enormous resources into blocking the equal rights amendment and legislation for reproductive rights, and into promoting anti-busing legislation, undoing affirmative action, and promoting defense spending and the arms race. The Mormon Church and Texas oil money provide many of the resources that drive the right wing. Fear of change attracts members to the conservative camp from near and distant territories, from Bible belt conservative Midwesterners to the neo-conservative staff of *Commentary* and the *National Review*, sons and daughters of immigrant Socialists who have made it up the ladder through hard work and brains and are both eager and explicit about protecting traditional values. If that means pulling up the ladder, making the society a bit less open, or rejecting their own children—well, that is just the price that will have to be paid.

A TURN AGAINST CHILDREN

Ideologists of the right—neo-conservatives who have supplied words and arguments for Ronald Reagan, the Reverend Jerry Falwell, and the

Mormon elders to use in their speeches—portray autonomous, self-directed women as the enemy and the danger. If women have individual freedom and the right to choose their lives as independent, self-directed individuals, men will, according to this view, revert to a primitive predatory sexual individualism and society and the family as we know it will collapse. It is important to note that the conservative position rejects the idea of individual identity in women but makes of men the true grotesques. Without the pawn of women's selfless dependency and children as the hostages that blackmail them into responsibility, men in George Gilder's view are atavistic animals without any allegiance to other individuals or to a community![39]

Children become pawns in the war of the sexes, objects to be used by women to hold men, to reassure men by their dependency and obeisance to male authority that they, the males, have a role in the world that merits self-esteem. Without the traditional husband-father-breadwinner role and the unique authority it has carried, the conservatives hold that men will feel no responsibility, no loyalty, no love or attachment to any individual other or social group.

The conservatives oppose child care legislation and count catsup as a vegetable in order to cut lunch program budgets in the schools. They see children as the private property of parents. Children are the individual responsibility of the people who produce them, there is no concept of the next generation, of children, as the responsibility of the whole community or society. There is no sense that once in the world, they are "all our children." Conservatives feel a keen proprietary interest in their own children and work hard to accumulate an estate that will protect the privilege of their heirs for generations. But they do not feel a responsibility for children born into families who have no resources or privilege: that is seen as the luck of the draw and is not questioned. Quite simply, the conservative view is that the poor and the underclass have too much sex and too many babies. If they can't take care of them, that's *their* problem.

Not surprisingly, the conservatives have led the way back to "tough love." During the youth rebellion, conservative ideologues wrote tracts attacking the young, blaming permissiveness and Dr. Spock for their "narcissism," and writing off the entire generation: to be precise, their own children. As one student pointed out, these were the people (the parents who rejected their counterculture children) who had rejected their own parents as they used their brains, drive, and an open opportunity structure to scramble into the affluent middle class. They often denied their past and their parents in order to make themselves acceptable in their new setting. When their children rejected the work ethic and achievement ideology that had served the parents so well (but at too high a cost from the point of view of the younger generation), they abandoned their children as well.[40]

The conservative blame the feminists for the destruction of the family and the moral collapse that underlies it. The feminist movement responds that it seeks primarily to create a world and a value system that will hold children and the rearing of children to be at the center of life and of highest value. However, the movement also contends that this world and system should not be established on the backs of women and at the expense of their full humanity. Men and women together create children, and they should share the responsibility of child-raising and family maintenance.

As with any important political or ideological revolution, the feminist movement has had its extreme elements and representatives. In the early days of the movement, some theorists maintained that the only way women could win their freedom and realize their individuality was by dismantling the family and developing new, more egalitarian forms of group life.[41] Some of this rhetoric devalued childbearing and children along with the patriarchal family structure, but it never became a dominant or official position of any large segment of the feminist movement. While "women's lib" was portrayed in the media as anti-family and anti-male, the fact is that in its writings and in its political stance, the movement has sought more humane arrangements for all people—children and men as well as women—and has emphasized the importance of all adults sharing in the significant task of raising the next generation.

The political controversies between feminists and the new right have been visible in public arenas, especially on television. Accusations and counter-accusations have been well aired for all to see and hear. Failures in taste and judgment—for example, pictorial presentation of fetuses in garbage bags and garbage cans—would not have such critical ramifications if they occurred in a lecture hall debate between adults before an adult audience. But their occurrence in the living rooms of American homes on television, with no means of discriminating among audiences or differentiating content on the basis of viewers' capacity to discount or filter their impact, endanger children. When a debater says that feminists want to kill or throw away children, adults either deny the assertion completely or filter its affective implications. But a child may take it as a statement of literal truth and draw out its implications: "If some mammas throw babies away, might my mamma throw me away?"

The omnipresence of television and the impossibility of controlling who watches what has reinforced the "erosion of childhood" that has begun to concern social observers and child advocates.[42] The thoughtless, unrestrained airing of any opinion or charge, without concern for its possible effects on persons at various developmental stages and stages

604   Elizabeth Douvan

of understanding, is one more reflection of our belief in the myth of absolute individualism, the myth that what one individual does has no implications for or effects on anyone else.[43]

THE ROLE OF EXPERTS

In the postwar period, when child-raising was a life-absorbing task for middle-class women, the role of the child-raising expert took on unprecedented importance. Raising children was the measure of parents' (read mothers') worth and could not be taken lightly. Mothers needed all the help they could get. Since middle-class couples were highly mobile and likely to live far from their own parents, young middle-class women bought and read Dr. Spock and other child-raising manuals by the millions. Even the works of Arnold Gesell and Frances L. Ilg—technical descriptions of normative patterns of development in young children— became best-sellers.[44]

In the period since 1963, as familistic values have been challenged and children have moved from the very center of life to somewhere in its flow, a great deal of criticism has been leveled at Dr. Spock and the "experts."[45] While at least some of the experts make easy, vulnerable targets (as we shall see below), it is important to note that the group represented by Spock filled an important need for young parents in postwar United States. They did not invent the need, although psychoanalysis certainly added to it. The fact is that young mothers, cut off from their home communities and access to advice from their own mothers and female kin, needed and found enormous comfort in these manuals. When a baby went into a febrile convulsion in the middle of the night or swallowed a funny looking mushroom in the garden, the assurance that Dr. Spock's index would list these emergencies and that help was at hand made the whole enterprise seem possible and manageable.

The manuals, and many of the experts, lacked a certain measure of humility and grace in their approach to psychological development. But we were at the beginning of the era of psychological technology, the era of "mental health" and "personal growth," and all things seemed more or less possible. Many young parents were critical of the way their parents had raised them, as young people have always been. But now, armed with greater knowledge of human development, they were optimistic about being able to do a better job.

In our post-familistic era, the child development experts have been lambasted both by the right wing and fundamentalist groups who think that analytic, rational thought about child development is somehow subversive, and by scholars (mainly historians) who have attacked the child development experts for their arrogance and for being either destructive of traditional authority or unconscious pushers of tradition and the status quo.[46]

The experts continue to carry significant authority for many young parents. For middle-class parents who now so deliberately choose to have children and for whom the role is very significant and valued, a good deal of worry and anxiety accompany the task of raising children. For many highly mobile young couples, experts and books are the only available sources of guidance, since their own parents and kin live too far away to be helpful in the day-to-day decisions and actions that constitute childrearing.

Our individualistic ethos also contributes to this reliance on experts rather than on one's kin and friends. Each parent is held responsible for what happens to her or his child, how the child develops. This privatized construction of child-raising creates a distance, reserve, and deference even among kin, who feel somehow that it is not their right to offer advice or criticism or to enter directly into the enterprise. The cultural assumptions that it is up to the parent and the parent alone to determine how the child will be raised and that no one else has either the right or responsibility to enter into the parent-child interaction, except in the most extreme conditions, are so pervasive that it is invisible until one experiences radically altered assumptions in another culture. In Scandinavia, for example, every adult feels free to protect and correct children in public spaces, and older adults are free to offer advice and criticism to younger parents if their children are thought to be either unprotected or a nuisance.[47]

Our individualistic beliefs, then, throw young parents onto the authority of experts. The same ethos pervades the academic-intellectual world of the experts and the knowledge and advice they create. The force of an extreme individualistic, competitive construction on the intellectual enterprise has many and varied effects. It tends to atomize knowledge, to convert ideas into property and emphasize their market aspects (for example, ownership, credit and attribution, primacy of "invention" or discovery), and to deemphasize the cumulative, collaborative, and social aspects of science and scholarship.[48]

Here let us explore briefly the emphasis on originality and primacy of discovery in the academic community. The need to be highly original and innovative in order to win tenure and status in the academy has had nefarious effects in many instances in the social sciences. Nowhere is this more obvious than in the field of child development and the advice literature that grows out of it. The geographer David Harvey has pointed to the problem of originality in the human sciences. Since, as he puts it, we are always dealing with the age-old and same human problems, young social scientists working for the Ph.D. must continually invent new languages in which to discuss and describe them. They must do this in order to make an "original" contribution as well as to give their advisors a sense of obsolescence so that the young can move in and take over the field.[49]

But the advisors in many areas are young enough so that they too must continually create "new" and original insights in order to justify and improve their own positions. The scramble for originality, then, leads to greater stretching, and not necessarily greater coherence or sense. Fads in the academy do little harm as long as they concern the interpretation of literary texts or Latin pronouns. But when they deal with weaning and toilet-training, sex education, and the nature of the learning process, the potential for danger grows. For example, a generation of babies born in the 1920s and 1930s came under the influence of John B. Watson and were raised by the clock on mechanical schedules so that they would not be spoiled by warmth or tenderness.[50]

In very recent times, with the intensifying of competition for "original" contributions, research in developmental psychology has uncovered the startling insight that the infant's relationship with the father makes a difference in the life and growth of the child's personality (an insight that many lay persons had assumed all along). In a final stroke of creativity, one expert emerged from his research with the conclusion that the father-infant relationship was *more* important to the child's development than the mother-infant tie.

The trend toward a monolithic concern with the child's cognitive development—to the exclusion of affective and social development—can be seen as a logical product of the individualistic, competitive ethos in academia. Cognitive development is readily accessible to study and lends itself to small, controlled experimental studies that fit the format of the dominant academic journals. Emotional and social development and the ways in which children learn about social relationships require a longer time perspective and the use of subtle and "softer" field methods of investigation.[51]

Several things follow from the preoccupation with experimental methods and the focus on cognition. They fragment behavior, decontextualizing and emphasizing its smallest units. This in turn gets translated in advice columns as the importance of the smallest bit of parental behavior. Not only is the good will and overall style of the parent important (as it was in Dr. Spock's system), but also each tiny act is now weighed with significance. No one reminds the young parents that their own parents managed to raise their children without the latest developmental discoveries, or that the discoveries are often established on the observation of twenty infants and group differences significant at the 5 percent level. What comes across to young parents now is that if they don't have a mobile hanging in the crib, the baby's cognitive growth will be truncated. A decline in SAT scores is invested with a concrete, literal significance and anxiety that seems more appropriate to, say, an increase in smallpox. In addition to increasing parents' anxiety, advice grounded in current academic findings and values reinforces the individualistic myth and competitive, self-centered, fragmented values that are already so dominant in the culture. Social scientists (and intellectuals at large) label the younger generation "narcissistic," and they decry the failure of social integration in our world. At the same time, they exemplify and promulgate the narrow, individualistic, competitive values from which narcissism grows.

The public schools and the teaching profession have been subjected to attack as another group of experts and as somehow responsible for undermining authority and conventional virtue. It is probably true that education nourishes secularization. But the schools are attacked for failing to provide children cognitive training as well as moral training.

The attack on public schools has coincided with the efforts to integrate them. The complex problems of school integration are treated as technical problems that should be resolved in a short time through the application of knowledge. When these efforts do not show immediate, palpable results, the schools are blamed for "softness" and for failure in the application of "standards of excellence." Tough policies are urged on school systems.[52]

The schools *are* hard pressed, and many children are leaving school unequipped for work or life in a complex society. But to see the schools as *only* failing and to attribute all of society's ills to educators' "softness" is to oversimplify matters grossly. School systems and teachers have been affected by and reflect all of the dominant value trends reviewed in this chapter: secularization and the "psychological revolution," professionalization and, perhaps most importantly, increased competitive individualism, the fragmenting of community and life. But the schools did not singlehandedly create the trends.

SUMMARY AND CONCLUSIONS

Two themes increasingly characterize attitudes about childhood and the experience of childhood in the United States. The first of these can be best described as a cultural ambivalence toward children that is grounded in our highly individualistic myth and value system. The second has to do with the erosion of a unique childhood experience based on clear and culturally credited differentiation among developmental stages.

Ambivalence in the Culture

Our culture provides two very different experiences of childhood depending primarily on social-class differences. The upper-middle-class

child, born to a couple who have chosen parenthood deliberately over
alternative life patterns, is the focus of enormous attention. With the
introduction of modern birth control technology and the softening of
familistic norms, the decision to have children represents for people in
this class an active choice to a degree previously unknown. The young
parents want to have children, and they have the resources and energy
to insure that their children will have every advantage. Since competitive
achievement through occupation is the guiding ethos in this class, advantage in the form of early cognitive stimulation, attendance at the
finest schools, and cultivation of talents becomes crucial to "successful
parenting" and the child's success in adulthood. Japan provides a model
of what childhood is like in such a system, except that in Japan pressure
for individual performance is balanced by a highly developed group
allegiance. Nonetheless, pressure for individual achievement begins in
nursery school and essentially never abates.

For the parents, providing the advantages that a middle-class child
needs becomes a major commitment of financial resources. Estimates of
the cost of raising a child to age eighteen appear regularly in the media,
and they have grown vastly. When a child becomes the focus of such a
large proportion of family resources, it is more likely that children will
be compared to alternative investments, that some universal measure
(either dollars or the parents' pleasure) will be invoked to accomplish
these comparative assessments, and that some proportion of adults will
decide the investment is not worth it. Children become commodities,
goods to be compared to other consumer goods. Some upper-middle-
class children feel objectified and pressured by the values of their parents
and their culture.

The other experience of childhood is that shared by all those children
whose parents are not able to provide them advantages or even, in many
cases, the bare necessities of life. Since our society rejects the notion that
the community is responsible for all children, the experience of these
children from poor families (often single-parent families and, most often,
female-headed, single-parent families) is often grim. Concessions to the
needs of these families are made with a tight fist and mean spirit: day
care is not assumed as a community service, and programs to protect
the health and diet of these children are among the first to be cut in
economy moves. Most families on assistance programs are there for
relatively short periods because of crisis circumstances; yet our society
treats them all as though they were cheats and freeloaders. Childhood
for the poor has never been protected. But the condition of poverty has
probably become more obvious, a more constant part of awareness in
recent times. The ubiquity of television and its presentation of "ideal"
American families have surely affected the experience of childhood in
poor families.

The media have also increased the visibility and effectiveness of groups devoted to the interests of poor children. The Carnegie Council on Children, the Children's Defense Fund, and similar groups are a visible feature on the political landscape. They lobby for legislation to improve the conditions under which children grow up, and they advocate for children in the public arena. Their activities bear witness to the fact that at least some powerful people in our society worry about the problems and misuse of children. They also testify to the fact there is much to worry about.

The Erosion of Childhood

Many factors have contributed to the decline in differentiation between children's and adult experiences. Dilution of traditional authority, the decreased importance of roles in the self-definitions of adults, and the increased focus on individual skill, talent, and taste as the bases for self-definition have all tended to reduce the difference. Increased incidence of divorce, family dissolution, and single-parent and impoverished families have reduced the possibility of protecting children from some of the harsher realities of life, thus making their experience more adult-like.

The increasing psychological orientation of the culture, the reliance on mental health technology and verbal therapy, and the heavy emphasis on cognition that characterizes developmental psychology have all contributed to the decreased differentiation of childhood from adulthood. If development is construed to mean memory and cognitive capacity, if we come to use the computer as our model for human psychic life, then clearly the difference between a child and an adult psyche is merely a matter of how much information has been put into them. This view underlies the current popularity of infant classes and cognitive training of children from the earliest months of life.[53]

No factor has been more forceful in homogenizing experience and eroding the difference between child and adult than television. When much of social experience and knowledge of social exchange was transmitted directly through apprenticeship or at least direct instruction by adults, it took a good part of childhood to learn the reality and the rules of adult behavior and exchange. It was possible under such conditions to censor children's access to certain knowledge, for example, sexual knowledge. When, however, television becomes a major source of knowledge transmission and when commercial interests rather than rational social policy dominates programming (determining how many hours of programming will be presented, the nature of the content, "what people want"), the possibility of a parent's conditioning and controlling what the child will know is radically reduced. Even the parent who bans television (on weeknights, for example) will not be able to control what the child sees at friends' houses or what she or he will learn at school from children whose viewing is not monitored.

Adulthood and particularly adult sexuality no longer have the aura of mystery about them. While earlier generations may have longed for "the secret password," the knowledge that would allow them to enter the world of adults, children in the present generation have access to the word, there are no secrets, and many children are not at all sure that "being grown-up" is such an attractive prospect.

Around the beginning of the period considered here, Philippe Aries[54] stated the influential thesis that childhood was an invention of the eighteenth century, a social construction that had not existed in earlier eras. Before the invention of childhood, Western society differentiated only infancy and adulthood and saw children simply as small adults. Paintings of the sixteenth century provide evidence for his thesis: children are dressed the same as adults; their bodies and faces are smaller than adults' but lack foreshortening and the other proportional features that distinguish children from adults.

Today it seems that our culture is eager to deny the difference between childhood and adulthood again. Or at least we are creating conditions under which the differentiation is being radically reduced. To some extent, a shift toward greater realism and less sentimentality and protectiveness was probably called for. The postwar focus on creating perfect children through a perfect environment was not a viable or helpful guide to parenthood and was bound to lead to a great deal of disillusionment. On the other hand, complete denial of developmental differences does not seem possible either. The most hopeful conclusion is that in a complex society such as ours fads tend to be kept from becoming dominant by the tough realities of life and by the good sense and faith of people in the validity of their own experience.

NOTES

1. David Elkind, *The Hurried Child: Growing Up Too Fast Too Soon* (Reading, Mass.: Addison-Wesley, 1981); Marie Winn, *Children Without Childhood* (New York: Pantheon, 1983).

2. Betty Friedan, *The Feminine Mystique* (New York: W. W. Norton, 1963).

3. For varied descriptions and analyses of this collapse of a dream, see Philip Slater, *The Pursuit of Loneliness* (Boston: Beacon, 1970); William H. Chafe, *The American Woman: Her Changing Social, Economic, and Political Roles, 1920 to 1970* (New York: Oxford University Press, 1972); Juliet Mitchell, *Women's Estate* (New York: Vintage, 1978); and Friedan, *Feminine Mystique*.

4. See, for example, the novels of John Updike and Joseph Heller and social analyses such as Kenneth Keniston, *All Our Children: The American Family Under Pressure* (New York: Harcourt Brace Jovanovich, 1977) , and David Gutmann,

"Female Ego Styles and Generational Conflict," in Judith Bardwick, et al., eds., *Feminine Personality and Conflict* (Westport, Conn.: Greenwood Press, 1980).

5. Jessie Bernard, *The Future of Marriage* (New York: Bantam, 1972); Carol Tavris and Carole Offir, *The Longest War: Sex Differences in Perspective* (New York: Harcourt Brace Jovanovich, 1977); Joseph Veroff, Elizabeth Douvan, and Richard Kulka, *The Inner American: A Self Portrait from 1957 to 1976* (New York: Basic, 1981); Daniel Yankelovich, *New Rules: Searching for Self-Fulfillment in a World Turned Upside Down* (New York: Random House, 1981).

6. Hugh Carter and Paul Glick, *Marriage and Divorce: A Social and Economic Study* (Cambridge, Mass.: Harvard University Press, 1976).

7. Richard Easterlin, "Does Economic Growth Improve the Human Lot? Some Empirical Evidence," *Nations and Households in Economic Growth* edited by Paul A. David and Melvin Reder (New York: Academic Press, 1974):89–125.

8. Barbara Ehrenreich has recently attributed the sexual revolution to men's sense of oppression under the extreme familistic pressure of the postwar period. See her *The Hearts of Men: American Dreams and the Flight from Commitment* (New York: Anchor, 1983).

9. See, for example, Christopher Lasch, *Haven in a Heartless World: The Family Besieged* (New York: Basic, 1977); and Michael Zuckerman, "Dr. Spock: The Confidence Man," in Charles E. Rosenberg, ed., *The Family in History* (Philadelphia: University of Pennsylvania, 1975), 179–207.

10. Slater, *Pursuit of Loneliness*; Philip Slater, *Earthwalk* (New York: Bantam, 1974); and Barrie Thorne and Marilyn Yalom, *Rethinking the Family: Some Feminist Questions* (New York: Longman, 1982).

11. The studies are reported in two volumes: Veroff, Douvan, and Kulka, *Inner American*, and *Mental Health in America* (New York: Basic, 1981).

12. Barrie Thorne, "Feminist Rethinking of the Family: An Overview," in Thorne and Yalom, *Rethinking the Family*. 1–14.

13. Veroff, Douvan, and Kulka, *Inner American*.

14. Mary Jo Bane, *Here to Stay: American Families in the Twentieth Century* (New York: Basic, 1976); and Keniston, *All Our Children*.

15. Joan Wallerstein and Joan Kelly, *Surviving the Break-Up: How Children and Parents Cope with Divorce* (New York: Basic, 1980); Mavis Hetherington, "Effects of Father Absence on Personality Development in Adolescent Daughters," *Developmental Psychology* 7 (1972): 313–326; Keniston, *All Our Children*; Robert Weiss, *Going It Alone: The Family Life and Social Situation of the Single Parent* (New York: Basic, 1979).

16. Keniston, *All Our Children*, and Heather Ross and Isabel Sawhill, *Time of Transition: The Growth of Families Headed by Women* (Washington, D.C.: Urban Institute, 1975).

17. Keniston, *All Our Children*.

18. Weiss, *Going It Alone*.

19. Elkind, *Hurried Child*; and Winn, *Children Without Childhood*.

20. This point is most clearly made by findings about children who have lost a parent through death. These children also "grow up a little sooner" and seem to benefit from their early assumption of responsibility. See, for example, Elizabeth Douvan and Joseph Adelson, *The Adolescent Experience* (New York: John Wiley & Sons, 1966).

21. Richard Sennett, *Families Against the City: Middle Class Homes of Industrial Chicago, 1872–1890* (New York: Vintage, 1970).

22. Lloyd deMause, ed., *The History of Childhood* (New York: Psychohistory Press, 1974); G. J. Barker-Benfield, *The Horrors of the Half-Known Life: Male Attitudes Toward Women and Sexuality in Nineteenth Century America* (New York: Harper & Row, 1976); and Quentin Bell, *Virginia Woolf: A Biography* (New York: Harcourt Brace Jovanovich, 1972).

23. Ralph E. Smith, *The Subtle Revolution: Women at Work* (Washington, D.C.: Urban Institute, 1979); Kathryn Kish Sklar, "Single-Parent Families," in Judith S. Ball and Mary Ann Krickus, eds., *Families and Work: Traditions and Transitions* (Washington, D.C.: AAUW, 1982), 9–11.

24. Linda Gordon, "Feminism, Reproduction, and the Family," in Thorne and Yalom, *Rethinking the Family*, 40–53; Sheila B. Kamerman and Arnold J. Kahn, *Child Care, Family Benefits, and Working Parents: A Study in Comparative Family Policy Analysis* (New York: Columbia University, 1981); Catherine Chilman, *Adolescent Sexuality in a Changing American Society* (New York: John Wiley & Sons, 1983).

25. Psychoanalysts have contributed to both the exaggerated individualistic myth and the political opposition to day care. Stressing the unique, irreplaceable quality of the mother-child relationship, Freudian theorists have lent their weight to the opponents of day care rather than urging provision of quality care for all those children whose mothers *must* work. At the same time, they consider themselves defenders of "every child's birthright." There is another irony in the position of the psychoanalysts: Having contributed as much as any movement or conceptual orientation to the culture's extreme individualism and preoccupation with individual gratification and "self-realization," the Freudians then lead the alarmed chorus that charges the culture, and youth in particular, with narcissism.

On the history of feminist political action, see, for example, Margaret Stacey and Marion Price, *Women, Power and Politics* (London: Tavistock, 1981); and Barrie Thorne, "Overview," in Thorne and Yalom, *Rethinking the Family*, 1–24.

26. Keniston, *All Our Children*.

27. Joseph Pleck, "Men's New Roles in the Family: Housework and Child Care," in Constantina Safilios-Rothschild, ed., *Family and Sex Roles*, forthcoming; Veroff, Douvan, and Kulka, *Inner American*.

28. Joseph Pleck, "Men's New Roles in the Family"; Veroff, Douvan, and Kulka, *Inner American*; Rhona Rapoport and Robert N. Rapoport, "Men, Women, and Equity," *Family Coordinator* 24, No. 4 (1975): 421–432.

29. Ivan Nye and Lois Hoffman, eds., *The Employed Mother in America* (Chicago: Rand McNally, 1963).

30. Elizabeth Douvan, "Changing Roles: Work, Marriage, and Parenthood," *Michigan Alumnus* 89, No. 2 (October 1982):4–7; Susan M. Partridge, *American Family Imagery in 1957 and 1976* (Ph.D. dissertation, University of Michigan, 1980).

31. Veroff, Douvan, and Kulka, *Inner American*.

32. Lillian Rubin, *Women of a Certain Age* (New York: Harper & Row, 1979).

33. Veroff, Douvan, and Kulka, *Inner American*.

34. Ibid.

35. Ronald Kessler and James McRae, "The Effect of Wives' Employment on the Mental Health of Men and Women," *American Sociological Review* 47 (1982): 216–227.

36. Veroff, Douvan, and Kulka, *Inner American*; Daniel Yankelovich, *New Rules* (New York: Random House, 1981).

37. Slater, *Pursuit of Loneliness*; Lasch, *Haven in a Heartless World*.

38. They are, then, the younger men who are *not* strained by their wives' work engagement (Veroff, Douvan, and Kulka, *Inner American*). They have been discussed extensively by Bernard, Pleck, and Douvan among others. See, for example, Jessie Bernard, "The Good Provider Role: Its Rise and Fall," *American Psychologist* 36, No. 1 (January 1981); Joseph H. Pleck, "Men's New Roles in the Family"; and Elizabeth Douvan, "Sex Differences in the Opportunities, Demands, and Developments of Youth," in R. Havighurst and P. Dreyer, eds., *Youth: Yearbook of the National Society for the Study of Education* (Chicago: University of Chicago, 1975), 27–45.

39. See, for example, George Gilder, *Naked Nomads* (New York: Quadrangle, 1974).

40. Midge Decter, *The New Chastity and Other Arguments Against Women's Liberation* (New York: Coward McCann and Geoghegan, 1972); Oscar Handlin and Mary Handlin, *Facing Life: Youth and the Family in American History* (Boston: Little, Brown & Co., 1971); Diana Baumrind, "Early Socialization and Adolescent Competence," in Stanley Dragastin and Glen Elder, eds., *Adolescence and the Life Cycle* (New York: John Wiley & Sons, 1975).

41. Shulamith Firestone, *The Dialectic of Sex* (New York: Morrow, 1970).

42. Elkind, *Hurried Child*; Winn, *Children Without Childhood*.

43. Slater, *Pursuit of Loneliness* and *Earthwalk*.

44. Benjamin Spock, *The Pocket Book of Baby and Child Care* (New York: Pocket, 1945, 1946, 1957, 1968); Arnold Gesell, Louise B. Ames, and Frances L. Ilg, *Infant and Child in the Culture of Today* (New York: Harper & Row, 1943).

45. Lasch, *Haven in a Heartless World*.

46. Ibid.; Zuckerman, "Dr. Spock: The Confidence Man."

47. All old cultures assume children to be a communal responsibility. Visitors to Israel, China, and villages anywhere in Europe are impressed with this marked difference from our own urban culture.

48. Howard Becker, in a lovely reversal of the dominant individualistic myth, has demonstrated the social nature of that most individual, idiosyncratic of human enterprises: the arts. See Becker, "Art as Collective Action," *American Sociological Review* 39, No. 6 (December 1974): 767–776.

49. David Harvey, *Social Justice and the City* (Baltimore: Johns Hopkins University Press, 1973).

50. John B. Watson, *Psychological Care of Infant and Child* (New York: Arno, 1972; original ed., 1928).

51. For an excellent recent discussion of the dominant competitive mode in academia, see Harold B. Gerard, "School Desegregation: The Social Science Role," *American Psychologist* 38, No. 8 (1983): 869–877.

52. David P. Gardner, et al., *A Nation at Risk: Report of the National Commission on Excellence in Education* (Washington, D.C.: U.S. Government Printing Office, April 1983).

53. Glenn Doman, *Teach Your Baby to Read: The Gentle Revolution* (New York: Random House, 1964); Joan Beck, *How to Raise a Brighter Child* (New York: Pocket, 1975); S. and T. Engelmann, *Give Your Child a Superior Mind* (New York: Cornerstone, 1981).

54. Philippe Aries, *Centuries of Childhood: A Social History of Family Life* (New York: Vintage, 1962).

BIBLIOGRAPHY

Aries, Philippe. *Centuries of Childhood: A Social History of Family Life.* Translated by Robert Baldick. New York: Vintage, 1962.

Bane, Mary Jo. *Here to Stay: American Families in the Twentieth Century.* New York: Basic, 1976.

Barker-Benfield, G. J. *The Horrors of the Half-Known Life: Male Attitudes Toward Women and Sexuality in Nineteenth Century America.* New York: Harper & Row, 1976.

Baumrind, Diana. "Early Socialization and Adolescent Competence." In *Adolescence and the Life Cycle*, edited by Stanley Dragastin and Glen Elder, pp. 117–146. New York: John Wiley & Sons, 1975.

Beck, Joan. *How to Raise a Brighter Child.* New York: Pocket Books, 1975.

Becker, Howard S. "Art As Collective Action." *American Sociological Review* 39, No. 6 (December 1974): 767–776.

Bell, Quentin. *Virginia Woolf: A Biography.* New York: Harcourt Brace Jovanovich, 1972.

Bernard, Jessie. *The Future of Marriage.* New York: Bantam, 1972.

———. *The Future of Motherhood.* New York: Dial, 1974.

———. "The Good Provider Role: Its Rise and Fall." *American Psychologist* 36, No. 1 (January 1981).

Bird, Carolyn. *Born Female: The High Cost of Keeping Women Down.* New York: Simon & Schuster, 1960.

Carroll, Berenice, ed. *Liberating Women's History: Theoretical and Critical Essays.* Urbana: University of Illinois Press, 1975.

Carter, Hugh, and Glick, Paul. *Marriage and Divorce: A Social and Economic Study.* Cambridge, Mass.: Harvard University Press, 1976.

Chafe, William H. *The American Woman: Her Changing Social, Economic, and Political Roles, 1920 to 1970.* New York: Oxford University Press, 1972.

Chilman, Catherine. *Adolescent Sexuality in a Changing American Society.* New York: John Wiley & Sons, 1983.

Chodorow, Nancy. *Reproduction of Mothering.* Berkeley: University of California Press, 1978.

Coleman, James. *Equality of Educational Opportunity.* Washington, D.C.: U.S. Government Printing Office, 1965.

Coles, Robert. *Children of Crisis.* Boston: Atlantic-Little, Brown & Co., 1967.

Decter, Midge. *The New Chastity and Other Arguments Against Women's Liberation.* New York: Coward McCann & Geoghegan, 1972.

Degler, Carl. *At Odds: Women and the Family in America from the Revolution to the Present.* New York: Oxford University Press, 1980.

deMause, Lloyd, ed. *The History of Childhood*. New York: Psychohistory Press, 1974.

Dinnerstein, Dorothy. *The Mermaid and the Minotaur: Sexual Arrangements and Human Malaise*. New York: Harper & Row, 1976.

Doman, Glenn J. *Teach Your Baby to Read: The Gentle Revolution*. New York: Random House, 1964.

Douvan, Elizabeth. "Changing Roles: Work, Marriage, and Parenthood." *Michigan Alumnus* 89, No. 2 (October 1982): 4–7.

———. "Sex Differences in the Opportunities, Demands, and Developments of Youth." In *Youth: Yearbook of the National Society for the Study of Education*, edited by Robert Havighurst and Philip Dreyer. Chicago: University of Chicago Press, 1975: 27–45.

———, and Adelson, Joseph. *The Adolescent Experience*. New York: John Wiley & Sons, 1966.

———; Weingarten, Helen; and Scheiber, Jane. *American Families (A Courses by Newspaper Reader)*. Dubuque, Iowa: Kendall/Hunt, 1980.

Easterlin, Richard. "Does Economic Growth Improve the Human Lot? Some Empirical Evidence." *Nations and Households in Economic Growth* edited by Paul Daird and Melvin Reder. New York: Academic Press, 1974: 89–125.

Ehrenreich, Barbara. *The Hearts of Men: American Dreams and the Flight from Commitment*. New York: Anchor, 1983.

Eisenstein, Zillah. *The Radical Future of Liberal Feminism*. New York: Longman, 1981.

Elkind, David. *The Hurried Child: Growing Up Too Fast Too Soon*. Reading, Mass.: Addison-Wesley, 1981.

Engelmann, S., and Engelmann, T. *Give Your Child a Superior Mind*. New York: Cornerstone, 1981.

Evans, Sara. *Personal Politics: The Roots of Women's Liberation in the Civil Rights Movement and the New Left*. New York: Alfred A. Knopf, 1978.

Firestone, Shulamith. *The Dialectic of Sex: The Case for Feminist Revolution*. New York: Morrow, 1970.

Fraiberg, Selma. *Every Child's Birthright: In Defense of Mothering*. New York: Basic, 1977.

Friedan, Betty. *The Feminine Mystique*. New York: W. W. Norton, 1963.

Gardner, David P., et al. *A Nation at Risk: Report of the National Commission on Excellence in Education*. U.S. Government Printing Office, 1983.

Gehlen, Frieda L. "Women Members of Congress: A Distinctive Role." In *A Portrait of Marginality*, edited by Marianne Githens and Jewel L. Prestage. New York: David McKay, 1977: 304–319.

Gerard, Harold B. "School Desegregation: The Social Science Role." *American Psychologist* 38, No. 8 (1983): 869–877.

Gesell, Arnold L.; Ames, Louise B.; and Ilg, Frances L. *Infant and Child in the Culture of Today*. New York: Harper & Row, 1943.

Gilder, George. *Naked Nomads: Unmarried Men in America*. New York: Quadrangle Books, 1974.

———. *Sexual Suicide*. New York: Quadrangle Books, 1973.

Gordon, Linda. "Feminism, Reproduction, and the Family." In *Rethinking the*

Family, edited by Barrie Thorne and Marilyn Yalom. New York: Longman, 1982: 40–53.

Gutmann, David. "Female Ego Styles and Generational Conflict." In *Feminine
Personality and Conflict*, edited by Judith Bardwick, et al. pp. 77–96. Westport, Conn.: Greenwood Press, 1980.

Handlin, Oscar, and Handlin, Mary. *Facing Life: Youth and the Family in American
History*. Boston: Little, Brown & Co., 1971.

Harvey, David. *Social Justice and the City*. Baltimore: Johns Hopkins University
Press, 1973.

Hetherington, Mavis. "Effects of Father Absence on Personality Development
in Adolescent Daughters." *Developmental Psychology* 7 (1972): 313–326.

Jencks, Christopher, et al. *Inequality: A Reassessment of the Effect of Family and
Schooling in America*. New York: Basic, 1972.

Kamerman, Sheila B., and Kahn, Arnold J. *Child Care, Family Benefits, and Working
Parents: A Study in Comparative Family Policy Analysis*. New York: Columbia
University, 1981.

Kanter, Rosabeth. *Work and Family in the United States*. New York: Russell Sage,
1977.

Keniston, Kenneth. *All Our Children: The American Family Under Pressure*. New
York: Harcourt Brace Jovanovich, 1977.

———. *The Uncommitted: Alienated Youth in American Society*. New York: Harcourt
Brace & World, 1965.

———. *Young Radicals; Notes on Committed Youth*. New York: Harcourt Brace &
World, 1968.

Kessler, Ronald, and McRae, James. "The Effect of Wives' Employment on the
Mental Health of Men and Women." *American Sociological Review* 47 (1982):
216–227.

Lasch, Christopher. *The Culture of Narcissism*. New York: W. W. Norton, 1979.

———. *Haven in a Heartless World: The Family Besieged*. New York: Basic, 1977.

Laslett, Peter. *Household and Family in Past Time*. London: Cambridge University
Press, 1972.

Mitchell, Juliet. *Women's Estate*. New York: Vintage, 1978.

Nye, Ivan, and Hoffman, Lois W. *The Employed Mother in America*. Chicago: Rand
McNally, 1963.

Pleck, Joseph H. "Husbands' Paid Work and Family Roles: Current Research
Issues." In *Research in the Interweave of Social Roles*, Vol. 3: *Families and
Jobs*. Greenwich, Conn.: JAI Press, 1983.

———. "Men's New Roles in the Family: Housework and Child Care." In *Family
and Sex Roles*, edited by Constantina Safilios-Rothschild. Forthcoming.

Rapoport, Rhona, and Rapoport, Robert N. "Men, Women, and Equity." *Family
Coordinator* 24 No. 4 (1975): 421–432.

Rapoport, Robert, and Rapoport, Rhona. *Working Couples*. New York: Harper
& Row, 1978.

Ross, Heather L., and Sawhill, Isabel V. *Time of Transitions: The Growth of Families
Headed by Women*. Washington, D.C.: Urban Institute, 1975.

Rubin, Lillian B. *Women of a Certain Age*. New York: Harper & Row, 1979.

Sennett, Richard. *Families Against the City: Middle Class Homes of Industrial Chicago,
1872–1890*. New York: Vintage, 1970.

Shorter, Edward. *The Making of the Modern Family*. New York: Basic, 1975.

Sklar, Kathryn K. "Single Parent Families." In *Families and Work: Traditions and Transitions*, edited by Judith S. Ball and Mary Ann Krickus, pp. 9–11. Washington, D.C.: American Association of University Women, 1982.

Slater, Philip E. *Earthwalk*. New York: Bantam, 1974.

———. *The Pursuit of Loneliness*. Boston: Beacon, 1970.

Smith, Ralph D., ed. *The Subtle Revolution: Women at Work*. Washington, D.C.: Urban Institute, 1979.

Spock, Benjamin. *The Pocket Book of Baby and Child Care*. New York: Pocket, 1945, 1946, 1957, 1968.

Stacey, Margaret, and Price, Marion. *Women, Power and Politics*. London: Tavistock, 1981.

Stack, Carol B. *All Our Kin: Strategies for Survival in a Black Community*. New York: Harper & Row, 1974.

Tavris, Carol, and Offir, Carole. *The Longest War: Sex Differences in Perspective*. New York: Harcourt Brace Jovanovich, 1977.

Thorne, Barrie, and Yalom, Marilyn. *Rethinking the Family*. New York: Longman, 1982.

Veroff, Joseph; Douvan, Elizabeth; and Kulka, Richard. *The Inner American: A Self-Portrait from 1957 to 1976*. New York: Basic, 1981.

———; Kulka, Richard A.; and Douvan, Elizabeth. *Mental Health in America*. New York: Basic, 1981.

Wallerstein, Joan, and Kelly, Joan. *Surviving the Break-Up: How Children and Parents Cope with Divorce*. New York: Basic, 1980.

Watson, John B. *Psychological Care of Infant and Child*. New York: Arno, 1972 (original 1928).

Weiss, Robert. *Going It Alone: The Family Life and Social Situation of the Single Parent*. New York: Basic, 1979.

Winn, Marie. *Children Without Childhood*. New York: Pantheon, 1983.

Wolfe, Tom. "The 'Me Decade' and the Third Great Awakening." *New York* 23 (August 1976): 26–40.

Yankelovich, Daniel. *New Rules: Searching for Self-Fulfillment in a World Turned Upside Down*. New York: Random House, 1981.

Zaretsky, Eli. *Capitalism, the Family and Personal Life*. New York: Harper & Row, 1976.

Zuckerman, Michael. "Dr. Spock: The Confidence Man." In *The Family in History*, edited by Charles E. Rosenberg, pp. 179–207. Philadelphia: University of Pennsylvania Press, 1975.

Chronology

1609   Virginia Company officials are authorized to kidnap Indian children in order to bring them up as Christians.[1]

1619   Shipment of poor children from England to Virginia is regularized.

1620   Privy Council grants Virginia Company authority to coerce children to ship out to Virginia.

1636   Lord Baltimore promises fifty-acre land grants to every immigrant child under the age of sixteen.

1641   Massachusetts adopts the *Body of Liberties* which prescribed capital punishment for rebellious children over 16.[2]

1642   Massachusetts statute requires parents and masters to teach their children to learn to read and to learn a trade.

        Virginia law establishes length of service of servants imported without indentures.

1646   Massachusetts courts assume responsibility for poor and idle children.

1647   Massachusetts General Court requires towns to maintain schoolmasters.

1648   Earliest recorded orphan's court in America held in Virginia.[3]

1651   New Haven court upholds binding out of children without father's consent.

1659   Anne Bradstreet writes poem concerning her children.

1660   Massachusetts laws contain a separate section pertaining to children and youth, and they describe offenses that applied only to young persons.[4]

1664   Council for Foreign Plantations recommends to Privy Council that compulsory shipping of children to Virginia be halted.

1671   Bill to halt involuntary shipping of children to Virginia fails to pass
        Parliament.

1682   Pennsylvania rules that parents, masters, and guardians must see that
        their children are educated and trained. The Crown disallows the law.

1690   *New England Primer* published.

1699   Cotton Mather publishes *A Family Well-Ordered*, an early book of chil-
        drearing advice and instruction to children.

        John Locke publishes *Some Thoughts Concerning Education*.

1700   James Janeway's *A Token for Children* is published.[5]

1721   Smallpox inoculation introduced in Boston.[6]

1729   Orphan home established at Ursuline Convent, New Orleans, first in
        present boundaries of United States.

1776   North Carolina Constitution authorizes establishment of public schools.

1777   Vermont constitution establishes public schools.

1779   Thomas Jefferson proposes a comprehensive system of public schools
        in Virginia.

1782   Noah Webster's *Speller* published.[7]

1785   U.S. Land Ordinance reserves a lot within every township "for the
        maintenance of public schools."

1790   Charleston, South Carolina, establishes country's first public orphanage.

1791   Alexander Hamilton recommends employment of women and children
        in manufacturing.

1793   *Respublica* v. *Kepple* (Pennsylvania) rules parents and guardians cannot
        bind out their children except as apprentices.

1795   New York state law authorizes use of New York City funds to support
        charity schools. State funds match these city funds.

1797   Society for the Relief of Poor Widows with Small Children founded in
        New York.

1805   Public School Society of New York City is founded to educate poor
        children not attending parochial charity schools.

1817   American Asylum for the Education and Instruction of the Deaf and
        Dumb opens in Hartford, Connecticut, with Thomas Hopkins Gallaudet
        as the first principal.

1821   New York law authorizes magistrates to send neglected children to
        almshouses.

1825   New York House of Refuge founded—first institution for juvenile de-
        linquents in the United States.

1827   Massachusetts makes the support of public schools by taxation compulsory.

1834   Pennsylvania makes public education general instead of confining it to the children of the indigent; entire system becomes tax supported.

1836   William Holmes McGuffey's First and Second Reader published.[8]

Massachusetts adopts compulsory school attendance law, the country's first.

1838   Case of *ex parte* Crouse (Pennsylvania) upholds legality of institutions for juvenile delinquents and the right of courts to commit children over parents' objections.

1842   Massachusetts and Connecticut limit working day for children under twelve to ten hours.

John Augustus saves children from jail by posting their bail, thus beginning the practice of probation.

1847   State Reform School for Boys established in Westborough, Massachusetts—the first state-funded institution for juvenile delinquents.

Lyman Cobb publishes his *The Evil Tendencies of Corporal Punishment.*[9]

1848   Pennsylvania bars children under twelve from factory work.

1851   First evaporated milk by Gail Borden of Brooklyn, New York.[10]

1853   New York Children's Aid Society founded.

1855   New York Children's Aid Society sends out first party of child emigrants.
1856   Massachusetts State Industrial School for Girls—the first such institution specifically for girls and the first on the "cottage plan" founded.

Kindergarten opened in Watertown, Wisconsin, under guidance of Mrs. Carl Schurz.[11]

1860   Indian boarding school founded on the Yakima Reservation, Washington Territory.

1863   New York Catholic Protectory founded (to protect Catholic children from proselytism of other juvenile institutions and agencies).

1868   Massachusetts Board of State Charities begins paying for children to board in private family homes.

1869   Massachusetts creates State Visiting Agent (thus making probation a state-funded rather than voluntary option).

Massachusetts founds the first permanent State Board of Health and Vital Statistics.

1874   New York Society for the Prevention of Cruelty to Children organized.

Padrone Act passed by Congress—outlawed traffic in Italian children brought to United States as beggars.

1880   Pediatric Section of American Medical Association organized with Abraham Jacobi as chairman.

1884   *Archives of Pediatrics*, first journal dealing with medical problems of children, founded.

New York outlaws contract labor of reform school children.

1888   Harvard University establishes a chair of pediatrics.

1889   American Pediatric Society founded.

1892   First infant milk depot established in New York City.

Ohio is first state to require physical education in the schools.

1894   Judge Ben Lindsey of Denver begins his work with juvenile delinquents.

1895   George Junior Republic established—required inmates to work for basic necessities.

1896   John Dewey founds "Laboratory School" at University of Chicago.

1897   National Congress of Mothers organized in Washington, D.C.[12]

1899   Illinois passes first juvenile court law. John Dewey publishes *School and Society*.

1903   New York City adopts medical inspection in schools. New York State requires working children to have certificates attesting to their legal age and good health; children under fourteen may not work during school hours.

1904   National Child Labor Committee founded.

G. Stanley Hall publishes *Adolescence*.

1905   *Commonwealth* v. *Fisher* (Pennsylvania) upholds legality of juvenile court.

1906   Playground and Recreation Association of America founded.

1909   American Association for the Study and Prevention of Infant Mortality meets in New Haven (American Child Hygiene Association in 1919).

William Healy founds Juvenile Psychopathic Institute in connection with the Chicago Juvenile Court.

First White House Conference on Care of Dependent Children recommends creation of the Federal Children's Bureau and resolves that poverty alone should not be a cause for removing children from families.

National Committee for Mental Hygiene founded.

National Kindergarten Association founded.

1910   Boy Scouts of America founded.

Campfire Girls founded.

1911   Arnold Gesell founds Clinic for Child Development at Yale.

Missouri and Illinois enact "mother's pension" laws.

1912   Girl Scouts of America founded.
       U.S. Children's Bureau created.

1914   Children's Bureau publishes *Infant Care*.
       William A. Healy publishes *The Individual Delinquent*.

1916   Congress passes Keating Owen Act—federal child labor law.

1917   Judge Baker Foundation opens in Boston—purpose is to deal with
       psychological problems of juvenile delinquents.

1918   U.S. Supreme Court in *Hammer* v. *Dagenhart* declares Keating Owen
       Act unconstitutional.
       Mississippi is last state to adopt compulsory school attendance law.

1919   White House Conference on Child Welfare Standards held.

1920   The nation's infant mortality rate is approximately 100 per 1,000 live
       births.[13]

1920   Child Welfare League of America established.

1921   Sheppard-Towner Act (federal-state program for maternal and infant
       health) enacted.

1923   American Child Health Association founded.

1927   *Child Development Abstracts* begins publication.

1929   Sheppard-Towner Act expires.

1930   White House Conference on Child Health and Protection held.

1931   Wickersham Commission reports on the condition of juvenile delin-
       quents who violate federal laws.

1933   Civilian Conservation Corps (CCC) created to provide jobs for unmar-
       ried young men ages 17–23.
       NRA codes prohibit child labor for children under age of 16.

1934   Children's Bureau presents "Security for Children" which becomes basis
       for children's titles of Social Security Act.

1935   President Roosevelt creates National Youth Administration to employ
       students and needy youth.
       Social Security Act includes provisions for grants to states for aid to
       dependent children, maternal and child health programs, crippled chil-
       dren's programs, and child welfare services.

1936   Walsh-Healy Act prohibits labor of boys under 16 and girls under 18
       in firms working on government contracts.

1938   Fair Labor Standards Act prohibits shipment in interstate commerce of goods produced where children under 16 (or 18 in hazardous occupations) have been employed.

Federal juvenile delinquency law provides that persons under age 17 accused of offenses against federal laws may be tried as juveniles.

1940   U.S. Supreme Court in case of *Minersville School District* v. *Gobitis* rules that state regulations requiring children to salute the flag do not violate the First Amendment.

White House Conference on Children in a Democracy notes inequalities among children, especially those in rural, low-income, migrant, and minority families.

1941   In the case of *U.S.* v. *Darby*, the Supreme Court upholds the child labor provisions of the Fair Labor Standards Act.

1942   Congress authorizes emergency grants to states for day care of children of working mothers.

1943   Supreme Court in case of *West Virginia State Board of Education* v. *Barnette* rules that children cannot be required to salute flag in school if their religion prohibits it.

1944   Supreme Court in case of *Prince* v. *Massachusetts* upholds state's exercise of *parens patriae* in order to promote "the general interest in youth's well being."

1946   National School Lunch Act passed.

1948   Children's Bureau establishes a clearinghouse for research and begins publishing *Research Relating to Children*.

1950   Mid-Century White House Conference on Children and Youth held.

1951   Federal Youth Corrections Act modifies parole and probation for youth.

1953   Cabinet-level Department of Health, Education, and Welfare is established.

Dr. Jonas Salk reports on success of polio research.[14]

1954   *Brown* v. *Board of Education of Topeka*.

1955   White House Conference on Education recommends expanded federal aid.

1957   In Little Rock, Arkansas, confrontation over integration of public schools takes place.

1959   United Nations adopts "Declaration of the Rights of the Child."

1960   Black students stage a "sit in" to desegregate lunch counter in Greensboro, North Carolina.

Children's Bureau and Woman's Bureau sponsor joint conference on day care and endorse day care as a necessary aspect of child welfare services.

Golden Anniversary White House Conference on Children and Youth held.

Congress creates Child Welfare Demonstration Grants Program administered by the Children's Bureau.

1962   In case of *Engel* v. *Vitale*, Supreme Court says that recital of official school prayer is unconstitutional.

Children's Bureau sponsors special conference on child abuse.

Congress authorizes creation of National Institute of Child Health and Human Development as a part of the National Institutes of Health.

1963   President John F. Kennedy establishes President's Council on Physical Fitness.

Congress adds programs to Social Security for the prevention of mental retardation.

1964   Congress passes Economic Opportunity Act, which creates the Job Corps and Head Start, among other programs for children and youth.

1965   Elementary and Secondary Education Act provides influx of federal funds for education.

1966   Child Nutrition Act adds breakfast to school meal programs.

Child Protection Act bans certain hazardous toys and other articles.

1967   Supreme Court in the case of In re Gault indicates that juveniles must receive both due process and equal protection in juvenile hearings.

Child Health Act broadens areas open to federal grants under Social Security Act.

1968   Supreme Court indicates in case of *Epperson* v. *Arkansas* that law banning teaching of evolution violates First Amendment.

1969   Case of *Tinker* v. *Des Moines Independent School District* holds that students are persons under the law.

1971   White House Conference on Youth passes resolution indicating that an individual has the right "to do her/his own thing, so long as it does not interfere with the rights of another."

Congresss passes Comprehensive Child Care Act, which would provide federal assistance for day care. It is vetoed by President Richard M. Nixon.

1972   Massachusetts Youth Service Department establishes program to abolish juvenile reformatories and replace them with community-based corrections.

1978   Birth in England of a baby resulting from implanting within the womb an egg fertilized outside it.[15]

1979   The nation's reported abortion rate is 358 per 1,000 live births.[16]

1984   The nation's infant mortality rate is 12.6 per 1,000 live births.[17]

NOTES

1. Unless otherwise noted, these dates are taken from Robert Bremner, et al., *Children and Youth in America, A Documentary History* (Cambridge, Mass.: Harvard University Press, 1970–1973). Vol. I, 817–821; Vol. II, 1523–1526; and Vol. III, 1987–2000.

2. Joseph M. Hawes, *Children in Urban Society; Juvenile Delinquency in the Nineteenth Century* (New York: Oxford University Press, 1971), 13.

3. Gorton Carruth, ed., *The Encyclopedia of American Facts and Dates* (4th ed., New York: Thomas Y. Crowell, 1966), 19.

4. Hawes, *Children in Urban Society*, 14.

5. Carruth, *Encyclopedia of American Facts and Dates*, 40.

6. Richard Morris and Jeffrey Morris, *Encyclopedia of American History* (6th ed., New York: Harper & Row, 1982), 806.

7. Carruth, *Encyclopedia of American Facts and Dates*, 96.

8. Ibid, 187, 189.

9. Ibid, 219.

10. Ibid, 213, 233.

11. Ibid, 247.

12. Ibid.

13. Kurt Snapper, "The American Legacy," in *200 Years of American Children* published by the Department of Health, Education and Welfare (Washington, D.C.: U.S. Government Printing Office, 1976), 26.

14. Morris and Morris, *Encyclopedia of American History*, 813, 814.

15. Ibid, 818.

16. Andrew Hacker, ed., *A Statistical Portrait of the American People* (New York: Viking Press, 1983).

17. U.S. Bureau of the Census. *Statistical Abstracts of the United States: 1984*, 105th edition (Washington, D.C., U.S. Government Printing Office, 1983): 77. The rate cited here is exclusive of fetal deaths.

List of Child-Helping Agencies

This list was compiled from the directory of member organizations published by the Child Welfare League of America[1] and a similar directory of associate agencies.[2] Not all listed agencies are included here; what we have included are representative examples of the various kinds of child-helping agencies and reasonable national coverage. Our bias will be for better known organizations found in larger cities. For further information, consult the directories cited in the notes. The list is alphabetical by state.

Alabama	Children's Aid Society 3600 S. Eighth Ave. Birmingham, Alabama 35222
	Bureau of Family and Children's Services 64 N. Union Street Montgomery, Alabama 36130
Alaska	Alaska Children's Service, Inc. 1200 E. 27th St. Anchorage, Alaska 99504
	Alaska Department of Health and Social Services State of Alaska Juneau, Alaska 99811
Arizona	Arizona Boy's Community, Inc. 4202 E. Union Hills Dr. Phoenix, Arizona 85028
	Florence Crittenton Services of Arizona, Inc. P.O. Box 5216 Phoenix, Arizona 85010
	State of Arizona Department of Economic Security 1717 W. Jefferson Phoenix, Arizona 85005
Arkansas	The United Methodist Children's Home, Inc. 2002 S. Fillmore Little Rock, Arkansas 72204

California	Los Angeles County Department of Adoptions 2550 W. Olympic Blvd. Los Angeles, California 90006
	Jewish Big Brothers Association of Los Angeles County 6505 Wilshire Blvd. Los Angeles, California 90048
Colorado	Colorado Christian Home, Inc. 4325 W. 29th Ave. Denver, Colorado 80212
	Denver Department of Social Services (City and County of Denver) Division of Services for Families, Children and Youth 1247 Santa Fe Dr. Denver, Colorado 80204
Connecticut	The Family Center, Inc. P.O. Box 965 Greenwich, Connecticut 06830
	Catholic Family Services, Archdiocese of Hartford 896 Asylum Ave. Hartford, Connecticut 06105
Delaware	Children's Bureau of Delaware 2005 Baynard Blvd. Wilmington, Delaware 19802
Florida	The Children's Home Society of Florida 3027 San Diego Rd. Jacksonville, Florida 32207
	Metropolitan Dade County Department of Youth and Family Development 1701 N.W. 30th Ave. Miami, Florida 33125
Georgia	Gate City Nursery Association 2080 Cascade Rd. S.W. Atlanta, Georgia 30311
	Metro-Atlanta Social Service Department The Salvation Army 675 Seminole Ave. N.E. Atlanta, Georgia 30306
Hawaii	Child and Family Service Community Service Center 200 N. Vineyard Blvd. Honolulu, Hawaii 96817
Illinois	Censerco, Ltd. Morgan-Washington Home (Girls) 403 S. State St. Bloomington, Illinois 61701
	Victory Hall for Boys 904 Hovey Ave. Normal, Illinois 61761
	Voluntary Interagency Association (coordinates five Chicago agencies) 310 S. Michigan Ave. Chicago, Illinois 60604
Indiana	Lutheran Social Services, Inc. 330 Madison St. Fort Wayne, Indiana 46802
	Family and Children's Center 1411 Lincoln Way West Mishawaka, Indiana 46544
Iowa	YMCA Boy's Home of Iowa P.O. Box 39 Johnston, Iowa 50131
	The Christian Home Association 500 N. 7th St. Council Bluffs, Iowa 51502

Kansas	United Methodist Youthville, Inc. 900 W. Broadway Newton, Kansas 67114
	Black Adoption Program and Service 1125 N. 5th Kansas City, Kansas 66101
	The Children's Division The Menninger Foundation P.O. Box 729 Topeka, Kansas 66601
Kentucky	Chosen Children Adoption Services 4010 Dupont Circle Louisvillle, Kentucky 40207
	Christian Church Children's Campus P.O. Box 45 Danville, Kentucky 40422
Louisiana	Children's Bureau of New Orleans 226 Carondelet St. New Orleans, Louisiana 70130
	Jewish Children's Regional Service (Jewish Children's Homes) P.O. Box 15225 New Orleans, Louisiana 70175
Maine	Community Counselling Center 187 Middle St. Portland, Maine 04101
	Maine Department of Human Services State House Augusta, Maine 04333
Maryland	Baltimore City Department of Social Services 1510 Guilford Ave. Baltimore, Maryland 21202
	Maryland Children's Aid and Family Service Society, Inc. 303 W. Chesapeake Ave. Towson, Maryland 21204
Massachusetts	Boston Children's Service Assn. 867 Boylston St. Boston, Massachusetts 02116
	Italian Home for Children, Inc. 1125 Centre St. Jamaica Plain, Massachusetts 02130
	Massachusetts Society for the Prevention of Cruelty to Children 43 Mt. Vernon St. Boston, Massachusetts 02108
	The New England Home for Little Wanderers 161 S. Huntington Ave. Boston, Massachusetts 02130
Michigan	Child and Family Services, Inc. 9880 E. Grand River Ave. Brighton, Michigan 48116
	Federation of Girls' Homes 548 E. Grand Blvd. Detroit, Michigan 48207
Minnesota	Children's Home Society of Minnesota 2230 Como Ave. St. Paul, Minnesota 55108
	Northwood Children's Home 714 College St. Duluth, Minnesota 55811
Mississippi	Mississippi State Department of Welfare Box 4321 Jackson, Mississippi 39216

Missouri	Family and Children Services of Kansas City, Inc. 3515 Broadway Kansas City, Missouri 64111
	Edgewood Children's Center 330 N. Gore Ave. Webster Groves, Missouri 63119
Montana	Department of Social and Rehabilitation Services P.O. Box 4210 Helena, Montana 59601
Nebraska	Nebraska Center for Children and Youth 5701 Walker Ave. Lincoln, Nebraska 68504
New Hampshire	Child and Family Services of New Hampshire P.O. Box 448 Manchester, New Hampshire 03105
New Jersey	Association for Children of New Jersey 744 Broad St. Newark, New Jersey 07102
	The Children's Home Society of New Jersey 929 Parkside Ave. Trenton, New Jersey 08618
New Mexico	New Mexico Department of Human Services P.O. Box 2348 Santa Fe, New Mexico 87503
New York	The Children's Aid Society 105 E. 22d St. New York, New York 10010
	The Salvation Army Social Services for Children 50 W. 23d St. New York, New York 10010
	Child Welfare League of America, Inc. 67 Irving Pl. New York, New York 10003
North Carolina	The Children's Home Society of North Carolina 740 Chestnut St. Greensboro, North Carolina 27405
Ohio	Ohio Boys' Town, Inc. 721 Eddy Road Cleveland, Ohio 44108
	Children's and Family Service The Family Center 535 Marmion Ave. Youngstown, Ohio 44502
Oklahoma	Bureau of Institutions and Community Services to Children and Youth P.O. Box 25352 Oklahoma City, Oklahoma 73125
	Sunbeam Family Services, Inc. 616 N.W. 21st St. Oklahoma City, Oklahoma 73103
Oregon	The Boys and Girls Aid Society of Oregon 2301 N.W. Glisan St. Portland, Oregon 97210
Pennsylvania	Children's Aid Society of Pennsylvania 311 S. Juniper St. Philadelphia, Pennsylvania 19107
	Federation Day Care Services Strahle and Horrocks Sts. Philadelphia, Pennsylvania 19152
	Philadelphia Society to Protect Children 419 S. 15th St. Philadelphia, Pennsylvania 19146

Rhode Island	Sophia Little Home 135 Norwood Ave. Cranston, Rhode Island 02905
	Department of Children and their Families 610 Mt. Pleasant Ave. Providence, Rhode Island 02908
South Carolina	The Children's Bureau of South Carolina 3700 Forest Dr. Columbia, South Carolina 29204
	Connie Maxwell Children's Home P.O. Box 1178 Greenwood, South Carolina 29646
South Dakota	Department of Social Services Division of Human Development Office of Children, Youth and Family Services Illinois St. Pierre, South Dakota 57501
Tennessee	Porter-Leath Children's Center 850 N. Manassas St. Memphis, Tennessee 38107
	Runaway House P.O. Box 40437 Memphis, Tennessee 38104
Texas	Juliette Fowler Home for Children P.O. Box 140129 Dallas, Texas 75214
	Children's Service Bureau 625 N. Alamo St. San Antonio, Texas 78215
Utah	The Children's Service Society of Utah 576 S. Temple Salt Lake City, Utah 84102
Vermont	Josephine B. Baird Children's Center 1110 Pine St. Burlington, Vermont 05401
	The Vermont Children's Aid Society, Inc. 72 Hungerford Terrace Burlington, Vermont 05401
Virginia	Family Service/Travelers Aid 222 19th St. W. Norfolk, Virginia 23517
	Friends' Association for Children 1004 St. John St. Richmond, Virginia 23220
Washington	The Casey Family Program 1402 Third Ave. Seattle, Washington 98101
West Virginia	Children's Home Society of West Virginia 1118 Kanawha Blvd. East Charleston, West Virginia 25330
Wisconsin	Children's Service Society of Wisconsin 610 N. Jackson St. Milwaukee, Wisconsin 53202
	Sunburst Youth Homes, Inc. 21 Winnebago Way Neillsville, Wisconsin 54456

NOTES

1. Child Welfare League of America, *Directory of Member Agencies* (New York: Child Welfare League of America, 1980).

2. Child Welfare League of America, *Associate Agencies* (New York: Child Welfare League of America, 1980).

Bibliography

Abbott, Grace. *The Child and the State.* 2 vols., Chicago, 1938.

Abbott, Jacob. *Gentle Measures for the Training of the Young.* New York, 1872.

Adams, Bess Porter. *About Books and Children: An Historical Survey of Children's Literature.* New York, 1953.

Adams, David Wallace. "Education in Hues: Red and Black at Hampton Institute, 1878–1893." *South Atlantic Quarterly* 76 (Spring 1977): 159–176.

———. "Schooling the Hopi: The Federal Indian Policy Writ Small, 1887–1917." *Pacific Historical Review* 48 (August 1979): 335–356.

Adams, Evelyn C. *American Indian Education: Government Schools and Economic Progress.* New York, 1971.

Albert, Judith Strong. "Transcendental School Journals in Nineteenth-Century America." *Journal of Psychohistory* 9 (Summer 1981): 105–126.

Albin, Mel, and Cavallo, Dominick, eds. *Family Life in America, 1620–2000.* St. James, N.Y., 1981.

Alcott, Louisa May. *Louisa May Alcott: Her life, Letters and Journals.* Edited by Ednah D. Cheney. Boston, 1888.

Allen, Frederick. "Horatio Alger, Jr." *Saturday Review of Literature* 18 (1938): 3–4, 16–17.

Allmendinger, David J. *Paupers and Scholars: The Transformation of Student Life in Nineteenth-Century New England.* New York, 1975.

Alper, Benedict S. "Progress in Prevention of Juvenile Delinquency." *Annals of the American Academy of Political and Social Science* 212 (November 1940): 202–208.

American Academy of Pediatrics. *Lengthening Shadows: A Report of the Council on Pediatric Practices of the American Academy of Pediatrics on the Delivery of Health Care to Children.* Evanston, Ill., 1971.

Anderson, John E. "Child Development: An Historical Perspective." *Child Development* 27 (June 1956): 181–196.

Antler, Joyce, and Antler, Stephen. "From Child Rescue to Family Protection: The Evolution of the Child Protection Movement in the United States." *Children and Youth Services Review* 1 (1979): 177–204.

Apple, Rima D. " 'To Be Used Only Under the Direction of a Physician': Commercial Infant Feeding and Medical Practice, 1870–1940." *Bulletin of the History of Medicine* 54 (Fall 1980): 402–417.

Aries, Philippe. *Centuries of Childhood: A Social History of Family Life.* Translated by Robert Baldick. New York, 1962.

Arnold, Arnold. *Pictures and Stories from Forgotten Children's Books.* New York, 1969.

Ashby, Leroy. "Straight from Youthful Heart's: *Lone Scout* and the Discovery of the Child, 1915–24." 9 *Journal of Popular Culture* (Fall 1975).

Axtell, James. *The European and the Indian, Essays in the Ethnohistory of Colonial America.* New York, 1981.

———. *The Indian Peoples of Eastern America: A Documentary History of the Sexes.* New York, 1981.

———. *The School upon a Hill: Education and Society in Colonial New England.* New Haven, 1974.

Bach, William G. "The Influence of Psychoanalytic Thought on Benjamin Spock's *Baby and Child Care.*" 10 *Journal of the History of the Behavioral Sciences* (1974): 91–94.

Bailyn, Bernard. *Education in the Forming of American Society.* Chapel Hill, 1960.

Baldwin, Bird T., et al. *Farm Children: An Investigation of Farm Children in Selected Areas of Iowa.* New York, 1930.

Bane, Mary Jo. *Here to Stay: American Families in the Twentieth Century.* New York, 1976.

———. "A Review of Child Care Books." 43 *Harvard Educational Review* (November 1973): 669–680.

Bardwick, Judith, et al., eds. *Feminine Personality and Conflict.* Westport, Conn., 1980.

Barenholtz, Bernard. *American Antique Toys: 1830–1900.* New York, 1980.

Barker-Benfield, G.J. *The Horrors of the Half-Known Life: Male Attitudes Toward Women and Sexuality in Nineteenth Century America.* New York, 1976.

Beales, Ross W., Jr. "In Search of the Historical Child: Miniature Adulthood and Youth in Colonial New England." 27 *American Quarterly* (1975): 379–398.

Beck, Joan. *How to Raise a Brighter Child.* New York, 1975.

Beck, Rochelle. "The White House Conferences on Children: An Historical Perspective." 43 *Harvard Education Review* (November 1973): 653–668.

Becker, Howard S. "Art as Collective Action," 39 *American Sociological Review.* (December, 1974): 767–776.

Bedell, Madelon. *The Alcotts: Biography of a Family.* New York, 1980.

———. "Introduction." Louisa May Alcott, *Little Women.* New York, 1983.

Beekman, Daniel. *The Mechanical Baby: A Popular History of the Theory and Practice of Child Raising.* Westport, Conn., 1977.

Bell, Winifred. *Aid to Dependent Children.* New York, 1965.

Benjamin, Gerald, ed. *Private Philanthropy and Public Elementary and Secondary Education.* New York, 1980.

Ben-Or, Joseph. "The Law of Adoption in the United States: Its Massachusetts Origins and the Statute of 1851." 130 *New England Historical and Genealogical Register* (1976): 259–272.

Bernard, Jessie. *The Future of Marriage*. New York, 1972.

———. "The Good Provider Role: Its Rise and Fall," 36 *American Psychologist*. *(January, 1981)*.

Berrol, Selma. *Immigrants at School: New York City, 1898–1914*. New York, 1978.

Best, John H., ed. *Historical Inquiry in Education: A Research Agenda*. Washington, D.C., 1983.

Billingsley, Andrew, and Giovanonni, Jeane M. *Children of the Storm: Black Children and American Child Welfare*. New York, 1972.

Bird, Carolyn, *Born Female: The High Cost of Keeping Women Down*. New York, 1960.

Blake, William. *The Illuminated Blake*. Edited by David V. Erdman. Garden City, N.Y., 1974.

Blau, Zena Smith. "Exposure to Child Rearing Experts: A Structural Interpretation of Class-Color Differences." In *The Black Family: Essays and Studies*, edited by Robert Staples. Belmont, Calif., 1971: 222–235.

Bloch, Ruth M. "American Feminine Ideals in Transition: The Rise of the Moral Mother, 1785–1815." *Feminist Studies* (1978): 101–126.

Bloom, Lynn. *Dr. Spock: Biography of a Conservative Radical*. Indianapolis, 1972.

Boll, Eleanor S. "The Child." 229 *Annals of the American Academy of Political and Social Science* (September 1943): 69–78.

Bolt, Richard A. "Progress in Saving Maternal and Child Life." 212 *Annals of the American Academy of Political and Social Science* (November 1940): 97–104.

Bowlby, John. *Maternal Care and Mental Health*. Geneva, 1951.

Boyer, Paul. *Urban Masses and Moral Order in America, 1820–1920*. Cambridge, Mass., 1978.

Boylan, Anne M. "The Role of Conversion in Nineteenth-Century Sunday Schools." 22 *American Studies* (1979): 35–48.

———. "Sunday Schools and Changing Evangelical Views of Children in the 1820s." 49 *Church History* (1979): 325–328.

Brace, Charles Loring. *The Crusade for Children: A Review of Child Life in New York During 75 Years, 1853–1928*. New York, 1928.

———. *The Dangerous Classes of New York and Twenty Years Work Among Them*. New York, 1872.

Bradbury, Dorothy E. *Five Decades of Action for Children: A History of the Children's Bureau*. Washington, D.C., 1962.

———, and Stoddard, George D. *Pioneering in Child Welfare: A History of the Iowa Child Welfare Research Station, 1917–1933*. Iowa City, 1933.

Brant, Sandra, and Cullman, Elissa. *Small Folk, A Celebration of Childhood in America*. New York, 1980.

Breckinridge, Sophonisba P. "Government's Role in Child Welfare." 212 *Annals of the American Academy of Political and Social Science* (November 1940): 42–50.

Bremner, Robert. "Other People's Children." 16 *Journal of Social History* (Spring 1983).

———, and Reichard, Gary, eds. *Reshaping America: Society and Institutions, 1945–1960*. Columbus, Ohio, 1982.

Bremner, Robert, et al. *Children and Youth in America*. 3 vols., Cambridge, Mass., 1970–1971.

Brenzel, Barbara. *Daughters of the State; A Social Portrait of the First Reform School for Girls in North America, 1856–1905*. Cambridge, Massachusetts, 1983.

———. "Domestication as Reform: A Study of the Socialization of Wayward Girls, 1856–1905." 50 *Harvard Education Review* (May 1980): 196–213.

Brigden, Susan. "Youth and the English Reformation." *Past and Present* no. 85(1982): 37–6.

Bronfenbrenner, Urie. "Reality and Research in the Ecology of Human Development." 119 *American Philosophical Society Proceedings* (December 1975): 439–469.

———. *Two Worlds of Childhood: U.S. and U.S.S.R.* New York, 1970.

Brown, D. Clayton. "Health of Farm Children in the South, 1900–1950." 53 *Agricultural History* (January 1979): 170–187.

Bunyan, John. *The Pilgrim's Progress from This World to That Which Is to Come*. Edited by James Blanton Wharey; 2d rev. ed. by Roger Sharrock. Oxford, 1960.

Butts, R. Freeman. *Public Education in the United States: From Revolution to Reform*. New York, 1978.

Byman, Seymour. "Child Raising and Melancholia in Tudor England." 6 *Journal of Psychohistory* (1978): 67–92.

Cable, Mary. *The Little Darlings, A History of Child Rearing in America*. New York, 1975.

Calvert, Karin Lee. "Children in American Family Portraiture, 1670–1810." 39 *William and Mary Quarterly* (1982): 87–113.

Campbell, D'Ann. "Judge Ben Lindsey and the Juvenile Court Movement, 1901–1904." 18 *Arizona and the West* (Spring 1976): 5-20.

Carpenter, Charles. *History of American School-Books*. Philadelphia, 1963.

Carpenter, Frederick T. "The American Myth: Paradise (To Be) Regained," 74 *Publications of the Modern Language Association* (1959): 599–606.

Carr, Lois Green. "The Development of the Maryland Orphans' Court." In *Law, Society, and Politics in Early Maryland: Proceedings of the First Conference on Maryland History, June 14–15, 1974*, edited by Aubrey C. Land, et al. Baltimore, 1977: 41–62.

Carroll, Bernice, ed. *Liberating Women's History: Theoretical and Critical Essays*. Urbana, Ill., 1975.

Carter, Hugh, and Glick, Paul. *Marriage and Divorce: A Social and Economic Study*. Cambridge, Mass., 1976.

Cavallo, Dominick. *Muscles and Morals: Organized Playgrounds and Urban Reform, 1880–1920*. Philadelphia, 1981.

Chafe, William. *The American Woman: Her Changing Social, Economic and Political Roles, 1920–1970*. New York, 1972.

Chapman, Paul Davis. "Schools as Sorters: Testing and Tracking in California, 1910–1925." 14 *Journal of Social History* (Fall 1980): 701–717.

Children's Books in the Rare Book Division of the Library of Congress. Totowa, N.J., 1975.

Child Study (November 1928). (Entire issue is devoted to the history of the Child Study Association of America.)

Chilman, Catherine. *Adolescent Sexuality in a Changing American Society*. New York, 1983.

Chodorow, Nancy. *The Reproduction of Motherhood*. Berkeley, 1978.

Church, Robert S. *Education in the United States: An Interpretive History*. New York, 1976.

Clark, Dennis. "Babes in Bondage: Indentured Irish Children in Philadelphia in the Nineteenth Century." 101 *Pennsylvania Magazine of History and Biography* (1977): 475–486.

Clement, Priscilla F. "Families and Foster Care: Philadelphia in the Late Nineteenth Century." 53 *Social Service Review* (March 1979): 406–420.

Clinton, Catherine. *The Plantation Mistress: Woman's World in the Old South*. New York, 1982.

Cohen, Ronald. "Schooling and Age Grading in American Society Since 1800: The Fragmentation of Experience." *Prospects: The Annual of American Cultural Studies*. Vol. 7, New York, 1982: 347–364.

————. "Schooling in Early Nineteenth Century Boston and New York." 1 *Journal of Urban History* (1974): 116–123.

————. "Urban Schooling in the Gilded Age and After." 2 *Journal of Urban History* (1976): 499–506.

————, and Mohl, Raymond. *The Paradox of Progressive Education: The Gary Plan and Urban Schooling*. Port Washington, N.Y., 1979.

Cohen, Sol, ed. *Education in the United States: A Documentary History*. 5 vols., New York, 1974.

————. "The Mental Hygiene Movement, the Development of Personality and the School: The Medicalization of American Education." 23 *History of Education Quarterly* (Summer 1983): 123–149.

Coleman, James. *Equality of Educational Opportunity*. Washington, D.C., 1965.

Coles, Robert. *Children of Crisis*. 5 vols., Boston, 1964–1978.

Cone, Thomas E. *History of American Pediatrics*. Boston, 1979.

————. *Two Hundred Years of Feeding Infants in America*. Columbus, Ohio, 1976.

Cott, Nancy F. *The Bonds of Womanhood: "Woman's Sphere" in New England, 1785–1835*. New Haven, 1977.

————. "Notes Toward an Interpretation of Antebellum Childrearing." 7 *Psychohistory Review* (1977–1978): 4–20.

————. "Passionlessness: An Interpretation of Victorian Sexual Ideology, 1790–1850." 14 *Signs* (1978): 219–236.

————. *Root of Bitterness: Documents in the Social History of American Women*. New York, 1972.

Cravens, Hamilton. *The Triumph of Evolution: American Scientists and the Heredity-Environment Controversy, 1900–1941*. Philadelphia, 1977.

Cremin, Lawrence A. *American Education, The Colonial Experience, 1607–1782*. New York, 1970.

————. *American Education, The National Experience, 1783–1876*. New York, 1980.

————. *The Transformation of the School: Progressivism in American Education, 1876–1957*. New York, 1961.

Darling, Richard L. *The Rise of Children's Book Reviewing in America, 1865–1881*. New York, 1968.

Darton, F.J. Harvey. *Children's Books in England: Five Centuries of Social Life*. 2d ed., Cambridge, 1958.

Davis, Glen. *Childhood and History in America*. New York, 1976.

Davis, Natalie Zemon. "The Reasons of Misrule: Youth Groups and Charivaris in Sixteenth Century France." 50 *Past and Present* (1971): 41–75.

Decter, Midge. *The New Chastity and Other Arguments Against Women's Liberation*. New York, 1972.

Degler, Carl. *At Odds: Women and the Family in America from the Revolution to the Present*. New York, 1980.

deMause, Lloyd, ed. *The History of Childhood*. New York, 1974.

Demos, John. "The American Family in Past Time." 43 *American Scholar* (1974): 422–446.

———. "Demography and Psychology in the Historical Study of Family-Life: A Personal Report." In *Household and Family in Past Time: Comparative Studies in the Size and Structure of the Domestic Group Over the Last Three Centuries in England, France, Serbia, Japan, and Colonial North America, with Further Materials from Western Europe*, edited by Peter Laslett and Richard Wall. Cambridge, 1972: 561–569.

———. "Developmental Perspectives on the History of Childhood." 2 *Journal of Interdisciplinary History* (1971): 315–327.

———. *A Little Commonwealth: Family Life in Plymouth Colony*. New York, 1970.

———, and Boocock, Sarane S., eds. *Turning Points: Sociological Essays on the Family*. Chicago, 1978.

———, and Demos, Virginia. "Adolescence in Historical Perspective." 31 *Journal of Marriage and the Family* (1969): 632–638.

Dennis, Wayne. *The Hopi Child*. New York, 1967 (reprint).

Dinnerstein, Dorothy. *The Mermaid and the Minotaur: Sexual Arrangements and Human Malaise*. New York, 1976.

Doman, Glenn J. *Teach Your Baby to Read: The Gentle Revolution*. New York, 1964.

Douglas, Ann. *The Feminization of American Culture*. New York, 1977.

Douvan, Elizabeth. "Changing Roles: Work, Marriage, and Parenthood," 89 *Michigan Alumnus* (October, 1982): 4–7.

———. "Sex Differences in the Opportunities, Demands, and Developments of Youth." In *Youth: Yearbook of the National Society for the Study of Education*, edited by Robert Havighurst and Philip Dreyer. Chicago, 1975: 27–45.

———, and Adelson, Joseph. *The Adolescent Experience*. New York, 1966.

Douvan, Elizabeth; and Weingarten, Helen; and Scheiber, Jane. *American Families (A Course by Newspaper Reader)*. Dubuque, Iowa, 1980.

Dragastin, Stanley, and Elder, Glen. eds. *Adolescence and the Life Cycle*. New York, 1975.

Dublin, Thomas. *Women at Work: The Transformation of Work and Community in Lowell, Massachusetts, 1826–1860*. New York, 1979.

———, ed. *Farm to Factory: Women's Letters, 1830–1860*. New York, 1981.

Dye, Nancy Schrom. "History of Childbirth in America." 6 *Signs* (1980): 97–108.

Eames, Wilberforce. *Early New England Catechisms*. New York, 1898.

Earle, Alice Morse. *Child Life in Colonial Days*. New York, 1899.

Easterlin, Richard. "Does Economic Growth Improve the Human Lot? Some

Empirical Evidence." in *Nations and Households in Economic Growth*. New York, 1974.

"The Early History of Children's Books in New England." 26 *New England Magazine* (1899): 147–160.

Edwards, Jonathan. *Images or Shadows of Things Divine*. Edited by Perry Miller. New Haven, 1948.

Ehrenreich, Barbara. *The Hearts of Men: American Dreams and the Flight from Commitment*. New York, 1983.

Eisler, Benita, ed. *The Lowell Offering: Writings of New England Mill Women (1840–1845)*. New York, 1977.

Elbert, Sarah. *So Sweet to Remember, Feminism and Fiction of Louisa May Alcott*. Philadelphia, 1983.

Elder, Glenn H. *Children of the Great Depression: Social Change in Life Experience*. Chicago, 1974.

———. "History and the Family: The Discovery of Complexity." 43 *Journal of Marriage and the Family* (1981): 489–519.

Elkind, David. *The Hurried Child: Growing Up Too Fast Too Soon*. Reading, Mass., 1981.

Elson, Ruth Miller. *Guardians of Tradition: American Schoolbooks of the Nineteenth Century*. Lincoln, Neb., 1964.

Engelmann, S., and Engelman, T. *Give Your Child a Superior Mind*. New York, 1981.

Evans, Sara. *Personal Politics: The Roots of Women's Liberation in the Civil Rights Movement and the New Left*. New York, 1978.

Farber, Bernard. *Guardians of Virtue: Salem Families in 1800*. New York, 1972.

Fass, Paula. *The Damned and the Beautiful: American Youth in the 1920s*. New York, 1977.

———. "The IQ: A Cultural and Historical Framework." 88 *American Journal of Education* (August 1980): 431–458.

Feinberg, Walter, and Rosemont, Henry, Jr., eds. *Work, Technology, and Education: Dissenting Essays in the Intellectual Foundations of American Education*. Urbana, Ill., 1975.

Felt, Jeremy P. "The Child Labor Provisions of the Fair Labor Standards Act." 22 *Labor History* (Fall 1970): 467–481.

———. *Hostages of Fortune: Child Labor Reform in New York State*. Syracuse, N.Y., 1965.

Filler, Louis. *Vanguards and Followers: Youth in the American Tradition*. Chicago, 1978.

Finkelstein, Barbara. "Educational History in the Pursuit of Justice." 8 *Reviews in American History* (March 1980): 122–128.

———. "In Fear of Childhood: Relationships Between Parents and Teachers in Nineteenth-Century America." 3 *History of Childhood Quarterly* (Winter 1976): 321–337.

———. "The Moral Dimensions of Pedagogy: Teaching Values in Popular Primary Schools in the Nineteenth Century." 15 *American Studies* (Fall 1974): 79–91.

———. "Pedagogy as Intrusion: Teaching Values in Popular Primary Schools in Nineteenth-Century America, 1820–1880." In *History, Education and*

Public Policy: Recovering the American Educational Past, edited by Donald Warren. Berkeley, Calif., 1978.

———. "Uncle Sam and the Children: History of Government Involvement in Childrearing." 3 *Review Journal of Philosophy and Social Science* (India) (1978): 139–153.

———. ed. *Regulated Children/Liberated Children: Education in Psychohistorical Perspective.* New York, 1979.

Firestone, Shulamit. *The Dialectic of Sex; The Case for Feminist Revolution.* New York, 1970.

Fleming, Sandford. *Children & Puritanism: The Place of Children in the Life and Thought of the New England Churches, 1620–1847.* New Haven, 1933.

Foley, Dan. *Toys Through the Ages.* New York, 1969.

Folks, Homer. *The Care of Destitute, Neglected, and Delinquent Children.* New York, 1901; reprint 1970.

Ford, Paul Leicester. *The New England Primer: A History of Its Origin and Development.* New York, 1897; reprint New York, 1962.

Fox, Vivian C. "Is Adolescence a Phenomenon of Modern Times?" *Journal of Psychohistory* (1977): 271–290.

———, and Quitt, Martin H. *Loving, Parenting and Dying: The Family Cycle in England and America, Past and Present.* New York, 1980.

Fraiberg, Selma. *Every Child's Birthright: In Defense of Mothering.* New York, 1977.

Franklin, Vincent P. *The Education of Black Philadelphia: The Social and Educational History of a Minority Community, 1900–1950.* Philadelphia, 1979.

Frazier, E. Franklin. *Negro Youth at the Crossways: Their Personality Development in the Middle States.* Washington, D.C., 1940.

Freeman, Estelle B. *Their Sisters' Keepers: Women's Prison Reform in America, 1830–1930.* Ann Arbor, Mich., 1981.

Freeman, Ruth S. *Yesterday's School Books.* Watkins Glen, N.Y., 1960.

Friedan, Betty. *The Feminine Mystique.* New York, 1963.

Friedberger, Mark. "The Decision to Institutionalize: Families with Exceptional Children in 1900." 6 *Journal of Family History* (Winter 1981): 396–409.

Friedenberg, Edgar Z. *The Vanishing Adolescent.* New York, 1959.

Frost, J. William. "As the Twig Is Bent: Quaker Ideas of Childhood." 60 *Quaker History* (1971): 67–87.

———. *The Quaker Family in Colonial America: A Portrait of the Society of Friends.* New York, 1973.

Fuchs, Estelle, and Havighurst, Robert J. *To Live on This Earth: American Indian Education.* Albuquerque, N. Mex., 1983 (reprint).

Fuller, Raymond G. "Child Labor—Continued." 212 *Annals of the American Academy of Political and Social Science* (November 1940): 146–152.

Fuller, Wayne E. *The Old Country School: The Story of Rural Education in the Middle West.* Chicago, 1982.

Gabert, Glen, Jr. *In Hoc Signo? A Brief History of Catholic Parochial Education in America.* Port Washington, N.Y., 1972.

Gardner, David P., et al. *A Nation at Risk: Report of the National Commission on Excellence in Education.* Washington, D.C., 1983.

Gerard, Harold B. "School Desegregation: The Social Science Role," 38 *American Psychologist.* (1983): 869–877.

Gesell, Arnold L., and Gesell, B. C. *The Normal Child and Primary Education*. Boston, 1912.

————, et al. *Infant and Child in the Culture of Today*. New York, 1943.

Gilbert, Sandra M., and Gubar, Susan. *The Mad Woman in the Attic*. New Haven, 1979.

Gilder, George. *Naked Nomads: Unmarried Men in America*. New York, 1974.

————. *Sexual Suicide*. New YOrk, 1973.

Gilje, Paul A. "Infant Abandonment in Early Nineteenth-Century New York." 8 *Signs* (Spring 1983): 580–590.

Githens, Mariane, and Jewel L. Prestage, eds. *A Portrait of Marginality*. New York, 1977.

Glassburg, David. "Restoring a 'Forgotten Childhood': American Play and the Progressive Era's Elizabethan Past." 32 *American Quarterly* (Fall 1980): 351–368.

Goddard, Henry H. *Juvenile Delinquency*. New York, 1921.

————. "The Problem of the Psychopathic Child." 57 *American Journal of Insanity* (1920): 511–516.

————. "Schools and Classes for Exceptional Children." 7 *Journal of Educational Psychology* (1916): 287–294.

————. *School Training of Defective Children*. New York, 1915.

————, and Hill, Helen F. "Delinquent Girls Tested by the Binet Scale." 8 *The Training School* (1911): 50–56.

————, et al. *The Bureau of Juvenile Research: Review of the Work, 1918–1920*. Mansfield, Ohio, 1921.

Goldstein, Ruth M., and Zornos, Edith. *The Screen Image of Youth: Movies About Children and Adolescents*. Metuchen, N.J., 1980.

Goodman, Paul. *Growing Up Absurd*. New York, 1959.

Goodrich, Samuel. *Recollections of a Lifetime*. New York, 1857.

Gordon, Ann D. "The Young Ladies' Academy of Philadelphia." In *Women of America: A History*, edited by Carol Berkin and Mary Beth Norton. Boston, 1979: 68–91.

Gordon, Michael. *The American Family in Social-Historical Perspective*. 2d ed., New York, 1978.

————. "Infant Care Revisited." 30 *Journal of Marriage and Family* (1968): 578–583.

————. *Juvenile Delinquency in the American Novel, 1905–1965: A Study in the Sociology of Literature*. Bowling Green, Ohio, 1971.

Gould, Stephen Jay. *The Mismeasure of Man*. New York, 1981.

Graebner, William. "The Unstable World of Benjamin Spock: Social Engineering in a Democratic Culture, 1917–1950." 67 *Journal of American History* (1980): 612–629.

Graham, Patricia. *Community and Class in American Education, 1865–1918*. New York, 1974.

"The Greek Padrone System in the United States." In U.S. Immigration Commission. *Report of the United States Immigration Commission* (popularly known as the "Dillingham Commission"). Washington, D.C., 1911.

Greven, Philip J., Jr. *Four Generations: Population, Land and Family in Colonial Andover, Massachusetts*. Ithaca, N.Y., 1970.

————. "Historical Demography and Colonial America: A Review Article." 24 *William and Mary Quarterly* (1967): 438–454.

————. *The Protestant Temperament: Patterns of Child-Rearing, Religious Experience, and the Self in Early America*. New York, 1977.

————. "Youth, Maturity, and Religious Conversion: A Note on the Ages of Converts in Andover, Massachusetts, 1711–1749." 108 *Essex Institute Historical Collections* (1972): 119–134.

————, ed. *Child-Rearing Concepts, 1620–1861: Historical Sources*. Itasca, Ill., 1973.

Grubb, W. Norton, and Lazerson, Marvin. *Broken Promises: How Americans Fail Their Children*. New York, 1982.

Gutman, Herbert. *The Black Family in Slavery and Freedom*. New York, 1976.

Hall, G. Stanley. *Adolescence: Its Psychology and Its Relations to Physiology, Anthropology, Sociology, Sex, Crime, Religion, and Education*. 2 vols., New York, 1904.

Halsey, Rosalie V. *Forgotten Books of the American Nursery*. Boston, 1911.

Handlin, Oscar, ed. *Children of the Uprooted*. New York, 1968.

————, and Handlin, Mary. *Facing Life; Youth and the Family in American History*. Boston, 1971.

Hareven, Tamara, ed. *Family and the Life Course in Historical Perspective*. New York, 1976.

Harvey, David. *Social Justice in the City*. Baltimore, 1973.

Hastings, Robert J. *A Nickel's Worth of Skim Milk, A Boy's View of the Great Depression*. Carbondale, Ill., 1972.

Hawes, Joseph M. *Children in Urban Society; Juvenile Delinquency in Nineteenth-Century America*. New York, 1971.

Hawthorne, Nathaniel. *The Wonder Book for Girls and Boys*. Boston and New York, 1900.

Healy, William. *The Individual Delinquent*. Boston, 1915.

————, and Bronner, Augusta F. *Delinquents and Criminals: Their Making and Unmaking*. New York, 1926.

Heartman, Charles F. *American Primers, Indian Primers, Royal Primers, and Thirty-seven Other Types of Non-New England Primers Issued Prior to 1830; A Bibliographical Checklist Embellished with Twenty-six Cuts, with an Introduction and Indexes*. Highland Park, N.J., 1935.

————. *The New England Primer Issued Prior to 1830*, n.p., 1922.

Heimert, Alan. "Puritanism, the Wilderness and the Frontier." 26 *New England Quarterly* (1953): 361–381.

Helton, Roy. "Are We doing Too Much for Our Children?" 212 *Annals of the American Academy of Political and Social Science* (November 1940): 231–240.

Hetherington, Mavis. "Effects of Father Absence on Personality Development in Adolescent Daughters" 7 *Developmental Psychology* (1972): 313-326.

Hilyer, Sister M. Inez. "Arapaho Child Life and Its Cultural Background." Bureau of American Ethnography, *Bulletin* No. 148. Washington, D.C., 1952.

Hiner, N. Ray. "Adolescence in Eighteenth-Century America." 3 *History of Childhood Quarterly* (1975): 253–280.

————. "The Child in American Historiography: Accomplishments and Prospects." 7 *Psychohistory Review* (1979): 13–23.

————. "Children's Rights, Corporal Punishment, and Child Abuse: Changing

American Attitudes, 1870–1920." 3 *Bulletin of the Menninger Clinic* (1979): 233–248.

———. "The Cry of Sodom Enquired into: Educational Analysis in Seventeenth-Century New England." 13 *History of Education Quarterly* (1973): 3–22.

———. "Wars and Rumors of Wars: The Historiography of Colonial Education as a Case Study in Academic Imperialism." 8 *Societas* (1978): 89–114.

———, and Hawes, Joseph M., eds. *Growing Up in America: Children in Historical Perspective*. Urbana, Ill., 1985.

Hogan, David. "Education and the Making of the Chicago Working Class, 1880–1930." *History of Education Quarterly* (Fall 1978).

Holl, Jack M. *Juvenile Reform in the Progressive Era*. Ithaca, N.Y., 1971.

Homan, Walter Joseph. *Children & Quakerism: A Study of the Place of Children in the Theory and Practice of the Society of Friends, Commonly Called Quakers*. New York, 1972 (reprint).

Horlick, Alan Stanley. *Country Boys and Merchant Princes: The Social Control of Young Men in New York*. Lewisburg, Pa., 1975.

Horn, James. "Servant Emigration to the Chesapeake in the Seventeenth Century." In *The Chesapeake in the Seventeenth Century: Essays on Anglo-American Society*, edited by Thad W. Tate and David L. Ammerman. Chapel Hill, 1979: 51–95.

Howe, Louise, ed. *The Future of the Family*. New York, 1972.

Hoxie, Frederick E. "Redefining Indian Education: Thomas J. Morgan's Program in Disarray." 24 *Arizona and the West* (Spring 1982): 5–18.

Humm, Rosamond Olmsted. *Children in America: A Study of Images and Attitudes*. Atlanta, 1978.

Jacoby, George. *Catholic Child Care in Nineteenth Century New York*. Washington, D.C., 1941.

Jencks, Christopher, et al. *Inequality: A Reassessment of the Effect of Family and Schooling in America*. New York, 1972.

Johanningmeier, Erwin V. *Americans and Their Schools*. Chicago, 1980.

Johnson, Clifton. *Old-Time Schools and School-Books*. New York, 1904; with a new introduction by Carl Withers. New York, 1963.

Jones, Kathleen W. "Sentiment and Science: The Late Nineteenth Century Pediatrician as Mother's Advisor." 17 *Journal of Social History* (Fall 1983): 79–96.

Jones, Landon. *Great Expectations: America and the Baby Boom Generation*. New York, 1980.

Kadushin, Alfred. *Child Welfare Services*. New York, 1974.

Kaestle, Carl F. *The Evolution of an Urban School System*. Cambridge, Mass., 1973.

———. *Pillars of the Republic: Common Schools and American Society, 1780–1860*. New York, 1983.

———. "Social Change, Discipline and the Common School in Early Nineteenth-Century America." 9 *Journal of Interdisciplinary History* (Summer 1978): 1–17.

———, and Vinovskis, Maris. *Education and Social Change in Nineteenth-Century Massachusetts*. Cambridge, Mass., 1980.

Kamerman, Sheila B., and Kanh, Arnold, Arnold J. *Child Care, Family Benefits and Working Parents: A Study in Comparative Family Policy Analysis.* New York, 1981.

Kammen, Michael. "Changing Perceptions of the Life Cycle in American Thought and Culture." 91 *Proceedings of the Massachusetts Historical Society* (1979): 35–66.

Kanter, Rosabeth. *Work and Family in the United States.* New York, 1977.

Kantor, Harvey, and Tyack, David, eds. *Work, Youth, and Schooling.* Stanford, Calif., 1982.

Karier, Clarence; Violas, Paul; and Spring, Joel. *Roots of Crisis: American Education in the Twentieth Century.* Chicago, 1973.

Katz, Michael. *Class, Bureaucracy, and Schools: The Illusion of Educational Change in America.* New York, 1975.

———. *The Irony of Early School Reform.* Cambridge, Mass., 1968.

Katznelson, Ira, et al. "Public Schooling and Working Class Formation: The Case of the United States." 90 *American Journal of Education* (February 1982): 111–143.

Kelly, R. Gordon. *Mother Was a Lady: Self and Society in Selected American Children's Periodicals, 1865–1890.* Westport, Conn., 1974.

Keniston, Kenneth. *All Our Children: The American Family Under Pressure.* New York, 1977.

———. *The Uncommitted: Alienated Youth in American Society.* New York, 1977.

———. *Young Radicals; Notes on Committed Youth.* New York, 1968.

Kerber, Linda K. *Women of the Republic: Intellect and Ideology in Revolutionary America.* Chapel Hill, 1980.

Kessler, Ronald, and MacRae, James. "The Effect of Wives' Employment on the Mental Health of Men and Women," 47 *American Sociological Review.* (1982): 216–227.

Kett, Joseph. "Adolescence and Youth in Nineteenth Century America." 2 *Journal of Interdisciplinary History* (1971): 283–298.

———. *Rites of Passage: Adolescence in America, 1790 to the Present.* New York, 1977.

Kiefer, Monica. *American Children Through Their Books.* Philadelphia, 1948.

Kiple, Kenneth F., and Kiple, Virginia H. "Slave Child Mortality: Some Nutritional Answers to a Perennial Puzzle." 10 *Journal of Social History* (1977): 284–309.

Knapp, Mary, and Knapp, Herbert. *One Potato, Two Potato: The Secret Education of American Children.* New York, 1976.

Kolodny, Annette. *The Lay of the Land.* Chapel Hill, 1975.

Komarovsky, Mirra. *Blue Collar Marriage.* New York, 1962.

Krug, Edward A. *The Shaping of the American High School, 1920–1941.* Madison, Wis., 1972.

Kuhn, Anne L. *The Mother's Role in Childhood Education: New England Concepts, 1830–1860.* New Haven, 1947.

Kuhoth, Jean Spealman. *Best Selling Children's Books.* Metuchen, N.J., 1973.

Larkin, Jack. "The View from New England: Notes on Every Day Life in Rural America to 1850." 34 *American Quarterly* (1982): 244–261.

Larsen, Charles. *The Good Fight: The Life and Times of Ben B. Lindsey.* Chicago, 1972.

Lasch, Christopher. *The Culture of Narcissism*. New York, 1979.

———. *Haven in a Heartless World: The Family Besieged*. New York, 1977.

———. *The New Radicalism in America, 1889–1963*. New York, 1965.

Laslett, Peter. *Household and Family in Past Time*. London, 1972.

Lasser, Carol. "A 'Pleasingly Oppressive' Burden: The Transformation of Domestic Service and Female Charity in Salem, 1800–1840." 116 *Essex Institute Historical Collections* (1980): 156–175.

Lazerson, Marvin. *Origins of the Urban School*. Cambridge, Mass., 1971.

———. "Urban Reform and the Schools: Kindergartens in Massachusetts, 1870–1915." In *Education in American History*, edited by Michael Katz. New York, 1973: 220–236.

———, and Grubb, W. Norton, eds. *American Education and Vocationalism: A Documentary History, 1870–1970*. New York, 1974.

———. *Broken Promises: How Americans Fail Their Children*. New York, 1982.

Lemons, J. Stanley. "The Sheppard-Towner Act: Progressivism in the 1920s." 55 *Journal of American History* (1969): 776–786.

Lenroot, Katherine F. "Child Welfare, 1930–40." 212 *Annals of the American Academy of Political and Social Science* (November 1940): 1–11.

Levenstein, Harvey. " 'Best for Babies' or 'Preventable Infanticide'? The Controversy Over Artificial Feeding of Infants in America, 1880–1920." 70 *Journal of American History* (June 1983): 75–94.

Levy, Barry. " 'Tender Plants:' Quaker Farmers and Children in the Delaware Valley, 1681–1735." 3 *Journal of Family History* (1978): 116–135.

Lewis, R.W.B. *The American Adam: Innocence, Tragedy and Tradition in the Nineteenth Century*. Chicago, 1955.

Lindley, Betty, and Lindley, Ernest K. *A New Deal for Youth: The Story of the National Youth Administration*. New York, 1938.

Littlefield, Emery. *Early Schools and School-books of New England*. New York, 1965.

Livermore, George. *The Origin, History and Character of the New England Primer*. New York, 1915.

Lomax, Elizabeth M.R. *Science and Patterns of Child Care*. San Francisco, 1978.

Lowrey, Lawson G., ed. *Institute for Child Guidance Studies, Selected Reprints*. New York, 1931.

———, and Sloane, Victoria, eds. *Orthopsychiatry, 1922–1948*. New York, 1948.

Lundberg, Emma O. *Unto the Least of These: Social Services for Children*. New York, 1947.

Lystad, Mary. *From Dr. Mather to Dr. Seuss*. Boston, 1980.

Mabee, Carleton. *Black Education in New York State: From Colonial to Modern Times*. Syracuse, N.Y., 1979.

McAdoo, Hariette Pipes, ed. *Black Families*. Beverly Hills, Calif., 1981.

McClintock, Inez, and McClintock, Marshall. *Toys in America*. Washington, D.C., 1961.

Maccoby, Eleanor. "Methods of Child-Rearing in Two Social Classes." In *Readings in Child Development*, edited by William Martin and Celia Stendler. New York, 1954: 380–396.

McConnell, Beatrice. "Child Labor in Agriculture." 236 *Annals of the American Academy of Political and Social Science* (November 1944): 92–100.

Macleod, Ann Scott. *A Moral Tale: Children's Fiction and American Culture, 1820–1860*. Hamden, Conn., 1975.

Macleod, David I. "Act Your Age: Boyhood, Adolescence, and the Rise of the Boy Scouts of America." 16 *Journal of Social History* (Winter 1982): 3–20.

———. *Building Character in the American Boy: The Boy Scouts, YMCA, and Their Forerunners, 1870–1920*. Madison, Wis., 1983.

McLoughliin, William G. "Evangelical Child-Rearing in the Age of Jackson: Francis Wayland's Views on When and How to Subdue the Wilfulness of Children." 9 *Journal of Social History* (1975): 21–43.

Magee, Elizabeth S. "Impact of the War on Child labor." 236 *Annals of the American Academy of Political and Social Science* (November 1944): 101–109.

Marks, Russell. *The Idea of I.Q.* Washington, D.C., 1981.

Martz, Louis L. *The Poetry of Meditation: A Study of English Religious Literature of the Seventeenth Century*. New Haven, 1962.

———, ed. *The Meditative Poem: An Anthology of Seventeenth-Century Verse*. New York, 1963.

Mateer, Florence. *Child Behavior: A Critical and Experimental Study of Young Children in the Method of Conditioned Reflexes*. Boston, 1918.

———. *The Unstable Child*. New York, 1924.

Mattessich, Paula. "Childlessness and Its Correlates in Historical Perspective: A Research Note." 4 *Journal of Family History* (Fall 1979): 299–307.

Maynard, Joyce. *Looking Back: A Chronicle of Growing Up Old in the Sixties*. New York, 1973.

Mead, Margaret. "Grandparents as Educators." 76 *Teachers College Record* (December 1974): 240–249.

———, and Wolfenstein, Martha, eds. *Childhood in Contemporary Cultures*. Chicago, 1955.

Mechling, Jay. "Advice to Historians on Advice to Mothers." 9 *Journal of Social History* (1975): 44–63.

Meigs, Cornelia. *Invincible Louisa: The Story of the Author of Little Women*. Boston, 1933.

———, et al., eds. *A Critical History of Children's Literature: A Survey of Children's Books in English*. Rev. ed., Toronto, 1969.

Mennel, Robert M. *Thorns and Thistles: Juvenile Delinquents in the United States, 1825–1940*. Hanover, N.H., 1973.

Mergen, Bernard. *Play and Playthings: A Reference Guide*. Westport, Conn., 1982.

Miller, Daniel R., and Swanson, Guy E. *The Changing American Parent: A Study in the Detroit Area*. New York, 1955.

Mitchell, Juliet. *Women's Estate*. New York, 1978.

Mohraz, Judy Jolley. *The Separate Problem: Case Studies of Black Education in the North, 1900–1930*. Westport, Conn., 1979.

Monroe, Paul. *The Founding of the American Public School System: A History of Education in the United States*. New York, 1964.

Morgan, Edmund Sears. *The Puritan Family: Essays on Religion and Domestic Relations in Seventeenth Century New England*. Boston, 1944.

———. *Virginians at Home: Family Life in the Eighteenth Century*. Charlottesville, Va., 1952.

Nasaw, David. *Schooled to Order: A Social History of Public Schooling in the United States.* New York, 1979.

National Congress of Parents and Teachers. *Parents and Teachers.* Boston, 1928.

National Research Council, Committee on Child Development. *Conference on Research in Child Development.* N.p., 1925.

Nietz, John. *Old Textbooks.* Pittsburgh, 1961.

Norris, Edward Opler. *Childhood and Youth in Jicarilla Apache Society.* Los Angeles, 1946.

Norton, Mary Beth. *Liberty's Daughters: The Revolutionary Experience of American Women, 1750–1800.* Boston, 1980.

Novak, Stephen J. *The Rights of Youth: American Colleges and Student Revolt, 1798–1815.* Cambridge, Mass., 1977.

Nye, Ivan, and Hoffman, Lois W. *The Employed Mother in America.* Chicago, 1963.

Olneck, Michael, and Lazerson, Marvin. "The School Achievement of Immigrant Children, 1900–1930." 14 *History of Education Quarterly* (Winter 1974): 453–482.

Payne, Alma. *Louisa May Alcott, A Reference Guide.* Boston, 1980.

Pearce, Roy Harvey. "The Significance of the Captivity Narrative." 19 *American Literature* (1947): 1–20.

———, ed. *Colonial American Writing.* New York, 1950.

Peck, Ellen, and Sanderowitz, Judith, eds. *Pronatalism: The Myth of Mom and Apple Pie.* New York, 1974.

Peterson, William. "The New American Family: Causes and Consequences of the Baby Boom." 21 *Commentary* (January 1956): 1–6.

Pettitt, George A. *Primitive Education in North America.* University of California Publications in Archaeology and Ethnology. Vol. 43, Berkeley, Calif., 1946.

Pickering, Samuel E., Jr. *John Locke and Children's Books in Eighteenth Century England.* Knoxville, Tenn., 1981.

Pickett, Robert S. *House of Refuge: Origins of Juvenile Reform in New York State, 1815–1857.* Syracuse, N.Y., 1969.

Platt, Anthony. *The Child Savers.* Chicago, 1969.

Pleck, Joseph H. "Husbands' Paid Work and Family Roles: Current Research Issues," in *Research in the Interweave of Social Roles*, Vol. 3: *Families and Jobs.* Greenwich, Conn., 1983.

———. "Men's New Roles in the Family: Housework and Child Care," in *Family and Sex Roles.* edited by Constantina Afilios-Rothschild, forthcoming.

Plumstead, A. W. *The Wall and the Garden; Selected Massachusetts Election Sermons, 1670–1675.* Minneapolis, 1968.

Polier, Justine Wise. *Everybody's Children, Nobody's Child: A Judge Looks at Under-privileged Children in the United States.* New York, 1941.

Pratt, Richard Henry. *Battlefield and Classroom: Four Decades with the American Indian, 1867–1904.* New Haven, 1964.

Prescott, Peter. *The Child Savers: Juvenile Justice Observed.* New York, 1981.

Radin, Norma, and Kamii, Constance K. "The Child Rearing Attitudes of Disadvantaged Negro Mothers and Some Educational Implications." 34 *Journal of Negro Education* (1965): 138–146.

Raichle, Donald R. "The Abolition of Corporal Punishment in New Jersey Schools."
    2 *History of Childhood Quarterly* (Summer 1974): 53–78.
Rapoport, Robert, and Rapoport, Rhona. *Working Couples.* New York, 1978.
Ravitch, Diane. *The Great School Wars, New York City, 1805–1973. A History of
    Public Schools as Battlefields of Social Change.* New York, 1974.
———. *The Revisionists Revised; A Critique of the Radical Attack on the Schools.* New
    York, 1978.
———. *The Troubled Crusade: American Education, 1945–1980.* New York, 1983.
Rayman, Ronald. "Joseph Lancaster's Monitorial System of Instruction and
    American Indian Education, 1815–38." 21 *History of Education Quarterly*
    (Winter 1981): 395–409.
"Recommendations of the White House Conference on Children and Youth,"
    14 *Social Security Bulletin* (February 1951): 10–14.
Reese, William J. *Progressivism and the Grass Roots: Social Change and Urban School-
    ing, 1840–1920.* London, forthcoming.
Reilly, Elizabeth Carroll. *A Dictionary of Colonial American Printers' Ornaments and
    Illustrations.* Worcester, Mass., 1975.
Reinier, Jacqueline. "Rearing the Republican Child: Attitudes and Practices in
    Post Revolutionary Philadelphia." 39 *William and Mary Quarterly* (1982):
    150–163.
Reller, Theodore L. "The School and Child Welfare." 212 *Annals of the American
    Academy of Political and Social Science* (November 1940): 51–58.
Rhodes, Sonya. "Trends in Child Development Research Import to Day-Care
    Policy." 53 *Social Service Review* (1979): 285-294.
Richards, William C., and Norton, William J. *Biography of a Foundation: The Story
    of the Children's Fund of Michigan, 1929–1954.* N.p., 1957.
Richardson, Anna E. "The Association's Program for Child Study and Parent
    Education." 18 *Journal of Home Economics* (October 1926): 572.
Riessman, Frank. *The Culturally Deprived Child.* New York, 1962.
Riis, Jacob. *The Children of the Poor.* New York, 1892.
Robinson, W. Stitt. "Indian Education and Missions in Colonial Virginia." 18
    Journal of Southern History (May 1952): 152–168.
Rodgers, Daniel T. "Socializing Middle Class Children: Institutions, Fables, and
    Work Values in Nineteenth-Century America." 13 *Journal of Social History*
    (Spring 1980): 354–367.
Romanofsky, Peter. "Saving the Lives of the City's Foundlings: The Joint Com-
    mittee and New York City Child Care Methods, 1860–1907." 61 *New York
    Historical Society Quarterly* (January-April 1977): 49–68.
Ronda, Bruce A. "Genesis and Genealogy: Bronson Alcott's Changing View of
    the Child." 84 *New England Historical and Genealogical Register* (October
    1981): 259–273.
Rooke, Patricia. "The Child Institutionalized in Canada, Britain, and the United
    States: A Transatlantic Perspective." 2 *Journal of Educational Thought* (Au-
    gust 1977): 156–171.
Rose, Wilie Lee. *Slavery and Freedom.* New York, 1982.
Roselle, Daniel. *Samuel Griswold Goodrich, Creator of Peter Parley: A Study of his Life
    and Works.* Albany, N.Y., 1968.

Rosenbach, A.S.W. *Early American Children's Books*. Portland, Maine, 1933; reprint New York, 1966.

Rosenberg, Chaim, and Paine, Herbert James. "Female Juvenile Delinquency: A Nineteenth-Century Followup." 19 *Crime and Delinquency* (1973): 72–78.

Rosenberg, Charles, ed. *The Family in History*. Philadelphia, 1975.

Ross, Dorothy. *G. Stanley Hall: The Psychologist as Prophet*. Chicago, 1972.

Ross, Elizabeth Dale. *The Kindergarten Crusade: The Establishment of Preschool Education in the United States*. Athens, Ohio, 1976.

Ross, Heather L., and Sawhill, Isabel V. *Time of Transitions: The Growth of Families Headed by Women*. Washington, D.C., 1975.

Rothman, David J. *Conscience and Convenience: The Asylum and Its Alternatives in Progressive America*. Boston, 1980.

———. *The Discovery of the Asylum: Social Order and Disorder in the New Republic*. Boston, 1971.

———. "Documents in Search of a Historian: Toward a History of Childhood and Youth in America." 2 *Journal of Interdisciplinary History* (1971): 367–377.

Rothman, Ellen. "Sex and Self-Control: Middle-Class Courtship in America, 1770–1870." 15 *Journal of Social History* (1982): 409–425.

Rothman, Sheila. "Other People's Children: The Day Care Experience in America." 30 *The Public Interest* (Winter 1973): 11–27.

———. *Woman's Proper Place: A History of Changing Ideals and Practices, 1870 to the Present*. New York, 1978.

Rubin, Lillian B. *Women of a Certain Age*. New York, 1979.

Rutman, Darrett B., and Rutman, Anita H. " 'Now-Wives and Sons-in-Law': Parental Death in a Seventeenth-Century Virginia County." In *The Chesapeake in the Seventeenth Century: Essays on Anglo-American Society*, edited by Thad W. Tate and David L. Ammerman. Chapel Hill, 1979: 153–182.

Ryan, Mary. *Cradle of the Middle Class: The Family in Oneida County, New York, 1790–1865*. New York, 1981.

Ryerson, Alice Judson. "Medical Advice on Child Rearing, 1550–1900." 31 *Harvard Educational Review* (1961): 302–323.

Ryerson, Ellen. *The Best-Laid Plans: America's Juvenile Court Experiment*. New York, 1978.

Samuel Wood and Sons. *Early New York Publishers of Children's Books*. New York, 1942.

Schlesinger, Elizabeth Bancroft. "Cotton Mather and His Children." 10 *William and Mary Quarterly* (1953): 181–189.

Schlossman, Steven. "Before Home Start: Notes Toward a History of Parent Education in America, 1897–1929." 46 *Harvard Educational Review* (1976): 436–467.

———. "Equity, Education, and Individual Justice: The Origins of the Juvenile Court." 52 *Harvard Educational Review* (February 1982): 77–83.

———. *Love and the American Delinquent: The Theory and Practice of "Progressive" Juvenile Justice, 1825–1920*. Chicago, 1977.

———. "Philanthropy and the Gospel of Child Development." 21 *History of Education Quarterly* (Fall 1981): 275–299.

————, and Wallach, Stephanie. "The Crime of Precocious Sexuality." 48 *Harvard Educational Review* (February 1978): 65–94.

Schnucker, R. V. "The English Puritans and Pregnancy, Delivery, and Breast Feeding." 1 *History of Childhood Quarterly* (1974): 637–658.

Scholten, Catherine M. " 'On the Importance of the Obstetrick Art': Changing Customs of Childbirth in America, 1760–1825." 34 *William and Mary Quarterly* (1977): 426–445.

Schultz, Stanley K. *The Culture Factory, Boston Public Schools, 1789–1860*. New York, 1973.

Scott, Donald M., and Wishy, Bernard, eds. *American Families: A Documentary History*. New York, 1982.

Scott, Rebecca. "The Battle Over the Child: Child Apprenticeship and the Freedman's Bureau in North Carolina." 10 *Prologue: The Journal of the National Archives* (Summer 1978): 101–113.

Sears, Robert. *Your Ancients Revisited: A History of Child Development*. Chicago, 1975.

————, et al. *Patterns of Child Rearing*. Stanford, Calif., 1957.

Sellin, Theodore. "Child Delinquency." 229 *Annals of the American Academy of Political and Social Science* (September 1943): 157–163.

Senn, Milton. *Insights on the Child Development Movement in the United States*. Chicago, 1975.

Sennett, Richard. *Families Against the City: Middle Class Homes of Industrial Chicago, 1872–1890*. New York, 1970.

Shalloo, J. P. "Understanding Behavior Problems of Children." 212 *Annals of the American Academy of Political and Social Science* (November 1940): 194–201.

Shapiro, Michael S. *Child's Garden: The Kindergarten Movement from Froebel to Dewey*. University Park, Pa., 1983.

Shipton, Clifford K. *Isaiah Thomas, Printer, Patriot and Philanthropist, 1749–1831*. New York, 1948.

Shirely, Mary M. "Children's Part in War." 14 *Smith College Studies in Social Work* (September 1943): 15–23.

Shorter, Edward. *The Making of the Modern Family*. New York, 1975.

Sklar, Kathryn K. "Single Parent Families." In *Families and Work: Traditions and Transitions*, edited by Judith S. Ball and Mary Ann Krickus. Washington, D.C., 1982: 9–11.

Slater, Peter Gregg. *Children in the New England Mind: In Death and Life*. Hamden, Conn., 1977.

————. " 'From the *Cradle* to the *Coffin*': Parental Bereavement and the Shadow of Infant Damnation in Puritan Society." 6 *Psychohistory Review* (1977–1978): 4–24.

Slater, Philip E. *Earthwalk*. New York, 1974.

————. *The Pursuit of Loneliness*. Boston, 1970.

Slotkin, Richard, and Olson, James F., eds. *So Dreadful a Judgment: Puritan Responses to King Phillip's War, 1676–1677*. Middletown, Conn., 1978.

Smith, Daniel Blake. "Autonomy and Affection: Parents and Children in Eighteenth Century Chesapeake Families." 6 *Psychohistory Review* (1977): 32–51.

———. *Inside the Great House: Planter Family Life in Eighteenth Century Chesapeake Society*. Ithaca, N.Y., 1980.

———. "Mortality and Family in the Colonial Chesapeake." 8 *Journal of Interdisciplinary History* (1978): 403–427.

———. "The Study of the Family in Early America: Trends, Problems, and Prospects." 39 *William and Mary Quarterly* (1982): 3–28.

Smith, Daniel Scott. "Child Naming Patterns and Family Structure Change: Hingham, Massachusetts, 1640–1880." *The Newberry Papers in Family and Community History*. Paper No. 76–75. Chicago, 1977.

———. "The Demographic History of Colonial New England." 32 *Journal of Economic History* (1972): 165–183.

———. "A Perspective on Demographic Methods and Effects in Social History." 39 *William and Mary Quarterly* (1982): 442–468.

Smith, Daniel Scott, and Hindus, Michael S. "Premarital Pregnancy in America, 1640–1971: An Overview and Interpretation." 5 *Journal of Interdisciplinary History* (1975): 537–570.

Smith, Dora V. *Fifty Years of Children's Books*. Champaign, Ill., 1963.

Smith, Ralph D., ed. *The Subtle Revolution: Women at Work*. Washington, D.C., 1979.

Smith-Rosenberg, Carroll. "The Female World of Love and Ritual: Relations Between Women in Nineteenth-Century America." 2 *Signs* (1975): 1–29.

———. "Puberty to Menopause: The Cycle of Femininity in Nineteenth-Century America." 1 *Feminist Studies* (Winter-Spring 1973): 58–72.

Soltow, Lee, and Stevens, Edward. *The Rise of Literacy and the Common School: A Socioeconomic Analysis to 1830*. Chicago, 1981.

Sommerville, C. John. "English Puritans and Children: A Social-Cultural Explanation." 6 *Journal of Psychohistory* (1978): 113–137.

———. *The Rise and Fall of Childhood*. Beverly Hills, Calif., 1982.

Spock, Benjamin. *The Pocket Book of Baby and Child Care*. New York, 1945.

Spodek, Bernard, ed. *Handbook of Research in Early Childhood Education*. New York, 1982.

Stacey, Margaret, and Price, Marion. *Women, Power, and Politics*. London, 1981.

Stack, Carol B. *All Our Kin: Strategies for Survival in a Black Community*. New York, 1974.

Stambler, Moses. "The Effect of Compulsory Education and Child Labor Laws on High School Attendance in New York City, 1898–1917." 8 *History of Education Quarterly* (Summer 1969): 189–214.

Stannard, David E. "Death and the Puritan Child." 26 *American Quarterly* (1974): 456–476.

Stansell, Christine. "Women, Children and the Uses of the Streets: Class and Gender Conflicts in New York City, 1850–1860." 8 *Feminist Studies* (1982): 309–335.

Staples, Robert, ed. *The Black Family: Essays and Studies*. Belmont, Calif., 1971.

Starkey, Marion L. "The Easiest Room in Hell." 92 *Essex Institute Historical Collections* (1956): 33–42.

Steffen, Charles G. "The Sewall Children in Colonial New England." 131 *New England Historical and Genealogical Register* (1977): 163–172.

Steinfels, Margaret O'Brien. *Who's Minding the Children? The History and Politics of Day Care in America.* New York, 1973.

Stendler, Celia. "Sixty Years of Child Training." 36 *Journal of Pediatrics* (January 1950): 122–134.

Stern, Madeleine. *Louisa May Alcott.* Norman, Okla., 1971.

Stevenson, George S., and Smith, Geddes. *Child Guidance Clinics: A Quarter Century of Development.* New York, 1934.

Strickland, Charles. "A Transcendentalist Father: The Child-Rearing Practices of Bronson Alcott." 3 *Perspectives in American History* (1969): 5–73.

Strout, Cushing. "Fathers and Sons: Notes on 'New Light' and 'New Left' Young People as a Historical Comparison." 6 *Psychohistory Review* (1977): 25–31.

Suitor, Jill. "Husbands' Participation in Childbirth: A Nineteenth-Century Phenomenon." 6 *Journal of Family History* (1981): 278–293.

Sulman, A. Michael. "The Humanization of the American Child: Benjamin Spock as a Popularizer of Psychoanalytic Thought." 9 *Journal of the History of the Behavioral Sciences* (1973): 258–265.

Sung, Betty Lee. *Transplanted Chinese Children.* Washington, D.C., 1979.

Sutton, John R. "Stubborn Children: Law and the Socialization of Deviance in the Puritan Colonies." 15 *Family Law Quarterly* (1981): 31–64.

Sutton-Smith, Brian, and Rosenberg, B. G. "Sixty Years of Historical Change in the Game Preferences of American Children." 74 *Journal of American Folklore* (1961): 17–46.

Szasz, Margaret Connell. " 'Poor Richard' Meets the Native: American Schooling for Young Indian Women in Eighteenth Century Connecticut." 49 *Pacific Historical Review* (May 1980): 215–235.

Takanishi, Ruby. "Federal Involvement in Early Education (1933–1973): The Need for Historical Perspectives." In *Current Topics in Early Childhood Education,* edited by Lilian G. Katz. Norwood, N.J., 1977: 139–163.

Tavris, Carol, and Offir, Carole. *The Longest War: Sex Differences in Perspective.* New York, 1977.

Tebbel, John W. *From Rags to Riches: Horatio Alger, Jr., and the American Dream.* New York, 1963.

Tennyson, Alfred Lord. *The Poems of Tennyson.* Edited by Christopher Ricks. London, 1969.

Terman, Lewis M. *The Measurement of Intelligence: An Explanation and a Complete Guide for the Use of the Stanford Revision ana Extension of the Binet-Simon Intelligence Scale.* Boston, 1916.

Thompson, Roger. "Adolescent Culture in Colonial Massachusetts." 9 *Journal of Family History* (1984): 127–144.

Thorne, Barrie, and Yalom, Marilyn. *Rethinking the Family.* New York, 1982.

Thwaite, Mary F. *From Primer to Pleasure in Reading.* Boston, 1972.

Tiffin, Susan. *In Whose Best Interest? Child Welfare Reform in the Progressive Era.* Westport, Conn., 1982.

Trattner, Walter I. *Crusade for the Children: A History of the National Child Labor Committee and Child Labor Reform in America.* Chicago, 1970.

———. *From Poor Law to Welfare State: A History of Social Welfare in America.* New York, 1974.

———. *Homer Folks: Pioneer in Social Welfare.* New York, 1968.

Trennert, Robert A. "Peaceably If They Will, Forcibly If They Must: The Phoenix Indian School, 1890–1901." 20 *Journal of Arizona History* (Autumn 1979): 314–317.

Troen, Selwyn K. "The Discovery of the Adolescent by American Educational Reformers, 1900–1920: An Economic Perspective." In *Schooling and Society: Studies in the History of Education,* edited by Lawrence Stone. Baltimore, 1976: 239–250.

———. *The Public and the Schools: Shaping the St. Louis School System, 1838–1920.* Columbia, Mo., 1975.

Tyack, David B. *The One Best System: A History of American Urban Education.* Cambridge, Mass., 1974.

———. "The Tribe and the Common School: Community Control in Rural Education." 24 *American Quarterly* (March 1972): 3–19.

———, and Berkowitz, Michael. "The Man Nobody Liked: Toward a Social History of the Truant Office, 1840–1940." 19 *American Quarterly* (Spring 1977): 31–54.

———, and Hansot, Elisabeth. *Managers of Virtue.* New York, 1982.

Tyson, Helen Glenn. "Care of Dependent Children." 212 *Annals of the American Academy of Political and Social Science* (November 1940): 168–178.

Ugland, Richard M. " 'Education for Victory': The High School Victory Corps and Curricular Adaptation During World War II." 19 *History of Education Quarterly* (Winter 1979): 435–451.

———. "Viewpoints and Morale of Urban High School Students During World War II—Indianapolis as a Case Study." 77 *Indiana Magazine of History* (June 1981): 150–178.

Uhlenberg, Peter. "Death and the Family." 5 *Journal of Family History* (1980): 313–320.

Valesh, Eva McDonald. "Child Labor." 14 *American Federationist* (March 1907): 157–173.

Vann, Richard T. "The Youth of *Centuries of Childhood,"* 21 *History and Theory* (1982): 279–297.

Veroff, Joseph; Douvan, Elizabeth; and Kulka, Richard. *The Inner American: A Self Portrait from 1957 to 1976.* New York, 1981.

Veroff, Joseph; Douvan, Elizabeth; and Kulka, Richard. *Mental Health in America.* New York, 1981.

Vinovskis, Maris A. "An Epidemic of Adolescent Pregnancy? Some Historical Considerations." 6 *Journal of Family History* (1981): 205–230.

———. "Quantification and the Analysis of American Antebellum Education." 13 *Journal of Interdisciplinary History* (Spring 1983): 761–786.

———, and Bernard, Richard M. "Beyond Catherine Beecher: Female Education in the Antebellum Period." 3 *Signs* (1978): 856–869.

Violas, Paul C. "The Indoctrination Debate and the Great Depression." 4 *The History Teacher* (May 1971): 25–35.

———. *The Training of the Urban Working Class: A History of Twentieth-Century American Education.* Chicago, 1978.

Wagner, Peter. "A Note on Puritans and Children in Early Colonial New England." 25 *Amerikastudien* (1980): 47–62.

Walkil, S. Parviz, et al. "Between Two Cultures: A Study in the Socialization of the Children of Immigrants." 43 *Journal of Marriage and the Family* (November 1981): 929–940.

Wallerstein, Joan, and Kelly, Joan. *Surviving the Break-Up: How Children and Parents Cope with Divorce.* New York, 1980.

Watson, John B. *Behaviorism.* New York, 1925.

———. *Psychological Care of Infant and Child.* New York, 1972 (reprint).

Webber, Thomas. *Deep Like the Rivers: Education in the Slave Quarter Community, 1831–1865.* New York, 1978.

Weber, Evelyn. *The Kindergarten: Its Encounter with Educational Thought in America.* New York, 1969.

Weiss, Nancy Pottishman. "The Mother-Child Dyad Revisited: Perceptions of Mothers and Children in 19th Century Child-Rearing Manuals." 34 *Journal of Social Issues* (1978): 29–45.

———. "Mother, the Invention of Necessity: Dr. Spock's *Baby and Child Care.*" 29 *American Quarterly* (1977): 519–546.

Weiss, Robert. *Going It Alone: The Family Life and Social Situation of the Single Parent.* New York, 1979.

Weitzman, Lenore, et al. "Sex Role Socialization in Picture Books for Preschool Children." 77 *American Journal of Sociology* (1972): 1125–1150.

Welch, d'Alte A. *A Bibliography of American Children's Books Printed Prior to 1821.* Worcester, Mass., 1972.

Wells, Robert V. *Revolutions in Americans' Lives: A Demographic Perspective on the History of Americans, Their Families, and Their Society.* Westport, Conn., 1982.

Welter, Barbara. *Dimity Convictions: The American Woman in the Nineteenth Century.* Athens, Ohio, 1976.

Wertz, Richard, and Wertz, Dorothy. *Lying-In: A History of Childbirth in America.* New York, 1977.

Whiting, Beatrice, ed. *Six Cultures: Studies of Child Rearing.* New York, 1963.

Wiggins, David K. "The Play of Slave Children in the Plantation Communities of the Old South, 1820–1860." 7 *Journal of Sport History* (Summer 1980): 21–39.

Wilson, Adrian. "The Infancy of the History of Childhood: An Appraisal of Philippe Aries." 19 *History and Theory* (1980): 132–154.

Winn, Marie. *Children without Childhood.* New York, 1983.

Wishy, Bernard. *Child and the Republic: The Dawn of Modern American Child Nurture.* Philadelphia, 1968.

Witmer, Helen. *Psychiatric Clinics for Children with Special Reference to State Programs.* New York, 1940.

Wohl, R. Richard. "The 'Country Boy' Myth and Its Place in American Urban Culture: The Nineteenth Century Contribution." 3 *Perspectives in American History* (1979): 75–156.

Wolfe, Tom. "The 'Me Decade' and the Third Great Awakening," 23 *New York* (August, 1976): 26–40.

Woody, Thomas. *A History of Women's Education in the United States.* New York, 1966 (reprint).

Wyatt-Brown, Bertram. "Child Abuse, Public Policy and Child Rearing in America, An Historical Approach." *Working Paper No. 2.* Center for the Study of Educational Policy and Human Values. College Park, Md., 1981.

Yankelovich, Daniel. *New Rules: Searching for Self-Fulfillment in a World Turned Upside Down.* New York, 1981.

Yarbrough, Anne. "Apprenticeship as Adolescents in Sixteenth-Century Bristol." 13 *Journal of Social History* (1979): 67–81.

Yezierska, Anzia. *Children of Loneliness.* New York, 1923.

Zainaldin, Jamil S. "The Emergence of a Modern Family Law: Child Custody, Adoption, and the Courts, 1796–1851." 73 *Northwestern University Law Review* (1979): 1038–1089.

Zaretsky, Eli. *Capitalism, the Family and Personal Life.* New York, 1976.

Zeitz, Dorothy. *Child Welfare, Principles and Methods.* New York, 1959.

Zelizer, Viviana A. "The Price and Value of Children: The Case of Children's Insurance." 86 *American Journal of Sociology* (1981): 1036–1056.

Zimand, Gertrude Folks. "The Changing Picture of Child Labor." 236 *Annals of the American Academy of Political and Social Science* (November 1944): 83–91.

Zuckerman, Michael. "Children's Rights: The Failure of Reform." *Policy Analysis* (Summer 1976).

———. "Dr. Spock: The Confidence Man." In *The Family in History,* edited by Charles Rosenberg. Philadelphia, 1975: 179–208.

———. "Penmanship Exercises for Saucy Sons: Some Thoughts on the Colonial Southern Family." 84 *South Carolina Historical Magazine* (July 1983): 152–166.

Index

Abbot, Jacob, 125–126
Abbott, Grace, 5, 276, 490
Abbott, John, 155
Abell, Aaron, 256
abortion, 404, 536
abundance, 544
academies, female: early nineteenth century, 161; eighteenth-century, 71; private secondary, in nineteenth century, 245
accidents, and colonial children, 69
Across Two Aprils (1964), 400
activists, young antiwar, 578 n.177
Adair, James, 313
Adam, 214
Adam of the Road (1942), 389
Adams, Abigal, 63, 91 n.18
Adams, David Wallace, 329
Adams, Evelyn C., 328
Adams, John, 63
Adam's Fall, 197
Adams family, 68
Addams, Jane, 278, 362
"adjustment" committees, juvenile, 507
administrators, professional schools for, 284
adolescence, 9, 250, 274, 278, 377, 392, 394, 401, 406, 424, 504, 509, 512, 513, 549, 561, 563, 564, 567; among boys, nineteenth century, 165; among colonial males and fe-

males, 75; disagreement on nature of, in Progressive period, 293; early nineteenth century, 159, 167–169, 172, 174; effects of class and ethnic differences on, 166; female, early nineteenth century, 160, 164, 169, 172, 174, 576 n.132; female, eighteenth century, 75–84; female, nineteenth century, 164–171; among immigrants, 354; male, 293; male, eighteenth century, 75; nineteenth-century definition of, 164; among nineteenth-century middle-class white males, 291–292; among Puritan youth, 35–38. *See also* teenagers; youth
adolescent behavior, 565
adolescent crisis, early nineteenth century, 166
adolescent girls, early nineteenth century, 166–167
adolescent rebellion, 563
adolescents, 394, 401, 403, 493, 504, 509, 513, 534, 561, 562, 565; depiction of, in colonial American portraits, 83; middle-class, 561; in nineteenth century, 70, 71, 74, 75
adoption, 65; and Catholic institutions, 294–295
adult behavior, rules of, 609
adult life, mysteries of, 560
adult life expectancy in seventeenth-

Hey, Big Spender, 403
higher education, 463; institutions of, controlled by native Americans, 328
high schools, 283, 360, 397, 401, 409, 505, 513, 549, 565; attendance, 245, 377; curriculum in, 285, 289, 554; emergence of, 292; enrollments, 1900–1940, 284–285; grades, 555; graduates, 555; life, 392; newspapers, 513; in nineteenth-century cities, 243; public, 245; small, 554; students in, 511, 513, 556, 565. *See also* schools
high school seniors, 558
highway construction, government, 547
hillbillies, 514
Hillis, Cora Bussey, 424, 435, 445; death of, 436
Hiner, N. Ray, 58, 62, 67, 74, 80–81, 85, 158; and history of childhood, 58
hired girls, early nineteenth century, 169
Hirschfelder, Arlene B., 312
Hiscoomes, Joel, 327
historians, 255, 504; Catholic, 240; of education in early nineteenth century, 113; revisionist, 276; view of child-saving movement, 276–277
historical interpretations of Depression, 510
historical methodology, eighteenth century, 76, 80–81, 98
historical novels, 383
historical sources, 59, 187, 247, 312–313, 344, 535; early nineteenth century, 173, 176; eighteenth century, 75, 80–81
historiography of American childhood, 3
history, 420, 553; American, 407
history of American childhood, overview, 6–11
History of Beasts, 207
history of childhood: and early American family, 15; new method-

ologies, 75; types of evidence, 58; recent discoveries, 57
history of education, 5
history of female childhood, need for study of, 175–176
history of the family, 5; and children, 5; relation to history of childhood, 57; trends in study of, 76
History of the Holy Jesus, 208
history of women: early nineteenth century, 159–160; and history of childhood, 174–175
history students, 506
hobbies, 395
Hoebel, E. Adamson, 318
Hofstadter, Richard, 275
Hogeland, Ronald, 156
Holl, Jack M., 281
Holli, Melvin G., 275
Hollywood, 504, 537, 561
Holocaust, 408
Holt, Luther Emmett, 417
home economics, 288; in Iowa, 450
homelessness, 251
homemakers, full-time, 596
home ownership, 541
Homer Price (1943), 388
Homestead, Pa., 273
home work: among immigrant children, 354
homiletics, seventeenth century, 186
homogeneous environments for children, nineteenth century, 116
homosexuality, 405
Hooker, Thomas, 36
hoola hoops, 558
Hoosier School Boy (1883), 386
Hopi, 313, 315, 317, 321, 326, 330
Hopkins, Harry, 505
Horn, Margo, 460
Horn Book, 391
The Horn Book Magazine, 379
horses, and native American children, 325
hospital admissions policies, 547
houses of refuge, 111, 255, 277; charter, in New York City, 119; early nineteenth century, 112, 162;

immigrant families, 359; school role in, 363; theories of, 359
interpersonal relations, 405
intimacy, early nineteenth century, 173
Inuit, 319, 325
Iowa, 441, 443, 445
Iowa Child Study Association, 435
Iowa Child Welfare Research Station, 434–437, 440–441, 445, 448, 451, 464
Iowa Federation of Women's Clubs, 435
Iowa State College, 435, 445, 450
Iowa University, 435, 448
Iowa Woman's Christian Temperance Union, 435
IQ, hereditarian theory of, 290
Irish, 253, 391, 395; in Boston, 346; Catholics, in nineteenth-century cities, 236; eighteenth century, 70–71, 88, 116; girls, early nineteenth century, 174
Iroquois, 319–320; child-rearing, Jesuit view of, 318–319; Longhouse Religion, 333; parents, view of babies, 311
Irving, Washington, 212
Italian children in New York City, 344
Italian governments, 263
Italian language, 359
Italian puppeteer, 406
Italy, 263
It's Like This, Cat (1963), 406
It's Not What You Expect (1973), 404, 407
Ives, Levi Silliman, 129–130, 259

Jack the Giant Killer, 205, 207
Jackson, Jesse, 398
Jacksonian era, 245
Jacobi, Abraham, 417
Jacobs, Wilbur R., 324
Jailhouse Rock, 562
James, character in *How Many Miles to Babylon?*, 403
James, Alice, 175

James, William, 388, 423
Jane, character in *Kallie's Corner*, 406
Janeway, James, 185
Janie (1944), 504
Japan, 494, 608; Japanese, 399
Jean and Johnny (1959), 396
Jefferson, Thomas, 72
Jencks, Jeremiah, 346
Jennings, Francis, 324, 328
Jesus, 398
Jewish families, Eastern European, 343
Jewish mother, role of, 363–364
Jews, 244, 403, 444; children of, 356; Eastern Europeans, 352; and school attendance, 352
jitterbug, 509
Jo, character in *Little Women*, 216–218
job opportunities, 247
Jody, character in *The Yearling*, 390
John, character in *The Star Beast*, 400
Johns Hopkins University, 432
Johnson, Henry, 131
Johnson, Lyndon, 601
Johnson County, Ind., 282
Johnstone, E. R., 426
joking relationship, among native Americans, 321
Jones, Landon, 510, 535–536, 558
Jones, Wissey, character in *The Child Buyer*, 555
Jo's Boys (1886), 382
Joseph, 198
Journal of Psych-Asthenics, 431
Juan and Juanita (1888), 386
Junior Miss, 504
junior municipalities, 281
Junior Republic Movement, 281; influence on public schools, 281; principles of, 281
juvenile alienation, 561
juvenile asylums, origins and purposes, 258
juvenile court, 9, 278, 290, 417, 429, 507; criticism of, 279; in Denver, 278; and families, 280; first, in Chicago, 278; in Iowa, 424; in Mil-

696   Index

Ravitch, Diane, 141 n. 44, 239–240,
    242
Rawling, Marjorie Kennan, 390
RCA Victor, 563
Reader's Digest, 542
Reading, Pa., 237
reading, 382; eighteenth century, 72;
    among immigrants, 362. *See also*
    literacy
reading materials, early nineteenth
    century, 132
Reagan, Ronald, 601
The Real Diary of a Real Boy (1903),
    384–385
Rebecca of Sunny Brook Farm (1903),
    382
Rebel Without a Cause, 561
recapitulation theory, 421, 424, 430;
    and child study movement, 290–
    291
records, 562; recording industry, 557
recreation, 492, 509; and play, 274
red-lining, 547
Reeder, Rudolph R., 490
reformatories, 255–256, 280, 298,
    417; access to, by Catholic parents,
    256; black children in, 269; Catho-
    lic, 256; for children, 256; and
    Civil War, 256; conditions in, post–
    Civil War, 256; congregate style,
    257–258, 278; contract labor in,
    post–Civil War, 256; cottage system
    in, 257–258, 265, 278; early nine-
    teenth century, 112; girls in, 257;
    juvenile, 255; overcrowding, dur-
    ing Civil War, 256; punitive, 280;
    rates of admission to, 256; school
    attendance in, 257; sex segregation
    in, 257
reformers, 252, 281; and children,
    117, 123–124; and child welfare,
    416; early nineteenth century, 118,
    123, 130, 134, 154; educational,
    early nineteenth century, 132; in
    Indian Service, 312; on latency age
    children, 130–134; progressive,
    418; types of, Progressive Era, 297;

and young children, ante-bellum
    period, 125. *See also* child-saving
reforms, 1890 to 1920, 275
reform schools, 9, 280; for delin-
    quents, 256; early nineteenth cen-
    tury, 162; number created in
    1824–1885, 255; as replacement
    for houses of refuge, 255; struc-
    ture and routine of, 280
refrigerators, 546
refuges, early nineteenth century,
    114
religion, 382; early nineteenth cen-
    tury, 114; Eastern, 600; immigrant,
    361
religious ideology, 62
religious orders, nineteenth century,
    243
religious orthodoxy, rejection of, by
    children of Jewish immigrants,
    359–360
religious revival, nineteenth century,
    201
religious societies, early nineteenth
    century, 141 n. 41
religious values, 589
rental-unit construction, 546
Report on Manufactures (1791), 167
The Reprobate's Reward, 209
reproduction, 600
Republican Mother, 157, 160–161,
    166
Republican party, 447
Republican virtue, early nineteenth
    century, 133
residential patterns, 244
resources, declining access of chil-
    dren to, eighteenth century, 78
Reynolds, Joshua, 205
rhetoric, in children's literature, 188
Rhode Island, 252
Ricardo, Ricky, 560
Richards, Caroline, 162
Richards, Laura E., 382
Richardson, Anne E., 450
Richardson, Samuel, 206
Richman, Julia, 351, 362
Rickover, Admiral Hyman, 554

Sing Sing prison, 460
Sinners in the Hand of an Angry God, 205
sisterhood: early nineteenth century, 172, 174; and historians, 174
sisters of charity, early nineteenth century, 118
Sklar, Kathyrn Kish, 156
Slater, Peter G., 27, 154
Slater, Philip, 402, 590
Slater, Samuel, 122
slave children: eighteenth-century conditions of, 78; and malnutrition, 68–69
slave family, 78, 365; eighteenth century, 77
slave girls, early nineteenth century, 164, 176
slavery, 11, 348, 364–366, 506; and children, 345; early nineteenth century, 164, 176; effect of, on girls, 176; eighteenth century, 77; and life of children, colonial period, 78; and two-parent families, 79
slaves, kin networks among, 79
slave work, eighteenth century, 79
Slavic community, Cleveland, 353
Sleator, William, 408
"Sleeping Beauty," 220
Slobodkin, Losi, 396
slums, 246, 276; clearance of, 547; as neighborhoods, 260
small adults, children as, 610
smallpox, 607; epidemics of, in eighteenth century, 68; inoculation against, eighteenth-century Boston, 68
small towns, 385; middle-class values in, 261; nostalgia for, 385
Smart, Christopher, 205
Smith, Billie G., 77, 79–80
Smith, Daniel Blake, 61, 64, 67, 76, 187
Smith, Dora V., 378
Smith, Dorothy, 85
Smith, Rev. Daniel, 127

Smith College School of Social Work, 461
Smith-Rosenberg, Carroll, 114–115, 165–166, 171–172
Smithsonian Institution, 323
Smoky the Cow Horse (1926), 388
Snow White, 512
Snyder, Zilpha Keatley, 408
social action, 275
social and economic change, 1880–1920, 274–275
social change, 402, 490, 512; and children, nineteenth century, 116
social classes, 540, 544–545, 607
social control, 278, 292, 361; among native Americans, 321; as motive of Progressives, 276–277
social critics, 589
Social Darwinism, 355, 421
social efficiency, and education, 283
social evils, 426, 436
social functions, 6; of eighteenth-century children, 7; of seventeenth-century children, 6
social history, eighteenth century, 76
social injustice, 276
Socialists, 553; and schools, 286
socialization, 187, 283, 540, 570–571 n. 32, 594, 598; early nineteenth century, 175; of girls, 175; as mode of child-rearing, 136 n. 7; sex-role, 573 n. 66
"socialized medicine," 494
social malaise, 509
social mobility, 352, 355, 392
"social parenthood," 501
social problems, 440
social psychology, 423
social reform, 425; social reformers, 275
social sciences, 439, 442, 449, 451; social scientists, 377, 589, 605, 607
Social Security, 499
Social Security Act, 489, 492, 494–495, 499–501, 547; Title IV, 496, 499, 548
Social Security Board, 497
social studies, 554

About the Contributors

ANDREW M. AMBROSE is currently working on a Ph.D. in American Studies at Emory University. His M.A. thesis, which he completed in 1979 at the University of Tennessee, is a study of the Tennessee Women's Christian Temperance Union and the state woman's suffrage movement between 1890 and 1920. He has also served as a Research Writer for the Georgia Department of Education project on Southern Women's History and as Research Historian for the Martin Luther King, Jr. National Historic Site and Preservation District.

LEROY ASHBY is Professor of History at Washington State University. He has published several articles on progressivism and is the author of *The Spearless Leader: Senator Borah and the Progressive Movement in the 1920's* (1972). His most recent work is *Saving the Waifs: Reformers and Dependent Children, 1890–1917* (1984).

ROSS W. BEALES, JR., is a member of the history faculty and Director of the Interdisciplinary Studies Program at the College of the Holy Cross, Worcester, Massachusetts. In addition to his work in the history of childhood and youth, he has published several articles in community and religious history as well as historical editing. He is currently working on a study of the family and community life of Ebenezer Parkman, an eighteenth-century New England minister.

SELMA BERROL is a Professor of History at Baruch College, City University of New York. She is a specialist in American immigration history with special emphasis on immigration and ethnicity in New York City. She is the author of *Immigrants at School: New York City, 1898–1914* (1978) and numerous articles on the public schools and immigrant children, German Jewish/Russian Jewish tensions, and related subjects.

ANNE M. BOYLAN is a Visiting Lecturer in History at the University of New Mexico. Her articles have appeared in *American Studies, Church History, Feminist Studies, Reviews in American History, Journal of Presbyterian History,* and *The History Teacher.* She is currently completing a book-length study on American Sunday Schools in the nineteenth century. She is also investigating women's benevolent organizations during the early nineteenth century.

PRISCILLA FERGUSON CLEMENT teaches U.S. social history and women's history at the University of Pennsylvania, Delaware County Campus. Her research has concentrated on children and poverty in nineteenth-century America, welfare and poverty in America, and juvenile delinquency. Her articles have appeared in *Pennsylvania Magazine of History and Biography, Newsletter of the Philadelphia City Archives,* and the *Social Service Review.*

RONALD D. COHEN teaches U.S. history at Indiana University Northwest in Gary, Indiana. He has published widely in scholarly journals and is the author of *The Family in Colonial America* (1976); *The Paradox of Progressive Education: The Gary Plan and Urban Schooling* (with Raymond Mohl, 1982); and *Gary: A Pictorial History* (with James Lane, 1982).

HAMILTON CRAVENS is Professor, Program in History of Technology and Science, Department of History, Iowa State University. He has published two books, *The Triumph of Evolution: American Scientists and the Heredity-Environment Controversy 1900–1941* (1978) and *Ideas in America's Cultures: From Republic to Mass Society* (1982), and numerous articles and papers. He is currently at work on several projects dealing with science and children in modern American culture and public policy.

ELIZABETH DOUVAN holds the Kellogg Chair in Psychology at the University of Michigan where she is Co-Director of Women's Studies and a member of the Institute for Social Research. Among her several publications are *The Adolescent Experience* (1966); *The Inner American: A Self-Portrait* (co-author, 1981); and *Mental Health in America: Patterns of Help Seeking from 1957–1976* (co-author, 1981). She is now editing a book on stages of family development.

BARBARA FINKELSTEIN is a member of the Department of Educational Policy, Planning, and Administration and Director of the Center for the Study of Educational Policy and Human Values at the University of Maryland. She is the author of numerous articles on the history of education, family, and childhood. She is the editor of *Regulated Children/ Liberated Children: Education in Psychohistorical Perspective* (1979).

ELIZABETH A. FRANCIS is a member of the Department of English and Director of Composition at the University of Nevada at Reno. She is the author of articles on Tennyson and the Rossettis, the editor of *Tennyson: Collection of Critical Essays* (1980), and the author of a forthcoming book, *Tennyson: A Reading of Fire and Dream.* She also serves as editor of *Children's Literature: An International Journal.*

SALLY ALLEN McNALL has taught American literature at the University of Arizona, the University of Missouri at Kansas City, the University of Kansas, and during a Fulbright year in New Zealand. Her publications include *Who Is in the House? A Psychological Study of Two Centuries of Popular Women's Fiction in America* (1981) and, with Scott G. McNall, *Plains Families* (1983). She worked on the National Education Association-funded oral history project "Images of Aging" (Lawrence Arts Center, Lawrence, Kansas 1981–1983).

CONSTANCE B. SCHULZ received her Ph.D. in early national American history from the University of Cincinnati. She has taught about the history of the family at the College of Wooster and at the University of Maryland, Baltimore County (UMBC). She is currently at Georgetown University. Her interest in material culture stems from collecting and preparing for publication *The History of Maryland Slide Collection* (Instructional Resources Corporation, 1981).

CHARLES E. STRICKLAND holds a joint appointment in History and Education at Emory University. He has published widely in American social, educational, and family history, including a study of the child-rearing practices of Bronson Alcott (1969). He is the editor of *Health, Growth and Heredity: G. Stanley Hall on Natural Education* (1965) and is the author of a forthcoming book, *Victorian Domesticity: Families in the Life and Art of Louisa May Alcott.*

MARGARET CONNELL SZASZ is a Visiting Scholar in the Department of History at the University of New Mexico, where she teaches American History and American Indian History. She has published several studies in Native American history, including *Education and the American Indian* (1974, 1977). Currently, she is working on a book on Indian education in colonial America.

ABOUT THE EDITORS

JOSEPH M. HAWES is Professor of History at Memphis State University. His previous works include *Children in Urban Society* and *Law and Order in American History*, as well as articles in *Paisano*, the *Journal of World History*, and the *Journal of the West*.

N. RAY HINER is Professor of History and Education at the University of Kansas. He is the author of numerous articles in scholarly journals and is coeditor (with Professor Hawes) of *Growing Up in America: Children in Historical Perspective* (1985), an anthology of articles on the history of childhood.